ANALYSIS OF DEVELOPMENT PROBLEMS

STUDIES OF THE CHILEAN ECONOMY

CONTRIBUTIONS
TO
ECONOMIC ANALYSIS

83

Honorary Editor

J. TINBERGEN

Editors

D.W. JORGENSON

J. WAELBROECK

NORTH-HOLLAND PUBLISHING COMPANY – AMSTERDAM • LONDON
AMERICAN ELSEVIER PUBLISHING COMPANY, INC. – NEW YORK

ANALYSIS OF DEVELOPMENT PROBLEMS:

Studies of the Chilean economy

Editors

R. S. ECKAUS and P. N. ROSENSTEIN-RODAN

Massachusetts Institute of Technology

1973

NORTH-HOLLAND PUBLISHING COMPANY – AMSTERDAM · LONDON
AMERICAN ELSEVIER PUBLISHING COMPANY, INC. – NEW YORK

Library of Congress Catalog Card Number: 73-75531

ISBN North-Holland for this series 0 7204 3100 x
ISBN North-Holland for this volume 0 7204 3185 9
ISBN American Elsevier for this volume 0 444 10518 2

Publishers:

NORTH-HOLLAND PUBLISHING COMPANY—AMSTERDAM
NORTH-HOLLAND PUBLISHING COMPANY, LTD.—LONDON

Sole distributors for the U.S.A. and Canada:
AMERICAN ELSEVIER PUBLISHING COMPANY, INC.
52 VANDERBILT AVENUE, NEW YORK, N.Y. 10017

PRINTED IN THE NETHERLANDS

PREFACE

The ODEPLAN of the Government of Chile and the Center for International Studies, MIT, carried on from 1968 to 1970 a joint program of policy-oriented economic research. The objective was to produce general methodologies useful for orienting future studies as well as substantive results which would be of assistance in understanding the current problems of the development of the Chilean economy. The research program generated a number of both types of studies, some of which are reproduced here. These studies not only provide insight into the characteristics of the Chilean economy but are also contributions to the analytical tool bag which development policymakers can carry to other countries.

A new government with a radically different economic philosophy has been inaugurated in Chile since the MIT ODEPLAN project was started and completed. The economic and social transformations associated with the change in government have been profound. Nonetheless, the basic facts of absolute and relative resource availabilities in Chile, which are fundamental determinants of its economic prospects and which, in one way or another, condition the results of all the substantive studies reported on here, have not changed. We therefore believe that the results of these studies continue to be timely and relevant for an understanding of the Chilean economy.

It is fair to say that one of the contributions of development economics to the economics profession more generally has been a greater appreciation of the various influences which create a divergence between the prices which actually prevail in markets and prices which would reflect the real scarcity value of resources. While the existence of such divergences has always been recognized, the conscious effort to improve resource allocation in less developed countries has led to a new appreciation of the importance of 'shadow prices' which do indicate real, relative scarcities. However, when nature or the independent workings of an economy do not perform the experiments which would reveal true shadow prices, approximate methods must be found for estimating them. These approximations, in turn, must take into account the special features of each economy. As could be expected, a number of alternative approaches to the estimation of shadow prices have developed. In this situation, in order to

clear the ground for the estimation of the real relative scarcity of foreign exchange in Chile, Edmar Bacha and Lance Taylor undertook a critical review
of the theory and methods of estimating that shadow price. This will be useful for other economists similarly facing the task of estimating shadow prices.

The evaluation of investment projects in less-developed countries typically
faces conditions which are different from those of more advanced countries:
the relative scarcity of capital is likely to be changing more rapidly and the
projects are unlikely to be 'marginal' but will be 'large' relative to the economy
as a whole. In such cases, the assumptions required to justify the conventional
discounting for project evaluation are less justified. Lance Taylor, in the second
paper, takes up these problems and shows how they can be dealt with.

The five papers in the second section of the book are interesting for their
empirical content as well as their methodologies. Francis Seton undertakes the
estimation of shadow wages in Chile. His conclusion that these wages are likely
to be substantially less than money wages indicates one of the problems that
burdens new projects in Chile. Taylor and Bacha project the future requirements for foreign exchange in Chile and find these to be relatively large partly
because the likelihood of significant progress in import substitution is small.
This conclusion indicates the importance of careful planning of investment
projects for export growth. For this reason they develop an estimate of the
shadow prices of foreign exchange. Sergio Bitar and Hugo Trivelli report on a
study of the private and social rates of return to capital in Chile. Its object was
to develop a rate which could be used in project evaluation. The next paper by
Lance Taylor also develops an estimate of the rate of return to capital, based
on a model of optimal growth in an open economy which distinguishes domestically produced and imported capital.

A substantial part of the ODEPLAN-MIT research program was devoted to
the development of multisectoral linear programming models for the Chilean
economy. In chapter 7 Peter Clark, Alejandro Foxley R. and Ana Maria Jul
demonstrate the usefulness of such multisectoral models, which are in most
respects highly aggregated, for the purpose of evaluating a particular investment
project. The advantages of a comprehensive model in taking into account all
the direct and indirect effects of the project and the direct and indirect effects
of various tax, subsidy and tariff proposals associated with the project are made
clear in the Clark, Foxley R., Jul paper.

Several studies included probe deeply into aspects of particular sectors of
the Chilean economy. In one study Jere Behrman makes a common assumption
that output from the agricultural sector is not sensitive to prices into a hypothesis to be tested. His results are skeptical with respect to that hypothesis. While
the structure of Chilean agriculture has been changing rapidly as a consequence

of land reform programs, the Behrman result deserves careful consideration as bearing on the effects of regulations which control agricultural prices. Again in his study of the magnitude and sources of excess capacity in Chile, Behrman confirms the sensitivity of responsiveness to price signals. The sources of the excess capacity which has prevailed widely in the Chilean economy have been found in large part to be the result of insufficient aggregate demand and price distortions.[1]

A theoretical analysis of trade strategy is undertaken by Bacha in chapter 10 to determine the implications for income of alternative commercial policies. He also introduces a 'preference for industry' which reflects government decision to favor industrialization and analyzes its implications. In chapter 11 Carlos Diaz-Alejandro describes the origins of the Andean common market and analyzes its likely contributions to the economic growth of its members with cautiously optimistic conclusions. A paper by Lance Taylor in the same section projects alternative future requirements for foreign exchange in Chile which would maintain equilibrium in the balance of payments, consistent with corresponding projections of alternative growth rates. Again the paper is interesting both for its substantive conclusions — which substantiate other estimates — and for its methodology in which the projections are made in the context of a model which does not rely on the usual assumptions about fixed linear relations between output and imports.

A multisectoral linear programming model was used by Clark and Foxley in chapter 13 to trace out a number of alternative efficient programs of development which embody alternative assumptions about technical and behavioral parameters and economic policy decisions. The paper thus demonstrates the manner in which such models can be used to assist in the choice of economic targets as well as indicating the strategy to be followed in the achievement of targets.

The paper by Behrman in Part V on the mechanism of Chilean inflation not only increases our insight into those inflationary processes but contributes more generally to an understanding of monetary influences. Behrman's conclusions give some weight to the influence of cost increases in Chilean inflation. However, it places more weight on the role of monetary influences and, like some other recent evaluations, concludes that the time lag of the effect of monetary policy on prices is relatively long.[2] The last paper, by Behrman and

---

[1] The significance of excess capacity in facilitating economic policy in the first year of the new government of Pres. Salvador Allende is emphasized in 'La economica Chilena en 1971 y perspectivas para 1972', ed. by Jorge Causs and Vittorio Corbo, *Informes de Coyuntura* No. 1, Instituto de Economia, Universidad Catolica de Chile.

[2] Milton Friedman, 'Have monetary policies failed?', *The American Economic Review, Papers and Proceedings* 62 (May, 1972) 14.

García, for Chile, is one of the few careful investigations of the common assertion that inflationary expectations are an important source of wage pressures. The results tend to corroborate that view.

Most of the studies in this volume were sponsored by the ODEPLAN— MIT project which was financed by the Ford Foundation through the Center for International Studies. Additional computational assistance for chapter 6 was supplied by the Development Research Group, Center for International Affairs, Harvard University. Chapter 5, written independently of the ODEPLAN—MIT project, was invited to appear in this volume because of the close association with the project of the authors and the subject matter. None of the supporting organizations bear any responsibility for the views expressed in the papers.

The editorial assistance of Claudia Cords is gratefully acknowledged.

R.S. Eckaus
P.N. Rosenstein-Rodan

CONTENTS

Preface

PART I. ESSAYS IN METHODOLOGY

PART II. ESTIMATES OF SHADOW PRICES

PART V. STUDIES OF THE EFFECTS OF INFLATION

PART I

ESSAYS IN METHODOLOGY

R.S. Eckaus, P.N. Rosenstein-Rodan (eds.), Analysis of development problems,
© *North-Holland Publishing Company*

FOREIGN EXCHANGE SHADOW PRICES *

A CRITICAL REVIEW OF CURRENT THEORIES

Edmar BACHA
University of Brasilia, Brasilia, D.F., Brasil

and

Lance TAYLOR
Harvard University, Cambridge, Mass., U.S.A.

I. Introduction

This is a review of currently accepted methods for calculating the shadow price of foreign exchange in developing countries. We wrote it in the field after spending some months dredging shadow price formulas from the literature, inventing new ones, rationalizing the whole lot in terms of foreign trade theory, and trying to decide which method was best for the shadow price estimates we were concurrently trying to make. We present a report on the theoretical side of this work here mainly in the utilitarian hope that we can save some future would-be shadow pricer all the essentially academic effort we put in, so that he can spend his time on more immediately productive activities. Also, we hope to stimulate further research about this important shadow price, so that future calculators can use methods more sophisticated than the ones herein—all of which fail to surpass the limitations of static, classic foreign trade theory. Generalization under dynamic and uncertain conditions and a more explicit treatment of the problems created by quantitative import restrictions are sorely needed. We hope that these improvements will be forthcoming in the near future.

Historically, most of the theoretical discussion about shadow prices has been among investment project analysts, and we too will concentrate on for-

* Thanks are due to Ernesto Fontaine, Arnold Harberger, and Francis Seton for commentary, and to Ana Maria Jul, Valentin Michelli and Diana Yañez for research help.

3

mulating rules for project selection. In many countries economists' investment rules have penetrated to the extent that even practical men are willing to use shadow prices in analyzing projects; the problem is that the practitioners usually are not quite sure how to estimate the shadow prices they want to use.

Unfortunately, economic theorists are not unanimous in their recommendations to the practical foreign exchange shadow pricer. They have pointed out three more or less distinct approaches to estimating the shadow exchange rate, which needn't necessarily give the same result. These will be described in the following sections of this paper. In summary, their basic recommendations are as follows:

(i) The foreign exchange shadow price should reflect the value in terms of welfare to the economy of an additional dollar (section II);

(ii) The shadow price should reflect the opportunity cost of a dollar in other uses (section III);

(iii) The shadow price should be the 'equilibrium' exchange rate – with varying assumptions about what the equilibrium rate may be (section IV).

After the descriptions of these approaches (and six shadow pricing rules they imply), we undertake in section V a critical analysis of their advantages and disadvantages in practical situations. Finally, we select the formula we consider to be appropriate for calculating 'the' foreign exchange shadow price, and describe how to use it in the investment decision.

II. The welfare approach

By this approach, we mean looking at an investment project as a perturbation to an economy already in equilibrium. One uses the equations describing the equilibrium to calculate whether or not some measure of economic welfare would increase after the 'small' displacement of the economy induced by the project. Usually this calculation reduces to an evaluation of the project's flows of inputs and outputs with a set of welfare-measuring shadow prices. If the balance from this shadow price accounting is positive, then the project is worth undertaking.[1]

A. Programming models

The natural extension of this evaluation technique is the attempt to deduce welfare-reflecting shadow prices from optimizing programming models. Al-

---

[1] An exposition of this line of thought in terms of a dynamic growth model appears in [ref. 182]. In this paper, we concentrate on static analysis.

though such price estimates have been made for a variety of countries, it is fair to say that they should be viewed with some scepticism. To explicate this, we have to consider in detail the distortions which lead us to try to revalue the exchange rate in the first place, and the problems these cause model-builders in specifying computable programs. Of the very many foreign trade distortions in developing countries, three seem to be particularly important:

(i) The existence of high tariffs and other restrictions on imports, not compensated by equivalent protection of exports. These are particularly important in countries exporting primary products where the mines or plantations are often so efficient that their exports are profitable even with an extremely overvalued local currency ('peso'). Other potential export industries cannot achieve such efficiency, but to give them adequate protection through subsidies or devaluation would be impossible in the short run because of the revenue loss this would entail the government.

(ii) A crucial bottleneck to economic growth created by rigid dependence on foreign-type goods in the economy. Especially for small countries, which cannot substitute many intermediate inputs and capital goods for the combined reasons of economies of scale in production and small domestic markets, lagging exports imply that additional foreign exchange would be extremely worthwhile in terms of a welfare function stressing economic growth.[2] The export lag may simply be due to the differential protection levels just mentioned, but low income elasticities of foreign demand and protectionism in the industrial countries should share some of the burden.

(iii) The reluctance of governments to devalue the currency in the face of domestic inflation. Devaluation is often undesirable because it increases quasi-rents and/or monopoly profits in the traditional export sector (often controlled by foreign-owned companies), and exerts upward pressure on prices of imported wage-goods.

To incorporate all of these effects into computable programming models is a difficult task. Linear models are ideally suited to evaluate (or exaggerate) the lack of substitutability implicit in point (ii), but cannot take into account the non-linear price-quantity interactions which would result from explicit consideration of the effects of tariffs and other trade restrictions on production levels mentioned in point (i). In addition, since existing tariffs necessarily enter into the input-output and productivity coefficients of the linear models, their rankings of sectors by 'comparative advantage' and implied costs of produc-

---

[2] An exhaustive theoretical discussion of this issue is given by McKinnon [ref. 132]. For empirical evidence on size of country vs. comparative success in import substituting intermediate and capital goods, see [ref. 1] and [ref. 180].

tion of foreign exchange are likely to be misleading in terms of world prices.[3] By extension, a model-produced foreign exchange shadow price becomes very difficult to interpret and accept.

One could in principle deal with the first type of problem by using convex programming models. However, in these models even ten sectors' worth of disaggregation stretches computational limits. This means that no global program can identify the three- and four-digit industries in which a country might have comparative advantage. Without the (often non-convex) production functions of these industries integrated into the models, the computer cannot produce a completely credible shadow price of foreign exchange.[4] Especially from nonlinear programming one can with good management derive indications about shadow prices, but certain results are impossible.

B. The Harberger—Schydlowsky—Fontaine shadow price [5]

If the general equilibrium programming models do not produce credible shadow prices (as is often the case in practice), then one has to fall back on analysis of the welfare effects of an investment project-perturbation in simpler models, based on the static, classic theory of foreign trade. In particular, if the economy has high import tariffs (with consequent overvaluation of the domestic peso), then displacement analysis of a small investment project generating exports or substituting (competitive) imports leads to a family of shadow price formulas proposed at various times by Harberger [refs. 89, 87], Schydlowsky [ref. 172] and Fontaine [ref. 69]. Here, we substitute the calculus for the authors' "little triangles" to derive these formulas in a simple monetary

---

[3] This same point will arise when we discuss Bruno-Krueger exchange rates, which also are based on domestic prices, in the next section. The solution there will be to value importable inputs at world prices in investment projects. One could in principle do the same thing with programming models, i.e. value their input—output coefficients in world terms by deflating domestic coefficients. However, this is empirically difficult and in addition fails to take into account the substitution among intermediate inputs which should result from availability of inputs at world prices, and by extension should influence the calculation of correct shadow prices.

[4] Actually, most models to date do even worse than the text hints. They do not formally include the possibility of electing levels of exports from the tens of sectors they typically include (although in many cases programmers do sensitivity analysis by varying exogenously specified export levels) so that the shadow prices which are produced lack allocational significance even in the sense of optimally selecting two-digit industries for export expansion.

[5] We are grateful to Ernesto Fontaine and Arnold Harberger for a number of friendly arguments about the contents of this subsection.

trade model, point out some correction terms which should be added, and then criticize the basic reasonableness of their consumers' surplus approach to measuring economic welfare under the assumed conditions.

For simplicity, we deal with a small three-sector economy with a floating exchange rate. The first sector competes with imports, the second sector exports, and the third sector produces goods which do not enter world trade under present commercial policy. If constant world prices for non-competitive intermediate imports, competitive imports and the export are respectively π_0, π_1, and π_2, domestic prices are given by

$$p_i = r(1+t_i)\,\pi_i = r\tau_i\pi_i \qquad (i = 0, 1)$$

$$p_2 = r(1+t_2)\pi_2 = r\varphi_2\pi_2 \,,$$

(1)

where the factors t_i stand for the effects of tariffs and subsidies in the transformation of world to domestic prices, $\tau_i = 1 + t_i$ is the "force" of tariff i, φ_2 is the force of the export tax or subsidy t_2, and r is the market exchange rate.

Assume perfect competition in the economy. The three industries produce their products z_i using perfectly mobile capital and labor as primary factor inputs according to the production functions

$$z_i = f^i(L_i, K_i)\,. \qquad (i = 1, 2, 3)$$

(2)

The usual full employment conditions are given by

$$\sum_i L_i = \bar{L}$$

(3)

$$\sum_i K_i = \bar{K}\,,$$

(4)

where $\bar{L}$ and $\bar{K}$ are the totals of labor and capital available to the economy.

We assume that each industry j uses the other industries' products as intermediate inputs according to fixed physical input-output coefficients a_{ij}, where $i = 0$ denotes non-competitive intermediate imported inputs, and $i = 1, 2, 3$ denote domestically produced or competitively imported intermediate inputs. We define "net prices" p_j^* as

$$p_j^* = p_j - \sum_{i=0}^{3} a_{ij} p_i \,. \qquad (j = 1, 2, 3)$$

(5)

The first-order production equilibrium conditions are then

$$p_i^* f_L^i = w \qquad\qquad (i = 1, 2, 3) \qquad\qquad (6)$$

$$p_i^* f_K^i = s, \qquad\qquad (i = 1, 2, 3) \qquad\qquad (7$$

where f_L^i and f_K^i are the derivatives of the production function in sector i with respect to labor and capital, w is the wage rate, and s is the rental on capital.

In the standard input-output matrix notation, the physical balance equations for domestic goods are

$$\begin{pmatrix} z_1^* \\ z_2^* \\ z_3^* \end{pmatrix} = (I - A) \begin{pmatrix} z_1 \\ z_2 \\ z_3 \end{pmatrix} = \begin{pmatrix} c_1 \\ c_2 \\ c_3 \end{pmatrix} - \begin{pmatrix} m_1 \\ 0 \\ 0 \end{pmatrix} + \begin{pmatrix} 0 \\ x_2 \\ 0 \end{pmatrix}, \qquad (8)$$

where A is the domestic input-output matrix, c_i are the sectoral final demand levels, m_1 is the level of competitive imports into sector 1, and x_2 is the level of exports of sector 2. Under the standard assumption of constant returns to scale, the net supply functions $z_i^*(p_0, p_1, p_2, p_3)$ will be homogeneous of degree zero in the prices $p_0 - p_3$.

In the foreign exchange market, the balance of payments in world prices is

$$\pi_2 x_2 = \pi_1 m_1 + \pi_0 a_0' z = \pi_1 m_1 + \pi_0 m_0 , \qquad\qquad (9)$$

where a_0' is the row vector of intermediate non-competitive import coefficients, z is the column vector of output levels, and m_0 is the total of non-competitive imports.

Define y as the sum of total final demand for goods and money valued at domestic prices,

$$y = \sum_i p_i c_i + c_M = p'c + c_M . \qquad\qquad (10)$$

The vector of demand levels c will depend on y, the vector of domestic prices $p' = p_1, p_2, p_3$, and the money supply M. Under the usual assumptions of individual utility maximization subject to a budget constraint, the demand functions for goods

$$c_i = c_i(p, y, M) \qquad\qquad (i = 1, 2, 3) \qquad\qquad (11a)$$

will be homogeneous of degree zero in prices and the supply of money. The demand for money

$$c_M = c_M(p, y, M) \tag{11b}$$

is usually assumed to be homogeneous of degree one.

Now suppose that the economy is in equilibrium, with the exchange rate and money supply chosen in such a way as to insure trade balance.[6] An opportunity to undertake a new export or import substitution project arises. The project, which we baptize $d\xi$, uses the primary factors in amounts $d\bar{K}$ and $d\bar{L}$, and produces a relatively small amount $d\Delta$ of foreign exchange. We are going to derive some expressions for the change $dy(=\Sigma_i p_i dc_i + dc_M = p'dc + dcM)$ induced in total final uses by the project $d\xi$, thereby making y into our measure of economic welfare.[7] In symbols, if $(dy/d\xi) \geqslant 0$, the project is worth undertaking.

To work out the effects of the project/perturbation on the economy, we begin by noting that the change in the balance of payments is

$$d\Delta + \pi_2 dx_2 = \pi_1 dm_1 + \pi_0 a_0' dz , \tag{12}$$

where

$$dm_1 = [\partial(c_1 - z_1^*)/\partial r] \, dr + [\partial(c_1 - z_1^*)/\partial M] \, dM \tag{13}$$

and

$$-dx_2 = [\partial(c_2 - z_2^*)/\partial r] \, dr + [\partial(c_2 - z_2^*)/\partial M] \, dM , \tag{14}$$

with the partial derivatives reflecting the *total* effects throughout the system of changes in r and M.[8]

---

[6] Note that all real variables in this model are determined by the prices, which in turn are determined by world prices as modified by tariffs, r and M. (The determination of the price of the domestic good, p_3, by the other variables can be demonstrated by applying Euler's theorem to the homogeneous-of-zero-degree-excess demand function $(c_3 - z_3^*)$, which must be equal to zero in equilibrium.) For further discussion of the type of full employment model developed here, see Krueger [ref. 119].

[7] Making total final uses into a welfare indicator is a practice which Fleming [ref. 67] introduced into international trade theory. An increase in y does correspond to an increase in social welfare when it is assumed that the economy is competitive, that increments in total welfare are the sum of increments in individual utility, and that the marginal utility of consumption of any good to any individual is measured by its price (i.e. individuals equate the marginal utility of each good to its price multiplied by the marginal utility of income, which is assumed to be equal for all persons). These are the classic postulates of consumers' surplus analysis, and total uses is the classic consumers' surplus welfare index.

[8] With given world prices, m and R determine the levels of the other variables in the model discussed here (see footnote 7). Hence, the derivatives in eqs. (13) and (14) reflect system-wide changes in the two 'independent' variables of the economy.

The equality between aggregate supply and demand in this economy can be written as

$$y = p'c + c_m$$
$$= p'z^* - p_0 a_0' z + M + p_0 m_0 + p_1 m_1 - p_2 x_2 . \tag{15}$$

The project makes two small real changes in the second line of eq. (15):

(i) It adds the (negative) amount $wd\overline{L} + sd\overline{K}$ of value added. This is easily shown to be equal to the change in value of final output $p'dz^* - p_0 a_0' dz = (p^*)'dz$ induced by the project's use of labor and capital previously used in the established industries.

(ii) It adds the amount $p_0 dm_0 + p_1 dm_1 - p_2 dx_2$, the domestic valuation of the trade changes produced by the foreign exchange $d\Delta$ generated by the project.

If the small change in the exchange rate and/or cash balances induced by the project is ignored, $dy/d\xi$ is therefore

$$\frac{dy}{d\xi} = \frac{p_0 dm_0 + p_1 dm_1 - p_2 dx_2}{d\Delta} \cdot \frac{d\Delta}{d\xi} + w\frac{d\overline{L}}{d\xi} + s\frac{d\overline{K}}{d\xi}$$

$$= \frac{p_0 dm_0 + p_1 dm_1 - p_2 dx_2}{\pi_0 dm_0 + \pi_1 dm_1 - \pi_2 dx_2} \cdot \frac{d\Delta}{d\xi} + w\frac{d\overline{L}}{d\xi} + s\frac{d\overline{K}}{d\xi} . \tag{16}$$

In this formula, the foreign exchange effect $(d\Delta/d\xi)$ of the project is revalued in terms of the domestic income it generates by the Harberger–Schydlowsky–Fontaine shadow price,

$$HSF_1 = \frac{r(\tau_0 \pi_0 dm_0 + \tau_1 \pi_1 dm_1 - \varphi_2 \pi_2 dx_2)}{\pi_0 dm_0 + \pi_1 dm_1 - \pi_2 dx_2} .$$

If there are n competitive import and m export goods, this shadow price formula obviously generalizes to

$$HSF_1 = \frac{r\left(\sum_{i=0}^{n} \tau_i \pi_i dm_i - \sum_{j=1}^{m} \varphi_j \pi_j dx_j\right)}{\sum_{i=0}^{n} \pi_i dm_i - \sum_{j=1}^{m} \pi_j dx_j} , \tag{17}$$

i.e. the weighted sum of domestic prices of traded goods, divided by a similar weighted sum of world prices, the weights in each case being the marginal changes in imports and exports induced by the project.[9]

This formula can be expressed in another, perhaps more elegant form if we assume that the money supply does not change and that non-competitive intermediate imports (and their differential dm_0) are negligible. Then from eqs. (12) – (14) we have that

$$dr = \frac{d\Delta}{\pi_1 \partial(c_1 - z_1^*)/\partial r + \pi_2 \partial(c_2 - z_2^*)/\partial r} . \tag{18}$$

The change in y induced by the additional foreign exchange is

$$dy = p_1 \frac{\partial(c_1 - z_1^*)}{\partial r} r \frac{dr}{r} + p_2 \frac{\partial(c_2 - z_2^*)}{\partial r} r \frac{dr}{r} .$$

If we substitute eq. (18) into this formula for dy, we get

$$dy = \frac{\dfrac{p_1 \partial(c_1 - z_1^*)}{\partial r} r + \dfrac{p_2 \partial(c_2 - z_2^*)}{\partial r} r}{\pi_1 \dfrac{\partial(c_1 - z_1^*)}{\partial r} r + \dfrac{\pi_2(c_2 - z_2^*)}{\partial r} r} .$$

With negligible non-competitive imports for intermediate uses, the world-price values of exports and imports become equal (see eq. (9)). Division of top and bottom of the above formula by this quantity, a sign reversal, and some cancellation of terms finally gives

$$\frac{dy}{d\xi} = \frac{-\tau_1 \eta_1 + \varphi_2 \epsilon_2}{-\eta_1 + \epsilon_2} r \frac{d\Delta}{d\xi} ,$$

where η_1 and ϵ_2 are the elasticities of excess demand for traded goods of the economy with respect to the exchange rate. If $u_i(v_j)$ are the shares of imports (exports) of sector $i(j)$ in total imports (exports), the above formula generalizes to

$$HSF_2 = \frac{-\displaystyle\sum_{i=1}^{n} \tau_i u_i \eta_i + \sum_{j=1}^{m} \varphi_j v_j \epsilon_j}{-\displaystyle\sum_{i=1}^{n} u_i \eta_i + \sum_{j=1}^{m} v_j \epsilon_j} r \tag{19}$$

[9] This version of the HSF shadow price is due to Harberger [ref. 89] and Schydlowsky [ref. 172]. Both implicity assume rigid export supply, i.e. $dx_j = 0$, all j.

which expresses the shadow price as a tariff-weighted average of the economy's foreign trade elasticities, multiplied by the market exchange rate.[10]

Aside from the obvious objection that all the terms assumed to be negligible need not be so in practice (this is especially unlikely for non-competitive intermediate imports), these formulas are not completely convincing on several grounds:

(i) They consider only marginal changes for *traded* goods in a situation where import quotas and prohibitions may play a much more important role in commercial policy than simple tariffs. In effect, HSF shadow prices are third best measures of the welfare increase created by an investment project — they take into account the distorting effects of tariffs, but not the possibility of initiating or expanding trade in goods subject to import controls. In an underdeveloped country which has for years promoted non-economical industries through prohibitive tariffs and prohibitions, this sort of calculation is unduly respectful of the established positions of completely protected infant industries which never grew up. A more complete evaluation of the trade prospects of an economy must take into account the abolition of prohibitions.[11]

(ii) The second objection to this type of analysis is classical: one has to assume a great deal about the state of the economy and about individual preferences to accept consumers' surplus as an adequate welfare index. The decision of course must be made in light of the specific situation, and also in light of the fact that consumers' surplus calculations at best consider *marginal* welfare changes. A shadow price taking into account the large welfare gains possible from opening the economy to trade seems more appropriate for many under-developed countries with highly restricted foreign trade sectors.[12]

(iii) Finally, the formula pays no attention to different cost structures among industries, and says nothing directly about comparative advantage. However, one main purpose of project selection broadly construed is the identification of sectors and industries having cost advantages which should be encouraged to expand. This necessarily involves looking closely at the supply

---

[10] This shadow price formula was proposed by Harberger [ref. 87] and Fontaine [ref. 69].

[11] Until recently in Chile, where we have some familiarity with trade statistics, 40% of importables in a 300-item sample taken by LAFTA were prohibited, and domestic prices on some prohibited imports like cars are 3–5 times the world level [ref. 8].

[12] In our discussion of the equilibrium exchange rate (below) we attempt to propose a shadow price which fills this need, and derive a formula to calculate such a price under a simple set of assumptions about the foreign exchange market. The formula (although not its rationale) turns out to be similar to eq. (19), except that we propose a geometric average of 'tariffs' and interpret the latter to mean average differences between world or domestic prices for some industry, regardless of whether the price differences result from ad valorem tariffs or from prohibitions and other such restrictions.

side of the economy in a way the demand-oriented HSF formula does not permit. Ways of doing this are discussed in the following section.

III. Costs of producing foreign exchange

The great advantage of analyzing supply in detail is that individual industries and investment projects can be compared and ranked in terms of their costs of producing foreign exchange. The current range of such costs is a valuable tool for investment analysis, especially in countries long insulated from world prices where foreign exchange effects are not often considered by the people who propose projects.

As with analysis of the last section, the problem of electing a cost base arises in the comparison of the proposals for ranking industries by 'comparative advantage' to be presented in this section. Basically, there are two approaches — the use of domestic costs (as Bruno [ref. 33] in his formalization of long-standing Israeli practice and Krueger [ref. 120] apparently recommend) and the use of costs measured in terms of world prices (as recommended in one variant by Balassa and Schudlowsky [ref. 11] Hufbauer [ref. 17] and others, and in another variant by Little and Mirrlees [ref. 128]). We treat these proposals in order.

A. Bruno–Krueger exchange rates

Bruno–Krueger (BK) rates follow from the production-side description of the economy used to derive the Harberger–Schydlowsky–Fontaine formula. Specifically, we assume that supply is determined by eqs. (2)–(7), except that there are n sectors instead of three. We also assume that domestic prices are given (without asking from whence they come) for the purpose of analyzing an entrepreneur's choice between production for domestic uses and production for export.

If we suppose perfect competition and the existence of linear homogeneous production functions, application of Euler's theorem gives the following equations for the exhaustion of value added by factor payments:

$$p_i^* z_i = p_i^* f_L^i L_i + p_i^* f_K^i K_i = w L_i + s K_i \, . \qquad (i = 1, 2, \ldots, n)$$

Dividing this equation by z_i gives

$$p_i^* = w l_i + s k_i \, , \qquad\qquad (i = 1, 2, \ldots, n) \qquad (20)$$

where l_i and k_i are the labor-output and capital-output ratios for sector i. If we let l and k be the vectors of these sectoral ratios, eqs. (20) can then be written using previously defined notation as

$$p'(I-A) - p_0 a_0' = wl' + sk' , \tag{21}$$

or

$$p' = p_0 a_0' (I-A)^{-1} + (wl' + sk')(I-A)^{-1} , \tag{22}$$

which expresses domestic goods prices in terms of factor costs.

Now suppose that a producer in sector i can sell his product abroad and receive $r\pi_i$ pesos, where r is the market exchange rate. This sale will be profitable if $r\pi_i \geqslant p_i$ or $r\pi_i \geqslant p'h_i$, where h_i is the 'unit' vector with unity as its ith coordinate, and all other coordinates equal to zero.

Using eq. (22) this condition becomes

$$r\pi_i \geqslant p_0 a_0'(I-A)^{-1} + (wl' + sk')(I-A)^{-1} \cdot h_i$$

or in modified form (with the additional assumption that the producer 'should not' be penalized by tariffs on non-competitive intermediate inputs, so $p_0 = r\pi_0$),

$$\frac{(wl' + sk')(I-A)^{-1} h_i}{\pi_i - \pi_0 a_0'(I-A)^{-1} h_i} < r . \tag{23}$$

Thus, the export sale will be profitable if the direct-and-indirect domestic value added in sector i is no greater than the revenue from the sale, net of direct-and-indirect non-competitive intermediate import requirements for domestic production.

The left side of eq. (23) is the Bruno–Krueger exchange rate for sector i. This formula ranks industries in the order in which they would enter into exportation as the exchange rate varies; the same sort of ranking can also be made for import substitution industries.

In a disequilibrium 'real world' economy, BK rates provide quite a natural method to rank investment projects, as is described very clearly by Bruno imself [ref. 33]. At the same time, the range of rates which results from existing industries and recent investment projects (both in export and import substitution) in principle brackets a 'planners' exchange rate, useful for valueing foreign exchange flows in present value calculations. In economies with overvalued currencies, BK costs of import substitution will typically be significantly above the corresponding export costs.[13] One might postulate

---

[13] See [ref. 8] for the Chilean estimates and Krueger's paper [ref. 120] for estimates for Turkey.

that a reasonable "planners" rate would lie somewhere between average export and import substitution rates. We discuss below how reasonable this supposition is.

B. Rates of effective protection

Balassa and Schydlowsky [ref. 11] pointed out most forcefully that the Bruno–Krueger rankings as presented here unduly penalize intermediate input-using industries by valuing *domestically* produced intermediate inputs at domestic prices. Often these inputs can be imported at far less cost than they can be produced domestically. Hence, charging industries for inputs at domestic prices can give estimates of costs of producing foreign exchange which are biased upwards. Because of this bias, an unmodified BK ranking of industries in terms of static comparative advantage can be misleading.

One way to overcome this bias is through use of BK rankings in which untraded but tradeable goods are switched from domestic costs in the numerator of eq. (23) to foreign costs in the denominator. Another, similar approach is to use effective protection (EP) calculations, which compare the value added of a domestic industry to what its value added 'would be' if importable intermediate inputs were available domestically at world prices. Since the number of variant rates of effective protection in the literature is now enormous, it is not so clear just which concept is most appropriate for the problem at hand. The approach we discuss here loosely follows Ethier [ref. 61], who gives the best theoretical discussion of effective protection.

We assume that input-output coefficients are *fixed* and express our shadow price as the ratio

$$H_j = p^*/\rho_j^* , \tag{24}$$

where the net prices are defined as

$$p_j^* = p_j - \sum_{i=0}^{n} a_{ij} p_i \tag{25}$$

and

$$\rho_j^* = \rho_j - \sum_{i=0}^{n} a_{ij} \rho_i , \tag{26}$$

and the ρ_j's are the prices which would rule under free trade conditions in the economy.

Note the following about these formulas:

(i) Non-competitive imports are included separately as a cost item in calculating net prices. In practice, these should be treated differently from competitive imports if possible, since they typically make up a significant proportion of costs and their tariffs (or scarcity prices) are often different from those of competitive imports.

(ii) Non-traded goods should be included in the formulas. This means that one must infer what relative prices of these goods 'would be' under free trade. A crude but practical way of doing this is to assume (a) that the free trade price in domestic terms of tradeable good i is given by the quantity $\rho_i = r^* \pi_i$, where π_i is the dollar world price of good i[14] and r^* is the equilibrium exchange rate discussed in the next section, and (b) that $\rho_i = p_i$ for non-tradeable goods. This ignores price shifts among non-tradeable goods, but at least takes into account the fact that under most circumstances trade liberation would be accompanied by policies directing its effect into exchange rate increases and *not* real wage reductions. Since most non-tradeable goods are labor-intensive and are usually not intensive users of traded intermediate inputs, assuming that their prices stay constant under trade liberation may not be inappropriate. (Using general equilibrium models, one could of course infer what the free-trade prices of all goods would be, using estimates of production and demand functions to aid the process. Space limitations prevent a full discussion here.)

(iii) As indicated above, these calculations are based on the assumption of fixed input-output coefficients. As Ethier shows, variable coefficients require the construction of a completely new system of shadow prices to evaluate the resource allocation implications of trade liberation. In practice, this is impossible, but one must realize that if input-output coefficients really are variable, then the usual effective protection calculations are subject to biases of unknown direction and magnitude.

Subject to these reservations, the ratio H_j can be used to rank industries and/or projects [15] according to their probable changes in value added after

---

[14] Usually, effective tariff calculators assume that domestic prices p_i only differ from world prices π_i by the factor $r(i + t_i)$, where t_i is the nominal ad valorem tariff on good *i*. In practice, this is rarely true, as Lewis and Guisinger [ref. 124] exemplify for Pakistan and we demonstrate for Chile in [ref. 8]. However, the concept of valuing inputs alternatively at domestic and world prices retains its validity, even though the prices are not related through discernible tariff rates.

[15] Note that the well-known problems with intermediate input- and factor-substitution do not loom so large in calculating effective tariffs of investment projects, since in practice one usually deals with at most a few specified technical alternatives in terms of equipment, rather than an exploration of the whole production function. From the underdeveloped buyer's point of view at least, fixed coefficients production models are realistic.

trade liberation. According to this criterion, a project is the better, the lower is its ratio H_j (i.e. the lower is the level of effective protection the project receives). Of course, there still remains the problem of evaluating a cut-off ratio. This will be discussed in the next two sections, but note here that the methods analogous to those suggested in connection with BK rate can be applied, i.e. the choice of the cut-off ratio on the basis of the range of levels of effective protection of imports and effective subsidization of exports observed in the economy. In analog to Bruno–Krueger, import substitution projects will typically have a much higher H_j than export projects; hence the suggestion that the cut-off ratio be put somewhere in the "middle" of these two ranges of rates.

C. The use of world prices in project analysis

Implicit in the use of EP calculations in project evaluation is the need for something like a foreign exchange shadow price, i.e. a cut-off ratio for criterion (24) or else a pure shadow price to multiply the world prices of the flows of tradeable goods in a present value calculation. In effect, the shadow price is used to revalue the flows of tradeables in domestic terms, to correct for the over-valued domestic currency.

In [ref. 128] Little and Mirrlees propose the opposite approach – using uncorrected world prices for tradeable goods and reducing (usually) the prices of non-tradeable goods to their estimated free trade levels. Taken at face value, this recommendation is practically impossible, since separate revaluations of all domestic goods in world terms would involve enormous computation. Little and Mirrlees finesse this problem by proposing a two-step shadow price calculation:

(i) Revaluation of wide ranges of domestic goods (including the consumption basket of labor) in terms of world prices by an estimate of the difference between world and domestic prices called the standard conversion factor. This quantity can be calculated as an economy-wide average effective rate of protection, for example.

(ii) A further revaluation of the cost of labor (as represented by its consumption basket) to take into account dualism within the economy.

In this guise, their procedure resembles using EP calculations in project evaluation, i.e., using world prices multiplied by a shadow exchange rate to evaluate tradeable goods, with possible additional revaluations of certain non-tradeable inputs such as labor. The main difference between the two approaches are: (i) one should not take the entire observed difference between world and domestic price levels as a measure of the shadow exchange rate or standard conversion factor — in fact in the next section we will recommend using rather less than the entire difference to take into account the compensating rise of the exchange rate (the magnitude of which will depend on demand and supply elasticities of the economy) which would accompany the abolition of protection — and (ii) Little—Mirrlees develop an elaborate theoretical model to justify their formula for the shadow price of labor, which we do not attempt. In many developing countries, the price distortions between tradeable and non-tradeable goods caused by tariffs and other trade restrictions appear to be worse than distortions within the non-tradeable sector caused by surplus labor, and we prefer to concentrate our attention on the former problem. For these countries, at least, we would recommend the use of shadow exchange rates in project evaluation, rather than the Little—Mirrlees procedure. The shadow exchange rate not only is less demanding in terms of the available data, but also correctly stresses external strangulation and the responses of economies to it as principal development constraints in much of the third world.

IV. Equilibrium and parity exchange rates

In the preceding section, we did not discuss the exchange rate per se, but it is clear that some sort of equilibrium rate is implicit in all the project ranking rules presented, i.e. the Bruno—Krueger, effective protection, and the Little—Mirrlees rankings all require some cutoff point, shadow price of foreign exchange, or standard conversion factor in the final decision about whether or not to undertake an investment project. We submit that the appropriate shadow price for these purposes is the equilibrium (free trade) exchange rate, and discuss its derivation in this section.

We define the exchange rate in the usual way — as the price of domestic currency in terms of foreign currency — and assume that it is determined in a floating foreign exchange market. Completeness would require the explicit incorporation of monetary variables in the models which follow. However, for our purposes it is simpler to keep money in the background and operate with the Robinson—Metzler model [refs. 167, 139] of the foreign exchange market. There is, fortunately, not much loss of generality in using the traditional model in place of alternative workable formulations. Kemp [ref. 110] criticized the Robinson—Metzler model, arguing that its assumption of no cross-price effects in the excess demand functions is untenable except in strictly defined partial equilibrium terms. However, Negishi [ref. 142] recently demonstrated in a general equilibrium context that the assumptions implicit in the Robinson—Metzler model are not necessarily more strict than those explicitly involved in

Kemp's monetary models (positive cross-price effects, in particular). Hence, continued use of the Robinson—Metzler model is justified by its simplicity.

In the following, we define the equilibrium exchange rate as that which prevails in a floating foreign exchange market when all import restrictions and export subsidies are removed. In subsection A, under the simplifying assumption of constant elasticity demand and supply curves, we derive an easily computable formula for this rate in the case of one import good, one export good and no export subsidies. (The appropriate generalization of this formula to the multisectoral case is also indicated.)

Another 'equilibrium' exchange rate which has many times been represented as useful in investment project analysis is the parity rate. In sub-section B, we discuss two variant parity rates; these two were chosen from the many in the literature since they have some relevance to recent attempts by the UN Economic Commission for Latin America (ECLA) to measure parity among South American countries.

The use of equilibrium exchange rates in project evaluation is discussed in section V.

A. The equilibrium (without tariff) exchange rate [16]

Since we are now interested in describing equilibrium in the foreign exchange market, we leave the elaborate specification of the production side of the economy of sections II and III, and work with demand and supply functions, accepting the Robinson—Metzler assumption that these functions for each good depend only on the good's own price. The model based on this hypothesis involves the following equations:
Balance of trade in foreign currency,

$$\pi_x x_d + \Delta = \pi_m m_s ; \tag{27}$$

Equality between export demand and supply functions,

$$x_d(\pi_x) = x_s(p_x) ; \tag{28}$$

Equality between import supply and demand functions

$$m_s(\pi_m) = m_d(p_m) ; \tag{29}$$

[16] The formula of this section was first worked out in 1968 and later published in ref. [7]. We are grateful to Francis Seton for suggesting a number of shortcuts to the original derivation, and also wish to point out that after this paper was finished it came to our attention that Bela Balassa has proposed a rather similar formula in a forthcoming book of effective protection studies.

Definition of domestic price of exports

$$p_x = \pi_x r ; \tag{30}$$

Definition of domestic price of imports;

$$p_m = \pi_m r \tau ; \tag{31}$$

where π_x is foreign price of exports; x_d, export demand; Δ, balance of trade deficit; π_m, foreign price of imports; m_s, import supply; x_s, export supply; m_d, import demand; p_x, domestic price of exports; r, market exchange rate; p_m, domestic price of imports; and τ, force of the ad valorem tariff equivalent to all protection given imports (= 1 + equivalent tariff[17]).

Our problem is to determine the revaluation in the exchange rate needed to re-establish the preexistent balance of trade when trade restrictions are removed.

Take total log differentials in the system $(27)-(31)$, to obtain, respectively;

$$(\mathrm{d}\pi_x/\pi_x + \mathrm{d}x_d/x_d)D = \mathrm{d}\pi_m/\pi_m + \mathrm{d}m_s/m_s \tag{32}$$

$$\eta_x(\mathrm{d}\pi_x/\pi_x) = \epsilon_x(\mathrm{d}p_x/p_x) \tag{33}$$

$$\epsilon_m(\mathrm{d}\pi_m/\pi_m) = \eta_m(\mathrm{d}p_m/p_m) \tag{34}$$

$$\mathrm{d}p_x/p_x = \mathrm{d}\pi_x/\pi_x + \mathrm{d}r/r \tag{35}$$

$$\mathrm{d}p_m/p_m = \mathrm{d}\pi_m/\pi_m + \mathrm{d}r/r + \mathrm{d}\tau/\tau , \tag{36}$$

where the trade deficit appears as the initial ratio between exports and imports, $D = \pi_x x/\pi_m m$; and where η_x = price elasticity of export demand; ϵ_x = price elasticity of export supply; η_m = price elasticity of import demand; and ϵ_m = price elasticity of import supply.

After successive substitution among eqs. $(32)-(36)$, we derive the fol-

---

[17] The usual microeconomic assumption that all excess demand functions are homogeneous of degree zero in all prices (and hence in money income) is implicit in the model $(27)-(31)$. Thus, despite its appearance, the model *is* specified in real terms, with all prices deflated by an appropriate general price index. For example, we could write eq. (30) as

$$p'_x/H = (\pi'_x/F) r' (F/H) ,$$

where a prime denotes money prices and H and F are the price indices in the home and foreign countries respectively. The problem of selection of price indices is discussed below in connection with parity exchange rates.

lowing differential equation relating the change in the exchange rate to the tariff change:

$$dr/r = -(d\tau/\tau)(1/1-q),$$
(37)

where

$$q = D(1+\eta_x)\,\epsilon_x(\epsilon_m - \eta_m)/(1+\epsilon_m)\,\eta_m(\eta_x - \epsilon_x).$$
(38)

Rearranging eq. (37) and integrating (under an approximate assumption of constant elasticities), we obtain after taking antilogs:

$$k = r^{(1-q)}\tau,$$
(39)

where k is a constant of integration. When τ is set to one in eq. (39), we find k as a function of r^*, the zero tariff exchange rate:

$$k = r^{*(1-q)}.$$
(40)

Substituting this expression into eq. (39), we get

$$r^* = r\tau^{1/(1-q)}$$
(41)

as our expression for the equilibrium exchange rate.

To apply this formula in practice, one would use an average of the difference between world and domestic prices to take into account all tariffs, restrictions, and prohibitions in estimating the force of the equivalent ad valorem tariff τ. Similarly, the elasticities entering into q should be interpreted as referring to volume indices of imports and exports, including goods which would enter into the home country's trade as the exchange rate changes.

In the case of a small country, the expression for q can easily be simplified and generalized to many sectors. Simplifying first, if the foreign supply of imports is perfectly elastic ($\epsilon_m = \infty$), then:

$$\lim_{\epsilon_m \to \infty} q = (1+\eta_x)\,\epsilon_x/(\eta_x - \epsilon_x)\,\eta_m.$$
(42)

If the foreign demand for exports is also perfectly elastic ($\eta_x = \infty$), then:

$$\lim_{\eta_x, \epsilon_m \to \infty} q = D\epsilon_x/\eta_m.$$
(43)

If the foreign offer curve is perfectly elastic and, in addition, $D = 1$, then the exponent $1/(1-q)$ is the familiar ratio $\eta_m/(\epsilon_x + \eta_m)$.

These formulas generalize to many sectors for a small country in the following way:

$$r^* = r\Pi_i \varphi_i^{(Dv_i\epsilon_i^x/\beta)} \Pi_i \tau_i^{(-u_i\eta_i^m/\beta)}$$

where

$$\beta = D \sum_i v_i \epsilon_i^x - \sum_i u_i \eta_i^m \, ,$$

and the large Π's are product signs and the other notation is as in eq. (19). In the multi-sectoral case, therefore, the equilibrium exchange rate reduces to a weighted geometric mean of tariffs and subsidies multiplied by the current exchange rate, the weights being related to import and export elasticities and shares of current imports and exports in total trade.

B. Parity exchange rates

Purchasing power parity exchange rates are alternatively defined as:
  (i) the exchange rate between two currencies which equates the market value of a representative basket of final goods in the two countries; or
  (ii) the rate which re-establishes the real value of country's official exchange rate as measured from a given base year by use of a general price index.

We consider definition (i) first. This rate is generally used for international comparisons of 'welfare' but also is found in project analyses as a correction for distortion in the official exchange rate caused by import restrictions and domestic inflation.

For simplicity, assume that a representative basket of final goods has only three components: an exportable, an importable, and a home good; and that transport costs, export subsidies, domestic commercialization rates and domestic taxes are all zero. We can then define a parity exchange rate as the following weighted geometric average:

$$r_p = (p_x/\pi_x)^\alpha (p_m/\pi_m)^\gamma (p_d/\pi_d)^{1-\alpha-\gamma} \, , \tag{44}$$

where r_p is the parity rate; the p's and π's are the prices of exportables, importables and home goods (from the home country's point of view) in the home country and foreign country respectively; and α and γ are expenditure weights.[18]

---

[18] Generally, the weights are those of the home country (for a Laspeyres index), the foreign country (a Paasche index), or something in between. ECLA is fond of using a geometric mean of the countries' weights to construct indices based on 'average international' market baskets.

To keep to essentials, assume away all but tariff-induced price distortions, and let:

$$p_x = (\pi_x/\tau_x)r$$

$$p_m = \pi_m \tau_m r$$

$$p_d = \pi_d g r \, ,$$

where the τ's are the forces of tariffs in the home and foreign countries; r is the official exchange rate; and g is an ad hoc factor accounting for international differences in prices of non-traded goods.

Applying these equations to the definition of the parity rate, we obtain

$$r_p = r \tau_x^{-\alpha} \tau_m^{\gamma} g^{1-\alpha-\gamma} \, . \tag{45}$$

As all tourists know intuitively and Balassa shows empirically [ref. 10] g is inversely related to per capita income.[19] Hence, if the foreign country is industrialized and the home country is underdeveloped, g will be smaller than one. Moreover, if the home country is industrialising via protectionism while the foreign country is, say, a member of the industrial Atlantic community, τ_x will be much nearer unity than τ_m. Finally, in these comparisons it will usually also be true that domestic consumption of the exportable good is negligible. Thus (particularly if the comparisons are made with the weights of the developing country), the formula for the parity exchange rate reduces to:

$$r_p = r \tau_m^{\alpha} g^{1-\gamma} \, . \tag{46}$$

In words, the relationship between the parity and the official exchange rate of an underdeveloped country is mostly a function of the height of its tariffs on importable goods and the cheapness of its non-traded goods.

In the studies by ECLA, where binary comparisons between Latin-American countries and the U.S.A. are made [refs. 190, 191], the effects of low wages in cheapening domestic goods dominate the high tariffs in all countries except Venezuela. As a consequence, Latin countries have currencies stronger in parity than official terms, and their dollar national incomes are correspondingly higher. This is an interesting result. It can, for example, be used to salve the consciences of industrial countries and to make underdeveloped countries feel better about their misery. However, beyond such international compari-

[19] The standard explanation for this finding is the following: non-traded goods are typically labor-intensive, so their low prices in developing countries simply reflect low domestic wage levels. If, in addition, the elasticity of substitution in the non-traded sector is low, more intensive use of capital cannot counteract high developed country wage levels. Hence, the observed fall of g with per capita income.

sons of 'welfare' parity exchange rates find little use. In particular, contrasting with the equilibrium exchange rate, the parity rate is devoid of allocational implications. Hence, we would strongly recommend that its use as a correction for tariff- and inflation-induced distortions in the official exchange rate be discontinued. The appropriate correction in these cases is given by the formula for the equilibrium exchange rate, whose computation offers no more difficulties than the misused parity rates.

According to the second interpretation, the parity exchange rate re-establishes the real value of a country's official exchange rate as measured from a given base year by use of an over-all price index.

In order to assess how appropriate this revaluation procedure is, we will use a modified form of our foreign exchange market model to derive a differential expression for the change in the market clearing exchange rate when prices and exogenous shift terms vary, but when import tariffs and export subsidies stay constant (perhaps at zero level). Only the small country case is analyzed here, although the conclusions apply as well to countries with monopoly power in trade.

At time v, the balance of payments is

$$B(v) = \pi_x(v) x_s(v) + \Delta(v) - \pi_m(v) m_d(v) .$$

The excess demand functions are (as usual) homogeneous of degree zero in all prices. We also assume that these functions depend on a shift variable b which reflects the impact of overall factor growth, technological progress, taste shifts, etc.:

$$x_s = x_s(p_x(v)/H(v), b(v))$$

$$m_d = m_d(p_m(v)/H(v), b(v)) ,$$

where H is a general domestic price index.

At any given time, domestic prices are related to world prices via the constant rates of tax and subsidy:

$$p_x = r(v) \pi_x(v) \varphi_x(0)$$

$$p_m = r(v) \pi_m(v) \tau_m(0) ,$$

where the world prices π_x and π_m for a small country are functions only of time (v).

Taking logarithmic derivatives with respect to time in the above equations, imposing d log $B/dv = 0$, and solving for d log r/dv ($= r''$), we obtain

$$r'' = H'' + \frac{(1+\eta_m)\pi_m'' - (1+\epsilon_x)D\pi_x'' - (D\alpha - \beta) b'' - (1-D) \Delta''}{D\epsilon_x - \eta_m} , \tag{47}$$

where α and β are the elasticities of export supply and import demand with respect to the shift variable b.

This is a general expression from which necessary conditions for parity adjustment of the type

$$r'' = H'' - F''$$

can be derived, where F'' is the rate of foreign inflation. The first condition is that the world prices of the tradeable goods change at the same rate,

$$\pi_x'' = \pi_m'' = F'' .$$

A second condition is that factor augmentation, technical progress, and other trend variables have a neutral effect on the trade balance (so that $D\alpha = \beta$). Further, if $D \neq 1$, then invariance of capital movements ($\Delta'' = 0$) and a stable foreign price level ($F'' = 0$) are required conditions for a parity-type adjustment of the exchange rate.

Once these rather stringent conditions are satisfied, the choice of an appropriate price index becomes largely a question of taste: a wholesale price index seems more relevant for supply decisions and capital goods demand, whereas a consumer price index has more meaning as a determinant of consumption goods demand. Hence, the excess demand functions (equal to domestic demand minus domestic supply) would involve both indexes in their arguments. In practice, a decision between the two indexes must in part be based on their reliability in particular cases.

Finally, note that the search for a 'normal' base year in the recent history of a country for parity calculations is nearly always fruitless. This means that there is no way of avoiding the work involved in calculating the equilibrium exchange rate for at least one year. Starting from this basis, the equilibrium rate in succeeding years can be computed with price indexes if the conditions specified above are satisfied.

V. Comparisons of the methods and a recommended evaluation rule

The review of method for calculating the shadow price of foreign exchange is complete. We now evaluate their relative usefulness in practical applications.

In the best of all possible worlds, there is no doubt which method for calculating shadow prices we would elect — the programming models. For intangible but compelling reasons of analytical elegance and the possibility of computing shadow prices in a technologically feasible future instead of inferring them from a statistically corrupted past, the programming approach is undeniably attractive. The trouble is that the calculation of useful shadow prices from models is also a Holy Grail, for the dual of any estimable and computable macroeconomic program is often much closer to being a mathematical arte-fact than a reflection of the real resource trade-offs within the economy. It seems clear to us that the programming models should continue to be devel-oped, for reasons of pedagogy, consistent prediction and future possibilities, but that the shadow prices they now produce should at best be taken as indic-ative and on the average not believed.[20]

For different reasons, we also have little faith in the Harberger—Schyd-lowsky—Fontaine shadow prices, which measure the effect of a foreign ex-change producing project on national income in domestic prices. These for-mulas are phrased in terms of changes in imports and exports of *currently traded* goods only, and accept the tariffs on these goods as the prices to be used in evaluating the consumers' surplus generated by an investment project. In our opinion, acceptance of import prohibitions as given, and the use of consumers' surplus welfare measures for developing countries where more often than not great welfare gains are potentially feasible through opening the tradeable goods sector to the world emphasize the wrong things. A more basic approach is to design a shadow price which takes into account the possi-bility of trade liberation. This is our basis for proposing below the use of an equilibrium exchange rate. (Note that such rates can be derived under a vari-ety of assumptions. For this paper we chose the simplest ones, which lead to a formula similar to the HSF shadow price. In some sense this is coincidence, for the conceptual bases of the two rates are different, and so are the methods of measurement of 'equivalent tariffs' which must be used in calculating shadow prices from the two formulas.)

The two cost-oriented methods are better guides to resource allocation than the welfare-oriented programming and HSF approaches. Both Bruno—

---

[20] To review briefly our argument in section II, we believe that calculation of shadow prices of foreign exchange by programming models is particularly difficult for the fol-lowing reasons: (i) The functional relationships are always estimated in tariff-distorted domestic prices, and hence cannot possibly give rise to shadow prices 'optimal' in terms of world prices. (There is of course no reason why world market prices should be optimal either, from the point of view of maximizing a planner's preference functional, but they *do* represent opportunity costs usually ignored in programming models.) (ii) In a long run, many substitution possibilities exist which are usually ignored by at least linear models, which in effect cannot take into account most of the non-linear functional relationships at the heart of international trade theory. (iii) Computable models cannot deal with the disaggregation and non-convexities inherent in a detailed treatment of the industries in which a country might have comparative advantage; hence the model's prices cannot reflect a resource allocation optimized in detail among these foreign-exchange generating activities.

Krueger exchange rates and effective tariffs rank industrial processes and activities according to export- or import-competing potential. The unmodified BK method amounts to computing the exchange rate at which a project becomes competitive in the world market if its domestic material inputs are valued in domestic prices. The effective tariff of a project indicates the exchange rate at which the project becomes competitive if all tradeable material inputs into the project are valued at world prices.

However, neither method answers the question whether or not we should accept a project which in order to become competitive requires an exchange rate $x\%$ higher than the market rate (where competitiveness can be understood in either the BK or EP sense). The methods themselves only give rankings of projects or industries, but one could presumably use the 'middle' of this range (typically located between the costs of recent export- and import-substitution projects) as the cut-off rate. However, this rate has no allocational significance, since it says nothing about which projects would be profitable if the trade restrictions distorting the exchange rate were really removed.

We now would like to suggest that a project should be accepted if the exchange rate which makes it competitive in the world market is not larger than the equilibrium exchange rate of the economy.[21] Competitiveness should be understood in the EP sense (i.e. all *tradeable* project inputs and products would be valued at world prices) because a BK evaluation without modification to take into account the possibility of importing tradeable inputs produced inefficiently at home punishes a project which has to use these inputs.[22]

This recommendation is fundamentally based on the key theorem in welfare economics calling for equality between world and domestic relative prices to guarantee a first best equilibrium position. We accept this equilibrium as a goal and recommend a rule for project evaluation which will lead to it. Specifically, the rule is that from now on a necessary condition for the approval of

[21] An alternative would be to accept the project if its competitive exchange rate did not exceed the Harberger–Schydlowsky–Fontaine shadow price. However, as stressed above, the HSF price ignores the effects of non-tariff trade restrictions on the exchange rate. Further, if estimated in form (17) without considering export changes (as would usually be done), the HSF shadow price would be unduly high as compared to the equilibrium rate.

[22] This is not to say that the unmodified Bruno–Krueger formula should be discarded out-of-hand as a resource allocation device. In many countries with overvalued currencies, there is general agreement that many industries are more costly than the import alternative and that this is a misallocation of resources. However, this consciousness is often based on valuation of tradeable inputs at domestic prices, not at 'extraneous' import prices. Hence, on tactical grounds, it is often preferable to argue against a project in BK terms. Fortunately, most projects which are rejected by effective protection calculations are even more strongly rejected by the BK test with its (usually) higher valuation of tradeable inputs.

an investment project is that the product of its required effective tariff and
the market exchange rate should not be greater than the equilibrium exchange
rate of the economy (calculated in terms of volume indices of importables and
exportables, as indicated in section IV). Eventually, as old capital wears out,
all activities in operation in the economy will have passed this test. Thus, no
resource reallocation would occur if at this point in time tariffs and other trade
restrictions were abolished and the exchange rate were allowed to adjust. In
other words, if domestic distortions and external effects were non-existent,
optimal resource allocation would have been achieved throughout the economy [23] (aside from possible imposition of optimal tariffs on certain goods,
which could be taken into account [24]). Given that both domestic distortions
and external effects seem to be important in any underdeveloped country,
carefully selected exceptions to the above rule should be made.

Naturally, our rule can be couched in terms more familiar to the project
analyst, such as the following: Consider for approval only those projects
having a positive present value in domestic currency (at a preassigned interest
rate which should also be chosen 'optimally')[25] when the dollar prices of its
tradeable outputs and inputs are converted into domestic currency by use of
equilibrium exchange rates (which may or may not vary in the life of the project). In some cases, additional revaluations of the prices of some non-tradeable
inputs may be deemed necessary.

From time to time, the equilibrium exchange rate should be recalculated,
either on the basis of the relevant elasticities and tariffs, or at least through the
use of parity type calculations based on the movement of the official exchange
rate and domestic and world price indices. Updating the equilibrium exchange

---

[23] Ideally, one would want to calculate a shadow price changing over future time in line
with the retirement of old capital and the (presumably) gradual reduction of tariffs and
other trade restrictions. In practice, this would amount to solving a rather complicated
programming problem, and for the reasons given above, we doubt that this could be undertaken. Because of this, we propose our more ad hoc pseudo-dynamic project evaluation
rule.

[24] Optimum resource allocation from a national point of view will generally require that
optimum tariffs be imposed on certain goods. In practice, one way to deal with this problem is always to use the small country formula in calculating the equilibrium exchange
rate. In some developing countries, this will require exclusion from the formula of those
products in which the country has some monopoly power (e.g. coffee in Brazil). The implicit assumption is that the optimum exchange rate system for these countries is dual:
the exchange rate for exports with price-inelastic demand is the current one, and the rate
for all other exports and all imports is the equilibrium rate.

[25] The literature on selecting an 'optimal' rate of interest is even larger than that on foreign
exchange shadow prices. A good summary is given by Henderson [ref. 93] while Little and
Mirrlees [ref. 128] and Marglin [ref. 134] present theoretical models of some applicability
to developing countries.

rate in this way would appear to be the only legitimate use of parity calcula-tions in project analysis.[26] As argued above, the use of parity rates as equilib-rium rates for project selection is a mistake, and the practice should be discon-tinued.

[26] This statement must be qualified by noting that the conditions under which parity type adjustments of the exchange rate are appropriate are very strict. Cases may be frequent where net capital movements are large and fluctuate widely, and/or where dollar prices of tradeables do not vary according to available foreign price indices. Under these conditions, one should try to estimate a new 'market clearing' exchange rate according to the general formula (47).

R.S. Eckaus, P.N. Rosenstein-Rodan (eds.), Analysis of development problems,
© North-Holland Publishing Company

TWO GENERALIZATIONS OF DISCOUNTING[*]

Lance TAYLOR
Harvard University, Cambridge, Mass., U.S.A.

I. Introduction

By now, it is certainly well established that discounting the flows of output
resulting from an investment project is the unambiguously correct rule for deciding whether or not to undertake the project — when it is 'small' and the
economy is adequately described by a one-sector Ramsey-type optimal accumulation model with malleable capital stock. Arrow and Kurz [ref. 4] give a
good discussion of this case.

What is less clear is the formulation of project evaluation criteria when
there are multiple capital goods in the system, particularly in the planning
model context where steady state growth properties are not guaranteed. Empirical evidence [ref. 181] indicates that relative capital goods prcies change
over time in such models, and also that the usual constant discount rate approximation is not valid. Under these conditions, a theoretical statement of
the correct conditions seems called for. Two sets of decision rules which
generalize discounting are therefore presented here. They are:

(i) A demonstration that ordinary discounting is *not* an optimal decision
rule when there are heterogeneous malleable capital goods in the system.
Rather, one must use shadow prices to evaluate the flows of output from the
project which depend in a complex way on the future marginal products of
all capital goods. Although these shadow prices cannot be expressed as familiar
discount integrals, they have a natural interpretation in terms of a multivariate
analog of discounting.

(ii) Formulas are also presented for optimal shadow prices in the case where
the investment project is itself large enough to influence future marginal products of capital. In this case, discounting is not a correct decision rule even in a
one-sector model, since it is basically a first-order procedure which cannot

---

[*] Thanks are due to David Jacobson for making available some of his research results on
differential dynamic programming, and to Edmar Bacha and Richard Eckaus for comments.

deal with feedbacks from the project onto the equilibrium prices of the economy.

These results are discussed in sections III and IV of this note. In section II, some very general rules for project analysis are indicated – all of the foregoing conclusions follow from specializations of these rules. They in turn follow naturally from the dynamic programming point-of-view, as is shown in the appendix.

II. General decision rules

The natural way to view an investment project in the context of an optimal growth model (or any other equilibrium system) is as a perturbation. That is, one can imagine solving an optimizing model containing whatever sort of descriptive relationships seem relevant – production functions, demand functions, etc. – and then re-solving with the particular flows of product resulting from a particular investment project added to the accounting relationships. Comparison of the optima with and without the project superimposed upon the general model indicates whether or not the project should be undertaken. Specifically, if the level of welfare is higher with the project included, then it is worth doing.

Given this approach, the whole point of project analysis is to calculate an approximation to the welfare change induced by the project. Of course, it is impossible to reprogram the whole economy for every new investment, but various decision rules can be used to short-cut this calculation and elect projects on more simple grounds. The most familiar rule is calculating the present discounted value (PDV) of a project, and checking whether it is positive or negative.

What I will do in this section (and in the appendix) is set up a general problem in optimal growth, and derive approximation formulas for the welfare effects of a project/perturbation imposed on an equilibrium solution of the model. The approximations are developed using a technique known as differential dynamic programming, originally proposed by D. Jacobson and D. Mayne for use in calculating numerical solutions to optimal control models.[1] The main differences between the formulas of this section and those of Jacobson and Mayne lie in the type of perturbation considered and in a restriction imposed here that the approximations must be based solely on values calculated in connection with the without-project solution.

---

[1] See Jacobson and Mayne [ref. 101] for complete description of the differential dynamic programming technique.

The problem of interest is the maximization of the gollowing welfare functional (of 'society' or, perhaps more realistically, of the Central Planning Office):

$$\int_{t_0}^{t_f} L(x, u, t)\, dt + F[x(t_f), t_f] \tag{1}$$

subject to the differential equations,

$$dx/dt = \dot{x} = f(x, u, t), \tag{2}$$

initial conditions,

$$x(t_0) = x_0 \text{ given}, \tag{3}$$

and terminal conditions,

$$G[x(t_f), t_f] = 0, \tag{4}$$

where the state variables x and control variables u are expressed as column vectors with m and n elements respectively, L and F are scalar-valued functions. f is an m-component vector function; and G is a vector function with $|p \leqslant m|$ components.[2]

In economic terms, the usual interpretations of all these variables and functions are the following: The state variables x are stocks of malleable capital (no restrictions have been placed on the rate of disposal of the capital stock) and the control variables correspond to flows of products or resources. The function L is a felicity function giving the welfare resulting from instantaneous levels of stock and flow variables and the vector-valued function f gives the rules for accumulation of stocks. The functions F and G represent alternative ways of specifying terminal stock levels — F gives a welfare weight to terminal stocks (e.g., a scrap value on capital stock), while G constrains the levels of terminal stocks to lie within some manifold or to certain point values.[3]

The solution to this problem can be expressed most simply in formal terms if the constraints (4) are adjoined Lagrange-wise to the welfare functional

---

[2] In many economic problems, it is reasonable to add constraints of the form $g(x, u, t) \leqslant 0$. The results which follow can be extended to this more general problem, but as the algebra is even more lushly foliated with matrices of several orders of derivatives than the appendix of this paper, this extension is omitted.

[3] The finite time horizon problem is discussed because it allows us to eschew complicated arguments about the existence of solutions, and because the finiteness or infiniteness of the optimal plan is not of much relevance to the things discussed here.

with a (transposed) multiplier vector k^t:

$$\int_{t_0}^{t_f} L(x, u, t) \, dt + F[x(t_f), t_f] + k' \, G[x(t_f), t_f] . \tag{1'}$$

Let $V^0(x, k, t)$ be the value of the optimized welfare functional when the problem is solved with x as the vector of initial values of the state variables, t as the initial time, and k as the multiplier on the terminal constraints. This optimal return function satisfies the boundary condition

$$V^0(x, k, t) = F(x, t) + k' G(x, t)$$
$$\text{on the hypersurface } G(x, t) \tag{5}$$

with k chosen in such a way that eq. (4) is satisfied. Its value at the particular point (x_0, t_0) with optimal choice of k is the value of the functional (1) when it is minimized with respect to (2)—(4).

It is well known that a general sufficiency condition for the solution of (1)—(4) is that the optimal return function satisfy the Hamilton—Jacobi—Bellman partial differential equation,[4]

$$\frac{-\partial V^0}{\partial t} = \underset{u}{\text{Min}} \, [L(x, u, t) + V_x^0 f(x, u, t)] \tag{6}$$

where V_x^0 is the vector of partial derivatives of V^0 with respect to x, written as a row. From this equation follow the usual optimality conditions for the control problem (1)—(4) including the condition for an (internal) minimum of the Hamiltonian function $H(x, u, V_x^0, t) = L(x, u, t) + V_x^0 f(x, u, t)$:

$$H_u = L_u + V_x^0 f_u = 0 , \tag{7}$$

where H_u and L_u are row vectors of partial derivatives with respect to u, and f is the $m \times n$ matrix of first derivatives of the m-vector f with respect to u. If one treats V_x^0 as a function of time along an optimal path, the Euler equations can also be deduced from eq. (6) in the form:

$$\dot{V}_x^0 = -H_x = -L_x - V_x^0 f_x \tag{8}$$

with associated boundary conditions,

$$V_x^0(t_f) = [F_x + k' G_x]_{t=t_f} . \tag{9}$$

---

[4] The Hamilton—Jacobi—Bellman dynamic programming eq. (6) is derived heuristically in a number of texts. The presentations of Arrow and Kurz [ref. 4], Bryson and Ho [ref. 36], and Dreyfus [ref. 56], are particularly to be recommended.

Eqs. (8) and (9) are identical to the equations satisfied by the costate variables in the solution to a control problem based on the Minimum Principle. Thus the costates can be interpreted as partial derivatives along an optimal trajectory of the optimal return function with respect to the state variables. The recommendation that these variables be used as shadow discount rates is made precisely because they have this interpretation.

To explore the implications of this recommendation, we introduce into the model a small amount of non-malleable capital in the form of an investment project which generates a vector of flows of product $r(t)$, whose time-phasing and product-mix cannot be varied.[5] If the project is undertaken, the capital-accumulation eq. (2) becomes

$$\dot{x} = f(x, u, t) + r(t) . \tag{2'}$$

Let W be the optimal return function for the problem with the project. By assumption, the problem without the project has been solved, and optimal values for the state variables (written henceforth as x^0), control variables (u^0) and the multipliers on the terminal constraints (k^0) are all known. The optimal solution to the with-project problem is described by the variables x, u, and k, defined as

$$x = x^0 + \delta x$$

$$u = u^0 + \delta u$$

$$k = k^0 + \delta k ,$$

where no restrictions have been put (yet) on the variations δx, δu, and δk.

Now the with-project return function $W(x, k, t)$ should satisfy an equation like eq. (6) for points x, u, and k along the new optimal trajectory. However, this new trajectory is unknown, so we can only write the equation corresponding to eq. (6) in terms of the expansion of W about its values on the without-project trajectory described by x^0, u^0, and k^0. When this expansion is carried through (as is done in the Appendix), a set of ordinary differential equations is derived for the matrices W_x and W_{xx} of the partial (first and second) derivatives of the optimal return function W of the with-project problem along the (x^0, u^0, k^0) trajectory. These equations are:

$$-\dot{W}_x = r' W_{xx} + H_x - H_u H_{uu}^{-1} (f_u' W_{xx} + H_{ux}) \tag{10}$$

---

[5] In some models (e.g. Little–Mirrlees [ref. 128]), a project perturbs the constraints in a non-linear way. The Taylor series expansions for the welfare effects of the projects which are developed below can be modified for non-linear perturbations in an obvious way.

and

$$-\dot{W}_{xx} = H_{xx} + f'_x W_{xx} + W_{xx} f_x - (W_{xx} f_u + H_{xu}) H_{uu}^{-1} (f'_u W_{xx} + H_{ux}), \quad (11)$$

and they have boundary conditions (at the terminal time) as follows,

$$W_x(t_f) = F_x[x^0(t_f), t_f] + k^{0'} G_x[x^0(t_f), t_f] \qquad (12)$$

$$W_{xx}(t_f) = F_{xx}[x^0(t_f), t_f] + k^{0'} G_{xx}[x^0(t_f), t_f] . \qquad (13)$$

At the same time, we may define a new variable $a(x^0, t)$,

$$a(x^0, t) = W(x^0, k^0, t) - V^0(x^0, k^0, t), \qquad (14)$$

the difference between the return W from following the optimal with-project trajectory forward from the point (x^0, t) and the return V^0 from following the nominal without-project trajectory forward from this point. At initial time, the value of $a(x_0, t_0)$ is a prediction of the change in welfare induced by the project, as will be exemplified shortly. At terminal time, obviously nothing can be gained over the nominal path, so the boundary condition,

$$a(x^0(t_f), t_f) = 0 \qquad (15)$$

necessarily holds.

In the appendix, it is shown that a satisfies the following differential equation,

$$-\dot{a} = W_x r - \tfrac{1}{2} H_u H_{uu}^{-1} H'_u , \qquad (16)$$

the basic relation for calculating the difference in welfare levels between the two problems.

III. First order decision rules

To make a first order approximation to the welfare change induced by the project, we ignore eq. (11) completely, and rewrite eqs. (10) and (16) without second order terms. This gives:

$$-\dot{a} = W_x r \qquad (16a)$$

and

$$-\dot{W}_x = H_x = L_x + W_x f_x \qquad (10a)$$

with the same boundary condition as before.

Not too surprisingly, the equation for $\dot{W}_x$ is the same as that for $\dot{V}_x^0$ in the without-project problem, while eq. (16a) simply evaluates the project's product flow with the shadow prices $W_x(t)$. In a model with only one state variable, this evaluation reduces to calculating the project's present discounted value, as can be easily shown.

If the project is acceptable, $a(x_0, t_0)$ should be non-negative. To check this, we write out the solution to the linear differential eq. (10a) as an exponential integral (assuming as usual that the felicity function $L(x, u, t)$ does not depend on the capital stock x_1), substitue into eq. (16a) and integrate again to derive the following condition for accepting the project:

$$a(x_0, t_0) = \int_{t_0}^{t_f} \exp \left[\int_{t_0}^{\tau} -f_1(v) \, dv \right] r(\tau) \, d\tau \geqslant 0 , \qquad (17)$$

where f_1 is the derivative of the accumulation function with respect to the unique state variable in the system. This is just the standard discounting rule (with a time-varying marginal product of capital) for deciding on an investment project. Hence, we conclude that *in a one-sector optimal growth model with malleable capital stock, the optimal decision rule about whether to accept a small investment project amounts to calculating the PDV of the project, and accepting it if the PDV is positive. The appropriate time-varying rate of discount is the marginal product of capital along the 'reference' (without-project) solution to the model.*

Still sticking to the linear analysis of the effects of the project, we now must consider the implications of the fact that eq. (10a) is a vector differential equation, with as many components as there are types of capital goods in the system. Written out fully, eq. (10a) in transposed form appears as follows:

$$\begin{bmatrix} -\dot{W}_1 \\ -\dot{W}_2 \\ \cdot \\ \cdot \\ \cdot \\ -\dot{W}_m \end{bmatrix} = \begin{bmatrix} L_1 \\ L_2 \\ \cdot \\ \cdot \\ \cdot \\ L_m \end{bmatrix} + \begin{bmatrix} f_1^1 & f_1^2 \ldots f_1^m \\ f_2^1 & \ldots \ldots \\ \cdot \\ \cdot \\ \cdot \\ f_m^1 & \ldots \ldots f_m^m \end{bmatrix} \begin{bmatrix} W_1 \\ W_2 \\ \cdot \\ \cdot \\ \cdot \\ W_m \end{bmatrix} , \qquad (18)$$

where subscripts denote differentiation with respect to the various components of the vector of capital stocks $x' = (x_1, x_2, \ldots, x_m)$ and the f^i are components to the vector function f.

In this form, it appears more or less obvious that *each* of the shadow prices W_i will in general depend over time on *all* of the other shadow prices and it-self. With just one capital good, we were able to express the capital shadow price W_1 as the exponential integral appearing in eq. (17). By analogy, one ought to be able to introduce some sort of exponential matrix function to use the same formal way in 'solving' eq. (18) with its coefficient matrix of margin-al products of capital. This we will do through the use of an $m \times m$ 'transition matrix' $\phi(t, t_0)$.[6]

Let f_x' stand for the matrix of derivatives of the f^i on the right side of eq. (18). Then if we take the minus sign in eq. (18) to the right side, the transition matrix of the resulting system satisfies the following matrix differential equa-tion,

$$\dot{\phi}(t, t_0) = -f_x'(t)\phi(t, t_0) \tag{19}$$

with initial boundary condition

$$\phi(t_0, t_0) = I \, (= \text{the identity matrix}) \, . \tag{20}$$

In effect, each column of $\phi(t, t_0)$ represents one of the m fundamental solu-tions of eq. (18) over time. In the one-variable system of the last section, the func-tion $\exp \int_{t_0}^{t} -f_1(\tau)\,d\tau$ served the same function. The following comparisons help illustrate the similarity of the two representations:

One-variable system:	*m-variable system:*
$\exp\left[\int_{t_1}^{t_2} -f_1(\tau)\,d\tau\right] \cdot \exp\left[\int_{t_0}^{t_1} -f_1(\tau)\,d\tau\right]$	$\phi(t_2, t_1) \cdot \phi(t_1, t_0)$
$= \exp\left[\int_{t_0}^{t_2} -f_1(\tau)\,d\tau\right]$	$= \phi(t_2, t_0)$
$\left\{\exp\left[\int_{t_0}^{t} -f_1(\tau)\,d\tau\right]\right\}^{-1} = \exp\left[\int_{t}^{t_0} -f_1(\tau)d\tau\right]$	$\phi^{-1}(t, t_0) = \phi(t_0, t) \, .$

Clearly, $\phi(t, t_0)$ performs a smoothing operation over time in the multi-variable system equivalent to that done by the exponential integral in the one-variable system. This stands out quite clearly when we write out the formal solution to eq. (18), starting from an initial value of W_x and again assuming that the non-homogeneous term L_x vanishes:

$$W_x' = \phi(t, t_0) W_x'(t_0) \, . \tag{21}$$

---

[6] Transition matrices are used in the formal analysis of linear vector differential equations. See, for example, Athans and Falb [ref. 6], Bryson and Ho [ref. 36], or Coddington and Levinson [ref. 47].

The generalization of eq. (17) corresponding to this solution is

$$a(x_0, t_0) = W_x(t_0) \int_{t_0}^{t_f} \phi(\tau, t_0) r(\tau) \, d\tau ,$$

where the integration is component-wise. In the case where $r(t)$ has only its first component non-zero (so that it uses and produces only the first type of capital good), the above expression reduces to

$$a(x_0, t_0) = \int_{t_0}^{t_f} \left[\sum_{j=1}^{m} W_j(t_0) \cdot \phi_{1j}(\tau, t_0) \right] r_1(\tau) \, d\tau ,$$

so that the appropriate shadow price for the first sector is a weighted sum of the first components of the m fundamental solutions of eq. (18). Since this will not correspond to an exponential integral, we may conclude that

Discounting is not an optimal decision rule when there are many hetero-geneous capital stocks, and must be replaced by a multivariate analog based on future marginal products of all capital goods in the system.[7]

We can illustrate this result with a simple two-sector model of the type being developed at the pilot stage by various economic programmers.[8] The model maximizes (or minimizes the negative of) a utility integral

$$\text{Min} \int_{t_0}^{t_f} L(c_1, c_2) \, dt$$

of the output of consumption goods in each of the sectors. The accumulation equations are

$$\dot{x}_1 = g^1(x_1 - y_1, y_2) - a_{12} g^2(y_1, x_2 - y_2) - c_1$$

$$\dot{x}_2 = -a_{21} g^1(x_1 - y_1, y_2) + g^2(y_1, x_2 - y_2) - c_2 ,$$

---

[7] This dependence of efficiency prices on all future marginal products of capital has, of course, been pointed out before by a number of authors — notably Dorfman, Samuelson, Solow [ref. 55] and Malinvaud [ref. 129]. The latter notes further that 'an' interest rate with the usual Fisherian properties can be defined by treating one commodity as a *numeraire.* However, from the point of view of project analysis, definition of a copper- or even a cannabis-based interest rate does not obviate the need to know all future relative prices of all capital goods. These are given in symmetric, no-favored-commodity form by eqs. (19) – (21). To my mind, interpretation of these equations as a multivariate generalization of discounting is more appropriate than attempting normalization in terms of some arbitrary commodity.

[8] For an example, see my attempt to calculate shadow prices for Chile in [ref. 181].

where y_1 and y_2 are control variables which assign the two types of capital stock between the two sectors and a_{12} and a_{21} are input–output coefficients.

The equations for $\dot{W}_x$ in this model are

$$
\begin{bmatrix} \dot{W}_1 \\ \dot{W}_2 \end{bmatrix} = \begin{bmatrix} -g_1^1 & a_{21}g_1^1 \\ a_{12}g_2^2 & -g_2^2 \end{bmatrix} \begin{bmatrix} W_1 \\ W_2 \end{bmatrix}
\tag{22}
$$

Suppose for illustrative purposes that the marginal products of capital g_1^1 and g_2^2 are constant over the planning period. Then the matrix on the right side of eq. (22) – call it G – will be constant. The Hawkins–Simon condition [ref. 55, pp. 215–218] assures us that the negative transpose of G will have two positive eigenvalues. Therefore, G itself will have two negative eigenvalues. Suppose that these are distinct, and call them λ_1 and λ_2; also call P the matrix which diagonalizes G:

$$
\begin{bmatrix} \lambda_1 & 0 \\ 0 & \lambda_2 \end{bmatrix} = P^{-1}GP.
$$

Then we can write the solution of eq. (22) as

$$
\begin{bmatrix} W_1(t) \\ W_2(t) \end{bmatrix} = P \begin{bmatrix} \exp(\lambda_1 t) & 0 \\ 0 & \exp(\lambda_2 t) \end{bmatrix} P^{-1} \begin{bmatrix} W_1(0) \\ W_2(0) \end{bmatrix}.
\tag{23}
$$

Thus, the appropriate shadow prices for project analysis are weighted sums of two exponential functions. For the 'reasonable' values of $g_1^1 = 0.2, g_2^2 = 0.1$, $a_{12} = 0.4$ and $a_{21} = 0.1$, the two eigenvalues turn out to have values of -0.207 and -0.092 respectively. For product flows induced far in the future by an investment project, therefore, the second value will dominate and 'the' appropriate discount rate will be about 9.2%. However, for near-future product flows in either of the two sectors, the appropriate shadow price will be some weighted average of present values at 20.7 and 9.2%. At a given time, neither of these shadow prices need have a value near the discounted marginal product of capital in any specific production function of the system.[9]

---

[9] The input–output coefficients are what tie the two sectors together in this example – if they were equal to zero, eq. (23) would already be a diagonal system, and it would be correct to discount product flows in each sector by the appropriate own-marginal product of capital. (Note that the two sectors' own-rates of interest need not be equal.) However, input–output relationships (and other interties between sectors like production externalities and common usage of scarce stock variables such as foreign exchange) *do* exist in the programmers' world, and it is appropriate to take them into account in formulating investment decision criteria.

IV. Optimal shadow prices for large projects

Finally, we discuss briefly in terms of the one-sector model the implications of the second-order approximation to the change in welfare imposed by a project. This discussion will focus on the qualitative properties of the relevant differential equations since little can be said quantitatively in the absence of numerical experimentation with specific equations.

The ruling equations in a one-sector model are

$$-\dot{a} = W_1 r - \tfrac{1}{2} H_u^2 H_{uu}^{-1} \tag{24}$$

$$-\dot{W}_1 = r W_{11} + H_1 - H_u H_{uu}^{-1} (f_u W_{11} + H_{u1}) \tag{25}$$

$$-\dot{W}_{11} = H_{11} + 2 W_{11} f_1 - (W_{11} f_u + H_{u1})^2 H_{uu}^{-1}, \tag{26}$$

where the subscripts '1' and 'u' refer respectively to differentiation with respect to the one state variable and the one control variable in the system.

The main qualitative characteristics of these equations are as follows:

(i) Eq. (24) in integrated form is

$$a(x_0, t_0) = \int_{t_0}^{t_f} [W_1 r - \tfrac{1}{2} H_u^2 H_{uu}^{-1}] \, dt,$$

which is similar to the equation discussed in the last section, except that a positive correction term $\tfrac{1}{2} H_u^2 H_{uu}^{-1}$ is subtracted from the term $W_1 r$ evaluating the project. This correction takes into account the improvement in the welfare function from the without-project to the with-project solution which would result from the change in the control variables.

(ii) Eq. (25) for $\dot{W}_1$ is the same as eq. (10a) for the without-project problem, except that a finite correction term involving the non-zero value of H_u for the with-project problem along the without-project optimal trajectory is subtracted (as in the equation for $\dot{a}$), and a term $r W_{11}$ involving the project is added. This latter addition reflects the influence of the project itself on optimal accumulation. The project changes the rate of change of the state-variable shadow price and this new price in turn affects the flow variable through the optimality condition (7). The point of the second-order approximation is just to take this feedback of exogenous capital accumulation onto the interest rate into account.

Eqs. (25) and (26) are interrelated, since W_1 enters into the determination of W_{11} via its presence in the derivatives of H with respect to the state variable in eq. (26). However, if we ignore this coupling and the term in eq. (25) involving H_u (which will be zero at the optimum), and also assume (as before) that $L_1 = 0$, then we can write the solution for W_1 in integrated form as

$$W_1(t) = W_1(t_f) \exp\left[\int_t^{t_f} f_1(\tau)\,d\tau\right] + \int_t^{t_f} \exp\left[\int_t^{\tau} f_1(v)\,dv\right] r(\tau) W_{11}(\tau)\,d\tau . \quad (27)$$

The second term of this equation takes into account the feedback of project on interest rate mentioned in the last paragraph. Clearly, it can be of either sign, depending at least on the sign of r. In the far future, r will presumably be positive, while inspection of eq. (26) and its associated boundary condition in the case where terminal capital stock is constrained to a certain level indicates that W_{11} will be negative. Hence the distant future shadow price of capital in the with-project solution will be less than in the without-project solution. Near-term effects are unfortunately both more interesting and harder to analyze.

Finally, we may note that eq. (27) cannot be manipulated to produce a discounting formula when its second term is non-negligible. Even in the one-sector model, the familiar decision rule breaks down in the case of 'sufficiently' large projects.

(iii) The weighting function W_{11} for r in its determination of the interest rate in eq. (27) is determined (with feedbacks from the shadow price W_1) by the Riccati eq. (26). Aside from the comments made in connection with the integral (27) for W_1, little can be said about this equation in qualitative terms, although it plays an important role in all second order analysis of optimal control problems. Nor can it be solved with a finite number of quadratures, and must therefore await computer analysis in specific cases.

Appendix

In this appendix, we derive the basic differential eqs. (10), (11), (16) and boundary conditions (12), (13), (15) for the change in welfare induced by the investment project. To do this, begin by writing a first order expansion (in W_x) of the Hamilton–Jacobi–Bellman eq. (6) about the nominal trajectory defined by the points x^0, u^0, k^0:

$$\frac{-\partial W(x^0 + \delta x, \, k^0 + \delta k, t)}{\partial t} \cong \operatorname*{Min}_{\delta u} \{L(x^0 + \delta x, \, u^0 + \delta u, \, t)$$

$$+ [W_x + \delta x' W_{xx} + \delta k' W_{kx}] \, [f(x^0 + \delta x, \, u^0 + \delta u, \, t) + r(t)]\} , \quad (A.1)$$

where W_x has been expanded to first order about $W_x(x^0, k^0, t)$. Also expanding the left side of eq. (A.1) about $W(x^0, k^0, t)$ we find (to second order)[10] that

$$\frac{-\partial W(x^0 + \delta x, k^0 + \delta k, t)}{\partial t} \cong \frac{-\partial}{\partial t}[W + W_x \delta x + W_k \delta k + \delta k' W_{kx} \delta x$$

$$+ \tfrac{1}{2}\delta x' W_{xx} \delta x + \tfrac{1}{2}\delta k' W_{kk} \delta k] = -\frac{\partial}{\partial t}[a + V^0 + W_x \delta x + W_k \delta k$$

$$+ \delta k' W_{kx} \delta x + \tfrac{1}{2}\delta k' W_{kk} \delta k + \tfrac{1}{2}\delta x' W_{xx} \delta x] , \qquad (A.2)$$

where the new variable $a(x^0, t) = W(x^0, k^0, t) - V^0(x^0, k^0, t)$ is defined as the difference between the return function W which results from applying optimal control forward from the point (x^0, t) and the return V^0 from applying nominal (without project) control forward from this point.

On the other side of eq. (A.1) the second order expansion gives

$$\underset{\delta u}{\text{Min}}\{L(x^0 + \delta x, u^0 + \delta u, t) + [W_x + \delta x' W_{xx} + \delta k' W_{kx}].$$

$$[f(x^0 + \delta x, u^0 + \delta u, t) + r(t)]\}$$

$$= \underset{\delta u}{\text{Min}}\{H(x^0 + \delta x, u^0 + \delta u, W_x, t) + [\delta x' W_{xx} + \delta k' W_{kx}].$$

$$f(x^0 + \delta x, u^0 + \delta u, t) + [W_x + \delta x' W_{xx} + \delta k' W_{kx}] r(t)\}$$

$$\cong \underset{\delta u}{\text{Min}}\{H + [\delta x' W_{xx} + \delta k' W_{kx}] f + [W_x + \delta x' W_{xx} + \delta k' W_{kx}] r$$

$$+ H_x \delta x + H_u \delta u + \delta x' W_{xx}[f_x \delta x + f_u \delta u] + \delta k' W_{kx}[f_x \delta x + f_u \delta u]$$

$$+ \delta u' H_{ux} \delta x + \tfrac{1}{2}\delta u' H_{uu} \delta u + \tfrac{1}{2}\delta x' H_{xx} \delta x\} \qquad (A.3)$$

with all terms again evaluated at (x^0, k^0, u^0).

---

[10] As before, W_x means the row vector of partial derivatives of W with respect to x, while W_{kx} is a matrix of cross partial derivatives with the number of rows equal to the dimensionality of k, and the number of columns equal to the dimensionality of x. The 'prime' sign indicates transposition. Note that W_x is only expanded to first order, while other functions are expanded to second order since W_{kx} and W_{xx} are already second order expressions in terms of the problem variables.

To the accuracy of the expansions, eq. (A.2) should equal eq. (A.3). To make use of this fact, we will remove δu from eq. (A.3) and then equate coefficients in δx and δk between eqs. (A.2) and (A.3) to get differential equations for the various derivative matrices W_x, W_{xx}, etc., and also for a.

To carry out these manipulations, begin by grouping terms in eq. (A.3) which contain δu:

$$\delta u' H_u' + \delta u' f_u' W_{xx} \delta x + \delta u' f_u' W_{xk} \delta k + \delta u' H_{ux} \delta x + \tfrac{1}{2} \delta u' H_{uu} \delta u . \qquad (A.4)$$

This is a sum of linear and quadratic terms in δu, with all coefficients evaluated along the without-project optimal solution. If we solved completely the with-project problem, these coefficients would change to their values at the points $(x^0 + \delta x, u^0 + \delta u, k^0 + \delta k)$, and complete minimization of eq. (A.3) with respect to δu would require that these non-linear coefficient changes be taken into account. This could be a difficult calculation. However, it is easy to make a Newton–Raphson type prediction of the change δu, by minimizing eq. (A.4) with constant coefficients. This gives

$$\delta u = - H_{uu}^{-1} \{ H_u' + (f_u' W_{xx} + H_{ux}) \delta x + f_u' W_{xk} \delta k \} \qquad (A.5)$$

as a basic feedback rule for changes in u as functions of changes in the state variables x and multiplier k.[11]

Now, after eq. (A.5) is used to remove δu from eq. (A.3), and coefficients are equated between eqs. (A.2) and (A.3), the following partial differential equations result:

$$- \partial (V^0 + a)/\partial t = H + W_x r + \tfrac{1}{2} H_u H_{uu}^{-1} H_u' \qquad (A.6)$$

$$- \partial W_x /\partial t = (f' + r') W_{xx} + H_x - H_u H_{uu}^{-1} (f_u' W_{xx} + H_{ux}) \qquad (A.7)$$

$$- \partial W_k /\partial t = (f' + r') W_{xk} - H_u H_{uu}^{-1} f_u' W_{xk}$$

$$- \partial W_{xx} /\partial t = H_{xx} + f_x' W_{xx} + W_{xx} f_x - (W_{xx} f_u + H_{xu}) H_{uu}^{-1} (f_u' W_{xx} + H_{ux})$$

$$- \partial W_{kx} /\partial t = W_{kx} [f_x - f_u H_{uu}^{-1} (f_u' W_{xx} + H_{ux})]$$

$$- \partial W_{kk} /\partial t = - W_{kx} f_u H_{uu}^{-1} f_u' W_{xk} . \qquad (A.8)$$

It will be useful to transform these into *ordinary* differential equations. This can be done for eq. (A.6) by noting that

$$\dot{W} = \partial W/\partial t + W_x \dot{x} = \partial W/\partial t + W_x f(x^0, u^0, t)$$

---

[11] Note that this feedback rule can always be calculated from the optimal solution of eqs. (1)–(4), since H_{uu} will be non-singular from the strengthened Legendre–Clebsch condition.

along the optimal solution to the without-project problem. When the definition of a is substituted into this equation, we get $\dot{V}^0 + \dot{a} = \partial(V^0 + a)/\partial t + W_x f(x^0, u^0, t)$ and further substitution into eq. (A.6) gives

$$- \dot{a} = \dot{V}^0 - W_x f + W_x r - \tfrac{1}{2} H_u H_{uu}^{-1} H_u' + H . \tag{A.9}$$

For the without-project problem, $\dot{V}^0 = - L(x^0, u^0, t)$. We can substitute this equality into eq. (A.9) and cancel the Hamiltonian H, to produce at last the ordinary differential equation

$$- \dot{a} = W_x r - \tfrac{1}{2} H_u H_{uu}^{-1} H_u' . \tag{16}$$

This is the basic relation giving the difference in the welfare levels between the two problems. Next, ordinary differential equations for $\dot{W}_x$ and $\dot{W}_{xx}$ and boundary conditions are derived. Regarding the former, note that

$$\dot{W}_x = \partial W_x/\partial t + \dot{x}' W_{xx} = \partial W_x/\partial t + f' W_{xx} \quad \text{and} \quad \dot{W}_{xx} = \partial W_{xx}/\partial t$$

to second order, and substitute in eqs. (A.7) and (A.8) to get

$$- \dot{W}_x = r' W_{xx} + H_x - H_u H_{uu}^{-1}(f_u' W_{xx} + H_{ux}) \tag{10}$$

$$- \dot{W}_{xx} = H_{xx} + f_x' W_{xx} + W_{xx} f_x - (W_{xx} f_u + H_{xu})H_{uu}^{-1}(f_u' W_{xx} + H_{ux}) . \tag{11}$$

Boundary conditions can be developed from the following approximate equality which must hold at terminal time t_f:

$$W(x^0 + \delta x, k^0 + \delta k, t_f) = F(x^0 + \delta x, t_f) + (k^0 + \delta k)' G(x^0 + \delta x, t_f)$$

$$\cong F + F_x \delta x + \tfrac{1}{2}\delta x' F_{xx} \delta x + (k^0)'(G + G_x \delta x + \tfrac{1}{2}\delta x' G_{xx} \delta x)$$

$$+ \delta k'(G + G_x \delta x) .$$

Expanding the left side to second order and equating coefficients, we find the boundary conditions:

$$a(t_f) = 0 \tag{15}$$

$$W_x(t_f) = F_x(x^0(t_f), t_f) + (k^0)' G_x(x^0(t_f), t_f) \tag{12}$$

$$W_{xx}(t_f) = F_{xx}(x^0(t_f), t_f) + (k^0)' G_{xx}(x^0(t_f), t_f) . \tag{13}$$

These conditions provide the starting information for the integration of eqs. (16), (10), and (11) backward in time to estimate the change in the welfare functional.

PART II

ESTIMATES OF SHADOW PRICES

R.S. Eckaus, P.N. Rosenstein-Rodan (eds.), Analysis of development problems,
© North-Holland Publishing Company

SHADOW WAGES IN CHILE*

Francis SETON
Nuffield College, Oxford, England

I. Introduction

This study attempts to test the feasibility and appropriateness of shadow-price calculations as suggested in the OECD Manual of Industrial Project Analysis[1] (I.M.D. Little and J.A. Mirrlees, Paris 1969) in the context of the Chilean economy. It is based on two short visits of less than 10 weeks' duration and cannot therefore pretend to the thoroughness which a fully committed and permanently operational research project could aim to achieve. However extensive and detailed the calculations offered, the numerical results should be regarded as illustrations and tests of plausibility rather than firm figures.

In what follows we shall restate the methodology of the Manual in barest outline (section I) and subsequently explain the modifications and special short-cuts adopted in applying it to the Chilean case. The reader who is acquainted with the Manual or prepared to take its theory for granted may skip section I and turn straight to section II.A on 'Definition and procedure'.

The final results of our estimating procedures in the shape of formulae and numerical averages appear in tables 10 and 11 below.

---

* Special acknowledgements are due to Professor Lance Taylor of Harvard and Mr. Maurice Scott of Nuffield College, Oxford, who have made most valuable suggestions on an earlier draft, and to Professor Bela Belassa of The Johns Hopkins University for his permission to use important tariff data from his book on 'The Structure of Protection in Developing Countries' (before publication by The Johns Hopkins Press). Expert help in computation was also received from Julio Cordoba and Patricio Anda in Chile, and from Sudhir Mulji and Clive Payne of Nuffield College Oxford. Stephen L. Black checked some of the calculations at MIT and drew my attention to certain errors which have now been rectified.
[1] Henceforth to be referred to simply as the 'Manual'.

II. The underlying theory of shadow-pricing

A. *Goods and services*

The central thesis of the Manual is that the true opportunity costs facing a nation in its choice between two goods (products, services, or resources) will not in general correspond to their price-ratios in domestic markets, but will be more adequately reflected in the terms on which the goods can be exchanged through foreign trade. If both are imports these terms are given by the ratio of the c.i.f. prices payable to foreign suppliers (i.e. exclusive of import duties and domestic trade- and transport-margins); if both are exports, by the ratio of the f.o.b. prices receivable from foreign buyers (i.e. disregarding export subsidies but including domestic margins); if one is an export and the other an import, by the ratio between the f.o.b. price of the first and the c.i.f. price of the second.[2] For ease of reference and to guard against the very common confusion with 'world market prices' we shall refer to these as (national) 'border prices'[3] and speak of 'BP valuations', 'BP dollars', or 'BP Escudos'[4] whenever domestic flows are revalued in these terms.[5]

It is important to understand that the choice of border-prices as the most suitable 'shadow values' for goods and services is in no way bound up with the view that foreign exchange must be the crucial bottleneck in an underdeveloped, or in any other, economy. We resort to border prices not because their use will push us into husbanding any particular resource or maximizing any particular objective, but because they are the clearest and the firmest indicators of the terms on which economic alternatives are currently on offer to the nation. To follow their verdict will do more than help us towards a Pareto

---

[2] If the nation bulks largely enough in world trade to affect these prices by its own additions to world demand or supply the proper ratios would be the *marginal* import-costs and export-revenues rather than the corresponding averages (prices). We shall, however, assume that this complication does not arise. In the case of Chile this is almost certainly justified: No import into the country lacks rival customers in sufficient strength to make its supply to Chile anything but perfectly elastic; and even the most specifically Chilean export – copper – is subject to sufficient competition from other suppliers to confront the country with a world demand that is to all intents and purposes fully elastic.

[3] The 'border-price' of any given good will in general differ substantially from one country to another and is therefore in a very real sense a 'national' value indicator.

[4] 'BP-Escudos' are simply 'BP-dollars' converted at the official rate of exchange and represent nothing but a change in *numéraire.*

[5] The possible existence of *two* border-prices (where a commodity is simultaneously exported and imported) does not seem important enough to warrant discussion here. A weighted average of the two will in practice be sufficiently near the mark.

optimum – a totally uncommitted state, but one in whose absence the position will always be worse than it *could* have been, whatever our ultimate objective may be.[6] This is perhaps not easily understood when we are faced with complex interdependent economies where output-flows may furnish inputs into other sectors as well as goods and services for final use (consumption or investment). A short and greatly simplified diagrammatic treatment may therefore be of help:

Assume an economy sub-divided into two sectors,[7] of which the first delivers its output (x_1) partly as an input to the second (u_1), partly for consumption $(y_1)^2$, and partly for exports abroad (e_1). The second sector produces an output x_2 which, jointly with an import flow of identical goods (m_2), supplies the productive needs of the first sector (u_2) and consumption demand at home (y_2).[8] If each output depends uniquely on the productive input on which it feeds, the flows within the economy must satisfy the equations

$$u_1 + y_1 + e_1 = x_1(u_2) \tag{1}$$

$$u_2 + y_2 - m_2 = x_2(u_1). \tag{2}$$

We assume, further, that exports and imports can be traded at foreign ('border') prices p_1 and p_2, and that foreign trade is in balance, i.e.

$$p_1 e_1 - p_2 m_2 = 0 \quad \text{or} \quad m_2 = (p_1/p_2)e_1. \tag{3}$$

Suppose now that we plan to satisfy a fixed consumption target y_1 (= OY_1 in fig. 1) of the first commodity. It will then be convenient to draw the production function $x_1(u_2)$ starting from point Y_1 in fig. 1, with u_2 as the vertical coordinate and x_1 as the horizontal distance from the line $Y_1 L$. Since the consumption demand to be satisfied is OY_1, the residue left over for productive use and exports $(u_1 + e_1)$ will uniquely depend on the production point chosen on $x_1(u_2)$, say P, and will be measured by the abscissa SP. If, moreover, it were decided to export a quantity TP, the input left over for sector 2

---

[6] The condition is of course optimal in a static sense only. But the correction necessitated by dynamic considerations (i.e. foreseeable changes over time) can be grafted on in particular cases without departing from basic principles. This may not be so if dynamic or 'scale' considerations are felt to be of overriding general importance; but the Manual does not take this view.

[7] The number of sectors could of course be multiplied at will without affecting the argument.

[8] For shortness the term 'consumption' is here used for any final use at home (i.e., consumption or domestic investment).

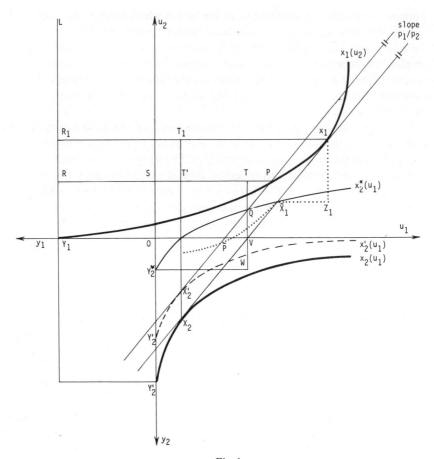

Fig. 1.

would stand at $ST (= Y_2^* W)$. In these conditions the domestic output of good 2 that can be produced will be measured by a distance such as WQ,[9] and its imports by the distance QT (which stands in the required foreign-price ratio p_1/p_2 with the exports TP already decided upon).

The total supply of good 2 is therefore measured by WT, and since $VT(= Y_1 R = u_2)$ of this was presumed to go on productive inputs for sector 1, the amount left over to satisfy consumption demand for good 2 will be

[9] Where $x_2^*(u_1)$ is the second industry's production function shifted parallelly to make it pass through the 'foreign trade point' Q.

$VW (= OY_2^*)$. In sum, if we choose production point P for the first sector and decide to export TP of its output, we can enjoy a consumption flow of OY_2^* in addition to our fixed target $OY_1 (= y_1 =$ consumer output from the first sector).

It is clear, however, that this is not the best that we can do for ourselves in the given situation: In the first place, even if the choice of production point P is maintained, we can get more y_2 by raising exports from PT to PT' (vertically above X_2', where the foreign-price line PQ is tangential to the parallelly shifted production curve x_2'); by doing so our consumption y_2 can be pushed up from OY_2^* to OY_2' without reducing the target for $y_1 (OY_1)$. In the second place, we could do even better by shifting our production point P further up to X_1, where the slope of the production function $x_1 (u_2)$ equals the price ratio p_1/p_2, since this would enable us to shift the foreign-price line as far to the *right* (and therefore the second production curve as far *downward*) as possible. Clearly, the optimal choice will be production at X_1 in conjunction with exports $X_1 T_1$, a situation where both production curves $x_1 (u_2)$ and $x_2 (u_1)$ are tangential to the same foreign-price line $X_1 X_2$ (with slope p_1/p_2); for this alone will maximize the consumption obtainable from the second sector (OY_2) while meeting the target for the first (OY_1). Any departure from such a position would entail a loss in the consumption of either good without gain in the consumption of the other.[10]

The Pareto optimum just described, therefore, requires adjustments in the pattern of production until the slopes of both production curves are idential and equal to the foreign-price ratio. Since the slopes in question measure the marginal productivity of each good in the production of the other, this piece of geometry simply means that production in each sector should be pushed to the point where marginal productivities fall into equality with the foreign price level of inputs ($dx_2/du_1 = p_1/p_2$ and $dx_1/du_2 = p_2/p_1$). Such a position will certainly be approached in the pursuit of maximum profit, as long as the costs of inputs and outputs facing entrepreneurs stand in the same ratios as their foreign prices. It is this which justifies the use of the latter as 'shadow prices' in project appraisal.

---

[10] This is not the place to go into the obvious assumptions we have made in drawing our diagram (mutual independence, convexity, continuity, etc. of production functions, and others). Some of these may be relaxed without affecting the conclusions; others are more crucial to our thesis. Suffice it to say here that in the view of the Manual the possible departures from these conditions will normally produce lesser distortions in the project appraisers' verdicts than would reliance on market- or other prices which did not, in the first instance at least, take their cue from the country's foreign trade.

The analysis of the last section is spelled out in algebraic terms in appendix A, where it is also generalized to apply to an indefinite number of sectors. Equally in appendix A we have extended the argument to sectors producing non-tradeable goods and services (construction, utilities, internal trade and transport, etc.). The problem of valuing these products within the framework of the Manual cannot be tackled without relating it to our general approach to importables and exportables. A full diagrammatic treatment along the lines of fig. 1 would therefore require three dimensions at least, and there is little point in attempting it here. We have however given our version in algebraic terms in appendix A for the benefit of readers who feel more at home in this field. Let us merely recall here that in the case of non-tradeables the Manual recommends the use of shadow prices reflecting *either* marginal claims on imports (through absorption of materials etc., which have to be imported at border prices) *or* marginal contributions to exports (through productive use in export industries). Under certain, rather stringent, conditions of optimality the two methods should give the same results. In practice they may not do so, but the choice between them is in any case likely to be dictated by the availability of data. We shall place reliance exclusively on the import side of the picture in this exercise. The procedure for the valuation of non-tradeables is explained in full detail in the section 'Definitions and Procedure' (II.A) and in the mathematical section immediately following (II.B).

When goods are tradeable but subject to quantitative restrictions the argument of the previous section breaks down. In terms of fig. 1, the optimum would have to lie on a 'translation' of the curve $x_1(u_2)$, with each of its points shifted southward by a distance corresponding to the permitted imports (say $X_1 Z_1$) and westward by the equivalent export volume ($Z_1 \bar{X}_1$). In fact it would lie on the one point of this shifted curve (shown dotted through $\bar{X}_1$) where tangentiality with a line parallel to $x_2(u_1)$ is achieved, i.e. possibly at $\bar{P}$. It is clear, however, that the slope of the two production curves at that point will not equal the border-price ratio p_1/p_2, and the search for the proper shadow prices is therefore immeasurably complicated. In such conditions the choices open to us in practice are all of a makeshift nature: we could treat the trade-restricted goods as if they were non-tradeable and value them at their derived foreign exchange costs at the margin; alternatively we could accept their border prices as if they were freely tradeable, with an upward adjustment to allow for some sort of 'tariff-equivalent' of the import quota. As will be explained later, we have adopted the second course, in line with conditions prevailing in the Chilean economy.

B. Labour

Assuming that workers do not save, each wage packet paid out by the project involves the economy in a real cost equal to the project-worker's consumption in terms of border prices, say c. This, however, may entail some increase in consumption levels b, [11] due to the shift of the worker from his previous, and presumably lower-paid, occupation. Since consumption increments are desirable per se, the Manual suggests that the real loss to the community is less than c by some quantity related to b, i.e. $c - b/s$, where s converts the consumption increment into what it *would have been worth in the hands of the wage-paying agency*.

We have departed from the Manual in our interpretation of b, as we do not believe that in Chilean conditions the sole, or even the main, source of recruitment for new projects will be agriculture. Nor do we believe that in Chilean conditions s should be made to depend mainly on the value of investment in terms of present consumption.[12] Our procedure will be to identify b as the wage-increase (in BP-terms) of the 'average' batch of workers as it might be recruited by the project from a variety of previous occupations (agricultural or not), and to replace the constant denominator s by a full-scale revaluation of b in terms of the 'general community purposes' (including investment) which are foregone by this immediate commitment to increased consumption. Since this may functionally depend on the previous consumption levels enjoyed, we shall write b_s instead of s.

Lastly, we believe that the new recruitment of labour in Chilean conditions may release funds due to the transfer of previously under-employed labour to the project (where we may be presume it to be fully employed), and that this benefit (e) must be deduced from the wage in estimating the true cost of project labour to the community. To the extent that the release occurs in the public sector the benefit will accrue to 'general community purposes' (by definition), and the deduction e must be made in full. To the extent that it occurs in the private sector it might (in the extreme case) benefit nothing but profit-earners' personal consumption and therefore be close to zero in value from the community's point of view.[13] Since e is likely to be fairly small and

---

[11] The Manual uses no single symbol for this increment.

[12] This is the conversion which would make b commensurable with c on the assumption that the only alternative to recruitung a new worker would have been to spend his wages on *investment*.

[13] We assume that the previous consumption level of profit earners was so high that further additions to it will have very low marginal values.

subject to error, it seems hardly worthwhile to heap guess upon guess. We shall therefore content ourselves with an arbitrary deduction mid-way between zero and its full value, and compute the Chilean shadow wage by the formula

$$\omega = c - b_s - \tfrac{1}{2} e.$$

In what follows section II will be devoted to the first element in this definition (c), i.e. to the 'cost of labour *to the project*', while section III will deal with the 'social adjustments' b_s and e, which make the cost of labour *to society* diverge from its cost to the individual project.

III. The cost of labour to the project (BP-content)

A. Definitions and procedure

Our first task is the computation of c,[14] the border-price value of all the goods and services purchased with the monthly wage. This entails the direct valuation of all 'tradeable' goods in the family budget in terms of their border prices, and the revaluation of all 'non-traded' items [15] in the nearest equivalent, i.e. the marginal import cost incurred in producing one more unit at home ('marginal border-cost').[16] We must therefore start with a clear separation of the two kinds of items. It is easy enough to identify 'tangible' commodities which are or could be transported across frontiers and to separate them from intangible servies which yield their benefit on the spot, while a few tangibles are so rarely traded that they can be relegated to the non-tradeable category without much searching of the heart (construction, gas, electricity, etc.). More difficult is the categorization of items subject to import quotas or prohibition which do possess a border price but are excluded from normal 'tradeables' by government *fiat*. In the Chilean case, however, we are saved from the dilemma of this choice by the fact that these items are dispersed over several of the aggregative sectors into which we must divide the economy for the purpose of computation (textiles, clothing, drink, etc.). It would clearly be against the spirit of the Manual to transfer these sectors to 'non-tradeables' wholesale,

---

[14] This quantity will obviously imply a conversion factor γ for the translation of current wage-payments into BP content, i.e., such that $c = \gamma w$, where w is in escudos and c in \$.
[15] Goods or services which do not enter the country's foreign trade and do not therefore possess a border price.
[16] An alternative would be the marginal loss in export earnings incurred by consuming one more unit at home. This, however, is in general more difficult to ascertain.

and impossible to pick out and split off the trade-restricted items into new sectors. We have therefore classified them as 'tradeable' in spite of this contamination, and we believe this is inevitable until disaggregation of the economy can be pushed to a level of detail which is at present beyond our reach.

In summary, our procedure classifies the first 28 sectors of the Chilean input–output table as 'tradeable' and therefore subject to direct revaluation at border prices. This accounts for nearly three quarters of urban family spending at retail prices. The remaining goods and services (less than 27% of family expenditure) were revalued in terms of their global cost-content of imports at c.i.f. prices, including the border-price valuation of such inputs as had been directly revalued. By 'global' we mean here both the direct and indirect requirement of given inputs, whether imported or not. The figure thus approaches the concept of (direct and indirect) import content, which has been current coinage ever since input–output techniques have come to be widely used. There are two crucial differences, however: (1) The 'tradeable' items enter the cost-structure of goods and services not at their 'import-content', but at their directly established border prices. We therefore propose to use the term *'border-price content'* (BP-content for short) for the final values we are seeking to establish. (2) The costs of wages and (as far as possible) of capital incurred in the production of each good or service are similarly revalued in BP-content before the final unit-values are established.

The whole list of unit-BP-contents, including that of labour, thus emerges as a self-consistent set from a calculation which in essence amounts to the solution of simultaneous equations. In these, however, the directly established border-prices, as well as all actual import-costs, enter as crucial parameters. This is as near to the intentions of the Manual as it seemed to us one could go in the Chilean context.

B. The mathematics

We now proceed to an operational definition of what we mean by 'border-price content'.

Let the current money flows between productive sectors $(1, 2, \ldots, n)$, factor-owners, and final users — as far as they are of interest to us — be represented in matrix form as follows:

$$Ax + \phi h + z = x$$

$$mx + \phi m_{10} \cdot \quad \cdot$$

$$lx \quad \cdot \quad \cdot = \phi \epsilon \tag{4}$$

$$Kx,$$

where A and K are the $n \times n$ matrices of input coefficients and capital coefficients respectively,[17] x, h, z are the n-dimensional (column-) vectors of gross outputs, consumption per worker's family, and other final purchases, and m and l are the import- and labour-costs per unit output respectively. Among the scalar values ϵ stands for total monthly expenditure per worker's family and ϕ for the number of families. m_{10} measures direct consumption imports per worker's family.

Note that all flows are expressed in current producer prices (in escudos) except imports, which are in c.i.f. dollars as paid at the frontier.

We now divide the n sectors into n_1 'tradeables' and n_2 'non-tradeables' and re-write our equations in partitioned form:

$$\begin{pmatrix} A_{11} & A_{12} \\ A_{21} & A_{22} \end{pmatrix} \begin{Bmatrix} x_1 \\ x_2 \end{Bmatrix} + \phi \begin{Bmatrix} h_1 \\ h_2 \end{Bmatrix} + \begin{Bmatrix} z_1 \\ z_2 \end{Bmatrix} = \begin{Bmatrix} x_1 \\ x_2 \end{Bmatrix}$$

$$[m_1 \ m_2] \begin{Bmatrix} x_1 \\ x_2 \end{Bmatrix} + \phi m_{10} \qquad . \qquad .$$

(5)

$$[l_1 \ l_2] \begin{Bmatrix} x_1 \\ x_2 \end{Bmatrix} \qquad . \qquad . = \Phi\epsilon$$

$$\begin{pmatrix} K_{11} & K_{12} \\ K_{21} & K_{22} \end{pmatrix} \begin{Bmatrix} x_1 \\ x_2 \end{Bmatrix} \qquad . \ . \qquad . \qquad .$$

where the subvectors x_1, x_2, h_1, h_2 etc. refer to the two subsets respectively and the partitions of the matrix A are conformable for multiplication (i.e. A_{11}, A_{22}, and K_{11}, K_{22} are square matrices of order n_1 and n_2 respectively).[18]

Now let p_1 stand for the vector of the n_1 border-pricing of tradeable products. Further, let v and λ stand for the 'border-price contents' of n products and of the wage-unit respectively, i.e. for the $n+1$ unit-values which it is our purpose to determine. We can then define the latter as follows:

$$p_1 \qquad\qquad\qquad\qquad\qquad\qquad = v_1 \ (n_1 \text{ identities})$$

$$p_1 A_{12} + v_2 A_{22} + m_2 + \lambda l_2 + p_1 K_{12} + v_2 K_{22} = v_2 \ (n_2 \text{ equations})$$

(6)

$$p_1 h_1 + v_2 h_2 + m_{10} \qquad\qquad\qquad\qquad = \lambda\epsilon \ (1 \text{ equation}) .$$

[17] The rows of K correspond to capital services supplied by the sectors in which the capital goods in question originated (e.g., engineering, construction, etc.).

[18] The rows of all K-matrices corresponding to sectors which do not supply capital equipment (i.e., the majority of sectors) will consist of zeros.

Thus the first n_1 ('tradeable') BP-contents are simply identified with the (known) border prices. The second n_2 ('non-tradeable') BP-contents are built up of the border prices of their tradeable inputs (current and capital), the BP-contents of their non-tradeable inputs, the border cost of their directly imported inputs, and the BP-content of the labour-costs they absorb. The latter, in turn, is defined in the last equation as the BP-content of all items consumed per unit of workers' expenditure.

We can simplify the equations slightly by writing B for $A + K$ and for all corresponding partitions, thus converting the second equation-set into $p_1 B_{12} + v_2 B_{22} + m_2 + \lambda l_2 = v_2$. This may be made explicit with respect to v_2:

$$v_2 = p_{12}^* + \lambda l_2^* + m_2^*, \tag{7}$$

where $p_{12}^* \equiv p_1 B_{12}(I - B_{22})^{-1}$, $l_2^* \equiv l_2(I - B_{22})^{-1}$, and $m_2^* \equiv m_2(I - B_{22})^{-1}$.

The vectors l_2^* and m_2^* will be recognized as the global (direct and indirect) unit-costs in labour and c.i.f. imports of non-tradeable products, while p_{12}^* measures that part of their costs which is incurred through the purchase of (border-priced) intermediate inputs. All coefficients make allowance for the capital services consumed in production, which need not therefore be added separately.

We can now substitute v_2 from eq. (7) in the last equation of (6), obtaining

$$\lambda \epsilon = p_1 h_1 + p_{12}^* h_2 + \lambda l_2^* h_2 + m_2^* h_2 + m_{10},$$

or, more concisely

$$\epsilon \lambda = p_{10} + p_{20} + \lambda l_{20} + m_{10} + m_{20}, \tag{8}$$

where

$$p_{10} \equiv p_1 h_1, \qquad l_{20} \equiv l_2^* h_2.$$

$$p_{20} \equiv p_{12}^* h_2, \qquad n_{20} \equiv m_2^* h_2.$$

Here the double-suffixed scalars refer to the various parts of total family consumption (in B.P.-content), with p_{10} and m_{10} denoting directly border-priced consumption of *tradeables* (home-produced and imported). The symbols p_{20}, l_{20}, and m_{20} stand for the total absorption of (border-priced) tradeables, labour, and imports involved in the consumption of *non-tradeables*.

If we are prepared to introduce further symbols for total tradeables- and import-contents ($p_0 \equiv p_{10} + p_{20}$ and $m_0 \equiv m_{10} + m_{20}$), the solution of the above equation may be written

$$\lambda = (p_0 + m_0)/(\epsilon - l_{20}) \tag{9}$$

Since we can compute the values p_0, m_0 and l_{20}, we can obtain the B.P.-content of labour from eq. (9), and by substituting this in eq. (8) the complete list of B.P.-contents of non-tradeables in the economy. The exact procedure is described in the following sections.

C. The computation

1. *Introductory*. In our attempt at translating the definitions and procedures of the last sections into actual figures we were severely limited by the nature of the statistics available. These consisted in the main of a study on nominal tariff rates for 1961, an agricultural survey covering the second half of the fifties, a 54-sector input–output table for 1962, and a detailed study of family budgets for the year ending October 1964.

The time interval of 21 months between the last two encompassed a severe spurt of inflation and was bound to be a constant source of uncertainty when the two sets of figures had to be 'married'. Broadly speaking we were reduced to assuming that the input coefficients of 1962 were still valid in 1963/4, at least *in real terms*, and that the only adjustment required was the scaling up across the board of $-*import* coefficients (per unit Escudo-output) in step with the devaluation of the domestic currency.

An even greater source of uncertainty is our forced reliance on tariff-data for 1961 in the context of family budgets from 1963/4. It is known that substantial changes in commercial policy occurred in the interval. However, no later tariff-data in anything like the required detail could be made available.

Almost equally serious was another defect in the data: the input-output table is at present only available in terms of *user*-prices, i.e. in terms of money flows which include payments for trade- and transport-services (as well as taxes) associated with the sale of the output in question. This inflates the contribution of the material production sectors properly so-called. It does so, moreover, in varying degrees, depending on the extent to which these sectors have to rely on outside specialist services to market their products. In this way the input-structure of each consuming sector (column of the table) will be distorted, and the coefficients implicit in the table cannot be accepted as correct representations of the technological constants on which the economy is based. Their direct use in our calculations would give rise to errors of a magnitude and direction that could only be guessed at. It was therefore decided to invest the time and effort required for at least a tentative conversion of the Chilean input-output table to *producer* prices. The procedure adopted for this purpose is more fully described in section 4 below and the results given in the appendix, tables I–III.

2. *The family budgets.* Table 1 shows the composition of family budgets as given by the Centre for Economic Research of the Catholic University of Chile from a sample of 2,300 urban families of employed and self-employed workers. We have ignored the distinction between so-called workers and employees among the employed ('obreros' and 'empleados') since this appears to follow irregular demarcation lines of little economic import. We have aggregated the raw data into the sectoral divisions of the input—output table and separated out both estimated imports and domestic trade- and transport-margins, as explained in the footnotes. The resulting expenditure list forms the basic material which must be subjected to revaluation at border-price content.

3. *Direct border domestic price ratios.* The Chilean Planning Office disposes of a study of nominal rates of protection in 1961 which offers estimates for the 28 'tradeable' sectors of the input—output table.[19] The nominal protection rate (t) is defined as the proportion by which the domestic producer price (d) exceeds the c.i.f. import price ex-tariff (b) for any commodity or sector, i.e.

$$t = b/d - 1 \, ,$$

where both prices are taken to be in home currency. In computing these ratios (column A of table 2) allowance was made for the great variety of Chilean protection measures other than tariffs, e.g. deposit schemes, fees, surcharges, etc. Tariff-equivalents were also computed for quota restrictions, and in special cases direct price comparisons were resorted to.

We have accepted the price-ratios implicit in these rates as the proper coefficients for the conversion of domestic into border prices, after deflation of escudo values into 1963/4 U.S. dollars, as explained in table 2.

4. *The input—output data.* Our next task is to compute the unit BP-contents for sectors 29 — 48 of the economy which produce non-tradable products. This can be done in accordance with eq. (7) in the mathematical section provided adequate data on the matrix $B (= A + K)$ can be assembled. Unfortunately all we dispose of is the 1962 A-matrix in terms of *user*-prices — a structure heavily contaminated with trade-, transport- and tax-margins which distorts the proper contributions of the productive sectors properly so-called to each other's output. It was therefore necessary to spend considerable time and effort to convert this matrix to a producer-price basis. To do so we have had to make drastic simplifying assumptions on the distribution of the total margins between the sectors into whose costs they enter. Briefly, we decided to impute them

---

[19] ODEPLAN: Tariff rates by Sectors of Origin, 1961 (derived from preliminary estimates by Teresa Jeanneret).

Table 1

Consumption expenditure per urban family in sample of 1963/4 (in current Escudos per month)[a]

I-O Number	Sector of origin	Expenditure of average urban family						Urban family expenditure on home goods and imports				
		Total by type of good or service	Of which: on direct imports				At user prices	At producer prices		By income-brackets[f]		
			Total	Trade	Transport	Including domestic margins	Average family (A-B)	Average family	Low	Med.–low	Med.–high	High
		A^b	B^c	C^d	D^d		E	F^e	G	H	I	J
1.	Agriculture	42.11	1.12	0.26	0.06		40.09	25.17	14.40	25.31	30.65	45.92
2.	Fisheries	4.64	–	–	–		4.64	2.13	1.37	2.02	2.74	3.73
9.	Food processing	115.53	10.17	1.72	0.14		105.36	80.51	39.43	63.67	90.32	117.43
10.	Drinks	5.44	0.07	0.02	–		5.37	2.78	0.99	2.91	4.62	9.21
11.	Tobacco	2.97	0.02	–	–		2.95	1.30	0.58	1.10	1.78	3.94
12.	Textiles	6.20	0.25	0.04	–		5.95	3.95	1.19	3.23	5.94	13.32
13.	Clothing & footwear	51.88	1.72	0.58	–		50.16	33.16	12.17	28.35	48.25	87.60
14.	Wood & cork	0.01	–	–	–		0.01	0.01	–	0.02	0.06	–
15.	Furniture, etc.	4.49	0.05	0.01	–		4.44	4.09	0.40	1.70	6.75	17.80
16.	Paper, etc.	0.26	0.01	–	–		0.25	0.18	0.06	0.14	0.27	0.60
17.	Printing, etc.	11.34	4.30	1.12	–		7.04	2.99	0.43	1.60	2.58	5.91
20.	Chemicals, etc.	19.42	0.77	0.25	–		18.65	8.16	1.91	4.28	13.26	34.80
21.	Coal & oil products	5.50	0.05	0.01	0.01		5.45	2.66	1.41	2.09	3.33	9.31
22.	Non-metallic minerals	0.81	0.06	–	–		0.75	0.58	0.17	0.60	0.90	1.16
24.	Metal working	1.30	0.30	0.06	–		1.00	0.65	0.18	0.45	1.07	1.51
25.	Mechanical engineering	3.35	0.01	–	–		3.34	2.36	0.02	0.42	3.45	13.88
26.	Electrical engineering	9.64	2.22	0.66	–		7.42	5.05	0.29	1.88	9.27	24.65
28.	Various manufactures	34.52	12.80	3.12	0.04		21.72	15.51	3.27	9.19	23.52	69.25
29.	Construction	3.27	–	–	–		3.27	3.23	0.08	0.84	3.14	17.40
30.	Electricity	6.93	–	–	–		6.93	6.35	3.35	5.86	8.58	14.33
31.	Gas	12.39	–	–	–		12.39	12.01	1.13	4.48	9.87	78.71
32.	Water & sanitation	2.51	–	–	–		2.51	3.41	1.83	3.26	4.35	7.34
33.	Internal trade	–	–	–	–		7.85[g]	77.29	21.14	57.66	103.21	240.47

Table 1 (continued)

38.	Housing	32.67	0.10	—	—	32.56	30.30	13.25	26.73	43.61	83.36
39.	Transport, etc.	19.03	0.54	—	—	18.74g	27.51h	10.11h	22.49h	35.86h	91.04h
40.	Education (private)	4.79	0.54	—	—	4.79	4.79	0.28	1.03	4.50	34.04
41.	Education (public)	6.52	—	—	—	6.52	7.75	0.87	3.41	11.20	39.46
42.	Health	9.86	—	—	—	9.86	9.86	2.54	5.80	15.11	38.39
44.	Professional services	4.60	—	—	—	4.60	4.25	0.87	2.52	4.65	8.98
45.	Entertainment	0.85	0.25	—	—	0.60	0.40	0.13	0.39	0.58	1.63
46.	Restaurants & hotels	2.14	0.30	—	—	1.84	1.72	0.51	1.45	2.78	7.87
47.	Laundries, barbers, etc.	8.53	—	—	—	8.53	8.39	0.66	3.55	13.48	44.86
50.	Total home goods	434.71	—	—	—	407.79	389.48	135.05	288.87	510.68	1173.61
51.	Total imports	—	—	—	—	27.01	12.96	4.57	9.70	17.37	40.48
52.	Total expenditure	434.71	35.11	7.85	0.25	434.70	402.44	139.62	298.57	528.05	1214.09

a Discrepancies due to rounding.

b Average of blue-collar workers ('obreros') and others ('empleados' and self-employed) from Universidad Católica de Chile, 'Algunos Resultados de la Encuesta de Presupuestos de Familias 1963/4' (mimeo), p.11, weighted at 45.5 and 54.5% respectively (proportions in which the two categories were reported in 1962 in the total population of the four cities sampled).

c Applying to col.A the percentages obtaining for personal consumption as a whole in 1962 (information in supplementation of input-ouput table).

d Applying to col.B the percentages listed for domestic goods in 1962 input-output table, after inflating by 23.02% and 5.15% for trade and transport respectively (to take account in higher margins on imported goods;

e Obtained from col. E by: (1) Deducting retail margins in proportion to estimates; (2) Applying to each figure the relevant clearing factor; (3) Adding to trade- and transport-rows their domestic margins as explained in app. B (page 89).

f Raw data from source of footnote b, trated in the same way as the average urban family (cols. A to F) except for slight adjustments in the presumed percentage of imports within each category (rising with income to give a total of 6.2, 6.5, 6.7, and 7.0% respectively, against an over-all average of 6.55%. Low = 0–225 E^o per month; Med.–low = 225–450 E^o per month; Med.–high = 450–750 E^o per month; High = over 750 E^o per month.

g Including margins on imported goods (clear of tax).

h After transferring to this cell all margins on domestic and imported goods (clear of tax).

Table 2
Estimates of border prices for tradeables.

	Nominal rate of protection[a] (%) A	Border price ratio (p) 1963/4[b] ($/E) B
1. Agriculture	43	0.3110
2. Fisheries	21	0.3675
3. Coal mining	37	0.3246
4. Iron mining	0	0.4447
5. Copper mining	2	0.4360
6. Nitrates	0	0.4447
7. Quarries, etc.	66	0.2678
8. Other mining	46	0.3048
9. Food industries	82	0.2443
10. Drinks	122	0.2003
11. Tobacco	106	0.2159
12. Textiles	182	0.1577
13. Clothing & footwear	255	0.1253
14. Wood & cork	35	0.3294
15. Furniture	129	0.1942
16. Paper, etc.	55	0.2869
17. Printing, etc.	72	0.2586
18. Leather	161	0.1704
19. Rubber	102	0.2201
20. Chemicals	94	0.2293
21. Oil & coal derivs	30	0.3421
22. Non-metallic minerals	139	0.1861
23. Basic metals	66	0.2679
24. Metal working	59	0.2797
25. Mechanical engineering	84	0.2417
26. Electrical engineering	105	0.2169
27. Transport equipment	84	0.2417
28. Various mfc.	125	0.1976

[a] Teresa Jeanneret, 'The structure of protection in Chile', A partly revised version is incorporated in *The structure of protection in developing countries* (Johns Hopkins Press), by Professor Bela Belassa, to whom I am indebted for permission to use the data. The nominal rate of protection (t) is defined as the proportion by which the domestic producer price (d) exceeds the c.i.f. import price (before tariff) expressed in home currency (b), after various adjustments for non-tariff protective measures have been made. In symbols: $t = b/d - 1$.
[b] Computed from the formula above as $p = rb/d = r/(1+t)$, where t is the value in column A and r is the dollar-escudo exchange rate of 1963/4 (0.44474).

proportionally to wholesale costs, after distributing retail trading margins in accordance with the ratios obtaining in the Norwegian economy (for which data in a similar breakdown could be made available). The result [20] cannot of course command complete confidence, but is in our view a substantial improvement on the uncorrected user-price matrix as a basis for our computations.

To establish the K-matrix we proceeded by estimating the value of fixed capital stocks in the 20 non-tradeable sectors [21] in a four-fold breakdown according to presumed origin (Mechanical Engineering, Electrical Engineering, Transport Equipment, and Construction). In most cases the totals could be obtained directly from Chilean data, but for the breakdown by type of capital we have had to rely heavily on structural data for the U.S. economy in the late thirties.

To convert the stock figures into annual flows of capital services we computed the size of the annuity which would exhaust the value of each asset stock over a period equal to its estimated life, on the assumption that the rate of interest was 12% p.a.[22] The average life of assets was estimated by us according to British tables, differentiated by type of asset and to some extent also by sector of use. For medium- and long-lived assets the result is in any case very insensitive to the exact length of life assumed.

In the case of working capital we found it best to deal separately with producers' and traders' stocks. The former was estimated from U.S. inventory-output ratios (by sectors) for 1939, in line with our estimates of fixed capital. For the latter we preferred to relate the estimates to Chilean trading margins rather than sectoral outputs, and computed the probable share of carrying costs in these margins from contemporary British data (after allowing for higher interest charges). In both cases the conversion of stocks into flows assumed an interest rate of 12%.

Finally, the absolute figures for fixed capital services were converted into input coefficients per unit output, and added to the coefficients of the other two tables to form the matrices K_{12} and K_{22}, as required in our calculations. By adding these to the corresponding partitions of the current input–output matrix A (appendix, table 1) we obtained the total matrix B which features in our eqs. (4) – (6). The system could then be solved for the border-price-contents v_2 and λ, as explained in the mathematical section.

---

[20] Displayed in full in appendix table 1.

[21] No data of this kind are required for tradeable sectors.

[22] This is somewhere near the average between bank interest and mortgage rates charged in Santiago and Valparaiso in the period under review. See Banco Central de Chile, *Boletin Mensual*, April 1965, pp. 434 and 488.

Table 3
The computation of border-price contents per unit output.

	Direct costs per unit output[a]			Global costs per unit output				Border-price content ($/E^o) per unit of:		
				Through 'non-priced inputs'[c]			Through 'priced' inputs[e]	Producer price[f]	Wholesale price[o]	Retail price[p]
	Labour (l)	Imports[b] (m)	Taxes (n)	Labour (l_2^*)	Imports[d] (m_2^*)	Taxes (n_2^*)		$(v)=(p)$	(q)	(r)
	A	B	C	D	E	F	G	F	G	H
1. Agriculture	0.5574	0.0074	0.0594				0.3110	0.3110	0.3024	0.3042
2. Fisheries	.6206	.0000	.1770				.3675	.3675	.3562	.3438
3. Coal mining	.8936	.0127	−.0141				.3246	.3246	.3099	.3103
4. Iron mining	.3700	.0364	.0062				.4447	.4447	.4243	.4243
5. Copper mining	.3357	.0289	.0359				.4360	.4360	.4547	.4547
6. Nitrates	.5220	.1087	−.0313				.4447	.4447	.4346	.4346
7. Quarries, etc.	.5758	.0059	.1167				.2678	.2678	.2692	.2692
8. Other mining	.4944	.0086	.0887				.3048	.3048	.3003	.3003
9. Food industry	.1116	.0410	.0555				.2443	.2443	.2378	.2077
10. Drinks	.1178	.0038	.1393				.2003	.2003	.2052	.2237
11. Tobacco	.1822	.0635	.0650				.2159	.2159	.1065	.1274
12. Textiles	.0482	.0636	.0648				.1577	.1577	.1556	.1662
13. Clothing and f'twear	.6062	.0038	.1096				.1253	.1253	.1141	.1708
14. Wood & cork	.3196	.0051	−.0367				.3294	.3294	.3093	.3097
15. Furniture, etc.	.4732	.0010	.0686				.1942	.1942	.1800	.2096
16. Paper, etc.	.1952	.0160	.0577				.2869	.2869	.2719	.2733
17. Printers, etc.	.4104	.0144	.0849				.2586	.2586	.2573	.2716
18. Leather industry	.1815	.207	.0811				.1704	.1704	.1688	.1787
19. Rubber	.1515	.0968	.1000				.2201	.2201	.2132	.2132
20. Chemicals	.1938	.0700	.1417				.2293	.2293	.2187	.2362
21. Oil & coal derivatives	.0666	.0729	.0522				.3421	.3421	.2609	.2626
22. Non-metallic minerals	.2560	.0198	.0433				.1861	.1861	.1892	.1922
23. Basic metals	.2862	.0525	.0214				.2679	.2679	.2623	.2623
24. Metal working	.3720	.0199	.0777				.2797	.2797	.2648	.2712
25. Mechanical engineering	.3642	.0175	.1064				.2417	.2417	.2321	.2361
26. Electrical engineering	.2427	.0297	.1324				.2169	.2169	.2110	.2184
27. Transport equipment	.3406	.0309	.1035				.2417	.2417	.2294	.2335
28. Various Mfc.	.2500	.0261	.0903				.1976	.1976	.1937	.2014

Table 3 (continued)

	Direct costs per unit output[a]			Global costs per unit output				Border-price content ($/E°) per unit of:		
				Through 'non-priced inputs'[c]			Through 'priced' inputs[e]	Producer price[f]	Wholesale price°	Retail price[p]
	Labour (l)	Imports[b] (m)	Taxes (n)	Labour (l_2^*)	Imports[d] (m_2^*)	Taxes (n_2^*)		$(v)=(p)$	(q)	(r)
	A	B	C	D	E	F	G	F	G	H
29. Construction	.3258	.0099	.0323	.4196	.0109	.6919	.0991	.2192	.2168	.2168
30. Electricity	.3159	.0190	.0648	.5528	.0261	.0956	.2753	.4453	.4080	.4080
31. Gas	.3606	.0166	-.0087	.5022	.0191	.0081	.2258	.3756	.3640	.3640
32. Water & sanitation	.9294	.0000	.0084	1.0971	.0040	.0270	.3925	.6821	.9260	.9260q
33. Trade	.6674	.0067	.0677	.7662	.0018	.0768	.0587	.2600	.2500q	.2500q
34. Banking	2.3319	.0000	.0100	2.6223	.0109	.0363	.0916	.7852	.6658	.6658
35. Insurance	.3698	.0000	.1094	.4959	.0022	.1198	.0247	.1560	.1265	.1265
36. Other finance	1.3444	.0000	.0383	1.6053	.0024	.0607	.0832	.5035	.8378	.8378
37. Real estate	.7796	.0000	.0008	.8573	.0018	.0097	.0402	.2652	.2435	.2435
38. Housing	.0000	.0000	.0018	.3969	.0095	.0404	.0885	.2013	.1873	.1873
39. Transport, etc.	.4572	.0093	.0794	.6243	.0128	.0987	.1144	.2897	.3367	.3367
40. Education (private)	.6502	.0038	.0041	.7745	.0067	.0173	.0538	.2621	.3114	.3114
41. Education (public)	1.3256	.0017	.0014	1.4420	.0046	.0136	.0395	.4195	.4193	.4193
42. Health (private)	.4816	.0029	.0179	.5889	.0050	.0277	.0527	.2110	.2110	.2110
43. Health (public)	.9230	.0011	.0600	1.0172	.0033	.0706	.0709	.3390	.3386	.3386
44. Professional services	.9531	.0000	.0146	1.0752	.0022	.0269	.0346	.3167	.2928	.2928
45. Entertainment	.5054	.0434	-.0042	.6719	.0458	.0092	.0460	.2667	.1767	.1767
46. Restaurants & hotels	.2001	.0000	.0615	.3099	.0016	.0737	.1260	.2083	.1946	.1946
47. Laundries, barbers, etc.	.9039	.0108	.0093	1.0013	.0130	.0207	.0439	.3176	.3125	.3125
48. Other services	.6486	.0000	.0145	.7109	.0012	.0211	.0435	.2298	.2984	.2984
50. Total consumed by av. urban family[g]										
a) In Escudos per month				138.0070[h]	16.3224[h]	11.6919	236.4189[i]	402.4400[j]	—	434.71[r]
b) In $ per month at c.i.f. prices				35.9287[k]	7.1819[l]	—	61.6606[m]	104.7734[n]	—	104.3061[s]

* For footnotes see next page.

Footnotes to table 3

a From input–output table, after multiplying labour- and import-coefficients by 1.50 and 0.44 respectively (see text). For labour coefficients see text.

b In c.i.f. dollars; from data supplied by ODEPLAN in connection with the input–output table.

c Direct and indirect costs incurred through purchase of 'non-border-priced' inputs (i.e. imports from sectors 28 – 48).

d In c.i.f. dollars.

e Costs incurred through direct and indirect purchase of 'border-priced' goods (1 – 28) in c.i.f. dollars. The first 28 entries are the directly computed border prices. The following 20 entries are the p_{12}^*-vector.

f In dollars per current escudo of final expenditure (at producer prices). The first 28 entries are the directly computed border-prices. The remaining entries are computed from columns D to G by $F = G + \lambda D + E$, where $\lambda = 0.2603$.

g Sum of above, weighted according to consumption expenditure of average urban family (table 1, col. F).

h Including direct imports.

i Residual, includes profits, rent, and interest.

j From table 1, 52F.

k = l_{20}

l Including direct imports, i.e. = $m_{10} + m_{20} = m_0$.

m = $p_{10} + p_{20} = p_0$.

n = $\lambda D + E + G$, with $\lambda = 0.2603$ (eq. (8)). The logic of the procedure also ensures that λ is equal to the ratio of the figures 50b/F and 50a/F, (i.e. $104.7734 \div 402.44$). The figure is identical with the result of revaluing average family expenditure at producer prices (table 1, col. F) in border-price content (col. F of this table) and adding the c.i.f. value of direct imports of 5.7024$ (= table 1, 51F multiplied by the conversion factor 0.44).

o Obtained from col. F by first inflating values in the ratio wholesale ÷ producer price (as estimated in app. B) and then adding tax-clear wholesale and transport-margins (app. B) revalued at 0.2600 and 0.2897 $/E° respectively (see figures 33F and 39F of this table).

p Obtained from col. G by first inflating values in the ratio retail ÷ wholesale price (as estimated in app. B) and then adding tax-inclusive retail margins revalued at 0.2500 $/E° (see figure 33G of this table). An allowance of 30% for retail margins on imports was included throughout.

q The figure was scaled down by about 4% to allow for taxes on retail trade (app. B).

r See table 1, 52A.

s Results of revaluing all items of average family expenditure at retail prices (table 1, col. A) at the border-price contents applicable to those prices (col. H of this table). This should be equal to total border-price content computed on the basis of producer prices, i.e. figure 50b/F, except for errors of rounding.

5. *The border-price content of goods and services.* The computation of the BP-contents for the twenty 'non-tradeable' sectors was done in accordance with eqs. (7) and (8), as shown in table 3. We started by listing the labour-, import- and tax-coefficients (*l, m, n*) for all 48 sectors of the economy, as derived from the producer-price matrix of appendix table C2. Although the purpose of this section requires a knowledge of only the last twenty of these, we decided to give the full list for the sake of completeness.

Before being entered in column A of table 3 the original labour coefficients (which refer to *hired* labour only) were scaled up in proportion to the ratio in which self-employment stood to hired employment in each sector.[23] The underlying assumption that the wage-element in the earnings of the self-employed is just about equal to the average wage of hired workers in the same sector seems justified in Chilean conditions. Any excess earnings over this may be credited to the non-labour elements in these earnings (rewards to entrepreneurship etc.) and merged with the profits and losses of ordinary employers (other than self-employed). This total we have chosen to neglect on the grounds that the *normal* profit component is already allowed for in our treatment of capital services (the matrix *K*), and that any supernormal profits beyond this will largely be compensated by losses elsewhere in the same sector.[24]

A further mark-up of 50% has been applied to all labour coefficients to allow for a 'social incubus' in the shape of wage-type incomes from State and employers' funds (maternity benefits, housing subsidies, etc.) which accrue to workers' families and undoubtedly add to the costs of labour from the community's point of view. Inevitably, our estimate of this incubus is hazardous in the extreme. It does, however, arise from a comparison of family expenditure with independent wage data and is probably of the right order of magnitude.

The import-coefficients were reduced to 44% of their escudo-values before being entered in column B, in line with official exchange-rates (0.8637 $ per escudo) in 1962 and the subsequent devaluation by 51% between that year and 1963/4.

The tax coefficients in column C of table 3 refer to indirect or 'business' taxes only and do not enter our final calculations, as they are not reflections of genuine resource costs. We do, however, list them (and the resulting global coefficients of column F) for the special interest they might present in other contexts.

---

[23] ODEPLAN, Evolución de la población ocupada per sectores economicos 1960 – 67, table 14, p. 18 et seq.
[24] We refer of course to the last 20 sections only. We shall, however, allow for special profits arising from the release of underemployed labour to new projects (see below).

Table 4

Border/user price ratios for consumption and the border-price content of wage and salary payments

	Average urban family	Of which: by income bracket			
		Low	Med.–low	Med.–high	High
1. BP content of home goods consumed ($)[b]	99.07	34.06	73.04	130.02	303.53
2. Direct consumption of imported goods (excl. margins) ($)[c]	5.70	2.01	4.27	7.64	17.81
3. BP content of total consumption expenditure ($)	104.77	36.07	77.31	137.87	321.34
4. Total consumption expenditure (E^O)[d]	402.44	139.62	298.57	528.05	1214.09
5. Border/Producer Price Ratio ($ per E^O)[e]	0.2603	0.2583	0.2590	0.2611	0.2647
6. Border/User Price Ratio ($ per E^O)[f]	0.2410	0.2391	0.2398	0.2417	0.2450
7. BP content of the wage salary unit ($ per E^O)[g]	0.3615	0.3586	0.3597	0.3626	0.3675

[a] Low: under 225 E^O/month, med.–low: 225–450 E^O/month, med.–high: 450 – 750 E^O/month, high: over 750 E^O/month.

[b] Consumption structures of table 1 at producer prices valued at BP contents as listed in table 5, col. F.

[c] Table 1, row 51 converted to 1963/4 $.

[d] Table 1, row 52.

[e] (3) ÷ (4).

[f] Row 5 multiplied by the average/user price ratios (0.9258), – see table 1, 52F ÷ 52E.

[g] Row 6 multiplied by the factor 1.5 (see text).

The 'global' input coefficients in columns D to G, and the resulting BP-contents are derived from columns A, B, and C with the aid of eqs. $(7) - (9)$, as explained in the footnotes.

In order to build up the total border-price contents of non-tradeables from these data we must first revalue the labour inputs of column D at the border-cost of workers' consumption λ, as shown in eqs. (7) and (9). As will be seen in table 4 (row 5), this figure emerges a 0.2603 dollars per escudo from the simultaneous solution of these two equations. When column D has been so revalued and added to the other two components (columns E and G), we obtain the final border/producer price ratios v_2 shown in the last 20 positions of column F. We then add the directly established border-prices of the first 28 sectors, and thus arrive at a complete listing of all the conversion coefficients we shall need at producer level. When these are applied to urban family expenditure item by item (col. F of table 1) we arrive at a total border cost of 104.7734 c.i.f. dollars per family per month. This must of course be equal to the corresponding escudo-outlay of 402.4400 per month when revalued at the rate of 0.2603 dollars per escudo. For ease of reference these explanations are repeated in summary form in the footnotes to table 4.

The purpose of all calculations in this study is first and foremost the estimation of the shadow wage of labour. The estimation of the border-price of family consumption (λ) is an important step towards that end. In arriving at this figure, however, we have had to estimate the BP-content of 48 major commodity-groups, and it would seem wasteful not to adapt these findings to other uses which project appraisers might wish to make of them at one time or other. With this object in view we have added two column to table 3 suggesting conversion coefficients for the revaluation of inputs in the form in which they are most likely to enter a new project, i.e. at wholesale prices (including taxes and margins) or at retail. It is the first of these which should be of the greatest use to project makers. The derivation of both sets of figures follows a fairly obvious pattern and is explained in the footnotes. It should be noted, however, that both columns G and H are subject to even greater errors than the border/producer price ratios which were the starting-point for their estimation.

6. *The border-price content of wages.* The BP-content of labour-pay (λ), which may be expressed as $(p_0 + m_0)/(\epsilon - l_{20})$[25], can be derived from the last two lines of table 3 which display the necessary ingredients:

ϵ = 402.4400 E°/month (row 50a/F)
l_{20} = 138.0070 E°/month (row 50a/D)
$P_0 = p_1 h_1 + p_{12}^* h_2$ = 61.6606 $/month (row 50b/G)
$m_0 = m_{10} + m_2^* h_2$ = 7.1819 $/month (row 50b/E)

Hence : $p_0 + m_0$ = 68.8425 $/month
$\epsilon - l_{20}$ = 264.3330 E°/month

Therefore: λ = 0.26034 $/E° as of 1963/4.

It will be remembered that the vectors h_1 and h_2 appearing in the calculation are the monthly expenditure-lists of the average urban family on tradeables and non-tradeables respectively.

[25] See eq. (9).

As explained before, we must now use the figure for λ just obtained to re-value the global (direct and indirect) labour cost of non-tradables (col. D of table 3) in terms of border-price content at c.i.f. dollars. When the result is added to the BP-content of imports and tradables (cols. E and G) we obtain the border prices of our twenty non-tradeables. This, in conjunction with the border prices of the 28 tradables (derived directly from tariff-data) gives us the complete list of border prices in c.i.f. dollars per escudo-unit for all 48 commodity-groups, as listed in col. F of table 3.

The figures can now be used to revalue urban family consumption at BP-content for the average household and for each of the four income brackets distinguished in the budget surveys. When applied to home-produced items only, this yields the figures in row 1 of table 4. On adding the c.i.f. values of *direct* consumption imports (row 2) we finally obtain the BP-content of total family expenditure, as listed in row 3. It should be clear that when these figures are divided by the corresponding escudo-sums (at producer prices), we must obtain the BP-contents of the average escudo-unit involved in family consumption (at producer level) in terms of $\$/E^o$. This has been done in row 5 of table 4.

As will be seen, the conversion factors change very little as we proceed from lower to higher income-groups. The slightly increasing trend which the figures seem to show is in accord with one's normal expectations, but our estimates of direct imports in the consumption pattern of individual income brackets is too hazardous to attach much importance to this result.

The sixth row of table 4 shows our estimates of the conversion-coefficients to be applied to expenditure-items when these are expressed in *user* prices. Finally, the last line of table 4 gives the factors to be applied to actual wage- or salary-payments in order to reach their BP-content, taking into account that each unit paid out in this way will on average entail 1.5 units of extra consumption due to the 'social incubus' discussed in the last section. Since the level of income makes so little difference, we shall not go far wrong if we apply a factor of 0.36 dollars per escudo to all wage- and salary-payments indiscriminately.

To this we add an allowance for average payments in kind,[26] and obtain the BP-content of all urban labour costs (in money and kind) as *0.3812 \$ per escudo*. This, then, is our estimate of the conversion factor γ by which

[26] From an internal paper of ODEPLAN's Manpower Division which suggests 7.125% of money wages as being the value of payments in kind in 1963/4 (our average). We have assumed that this was made up of housing, utilities, education, and medical care in the proportions used by all consumers and government, and have revalued each of these categories at their BP-content from table 3.

the project-worker's money wage must be multiplied to yield the BP-content of his consumption ($c = \gamma w$). To avoid the suggestion of spurious accuracy we shall round γ down to *0.38* throughout.

IV. The social adjustments

A. The computation

Having arrived at an estimate of the total cost of labour in terms of border prices as it faces the employing agency (whether public or private), we must now turn to the evaluation of that portion of it which represents an implied benefit to the community as a whole. This of course must be deducted from employers' cost to arrive at the shadow price of labour (i.e. its net cost to the community).

Let us recall from section I. B, that the benefit in question consists of

(1) all net consumption increments consequent upon the employment of an extra project worker, a quantity we have denoted by b, revalued as b_s (to allow for the smaller value of this extra consumption compared with the alternative social purpose that might have been pursued if funds had *not* been diverted to the employment of labour);

(2) all releases of fund (e) due to the abstraction of the worker from some other occupation where his marginal product may have fallen short of his institutionally determined wage; this we decided to deduct at half its par value (section I.B).

Both the values b_s and e evidently depend on the branch (or branches) of the economy from which the workers are likely to be abstracted by virtue of the project being undertaken, and it is to this that we must now turn.

1. The probable origin of new project labour. In the treatment of the Manual the ultimate source of project labour is identified with agriculture. This may be plausible enough in the case of many underdeveloped countries. It is less so in the case of Chile. Our general impression in that country has been that labour- and wage-legislation have reached a stage where many enterprises find themselves employing more labour than its marginal product would warrant, i.e. institutional wages often appear to exceed marginal products. In these conditions it is doubtful whether workers departing voluntarily from a given branch to take up work on a new project will actually be replaced there — or replaced to the full extent of the loss. In this way the chain of departures and replacements, though it might eventually reach down to agriculture, will lose many links on the way, and the ultimate net suppliers of labour may be a number of intermediate branches in addition to agriculture.

In conformity with the implicit hypothesis of the Manual we assume that unless a new project is specifically designed to relieve unemployment it will not have a net impact on the total pool of workless in the country. For all those individual unemployed who might be drawn into the project new contingents of about equal strength will normally join the unemployed, due to additional urban inflows attracted by the mere existence of the project or due to the reduced employment opportunities in competing branches which the project will create. The new recruitment must therefore be assumed to diminish employment in existing productive sectors compared with that which would have obtained in the absence of the project.

In the nature of things we had to estimate the pattern of this 'ultimate' labour supply in a very roundabout way:

From the structure of incremental demand for output between 1960 and 1967 (as shown in the first half of table 5) we computed the total new demand for labour which would have resulted in the various sectors [27] if production methods and technology had remained unaltered at the 1962 level.[28] The result (row 7 of table 5) was compared with the *actual* increases in employment, and all shortfalls of the latter below the former were taken as a measure of the sector's relative 'tendency to lose labour' in the wake of technological progress or other supply-determined changes. We then accepted the branch-structure of this tendency (last row of table 5) as the best clue we were likely to get concerning the ultimate 'origins' of a typical batch of 100 workers recruited for a new project: 37 of them are likely to be drawn from agriculture, 12 from mining, etc., as table 5 indicates.[29] Further details of the underlying model and computations are given in appendix B and the footnotes to table 5.

2. Sectoral wage-levels and consumption increments from project-induced shifts in employment. We can best summarize our hypotheses in two tables, showing respectively our estimate of comparative wage-levels (table 6) and the corresponding income rises following from employment shifts between the sectors (table 7) as induced by the recruitment of labour to new projects.

The average pay for 1963/4 in industrial sectors was estimated by us from the Chilean input—output table and independent wage data. In the case of

[27] Directly and indirectly.
[28] This was computed with the aid of the input—output table.
[29] It should be noted that this is not meant to show the previous employment record of the 100 actual individuals recruited, but merely the ultimate net affect of their recruitment on the employment structure of the country.

The structure of incremental demand between 1960 and 1967.

	Total demand [a] A	Of which:							
		Agr. [b] B	Mining C	Mfc. [c] D	Constr. E	Trade F	Trans't G	Dom. service H	Other services I
Incremental demand for output (in mil. escudos of 1962):									
1. Personal consn. [d]	1475	136	–	896	11	225	81	: :	126
2. Govt. Expend're [e]	176	1	–	32	1	1	–	: :	140
3. Gross fixed cp'l. $F'n$ [f]	143	–	–	43	100	–	–	: :	–
4. Exports [g]	286	21	247	18	–	–	–	: :	–
5. Total final demand	2080	158	247	989	112	226	81	: :	266
Incremental labour (in thous. man-years):									
6. Direct 'induced' demand [h]	525	112	33	122	24	46	23	93 [i]	72
7. Global 'induced' demand [j]	737	174	39	190	27	154	50	23 [n]	80
8. Actual empl't [k]	490	54	1	125	10	109	35	– 13	169
9. 'Redundancy' (7–8) [l]	326 [l]	120	38	65	17	35	15	36	–1
10. Structure of 'redundancy' (%) [m]	100 [m]	37	12	20	5	10	5	11	– [m]

a From ODEPLAN, 'Cuentas Nacionales de Chile 1960–1967', pp. 33 et seq. The data are in constant escudos of 1965 and were converted by us into 1962 escudos by deflating by the rise in wholesale prices between the two years (296.62%, see ODEPLAN, 'Statistical profile of Chile', 1969 ed., p. 14).

b Incl. Fisheries.

c Manufacturing and utilities.

d Breakdown of figure A in proportion to family budgets (see table 1, col. F) corrected for rural consumption.

e Breakdown of figure A from 1962 input–output table.

f Construction and home-produced machinery and equipment only; see first source of footnote a.

g Breakdown of figure A from ODEPLAN, 'Statistical Profile of Chile', 1969 ed., p. 57.

h Applying to row 5 the sectoral labour-coefficients of 1962 computed from gross outputs (input–output table condensed) and employment data from ODEPLAN, 'Evolucion de la Poblacion Ocupada por Sectores Economicos 1960–1967', p. 15.

i Assuming expansion in proportion to total consumer expenditure at constant prices as a first hypothesis.

j Direct and indirect labour demand to cover intermediate as well as final requirements = row 6 pre-multiplied by matrix G (appendix B)

k From source of footnote h, pp. 14 and 17.

l Defined as shortfall in actual employment-rise below the figure which autonomous (final) demand increases would have lead one to expect (row 7). 'Other services' as 'labour-gaining' branches are excluded.

m For 'labour-losing' branches only, i.e. excluding 'Other services'.

n Figure 6H arbitrarily reduced by 75% to allow for observable social trends.

Table 6
Wages and labour costs in agriculture and industry.

	Total wages & salaries 1962[a] (mill. E°)	No. of hired workers 1962[b] (thous.)	Av. mthly pay 1962[c] (E°)	Av. mthly pay 1963/4[d] (E°)	Mthly labour cost 1963/4[e] (E°)	BP-content of labour cost[f] ($)
	A	B	C	D	E	F
1. Agric. etc.	168.8	438.3	32.08	51.3	84.09	30.3
2. Of which: voluntario	–	–	–	–	38.40	13.8[g]
3. Mining	162.5	87.8	154.21	275.22	294.83	104.6
4. Mfc. & utilities	402.2	353.7	94.75	169.10	181.15	64.3
5. Construction	108.0	109.6	82.14	146.60	157.04	55.7
6. Trade	205.0	131.7	129.71	231.50	248.00	88.0
7. Transport	174.1	109.4	132.62	236.69	253.55	89.9
8. Domestic service	49.2	202.4	20.25	36.14	72.38	27.5
9. Gov't. service	239.0	110.9	179.60	320.53	343.37	121.8
10. Other services	441.9	222.6	165.44	295.26	316.30	112.2
11. Urban excl. dom. service	1732.7	1125.7	128.3	229.0	245.3	87.0
12. Urban excl. all services	1051.8	792.2	110.6	197.4	211.5	75.0

[a] From condensation of input–output table.

[b] ODEPLAN, 'Evolución de la Poblacion Ocupada por Sectores Económicos 1960–67' pp.15 and 49.

[c] A ÷ B converted to monthly basis.

[d] 1962 increased by 78.47% (Peter Gregory, *Industrial wages in Chile*, Ithaca, N.Y., p. 42) in line with wages in manufacturing, except for agriculture where a 60% growth rate was assumed (based on information that the index of growth was 10% below that of urban industries).

[e] Adding to D estimated payments in kind, valued at 80.2% of cash wages in agriculture (Alberto Valdés, 'Wages and schooling of agricultural workers in Chile', May 1968, typescript) and 7.125% of cash wages in urban sectors (see section 7). In the case of domestic service we arbitrarily assumed a ratio of 50%.

[f] Applying BP-ratios of 0.36 per E° to col. E for agriculture (see text) and 0.38 $ per E° to col. D for all other branches (see section 8) except domestic services where the coefficient was applied to col.E.

[g] Estimate of the marginal product of labour in agriculture.

Table 7
Increased consumption per man employed in new projects (in BP-content as percent of new consumption levels).

Sector where new project is located: Recruited from:	Relative levels of consumption[a]						Cons-rise through shift to[b]						Estimated structure of recruitment[d]
	Mining A	Mfc. & util. B	Constr. C	Trade D	Trans't. etc. E	Unspecified[c] F	Mining G	Mfc. & util. H	Constr. I	Trade J	Trans't. etc. K	Unspecified[c] L	M
1. Agriculture etc.[e]	13.2	21.5	24.8	15.7	15.4	18.3	86.8	78.5	75.2	84.3	84.6	81.7	37
2. Mining	100.0	162.7	187.8	118.9	116.4	139.5	0.0	-62.7	-87.8	-18.9	-16.4	-39.5	12
3. Manufacturing and utilities	61.5	100.0	115.4	73.1	71.5	85.7	38.5	0.0	-15.4	26.9	14.3	14.3	20
4. Construction	53.2	86.6	100.0	63.3	62.0	74.3	46.8	13.4	0.0	36.7	38.0	25.7	5
5. Trade	84.1	136.8	158.0	100.0	97.9	117.3	15.9	36.8	-58.0	0.0	2.1	-17.3	10
6. Transport	85.9	139.8	161.4	102.2	100.0	119.9	14.1	39.8	-61.4	-2.2	0.0	-19.9	5
7. Domestic service	26.2	42.8	49.4	31.2	30.6	36.7	73.8	57.2	50.6	68.8	69.4	63.3	11
8. Unspecified[c]	71.7	116.9	134.6	85.2	83.4	100.0	28.3	16.9	-34.6	14.8	16.6	0.0	–
9. Consumption rise from all recruitment[f](% of new consumption levels)	–	–	–	–	–	–	52.6	22.8	10.9	43.6	44.8	33.9	–

a Table 6 (col. F) based on the absolute level of each sector in turn (= 100).
b 100.0% minus the corresponding column in first half of the table.
c Urban sectors excluding all services (gov't, domestic, and others).
d See table 5, row 10.
e Assuming voluntario wages, i.e. consumption of the marginal product only.
f Rows 1–7 weighted by column M.

agriculture a separate estimate had to be made to ascertain the marginal product of labour, as it is this rather than the *average* wage which is needed to ascertain the proper consumption increment accruing to the community.[30] We
took it that the marginal product in question could best be approximated by
the wage of the lowest-paid category of agricultural workers,[31] so-called *voluntario* labour, and based ourselves on a sample survey of 48 farms[32] which
puts the voluntario's remuneration (in money and in kind) at 45.7% of the
cost of 'avergae farm labour'. Our wage-estimates were then converted to BP-
content, and for the rest the two tables may be left to speak for themselves.[33]

3. *The social valuation of consumption shifts.* In the last row of table 7 we
gave our estimates of the total consumption increment to be expected from
the shift of one worker to a new project, measured as a proportion p of his
new consumption level. When this is multiplied by his project-wage c (at f.p.-
valuation) we obtain the absolute border-price content of the consumption increment b, i.e. $b = pc$.

   In this section we shall be concerned with the revaluation of b in terms of
'general government purposes' as explained in section I. C in fact with the
translation of b into b_s for use in our basic formula for the shadow wage
$\omega = c - b_s \doteq \frac{1}{2}e$. For this purpose we need to take a view on two points: (1)
The government's degree of preference for generalized command over re-
sources in its own hands compared with the outright commitment of those

---

[30] A worker shifting directly from agriculture to a new project would experience a consumption increment of $c - a$, where c is the project-wage and a the average wage in agriculture. In addition, however, he will release resources equal to the excess of his previous
consumption (a) over his marginal product (m), i.e., $a - m$, which we assume to accrue to
the workers *remaining* on the land. The total consumption increment induced by his departure is therefore, $c - m$, i.e., $(c - a) + (a - m)$.

[31] As paid during the period of their actual employment each year.

[32] Alberto Valdés E., 'Wages and schooling of agricultural workers in Chile', May 1968.

[33] For the sake of simplicity we proceeded in table 7 as if every worker transferred from
branch A to branch B had his wages raised from the *average* level obtaining in the first to
the *average* level obtaining in the second. In what follows we allow departures from this,
but continue to assume that the wage rises for all skill categories or grades moving from
A to B remain in the same proportion p which obtains between the averages. In other
words we assume that a batch of workers newly recruited by, say, the construction industry into a grade earning $x\%$ above the average will have been drawn from similar grades
in other branches, i.e., from wage-scales earning $x\%$ above the average of the branch in
which they were previously occupied. This assumption allowed the fixed proportions p
(row 9 of table 7) to be applied to *all* wage-levels of the project industry when computing
the consumption effects of its new recruitment.

resources to personal 'utilities' in the shape of consumption increments, and
(2) The way in which the personal 'utilities' afforded by given increments might
vary with the income level of the recipient.

The mathematical details of our procedure and computation are set out in
appendix C. All we need say here is that we assume some regular way in which
the typical workers' marginal utility will diminish with his income level.[34] We
then assume that the community (= government) will so value his incremental
income that the sum of marginal utilities accruing from it would be equal to
the net revenue which the government might expect from pushing taxation
beyond its present level to just the extent which would deprive him of such
an increment. This is based on the notion that the government will have acted
rationally in adjusting total taxation in such a manner that it is indifferent
between the marginal benefits that would accrue to itself from further taxation and the consumption benefits that this would cost its presumptive victims.
Were it not so, we take it, the government would tax either less or more than
it does at present.

If this method is accepted, the social valuation of income increments will
come to depend on the previous income-level of the recipient, as well as certain parameters of the assumed utility function and the existing income distribution of workers in the economy. We have attempted to devise our model
in such a way that no undue strain is put on the normal statistical resources
of a less developed country. The reader will, however, need to form his own
judgment, in the light of the details provided in Appendix B.

Table 8 shows our estimates of b_s, the social valuation of income increments
that would result from the recruitment of a 'typical' batch of workers to a
new project, in its dependence on the sectors in which the project is located
(i.e. the prevailing wage to which these workers would be raised).

As may be seen in the last section of table 8, the assumption of marginal
utilities falling in strict proportion to income-rises ($r = 0$, row L) implies that
the government values its general command over resources ('money in its own
hands') dollar for dollar on a par with personal consumption increments
('money in workers' bands'), provided the latter are of a magnitude and to a
level enjoyed by the 'average' worker recruited to the 'average' project. This
is apparent from the near-equality of the actual cost b with its first valuation
b_s in the case of the 'unspecified' (= average urban) sector, i.e. from figures
K6 and L6 of table 8. Consumption increments from recruitment to *lower*-

---

[34] This will in fact be a function relationship of the type $u(x) = k/x^{r+1}$, where x stands
for income and k and r are constants to be determined. We are, in fact, taking several
alternative values for r which might be held to mark out the extremes of a plausible range
(see appendix B).

Table 8
The BP-contents of consumption increments b following recruitment to different wage-levels (w) and their social valuations b_s under three hypotheses. [a]

Recruitments to projects in: →	Mining 1	Mfg. & Util. 2	Construction 3	Trade 4	Transport 5	Unspecified[b] 6
A. Av. wage (E^o/mth)[c] w	275	169	147	232	237	197
B. Wage rise on recruitm't.t_r(%)[d] P	52.6	22.8	10.9	43.6	44.8	33.9
C. Pre-recruitm't. level (%)[e] q	47.4	77.2	89.1	56.4	55.2	66.1
D. $\log 1/q$	0.7465	0.2588	0.1154	0.5727	0.5942	0.4140
E. $(1-\sqrt{q})/\sqrt{q}$	0.4525	0.1381	0.0594	0.3316	0.3460	0.2300
F. P/q	1.110	0.295	0.122	0.773	0.812	0.513
BP-cons'n. increments for wage w^f						
G. Actual $b = \gamma p w^g$	0.200w	0.087w	0.041w	0.165w	0.170w	0.129w
H. Valuations $b_s = B_0/w^0 (r=0)^h$	45.0	16.3	7.3	36.0	37.4	26.0
I. Valuations $b_s = B_1/w^{\frac{1}{2}}(r=\frac{1}{2})^i$	619/√w	189/√w	81/√w	454/√w	474/√w	315/√w
J. Valuations $b_s = B_2^{\frac{1}{2}}/w_1(r=1)^j$	8115/w	2157/w	892/w	5651/w	5936/w	3751/w
BP-cons'n. increments for av. wage w^k						
K. Actual b	55.0	14.7	6.0	38.3	40.3	25.4
L. Valuations $b_s(r=0)$	45.0	16.3	7.3	36.0	37.4	26.0
M. Valuations $b_s(r=\frac{1}{2})$	37.3	14.5	6.7	29.8	30.8	22.4
N. Valuations $b_s(r=1)$	29.5	12.8	6.0	24.4	25.0	19.0

a The hypotheses differ in regard to the assumed rate at which the marginal utilities of workers (u) diminish as their income (x) rises, i.e.
hypothesis 1 ($r=0$): $u = k/x$;
hypothesis 2 ($r=\frac{1}{2}$): $u = k/\sqrt{x}$, where k is adjusted to each hypothesis, see eqs. (18) and (18a).
hypothesis 3 ($r=1$): $u = k/x^2$
b Average in total urban non-service sphere.
c Table 6, col. D.
d Based on wages after recruitment to the new sector; table 7, row 9.
e $q = 1-p$.
f Application of formulae (23) for $\tau = 0.9$, $\bar{x} = 69.9$, $\xi_1 = 0.8000$, $\xi_{\frac{1}{2}} = 0.6300$, $\gamma = 0.38$; see text and footnotes to this table.
g $\gamma = 0.38$ see section 8.
h $B_0 = \tau \times n1/q = 0.9 \times 69.9 \times$ row D; see text.
i $B_{\frac{1}{2}} = \xi_{\frac{1}{2}}/\sqrt{\tau}.\bar{x}^{3/2}.(1-\sqrt{q})/\sqrt{q} = (2 \times 0.9 \times 0.80/\sqrt{.38}).(69.9)^{3/2}.$ row E; see text.
j $B_1 = \xi_1/\sqrt{\tau}^2.p/q = (0.9 \times 0.63/\sqrt{.38}).(69.9)^2.$ row F; see text

paid sectors (manufacturing and construction) will be valued more *highly* than money in government hands (compare L2 and L3 with the corresponding *b*-values in row K); a rational government would therefore prefer to give subsidies (or remit taxation) for such increments rather than spend equal amounts for other purposes, but would be debarred from doing so by our requirement that marginal tax-changes must be non-distributive. Consumption-gains on transfer to *higher*-paid sectors, however, are valued *below* the government's own money (see L1, L4, and L5), since these involve faster decreases in utility-returns.

The assumption of marginal utilities falling more radically, i.e. with the square of income-rises ($r = 1$) implies that the government values nearly all consumption-gains (reaching average sector levels) below their costs in terms of its own money (compare rows N and K)[35] — with discounts ranging from 0% for the lowest-paid sector (construction) to nearly 50% for the highest (mining). The latter case would correspond to a value of *s* equal to 2 in terms of the Manual.[36]

Between these two extremes lies the assumption of marginal utilities falling with the cube of the square-root of income-rises ($r = \frac{1}{2}$), which implies government indifference between consumption-rise to the average level of *manufacturing* wages and its own general purpose spending (compare M2 with K2). This would correspond to an *s*-value equal to 1 in terms of the Manual. All other average consumption-rises, except for those to the level of the construction industry, are valued by the government *below* par (compared with its own money). This time the discount ranges from 0 to just over 30% (in mining). It would be about 12% for the average non-agricultural project (col. 5), which corresponds to an *s*-value of nearly 1.14 in terms of the Manual.

It will be remembered that if the project-worker's wage *w* exceeds the average level of the sector to which he has been recruited ($\overline{w}$), his consumption-gain is still assumed to be the same *in percentage terms* as that which we regard as typical for the sector in question (i.e. *p*). This, however, will now represent a greater *absolute* amount *b*, thus implying lower utility-returns for each extra dollar earned, and hence a lower social valuation of the total gain (b_s). The valuation will be inversely proportional to the wage-level reached (*w*) if hypothesis $r = 1$ is adopted (row J), or to its square root under hypothesis $r = \frac{1}{2}$ (row I).

---

[35] The one inconsequential exception is the construction sector.

[36] It will be remembered that the Manual suggested that consumption-increments *b* be made commensurable with savings funds by dividing them by a constant deflator *s*, i.e., $b_s = b/s$.

Table 9

Funds saved per man employed in new projects due to release from urban under-employment (in BP-content as % of new consumption level c).

| Sector where new project is located: | Relative wage-levels[a] | | | | | | Structure of recruitment (% of total)[c] |
	Mining A	Mfc. & util. B	Constr'n. C	Trade D	Trans't etc. E	Unspec'd[b] F	G
Recruited from sector:							
1. Mining	100.0	162.7	187.8	118.9	116.4	139.5	12
2. Mfc. & util.	61.5	100.0	115.4	73.1	71.5	85.5	20
3. Construction	53.2	86.6	100.0	63.3	62.0	74.3	5
4. Trade	84.1	136.8	158.0	100.0	97.9	117.3	10
5. Transport, etc.	85.9	139.8	161.4	102.2	100.0	119.9	5
6. Wages earned in previous empl't. in above sectors (as % of c)[d]	39.7	64.5	74.5	47.2	46.2	55.3	–
7. Assumed excess of wages over marg'l. product (% of c)[e]	10	15	20	10	10	15	–
8. Funds saved e (as % of c)[f]	4.0	9.6	15.0	4.7	4.6	8.2	–
9. Social valuation of e (% of c)[g]	2.0	4.8	7.5	2.4	2.3	4.1	–
10. 100.0 – (9) (%)	98.0	95.2	92.5	97.6	97.7	95.9	–
11. Coefficient A[h]	0.372	0.362	0.351	0.371	0.371	0.364	–

[a] Table 7, cols. A – F.
[b] Average urban sector excluding service sphere.
[c] Table 7, col. M.
[d] Sum of first 5 rows weighted by percentages in col. G.
[e] See text.
[f] Row 6 × row 7.
[g] One half of row 8 (see text).
[h] A = coeff. γ (0.38) multiplied by percentages in row 10.

4 . *Saving from reduced urban under-employment.* In line with our previous analysis we assume that each batch of 100 new project-workers will contain 52 recruits from five urban sectors[37] in which some degree of under-employment exists. This will 'liberate' resources valued at e border-price dollars to the extent that their previous consumption exceeded their marginal products. In table 9 (row 7) we have guessed at this excess in the various sectors by making 'freehand' adjustment for known or suspected discrepancies from an overall estimated average of 15%.[38] Just how tenuous this estimate is can easily be seen by applying it to other countries in other periods. In the Chilean context there may be more to be said for it than elsewhere, and we can do no better than present it as our best guess in the time available.

The figure for e is then computed in row 8 of table 9 and 'socially valued' at one half its original size. This is in line with our reasoning in section I(C) which put the shadow wage (ω) equal to $c - b_s - \frac{1}{2}e$. Disregarding consumption gains (b_s), we see that the reduction of c may be put in the form

$$c - \tfrac{1}{2}e = (1 - \tfrac{1}{2}\tfrac{e}{c})c = Aw ,$$

where the coefficient A stands for the expression $(1 - \tfrac{1}{2}e/c)\gamma$. This, then, is the conversion factor by which escudo-wages should be multiplied to yield the shadow wage before the allowance for consumption shifts (b_s) is deducted from the result.

V. Summary of results

We are now in a position to integrate into a single figure the three basic elements of the shadow wage which we have separately estimated in the preceding sections, i.e.

[37] Twelve from mining, 20 from manufacturing or utilities, 5 from construction, 10 from trade, and 5 from transport (see table 7, col. M). The funds saved through recruitment from agriculture are assumed to accrue wholly to consumption and have already been dealt with at length. The only other recruits – those from domestic service – are not assumed to have been under-employed before and do not therefore give rise to benefits of this sort.

[38] A rough calculation suggests that average labour productivity rose by 25% between 1960 and 1967, while real wages and salaries rose by 47%. If the former percentage may be taken as equal to the growth in the *marginal* product of labour, it follows that this has risen about 15% more slowly than real wages in the seven years under review. We shall now assume quite arbitrarily that the length of service of the average worker in a given occupation is approximately seven years and that at the time of his engagement his real wage was equal to his marginal product. If both his wage and his productivity follow the national trend, he will after seven years end up with a marginal product some 15% below his real wage.

Table 10
Shadow wages (ω)ᵃ.
Sectoral estimates for two hypothesesᵇ and wage-levels.

		General formula for ω (in BP-dollars), given money-wage w (in E⁰)ᵈ $Aw - B/w^f$		Average sector levels			Double averages (for $\bar{\bar{w}} = 2\bar{w}$)	
				Money wage (E⁰/month) $\bar{w}$	BP-contentᵉ ($/month) $\bar{c}$	Shadow wageᶠ ($/mth)(% of c) $\bar{\omega}$	BP-content $\bar{\bar{c}}$	Shadow wageᵍ ($/mth)(% of c) $\bar{\bar{\omega}}$
		Aw	B/w^f					
1. Miningᶜ	$r = \frac{1}{2}$	$0.372w$	$619/\sqrt{w}$	275	104	64.7 (62%)	208	178 (86%)
	$r = 1$	$0.372w$	$8115/w$			72.5 (70%)		189 (91%)
2. Manufacturing & utilities	$r = \frac{1}{2}$	$0.362w$	$189/\sqrt{w}$	169	64	46.5 (73%)	128	112 (88%)
	$r = 1$	$0.362w$	$2157/w$			48.2 (75%)		115 (90%)
3. Construction	$r = \frac{1}{2}$	$0.351w$	$81/\sqrt{w}$	147	56	45.3 (81%)	112	99 (88%)
	$r = 1$	$0.351w$	$892/w$			45.9 (82%)		101 (90%)
4. Trade	$r = \frac{1}{2}$	$0.371w$	$454/\sqrt{w}$	232	88	56.2 (64%)	176	151 (86%)
	$r = 1$	$0.371w$	$5936/w$			61.6 (70%)		160 (91%)
5. Transport etc.	$r = \frac{1}{2}$	$0.371w$	$474/\sqrt{w}$	237	90	57.2 (64%)	180	154 (86%)
	$r = 1$	$0.371w$	$5936/w$			63.0 (70%)		164 (91%)
6. Average non-agricultural project	$r = \frac{1}{2}$	$0.364w$	$315/\sqrt{w}$	197	75	49.6 (66%)	150	128 (85%)
	$r = 1$	$0.364w$	$3751/w$					

ᵃ All figures are rounded to avoid spurious accuracy.
ᵇ The two hypotheses differ in regard to the assumed rate at which the marginal utilities of workers (u) diminish as their income (x) rises, i.e.
hypothesis $r = \frac{1}{2}$: $u = k/\sqrt{x}$, where k is adjusted to each hypothesis; see eqs. (18) and (18a).
hypothesis $r = 1$: $u = k/x$
ᶜ Project in 'urban non-service sphere'; i.e. average of sectors 1– 5.
ᵈ A- and B-values from tables 7 and 9.
ᵉ $c = \gamma w = 0.38w$ (see section 8).
ᶠ Substituting $\bar{w}$ for w in the first column. The figures in brackets show percentages of BP-content c.
ᵍ Substituting $\overline{2w}$ for w in the first column.

c, the frontier-price content of the direct cost of labour to the project
(= consumption per worker),

b_s, the social value of the consumption-increment occasioned by the recruitment of each worker to the project, and

e, the saving due to reduced under-employment in the sector(s) from which the worker has been recruited.

These elements, it will be remembered, make up the shadow wage according to the formula

$$\omega = c - \tfrac{1}{2}e - b_s \, ,$$

or, combining the first two elements and expressing the last as explained in the previous section:

$$\omega = Aw - B_r/w^r \text{ (for } r = \tfrac{1}{2} \text{ or } 1 \text{, according to our hypothesis concerning the}$$
speed with which personal utility falls as income grows),

where *w* stands for the money wage, and the constants are explained in the appendix.

Table 10 presents a conspectus of the numerical results of the two preceding tables in which the values for *A* and *B* were computed.

The first column of table 10 shows how our version of the shadow wage may be computed, given (1) the hypothesis we choose to adopt ($r = \tfrac{1}{2}$ or 1), (2) the sector in which the project is located, (3) the previous money-wage (*w*) or the worker.

As may be seen from the columns headed $\bar{\omega}$ and $\bar{\bar{\omega}}$, the choice of one or other of our hypotheses makes comparatively little difference to the outcome. For the 'average' project (row 6), the assumption of faster diminishing utility-returns from rising incomes ($r = 1$) increases the shadow wage by less than 7%, and the gap is reduced to under 5.5% as the wage level increases (compare $\bar{\omega}$ with $\bar{\bar{\omega}}$). The difference is greater for the higher-paid sectors (mining and trade and transport), and considerably less for lower-paid branches (manufactures and construction).

The shadow price would have been affected much more radically (in a downward direction) if we had adopted the hypothesis $r = 0$, which we discarded as implausible. Compared with the assumption $r = \tfrac{1}{2}$ this would have depressed the result by a maximum of 16% (in the case of mining) and by slightly over 10% for the average project. Again the reduction would be smaller as the wage-level increased.

Some doubt may attach to the 'sector in which the project is located'. It would be in the spirit of this study to interpret this as the branch of production

which may reasonably be supposed to govern the general conditions of pay of
the workers employed. If the labour force attached to the project can be classified as, say, 'construction labour' in the sense of being governed by the wage-
levels and a wage-structure typical of the construction industry, the project
would be said to be wholly 'located' in that sector. If, however, the labour
falls naturally into different groupings, professional or otherwise, then each
worker's labour must be valued at the shadow price appropriate to the sector
to which his group is most closely akin (as far as wage-levels and structure are
concerned). It is not anticipated that this differentiation will normally cause
much difficulty. In the last resort any labour which cannot be allocated in this
way might be treated as 'average non-agriculture' (sector 6).[39]

Comparison of columns ω and $\bar{\omega}$ makes it clear that the 'social adjustments'
(allowances for increased consumption and savings) remove the shadow wage
quite radically from the BP-content of wages, but do so to a much smaller extent as wage-levels rise. This is of course to be expected, since in accordance
with our hypotheses consumption-rises are valued much lower when they occur at higher income levels. At the average sectoral wage-level the adjustments
cause reductions ranging between 18 and 38%, depending on sector and hypothesis; at twice the average level they fall to a range between 8 and 14%. Perhaps we may hazard the guess that a new project will normally pay wages
somewhat exceeding the average of each professional group and that the typical shadow wage is therefore likely to lie within a range of, say, 15 – 30% of
the worker's consumption in BP-dollars. While this may be helpful in suggesting
general orders of magnitude, it does not absolve us from computing the shadow
wage according to the formula in each particular case.

Where the project wages offered fall below the sectoral averages the social
adjustments have more substantial effects and the shadow wage may come to
lie as much as 50 or even 75% below the BP-consumption level. In extreme
cases the reduction could be of 100% of more. There is of course nothing in-
herently absurd about negative shadow wages when the consumption rises are
from abysmally low levels and therefore socially more valuable than the wage
costs incurred. Nevertheless in such extreme cases the assumption of previous
consumption-levels as low as our fixed sectoral percentages would imply may
become blatantly implausible, and it is therefore suggested that we set a lower
limit of *zero* dollars to all shadow wages computed by our formulae. In other

---

[39] Let us recall that the differentiation by sectoral type of labour flows from the assumption that workers newly employed as, say, 'mining labour' will – whatever their wages –
experience consumption rises from a previous level which was on average 52.6% lower,
while 'construction labour' will only better their lot by 10.9% on average. Similar percentage rises apply to all other sectoral types of labour.

Table 11
Summary coefficients (α) for the conversion of current escudo-wages (w) into shadow-wages in dollars (ω).[a]

Sector and level (β) / Year (γ)	For wages at the average level of each sector					For wages at double av. level
	Mining (0.660)	Mfc. (0.745)	Constr'n. (0.815)	Trade & transp't. (0.670)	Average non-agr. (0.685)	All sectors (0.885)
1963/4 (0.380)	0.251	0.283	0.310	0.255	0.260	0.336
1965 (0.272)	0.180	0.203	0.222	0.182	0.186	0.241
1966 (0.216)	0.143	0.161	0.176	0.145	0.148	0.191
1967 (0.168)	0.111	0.125	0.137	0.113	0.115	0.149
1968 (0.126)	0.083	0.094	0.103	0.084	0.086	0.112
1969 (Prov) (0.098)	0.065	0.073	0.080	0.066	0.067	0.087

[a] The table gives the value of α in \$ per E^o to be used in the conversion formula $\omega = \alpha w$. The bracketed values for γ are the conversion coefficients to BP-contents for wages in various years (see text). The values for β under the sector headings (bracketed) are the social adjustment coefficients to be applied to the BP-content (mid-point values of the percentages in the $\bar{\omega}$- and $\underline{\omega}$-columns of table 10). The α-values in the body of the table are the products of the relevant β and γ, i.e. $\alpha = \beta\gamma$.

words, whenever the formulae result in a negative shadow wage, we substitute zero and leave it at that. This will normally occur when the money wage is at or below one half of the sectoral average — a contingency which is not very likely owing to the extreme skewness of the typical income distribution.

The bracketed figures (say β) in the shadow wage column of table 10 show the percentages by which the cost of labour to the project c (at BP-valuation) must be multiplied to yield the relevant shadow-price, i.e. $\omega = \beta c$. Since c is itself a constant multiple of the escudo money wage w (i.e. $c = \gamma w$), we may write the shadow-wage as a direct multiple of the latter:

$$\omega = \alpha w, \quad \text{where} \quad \alpha \equiv \beta \gamma .$$

If, furthermore, we are prepared to accept a β-factor midway between the two extremes of each sector, we can summarize the suggested conversion procedure in a more succint tabulation of the single coefficient α for each sector and for two critical wage-levels, as has been done in table 11. To this we have added a time-series of estimates between 1963/4 and 1969, arrived at by simple adjustment for exchange depreciation from year to year.

It is suggested that in cases where the escudo rate departs significantly from the average rate of the relevant sector, the appropriate α-coefficient should be computed by rough interpolation between the values for the two critical levels as quoted in table 11. Suppose, for instance, we wish to convert the wages of a worker in manufacturing industry in 1965 whose skill-rating, seniority, etc. earns him 33% above the average manufacturing wage. Table 11 tells us that the appropriate α-coefficient would be between 0.203 \$ per E° (at average wage-level) and 0.241 \$ per E° (at twice the average level). Accordingly, we should be sufficiently near the truth if we accepted a coefficient one-third of the way between the two, i.e. $\alpha = 0.216$.

It is scarcely necessary to repeat, however, that the validity of these coefficients depends on the stability of all the constants of structure, tariff-levels, and relative wage-ratios which entered into our estimation procedure. Few experienced economists would be prepared to rely on this. We must conclude with the observation, therefore, that shadow-price calculations are likely to be out of date within a short period of time, and ought to be repeated at three year intervals at the very least — and earlier if important changes are known to have taken place.

Appendix A: Border prices and the static Pareto optimum

Assume an economy of $n + 1$ sectors producing outputs $x_0, x_1, x_2, \ldots, x_n$, which are functionally dependent on inputs from each other (u_{ij}) and delivering final goods for domestic consumption or investment in quantities $y_0, y_1, \ldots,$ y_n. Its intersectoral flows may be shown in *tableau*-form as follows:

$$
\begin{aligned}
&\cdot \quad u_{01} + u_{02} \ldots + u_{0n} + y_0 = x_0 \,(\, . \quad , u_{10}, u_{20}, \ldots u_{n0}\,) \\
&u_{10} \quad\cdot\quad + u_{12} \ldots + u_{1n} + y_1 = x_1 \,(u_{01}, \quad \cdot \quad , u_{21}, \ldots u_{n1}\,) \\
&u_{20} + u_{21} \quad\cdot\quad \ldots + u_{2n} + y_2 = x_2 \,(u_{02}, u_{12}, \quad \cdot \quad \ldots u_{n2}\,) \\
&\vdots \quad \vdots \quad \vdots \,\vdots\,\vdots \quad \vdots \quad \vdots \quad \vdots \\
&u_{m0} + u_{m1} + u_{m2} \ldots + u_{mn} + y_m = x_m \,(u_{0m}, u_{1m}, u_{2m}, \ldots u_{nm}) \\
&u_{n0} + u_{n1} + u_{n2} \ldots \quad\cdot\quad + y_n = x_n \,(u_{0n}, u_{1n}, u_{2n}, \ldots \quad \cdot \quad)
\end{aligned}
\tag{A.1}
$$

Let us suppose that firm targets for all final outpurs (y_i) *other than* y_n are fixed beforehand, and that we wish to enquire what pattern of inputs and outputs must be adopted (with the given production functions) if the remaining element y_n is to be maximized. By virtue of the last equation this may be stated as a constrained maximum problem as follows:

Maximise $x_n(u_{0n}, \ldots) - u_{n0} - \Sigma u_{ni}$

Subject to
$$
\left\{
\begin{aligned}
&\Sigma u_{0i} + y_0 - x_0 = 0 \\
&u_{10} + \Sigma u_{1i} + y_1 - x_1 = 0 \\
&\vdots \quad \vdots \quad \vdots \quad \vdots \quad \vdots \\
&u_{n0} + \Sigma u_{mi} + y_m - x_m = 0
\end{aligned}
\right.
\tag{A.2}
$$

where all Σ's indicate summation from $i = 1$ to $i = n(u_{ii} = 0)$ and all x's are functions of inputs as in eq. (A.1).

or in Lagrangian form:

Maximise $L \equiv$
$$
\left\{
\begin{aligned}
&x_n - u_{n0} - \Sigma u_{ni} \\
&-\lambda_0 (\, . \; \Sigma u_{0i} + y_0 - x_0) \\
&-\lambda \,(u_{10} + \Sigma u_{1i} + y_1 - x_1) \\
&\vdots \\
&-\lambda_m (u_{m0} + \Sigma u_{mi} + y_m - x_m)
\end{aligned}
\right.
\tag{A.3}
$$

where the λ's are known as Lagrangian multipliers.

Subject to the usual second-order conditions (which we assume fulfilled) the solution is obtained by setting all partial derivatives of L equal to zero $(\partial L/\partial u_{ij} \equiv L_{ij} = 0)$:

$$L_{10} = -\lambda_1 + \lambda_0 x_{01} = 0, \ldots L_{n0} = -1 + \lambda_0 x_{0n} = 0$$

$$L_{01} = -\lambda_0 + \lambda_1 x_{10} = 0, \qquad\qquad \ldots L_{n1} = -1 + \lambda_1 x_{1n} = 0$$

$$\cdot \qquad\qquad \cdot \qquad \cdot \qquad\qquad\qquad \cdot \quad \cdots \qquad \cdot \qquad\qquad \cdot$$

$$\cdot \qquad\qquad \cdot \qquad \cdot \qquad\qquad\qquad \cdot \quad \cdots \qquad \cdot \qquad\qquad \cdot$$

$$\cdot \qquad\qquad \cdot \qquad \cdot \qquad\qquad\qquad \cdot \quad \cdots \qquad \cdot \qquad\qquad \cdot$$

$$L_{0m} = -\lambda_0 + \lambda_{11} x_{m0} = 0, L_{1m} = -\lambda_1 + \lambda_m x_{m1} = 0, \ldots L_{nm} = -1 + \lambda_m x_{mn} = 0$$

$$L_{0n} = -\lambda_0 + x_{n0} \qquad = 0, L_{1n} = -\lambda_1 + x_{n1} \qquad = 0, \ldots,$$

where x_{ij} stands for the partial derivative of the production function $(\partial x_i / \partial u_{ij})$, i.e. the marginal productivity of good j in the ith sector.

From these conditions it follows that in the production of good i the marginal productivity of good o must equal λ_o / λ_i (see first column), that of good 1 must equal λ_1 / λ_i (second column), etc., and that of good n must equal $1/\lambda_i$ (last column). In general, therefore, we may write:

$$x_{ij} = \lambda_j / \lambda_i = 1/x_{ji} . \tag{A.4}$$

This condition, which will be referred to as the 'reciprocity rule', may be restated in words as: The marginal productivity of j in the production of i must equal the reciprocal of the marginal productivity of i in the production of j.

Let us now single out one of the products, say good o, as a universal yardstick of reference in productivity calculations and write eq. (A.4) as:

$$x_{ij} = \frac{\lambda_j / \lambda_0}{\lambda_i / \lambda_0} = \frac{x_{i0}}{x_{j0}} . \tag{A.5}$$

In this form the condition may be referred to as the 'roundabout rule', whereby the marginal gain of i from sacrificing one unit of j *directly* in its production (x_{ij}) is required to equal the gain which would result from sacrificing the same quantity *indirectly* by shifting the requisite units of the standard input (o) from the production of j to that of i. In other words, it must not make any difference whether j is given up for i *directly* (as technology dictates) or in a roundabout way by reallocating third resources in favour of i. An 'optimum' is thus a situation where switches from one given product to another can only be made at a single rate of substitution, however roundabout the way in which this is arranged for.

Let us now assume that sector o represents foreign trade, i.e. an industry 'consuming' exports (net of competitive imports) and 'producing' foreign exchange — with part of the latter used to pay for the complementary (= non-home-produced) imports needed in current production. In other words:

u_{0i} ≡ complementary imports used in the production of i in terms of foreign currency.

u_{i0} ≡ export net of competitive import in physical units.

x_0 ≡ $p_1 u_{10} + p_2 u_{20} \ldots + p_n u_{n0}$ ≡ foreign currency receipts (at border prices p_i) from exports net of competitive imports.

y_0 ≡ surplus on trade account (balance of trade) in foreign currency.

By virtue of the special linear form of the 'production function' x_0, the marginal productivity of any input into sector o ($x_{0i} \equiv \partial x_0 / \partial u_{i0}$) reduces to its foreign trade price p_i ('border price') which we assume to be constant in all cases. The 'roundabout rule' (A.5) may therefore be restated as

$$x_{ij} = 1/x_{ji} = p_i/p_j , \tag{A.7}$$

or more simply

$$p_j x_{ij} = p_i \qquad \text{and} \tag{A.8}$$

$$p_i x_{ij} = p_j . \tag{A.9}$$

Optimality thus requires that the 'marginal dollar cost' of good i ($p_j x_{ij}$ for all j) be equal to its dollar price p_i, and that the 'marginal dollar productivity' of good j (p_i/x_{ij} for all i) be equal to its dollar cost p_j. Such a position will evidently be achieved if profit-maximizers are faced with inputs and outputs selling at border prices, and the latter are therefore the proper shadow prices to be used in profitability calculations within a static framework.

For our purposes the usefulness of these apparently well-worn statements lies in the way in which we have derived them: The 'roundabout rule' (A.5) is valid whatever interpretation we choose to give to the 'standard sector' o. We might have cast any of the normal branches of industry in that role, but the point is that this would have provided little guidance to project appraisers unless the marginal productivities in the chosen branch were *more firmly knowable* (because less contingent on output variations) than those of other branches. It is no help to be told that the iron industry should use coke until its marginal productivity equals the ratio of marginal productivities which, say, electric power enjoys in iron- and in coke-works; for this ratio will itself vary as the iron and the coke industries follow similar prescriptions in respect of their inputs. We can be saved from this difficulty only by the selection of a 'standard sector' whose production function is *linear in all inputs,* so that their marginal productivity ratios are constants which can be taken as guidelines independently of the effects of adjustment processes. The only sector, however, to which such a 'production function' can be plausibly attributed is foreign trade (for a country facing practically perfect foreign elasticities), and it is this which provides the justification for the use of border prices in our context.

In the case of a non-traded good i the condition (A.8) will of course be unusable for lack of a border price p_i. It will, however, normally be possible to find a number of traded inputs used in its production which do have such prices, say $j = r, s$, and we know from the 'roundabout rule' (A.7) that

$$p_r x_{ir} = p_s x_{is} = p_i' . \tag{A.10}$$

There is nothing to prevent us, therefore, from computing the marginal dollar cost of i in terms of its input r or s and identifying this as a surrogate border price p_i', to be used in profitability calculations exactly as if it were a true border price. This is in essence what the Manual suggests, although as a consequence of widespread complementarity in production we will normally have to make do with the marginal dollar cost of a whole *bundle* of inputs.

Alternatively, we might select a number of products, say $i = t, u$, into which our non-traded good j enters as an input, and compute its marginal dollar *productivities* in these branches:

$$p_t / x_{tj} = p_u / x_{uj} = p_j'' . \tag{A.11}$$

We could then use the figure p_j'' as an alternative surrogate for the missing border price.

In line with what has been said before, however, these surrogates will only be useful to the extent that the auxiliary goods selected (r, s, t, u) relate themselves to the non-traded sector i or j in a way that is already optimal or at least subject to minimal change (in the face of varying scales of production), so that their discoverable marginal productivities (or costs) may be accepted as constants.

Appendix B: The computation of demand-induced labour requirements (table 5)

We assume that during the seven years 1960−1967 final demand increased by 2080 mil. escudos at constant 1962 prices, and that this was distributed over seven major sectors of the economy as shown in row 5 of table 5. If this row is written as a column vector y, and if the inter-sector input coefficients

Table B1
The condensed matrix of current input coefficients (A) and employment coefficients for 1962 (at user prices).

	Agr.	Mining	Mfc. & Ut's.	Constr.	Trade	Tr'prt.	Services
	1	2	3	4	5	6	7
1. Agr.	0.05914	0.00036	0.10733	0.00008	0.00020	0.00448	0.01583
2. Mining	0.01000	0.00482	0.01772	0.05861	0.00004	0.01913	0.00062
3. Mfc. & ut's.	0.06416	0.10013	0.21458	0.35662	0.04473	0.24980	0.15819
4. Constr.	–	–	0.00020	–	0.00377	0.00406	0.02865
5. Trade	0.20710	0.02885	0.17639	0.00875	0.22426	0.00766	0.00995
6. Tr'prt.	0.05539	0.05876	0.02541	0.01979	0.02492	0.02630	0.00859
7. Services	–	0.01106	0.00288	0.01763	0.01688	0.02650	0.01013
8. Output (mil. E^0)	950.135	671.757	4279.674	570.824	1326.359	431.414	1440.334
9. No. employed & self-employed[a]	676.6	90.8	761.9	124.5	270.7	136.5	392.9
10. Labour per unit output[b] (units per thous E^0) (n)	0.7121	0.1351	0.1232	0.2181	0.2041	0.2778	0.2727

[a] ODEPLAN, Evolucion de la poblacion ocupado per sectores ecinimicos 1960 – 67, p.15.
[b] Row 9 ÷ row 8.

Table B2
Leontief inverse of the condensed matrix $(I-A)^{-1}$.

	Agr.	Mining	Mfc. & ut's.	Constr.	Trade	Tr'prt.	Services
	1	2	3	4	5	6	7
1. Agr.	1.07873	0.01924	0.15215	0.05725	0.01176	0.04590	0.04375
2. Mining	0.01477	1.00927	0.02637	0.06925	0.00295	0.02718	0.00735
3. Mfc.&ut's.	0.13419	0.16002	1.32903	0.49530	0.09552	0.35388	0.23300
4. Constr.	0.00176	0.00104	0.00211	1.00149	0.00581	0.00559	0.02946
5. Trade	0.31990	0.07994	0.34450	0.14252	1.31480	0.10450	0.07847
6. Tr'prt.	0.07405	0.06838	0.05389	0.04457	0.03732	1.04356	0.02056
7. Services	0.00802	0.01495	0.01152	0.02368	0.02383	0.03115	1.01540

are ranged in the matrix A (of order 7×7), the consequent incremental output requirements x must satisfy the equation

$$Ax + y = x, \quad \text{or} \quad x = (I - A)^{-1}y. \tag{B.1}$$

Suppose now that every unit-increment of output in sector i requires an increase of n_i man-years in the labour-inputs of that sector. The list of *directly* demand-induced labour requirements d may then be written

$d = \hat{n}y$, where $\hat{w}$ stands for the diagonal matrix of the w_i

or $\hspace{10cm}$ (B.2)

$$y = \hat{n}^{-1}d.$$

At the same time the *global* (direct and indirect) increments in labour requirements, say g, will obviously be

$$g = \hat{n}x. \tag{B.3}$$

By substituting (B.2) and (B.3) in (B.1) we find

$$g = Gd, \quad \text{where} \quad G \equiv \hat{n}(I - A)^{-1}\hat{n}^{-1}. \tag{B.4}$$

Below we reproduce the condensed 7×7 table of input coefficients A, and the derivative matrices $(I - A)^{-1}$ and G, together with the vector of employment-coefficients w. Row 6 of table 5 is computed by multiplying these coefficients by the final demand-increments of row 5. Row 7 is then calculated by pre-multiplying the result by the matrix G below.

Table B3
The matrix of employment multipliers (G). $G \equiv \hat{n}(I-A)^{-1}\hat{n}^{-1}$.

	Agr. 1	Mining 2	Mfc. & ut's. 3	Constr'n. 4	Trade 5	Trans't. etc. 6	Services 7
1. Agr.	1.07872	0.10141	0.87943	0.18692	0.04103	0.11766	0.11424
2. Mining	0.00280	1.00927	0.02892	0.04290	0.00195	0.01322	0.00364
3. Mfc. & ut's.	0.02322	0.14592	1.32902	0.27978	0.05766	0.15694	0.10527
4. Constr'n.	0.00054	0.00168	0.00373	1.00149	0.00621	0.00439	0.02356
5. Trade	0.09169	0.12077	0.57071	0.13337	1.31480	0.07677	0.05873
6. Transport, etc.	0.02889	0.14061	0.12152	0.05677	0.05066	1.04356	0.02095
7. Services	0.00307	0.03018	0.02550	0.02961	0.03184	0.03058	1.01340
Demand-induced employment increments 1960–67 (thous. man- years):							
8. Direct empl't.[a]	112	33	122	24	46	23	72
9. Global empl't.[b]	249	39	190	27	154	50	80
10. Row 9 adjusted	174[c]	39	190	27	154	50	80

[a] $d = \hat{n}y$, i.e. row 9 of table B1 multiplied by row 5 of table 5 $\equiv$ row 6 of table 5.

[b] $g = Gd$, i.e. row 8 pre-multiplied by the matrix in lines 1 to 7.

[c] The figure in row 9 was arbitratily reduced by 30% to allow for the relative inelasticity of consumer demand for agricultural products.

Appendix C: The social valuation of incremental consumption

Our first assumption is that a typical worker's marginal utility from the last income-unit he spends (u) diminishes in some regular manner as his total income x increases. It is hardly a great departure from generality to postulate some relationship of the sort:

$$u(x) = k/x^{r+1} , \tag{C.1}$$

where r is some fixed parameter (presumably zero or positive) and k a constant of scale. If r were zero, the marginal utility of a man with twice the income of another would be just half as big as the latter's. One would normally assume, however, that marginal utility falls *faster* than income increases, i.e. that r is greater than zero. We shall end up by postulating experimentally that r equals $\frac{1}{2}$ or 1, i.e. that marginal utility falls with the *square* of income rises. Many might regard this as the outside limit of what is plausible. We shall therefore conduct the theoretical analysis without committing ourselves to any particular value of r, and offer concrete figures for $r = 1$, $r = \frac{1}{2}$ and $r = 0$ (which is presumably the *lower* limit of what is plausible).

The scale constant k cannot have a definite meaning from the consumer's own point of view since this would suppose that one could fix the size of his subjective 'utils'. It can, however, be assigned a *social* value if we assume that society (in the shape of the government) sets store by individual consumption in general and values each 'util' of it at some ascertainable rate. This rate must of course be deduced from some explicit aspect of government policy, and in what follows we explore one particular way in which this might be done.

Suppose the government decided to withdraw an extra dose of resources from workers' consumption in order to spend it on its own purposes (investment, defence, foreign currency reserves, etc.). It could obviously do this with the least loss of personal utility by levying the whole of the tax on those in the higher income bracket. We assume, however, that it will be inhibited from doing this by the fear of creating severe disincentives, and that, instead it will arrange the withdrawal through some package deal of direct and indirect taxation which will diminish *every* worker's consumption by the same proportion t. This may seem to run counter to the accepted methods of progressive taxation; it becomes more plausible, however, when we bear in mind the regressive effects of many indirect taxes and the fact that we assume only a *marginal* increase in total taxation for purely revenue purposes, i.e. we assume that the government will not wish to make the tax-increase into an occasion for a change in distribution policy, and that proportional taxation appear to it as the only 'neutral' policy.

With such a proportional tax element, and a cost of tax-collection of $1-\tau$ per unit tax[40], the government's revenue increment will be measured by

$$T = \tau \int_0^\infty tx f(x) \, dx = \tau t n x \,,$$

where $f(x) \equiv$ frequency of income x, $\bar{x} \equiv$ arithmetic mean income, and $n \equiv$ total number of incomes.

In doing this the government diminishes each worker's income from x to $(1-t)x$, and therefore lowers their total utilities by

$$U = \int_0^\infty f(x) \int_{(1-t)x}^x \frac{k}{y^{r+1}} \, dy \, dx = \frac{k}{r} \int_0^\infty f(x) \left| -\frac{1}{x^r} \right|^x_{(1-t)x} \, dx =$$

$$= \frac{1-(1-t)^r}{(1-t)^r} \frac{kn}{r\bar{x}_r} \,, \quad \text{for } r \neq 0 \,, \tag{C.3}$$

where $\bar{x}_r$ is defined as the harmonic mean (of incomes) of degree r, i.e.

$$1/\bar{x}_r = \frac{1}{n} \int_0^\infty \frac{f(x)}{x^r} \, dx \,.$$

The harmonic mean of degree 1 is of course the familiar harmonic mean of elementary statistics, and that of degree zero is equal to unity.

If r were equal to zero, the result of the integration above would involve logarithms, i.e.

$$U = \int_0^\infty f(x) \int_{(1-t)x}^x \frac{k}{y} \, dy \, dx = k \int_0^\infty f(x) \left| \lg x \right|^x_{(1-t)x} \, dx = kn \lg \frac{1}{1-t} \,. \tag{C.3a}$$

Our argument now runs as follows: Since the government taxes workers just to the present limit and refrains from withdrawing the *next* dose of resources from their consumption, we can assume that the extra command over resources which it could obtain in this way (i.e. T) does not appear to it to be of greater value than the personal utilities that would be lost (i.e. U). If it appeared *less* valuable, the government would presumably *diminish* taxation from its present level — if *more*, it would *increase* it. Assuming therefore that the government is rational, and not otherwise constrained, we may postulate that in its view the total utility U is exactly equal to its opportunity cost in revenue T, i.e. that

$$T = U \,. \tag{C.4}$$

[40] To be explained below.

By virtue of the previous three equations this implies the following values for k (in the government's view):

$$k = \frac{tr}{1/(1-t)^{r}-1}\, \tau\bar{x}\,\dot{x}_r, \quad \text{for} \quad r \neq 0, \text{and} \tag{C.5}$$

$$k = \frac{t}{\lg 1/(1-t)}\, \tau\bar{x} \quad \text{for} \quad r = 0 . \tag{C.5a}$$

Moreover, since we are considering *marginal* decisions, i.e. the option of changing consumption by a very *small* proportion t, we may assume that the fractions on the right-hand sides above will take on their limiting values (for t tending to zero). This can be shown to be unity in both cases,[41] and we can therefore write the single equation

$$k = \tau\bar{x}\,\dot{x}_r \quad (\text{where } x_0 \text{ would be} = 1) . \tag{C.6}$$

The utility function can be re-written in terms of the *social* valuation of utils as

$$u(x) = \frac{\tau\bar{x}\,\dot{x}_r}{x^{r+1}} = \frac{\tau\xi_r\bar{x}^{r+1}}{x^{r+1}} , \tag{C.7}$$

where ξ_r is the ratio of the relevant harmonic mean $\dot{x}_r$ to the arithmetic mean, raised to the equivalent power, i.e.

$$\xi_r \equiv \dot{x}_r/\bar{x}^r$$

which is a characteristic of the country's income distribution.[42]

We are now in a position to measure the social valuation of an increase in income (= consumption) to any pre-assigned level c from a previous level $100p\%$ below it, i.e. from qc to c (where $q \equiv 1-p$). With the social utility function this value is evidently

$$b_s = \int_{qc}^{c} \frac{\tau\xi_r\bar{x}^{r+1}}{x^{r+1}}\, dx = \frac{\tau\xi_r\bar{x}^{r+1}}{rc^r}\, \frac{1-q^r}{q^r} \quad \ldots \text{ for } r \neq 0$$

$$= \tau\bar{x}\, \lg(1/q) \quad \ldots \text{ for } r = 0 . \tag{C.8}$$

[41] $\displaystyle \lim_{t \to 0} \frac{tr}{1/(1-t)^r-1} = \lim_{t \to 0} \frac{r}{r/(1-t)^{r+1}} = 1, \quad \lim_{t \to 0} \frac{t}{\lg 1/(1-t)} = \lim_{t \to 0} \frac{1}{1/(1-t)} = 1$

[42] ξ_r has been defined as a pure number, i.e. as a ratio between two parameters of the same dimensionality (= rth power of the income unit). This makes it independent of the scales of measurement used.

For the particular 'extreme' cases $r = 0$, and $r = 1$, we may therefore write in summary

$$b_s^0 = \tau \bar{x} \lg (1/q) , \quad \text{and} \tag{C.9}$$

$$b_s^1 = (p/q) \tau \xi_1 \bar{x}^2 / c . \tag{C.10}$$

The assumption of inverse proportionality in the utility function ($r = 0$) implies that the consumption increment has a social value independent of the consumption level (c), and uniquely dependent on the *proportion* (p) by which that level has been increased[43]. The alternative assumption $r = 1$, i.e. utility falling with the *square* of income, implies the dependence of b_s on both the proportional consumption increase and the consumption *level* which is being affected (c) — the latter influencing the valuation in inverse proportion.

Since c may be expressed in terms of the money wage w, i.e. $c = \gamma w$[44], it will be convenient to write our general formula more simply as

$$b_s^r = B_r / w^r , \tag{C.11}$$

where

$$B_r \equiv \frac{\tau \xi_r \bar{x}^{r+1}}{r \gamma^r} \frac{1-q^r}{q^r} \quad \text{for } r \neq 0, \quad \text{and}$$

$$b_s = B_0 / w^0 \equiv \tau \bar{x} \lg (1/q) \text{ for } r = 0 . \tag{C.12}$$

The particular formula for $r = 1$ becomes of course

$$b_s^1 = B_1 / w , \quad \text{with} \quad B_1 \equiv (p/q) \tau \xi_1 \bar{x}^2 / \gamma , \tag{C.13}$$

and that for $r = \frac{1}{2}$

$$b_s^{\frac{1}{2}} = B_{\frac{1}{2}} / \sqrt{w}, \quad \text{with} \quad B_{\frac{1}{2}} \equiv (1 - \sqrt{q}) / \sqrt{q} \cdot 2\tau \xi_{\frac{1}{2}} \bar{x}^{\frac{3}{2}} / \sqrt{\gamma} . \tag{C.14}$$

It must now be our concern to find appropriate numerical values for the parameters.

(1) *Tax losses* ($\tau = 90\%$). We have assumed that the government normally reckons with a 'loss' of 10% of all tax payments before they reach its own coffers, i.e. $\tau = 90\%$. The loss will take the form of administrative costs in operating and controlling the tax-system and in some 'leakage' due to inevitable

[43] Remember that $q = 1 - p$.
[44] Where γ is the BP-content of the wage-unit ($= 0.38$, see section 6).

deficiencies in competence or probity[45]. The figure of 90% is of course entirely impressionistic. Any alternative that might be preferred would alter our
findings in strict proportion to the change; but it would be highly unrealistic
not to put in some figure of the kind, and a 'loss' of 10% appears at least not
implausible for a country in Chile's current stage of development.

(2) *The average cost of labour* ($\bar{x}$ = 69.9 *dollars per month*). This was estimated by weighting the border-price content of sectoral labour costs (col. F
of table 6) in proportion to the employed and self-employed labour-force as
projected for 1964 by the Chilean Planning Office[46]. Our benchmark year of
1963/4 extends into the first 9 months of 1964 and is therefore sufficiently
coincident with the latter year to ignore discrepancies in calculations of this
kind.

(3) *The harmonic/arithmetic mean ratio of incomes* (ξ_1 = 0.6300). This
may be taken as a characteristic of a country's income distribution, depending
largely on its dispersion, skewness, and 'degree of inequality'. The few experiments we were able to make suggest that it is fairly stable: It was found to be
0.593 and 0.612 in the United Kingdom for 1959 and 1966 respectively; in
the U.S.A. it fell from 0.562 in the mid-thirties to 0.548 in 1959. Unfortu·
nately we were unable to locate sufficient data on the Chilean distribution[47].
We therefore made use of the Argentinian distribution in 1961 which is readily
available in great detail[48] and probably sufficiently near the Chilean pattern
to serve as a proxy. It has the added advantage of distinguishing employed,
self-employed, property-, and retirement incomes, all of which will obviously
have distribution characteristics of their own. We found the value ξ_1 = 0.6300
for the combined distribution of incomes from employment and self-employment. The ratio is a pure number[49] and can therefore be applied to Chilean
data without change of unit.

(4) *The square-root harmonic/arithmetic mean ratio* ($\xi_{\frac{1}{2}}$ = 0.8000). This was
computed from the same Argentinian income distribution by dividing the
square-root harmonic mean (10.28 $\sqrt{}$thous. pesetas) by the square root of the
arithmetic mean (12.85 $\sqrt{}$thous. pesetas).

---

[45] The figure is intended to measure actual money losses on the way from tax-payer to
government. No notional discount for unpopularity of taxation, diminished electoral
chances, etc. is included, since this is subsumed (in intention at least) in the general adjustment for social valuation.
[46] ODEPLAN, 'Evolución de la población ocupada por sectores económicos 1960–1967',
p. 16.
[47] The data for Chile, as collected by the Chilean Development Corporation (CORFO),
are not adeuqate to our purposes as they do not distinguish the self-employed from the
general employing class (profit earners). Moreover, the income-variable is quoted in terms
of multiples of minimum wages (which may vary between sectors).
[48] U.N. Economic Bulletin for Latin America, April 1966.
[49] The dimension of both geometric and arithmetic means is the same income unit.

Appendix. Table C1
Matrix of input—output flows at producer prices (estimated) (current escudos of 1962).

	1 Agr.	2 Fish.	3 Coal	4 Iron	5 Copper	6 Nitrate	7 Quarries	8 Other
1. Agriculture	46093	0	2	0	167	32	0	0
2. Fisheries	0	0	0	0	0	0	0	0
3. Coal mining	0	0	639	0	1007	106	75	84
4. Iron mining	0	0	0	0	0	0	0	0
5. Copper ming	0	0	0	0	0	0	0	0
6. Nitrate mining	8684	0	0	0	0	0	0	0
7. Quarries, etc.	0	0	0	0	0	0	0	0
8. Other mining	180	0	0	0	489	40	0	0
9. Food industries	10966	58	18	0	0	0	0	89
10. Drinks	0	0	0	0	0	0	0	0
11. Tobacco	0	0	0	0	0	0	0	0
12. Textiles	140	663	14	0	54	83	0	0
13. Clothing, ftwr.	0	50	117	0	380	118	0	14
14. Wood, etc.	0	128	574	119	1024	306	0	30
15. Furniture	0	0	6	0	8	39	0	12
16. Paper, etc.	0	0	8	0	50	0	0	0
17. Printing, etc.	0	10	97	141	226	209	12	234
18. Leather, etc.	0	0	1	0	25	0	0	0
19. Rubber	1233	0	24	0	135	28	0	37
20. Chemicals	11275	562	666	930	8021	1473	112	258
21. Oil coal dev.	8081	815	152	354	6699	266	280	109
22. Non-metals	0	0	518	0	1819	122	0	38
23. Basic metals	0	0	64	222	8765	127	0	47
24. Metal works	0	0	775	1110	1589	307	366	57
25. Mech. engineering	4592	0	16	1034	2455	199	79	16
26. Elec. engineering	0	53	103	0	906	70	0	54
27. Vehicles	5738	961	23	1125	1158	85	0	0
28. Other manufacts.	0	8	613	169	1392	42	0	172
29. Construction	0	0	0	0	0	0	0	0
30. Electricity	2048	67	1295	199	1184	28	27	290
31. Gas	0	0	0	0	31	0	8	0
32. Water, etc.	0	0	0	0	0	0	7	0
33. Trade	12852	332	636	1835	9110	1897	241	367
34. Banking	5567	0	92	0	0	388	31	0
35. Insurance	1965	563	58	221	405	41	109	337
36. Other finance	0	0	0	0	0	0	0	0
37. Real estate	0	0	0	0	0	0	0	0
38. Housing	0	0	0	0	0	0	0	0
39. Transport, etc.	8449	326	485	930	6229	1379	160	186
40. Education prvt.	0	0	0	0	0	0	0	0
41. Education public	0	0	0	0	0	0	0	0
42. Health prvt.	0	0	0	0	0	0	0	0
43. Health public	0	0	0	0	0	0	0	0
44. Producers serv.	0	0	0	0	570	0	50	5893
45. Entertainment	0	0	0	0	0	0	0	0
46. Catering	0	0	0	0	0	0	0	0
47. Laundry, etc.	0	0	0	0	0	0	0	0
48. Other services	0	0	0	0	396	0	0	0
49. Imports	11491	0	956	5215	27463	11541	285	912
50. Total interim	139454	4591	7950	13604	81756	18926	1840	9237
51. Wages + salaries	166622	2167	19457	14085	90704	16262	6724	15243
52. Employers cont.	24631	542	5828	4564	18383	5381	2115	4235
53. Other gross	350688	15392	-156	30698	209028	6142	10545	18130
54. Gross output	681395	22695	33079	62951	399871	46711	21132	46845

Appendix. Table C1 (continued)

	9 Food	10 Drinks	11 Tobacco	12 Tex'les.	13 Clth'g.	14 Wood	15 Furn.	16 Paper
1. Agriculture	272841	63561	3534	12745	1270	7936	66	6946
2. Fisheries	3265	0	0	0	0	0	0	0
3. Coal mining	2474	487	0	439	64	86	0	37
4. Iron mining	0	0	0	0	0	0	0	0
5. Copper mining	0	0	0	0	0	0	0	0
6. Nitrate mining	0	0	0	0	0	0	0	0
7. Quarries, etc.	0	0	0	0	0	0	0	0
8. Other mining	0	0	0	179	0	0	0	393
9. Food industries	132351	5552	4	296	1533	0	0	556
10. Drinks	226	4428	0	0	0	0	0	0
11. Tobacco	0	0	0	0	0	0	0	0
12. Textiles	5551	0	0	52292	109480	47	8290	32
13. Clothing, ftwr.	698	84	0	4	7303	0	0	0
14. Wood, etc.	3350	866	1	7	1340	33304	11923	20
15. Furniture	0	0	0	0	0	0	48	0
16. Paper, etc.	3757	285	709	201	1473	15	72	10735
17. Printing, etc.	1382	591	13	61	31	0	0	6
18. Leather, etc.	88	0	0	4	26379	36	360	0
19. Rubber	0	0	0	111	2148	0	0	2
20. Chemicals	3343	1747	104	5042	1053	929	4442	931
21. Oil coal dev.	3385	447	102	2210	296	651	232	1954
22. Non-metals	549	6233	0	2	68	55	2414	78
23. Basic metals	542	48	224	13	298	181	11781	93
24. Metal works	7586	3169	0	34	2389	401	3589	51
25. Mech. engineering	723	77	31	973	93	54	25	1913
26. Elec. engineering	228	81	32	412	83	59	26	213
27. Vehicles	226	255	50	50	118	268	29	69
28. Other manufacts.	2366	1	0	132	3288	27	1183	0
29. Construction	0	0	0	0	0	0	0	0
30. Electricity	3685	1086	54	2395	1163	825	784	2169
31. Gas	208	66	0	22	210	9	95	16
32. Water, etc.	43	1	0	20	0	0	0	0
33. Trade	48495	10644	1174	11648	9705	2635	2682	3169
34. Banking	466	47	0	745	47	171	47	248
35. Insurance	1222	1766	18	1242	199	457	118	40
36. Other finance	0	0	0	0	0	0	0	0
37. Real estate	0	0	0	0	0	0	0	0
38. Housing	0	0	0	0	0	0	0	0
39. Transport, etc.	35316	7258	695	5033	1512	10274	4418	1993
40. Education prvt.	0	0	0	0	0	0	0	0
41. Education public	0	0	0	0	0	0	0	0
42. Health prvt.	0	0	0	0	0	0	0	0
43. Health public	0	0	0	0	0	0	0	0
44. Producers serv.	2213	458	91	602	857	302	251	159
45. Entertainment	0	0	0	0	0	0	0	0
46. Catering	0	0	0	0	0	0	0	0
47. Laundry, etc.	0	0	0	0	0	0	0	0
48. Other services	0	0	0	0	0	0	0	0
49. Imports	73410	1604	3799	3307	1151	295	2404	169
50. Total interim	609809	110838	10636	134588	175707	59874	51182	34228
51. Wages-salaries	54888	14177	3202	36770	39642	18507	19974	8275
52. Employers cont.	12259	3234	542	8097	7668	4043	4302	1836
53. Other gross	110716	56058	11939	81271	155802	16166	37861	21977
54. Gross output	787672	184307	26318	260726	378829	98589	113270	66317

Appendix. Table C1 (continued)

	17 Printing	18 Leather	19 Rubber	20 Chem.	21 Oil coal dev.	22 Non-metals	23 Basic metals	24 Metal works
1. Agriculture	2	609	80	721	5	693	171	39
2. Fisheries	0	0	0	0	0	68	0	0
3. Coal mining	1	7	172	289	0	4055	4783	47
4. Iron mining	0	0	0	0	0	6	5486	0
5. Copper mining	1988	0	0	0	0	0	8993	0
6. Nitrate mining	0	0	0	0	0	0	0	0
7. Quarries, etc.	0	0	0	0	1	1635	607	71
8. Other mining	0	0	40	362	17136	3257	207	20
9. Food industries	0	12003	1	714	49	0	0	0
10. Drinks	0	0	0	0	0	0	0	0
11. Tobacco	0	0	0	0	0	0	0	0
12. Textiles	17	1308	743	237	0	1	108	539
13. Clothing, ftwr.	0	0	0	146	55	49	22	58
14. Wood, etc.	0	19	1	483	3	110	106	645
15. Furniture	0	0	0	0	24	0	0	1
16. Paper, etc.	9180	94	48	2998	29	2698	15	305
17. Printing, etc.	0	0	1	314	0	12	1	22
18. Leather, etc.	9	4507	68	74	0	0	0	8
19. Rubber	19	0	629	4	32	172	3	60
20. Chemicals	1317	1390	831	19160	329	1959	340	981
21. Oil coal dev.	102	260	164	2388	50	2317	1834	794
22. Non-metals	0	94	131	1638	247	7393	309	3359
23. Basic metals	75	79	254	1176	258	842	19140	24262
24. Metal works	17	626	82	909	1259	252	249	3791
25. Mech. engineering	66	34	61	163	153	763	370	413
26. Elec. engineering	84	25	64	171	343	471	384	317
27. Vehicles	21	4	55	180	44	214	202	77
28. Other manufacts.	93	522	38	51	63	40	21	279
29. Construction	0	0	0	0	0	0	0	0
30. Electricity	628	403	588	1542	84	1002	3901	1782
31. Gas	29	8	7	786	0	936	507	302
32. Water, etc.	0	0	0	0	0	3	0	0
33. Trade	1150	1287	1911	8209	2734	3163	5000	3334
34. Banking	47	62	47	3605	0	109	481	357
35. Insurance	936	520	490	2438	649	426	1863	179
36. Other finance	0	0	0	0	0	0	0	0
37. Real estate	0	0	0	0	0	0	0	0
38. Housing	0	0	0	0	0	0	0	0
39. Transport, etc.	592	624	519	2754	6235	5206	6500	2533
40. Education prvt.	0	0	0	0	0	0	0	0
41. Education public	0	0	0	0	0	0	0	0
42. Health prvt.	0	0	0	0	0	0	0	0
43. Health public	0	0	0	0	0	0	0	0
44. Producers serv.	98	116	89	353	1262	328	352	263
45. Entertainment	0	0	0	0	0	0	0	0
46. Catering	0	0	0	0	0	0	0	0
47. Laundry, etc.	0	0	0	0	0	0	0	0
48. Other services	0	0	0	0	0	0	0	0
49. Imports	1695	2149	8738	24550	16755	5562	17438	5329
50. Total interim	18164	26760	15850	76415	47798	43744	79381	50171
51. Wages + salaries	13470	4090	3481	19415	4507	20015	27655	24374
52. Employer cont.	3193	911	795	4589	1080	4480	6205	5368
53. Other gross	16978	14004	19610	53890	47728	55400	33164	37827
54. Gross output	51805	45765	39737	154308	101093	123639	146405	117740

Appendix. Table C1 (continued)

	25 Mech. eng'ng.	26 Elec. eng'ng.	27 Vehicles	28 Other mfcs.	29 Constr.	30 Elec.	31 Gas	32 Water etc.
1. Agriculture	107	2	24	2260	35	0	0	0
2. Fisheries	0	0	0	25	0	0	0	0
3. Coal mining	2	6	61	3	0	3592	3571	0
4. Iron mining	0	0	0	0	0	0	0	0
5. Copper mining	0	0	0	0	0	0	0	0
6. Nitrate mining	0	0	0	0	0	0	0	0
7. Quarries, etc.	0	13	20	1	18763	0	0	14
8. Other mining	0	28	0	113	0	0	1	0
9. Food industries	0	1	0	54	0	7	0	0
10. Drinks	0	0	0	0	0	0	0	0
11. Tobacco	0	0	0	0	0	0	0	0
12. Textiles	439	787	907	1221	2	18	19	9
13. Clothing, ftwr.	0	0	48	5	0	93	52	13
14. wood, etc.	176	257	145	730	19995	59	11	26
15. Furniture	0	651	733	0	2726	112	5	26
16. Paper, etc.	24	260	11	438	817	24	0	5
17. Printing, etc.	0	140	0	76	38	492	75	25
18. Leather, etc.	3	32	32	0	117	180	1	7
19. Rubber	165	264	946	202	331	135	1	37
20. Chemicals	889	1340	2050	1026	9189	69	121	64
21. Oil coal dev.	292	214	1008	186	3473	1172	436	25
22. Non-metals	165	314	211	141	71083	77	286	137
23. Basic metals	10721	6369	13247	5986	28751	133	658	156
24. Metal works	3465	1663	2330	306	22384	457	94	125
25. Mech. Engineering	9197	303	183	29	1941	57	27	349
26. Elec. engineering	678	2040	327	240	2852	338	20	49
27. Vehicles	104	16	8266	22	1271	241	51	226
28. Other manufacts.	210	421	540	1713	3292	309	60	64
29. Construction	0	0	0	0	0	464	94	295
30. Electricity	665	739	1317	495	558	18343	192	363
31. Gas	93	23	231	31	0	43	25	0
32. Water, etc.	0	0	0	0	236	126	12	0
33. Trade	4418	3673	5357	2319	19470	1905	465	150
34. Banking	248	109	140	341	667	536	13	25
35. Insurance	2	48	224	130	2009	72	140	98
36. Other finance	0	0	0	0	2884	0	0	0
37. Real estate	0	0	0	0	0	0	0	0
38. Housing	0	0	0	0	0	0	0	0
39. Transport, etc.	969	755	1518	1259	36783	3983	1283	372
40. Education prvt.	0	0	0	0	0	108	10	0
41. Education public	0	0	0	0	0	0	0	0
42. Health prvt.	0	0	0	0	0	555	44	0
43. Health public	0	0	0	0	0	0	0	0
44. Producers serv.	182	163	304	152	152	5319	962	63
45. Entertainment	0	0	0	0	0	96	3	0
46. Catering	0	0	0	0	4026	554	0	45
47. Laundry, etc.	0	0	0	0	0	23	4	0
48. Other services	0	0	0	0	0	146	21	54
49. Import	3304	5315	10127	3986	12649	4092	614	0
50. Total interim	36518	25945	50307	23488	271662	39573	8592	2763
51. Wages + salaries	15417	10470	26992	6119	108036	19813	3901	7045
52. Employers cont.	3438	2452	6328	1371	23895	4730	1764	868
53. Other gross	27827	39710	60549	36274	161009	30727	1950	1050
54. Gross output	83200	78577	144176	67252	564602	94913	16227	11725

Appendix. Table C1 (continued)

	33 Trade	34 Banking	35 Ins'ce	36 Other finance	37 Real est.	38 Housing	39 Tr'spt.	40 Educ. prvt.
1. Agriculture	52	0	0	241	0	0	1807	1046
2. Fisheries	0	0	0	0	0	0	0	108
3. Coal mining	1	0	19	47	0	0	8946	75
4. Iron mining	0	0	0	0	0	0	0	0
5. Copper mining	0	0	0	0	0	0	0	0
6. Nitrate mining	2	0	0	0	0	0	0	0
7. Quarries, etc.	0	0	0	0	0	0	2	0
8. Other mining	0	0	0	0	0	0	0	0
9. Food industries	0	0	0	16	0	0	302	4587
10. Drinks	0	0	0	0	0	0	199	0
11. Tobacco	0	0	0	0	0	0	0	0
12. Textiles	4062	32	1	23	2	0	365	0
13. Cloting, ftwr.	1393	148	1	41	0	0	22	166
14. wood, etc.	187	4	0	5	0	0	1627	80
15. Furniture	6	51	13	81	6	0	76	284
16. Paper, etc.	8590	946	21	517	81	0	214	684
17. Printing, etc.	19630	3106	205	1196	466	0	1502	2257
18. Leather, etc.	0	3	0	1	0	0	73	0
19. Rubber	3712	24	0	60	6	0	11835	112
20. Chemicals	3072	64	25	213	37	0	940	398
21. Oil coal dev.	2859	115	5	109	4	0	23294	1312
22. Non-metals	32	0	0	0	0	0	254	240
23. Basic metals	0	0	0	0	0	0	2744	6
24. Metal works	856	0	2	0	0	0	1634	0
25. Mech. engineering	5	287	0	42	19	0	179	28
26. Elec. engineering	2782	83	48	76	0	0	1383	131
27. Vehicles	5389	39	5	258	8	0	42190	34
28. Other manufacts.	2233	576	57	309	38	0	1208	670
29. Construction	3971	1209	98	1472	0	91636	1971	4424
30. Electricity	4202	539	140	111	32	0	3334	376
31. Gas	1103	260	41	75	0	0	80	415
32. Water, etc.	383	43	8	26	3	0	272	223
33. Trade	10963	337	28	217	20	0	12221	699
34. Banking	5830	760	15	233	0	0	434	79
35. Insurance	4647	10	48	146	11	1196	2637	204
36. Other finance	0	351	0	572	0	3148	0	0
37. Real estate	0	0	1	0	0	7160	0	0
38. Housing	0	0	0	0	0	0	0	0
39. Transport, etc.	13632	3720	478	823	185	0	27195	3567
40. Education prvt.	0	115	0	0	0	0	0	0
41. Education public	0	0	0	0	0	0	0	0
42. Health prvt.	0	0	1230	4	0	0	4	369
43. Health public	0	0	107	0	0	0	0	0
44. Producers serv.	9354	706	695	928	13	0	2772	0
45. Entertainment	2535	23	0	50	0	0	0	0
46. Catering	7997	1405	81	1950	0	0	8928	190
47. Laundry, etc.	0	239	17	9	0	0	121	462
48. Other services	1	0	4	48	0	0	351	0
49. Imports	0	461	0	0	0	0	12074	1071
50. Total interim	119481	15654	3312	9900	848	103141	171290	24298
51. Wages + salaries	204982	46881	7273	16260	3124	0	174138	52434
52. Employers cont.	40846	19100	1346	2347	1180	0	25413	6467
53. Other gross	668306	-51275	20046	-10366	2160	275427	200418	40321
54. Gross output	1033615	30359	32057	18141	7312	378567	571159	123419

Appendix. Table C1 (continued)

	41 Educ. public	42 Health prvt.	43 Health public	44 Prod. serv.	45 Ent'mnt.	46 Cat'ng.	47 Laundry etc.	48 Other ser.
1. Agriculture	654	874	1036	0	0	12127	0	4
2. Fisheries	67	89	110	0	0	1458	0	0
3. Coal mining	3	0	0	0	0	538	0	0
4. Iron mining	0	0	0	0	0	0	0	0
5. Copper mining	0	0	0	0	0	0	0	0
6. Nitrate mining	0	0	0	0	0	0	0	0
7. Quarries, etc.	0	0	0	0	0	0	0	0
8. Other mining	1	0	0	0	0	0	0	0
9. Food industries	2792	3820	9677	0	0	56733	0	1922
10. Drinks	0	0	0	0	0	36644	0	0
11. Tobacco	0	0	0	0	0	0	0	0
12. Textiles	25	268	484	0	0	0	0	0
13. Clothing, ftwr.	60	215	929	0	0	390	91	76
14. Wood, etc.	19	82	113	0	0	0	0	4141
15. Furniture	47	68	372	0	0	125	0	0
16. Paper, etc.	201	20	228	56	28	0	138	0
17. Printing, etc.	1325	256	753	1448	2105	329	271	210
18. Leather, etc.	0	0	4	0	4	0	0	0
19. Rubber	12	72	87	15	0	0	0	56
20. Chemicals	44	6765	5753	0	99	791	2869	90
21. Oil coal dev.	146	434	1331	11	28	2332	411	118
22. Non-metals	79	36	489	0	0	33	0	0
23. Basic metals	5	0	17	0	0	0	0	69
24. Metal works	81	134	70	0	0	0	0	0
25. Mech. engineering	97	183	111	0	118	0	54	0
26. Elec. engineering	19	0	11	0	260	0	111	0
27. Vehicles	200	2	595	21	0	42	113	141
28. Other manufacts.	339	1113	930	487	435	154	157	72
29. Construction	296	2544	5057	544	1	103	128	15
30. Electricity	362	131	1643	145	99	1692	419	94
31. Gas	194	126	280	0	0	1649	56	0
32. Water, etc.	165	141	204	0	45	326	68	11
33. Trade	309	1591	1598	151	180	15567	535	499
34; Banking	0	7	0	502	75	87	30	13
35. Insurance	13	84	19	17	13	539	153	0
36. Other finance	0	0	0	0	0	0	0	0
37. Real estate	0	0	0	0	0	0	0	0
38. Housing	0	0	0	0	0	0	0	0
39. Transport, etc.	803	2257	2156	1661	958	9358	1795	1353
40. Education prvt.	13	0	0	0	0	0	0	0
41. Education public	0	0	0	0	0	0	0	0
42. Health prvt.	0	0	0	0	14	0	0	0
43. Health public	0	0	0	0	0	0	0	0
44. Producers serv.	6	4	209	0	2214	184	87	436
45. Entertainment	0	0	0	0	0	136	44	0
46. Catering	321	0	419	1001	740	190	0	66
47. Laundry etc.	0	2327	8	0	0	283	0	0
48. Other services	0	0	0	0	0	0	14	0
49. Import	536	665	276	0	3783	0	1116	0
50. Total interim	9236	24307	34928	6058	11198	141761	8489	9386
51. Wages + salaries	126312	30370	72333	16848	9642	23682	8696	28090
52. Employers cont.	4358	3672	3259	2042	1167	2866	1047	2879
53. Other gross	2974	44707	6890	20386	16348	82504	26968	11820
54. Gross output	142880	103056	117410	45329	38356	250813	45400	52175

Appendix. Table C1 (continued)

	49 Total interm.	50 H'hold cons.	51 Gvt. cons.	52 Fixed inv't.	53 Stock bld'g.	54 Ex-ports	55 Gross output
1: Agriculturé	437782	185053	3985	32128	420	22028	681395
2. Fisheries	5180	17119	254	0	0	142	22695
3. Coal mining	29697	3546	52	0 -	-242	27	33079
4. Iron mining	5492	0	0	0	916	56542	62951
5. Copper mining	10981	0	0	0	3540	385350	399871
6. Nitrate mining	8686	0	0	0	1362	36663	46711
7. Quarries, etc.	21126	0	2	0	0	3	21132
8. Other mining	22444	0	1	21506	2278	616	46845
9. Food industries	244099	518658	10503	0	-5225	19637	787672
10. Drinks	41496	142116	0	0	241	454	184307
11. Tobacco	0	25778	0	0	525	16	26318
12. Textiles	186239	48722	359	0	25166	239	260726
13. Clothing, ftwr.	12843	391023	9494	0	-34956	416	378820
14. Wood, etc.	82018	6000	790	0	7905	1876	98589
15. Furniture	5518	83555	2049	17239	4888	1	113270
16. Paper, etc.	45942	8391	1579	0	3962	6442	66317
17. Printing, etc.	39267	10667	4653	0	-2895	113	51805
18. Leather, etc.	31993	14351	58	0	-1529	893	45765
19. Rubber	22710	11224	/735	0	5044	4	39737
20. Chemicals	103077	34937	1879	0	10207	4210	154308
21. Oil coal dev.	73244	24767	1808	0	1176	67	101093
22. Non-metals	98644	24973	660	0	-694	56	123639
23. Basic metals	137358	0	408	0	2424	6215	146405
24. Metal works	62188	36530	1682	9831	6755	814	117740
25. Mech. engineering	27642	34870	342	19208	1006	132	83200
26. Elec. engineering	15646	50936	1067	11728	-909	114	78577
27. Vehicles	70226	59225	3028	7081	3003	1613	144176
28. Other manufacts.	25887	38887	1410	253	548	267	67252
29. Construction	114321	0	4641	445640	0	0	564602
30. Electricity	63096	27409	4370	0	0	38	94913
31. Gas	7944	7514	741	0	0	28	16227
32. Water, etc.	2366	8854	481	0	0	24	11725
33. Trade	226790	739908	5448	53111	2540	5818	1033615
34. Banking	22700	4438	3222	0	0	0	30359
35. Insurance	28658	2822	296	0	0	281	32057
36. Other finance	6956	6777	4408	0	0	0	18141
37. Real estate	7161	151	0	0	0	0	7312
38. Housing	0	378234	0	0	0	333	378567
39. Transport, etc.	226454	257375	5681	9850	2327	69472	571159
40. Education prvt.	246	122205	877	0	0	91	123419
41. Education public	0	3529	139381	0	0	0	142880
42. Health prvt.	4493	98487	0	0	0	76	103056
43. Health public	107	10417	106886	0	0	0	117410
44. Producers serv.	39822	3882	1519	0	0	106	45329
45. Entertainment	3244	25548	541	0	0	9023	38356
46. Catering	27725	185209	4187	0	0	33712	250813
47. Laundry, etc.	3553	41822	26	0	0	0	45400
48. Other services	1035	50709	196	0	0	35	52175

Appendix. Table C2
Matrix of input—output coefficients at producer prices (estimated) (current escudos of 1962).

	1 Agr.	2 Fish.	3 Coal	4 Iron	5 Copper	6 Nitrate	7 Quarried	8 Other
1. Agriculture	0.0676	0.0000	0.0000	0.0000	0.0004	0.0007	0.0000	0.0000
2. Fisheries	0.0000	0.0000	0.0000	0.0000	0.0000	0.0000	0.0000	0.0000
3. Coal mining	0.0000	0.0000	0.0193	0.0000	0.0025	0.0023	0.0036	0.0018
4. Iron mining	0.0000	0.0000	0.0000	0.0000	0.0000	0.0000	0.0000	0.0000
5. Copper mining	0.0000	0.0000	0.0000	0.0000	0.0000	0.0000	0.0000	0.0000
6. Nitrate mining	0.0127	0.0000	0.0000	0.0000	0.0000	0.0000	0.0000	0.0000
7. Quarries, etc.	0.0000	0.0000	0.0000	0.0000	0.0000	0.0000	0.0000	0.0000
8. Other mining	0.0003	0.0000	0.0000	0.0000	0.0012	0.0009	0.0000	0.0000
9. Food industries	0.0161	0.0025	0.0005	0.0000	0.0000	0.0000	0.0000	0.0019
10. Drinks	0.0000	0.0000	0.0000	0.0000	0.0000	0.0000	0.0000	0.0000
11. Tobacco	0.0000	0.0000	0.0000	0.0000	0.0000	0.0000	0.0000	0.0000
12. Textiles	0.0002	0.0292	0.0004	0.0000	0.0001	0.0018	0.0000	0.0000
13. Clothing, ftwr.	0.0000	0.0022	0.0035	0.0000	0.0009	0.0025	0.0000	0.0003
14. Wood, etc.	0.0000	0.0056	0.0174	0.0019	0.0025	0.0065	0.0000	0.0006
15. Furniture	0.0000	0.0000	0.0002	0.0000	0.0000	0.0008	0.0000	0.0003
16. Paper, etc.	0.0000	0.0000	0.0002	0.0000	0.0001	0.0000	0.0000	0.0000
17. Printing, etc.	0.0000	0.0004	0.0029	0.0022	0.0005	0.0045	0.0006	0.0050
18. Leather, etc.	0.0000	0.0000	0.0000	0.0000	0.0001	0.0000	0.0000	0.0000
19. Rubber	0.0018	0.0000	0.0007	0.0000	0.0003	0.0006	0.0000	0.0008
20. Chemicals	0.0165	0.0247	0.0201	0.0148	0.0201	0.0315	0.0053	0.0055
21. Oil coal dev.	0.0119	0.0359	0.0046	0.0056	0.0168	0.0057	0.0132	0.0023
22. Non-metals	0.0000	0.0000	0.0157	0.0000	0.0045	0.0026	0.0000	0.0008
23. Basic metals	0.0000	0.0000	0.0019	0.0035	0.0218	0.0027	0.0000	0.0010
24. Metal works	0.0000	0.0000	0.0234	0.0176	0.0040	0.0066	0.0173	0.0012
25. Mech. engineering	0.0069	0.0000	0.0005	0.0164	0.0062	0.0043	0.0037	0.0004
26. Elec. engineering	0.0000	0.0023	0.0031	0.0000	0.0022	0.0015	0.0000	0.0011
27. Vehicles	0.0084	0.0423	0.0007	0.0179	0.0029	0.0018	0.0000	0.0000
28. Other manufacts.	0.0000	0.0003	0.0185	0.0027	0.0035	0.0009	0.0000	0.0037
29. Construction	0.0000	0.0000	0.0000	0.0000	0.0000	0.0000	0.0000	0.0000
30. Electricity	0.0030	0.0029	0.0391	0.0082	0.0029	0.0006	0.0013	0.0062
31. Gas	0.0000	0.0000	0.0000	0.0000	0.0001	0.0000	0.0004	0.0000
32. Water, etc.	0.0000	0.0000	0.0000	0.0000	0.0000	0.0000	0.0003	0.0000
33. Trade	0.0189	0.0146	0.0192	0.0291	0.0228	0.0406	0.0114	0.0078
34. Banking	0.0082	0.0000	0.0028	0.0000	0.0000	0.0083	0.0014	0.0000
35. Insurance	0.0029	0.0248	0.0018	0.0035	0.0010	0.0009	0.0051	0.0072
36. Other finance	0.0000	0.0000	0.0000	0.0000	0.0000	0.0000	0.0000	0.0000
37. Real estate	0.0000	0.0000	0.0000	0.0000	0.0000	0.0000	0.0000	0.0000
38. Housing	0.0000	0.0000	0.0000	0.0000	0.0000	0.0000	0.0000	0.0000
39. Transport, etc.	0.0124	0.0144	0.0147	0.0148	0.0156	0.0295	0.0076	0.0040
40. Education, prvt.	0.0000	0.0000	0.0000	0.0000	0.0000	0.0000	0.0000	0.0000
41. Education public	0.0000	0.0000	0.0000	0.0000	0.0000	0.0000	0.0000	0.0000
42. Health prvt.	0.0000	0.0000	0.0000	0.0000	0.0000	0.0000	0.0000	0.0000
43. Health public	0.0000	0.0000	0.0000	0.0000	0.0000	0.0000	0.0000	0.0000
44. Producers serv.	0.0000	0.0000	0.0000	0.0000	0.0014	0.0000	0.0024	0.1258
45. Entertainment	0.0000	0.0000	0.0000	0.0000	0.0000	0.0000	0.0000	0.0000
46. Catering	0.0000	0.0000	0.0000	0.0000	0.0000	0.0000	0.0000	0.0000
47. Laundry, etc.	0.0000	0.0000	0.0000	0.0000	0.0000	0.0000	0.0000	0.0000
48. Other services	0.0000	0.0000	0.0000	0.0000	0.0012	0.0000	0.0000	0.0000
49. Imports	0.0169	0.0000	0.0289	0.0828	0.0687	0.2471	0.0135	0.0195
50. Total interim	0.2047	0.2024	0.2403	0.2161	0.2045	0.4052	0.0870	0.1972
51. Wages + salaries	0.2445	0.0955	0.5882	0.2237	0.2269	0.3481	0.3182	0.3254
52. Employers cont.	0.0361	0.0239	0.1762	0.0725	0.0460	0.1152	0.1001	0.0904
53. Other gross	0.5147	0.6782	-0.0047	0.4876	0.5226	0.1315	0.4947	0.3870
54. Gross output	1.0000	1.0000	1.0000	1.0000	1.0000	1.0000	1.0000	1.0000

Appendix, Table C2 (continued)

	9 Food	10 Drinks	11 Tobacco	12 Tex'les.	13 Clth'g.	14 Wood	15 Furn.	16 Paper
1. Agriculture	0.3464	0.3449	0.1343	0.0489	0.0034	0.0805	0.0636	0.1047
2. Fisheries	0.0041	0.0000	0.0000	0.0000	0.0000	0.0000	0.0000	0.0000
3. Coal mining	0.0031	0.0026	0.0000	0.0017	0.0002	0.0009	0.0000	0.0006
4. Iron mining	0.0000	0.0000	0.0000	0.0000	0.0000	0.0000	0.0000	0.0000
5. Copper mining	0.0000	0.0000	0.0000	0.0000	0.0000	0.0000	0.0000	0.0000
6. Nitrate mining	0.0000	0.0000	0.0000	0.0000	0.0000	0.0000	0.0000	0.0000
7. Quarries, etc.	0.0000	0.0000	0.0000	0.0000	0.0000	0.0000	0.0000	0.0000
8. Other mining	0.0000	0.0000	0.0000	0.0007	0.0000	0.0000	0.0000	0.0059
9. Food industies	0.1680	0.0301	0.0001	0.0011	0.0040	0.0000	0.0000	0.0084
10. Drinks	0.0003	0.0240	0.0000	0.0000	0.0000	0.0000	0.0000	0.0000
11. Tobacco	0.0000	0.0000	0.0000	0.0000	0.0000	0.0000	0.0000	0.0000
12. Textiles	0.0070	0.0000	0.0000	0.2006	0.2890	0.0005	0.0555	0.0005
13. Clothing ftwr.	0.0009	0.0005	0.0000	0.0000	0.0193	0.0000	0.0000	0.0000
14. Wood, etc.	0.0043	0.0047	0.0001	0.0000	0.0035	0.3378	0.1053	0.0003
15. Furniture	0.0000	0.0000	0.0000	0.0000	0.0000	0.0000	0.0004	0.0000
16. Paper, etc.	0.0048	0.0015	0.0270	0.0008	0.0039	0.0002	0.0006	0.1619
17. Printing, etc.	0.0018	0.0032	0.0005	0.0002	0.0001	0.0000	0.0000	0.0001
18. Leather, etc.	0.0001	0.0000	0.0000	0.0000	0.0696	0.0004	0.0032	0.0000
19. Rubber	0.0000	0.0000	0.0000	0.0004	0.0057	0.0000	0.0000	0.0000
20. Chemicals	0.0042	0.0095	0.0040	0.0193	0.0028	0.0094	0.0392	0.0140
21. Oil coal dev.	0.0043	0.0024	0.0039	0.0085	0.0008	0.0066	0.0020	0.0295
22. Non-metals	0.0007	0.0338	0.0000	0.0000	0.0002	0.0006	0.0213	0.0012
23. Basic metals	0.0007	0.0003	0.0085	0.0001	0.0008	0.0018	0.1040	0.0014
24. Metal works	0.0096	0.0172	0.0000	0.0001*	0.0063	0.0041	0.0317	0.0008
25. Mech. engineering	0.0009	0.0004	0.0012	0.0037	0.0002	0.0005	0.0002	0.0289
26. Elec. engineering	0.0003	0.0004	0.0012	0.0016	0.0002	0.0006	0.0002	0.0032
27. Vehicles	0.0003	0.0014	0.0019	0.0002	0.0003	0.0027	0.0003	0.0010
28. Other manufacts.	0.0030	0.0000	0.0000	0.0005	0.0087	0.0003	0.0104	0.0000
29. Construction	0.0000	0.0000	0.0000	0.0000	0.0000	0.0000	0.0000	0.0000
30. Electricity	0.0046	0.0059	0.0021	0.0092	0.0031	0.0084	0.0069	0.0327
31. Gas	0.0003	0.0004	0.0000	0.0001	0.0006	0.0001	0.0008	0.0002
32. Water, etc.	0.0001	0.0000	0.0000	0.0001	0.0000	0.0000	0.0000	0.0000
33. Trade	0.0615	0.0578	0.0446	0.0447	0.0256	0.0267	0.0237	0.0478
34. Banking	0.0006	0.0003	0.0000	0.0029	0.0001	0.0017	0.0004	0.0037
35. Insurance	0.0016	0.0096	0.0007	0.0048	0.0005	0.0046	0.0010	0.0006
36. Other finance	0.0000	0.0000	0.0000	0.0000	0.0000	0.0000	0.0000	0.0000
37. Real estate	0.0000	0.0000	0.0000	0.0000	0.0000	0.0000	0.0000	0.0000
38. Housing	0.0000	0.0000	0.0000	0.0000	0.0000	0.0000	0.0000	0.0000
39. Transport, etc.	0.0448	0.0394	0.0264	0.0193	0.0040	0.1042	0.0390	0.0301
40. Education prvt.	0.0000	0.0000	0.0000	0.0000	0.0000	0.0000	0.0000	0.0000
41. Education public	0.0000	0.0000	0.0000	0.0000	0.0000	0.0000	0.0000	0.0000
42. Health prvt.	0.0000	0.0000	0.0000	0.0000	0.0000	0.0000	0.0000	0.0000
43. Health public	0.0000	0.0000	0.0000	0.0000	0.0000	0.0000	0.0000	0.0000
44. Producers serv.	0.0028	0.0025	0.0034	0.0023	0.0023	0.0031	0.0022	0.0024
45. Entertainment	0.0000	0.0000	0.0000	0.0000	0.0000	0.0000	0.0000	0.0000
46. Catering	0.0000	0.0000	0.0000	0.0000	0.0000	0.0000	0.0000	0.0000
47. Laundry etc.	0.0000	0.0000	0.0000	0.0000	0.0000	0.0000	0.0000	0.0000
48. Other services	0.0000	0.0000	0.0000	0.0000	0.0000	0.0000	0.0000	0.0000
49. Import	0.0932	0.0087	0.1443	0.1445	0.0087	0.0117	0.0023	0.0363
50. Total interim	0.7742	0.6014	0.4041	0.5162	0.4638	0.6073	0.4514	0.5161
51. Wages + salaries	0.0697	0.0769	0.1217	0.1410	0.1046	0.1877	0.1763	0.1248
52. Employers cont.	0.0156	0.0175	0.0206	0.0311	0.0202	0.0410	0.0380	0.0277
53. Other gross	0.1406	0.3042	0.4536	0.3117	0.4113	0.1640	0.3343	0.3314
54. Gross output	1.0000	1.0000	1.0000	1.0000	1.0000	1.0000	1.0000	1.0000

Appendix. Table C2

	17 Printing	18 Leather	19 Rubber	20 Chem.	21 Oil coal dev.	22 Non-metals	23 Basic metals	24 Metal works
1. Agriculture	0.0000	0.0133	0.0020	0.0047	0.0000	0.0056	0.0012	0.0003
2. Fisheries	0.0000	0.0000	0.0000	0.0000	0.0000	0.0005	0.0000	0.0000
3. Coal mining	0.0000	0.0002	0.0043	0.0019	0.0000	0.0328	0.0325	0.0004
4. Iron mining	0.0000	0.0000	0.0000	0.0000	0.0000	0.0000	0.0375	0.0000
5. Copper mining	0.0402	0.0000	0.0000	0.0000	0.0000	0.0000	0.0643	0.0000
6. Nitrate mining	0.0000	0.0000	0.0000	0.0000	0.0000	0.0000	0.0000	0.0000
7. Quarries, etc.	0.0000	0.0000	0.0000	0.0000	0.0000	0.0132	0.0041	0.0006
8. Other mining	0.0000	0.0000	0.0010	0.0023	0.1695	0.0263	0.0014	0.0002
9. Food industies	0.0000	0.2623	0.0000	0.0046	0.0005	0.0000	0.0000	0.0000
10. Drinks	0.0000	0.0000	0.0000	0.0000	0.0000	0.0000	0.0000	0.0000
11. Tobacco	0.0000	0.0000	0.0000	0.0000	0.0000	0.0000	0.0000	0.0000
12. Textiles	0.0003	0.0286	0.0187	0.0015	0.0000	0.0000	0.0007	0.0046
13. Clothing, ftwr.	0.0000	0.0000	0.0000	0.0009	0.0005	0.0004	0.0001	0.0005
14. Wood, etc.	0.0000	0.0004	0.0000	0.0031	0.0000	0.0009	0.0007	0.0055
15. Furniture	0.0000	0.0000	0.0000	0.0000	0.0002	0.0000	0.0000	0.0000
16. Paper, etc.	0.1772	0.0020	0.0012	0.0194	0.0003	0.0218	0.0001	0.0026
17. Printing, etc.	0.0000	0.0000	0.0000	0.0020	0.0000	0.0001	0.0000	0.0002
18. Leather, etc.	0.0002	0.0985	0.0017	0.0005	0.0000	0.0000	0.0000	0.0001
19. Rubber	0.0004	0.0000	0.0158	0.0000	0.0003	0.0014	0.0000	0.0005
20. Chemicals	0.0254	0.0304	0.0209	0.1242	0.0033	0.0158	0.0021	0.0083
21. Oil coal dev.	0.0020	0.0057	0.0041	0.0155	0.0005	0.0187	0.0125	0.0067
22. Non-metals	0.0000	0.0020	0.0033	0.0106	0.0024	0.0598	0.0021	0.0285
23. Basic metals	0.0014	0.0017	0.0064	0.0076	0.0025	0.0068	0.1307	0.2061
24. Metal works	0.0003	0.0137	0.0021	0.0059	0.0125	0.0020	0.0017	0.0322
25. Mech. engineering	0.0013	0.0007	0.0015	0.0011	0.0015	0.0062	0.0025	0.0035
26. Elec. engineering	0.0016	0.0008	0.0016	0.0011	0.0034	0.0038	0.0026	0.0027
27. Vehicles	0.0004	0.0001	0.0014	0.0012	0.0004	0.0017	0.0016	0.0007
28. Other manufacts.	0.0018	0.0114	0.0010	0.0003	0.0006	0.0003	0.0001	0.0024
29. Construction	0.0000	0.0000	0.0000	0.0000	0.0000	0.0000	0.0000	0.0000
30. Electricity	0.0121	0.0088	0.0148	0.0100	0.0008	0.0081	0.0256	0.0151
31. Gas	0.0006	0.0002	0.0002	0.0051	0.0000	0.0076	0.0005	0.0026
32. Water, etc.	0.0000	0.0000	0.0000	0.0000	0.0000	0.0000	0.0000	0.0000
33. Trade	0.0222	0.0281	0.0481	0.0532	0.0270	0.0256	0.0342	0.0283
34. Banking	0.0009	0.0014	0.0012	0.0234	0.0000	0.0009	0.0003	0.0030
35. Insurance	0.0181	0.0114	0.0123	0.0158	0.0064	0.0034	0.0127	0.0015
36. Other finance	0.0000	0.0000	0.0000	0.0000	0.0000	0.0000	0.0000	0.0000
37. Real estate	0.0000	0.0000	0.0000	0.0000	0.0000	0.0000	0.0000	0.0000
38. Housing	0.0000	0.0000	0.0000	0.0000	0.0000	0.0000	0.0000	0.0000
39. Transport, etc.	0.0114	0.0136	0.0131	0.0178	0.0617	0.0421	0.0444	0.0215
40. Education prvt.	0.0000	0.0000	0.0000	0.0000	0.0000	0.0000	0.0000	0.0000
41. Education public	0.0000	0.0000	0.0000	0.0000	0.0000	0.0000	0.0000	0.0000
42. Health prvt.	0.0000	0.0000	0.0000	0.0000	0.0000	0.0000	0.0000	0.0000
43. Health public	0.0000	0.0000	0.0000	0.0000	0.0000	0.0000	0.0000	0.0000
44. Producers serv.	0.0019	0.0025	0.0022	0.0023	0.0125	0.0027	0.0024	0.0025
45. Entertainment	0.0000	0.0000	0.0000	0.0000	0.0000	0.0000	0.0000	0.0000
46. Catering	0.0000	0.0000	0.0000	0.0000	0.0000	0.0000	0.0000	0.0000
47. Laundry etc.	0.0000	0.0000	0.0000	0.0000	0.0000	0.0000	0.0000	0.0000
48. Other services	0.0000	0.0000	0.0000	0.0000	0.0000	0.0000	0.0000	0.0000
49. Imports	0.0327	0.0470	0.2199	0.1591	0.1657	0.0450	0.1194	0.0453
50. Total interim	0.3525	0.5847	0.3989	0.4952	0.4728	0.3538	0.5453	0.4261
51. Wages + salaries	0.2600	0.0894	0.0876	0.1258	0.0446	0.1619	0.1889	0.2070
52. Employers cont.	0.0616	0.0199	0.0200	0.0297	0.0105	0.0362	0.0424	0.0456
53. Other gross	0.3259	0.3060	0.4935	0.3492	0.4721	0.4481	0.2234	0.3213
54. Gross output	1.0000	1.0000	1.0000	1.0000	1.0000	1.0000	1.0000	1.0000

Appendix. Table C2 (continued)

	25 Mech. eng'ng.	26 Elec. eng'ng.	27 Vehicles	28 Other mfcs.	29 Constr.	30 Elec.	31 Gas	32 Water etc.
1. Agriculture	0.0013	0.0000	0.0002	0.0336	0.0001	0.0000	0.0000	0.0000
2. Fisheries	0.0000	0.0000	0.0000	0.0004	0.0000	0.0000	0.0000	0.0000
3. Coal mining	0.0000	0.0001	0.0004	0.0000	0.0000	0.0378	0.2200	0.0000
4. Iron mining	0.0000	0.0000	0.0000	0.0000	0.0000	0.0000	0.0000	0.0000
5. Copper mining	0.0000	0.0000	0.0000	0.0000	0.0000	0.0000	0.0000	0.0000
6. Nitrate mining	0.0000	0.0000	0.0000	0.0000	0.0000	0.0000	0.0000	0.0000
7. Quarries, etc.	0.0000	0.0002	0.0001	0.0000	0.0332	0.0000	0.0000	0.0012
8. Other mining	0.0000	0.0004	0.0000	0.0017	0.0000	0.0000	0.0000	0.0000
9. Food industies	0.0000	0.0000	0.0000	0.0008	0.0000	0.0001	0.0000	0.0000
10. Drinks	0.0000	0.0000	0.0000	0.0000	0.0000	0.0000	0.0000	0.0000
11. Tobacco	0.0000	0.0000	0.0000	0.0000	0.0000	0.0000	0.0000	0.0000
12. Textiles	0.0053	0.0100	0.0063	0.0182	0.0000	0.0002	0.0012	0.0008
13. Clothing, ftwr.	0.0000	0.0000	0.0003	0.0001	0.0000	0.0010	0.0032	0.0011
14. Wood, etc.	0.0021	0.0033	0.0010	0.0109	0.0354	0.0006	0.0007	0.0022
15. Furniture	0.0000	0.0083	0.0051	0.0000	0.0048	0.0012	0.0003	0.0022
16. Paper, etc.	0.0003	0.0033	0.0001	0.0065	0.0014	0.0003	0.0000	0.0004
17. Printing, etc.	0.0000	0.0018	0.0000	0.0011	0.0001	0.0052	0.0046	0.0022
18. Leather, etc.	0.0000	0.0004	0.0002	0.0000	0.0002	0.0019	0.0001	0.0006
19. Rubber	0.0020	0.0034	0.0066	0.0030	0.0006	0.0014	0.0001	0.0031
20. Chemicals	0.0107	0.0171	0.0142	0.0153	0.0183	0.0007	0.0075	0.0055
21. Oil coal dev.	0.0035	0.0027	0.0070	0.0028	0.0062	0.0123	0.0269	0.0022
22. Non-metals	0.0020	0.0040	0.0015	0.0021	0.1259	0.0008	0.0176	0.0117
23. Basic metals	0.1289	0.0811	0.0919	0.0890	0.0509	0.0014	0.0406	0.0183
24. Metal works	0.0416	0.0212	0.0162	0.0046	0.0396	0.0048	0.0058	0.0107
25. Mech. engineering	0.1105	0.0039	0.0013	0.0004	0.0034	0.0006	0.0016	0.0297
26. Elec. engineering	0.0081	0.0260	0.0023	0.0036	0.0051	0.0036	0.0013	0.0042
27. Vehicles	0.0012	0.0002	0.0573	0.0003	0.0023	0.0025	0.0031	0.0193
28. Other manufacts.	0.0025	0.0054	0.0037	0.0255	0.0058	0.0033	0.0037	0.0055
29. Construction	0.0000	0.0000	0.0000	0.0000	0.0000	0.0049	0.0058	0.0251
30. Electricity	0.0080	0.0094	0.0091	0.0074	0.0010	0.1933	0.0118	0.0309
31. Gas	0.0011	0.0003	0.0016	0.0005	0.0000	0.0004	0.0016	0.0000
32. Water, etc.	0.0000	0.0000	0.0000	0.0000	0.0004	0.0013	0.0008	0.0000
33. Trade	0.0531	0.0467	0.0372	0.0345	0.0345	0.0201	0.0287	0.0128
34. Banking	0.0030	0.0014	0.0010	0.0051	0.0012	0.0056	0.0008	0.0022
35. Insurance	0.0000	0.0006	0.0016	0.0019	0.0036	0.0008	0.0086	0.0033
36. Other finance	0.0000	0.0000	0.0000	0.0000	0.0051	0.0000	0.0000	0.0000
37. Real estate	0.0000	0.0000	0.0000	0.0000	0.0000	0.0000	0.0000	0.0000
38. Housing	0.0000	0.0000	0.0000	0.0000	0.0000	0.0000	0.0000	0.0000
39. Transport, etc.	0.0116	0.0096	0.0105	0.0187	0.0651	0.0420	0.0791	0.0317
40. Education prvt.	0.0000	0.0000	0.0000	0.0000	0.0000	0.0011	0.0006	0.0000
41. Education public	0.0000	0.0000	0.0000	0.0000	0.0000	0.0000	0.0000	0.0000
42. Health prvt.	0.0000	0.0000	0.0000	0.0000	0.0000	0.0058	0.0027	0.0000
43. Health public	0.0000	0.0000	0.0000	0.0000	0.0000	0.0000	0.0000	0.0000
44. Producers serv.	0.0022	0.0021	0.0021	0.0023	0.0094	0.0101	0.0114	0.0054
45. Entertainment	0.0000	0.0000	0.0000	0.0000	0.0000	0.0010	0.0002	0.0000
46. Catering	0.0000	0.0000	0.0000	0.0000	0.0071	0.0058	0.0000	0.0028
47. Laundry etc.	0.0000	0.0000	0.0000	0.0000	0.0000	0.0002	0.0002	0.0000
48. Other services	0.0000	0.0000	0.0000	0.0000	0.0000	0.0015	0.0013	0.0046
49. Import	0.0397	0.0676	0.0702	0.0593	0.0224	0.0431	0.0378	0.0000
50. Total interim	0.4389	0.3302	0.3489	0.3493	0.4812	0.4176	0.5295	0,2356
51. Wages + salaries	0.1853	0.1332	0.1872	0.0910	0.1913	0.2087	0.2404	0.6008
52. Emploers cont.	0.0413	0.0312	0.0439	0.0204	0.0423	0.0498	0.1099	0.0740
53. Other gross	0.3345	0.5054	0.4200	0.5394	0.2852	0.3239	0.1202	0.0896
54. Gross output	1.0000	1.0000	1.0000	1.0000	1.0000	1.0000	1.0000	1.0000

Appendix. Table C2 (continued)

	33 Trade	34 Banking	35 Ins'ce	36 Other finance	37 Real est.	38 Housing	39 Tr'spt.	40 Educ. prvt.
1. Agriculture	0.0000	0.0000	0.0000	0.0133	0.0000	0.0000	0.0032	0.0085
2. Fisheries	0.0000	0.0000	0.0000	0.0000	0.0000	0.0000	0.0000	0.0009
3. Coal mining	0.0000	0.0000	0.0006	0.0026	0.0000	0.0000	0.0122	0.0006
4. Iron mining	0.0000	0.0000	0.0000	0.0000	0.0000	0.0000	0.0000	0.0000
5. Copper mining	0.0000	0.0000	0.0000	0.0000	0.0000	0.0000	0.0000	0.0000
6. Nitrate mining	0.0000	0.0000	0.0000	0.0000	0.0000	0.0000	0.0000	0.0000
7. Quarries	0.0000	0.0000	0.0000	0.0000	0.0000	0.0000	0.0000	0.0000
8. Other mining	0.0000	0.0000	0.0000	0.0000	0.0000	0.0000	0.0000	0.0000
9. Food industries	0.0000	0.0000	0.0000	0.0009	0.0000	0.0000	0.0005	0.0372
10. Drinks	0.0000	0.0000	0.0000	0.0000	0.0000	0.0000	0.0003	0.0000
11. Tobacco	0.0000	0.0000	0.0000	0.0000	0.0000	0.0000	0.0000	0.0000
12. Textiles	0.0039	0.0010	0.0000	0.0012	0.0002	0.0000	0.0006	0.0000
13. Clothing, ftwr.	0.0013	0.0049	0.0000	0.0023	0.0000	0.0000	0.0000	0.0013
14. Wood, etc.	0.0002	0.0001	0.0000	0.0003	0.0000	0.0000	0.0028	0.0006
15. Furniture	0.0000	0.0017	0.0004	0.0045	0.0008	0.0000	0.0001	0.0023
16. Paper, etc.	0.0083	0.0312	0.0006	0.0285	0.0089	0.0000	0.0004	0.0055
17. Printing, etc.	0.0190	0.1023	0.0064	0.0659	0.0637	0.0000	0.0026	0.0183
18. Leather, etc.	0.0000	0.0001	0.0000	0.0000	0.0000	0.0000	0.0001	0.0000
19. Rubber	0.0036	0.0008	0.0000	0.0033	0.0008	0.0000	0.0207	0.0009
20. Chemicals	0.0030	0.0021	0.0008	0.0117	0.0050	0.0000	0.0016	0.0032
21. Oil coal dev.	0.0028	0.0038	0.0002	0.0060	0.0005	0.0000	0.0408	0.0106
22. Non-metals	0.0000	0.0000	0.0000	0.0000	0.0000	0.0000	0.0004	0.0019
23. Basic metals	0.0000	0.0000	0.0000	0.0000	0.0000	0.0000	0.0048	0.0000
24. Metal works	0.0008	0.0000	0.0001	0.0000	0.0000	0.0000	0.0029	0.0000
25. Mech. engineering	0.0000	0.0094	0.0000	0.0023	0.0026	0.0000	0.0003	0.0002
26. Elec. engineering	0.0027	0.0027	0.0015	0.0042	0.0000	0.0000	0.0024	0.0011
27. Vehicles	0.0052	0.0013	0.0002	0.0142	0.0011	0.0000	0.0739	0.0003
28. Other manufacts.	0.0022	0.0190	0.0018	0.0171	0.0052	0.0000	0.0021	0.0054
29. Construction	0.0038	0.0398	0.0031	0.0811	0.0000	0.2421	0.0035	0.0358
30. Electricity	0.0041	0.0177	0.0044	0.0061	0.0044	0.0000	0.0058	0.0030
31. Gas	0.0011	0.0086	0.0013	0.0041	0.0000	0.0000	0.0001	0.0034
32. Water, etc.	0.0004	0.0014	0.0003	0.0014	0.0004	0.0000	0.0005	0.0018
33. Trade	0.0106	0.0111	0.0009	0.0120	0.0027	0.0000	0.0241	0.0057
34. Banking	0.0056	0.0250	0.0005	0.0129	0.0000	0.0000	0.0008	0.0006
35. Insurance	0.0045	0.0003	0.0015	0.0080	0.0014	0.0032	0.0046	0.0016
36. Other finance	0.0000	0.0116	0.0000	0.0316	0.0000	0.0083	0.0000	0.0000
37. Real estate	0.0000	0.0000	0.0000	0.0000	0.0000	0.0189	0.0000	0.0000
38. Housing	0.0000	0.0000	0.0000	0.0000	0.0000	0.0000	0.0000	0.0000
39. Transport, etc.	0.0132	0.1225	0.0149	0.0454	0.0226	0.0000	0.0476	0.0289
40. Education prvt.	0.0000	0.0038	0.0000	0.0000	0.0000	0.0000	0.0000	0.0000
41. Education public	0.0000	0.0000	0.0000	0.0000	0.0000	0.0000	0.0000	0.0000
42. Health prvt.	0.0000	0.0000	0.0384	0.0002	0.0000	0.0000	0.0000	0.0030
43. Health public	0.0000	0.0000	0.0000	0.0000	0.0000	0.0000	0.0000	0.0000
44. Producers serv.	0.0090	0.0233	0.0217	0.0512	0.0018	0.0000	0.0049	0.0000
45. Entertainment	0.0025	0.0008	0.0000	0.0027	0.0000	0.0000	0.0000	0.0000
46. Catering	0.0077	0.0463	0.0025	0.1075	0.0000	0.0000	0.0156	0.0015
47. Laundry, etc.	0.0000	0.0079	0.0005	0.0005	0.0000	0.0000	0.0002	0.0027
48. Other services	0.0000	0.0000	0.0002	0.0027	0.0000	0.0000	0.0008	0.0000
49. Import	0.0000	0.0152	0.0000	0.0000	0.0000	0.0000	0.0211	0.0087
50. Total interim	0.1156	0.5156	0.1058	0.5472	0.1201	0.2724	0.2997	0.1969
51. Wages + salaries	0.1983	1.5442	0.2269	0.8963	0.4273	0.0000	0.3047	0.4248
52. Employers cont.	0.0395	0.6291	0.0420	0.1294	0.1573	0.0000	0.0445	0.0516
53. Other gross	0.6466	-1.6890	0.6253	-0.5729	0.2953	0.7274	0.3507	0.3267
54. Gross output	1.0000	1.0000	1.0000	1.0000	1.0000	1.0000	1.0000	1.0000

Appendix. Table C2 (continued)

	41 Educ. public	42 Health prvt.	43 Health public	44 Prod. serv.	45 Ent'mnt.	46 Cat'ing	47 Laundry etc.	48 Other ser.
1. Agriculture	0.0046	0.0085	0.0088	0.0000	0.0000	0.0484	0.0000	0.0001
2. Fisheries	0.0005	0.0009	0.0009	0.0000	0.0000	0.0000	0.0058	0.0000
3. Coal mining	0.0000	0.0000	0.0000	0.0000	0.0000	0.0021	0.0000	0.0000
4. Iron mining	0.0000	0.0000	0.0000	0.0000	0.0000	0.0000	0.0000	0.0000
5. Copper mining	0.0000	0.0000	0.0000	0.0000	0.0000	0.0000	0.0000	0.0000
6. Nitrate mining	0.0000	0.0000	0.0000	0.0000	0.0000	0.0000	0.0000	0.0000
7. Quarries, etc.	0.0000	0.0000	0.0000	0.0000	0.0000	0.0000	0.0000	0.0000
8. Other mining	0.0000	0.0000	0.0000	0.0000	0.0000	0.0000	0.0000	0.0000
9. Food industies	0.0195	0.0371	0.0824	0.0000	0.0000	0.0000	0.2262	0.0368
10. Drinks	0.0000	0.0000	0.0000	0.0000	0.0000	0.1461	0.0000	0.0000
11. Tobacco	0.0000	0.0000	0.0000	0.0000	0.0000	0.0000	0.0000	0.0000
12. Textiles	0.0002	0.0026	0.0039	0.0000	0.0000	0.0000	0.0000	0.0000
13. Clothing, ftwr.	0.0004	0.0021	0.0079	0.0000	0.0000	0.0016	0.0020	0.0015
14. Wood, etc.	0.0001	0.0008	0.0010	0.0000	0.0000	0.0000	0.0000	0.0793
15. Furniture	0.0003	0.0007	0.0032	0.0000	0.0000	0.0005	0.0000	0.0000
16. Paper, etc.	0.0014	0.0002	0.0019	0.0012	0.0007	0.0000	0.0030	0.0000
17. Printing, etc.	0.0093	0.0025	0.0064	0.0319	0.0549	0.0013	0.0060	0.0040
18. Leather, etc.	0.0000	0.0000	0.0000	0.0000	0.0001	0.0000	0.0000	0.0000
19. Rubber	0.0001	0.0007	0.0007	0.0003	0.0000	0.0000	0.0000	0.0010
20. Chemicals	0.0003	0.0656	0.0490	0.0000	0.0026	0.0032	0.0632	0.0018
21. Oil coal dev.	0.0010	0.0042	0.0113	0.0002	0.0007	0.0093	0.0091	0.0023
22. Non-metals	0.0006	0.0003	0.0042	0.0000	0.0000	0.0001	0.0000	0.0000
23. Basic metals	0.0000	0.0000	0.0001	0.0000	0.0000	0.0000	0.0000	0.0014
24. Metal works	0.0006	0.0013	0.0006	0.0000	0.0000	0.0000	0.0000	0.0000
25. Mech. engineering	0.0007	0.0018	0.0009	0.0000	0.0031	0.0000	0.0019	0.0000
26. Elec. engineering	0.0001	0.0000	0.0001	0.0000	0.0068	0.0000	0.0024	0.0000
27. Vehicles	0.0014	0.0000	0.0051	0.0005	0.0000	0.0002	0.0025	0.0026
28. Other manufacts.	0.0024	0.0108	0.0079	0.0107	0.0113	0.0006	0.0035	0.0014
29. Construction	0.0021	0.0247	0.0431	0.0120	0.0000	0.0004	0.0028	0.0002
30. Electricity	0.0025	0.0013	0.0140	0.0032	0.0026	0.0067	0.0092	0.0018
31. Gas	0.0014	0.0012	0.0022	0.0000	0.0000	0.0066	0.0012	0.0000
32. Water, etc.	0.0012	0.0014	0.0017	0.0000	0.0012	0.0013	0.0015	0.0002
33. Trade	0.0022	0.0154	0.0136	0.0033	0.0047	0.0621	0.0118	0.0096
34. Banking	0.0000	0.0001	0.0000	0.0111	0.0019	0.0003	0.0007	0.0002
35. Insurance	0.0001	0.0008	0.0002	0.0004	0.0003	0.0022	0.0034	0.0000
36. Other finance	0.0000	0.0000	0.0000	0.0000	0.0000	0.0000	0.0000	0.0000
37. Real estate	0.0000	0.0000	0.0000	0.0000	0.0000	0.0000	0.0000	0.0000
38. Housing	0.0000	0.0000	0.0000	0.0000	0.0000	0.0000	0.0000	0.0000
39. Transport, etc.	0.0056	0.0219	0.0184	0.0366	0.0250	0.0373	0.0395	0.0260
40. Education prvt.	0.0001	0.0000	0.0000	0.0000	0.0000	0.0000	0.0000	0.0000
41. Education public	0.0000	0.0000	0.0000	0.0000	0.0000	0.0000	0.0000	0.0000
42. Health prvt.	0.0000	0.0000	0.0000	0.0000	0.0004	0.0000	0.0000	0.0000
43. Health public	0.0000	0.0000	0.0000	0.0000	0.0000	0.0000	0.0000	0.0000
44. Producers serv.	0.0000	0.0000	0.0018	0.0000	0.0577	0.0005	0.0019	0.0083
45. Entertainment	0.0000	0.0000	0.0000	0.0000	0.0000	0.0005	0.0010	0.0000
46. Catering	0.0022	0.0000	0.0036	0.0221	0.0193	0.0008	0.0000	0.0013
47. Laundry, etc.	0.0000	0.0226	0.0001	0.0000	0.0000	0.0011	0.0000	0.0000
48. Other services	0.0000	0.0000	0.0000	0.0000	0.0000	0.0000	0.0003	0.0000
49. Imports	0.0038	0.0065	0.0024	0.0000	0.0986	0.0000	0.0246	0.0000
50. Total interim	0.0646	0.2359	0.2975	0.1337	0.2920	0.5652	0.1915	0.1798
51. Wages + salaries	0.8840	0.2947	0.6161	0.3761	0.2514	0.0944	0.1914	0.5384
52. Employers cont.	0.0305	0.0356	0.0278	0.0450	0.0304	0.0114	0.0231	0.0552
53. Other gross	0.0208	0.4338	0.0587	0.4497	0.4262	0.3289	0.5938	0.2266
54. Gross output	1.0000	1.0000	1.0000	1.0000	1.0000	1.0000	1.0000	1.0000

Appendix. Table C3
Coefficients of global input requirements (direct and indirect) at producer prices (estimated) (current escudos of 1962).

	1. Agr.	2 Fish.	3 Coal mining	4 Iron mining	5 Copper mining	6 Nitrate mining	7 Quarries etc.	8 Other mining
1. Agriculture	1.0812	0.0048	0.0048	0.0011	0.0018	0.0032	0.0004	0.0023
2. Fisheries	0.0001	1.0000	0.0000	0.0000	0.0000	0.0000	0.0000	0.0000
3. Coal mining	0.0008	0.0010	1.0233	0.0011	0.0044	0.0035	0.0042	0.0026
4. Iron mining	0.0001	0.0002	0.0005	1.0005	0.0012	0.0003	0.0002	0.0001
5. Copper mining	0.0003	0.0005	0.0010	0.0011	1.0019	0.0008	0.0004	0.0006
6. Nitrate mining	0.0138	0.0001	0.0001	0.0000	0.0000	1.0000	0.0000	0.0000
7. Quarries, etc.	0.0000	0.0001	0.0003	0.0001	0.0002	0.0001	1.0001	0.0001
8. Other mining	0.0029	0.0067	0.0020	0.0014	0.0047	0.0026	0.0025	1.0007
9. Food industries	0.0214	0.0038	0.0015	0.0004	0.0005	0.0009	0.0002	0.0034
10. Drinks	0.0002	0.0001	0.0002	0.0001	0.0001	0.0002	0.0001	0.0005
11. Tobacco	0.0000	0.0000	0.0000	0.0000	0.0000	0.0000	0.0000	0.0000
12. Textiles	0.0010	0.0381	0.0030	0.0008	0.0010	0.0039	0.0003	0.0005
13. Clothing, ftwr.	0.0002	0.0024	0.0039	0.0001	0.0010	0.0028	0.0001	0.0004
14. Wood, etc.	0.0036	0.0091	0.0279	0.0035	0.0046	0.0107	0.0004	0.0014
15. Furniture	0.0001	0.0003	0.0003	0.0001	0.0001	0.0009	0.0000	0.0003
16. Paper, etc.	0.0017	0.0015	0.0031	0.0016	0.0016	0.0033	0.0007	0.0027
17. Printing, etc.	0.0019	0.0015	0.0045	0.0032	0.0016	0.0067	0.0013	0.0096
18. Leather, etc.	0.0001	0.0002	0.0005	0.0000	0.0002	0.0003	0.0000	0.0001
19. Rubber	0.0026	0.0010	0.0017	0.0008	0.0010	0.0017	0.0003	0.0012
20. Chemicals	0.0219	0.0308	0.0257	0.0183	0.0241	0.0375	0.0067	0.0072
21. Oil coal dev.	0.0146	0.0385	0.0081	0.0076	0.0190	0.0086	0.0142	0.0034
22. Non-metals	0.0006	0.0007	0.0185	0.0010	0.0056	0.0037	0.0008	0.0014
23. Basic metals	0.0035	0.0065	0.0122	0.0145	0.0293	0.0075	0.0055	0.0028
24. Metal works	0.0014	0.0019	0.0260	0.0198	0.0053	0.0079	0.0185	0.0018
25. Mech. engineering	0.0087	0.0005	0.0012	0.0188	0.0072	0.0053	0.0044	0.0006
26. Elec. engineering	0.0004	0.0030	0.0040	0.0006	0.0028	0.0021	0.0003	0.0014
27. Vehicles	0.0115	0.0470	0.0034	0.0208	0.0051	0.0053	0.0010	0.0011
28. Other manufacts.	0.0006	0.0009	0.0201	0.0032	0.0040	0.0016	0.0003	0.0054
29. Construction	0.0006	0.0004	0.0007	0.0003	0.0003	0.0008	0.0003	0.0018
30. Electricity	0.0056	0.0062	0.0524	0.0061	0.0051	0.0032	0.0028	0.0092
31. Gas	0.0003	0.0004	0.0005	0.0003	0.0004	0.0004	0.0005	0.0001
32. Water, etc.	0.0000	0.0000	0.0001	0.0000	0.0000	0.0001	0.0003	0.0000
33. Trade	0.0263	0.0231	0.0276	0.0348	0.0293	0.0468	0.0140	0.0109
34. Banking	0.0100	0.0012	0.0044	0.0009	0.0010	0.0099	0.0019	0.0018
35. Insurance	0.0040	0.0263	0.0032	0.0045	0.0023	0.0023	0.0056	0.0078
36. Other finance	0.0001	0.0000	0.0001	0.0000	0.0000	0.0001	0.0000	0.0000
37. Real estate	0.0000	0.0000	0.0000	0.0000	0.0000	0.0000	0.0000	0.0000
38. Housing	0.0000	0.0000	0.0000	0.0000	0.0000	0.0000	0.0000	0.0000
39. Transport, etc.	0.0197	0.0227	0.0263	0.0197	0.0219	0.0371	0.0109	0.0116
40. Education, prvt.	0.0000	0.0000	0.0001	0.0000	0.0000	0.0000	0.0000	0.0000
41. Education public	0.0000	0.0000	0.0000	0.0000	0.0000	0.0000	0.0000	0.0000
42. Health prvt.	0.0002	0.0010	0.0004	0.0002	0.0001	0.0001	0.0002	0.0004
43. Health public	0.0000	0.0001	0.0000	0.0000	0.0000	0.0000	0.0000	0.0000
44. Producers serv.	0.0015	0.0027	0.0018	0.0011	0.0030	0.0016	0.0033	0.1265
45. Entertainment	0.0001	0.0001	0.0001	0.0001	0.0001	0.0001	0.0000	0.0000
46. Catering	0.0011	0.0008	0.0012	0.0012	0.0007	0.0007	0.0005	0.0032
47. Laundry, etc.	0.0001	0.0001	0.0001	0.0000	0.0000	0.0001	0.0000	0.0000
48. Other services	0.0000	0.0000	0.0001	0.0000	0.0010	0.0000	0.0000	0.0000

Appendix. Table C3 (continued)

	9 Food	10 Drinks	11 Tobacco	12 Text'ls.	13 Clth'ng ftwr.	14 Wood etc.	15 Furn.	16 Paper etc.
1. Agriculture	0.4537	0.3983	0.1496	0.0679	0.0381	0.1336	0.0212	0.1411
2. Fisheries	0.0050	0.0002	0.0000	0.0000	0.0001	0.0000	0.0000	0.0001
3. Coal mining	0.0058	0.0060	0.0012	0.0036	0.0021	0.0048	0.0078	0.0041
4. Iron mining	0.0003	0.0003	0.0004	0.0001	0.0002	0.0003	0.0050	0.0004
5. Copper mining	0.0007	0.0008	0.0008	0.0003	0.0004	0.0007	0.0066	0.0008
6. Nitrate mining	0.0058	0.0051	0.0019	0.0009	0.0005	0.0017	0.0003	0.0018
7. Quarries, etc.	0.0001	0.0006	0.0001	0.0000	0.0001	0.0001	0.0009	0.0001
8. Other mining	0.0029	0.0033	0.0018	0.0033	0.0016	0.0036	0.0030	0.0142
9. Food industries	1.2118	0.0457	0.0038	0.0037	0.0316	0.0041	0.0026	0.0157
10. Drinks	0.0007	1.0249	0.0002	0.0002	0.0002	0.0006	0.0003	0.0003
11. Tobacco	0.0000	0.0000	1.0000	0.0000	0.0000	0.0000	0.0000	0.0000
12. Textiles	0.0125	0.0016	0.0006	1.2516	0.3726	0.0019	0.0710	0.0020
13. Clothing, ftwr.	0.0014	0.0008	0.0001	0.0002	1.0198	0.0002	0.0003	0.0003
14. Wood, etc.	0.0088	0.0085	0.0005	0.0006	0.0063	1.5115	0.1607	0.0015
15. Furniture	0.0001	0.0001	0.0001	0.0001	0.0001	0.0002	1.0005	0.0002
16. Paper, etc.	0.0097	0.0060	0.0335	0.0033	0.0070	0.0022	0.0040	1.1956
17. Printing, etc.	0.0051	0.0060	0.0021	0.0025	0.0019	0.0025	0.0020	0.0031
18. Leather, etc.	0.0003	0.0001	0.0000	0.0001	0.0788	0.0007	0.0037	0.0002
19. Rubber	0.0028	0.0024	0.0013	0.0017	0.0068	0.0043	0.0020	0.0019
20. Chemicals	0.0168	0.0214	0.0087	0.0299	0.0163	0.0206	0.0512	0.0239
21. Oil coal dev.	0.0153	0.0120	0.0087	0.0139	0.0069	0.0200	0.0111	0.0409
22. Non-metals	0.0020	0.0382	0.0004	0.0007	0.0011	0.0019	0.0252	0.0025
23. Basic metals	0.0075	0.0082	0.0119	0.0027	0.0056	0.0093	0.1324	0.0112
24. Metal works	0.0135	0.0200	0.0008	0.0013	0.0089	0.0082	0.0353	0.0045
25. Mech. engineering	0.0055	0.0044	0.0037	0.0061	0.0026	0.0024	0.0020	0.0403
26. Elec. engineering	0.0012	0.0014	0.0018	0.0026	0.0014	0.0019	0.0017	0.0051
27. Vehicles	0.0109	0.0103	0.0065	0.0039	0.0028	0.0196	0.0075	0.0072
28. Other manufacts.	0.0044	0.0010	0.0004	0.0013	0.0107	0.0015	0.0117	0.0011
29. Construction	0.0010	0.0009	0.0005	0.0008	0.0005	0.0012	0.0008	0.0011
30. Electricity	0.0119	0.0126	0.0059	0.0163	0.0112	0.0195	0.0190	0.0519
31. Gas	0.0007	0.0011	0.0002	0.0004	0.0009	0.0005	0.0020	0.0007
32. Water, etc.	0.0002	0.0001	0.0000	0.0002	0.0001	0.0001	0.0001	0.0001
33. Trade	0.0910	0.0774	0.0528	0.0425	0.0522	0.0522	0.0455	0.0702
34. Banking	0.0080	0.0050	0.0021	0.0056	0.0027	0.0051	0.0035	0.0074
35. Insurance	0.0049	0.0126	0.0020	0.0073	0.0043	0.0093	0.0057	0.0028
36. Other finance	0.0001	0.0001	0.0000	0.0001	0.0000	0.0001	0.0000	0.0001
37. Real estate	0.0000	0.0000	0.0000	0.0000	0.0000	0.0000	0.0000	0.0000
38. Housing	0.0000	0.0000	0.0000	0.0000	0.0000	0.0000	0.0000	0.0000
39. Transport, etc.	0.0704	0.0581	0.0342	0.0314	0.0196	0.1734	0.0736	0.0501
40. Education, prvt.	0.0000	0.0000	0.0000	0.0000	0.0000	0.0000	0.0000	0.0001
41. Education public	0.0000	0.0000	0.0000	0.0000	0.0000	0.0000	0.0000	0.0000
42. Health prvt.	0.0003	0.0006	0.0001	0.0004	0.0002	0.0005	0.0003	0.0004
43. Health public	0.0000	0.0000	0.0000	0.0000	0.0000	0.0000	0.0000	0.0000
44. Producers serv.	0.0055	0.0051	0.0048	0.0048	0.0048	0.0074	0.0053	0.0071
45. Entertainment	0.0002	0.0002	0.0001	0.0002	0.0001	0.0002	0.0001	0.0002
46. Catering	0.0023	0.0020	0.0012	0.0015	0.0010	0.0037	0.0019	0.0022
47. Laundry, etc.	0.0001	0.0001	0.0000	0.0001	0.0000	0.0001	0.0001	0.0001
48. Other services	0.0001	0.0001	0.0000	0.0001	0.0000	0.0002	0.0001	0.0001

F. Seton, Shadow prices in Chile

Appendix. Table C3 (continued)

	17 Print. etc.	18 Leather etc.	19 Rubber	20 Chem'ls.	21 Oil coal dev.	22 Non- metals	23 Basic metals	24 Metal works
1. Agriculture	0.0259	0.1520	0.0048	0.0135	0.0017	0.0111	0.0030	0.0036
2. Fisheries	0.0000	0.0015	0.0000	0.0001	0.0000	0.0006	0.0000	0.0000
3. Coal mining	0.0021	0.0035	0.0062	0.0058	0.0019	0.0395	0.0422	0.0125
4. Iron mining	0.0002	0.0004	0.0004	0.0005	0.0003	0.0006	0.0433	0.0093
5. Copper mining	0.0407	0.0008	0.0007	0.0011	0.0007	0.0009	0.0711	0.0154
6. Ni trate mining	0.0003	0.0019	0.0001	0.0002	0.0000	0.0001	0.0000	0.0000
7. Quarries, etc.	0.0001	0.0001	0.0001	0.0003	0.0001	0.0142	0.0049	0.0021
8. Other mining	0.0034	0.0027	0.0024	0.0009	0.1704	0.0325	0.0053	0.0039
9. Food industies	0.0033	0.3537	0.0013	0.0081	0.0018	0.0013	0.0009	0.0008
10. Drinks	0.0002	0.0004	0.0002	0.0004	0.0004	0.0003	0.0003	0.0003
11. Tobacco	0.0000	0.0000	0.0000	0.0000	0.0000	0.0000	0.0000	0.0000
12. Textiles	0.0012	0.0441	0.0244	0.0035	0.0008	0.0010	0.0019	0.0071
13. Clothing, ftwr.	0.0002	0.0006	0.0002	0.0014	0.0007	0.0007	0.0006	0.0008
14. Wood, etc.	0.0008	0.0041	0.0006	0.0061	0.0009	0.0031	0.0034	0.0098
15. Furniture	0.0001	0.0001	0.0001	0.0001	0.0004	0.0001	0.0002	0.0001
16. Paper, etc.	0.2133	0.0077	0.0033	0.0303	0.0018	0.0293	0.0018	0.0056
17. Printing, etc.	1.0017	0.0031	0.0018	0.0072	0.0030	0.0020	0.0025.	0.0022
18. Leather, etc.	0.0003	1.1094	0.0020	0.0008	0.0001	0.0001	0.0002	0.0002
19. Rubber	0.0012	0.0016	1.0168	0.0012	0.0022	0.0030	0.0018	0.0018
20. Chemicals	0.0348	0.0458	0.0259	1.1444	0.0059	0.0223	0.0075	0.0132
21. Oil coal dev.	0.0115	0.0138	0.0066	0.0217	1.0045	0.0250	0.0200	0.0142
22. Non-metals	0.0012	0.0042	0.0043	0.0139	0.0035	1.0652	0.0043	0.0328
23. Basic metals	0.0063	0.0110	0.0098	0.0143	0.0086	0.0135	1.1569	0.2491
24. Metal works	0.0020	0.0205	0.0031	0.0083	0.0139	0.0050	0.0056	1.0355
25. Mech. engineering	0.0090	0.0033	0.0022	0.0031	0.0021	0.0088	0.0050	0.0057
26. Elec. engineering	0.0030	0.0018	0.0022	0.0022	0.0041	0.0050	0.0041	0.0043
27. Vehicles	0.0034	0.0056	0.0035	0.0049	0.0062	0.0069	0.0085	0.0053
28. Other manufacts.	0.0025	0.0148	0.0016	0.0017	0.0021	0.0018	0.0021	0.0035
29. Construction	0.0006	0.0009	0.0006	0.0018	0.0009	0.0007	0.0010	0.0008
30. Electricity	0.0256	0.0184	0.0209	0.0185	0.0044	0.0162	0.0424	0.0304
31. Gas	0.0010	0.0008	0.0005	0.0064	0.0002	0.0084	0.0043	0.0040
32. Water, etc.	0.0001	0.0001	0.0001	0.0001	0.0001	0.0001	0.0001	0.0001
33. Trade	0.0392	0.0657	0.0547	0.0687	0.0330	0.0363	0.0490	0.0450
34. Banking	0.0033	0.0051	0.0026	0.0284	0.0010	0.0024	0.0050	0.0051
35. Insurance	0.0195	0.0156	0.0138	0.0194	0.0085	0.0054	0.0161	0.0059
36. Other finance	0.0000	0.0001	0.0000	0.0003	0.0000	0.0000	0.0001	0.0001
37. Real estate	0.0000	0.0000	0.0000	0.0000	0.0000	0.0000	0.0000	0.0000
38. Housing	0.0000	0.0000	0.0000	0.0000	0.0000	0.0000	0.0000	0.0000
39. Transport, etc.	0.0249	0.0428	0.0192	0.0338	0.0698	0.0554	0.0633	0.0434
40. Education, prvt.	0.0000	0.0000	0.0000	0.0001	0.0000	0.0000	0.0001	0.0001
41. Education public	0.0000	0.0000	0.0000	0.0000	0.0000	0.0000	0.0000	0.0000
42. Health prvt.	0.0009	0.0007	0.0007	0.0009	0.0004	0.0003	0.0009	0.0004
43. Health public	0.0001	0.0001	0.0000	0.0001	0.0000	0.0000	0.0001	0.0000
44. Producers serv.	0.0045	0.0062	0.0040	0.0062	0.0350	0.0086	0.0056	0.0051
45. Entertainment	0.0001	0.0002	0.0002	0.0002	0.0001	0.0001	0.0002	0.0001
46. Catering	0.0012	0.0017	0.0011	0.0027	0.0022	0.0016	0.0020	0.0016
47. Laundry, etc.	0.0001	0.0001	0.0001	0.0003	0.0000	0.0000	0.0001	0.0001
48. Other services	0.0001	0.0001	0.0001	0.0001	0.0001	0.0001	0.0002	0.0001

Appendix. Table C3 (continued)

	25 Mech. Eng'ng.	26 Elec. Eng'ng.	27 Vehicles	28 Other mfcs.	29 Constr.	30 Elec.	31 Gas	32 Water etc.
1. Agriculture	0.0038	0.0032	0.0021	0.0424	0.0100	0.0040	0.0033	0.0031
2. Fisheries	0.0000	0.0000	0.0000	0.0004	0.0002	0.0001	0.0000	0.0001
3. Coal mining	0.0080	0.0051	0.0062	0.0052	0.0093	0.0495	0.2301	0.0040
4. Iron mining	0.0068	0.0039	0.0045	0.0041	0.0028	0.0003	0.0021	0.0011
5. Copper mining	0.0113	0.0066	0.0074	0.0068	0.0048	0.0009	0.0037	0.0020
6. Nitrate mining	0.0000	0.0000	0.0000	0.0005	0.0001	0.0001	0.0000	0.0000
7. Quarries, etc.	0.0009	0.0007	0.0007	0.0005	0.0354	0.0003	0.0008	0.0024
8. Other mining	0.0021	0.0019	0.0023	0.0034	0.0066	0.0034	0.0067	0.0016
9. Food industries	0.0007	0.0008	0.0007	0.0025	0.0034	0.0043	0.0016	0.0022
10. Drinks	0.0002	0.0002	0.0002	0.0002	0.0015	0.0014	0.0004	0.0008
11. Tobacco	0.0000	0.0000	0.0000	0.0000	0.0000	0.0000	0.0000	0.0000
12. Textiles	0.0088	0.0145	0.0099	0.0241	0.0017	0.0018	0.0041	0.0027
13. Clothing, ftwr.	0.0003	0.0002	0.0006	0.0003	0.0003	0.0016	0.0043	0.0013
14. Wood, etc.	0.0049	0.0073	0.0034	0.0176	0.0560	0.0040	0.0087	0.0066
15. Furniture	0.0002	0.0086	0.0055	0.0001	0.0050	0.0016	0.0005	0.0026
16. Paper, etc.	0.0027	0.0064	0.0018	0.0101	0.0076	0.0033	0.0035	0.0026
17. Printing, etc.	0.0025	0.0037	0.0016	0.0033	0.0027	0.0089	0.0076	0.0037
18. Leather, etc.	0.0001	0.0006	0.0004	0.0001	0.0004	0.0028	0.0005	0.0009
19. Rubber	0.0033	0.0043	0.0079	0.0042	0.0031	0.0034	0.0028	0.0046
20. Chemicals	0.0166	0.0227	0.0195	0.0211	0.0248	0.0046	0.0168	0.0094
21. Oil coal dev.	0.0093	0.0067	0.0113	0.0078	0.0161	0.0192	0.0347	0.0064
22. Non-metals	0.0050	0.0061	0.0032	0.0033	0.1365	0.0035	0.0246	0.0169
23. Basic metals	0.1816	0.1050	0.1196	0.1086	0.0754	0.0077	0.0551	0.0303
24. Metal works	0.0501	0.0240	0.0192	0.0061	0.0442	0.0088	0.0137	0.0151
25. Mech. engineering	1.1256	0.0054	0.0023	0.0019	0.0060	0.0014	0.0029	0.0342
26. Elec. engineering	0.0106	1.0275	0.0033	0.0033	0.0046	0.0053	0.0031	0.0054
27. Vehicles	0.0049	0.0027	1.0634	0.0041	0.0108	0.0087	0.0120	0.0245
28..Other manufacts.	0.0039	0.0064	0.0048	1.0269	0.0073	0.0060	0.0092	0.0067
29. Construction	0.0008	0.0006	0.0005	0.0008	1.0013	0.0072	0.0069	0.0259
30. Electricity	0.0202	0.0180	0.0181	0.0157	0.0095	1.2443	0.0305	0.0420
31. Gas	0.0023	0.0010	0.0024	0.0012	0.0018	0.0009	1.0022	0.0005
32. Water, etc.	0.0001	0.0001	0.0001	0.0001	0.0005	0.0017	0.0009	1.0001
33. Trade	0.0732	0.0883	0.0493	0.0467	0.0521	0.0323	0.0441	0.0232
34. Banking	0.0054	0.0031	0.0026	0.0072	0.0034.	0.0081	0.0030	0.0034
35. Insurance	0.0035	0.0031	0.0042	0.0047	0.0070	0.0022	0.0114	0.0047
36. Other finance	0.0001	0.0000	0.0000	0.0001	0.0053	0.0001	0.0001	0.0002
37. Real estate	0.0000	0.0000	0.0000	0.0000	0.0000	0.0000	0.0000	0.0000
38. Housing	0.0000	0.0000	0.0000	0.0000	0.0000	0.0000	0.0000	0.0000
39. Transports, etc.	0.0293	0.0217	0.0228	0.0331	0.0916	0.0625	0.0991	0.0438
40. Education, prvt.	0.0000	0.0000	0.0000	0.0000	0.0000	0.0014	0.0006	0.0001
41. Education public	0.0000	0.0000	0.0000	0.0000	0.0000	0.0000	0.0000	0.0000
42. Health prvt.	0.0003	0.0002	0.0003	0.0003	0.0003	0.0074	0.0033	0.0004
43. Health public	0.0000	0.0000	0.0000	0.0000	0.0000	0.0000	0.0000	0.0000
44. Producers serv.	0.0048	0.0040	0.0041	0.0044	0.0131	0.0145	0.0147	0.0074
45. Entertainment	0.0002	0.0002	0.0001	0.0001	0.0002	0.0014	0.0003	0.0001
46. Catering	0.0015	0.0011	0.0011	0.0014	0.0101	0.0093	0.0026	0.0055
47. Laundry, etc.	0.0001	0.0000	0.0000	0.0001	0.0001	0.0006	0.0004	0.0001
48. Other services	0.0001	0.0001	0.0001	0.0001	0.0001	0.0020	0.0014	0.0047

Appendix. Table C3 (continued)

	33 Trade	34 Banking	35 Ins.	36 Other finance	37 Real estate	38 Housing	39 Transp't. etc.	40 Educ. prvt.
1. Agriculture	0.0043	0.0212	0.0025	0.0484	0.0032	0.0029	0.0089	0.0289
2. Fisheries	0.0001	0.0004	0.0001	0.0008	0.0000	0.0000	0.0001	0.0011
3. Coal mining	0.0010	0.0062	0.0015	0.0071	0.0008	0.0023	0.0146	0.0028
4. Iron mining	0.0001	0.0005	0.0001	0.0006	0.0001	0.0007	0.0007	0.0002
5. Copper mining	0.0010	0.0050	0.0004	0.0037	0.0025	0.0013	0.0013	0.0011
6. Nitrate mining	0.0001	0.0003	0.0000	0.0006	0.0000	0.0000	0.0001	0.0004
7. Quarries, etc.	0.0002	0.0016	0.0002	0.0031	0.0000	0.0086	0.0003	0.0013
8. Other mining	0.0009	0.0032	0.0003	0.0034	0.0007	0.0016	0.0078	0.0027
9. Food industies	0.0028	0.0163	0.0032	0.0351	0.0006	0.0011	0.0059	0.0464
10. Drinks	0.0013	0.0079	0.0005	0.0173	0.0001	0.0005	0.0030	0.0004
11. Tobacco	0.0000	0.0000	0.0000	0.0000	0.0000	0.0000	0.0000	0.0000
12. Textiles	0.0059	0.0050	0.0005	0.0048	0.0007	0.0005	0.0026	0.0016
13. Clothing, ftwr.	0.0015	0.0054	0.0002	0.0029	0.0000	0.0001	0.0003	0.0015
14. Wood, etc.	0.0008	0.0046	0.0006	0.0078	0.0005	0.0136	0.0058	0.0041
15. Furniture	0.0001	0.0022	0.0005	0.0053	0.0008	0.0013	0.0007	0.0025
16. Paper, etc.	0.0149	0.0630	0.0027	0.0533	0.0222	0.0027	0.0021	0.0117
17. Printing, etc.	0.0206	0.1086	0.0075	0.0734	0.0642	0.0025	0.0041	0.0192
18. Leather, etc.	0.0002	0.0007	0.0000	0.0004	0.0000	0.0001	0.0003	0.0002
19. Rubber	0.0042	0.0046	0.0005	0.0058	0.0015	0.0008	0.0231	0.0020
20. Chemicals	0.0052	0.0114	0.0048	0.0229	0.0086	0.0064	0.0054	0.0075
21. Oil coal dev.	0.0047	0.0151	0.0017	0.0154	0.0029	0.0041	0.0452	0.0143
22. Non-metals	0.0009	0.0072	0.0009	0.0133	0.0003	0.0332	0.0021	0.0075
23. Basic metals	0.0025	0.0122	0.0015	0.0147	0.0023	0.0184	0.0178	0.0854
24. Metal works	0.0016	0.0046	0.0007	0.0064	0.0006	0.0108	0.0062	0.0029
25. Mech. engineering	0.0008	0.0140	0.0003	0.0059	0.0038	0.0016	0.0010	0.0014
26. Elec. engineering	0.0031	0.0046	0.0017	0.0061	0.0004	0.0017	0.0034	0.0017
27. Vehicles	0.0072	0.0144	0.0019	0.0230	0.0034	0.0029	0.0835	0.0041
28. Other manufacts.	0.0028	0.0221	0.0027	0.0207	0.0057	0.0020	0.0034	0.0064
29. Construction	0.0044	0.0434	0.0046	0.0859	0.0002	0.2431	0.0041	0.0363
30. Electricity	0.0071	0.0312	0.0065	0.0166	0.0080	0.0026	0.0115	0.0864
31. Gas	0.0013	0.0096	0.0014	0.0057	0.0001	0.0005	0.0006	0.0036
32. Water, etc.	0.0004	0.0017	0.0003	0.0018	0.0004	0.0002	0.0006	0.0019
33. Trade	1.0154	0.0334	0.0040	0.0398	0.0076	0.0131	0.0330	0.0152
34. Banking	0.0064	1.0278	0.0010	0.0164	0.0006	0.0010	0.0017	0.0015
35. Insurance	0.0054	0.0046	1.0020	0.0122	0.0030	0.0050	0.0064	0.0031
36. Other finance	0.0001	0.0125	0.0000	1.0332	0.0000	0.0099	0.0000	0.0002
37. Real estate	0.0000	0.0000	0.0000	0.0000	1.0000	0.0189	0.0000	0.0000
38. Housing	0.0000	0.0000	0.0000	0.0000	0.0000	1.0000	0.0000	0.0000
39. Transport, etc.	0.0186	0.1509	0.0195	0.0769	0.0269	0.0234	1.0597	0.0402
40. Education, prvt.	0.0000	0.0039	0.0000	0.0001	0.0000	0.0000	0.0000	1.0000
41. Education public	0.0000	0.0000	0.0000	0.0000	0.0000	0.0000	0.0000	0.0000
42. Health prvt.	0.0003	0.0004	0.0385	0.0008	0.0002	0.0002	0.0003	0.0032
43. Health public	0.0000	0.0000	0.0033	0.0000	0.0000	0.0000	0.0000	0.0000
44. Producers serv.	0.0102	0.0279	0.0222	0.0569	0.0025	0.0038	0.0077	0.0018
45. Entertainment	0.0025	0.0010	0.0000	0.0030	0.0000	0.0001	0.0001	0.0001
46. Catering	0.0088	0.0527	0.0035	0.1155	0.0006	0.0034	0.0172	0.0027
47. Laundry, etc.	0.0001	0.0082	0.0014	0.0008	0.0000	0.0000	0.0003	0.0038
48. Other services	0.0000	0.0003	0.0002	0.0028	0.0000	0.0001	0.0007	0.0001

Appendix. Table C3 (continued)

	41 Educ. public	42 Health prvt.	43 Health public	44 Prods. serv.	45 Ent'mnt.	46 Catering	47 Laundry etc.	48 Other serv.
1. Agriculture	0.0150	0.0284	0.0507	0.0069	0.0069	0.2142	0.0022	0.0282
2. Fisheries	0.0006	0.0011	0.0014	0.0002	0.0002	0.0070	0.0000	0.0002
3. Coal mining	0.0008	0.0017	0.0031	0.0012	0.0010	0.0070	0.0015	0.0013
4. Iron mining	0.0001	0.0002	0.0003	0.0001	0.0001	0.0002	0.0001	0.0001
5. Copper mining	0.0005	0.0005	0.0008	0.0016	0.0025	0.0005	0.0005	0.0004
6. Nitrate mining	0.0002	0.0004	0.0006	0.0001	0.0001	0.0027	0.0000	0.0004
7. Quarries, etc.	0.0001	0.0009	0.0016	0.0005	0.0001	0.0002	0.0002	0.0000
8. Other mining	0.0004	0.0018	0.0033	0.0007	0.0007	0.0034	0.0025	0.0010
9. Food industries	0.0246	0.0461	0.1022	0.0069	0.0064	0.2826	0.0010	0.0456
10. Drinks	0.0004	0.0002	0.0008	0.0036	0.0032	0.1503	0.0002	0.0004
11. Tobacco	0.0000	0.0000	0.0000	0.0000	0.0000	0.0000	0.0000	0.0000
12. Textiles	0.0008	0.0054	0.0099	0.0006	0.0007	0.0045	0.0014	0.0014
13. Clothing, ftwr.	0.0005	0.0024	0.0084	0.0001	0.0001	0.0022	0.0022	0.0016
14. Wood, etc.	0.0007	0.0039	0.0059	0.0013	0.0007	0.0039	0.0010	0.1206
15. Furniture	0.0004	0.0008	0.0035	0.0001	0.0001	0.0006	0.0001	0.0000
16. Paper, etc.	0.0040	0.0039	0.0070	0.0094	0.0137	0.0047	0.0073	0.0018
17. Printing, etc.	0.0096	0.0039	0.0080	0.0336	0.0576	0.0052	0.0072	0.0050
18. Leather, etc.	0.0001	0.0003	0.0008	0.0000	0.0002	0.0003	0.0003	0.0002
19. Rubber	0.0004	0.0017	0.0020	0.0014	0.0009	0.0024	0.0012	0.0023
20. Chemicals	0.0015	0.0791	0.0603	0.0023	0.0060	0.0128	0.0734	0.0048
21. Oil coal dev.	0.0021	0.0084	0.0164	0.0032	0.0034	0.0180	0.0129	0.0059
22. Non-metals	0.0011	0.0050	0.0116	0.0020	0.0006	0.0067	0.0015	0.0007
23. Basic metals	0.0015	0.0057	0.0079	0.0033	0.0037	0.0047	0.0035	0.0037
24. Metal works	0.0012	0.0040	0.0050	0.0011	0.0009	0.0068	0.0014	0.0015
25. Mech. engineering	0.0011	0.0029	0.0024	0.0007	0.0042	0.0025	0.0027	0.0005
26. Elec. engineering	0.0003	0.0007	0.0010	0.0005	0.0074	0.0010	0.0030	0.0004
27. Vehicles	0.0024	0.0034	0.0093	0.0043	0.0029	0.0088	0.0067	0.0072
28. Other manufacts.	0.0027	0.0119	0.0094	0.0116	0.0127	0.0024	0.0041	0.0020
29. Construction	0.0022	0.0252	0.0437	0.0127	0.0011	0.0014	0.0033	0.0008
30. Electricity	0.0041	0.0040	0.0212	0.0063	0.0062	0.0147	0.0139	0.0050
31. Gas	0.0014	0.0018	0.0028	0.0004	0.0003	0.0071	0.0017	0.0001
32. Water, etc.	0.0012	0.0015	0.0018	0.0001	0.0012	0.0014	0.0016	0.0002
33. Trade	0.0057	0.0277	0.0313	0.0098	0.0118	0.0990	0.0196	0.0190
34. Banking	0.0003	0.0027	0.0026	0.0118	0.0032	0.0036	0.0028	0.0011
35. Insurance	0.0006	0.0031	0.0026	0.0016	0.0020	0.0063	0.0052	0.0014
36. Other finance	0.0000	0.0002	0.0003	0.0002	0.0000	0.0001	0.0001	0.0000
37. Real estate	0.0000	0.0000	0.0000	0.0000	0.0000	0.0000	0.0000	0.0000
38. Housing	0.0000	0.0000	0.0000	0.0000	0.0000	0.0000	0.0000	0.0000
39. Transport, etc.	0.0088	0.0333	0.0352	0.0446	0.0331	0.0685	0.0468	0.0453
40. Education, prvt.	0.0001	0.0000	0.0000	0.0001	0.0000	0.0000	0.0000	0.0000
41. Education public	1.0000	0.0000	0.0000	0.0000	0.0000	0.0000	0.0000	0.0000
42. Health prvt.	0.0001	1.0002	0.0002	0.0001	0.0005	0.0003	0.0003	0.0001
43. Health public	0.0000	0.0000	1.0000	0.0000	0.0000	0.0000	0.0000	0.0000
44. Producers serv.	0.0105	0.0017	0.0043	1.0011	0.0586	0.0043	0.0035	0.0091
45. Entertainment	0.0000	0.0001	0.0001	0.0001	1.0000	0.0008	0.0010	0.0000
46. Catering	0.0025	0.0029	0.0051	0.0236	0.0211	1.0030	0.0012	0.0024
47. Laundry, etc.	0.0000	0.0226	0.0001	0.0001	0.0001	0.0012	1.0000	0.0000
48. Other services	0.0000	0.0001	0.0001	0.0001	0.0000	0.0001	0.0004	1.0000

R.S. Eckaus, P.N. Rosenstein-Rodan (eds.), Analysis of development problems,
© North-Holland Publishing Company

GROWTH AND TRADE DISTORTIONS IN CHILE, AND THEIR IMPLICATIONS IN CALCULATING THE SHADOW PRICE OF FOREIGN EXCHANGE [*]

Lance TAYLOR

Harvard University, Cambridge, Mass., USA

and

Edmar BACHA

University of Brasilia, Brasilia, D.F., Brasil

I. Introduction

In this paper we attempt to deal with three inter-related problems—forecasting Chile's foreign exchange needs in the medium term, assessing the feasibility of meeting these needs in the face of rather severe trade distortions, and estimating an appropriate shadow price for foreign exchange on the basis of quantitative estimates of the extent of these distortions.

As we will spell out as we go along, there are substantial analytical and empirical difficulties in trying to do all these things. The analytical problems are dealt with at length elsewhere [refs. 8, 18] and we concentrate on empirical problems here. The main results of the paper are estimates of the shadow price of foreign exchange (or, in our interpretation, the equilibrium exchange rate) for Chile, which appear in table 9.

Why estimate the shadow price of foreign exchange in the first place? Clearly, one has limited resources to devote to shadow price estimation, and one must choose one's targets carefully in light of existing distortions in the economy and the possibilities of making a significant impact on economic welfare through shadow price corrections in investment project evaluation.

[*] A first draft of this paper was presented at a seminar on public sector project evaluation organized by ODEPLAN for public and private sector executives in April 1970. We are grateful to Gabriel Diaz, Ana Maria Jul, Valentin Michelli and Victor Perez for research help, and to the Harvard University Center for International Affairs and Fundação Getulio Vargas for research support after we left Chile.

121

On both these grounds, shadow exchange rate corrections in Chile are important.

Economic growth forecasts indicate that Chile's foreign exchange needs during the next decade will be very high, justifying a careful screening of investment projects in terms of their costs of saving or generating additional foreign exchange. And the distortions imposed on the economy (especially on the election between export and import-substitution investments) by the protectionist policies pursued over the last four decades necessitate a fairly substantial increase of the price of the dollar to achieve an efficient resource allocation. Because of these reasons, there has been extensive work at ODEPLAN and elsewhere on calculation of the shadow exchange rate, and related matters. The results of these investigations are summarized here.

The organization of the paper is as follows: in the next section, we give a summary of projections which have been made of Chile's foreign exchange needs during the next decade. This will be followed by a review of the comparative costs of generating foreign exchange in different branches of the Chilean economy, with evidence coming from a variety of sources. This cost analysis will lead finally to the conclusion that the escudo is over-valued in terms of the dollar, and a foreign exchange shadow price which can compensate for this overvaluation in investment project analysis will be presented.

II. Projections of foreign exchange use

Several models have been developed to forecast Chile's foreign exchange needs in the 1970's. These will be reviewed in due course, but first it is worthwhile to make some order-of-magnitude projections of what these requirements are likely to be.

As a preliminary, we may characterize the current foreign exchange scene as follows: Chile now exports (and imports) about US $ 1000 million per year, with imports amounting to about 14% of GDP. Imports of intermediate inputs to production make up a bit more than one-half of total goods imports, capital goods make up almost one third of these imports, and consumer goods are the balance. The intermediate imports (in c.i.f. values) are about seven percent of GDP, while capital goods imports make up more than one-third of total gross capital formation. In recent years, exports of copper and other minerals have made up 70% or more of total exports.

What are the possible future paths of evolution from this situation? To make projections it is necessary to start from some assumptions about what is likely to remain constant, and what is likely to change in the relationships among import-export and domestic variables.

A very basic assumption is that capital goods imports are unlikely to decline as a share of gross capital formation. One reason for assuming this is that the production of capital equipment which does take place in Chile is very expensive in terms of world prices (as will be discussed more thoroughly below), and it may not be economical to expand it further. Another reason is that very few small countries (including even the most advanced ones), have succeeded in reducing their import component of capital formation to below about 30%.[1]

Secondly, we assume that intermediate imports also will not be substituted to a great extent, except at high cost. This is *not* consistent with the investigation of Lilia Rodriguez [ref. 168] who found on the basis of survey information that somewhat more than one-half of intermediate imports are 'competitive' and could be substituted. However, her definition of competitiveness is ample, referring to all technical possibilities. The practice is rather more difficult, and for this reason no drastic reduction in the importance of this type of imports is postulated.

Thirdly, suppose for the moment that exports can only grow proportionately to GDP. This means that in the absence of foreign capital inflows, foreign exchange availability in any moment will be about 15% of GDP (from exports), *less* intermediate imports (7%), *less* factor payments abroad (about 3%). This leaves 5% of GDP in foreign exchange available for capital goods and consumption imports. On the other hand, capital goods imports make up one third of investment, so that if *all* consumption imports were suppressed investment would still be limited on the foreign exchange side to 15% of GDP. If the capital-output ratio is three, then *the maximum rate of growth of GDP on the assumption that exports make up a constant fraction of GDP and not allowing imports of consumption goods and capital inflows is five percent.* Clearly, exports plus foreign capital inflows plus import substitution would have to grow more rapidly than GDP if the rate of economic growth in Chile is to accelerate over past levels.

There are a number of things wrong with the calculation we have just gone through, most of which are related to the rigidity of its hypotheses of proportionality of different variables. However, its basic result — that rapid export growth or further import substitution is a necessary condition for high growth rates — is verified by more complex models.

Three models of the requisite type will be reviewed here. The first of these is the ODEPLAN two-gap model [refs. 70, 72], and the second is the linear programming model of the Chilean Economy developed by the Global programming group at ODEPLAN [ref. 150]. The most recent foreign exchange

---

[1] For empirical verification of the great importance of capital goods imports in small countries, see Adams [ref. 1] and Taylor [ref. 180].

gap forecasts of these models are briefly summarized below. A third neoclassical model [ref. 183] was also developed to emphasize the fact that substantial 'trade improvement'[2] is a necessary condition for rapid economic advance — even under strong assumptions allowing maximum possibilities of substituting domestic for foreign production.

This model assumes that production possibilities for domestic uses and trade improvement (non-traditional exportation and import substitution) are described by a three-factor neoclassical production function, the factors being labor, domestic-type capital and foreign-type capital. Accumulation of domestic-type capital is what is left of production after consumption of domestic goods, production for trade improvement, exogenous expenditure (mainly government) and capital depletion are subtracted. The amount of accumulation of foreign-type capital is foreign exchange supply (production for trade improvement plus exogenously determined mineral exports, both valued at world prices) less intermediate and consumption imports and exogenous foreign exchange flows abroad. Intermediate imports are assumed to be proportional to domestic output levels, while consumption imports are determined by total consumption demands and price elasticities.

For this paper, the model was used to work out the rates of growth of mineral exports and production for trade improvement needed to support different rates of growth of per capita consumption on the assumption that trade improvement is of equal value both in domestic and world prices.[3] Fig. 1 shows the various growth rates of traditional exports and trade improvement needed to support rates of growth of per capita consumption of 3% and 4% per year. These rates of consumption growth are (optimistically speaking) feasible in terms of historical average savings rates.[4] (The solid and dashed lines in the graph refer to different assumptions about the rate of exogenous technical progress in the economy—the value of 2.5% per year is roughly consistent

---

[2] By 'trade improvement' (the phrase comes from Chenery and MacEwan [ref. 40] we mean new production either for import substitution or export.

[3] This assumption understates required production for trade improvement, since it amounts to assuming that Chilean prices are equal to world prices at the current exchange rate, i.e. Chilean non-traditional exports are competitive in the world market without subsidy. As we will see below, this is in general not true.

[4] Fig. 1 is based on solutions to the model assuming a direct partial elasticity of substitution of 2.0 between domestic type capital (plant) and foreign-type capital (equipment). This assumption is consistent with values estimated for this parameter in the USA by Sato [ref. 170] and allows 'much' more possibility of substitution against foreign-type capital than the zero-elasticity production functions of two-gap models.

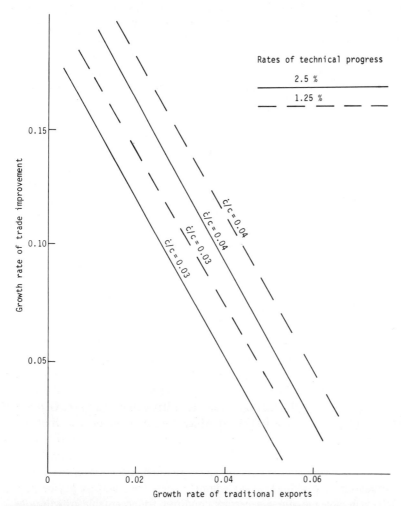

Fig. 1. Growth rates of trade improvement needed to support different consumption growth rates ($\dot{c}/c$).

with the findings of Harberger and Selowsky [ref. 92], while the value of 1.25% is closer to the estimate of Bruton [ref. 35] as corrected by Michalopolous [ref. 140].)

From fig. 1 it is clear that relatively high growth rates of production for trade improvement (or massive foreign capital inflows) will be required to support the assumed rates of consumption growth, even when

sustained growth rates of the *value* of mineral exports are relatively
high. For example, on the pessimistic (and probably more realistic) assumption
about technical progess, a rate of growth of mineral exports of 5% [5] implies
that production for trade improvement has to grow at about $7\frac{1}{2}$% per year to
support a per capita consumption growth rate of 4%. Either in terms of import
substitution or exportation, this rate of growth would be a non-trivial achievement, and it would have to be exceeded if technical progress occurs less rapidly than the historical trend or if copper prices fall off.

The rates of growth of GDP underlying the consumption growth rates of
fig. 1 are not astronomical, ranging between 5% and 6%. Using the ODEPLAN
two-gap model, Foxley et al. [ref. 72] calculated that foreign trade and savings
needs would be satisfied in 1980 if GDP grows at exactly 6% per year and
exports and imports grow at the following alternative rates:[6]

Export growth:	Import growth:
6.0%	6.4%
5.5%	5.9%
5.0%	5.3%
4.5%	4.6%

If imports grow at the high rate (the most probable happening, since a rate
of growth of imports substantially less than the rate of growth of GDP is an
unlikely prospect) and mineral exports grow at 5%, then these figures imply
that non-traditional exports will have to grow at 8% per year to fill foreign
exchange needs in 1980. This result is also broadley confirmed by the ODEPLAN
linear programming model [ref. 150], which permits a rate of growth of GDP
on the order of 6% per year with an overall export growth rate of $4\frac{1}{2}$%, but
only when the balance of payments deficit is on the order of $ 200 million
annually. This figure implies that the linear program concurs with the other
two models in forecasting that trade improvement (or a massive payments
deficit) is in large measure a necessary condition for acceptable growth rates
in the 1970's.

III. Costs of trade improvement

What problems will Chile face in generating the postulated amounts of trade
improvement?

---

[5] In terms of five-year growth rates (taking into account the projected hump in copper
production in 1971), this is probably a reasonable estimate.
[6] See Foxley et al., [ref. 71], table 3.

Given the large absolute amounts of trade improvement required, it is obvious that investments in import substitution and export promotion will have to be carefully selected and designed to give maximum yields in terms of foreign exchange at minimum cost, even under the unlikely best of conditions (for example—no drastic fall of copper prices from their present levels). However, adopting comparative cost criteria in investment requires knowledge of current costs, for use in making rules about when to reject inefficient investments. Further, cost and price data are useful in indicating the point from which Chile must start in any attempts to compete in world markets—if the country is priced out of market by large amounts in certain products, common sense would suggest that further expansion of their production be curtailed.

As it turns out, Chile does have high domestic prices, the result of a long history of trade restriction and the consequent overvaluation of the escudo. There is no one good set of evidence which can be cited to justify this assertion, but a number of indirect calculations have been made which tend to verify it. These are reviewed in some detail in this section, since they are of relevance to the calculations of foreign exchange shadow prices further on.

A. Direct price comparisons

In a country which has long practiced trade restrictions through high and diverse tariffs, import quotas and prohibitions, multiple exchange rates, special import regimes, and import deposits at various rates and real costs of capital, tracing the relationship between domestic and c.i.f. import prices is exceptionally difficult. For this reason, direct price comparisons at the wholesale level would be the best basis for computing indices of domestic overvaluation. We have attempted to do this, but not with complete success. The only reasonably complete price survey we could find was rather old (dating from 1960—62) and was taken at the *consumer* level by ECLA to compute parity exchange rates [refs. 190, 191]. We used this data to compute ratios between Chilean users' prices (in Santiago) and minimum users' prices in the capitals of the South American countries sampled by ECLA. This ratio will approximate the ratio between domestic and international prices c.i.f.-Santiago insofar as the following assumptions are not greatly violated:

(i) No price discrimination between domestic and foreign demand in the sample countries;

(ii) Similar domestic commercialization rates (proportional differences between wholesale and users' prices) in all countries;

(iii) Transport costs between Latin-American sources and Chile approximately equal to the positive difference between true international prices and minimum sample prices.

Table 1
Chile: Users' prices of groups of tradable products in terms of minimum prices in Lafta countries, at the official exchange rates, June 1962.

Group of products	Relative price in Chile	Weight	Country of comparison
Meat, poultry	298	9.90	Argentina
Fish	200	0.79	Ecuador
Milk products	253	5.23	Argentina
Cereals	134	10.19	Argentina
Fruits	197	1.10	Ecuador
Vegetables	205	9.12	Peru
Sugar	201	1.91	Peru
Fats, oils	312	2.52	Argentina
Other foods	285	2.50	Colombia
Non-alcoh. beverages	244	1.24	Mexico
Alcoholic beverages	282	8.84	Argentina
Tobacco	380	1.32	Peru
Clothing	269	11.02	Ecuador
Footwear	144	4.73	Ecuador
Textiles	225	3.31	Colombia
Household utensils	345	4.81	Brazil
Furniture	238	0.88	Peru
Electrical appliances	318	0.88	Argentina
Operation private transportation	217	1.32	Venezuela
Toilet articles	365	0.44	Brazil
Pharmac. products	168	1.53	Brazil
Books, toys	211	1.72	Brazil
Agricultural machinery	123	0.57	Venezuela
Industrial machinery	141	5.66	Mexico
Office equipment	254	0.28	Argentina
Road trans. equipment	189	2.56	Mexico
Other vehicles	144	0.57	Mexico
Construction materials	134	5.09	Ecuador
Average	228	100.00	

Notes: The table was constructed from published and unpublished data gathered by ECLA in 1960–62 in all Latin-American countries. See: ECLA, Medición del nivel de precios y el poder adquisitivo de la moneda en América Latina, 1960–62 (E/CN. 12/653, 30 August 1967), especially Cuadro VII-b, p. 197. The official exchange rates used are presented in IMF, International financial statistics, 1 (January 1963) 16. The weights for consumer goods are estimated from Chilean per-capita consumption; the demand distribution between consumer and capital goods and the weights for capital goods are derived from average final demand figures for all Latin-American countries (all weights from unpublished information by ECLA).

The credibility of these hypotheses is difficult to evaluate, but it is clear that the ECLA results must be used to make only tentative inferences. However, when one notes from table 1 that Chile has the dubious distinction of *not* having the lowest purchasers' price in the sample for *any* of the 28 groups of goods therein, and that Chilean prices are on the average 228% of minimum Latin prices, the implications of the price comparisons are clear: At least in the first part of the last decade, Chilean prices on the average for a wide variety of goods were very far from being competitive.

More recent detailed evidence on this matter is not available. However, some price comparisons made in 1969 by the Chilean Steel Institute tend to support the interferences drawn from the ECLA prices (table 2), as does most casual store-window observation. There seems to be little doubt that Chilean prices are high. The main question to be asked, however, is what we can infer from these prices and other data about costs of production in Chile? To this type of analysis we now turn.

Table 2
Comparison between recent Chilean and international prices of selected products in the metal products and machinery sectors, first semester 1969 (exchange rate: U.S. $1 = E^{0}8.16)

Product description	Price in Chile U.S. $	International price U.S. $	Price index in Chile
1. Electric sewing machine	366	120	305
2. Automatic washing machine	510	200	255
3. Home refrigerator	498	80	623
4. Gas stove	177	63	281
5. Air conditioner	1,156	150	771
6. Electric iron	27	8	338
7. TV set	415	110	377
8. Bicycle	133	27	493
9. Floor waxer	185	49	378
10. Disc for agricultural implements	17	10	170
11. Industrial abrasive wheel	281	95	296
12. Electric drill-press	593	140	424
13. Three-phase electric motor, $\frac{1}{2}$ HP	101	33	306

Note: The basis for international prices is c.i.f.-Valparaiso. Exceptions are the iron and the floor waxer, the international prices of which are the wholesale prices in Colombia and Venezuela, respectively. Products in Chile are priced either ex-factory or at the wholesale level, with the exception of the washing machine, which is priced at the consumers' level. The data presented is based on an original survey by the Chilean Steel Institute.

B. Comparative costs: Bruno–Krueger exchange rates

The Bruno–Krueger exchange rate (or domestic resource cost) for a sector is defined as the ratio of total domestic costs of production (payment for labor, domestic capital services, home-produced intermediate inputs, etc.) to the value of the sector's product in world prices, net of costs of intermediate imports and imported capital services. Thus, Bruno–Krueger sector rates give a measure of the comparative costs to the country of diverting resources to either import substitution or export promotion in the various sectors.

In [ref. 8] it is shown that the algebraic formula for the Bruno–Krueger exchange rate BK_i in sector i is

$$BK_i = \frac{c'(I-A)^{-1} h_i}{\pi_i - \pi_0 \, a'_0 (I-A)^{-1} h_i}, \tag{1}$$

where c' is a row vector of domestic costs per unit of gross output by sector, A is the input–output matrix for domestic inputs, π_i is the foreign price of product i, π_0 is an index of imported input prices, a'_0 is a row vector of non-competitive intermediate import and capital use coefficients, and h_i is a vector with unity as its ith element and with other elements equal to zero.

In ODEPLAN, we calculated Bruno–Krueger exchange rates for various industries using the 1962 Chilean input–output matrix [ref. 147], while Victor Perez at the Centro de Planeamiento of the University of Chile made direct cost calculations for a number of recent investment projects. We present the input–output results first.

In these calculations, two different assumptions were made about costs. The first was the theoretically incorrect supposition that domestic costs are adequately represented by value added less indirect taxes, while foreign capital costs are negligible. In this case the vector c' in the above formula is made up of ratios of this cost measure to gross value of output by sector.

The second, theoretically correct but empirically difficult, assumption was that domestic costs are made up of labor payments plus a 'normal' gross rate of return to domestically-produced capital used in the production process, while foreign costs include both intermediate imports and a gross rate of return to foreign-produced capital goods. In symbols, this costing procedure gives the following version of the Bruno–Krueger rate:

$$BK_i = \frac{(wl' + sk'_1)(I-A)^{-1} h_i}{\pi_i - (\pi_0 a'_0 + s\pi_2 k'_2)(I-A)^{-1} h_i}, \tag{2}$$

Table 3
Bruno–Krueger export shadow prices for Chile

Sector of ODEPLAN 1962 input–output matrix	Production costs based on	
	Value added	Labor payments and 20% return to capital
1. Agriculture, livestock, forestry and hunting [a]	1.108	1.107
4. Iron mining [a]	0.899	1.803
5. Copper mining [a]	0.943	0.599
6. Nitrate mining [a]	0.958	negative
7–8. Other mining and quarrying [a]	0.946	0.819
9. Food products [a]	1.090	0.973
13. Footwear and clothing	1.116	0.517
14. Wood and cork	1.137	1.608
15. Furniture	1.121	0.728
16. Paper and paper products [a]	1.103	1.644
18. Leather and leather products	0.932	0.545
20. Chemical products	1.029	0.750
23. Basic metals [a]	1.196	3.804
25. Non-electrical machinery	0.898	0.592
26. Electrical machinery	0.995	0.499
27. Transport equipment	0.928	0.563
28. Other manufactures	0.971	0.408

[a] Sectors with more than U.S. $ 10 million of exports in 1967.
Sources: The two shadow prices are ratios of the costs of producing U.S. $ 1 of exports according to the 1962 technology of the ODEPLAN input–output matrix (in users' prices) to the 1962 exchange rate. The two estimates are based respectively on formulas (1) and (2) of the text. Drawback payments in 1968 were used to estimate differentials between world and Chilean prices.

where in addition to previously defined symbols, w is the wage rate, l' is a vector of labor-output ratios, k'_1 is a vector of domestic capital-output ratios, s is the gross rate-of-return to capital, k'_2 is a vector of foreign capital-output ratios, and π_2 is an index of prices of foreign capital goods.

Tables 3 and 4 give Bruno–Krueger shadow prices for a number of important export and import-substituting sectors of the Chilean economy. These results were calculated according to the following assumptions:

(i) The cost structure of production in a sector for either import substitution or export promotion is the same; however, the international values of goods which substitute imports or are exported may vary.

(ii) The 'drawback' (export subsidy) payments which have been given since 1967 as part of Chile's export promotion policy provide an adequate index

Table 4
Bruno–Krueger import shadow prices for Chile

	Production costs based on:	
Sector of ODEPLAN 1962 input–output matrix	Value added	Labor payments and 20% return to capital
1. Agriculture, livestock, forestry and hunting	2.25	2.50
9. Food products	1.66	2.53
10. Beverages	1.88	2.59
11. Tobacco	0.90	0.47
12. Textiles	3.89	negative
13. Footwear and clothing	3.56	19.16
14. Wood and cork	1.25	2.10
15. Furniture	2.06	2.41
16. Paper and paper products	1.37	6.83
17. Printing and publishing	1.60	2.97
18. Leather and leather products	2.39	21.09
19. Rubber products	1.71	0.77
20. Chemical products	1.76	3.56
21. Petroleum and coal products	0.82	0.47
22. Non-metallic mineral products	2.17	negative
23. Basic metals	1.67	negative
24. Metallic products	1.36	2.17
25. Non-electrical machinery	1.53	1.50
26. Electrical machinery	1.71	1.31
27. Transport equipment	1.45	1.18
28. Other manufactures	1.99	1.75

Sources: The two shadow prices are ratios of the costs of substituting U.S. $ 1 of imports according to the 1962 technology of the ODEPLAN input–output matrix (in users' prices) to the exchange rate for 1962. The two estimates are based respectively on formulas (1) and (2) of the text. Teresa Jeanneret's nominal tariff rates for 1961 [ref. 102] were used to estimate differentials between world and Chilean prices.

of the differences between internal and f.o.b. prices of exportable products from individual input–output table sectors (two-digit industries). At least for most sectors with non-negligible exports (noted in table 3), this is not a bad assumption, since 'drawbacks' are given according to manufacturers' cost estimates.

(iii) Teresa Jeanneret's estimates of tariff rates on final goods for 1961 [ref. 102] were used to infer the difference between internal and c.i.f. prices of importables. These estimates suffer greatly from being out-of-date, and in addition may be underestimates of true price differentials. However, Jeanneret's tariffs are the only available price estimates classified consistently with the Chilean input—output table, and in addition cover a far wider range of products than our other price indicators. Using ECLA data presented in table 1, we attempted to calculate an alternative set of input—output matrix-consistent tariffs. Unfortunately, these calculations proved to be so sensitive at the sector level to different assumed weighting schemes (perhaps because of the smallness of the samples) that we had to give the project up.

(iv) Average capital-output ratios, based on the period 1962—67, were used in eq. (2). Like most data of their kind, these are subject to serious reservations, but they at least seem consistent with the aggregate development of the Chilean economy as summarized in ODEPLAN's programming models. The rate of return used in eq. (2) was 20%, a level consistent with the estimates of gross rates of return to fixed capital which have been made for Chile. Total labor payments (including employer's contributions to pension funds) were used to estimate labor costs in eq. (2).

Besides these assumptions, we should also note that the calculations are subject to the qualifications that the input—output matrix is quite old and is in users' prices. The present calculations should therefore be re-done with the 1967 input—output matrix when it appears (hopefully in producers' prices), to put them on a more firm statistical basis.

With all these *caveats* listed, we can now turn to a tentative interpretation of the results in tables 3 and 4, which show sectoral Bruno—Krueger exchange rates divided by the exchange rate in 1962. The tables support the following inferences:

(i) Import substitution is on the average a great deal more expensive than exportation in terms of foreign exchange costs.[7] Of course, this finding results from the difference between the import and export price deflators, but it is still striking to note the range in costs between efficient export activities such as mining and relatively inefficient import-substituting industries such as textiles.

(ii) When costs of foreign capital are considered, the range of costs of exportation still lies below the import substitution range , except in the case of nitrate mining (which besides using foreign-made capital intensively, spends over 20% of its gross value of production on intermediate imports) and the capital-intensive basic metals industry. However, even the relatively capital-intensive pulp and paper industry still generates foreign exchange more cheaply than most import substituting sectors.

---

[7] This is the usual result of this type of calculation for economies with overvalued exchange rates. See Krueger's original paper [ref. 119] for another example, Turkey.

(iii) The most costly sectors appear to be those where import substitution has advanced the furthest, notably textiles and clothing. (This result can also be read from the price comparisons above.) Also, when capital costs are considered, expansion of the heavy industry sectors 22 and 23 appears from these calculations to have been a rather expensive exercise in import displacement.

(iv) As a final conclusion, one might hazard a guess from the results of these aggregate calculations that there is room for export expansion with a domestic to foreign cost ratio not exceeding 1.25—1.5 times the nominal exchange rate, a result consistent with the estimate to be presented below of the Chilean equilibrium exchange rate. On the other hand, much additional import substitution should show a domestic/foreign cost ratio as least two times the nominal exchange rate, with costs running far higher in certain sectors.

To check these last suppositions, we turn to some Bruno—Krueger exchange rates calculated from the cost structures given by Chilean manufacturers when requesting export drawbacks, and from recent investment projects in import substitution.[8] These estimates appear in tables 5 and 6 (with names somewhat altered to preserve anonymity). The average domestic resource cost of the export industries (weighted by their net savings of foreign exchange) is 1.138 times the current exchange rate, while the average cost of the import substitution industries is 1.382 times the exchange rate. Once again, exports

Table 5
Bruno—Krueger shadow prices for Chilean export industries

Industry	Shadow price [a]	Net foreign exchange earnings [b]
Preserved shellfish	0.860	$ 248,171
Fish derivatives	1.349	1,038,088
Steel products	1.204	470,129
Wool	1.191	3,359,945
Chemical products derived from copper	1.509	15,034
Low voltage electrical products	1.457	276,602
Malt	0.721	1,360,714
Organic chemicals	2.449	89,044
Average	1.343	
Average weighted by net foreign exchange gains	1.138	

[a] Relative to the current exchange rate
[b] For a 'typical' year
Source: [ref. 157].

[8] These results are taken from the Honor's thesis (memoria) of Victor Perez at the Centro de Planeamiento, Universidad de Chile [ref. 157].

Table 6

Bruno–Krueger shadow prices for recent Chilean import substitution projects

Project	Shadow price [a]	Net foreign exchange savings [b]
Electric condensors	1.009	$ 755,553
Compressors	1.672	255,718
Petrochemical derivatives	1.116	3,192,975
Plastics products	1.665	509,868
Agricultural machinery	1.400	538,225
Medium voltage electrical products	1.996	323,349
Hydraulic pumps	2.171	430,404
Cutting tools [c]	0.882	569,331
Intermediate chemicals [c]	1.990	1,063,000
Average	1.545	
Average weighted by net foreign exchange savings	1.382	

[a] Relative to the current exchange rate.

[b] For the year in which the project report forecasts the biggest net foreign exchange savings.

[c] The level of production of these commodities permits the exportation of small quantities (to Peru).

Source: [ref. 157].

appear as the cheaper method for earning foreign exchange, especially when one notes that there are no drawback-receiving export industries with higher costs than those of table 5, while a number of recent import substitution activities have costs far higher than those of table 6.[9]

C. Comparative costs: rates of effective protection

As pointed out most forcefully by Balassa and Schydlowsky [ref. 11] and discussed in detail in [ref. 8], the Bruno–Krueger ranking unduly penalizes intermediate input-using industries by valuing *domestically* produced intermediate inputs at domestic prices.

One way to overcome this bias is through the use of effective protection-type calculations. Since the number of variant rates of effective protection in the literature is now enormous, it is not so clear just which concept is most appropriate for the problem at hand. The variant we use here is due to

[9] The best known example is, of course, automobile assembly. See Johnson [ref. 106] for a not completely up-to-date but nonetheless enlightening discussion of the high costs encountered in this Chilean industry.

Hufbauer [ref. 97], and captures the essentials of the situation, although it
lacks the refinement of reestimation of non-tradeable goods' prices discussed
in [ref. 8].

In symbols, the Hufbauer formula is as follows: Classify the indices i of the
input—output coefficients a_{ij} into two sets, set I corresponding to tradable
intermediate inputs[10] and set II corresponding to non-tradable intermediate
inputs. Then we can define a 'net price' p^* which is the revenue from a one
escudo sale in sector j, net of the cost of tradable intermediate inputs:

$$p_j^* = p_j - \sum_{i \in I} a_{ij} p_i - a_{0j} p_0 \tag{3}$$

at the same time, we can calculate a price π^* net of tradable intermediate
inputs valued at world terms

$$\pi_j^* = \pi_j - \sum_{i \in I} a_{ij} \pi_i - a_{0j} \pi_0. \tag{4}$$

The ratio of these two net prices,

$$H_j = p^*/\pi^* \tag{5}$$

can be used to rank industries and/or projects according to their differences
in value-added-plus-value-of-non-traded-inputs in world and domestic terms.
According to this criterion a project is the better, the lower is its ratio H_j.
In analog to Bruno—Krueger, import substitution projects will typically have
a much higher H_j than export projects.

Empirically, there has been only one study of rates of effective protection
in Chile — the important work of Teresa Jeanneret for 1961 [ref. 102]. Here,
we present results very similar to hers for the protection given import substitution,[11] and in addition evaluate the effects of the recently introduced export subsidy ('drawback') program in offsetting the taxation imposed on
Chilean export production through protection of intermediate inputs.

Estimates are presented in tables 7 and 8 of rates of effective protection
(effective promotion) of import substitution (exportation). As with the Bruno—
Krueger exchange rates, we assume the domestic cost structures for the two
activities in each sector are the same.

The effective protection calculations are to be understood in terms of the

---

[10] Non-competitive intermediate import coefficients are denoted by a_{0j}.

[11] The results reported here are based on Jeanneret's tariff rates, but use the Hufbauer
protection formula instead of other formulas used by Jeanneret, and in addition take
into account differences between world and domestic prices for goods actually imported
for intermediate uses (involving the terms with a_{0j} in the above formulas) which Jeanneret
omitted.

Table 7
Rates of effective promotion of Chilean export sectors

Sector of ODEPLAN 1962 input–output matrix	Taxation due to tariffs on intermediate inputs	Rate of export drawback (relative to f.o.b. price)	Effective promotion with drawback	Shadow price of foreign exchange
1. Agriculture, livestock, forestry and fishing [a]	− 0.056	0.185	0.128	1.147
4. Iron mining [a]	− 0.138	0.0	− 0.138	0.879
5. Copper mining [a]	− 0.118	0.0	− 0.118	0.895
6. Nitrate mining [a]	− 0.128	0.0	− 0.128	0.886
8. Other mining [a]	− 0.157	0.060	− 0.070	0.935
9. Food products [a]	− 0.595	0.270	0.030	1.030
13. Footwear and clothing	− 0.286	0.290	0.045	1.047
14. Wood and cork	− 0.039	0.238	0.181	1.221
15. Furniture	− 0.156	0.300	0.152	1.179
16. Paper and paper products [a]	− 0.272	0.270	0.123	1.140
18. Leather and leather products	− 0.528	0.150	− 0.247	0.802
20. Chemical products	− 0.218	0.241	0.123	1.141
23. Basic metals [a]	− 0.193	0.283	0.173	1.209
25. Non-electrical machinery	− 0.269	0.121	− 0.095	0.913
26. Electrical machinery	− 0.191	0.257	0.093	1.103
27. Transport equipment	− 0.268	0.210	0.007	1.007
28. Other manufactures	− 0.174	0.180	0.040	1.042

[a] Sectors with export of more than U.S. $ 10 million in 1967.
Sources: Shadow prices of foreign exchange calculated according to formula (5) of the text. Rates of effective promotion and taxation due to tariffs are calculated with respect to domestic value added. Calculations are based on ODEPLAN's 1962 input–output matrix (including unpublished estimates of both c.i.f. and domestic value of imported intermediate goods), Teresa Jeanneret's estimated tariffs on intermediate imports in 1961 [ref. 102] and Drawback payments in 1968.

net protection a sector receives after purchase of intermediate inputs (a positive number). Similarly, the effective promotion of exportation is positive if export subsidy payments more than counteract the effects of taxation of intermediate inputs.

(i) Once again, the difference in costs of producing foreign exchange between import substitution and export activities shows up clearly. None of the major export sectors has a shadow price of foreign exchange greater than about 1.2, a value exceeded by almost all import-substituting sectors.

(ii) Although the taxation due to tariffs on intermediate imports in many

Table 8
Rates of effective protection of Chilean import sectors.

Sector of ODEPLAN 1962 input—output matrix	Protection from tariffs on intermediate inputs	Nominal tariff rate [a]	Rate of effective protection	Shadow price of foreign exchange
1. Agriculture, livestock, forestry and hunting	− 0.056	1.238	0.592	2.452
9. Food products	− 0.595	0.820	0.684	3.165
10. Beverages	− 0.148	1.218	0.621	2.638
11. Tobacco	− 0.148	1.057	0.008	1.008
12. Textiles	− 0.372	1.818	0.822	5.620
13. Footwear and clothing	− 0.286	2.549	0.761	4.188
14. Wood and cork	− 0.039	0.352	0.232	1.303
15. Furniture	− 0.156	1.294	0.559	2.269
16. Paper and paper products	− 0.272	0.552	0.331	1.494
17. Printing and publishing	− 0.124	0.718	0.435	1.769
18. Leather and leather products	− 0.528	1.612	0.764	4.246
19. Rubber products	− 0.336	1.019	0.577	2.366
20. Chemical products	− 0.218	0.937	0.516	2.065
21. Petroleum and coal products	− 0.156	0.049	− 0.350	0.741
22. Non-metallic mineral products	− 0.191	1.390	0.641	2.787
23. Basic metals	− 0.193	0.655	0.427	1.744
24. Metallic products	− 0.223	0.592	0.310	1.450
25. Non-electrical machinery	− 0.269	0.844	0.421	1.726
26. Electrical machinery	− 0.191	1.052	0.479	1.919
27. Transport equipment	− 0.268	0.839	0.404	1.677
28. Other manufactures	− 0.174	1.249	0.564	2.294

[a] Relative to c.i.f. prices.
Sources: Shadow prices of foreign exchange calculated according to formula (5) of the text. Rates of effective protection and taxation due to tariffs are calculated with respect to domestic value added. Calculations are based on ODEPLAN's 1962 input—output matrix (including unpublished estimates of both c.i.f. and domestic value of intermediate imports), and Teresa Jeanneret's estimated tariffs on intermediate and final imports in 1961.

export sectors is substantial (first column of table 7), it appears to be offset in most cases by the export subsidies. (The positive values in the third column of table 7 indicate negative effective taxation, or effective promotion.) On the other hand, effective export subsidies are generally far below the levels of effective protection of manufacturing sectors, and it is by no means obvious that the drawbacks are sufficiently large to induce producers to venture seriously outside the protected domestic market.[12]

(iii) In terms of relative incentives, it appears that agricultural exports are as well protected as those of the industrial sectors. On the other hand, import substitution in agriculture receives much less protection than the same activity in many industries. There is much variation among rates of effective protection for the various industrial sectors. Similar patterns are found both in the effective protection and Bruno—Krueger calculations — for example the high protection given textiles and clothing.

(iv) Judging from the sectors which have more than $ 10 million in exports, it appears that the effective subsidy rates of 10—20% of domestic value added may lead to a fairly healthy export response. This compares to rates of effective protection exceeding 50% of domestic value added (or 100% of value added in world terms) in many domestic manufacturing sectors. The mid-point of this range — a domestic cost of foreign exchange production 30—40% above the nominal exchange rate — is consistent with the general results from the Bruno—Krueger calculations and the calculation in the next section of the equilibrium exchange rate for Chile.

IV. Shadow price calculations

To review briefly: we calculated in section II that import substitution and/ or promotion of non-traditional exports will have to take place at a high rate during the decade of the 1970's as a necessary condition for an acceptable growth performance in Chile. In section III, analysis of cost revealed that in the 1960's at least, there were ample prospects for some import substitution and numerous export promotion schemes at costs on the order of 1.2—1.5 times the current exchange rate.

[12] International evidence is always of doubtful applicability in specific local situations, but it is worth noting that Pakistan gives export subsidies approaching 100% of value added [ref. 97], while Colombia has experimented with special export exchange rates pegged well above the nominal rate [ref. 131]. Both countries have had good results in fomenting exports, and the Chilean experience with the comparatively timid incentive given to date suggests that this country also might have more healthy growth of exports with more active support policies. Non-traditional exports have been increasing consistently in recent years, with little protection aside from Chile's relatively modest drawback program. (For details on recent export promotion activities, see Jul [ref. 109].) A more active policy pursued for a relatively long period (such as a decade) might well lead to the kind of sustained export growth which has characterized Pakistan, Korea, Japan, Israel, and a few other developing countries.

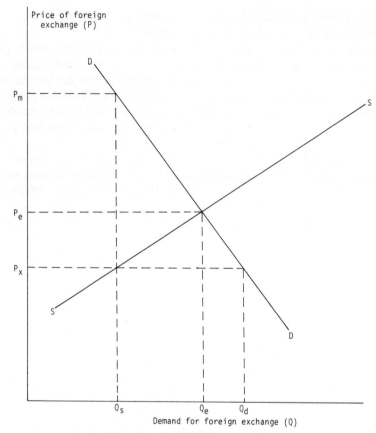

Fig. 2. The foreign exchange market.

What can we infer from these results about the evaluation of investment projects?

First – note that the high requirements for trade improvement require something approaching a completely efficient allocation of scarce resources. This means that an Escudo spent in one use should bring returns not exceeded by possible returns in other uses. For example, an escudo should not be spent to substitute U.S. $ 0.05 worth of imports when it perfectly well can be used to generate U.S. $ 0.08 of foreign exchange through exports. Import substitution and export promotion projects should be compared to each other in evaluation, and should not be treated as separate kinds of investment. They really do the same thing.

Second – The comparative cost results indicate that import substitution tends to be more expensive than exportation in terms of domestic resources. The reason for this is fairly easily seen in terms of a well-known diagram (fig. 2) relating the demand and supply of foreign exchange. At the usual demand-supply equilibrium point, the price of foreign exchange is P_e, and its demand (from curve $D-D$) and supply (from curve $S-S$) are equal at the level Q_e. In Chile, the effect of protectionist policies has been to make the after-tariff price of imports something like P_m, while the actual market price of the dollar is P_x. Thus, both imports and exports are at levels inferior to those which would be observed with a more free foreign trade situation. Since the domestic cost of imports is P_m, in general costs of industries substituting imports will be at about this level. On the other hand, since exporters only gain P_x, costs of export projects are about at this level. With free trade, the exchange rate would rise above P_x and the export and import substitution projects which now cost about 1.2–1.5 times the exchange rate would become profitable at ruling market prices.

The above analysis suggests that the equilibrium exchange rate P_e is a good first approximation to the appropriate shadow price for project evaluation. One would certainly not use a rate higher than this, because projects which would lose money even in a non-distorted market would still be profitable in shadow price calculations. On the other hand, a lower rate than P_e would discriminate against otherwise feasible projects (particularly those for import substitution). For this reason (and others presented in [ref. 8]) the no trade-restriction exchange rate is our proposal for the shadow price of foreign exchange.[13]

How do we calculate this exchange rate?

At once, note that the calculation should be of a fairly 'long-term' nature, in the sense that cyclical effects should not influence the results. For example, the fact that the Central Bank accumulates reserves because of the high price of copper does not substantially alter the assertion that the escudo is over-valued because of the level of import protection in Chile. When the price of copper falls back to a 'normal' forty cents per pound, accumulation of dollars by the Central Bank will stop, and the surplus on balance of payments will revert to a level closer to zero.

Second, a balance-of-payments policy has to be assumed to calculate an equilibrium exchange rate. We suppose here that the decifit or surplus on current account will be approximately zero.

Third, a certain level of import protection and export subsidies has to be

---

[13] Uncritical use of P_e is of course subject to some reservations, as discussed in [ref. 8]. However, we *do* feel that P_e is a valid first approximation to 'the' shadow price, and re-commend its use for that reason.

assumed. We estimated protection levels with the ECLA prices of table 1, and assumed no drawbacks. The latter assumption is not too misleading (since export drawbacks still cover only a small fraction of total exports), and our justifications for using the old price data and the way it was brought up to date are given below.

Finally, we note that monetary policy is not explicitly considered in our calculation of the equilibrium exchange rate, since we used a partial equilibrium ('Robinson–Metzler') model in which imports and exports depend only on their own prices. This is an omission which one ideally would like to correct, but as indicated in {ref. 8], models of the foreign exchange market proposed to date which incorporate monetary effects explicitly make other restrictive assumptions which are on balance as limiting as the Robinson–Metzler hypothesis. Given this limitation, we chose to work with the traditional model. From it, we derive the following expression for the equilibrium exchange rate r^*,

$$r^* = r\,\tau^{1/(1-q)},$$ (6)

where

$$q = D(1 + \eta_x)\,\epsilon_x(\epsilon_m - \eta_m)/(1 + \epsilon_m)\eta_m\,(\eta_x - \epsilon_x).$$ (7)

and where the symbols are defined as follows: D, balance of trade deficit in ratio terms; r, market exchange rate; τ, 'force' of tariff (= 1 + tariff); η_x, price elasticity of export demand; ϵ_x, price elasticity of export supply; η_m, price elasticity of import demand; and ϵ_m, price elasticity of import supply.

On the basis of the ECLA price sample described above, we have an average tariff of 128% to use in calculating the equilibrium exchange rate.[14] On the elasticity side, we note that Chile's many trade restrictions have the effect of minimizing price responsiveness as estimated from time series. Under these circumstances, we thought it worthwhile to make subjective estimates of the relevant eleasticities on the basis of an intuitive appraisal of Chile's foreign trade sector.[15]

To begin, note that the experience of Western industrial countries suggests that import demand elasticities under conditions of free trade are fairly high. Using an average figure – which seems to be valid for Western countries·in general – we assume that the import demand elasticity in Chile is equal to 2.0 (see Balassa [ref. 12] for the relevant international data and sources).

[14] During the observation period, the ratio of Chilean exports to imports was practically one. Thus we let $D = 1$ in the above calculation of $1/(1 - q)$.
[15] Subjective appraisals generally provide the final estimates of foreign trade price elasticity even in studies of the developed countries, e.g. Floyd [ref. 68] and Balassa and associates [ref. 12].

We also believe that supply elasticities are likely to be high. Fig. 2 and the experience of small countries in the world economy which adopt a relatively free trade policy suggest that the export sector in Chile would be much bigger if import restrictions were abolished. A glance at particular export industries suggests the same conclusion. Supply responsiveness in copper production (about 70% of exports) is likely to be relatively high now that the long standing and paralyzing conflict between the Chilean government and the U.S. copper companies is being resolved with the 'Chileanization' of the mines. Also, several potential export industries are already entering the world market as the result of the export promotion policy. Such industries — producing wine, fresh and canned fruits, wool, fish products, pulp, paper, and specialized parts and components in the metal products and electronics sectors — are likely to be highly responsive to price. Hence, it is not farfetched to assume export supply elasticities on the order of 3.0.

Regarding the foreign elasticities, assuming that import supply is infinitely elastic seems reasonable. On the demand side, it is best to consider separately copper and the rest of exports. For the former, it must be noted that even after the present expansion of the mines is completed. Chile's share in world production will be smaller than 20%. If both the absolute value of the world copper consumption elasticity and the world production elasticity are as small as 0.5, then a well-known formula tells us that Chile's demand elasticity will still be equal to − 4.5. For the rest of Chile's export products, the elasticities must be much higher, since the country's market share is negligible in everything besides copper. We can comfortably assume an overall price elasticity of demand for Chilean exports on the order of − 9.0.

We thus arrive at the following figures: $\eta_x \cong -9.0$, $\epsilon_x \cong 3.0$, $\eta_m \cong -2.0$, $\epsilon_m \cong \infty$ and $D \cong 1.0$. Applying these guesses in eq. (7) we conclude that $1/(1-q)$ is equal to 0.5, and combining this estimate with our previously estimated value of 2.28 for τ, we conclude from eq. (6) that in June, 1962, the Chilean equilibrium exchange rate was 51% above the official rate.

The most desirable way to bring this calculation up to date would be through the use of more recent tariff estimates. The sum effect of tariffs and other import restrictions is likely to have changed since the early 1960's, but no detailed indicator of these changes is available.[16] Moreover, alternative approximate estimators of aggregate tariff changes yield totally inconsistent results, as shown below:[17]

---

[16] A forthcoming joint study of the Brookings Institution and economic research institutes in the LAFTA countries will contain estimates of parity exchange rates for 1968 in the area. The basic data of this study could be used to update our tariff estimates.

[17] Sources for these estimates are (i) ODEPLAN, and (ii) monthly bulletins of the Central Bank.

Index of tariff rates based on:	1962	1963	1964	1965	1966	1967	1968
(i) Ratio between tariff receipts and imports	100	71	57	63	74	91	71
(ii) Ratio between post-tariff escudo unit value and dollar unit value of imports	100	98	111	94	96	n.a.	n.a.

Under these circumstances, we can only call on the principle of insufficient reason to assume that any tariff changes that might have occurred in recent years are adequately measured by the evolution of the relationship between the parity exchange rate (based in June 1962) and market exchange rate. In other words, we assume that the equilibrium exchange rate moves in accordance with the difference between a domestic and foreign price index only. The market clearing exchange rate, on the other hand, has to compensate not only overall price movements but also any change in tariffs or import restrictions. Thus, if the market rate increases by more than the parity rate does, this means that tariffs and other import restrictions are going down. Naturally, the market rate may move at a speed different from the parity rate for a num-

Table 9
Equilibrium exchange rates in Chile, 1962—69 (escudos per dollar).

Year	Official [a] exchange rate in current prices	Ratio between the wholesale price indexes of Chile and the US (June 62 = 1.00)	Equilibrium [b] exchange rate: $1/(1 - q) = 0.5$ and $\tau = 2.28$	Ratio between equilibrium and official exchange rates
June 1962	1.05	1.00	1.59	1.51
1962	1.14	1.04	1.66	1.45
1963	1.88	1.60	2.54	1.35
1964	2.37	2.40	3.82	1.61
1965	3.13	2.96	4.70	1.50
1966	3.95	3.48	5.54	1.40
1967	5.10	4.16	6.62	1.30
1968	6.80	5.32	8.46	1.24
April 1969	8.37	6.57	10.45	1.25

[a] Average buying rate in the bank market.
[b] The equilibrium exchange rate for June 1962 was obtained according to the formula $1.05 (2.28)^{0.5} = 1.59$. The rate for the remainning years is equal to 1.59 times the ratio between the wholesale price idexes of Chile and the U.S.A.
Sources: Banco Central de Chile, Boletín mensual, and IMF, International financial statistics.

ber of other reasons, such as changes in capital movements or shifts in the export and/or import functions. In [ref. 8] a more refined formula than the parity rate for changes through time in the equilibrium exchange rate is developed, taking into account these other factors affecting the balance of payments. However, we have not been able to implement empirically this new formula which seems very sensitive to particular assumptions made about price-elasticities and to changes in capital movements which are both volatile and hard to measure.

Given this problem, we have simply used changes in the nominal exchange rate and price indices to update our equilibrium exchange rate estimate.[18] We first constructed an index for the real value of the equilibrium exchange rate, using as a deflator the ratio between the wholesale price index in Chile and the corresponding U.S. index. The deflated equilibrium rate was then divided by the official rate to give a year-to-year estimate of the foreign exchange shadow price. From the detailed calculation in table 9 it appears that Chile's exchange rate has improved considerably since 1962. In 1969, the overvaluation of the escudo was on the order of 25% as opposed to 51% in 1962. Observe, however, that the 12% increase in the U.S. wholesale price index over the period made a significant contribution to this improvement.

V. Conclusions

The main theme of this paper has been that investment in trade improvement should be assigned according to the comparative cost principle of resource allocation, i.e. *that the usefulness of an escudo of investment should be measured in terms of the dollars it produces, regardless of whether the investment takes place in import substitution or exportation.* Further, the investment will be justified in terms of shadow price calculations, if it is profitable when all its internationally tradable products and inputs are converted from dollar to escudo-valuation with a shadow exchange rate about 1.25—1.30 times the level of the official exchange rate, and non-tradable inputs are valued at domestic prices.

To this general principle, few qualifications can be added. However, it is still important to note that

(i) Revaluation (and probable reduction) of the shadow exchange rate

[18] This type of parity adjustment can be justified rigorously only under strict conditions, as we indicate in [ref. 8]. Here, we can only plead lack of data as our justification for making these estimates.

should be undertaken in line with the reduction in tariffs and other protective measures which will take place in the future as a response to Chile's entry into the *Grupo Andino*. In particular, when it is clear what plans of tariff reduction will be followed, a thorough study of effective protection of industry and recalculation of the equilibrium exchange rate under the new conditions should take place.

(ii) With a value of 1.25–1.30 for the shadow exchange rate, it is very possible that many socially desirable trade improvement projects will not be profitable under current market prices. This is to be expected in import substitution but the fact that desirable export projects may not be profitable at the current exchange rate is often taken as surprising. As a not uncommon example, we may cite a Minister of Economics, who said recently that[19] 'We consider that . . . policies stimulating exports need not be permanent. On the contrary, they should serve as supports when a new line of exports is entering the market, but then should be reduced gradually. Thus we will avoid supporting exports that cannot reasonably compete in foreign markets.'

Despite the Minister's last sentence, our accumulated evidence indicates that there is no reason at all to expect acceptable export projects to be competitive in the long run *at the current exchange rate*. In terms of fig. 2, there are projects which are not profitable at the current price of the dollar P_x, but which would become profitable as the price moves toward its equilibrium value P_e. And in terms our cost data, although it is clear that in some industries exports are profitable even with the undervalued dollar of today, the same cannot be said of all lines of production.

Thus, the correct way to restate the Minister is that *exportation and substitution of imports should be protected only up to the point where they cease to be competitive in foreign markets when their tradable costs and returns are valued at the equilibrium exchange rate which is about 1.3 times the current exchange rate.*

Of course, this type of protection has been given in the past as a matter of course to import substitution projects which would not have been competitive in world markets even at exchange rates two or three times as high as the official rate. More modest protection can be given to acceptable import substitution projects in the future. A more serious problem will be arranging protection of exportation in the critical years before tariff reductions will have made unnecessary the use of a shadow price for foreign exchange.

[19] El Mercurio, September 24, 1969.

R.S. Eckaus, P.N. Rosenstein-Rodan (eds.), Analysis of development problems,
© North-Holland Publishing Company

THE COST OF CAPITAL IN THE CHILEAN ECONOMY*

Sergio BITAR

Catholic University of Chile, Santiago, Chile

and

Hugo TRIVELLI

Harvard University, Cambridge, Mass., U.S.A.

I. Introduction

The government economic planning organizations in Chile increased their influence over government decisions during the decade of the 1960's. This was accomplished by formulating concrete propositions leading to the solution of the specific problems which the political authorities face daily.

One of the means which was used to achieve this objective was the undertaking of the evaluation of the most important investment projects in the country. In Chile, there have been two conditions which have facilitated the task: The progressive control of the state over an increasing percentage of the total investment in the country, and the relatively widespread knowledge of the techniques of project evaluation in the state-owned agencies, banks and firms.

Nevertheless, until 1970, the role of the planning offices in the field of investment project evaluation was restricted to the analysis of a few special cases about which there existed divergent opinions. Some of the sectoral agencies and large state-owned firms have made some efforts in evaluating projects, but within the confines of their area or activity, and without employing any mechanism of comparison between projects developed by different organizations.

One of the main obstacles to the creation of such a mechanism arises from

---

* This paper is based mainly on the article by the same authors: 'Calculo de Rentabilidades Financieras y Economicas de Empresas Industriales Chilenas', *Cuadernos de Economíca*, No. 19, Dec. 1969, Universidad Católica de Chile.

the lack of common criteria of evaluation and particularly, from the lack of precedents for setting initial approximations to the value of the social rate of discount, the social cost of labor and the social cost of foreign exchange.

This study describes some efforts undertaken to quantify the social cost of capital in Chile in order to establish a rate of discount. Determining the value of that rate for a certain period of time is a complex task which must take a series of factors into account, both economic and non-economic. No quantitative methods exist which could replace the political judgment which finally must be the basis for a decision. Nevertheless, quantitative studies can indicate some orders of magnitude.

The economic literature has been overly abundant in the estimation of the cost of capital and several methods of quantification, each one based on various hypotheses, have been proposed. These methods could be classified in two main groups: (1) those based on the social time preference (STP) of the consumer and thus of society as an aggregation of individuals (or a certain weighted average of individual preferences); (2) those based on the opportunity cost of capital (OCC).

With equilibrium prevailing in the market, both kinds of methods are like the two sides of a coin and should produce results of similar value. But, if there is no such equilibrium, due to a series of imperfections in the economic system, it becomes necessary to choose the method of calculation which most satisfactorily fulfills the properties attributed to the rate of discount. This rate, in order to generate optimum social decisions, should match the social productivity of the investment with the supply of savings, which is regulated politically.

Those procedures which attempt to measure the time preference of society are independent of the yield of capital; on the other hand, they emphasize the subjective attitude of each individual towards the future. The quantitative problem lies in estimating such a subjective attitude, a task which is undoubtedly subjective as well, since the quantification model is left to the imagination of the economist to a certain extent. Several methods have been proposed and one can cite those of Eckstein [refs. 58,59] and Frisch [ref. 74] which introduce other variables such as the level of per capita income and the expected rate of growth.

The methods based on the OCC stand on firmer ground due to the objectivity of the required data. They rest on the hypothesis that society, when it uses resources in one particular project, is losing benefits in other projects. Those other benefits are gauged by the OCC, and a new project, in order to be worth undertaking, must show a rate of return higher than the OCC. This type of procedure has been described by such authors as Harberger [refs. 85,86] Olivier [ref. 152] Papanek and Quereski [ref. 156]. Some adjustments have also been introduced which take into account the impact on savings, risk, expected inflation, etc. [ref. 173].

Harberger, in a recent paper [ref. 10], tries to solve the contradictions between the STP and the OCC. He proposes to calculate the rate of discount as a weighted average between marginal productivity of capital in the private sector and the STP, measured by the after-tax interest rate received by the marginal saver.

Marglin [ref. 135] after reviewing both procedures, rejects them. Regarding the methods of measuring the rate of discount by STP, he discusses the hypothesis of the rational behavior of the consumer and the savings of individuals in less developed economies. He also points out the eventual divergence between consumer preferences and those of society. Regarding the OCC method of calculating the rate of discount, he indicates that this method is supported by a very limited set of hypotheses: (a) Over-all investment budget is fixed independently of project decisions; (b) There are only two time periods to take into consideration. Finally, Marglin states that '... there is thus no escape from the need for the Government to make a value judgment about the relative weight to be accorded to aggregate consumption benefits and costs at different times ...'. He suggests that the internal rate of return of the projects be calculated in order to facilitate the task of the government in fixing a value for the rate of discount. Nevertheless, this conclusion does not bring the problem much closer to a solution than it was in the initial stage.

Knowing the methods of calculation now employed in Chile, it seems preferable not to avoid an estimation. Any reasonable approximation of the rate of discount could produce better results than those obtained from the present methods. Of course, it must be understood that the values which are set are only an initial approximation and in the future can be modified by an iterative process [ref. 130].

Keeping this in mind, this study shows the results obtained from an analysis of the social rate of return of industrial investments in Chile. This study is mainly based on a work by Harberger [ref. 85]. Moreover, several other facts appear at the end regarding the rate of return of investments in education and irrigation.

II. Social rate of return in the industrial sector

In this study, the private and social rates of return of 117 Chilean stock companies (Sociedades Anonimas) have been computed. These firms operate in the industrial sector. The figures cover the 1960—65 time period.

Different methods have been employed to estimate the rate of return for each firm. These are described later. By the term 'private rate of return' is understood the rate of return estimated from the point of view of the private entrepreneur, whereas the 'social rate of return' is an attempt at estimation from the point of view of the whole nation.

The information needed to estimate the 'social rate of return' includes data which ordinarily is not available. In this first attempt at calculation, the balance sheets of the firms, filed at the Superintendency of Stock Companies (Superintendencia de Sociedades Anonimas), have been consulted. The format of these balance sheets varies from one firm to another and may change in a given firm from one year to the next.The names of the entries, as well as the particulars which accompany them, are not homogeneous. These facts make comparison of data between firms much more difficult. Nevertheless, the considerations formulated in each are explaind in detail in order to demonstrate clearly the significance of the results.

Data was obtaind for 117 stock companies, which were chosen in the following way:

(a) Consulting the industrial list of 1964, the National Planning Office (ODEPLAN) classified the firms by the number of workers they employed. Those firms employing 100 or more workers were chosen from the list.

(b) Of these enterprises stock companies were selected including 323 firms, since systematic data from the Superintendency of Stock Companies was only for them.

(c) Next, only those companies fulfilling two added requirements were chosen:

(i) Total assets greater than 1 million escudos in 1965

(ii) Having submitted complete balance sheets for 3 or more consecutive years since 1960.

The final group of firms consisted of the 117 firms (Stock Companies) mentioned above.

The gross value of output of these 117 firms represents 12.6% of the total gross value of output of the industrial sector in Chile in 1964.

III. Methodology

By means of the collected data, a 'private' and a 'social' rate of return were calculated. The first rate measured the yield of an investment for the entrepreneur. The second one tries to quantify the benefits which society receives from the investments made by private industry.

The difference between these two rates will soon become apparent when the procedures of calculation to be followed in each case are indicated and when the costs, benefits and their significance are analyzed.

First, it can be questioned whether the market prices indicate the 'scarcity' of a particular product. The market price of some production factors (labor, capital, foreign exchange) does not always reflect their relative scarcity.

Second, some of the debits which the private entrepreneur incurs, and which are consequently computed as costs, such as taxes, cannot be seen in the same light by the nation, but must be regarded as a transfer payment.

A. The private rate of return

As explained, the yearly profit which appears in the balance sheet reflects the yield of the private entrepreneur. Likewise, the capital plus the reserves appearing in the same balance sheets represent the capital invested by the private entrepreneur (or firm). Accordingly, the following has been calculated as an index:

$$\frac{\text{yearly profit}}{\text{capital + reserves}} \; ; \text{for each year and each firm.}$$

B. The social rate of return

The theoretical definitions of this rate is problematical and its quantification, with the quality of the avaible data, is even more complex. However, this data has been treated in a way which always insures an estimation lower than the actual value of the rate. Consequently, the values reached by the calculation are lower or, at the most, equal to the 'true' values.

With the quantification of this rate, an attempt has been made to measure the relationship between the profits generated by the firm, measured from a national viewpoint, and the capital investments made by society. In order to make a systematic analysis of the problem, we will deal with the hypotheses and corrections introduced by: revenues, costs, and the investment.

1. The revenues. The social revenues, from the national viewpoint, are supposed to be measured by the price of each commodity. This assumption implies acceptance of the fact that this price measures the marginal satisfaction of the consumer who purchases the commodity, and moreover, that an optimum distribution of income exists, such that, whoever the consumer of

each commodity may be, the social welfare is not affected. In the case of an intermediate commodity, the price reflects its marginal productivity. Thus, the price measures all the benefits which society derives from a commodity. This hypothesis is valid only if the variation in the level of output of the firm is marginal when compared to the total output of that commodity.

2. *The costs.* The costs of raw materials, wages, intermediate goods, etc., have been calculated by their market prices, based on the assumption that these prices represent the marginal productivity of the commodities. This assumption has two additional implications:

(a) That the demand of the firm for inputs is marginal compared to the production of such commodities.

(b) That there be a full utilization of resources.

This study is based on the figures of the balance sheets, mentioned in the preceding pages, which have been submitted to some corrections.

First, the taxes paid by the firm have not been regarded as a production cost, but as a transfer from the firm to the government. As far as the nation is concerned, the taxes paid have been deducted from the cost in order to estimate the social rate of return.

In the calculation, only those taxes incurred by the firm in the stage of production, have been deducted; however, the taxes incorporated into the cost of the intermediate commodities have not been deducted, since they constitute part of the added value generated by the firm which produced them.

Unfortunately, not all of the taxes generated by the firm appear in the balance sheets under tax expenses. Thus, only part of the total taxes has been considered in the correction. Consequently, the costs after correction prove to be higher than those which would have been obtained by deducting the sum total of the taxes, and therefore, the profits and social rate of return have been underestimated.

The entrepreneurs regard social security as part of the cost of labor. From the national economic point of view, social security could be analyzed like taxes, since it could also be regarded as a transference. Nevertheless, some objections to this approach can be pointed out. Social security permits the financing of institutions whose aim is to supply direct services to the workers, and such expenditures would be an indirect kind of salary. In this calculation, social security has not been deducted from the costs of the firm.

3. *Yearly profits and social capital.* Yearly profits have been corrected by the inclusion of the tax expenses, mentioned earlier in this study, and had to

be deducted from the accountable costs of the firm. Nevertheless, depending on how the social capital is regarded, new corrections concerning financial expenditures should be introduced.

For society, the effort in terms of investment must take into account the total resources assigned to a firm, and not only the capital handled by the private entrepreneur. The tangible capital (fixed assets plus inventories) and the total assets could be distinguished from the total of the assigned capital.

The yearly profits should be attributed to the total of the capital available to a firm. Much of the yearly profits can be attributed to the tangible capital, but also another part of the profit is due to the working capital (available plus convertible assets, not including the inventories).

Therefore, if one wishes to calculate the social rate of return of the tangible assets, a part representative of the other more liquid assets should be deducted from the total yearly profits.

The profit, from a social point of view (as opposed to the private), must be a profit from which there has been no deduction of the interest paid on short-term loans or, in general, for the debts incurred in financing the assets. In a social approach to the problem, it is important to know the amount of investment and the profits obtained, independently of the source of such means of investment.

The private expenses have already been deducted from the yearly profits and should be re-incorporated in order to obtain the social profit.

In this calculation, the net social profit will be equal to the yearly profit plus the tax expenses and the financial expenses.

$$NSP = YP + TE + FE .$$

Nevertheless, the financial expenses which appear in the accounts of losses and profits represent only a part of the financial expenses incurred by the firm. Some of these expenses arise from debts contracted directly with banks. But when suppliers contribute the financing, there is generally a rise in the price of commodities, which causes a reduction in profit. This price increase is equal to the financial expenses, but it is not entered into the accounts as such.

It has already been stated that the *NSP* should be considered as a whole or in part, depending on whether the tangible assets or the total assets are taken into consideration. In order to determine the rate of return on the tangible assets, a certain amount, representative of the part (of the total profits) generated by the more liquid assets, should be deducted from the total profits. This amount could be calculated as a percentage of those assets, a percentage which could be considered equal to the interest rate of short-term loans.

$NSP^* = NSP - i$ (available assets + convertible assets − inventories) .

This $(NSP)^*$ would be related to tangible assets (fixed assets plus inventories).

In the second calculation, the NSP would be related to the total assets. This is based on the assumption that these assets measure the total investment which society makes to obtain that profit.

In practice, fixing a value for i proves to be very arbitrary. If the many values of the real rate of interest for the 1960–65 time period are analyzed, considerable fluctuations can be detected.

A decision was made to calculate the social rate of return of the firms on the basis of the quotient between the NSP and the total assets, for each year. At the same time, the quotient between the NSP and the fixed assets plus inventories was calculated, in order to compare the results.

4. *The calculation of the internal rate of return.* The social rate of return has also been calculated by means of the internal rate of return. This rate has greater economic significance, since it provides an estimate of a reference rate for the social rate of discount. It makes it possible to obtain a single figure for the period of activity under consideration in each firm.

For the calculation of the internal rate of return, the following figures are required: initial investment, net profit for each year, and residual value.

The yearly profits are 'cash' profits from which the yearly depreciation has not been deducted.

Therefore, one must deal with the gross social profit, in which:

$GSP = NSP +$ yearly depreciation .

The initial investment corresponds to the total net assets of the first year and the residual value corresponds to the total net assets of the final year, as it appears in the account books. For the calculation the escudos of a particular year, deflated by the index of whole-sale prices were used. The internal rate of return is defined as the value of the social rate of discount which sets to zero the present discounted value of the benefits. With r designated to represent the value of the internal rate of return, we arrive at the following equation:

$$I_i = \sum_{1}^{n} \frac{P_t}{(1+r)^t} + \frac{I_f}{(1+r)^n} ,$$

in which I_i = initial investment, I_f = residual value, and P_t = profits in the year t.

This equation is based on the supposition that no investments are made in the period of time from year 1 to year n. A more general equation must be outlined to include them. This is accomplished by taking into account the increase of investments ΔI_t in the corresponding years. The sum total of these up-to-date increases plus the initial investment constitute the total realized investment. In order to establish the successive annual investments, a comparison has been made between the total gross assets of one year and the total assets of the preceding year, measured in prices of the same year. Assuming that the firm does not make any new investments and the general situation of the capital market remains unchanged, the total assets of the year $(t+1)$ should be inferior to the assets of the year t, by a sum equal to the yearly depreciation. It is evident that changes in the tangible assets as well as financial assets can occur. An increase of either one of them, over the corresponding value of the previous year, will be considered as an investment.

Regarding the tangible assets, a comparison has been made between:

$$(TA)_t \quad \text{and} \quad (TA)_{t+1} + D_t ,$$

where TA = tangible assets and D = depreciation.

Regarding financial assets, comparing:

$$(FA)_t \quad \text{with} \quad (FA)_{t+1} ,$$

where FA = financial assets.

Therefore, the difference between

$$(\text{tot. } A)_{t+1} + D_t \quad \text{and} \quad (\text{tot. } A)_t ,$$

where tot. A = total assets and D = depreciation, is regarded as an investment.

The method of calculation prescribed so far runs into practical difficulties, mainly due to the arbitrary accounting of depreciation and the irregular procedures for revaluing assets. Both factors affect the value of the initial investment, the residual value and intermediate investments.

The total assets of the first year have been regarded as a measure of the initial investment. The value of this asset depends on the revaluation policy employed in dealing with the tangible assets, and the amount of depreciation of these assets, up to that year.

Revaluation by an amount less than the increase in the index of wholesale prices used in this calculation, would lead to an underestimation of the intermediate investments and the residual value.

While bearing in mind these limitations, a more simple method of calculation, compatible with the nature of the available data, was adopted. Summing up, the internal rate of return was calculated by the equation:

$$(\text{tot. } A)_0 + \sum_{t=1}^{n} \frac{\Delta I_t}{(1+r)^t} = \sum_{1}^{n} \frac{P_t}{(1+r)^t} \frac{(\text{tot. } A)_n}{(1+r)^n}.$$

IV. Results of the industrial sector

A. Indexes of the rate of return

The following indexes have been calculated to measure the rates of return:

(a) $YP/(C+R)$, where YP = yearly profits, C = capital, and R = reserves.

(b) $NSP/\text{tot. } A$, year by year and firm by firm.

(c) $NSP/(FA + \text{invent.})$, year by year and firm by firm, where FA = fixed assets.

(d) The internal rate of return for each firm. This was calculated in two ways, depending on how the additional investments during the 1960–65 time period were handled.

Due to the underestimation of the assets, the calculation of the ΔI revealed negative figures for some years. This occurs, for example, in 1963, in almost all the firms.

The first calculation was made keeping the figures exactly as they appeared in the calculation of the ΔI, assuming that the percentage of the assets which was not revalued, would be regained in subsequent years. (*IRR* 1 – internal rate of return 1.)

In the second calculation, all the negative values of ΔI were considered equal to zero; that is, it was assumed that no investments would be withdrawn. (*IRR* 2 – internal rate of return 2.)

Based on the aforementioned indexes, a calculation was made of the average value of the firms, corresponding to each sector of the United Nations industrial classification, and of the average value of the totality of firms.

These averages were obtained by weighing the contribution of each firm, according to its participation in the total investment, of the sector or of all the firms, depending on which average we are dealing with.

The results appear in tables 1 and 2.

B. Variance

In order to measure the spread of the figures, based on the averages of the tables, a variance was calculated by sector, and then the total variance and the standard deviations were calculated.

Table 1

Sector	Group	NSP/tot. A (%)	NSP/(FA+invent.) (%)	YP/(C+R) (%)	IRR 2 (%)	IRR 1 (%)
Food	20	12.4	18.4	10.7	10.2	13.2
Beverages	21	32.7	35.9	10.4	34.8	36.1
Tobacco	22	–	–	–	–	–
Textiles	23	10.1	14.9	7.2	11.2	12.4
Cloth. & shoe industry	24	17.4	31.8	14.3	19.0	20.2
Wood	25	9.7	12.9	7.7	8.8	10.7
Furniture	26	–	–	–	–	–
Paper	27	–	–	–	–	–
Printing	28	16.9	24.0	14.5	15.6	16.1
Leather	29	16.5	32.2	10.4	19.0	21.4
Rubber	30	22.1	32.6	14.4	26.2	26.5
Chem. products	31	11.8	17.5	9.9	9.9	13.7
Oil and coal	32	–	–	–	–	–
Non-metallic minerals	33	12.0	17.8	9.8	12.8	14.7
Primary metals	34	11.7	16.7	14.2	10.6	13.2
Metal products	35	14.9	21.9	15.2	13.0	13.4
Machinery	36	–	–	–	–	–
Electrical machinery	37	14.9	23.1	18.1	13.5	14.9
Transportation	38	11.5	31.2	14.5	0.5	12.7
Miscellaneous	39	7.2	10.3	5.7	3.1	8.0
Total average		13.9	20.2	10.5	13.7	15.7

Table 2

Group	NSP/tot. assets						
	60	61	62	63	64	65	Gen. avr.
20	12.6	11.7	11.4	10.9	15.9	11.9	12.4
21	31.5	36.7	32.7	29.8	30.9	34.5	32.7
22	–	–	–	–	–	–	–
23	8.9	7.5	10.0	10.2	11.0	11.5	10.1
24	18.1	16.8	17.2	18.9	19.3	14.8	17.4
25	7.5	7.8	10.2	11.3	12.0	9.3	9.7
26	–	–	–	–	–	–	–
27	–	–	–	–	–	–	–
28	17.2	14.0	15.3	13.5	19.3	19.2	16.9
29	22.9	13.6	16.5	13.6	16.6	19.4	16.5
30	25.5	21.7	20.4	20.5	21.2	23.4	22.1
31	11.8	9.8	8.4	13.1	13.4	14.0	11.8
32	–	–	–	–	–	–	–
33	14.2	11.8	12.7	12.6	11.0	10.6	12.0
34	10.9	7.0	7.9	12.5	13.4	15.9	11.7
35	11.6	10.4	10.9	17.9	18.2	15.3	14.9
36	–	–	–	–	–	–	–
37	10.0	12.0	15.0	18.1	15.0	14.3	14.9
38	8.0	9.3	12.7	15.0	14.5	8.6	11.5
39	11.1	1.9	3.9	9.2	8.4	9.4	7.2
Total average	14.4	14.0	13.6	14.8	16.8	14.6	13.9

Group	NSP/(FA+invent.)						
20	18.1	16.6	18.9	16.3	22.9	17.1	18.4
21	34.6	40.7	36.7	31.8	33.2	38.3	35.9
22	–	–	–	–	–	–	–
23	12.7	10.9	14.4	14.6	16.3	18.1	14.9
24	36.7	34.0	33.6	32.3	36.1	24.5	31.8
25	10.8	10.5	13.6	14.9	15.3	12.1	12.9
26	–	–	–	–	–	–	–
27	–	–	–	–	–	–	–
28	23.8	19.0	21.5	18.9	29.0	27.2	24.0
29	46.9	18.0	61.5	23.7	32.8	40.3	32.2
30	36.0	29.2	28.8	29.6	34.6	36.8	32.6
31	17.9	14.6	12.8	19.9	19.9	19.3	17.5
32	–	–	–	–	–	–	–
33	21.9	17.7	19.6	20.9	15.4	14.1	17.8
34	14.6	11.1	10.2	16.5	20.5	23.5	16.7
35	18.8	17.9	14.9	26.4	25.9	21.5	21.9

Table 2 (cont.)

| Group | NSP/(FA+invent.) | | | | | | |
	60	61	62	63	64	65	Gen. avr.
36	–	–	–	–	–	–	–
37	14.4	18.6	22.2	26.8	24.1	23.0	23.1
38	24.9	30.4	30.4	37.8	43.0	20.0	31.2
39	16.4	3.8	5.4	12.6	11.6	12.6	10.3
Total average	20.6	20.6	19.7	21.6	25.5	20.2	20.2

| Group | YP/(C+R) | | | | | | | | |
	60	61	62	63	64	65	Gen.	IIR 1	IIR 2
20	9.7	9.6	10.9	10.3	15.5	7.8	10.7	13.2	10.2
21	13.5	14.9	12.3	9.7	6.3	7.3	10.4	36.1	34.8
22	–	–	–	–	–	–	–	–	–
23	5.2	4.4	7.5	8.2	8.5	8.8	7.2	12.4	11.2
24	12.9	11.1	12.1	16.7	15.3	16.2	14.3	20.2	19.0
25	5.4	5.0	8.5	10.4	9.7	7.1	7.7	10.7	8.8
26	–	–	–	–	–	–	–	–	–
27	–	–	–	–	–	–	–	–	–
28	15.0	11.3	13.6	12.0	18.2	14.9	14.5	16.1	15.6
29	8.3	6.6	7.5	8.0	17.8	12.5	10.4	21.4	19.0
30	18.7	13.9	14.0	12.5	13.6	14.7	14.4	26.5	26.2
31	8.8	7.1	6.7	12.1	11.8	11.8	9.9	13.7	9.9
32	–	–	–	–	–	–	–	–	–
33	11.3	10.0	9.9	10.2	9.4	8.3	9.8	14.7	12.8
34	11.3	7.2	8.5	14.1	21.8	19.9	14.2	13.2	10.6
35	12.5	11.8	11.0	22.0	17.1	13.6	15.2	13.4	13.0
36	–	–	–	–	–	–	–	–	–
37	7.7	10.0	16.6	29.5	18.6	17.3	18.1	14.9	13.5
38	18.8	15.5	2.6	3.4	38.6	13.7	14.5	12.7	0.5
39	12.2	1.0	2.5	9.3	7.5	6.8	5.7	8.0	3.1
Total average	11.4	8.9	9.7	12.0	10.3	10.1	10.5	15.7	13.7

In both cases, the participation of each firm in the total investment was weighed.

The following are the standard deviations for the total averages:

Standard deviations (in %)

IRR 1	IRR 2	NSP tot. assets	NSP FA + invent.	YP C + R
9.0	10.0	7.0	10.0	7.0

C. Classification of investments by levels of the internal rate of return

In order to estimate the range of values of the rate of return in which most of the investments lie, the percentages of the investments in the different rate of return categories were calculated as follows:

Percentages of the total investment comprised in the range of value of the internal rate of return

1. For *IRR* 2

	i.r.r.	10% : 47.3% of TI
10%	i.r.r.	12% : 6.6% of TI
12%	i.r.r.	15% : 9.0% of TI
15%	i.r.r.	: 37.1% of TI

2. For *IRR* 1

i.r.r. < 10% : 27.4% of TI
10% < i.r.r. < 12% : 3.3% of TI
12% < i.r.r. < 15% : 31.1% of TI
15% < i.r.r. : 38.2% of TI

D. Sensitivity of the internal rate of return to variations in taxes

The taxes which were identified on the balance sheets of the firms and were used in calculating the 'social profit', represent a fraction of the total paid taxes. The sales taxes and the customs duties have not been taken into account, as they were not separated from the rest of the costs.

In order to estimate the fluctuation of the total average of the rate of return, taking into account a variation in taxes, this rate of return was calculated on the supposition that the sum total of paid taxes corresponds to twice the amount of those taxes clearly identified on the balance sheets. Consequently, it is a question of making a very rough adjustment, in order to appreciate the sensibility of the rate of return to the taxes.

An internal rate of return (*IRR* 1) of 22.8% was obtained as an average of all the firms. When the taxes were doubled, the internal rate of return rose 45% over the previous internal rate of return (*IRR* 1).[1]

V. Discussion of the results

The most important result is the determination of the average value of the rate of return of all the investments, during the whole time period. Nevertheless, since the calculation has been made firm by firm and year by year, the same figures could be used to carry out additional analysis.

A considerable fluctuation can be observed in the variation, over a given period of time, of the rates of return of a particular firm, without the existence of a clear tendency towards change in all the rates of return of certain years. The values of the average rates of return of each sector show no such tendency.

On the other hand, the rates of return calculated from year to year are affected by a great number of short-term factors, such as the underestimation of assets, which was most acute in 1963. Consequently, it is more significant to analyse the results of an average of the rates of return of the firm, during a longer period of time, in this case of six years, which makes up for short-term distortions.

These averages of the rates of return for each firm have been weighed individually, in order to compute the average of the rates of return of all those companies belonging to the same sector. Since the method of analysis of the set of firms has not been sufficiently developed to reveal their productive structure, the resultant rates of return for each sector have little validity, as a basis for making comparisons between sectors. Nevertheless, in some cases, the firms of a particular sector have turned out to be homogeneous, in that they produce similar products, and have similar rates of return. The basically heterogeneous sectors are: foods, chemicals, and miscellaneous. The most homogeneous sectors are: beverages, textiles, clothing and wood. A more significant comparison can be made with the homogeneous ones.

A. Underestimation of the social rate of return

In the various stages of the calculation, an attempt has always been made

---

[1] The illustration of the results and calculations is not included in this study, but can be found in a recent publication [ref. 30].

to underestimate the social rate of return. The lack of data has admitted only partial corrections of profits, which insures an underestimation. However, this underestimation can be excessive. The tax expenses as well as the private expenses dealt with in the calculation could reach only a small proportion of the total. For the most part, only taxes on corporate profits and property taxes have been included in the tax expenses, excluding the customs duties and the sales taxes, which are often higher than the other taxes. On the other hand, the taxes included in the calculation are often at least as substantial as the profits. Consequently, if the taxes not included are as sizable as those included, the social profits would increase by 50%, if they were added. The private expenses have less influence. Those private expenses related to suppliers, which contribute directly to an increase in prices and which, therefore, do not appear as private expenses on the balance sheets, have been excluded from the calculation.

However, some studies of the Economic Institute (1961 Survey) and of CORFO (1957), confirm the existence of an underestimation of assets in the area of 37%.

This underestimation is mostly applicable to the fixed assets and, for this reason, will have a lesser effect on the assets. If we accept a ratio of FA/tot. assets near one-half on an average, the effect of the underestimation would reach 20% above the total. This effect of underestimation of the assets is partly compensated for, because high customs duties, which have not been excluded from this calculation, are included in the value of currently imported equipment and machinery, and consequently, this means that there is an overestimation of the cost of such equipment for society. The profits seem then to have been underestimated by an amount higher than the total assets, and this would occasion an underestimation of the rate of return.

In any event, an error in the valuation of the assets occurs more infrequently when calculations are based on the internal rate of return, because such assets appear as an investment in the first year and as a residual value in the final year; that is, they seem to influence in opposite directions, and therefore, tend to compensate one another. The underestimation which would be inherent in the internal rate of return would be even more important.

B. The private rate of return and the social rate of return

The figures obtained show that, on an average, the social rate of return is higher than the private rate of return; however, if due importance is given to the sectoral figures, it can be noted that in the sectors of primary metals (not including CAP)[2] metal products, electric machinery, and transportation, the private is higher than the social rate of return.

C. Average values and marginal values

The most important limitation of these results, for the purpose of estimating a rate of discount based on the marginal productivity of the capital (its opportunity cost), and which is used to compare the different investment projects economically, is related to its properties as an average. The use of the rate of discount is marginal in nature, and so one attempts to use this rate in comparing projects which have a marginal effect on the rest of the sector to which they belong. Therefore, an average value is only a rough approximation. Unfortunately, no alternate methods exist, which are both trustworthy and easily accomplished.

D. Summary

The average of the figures calculated for the 117 firms, is 10.5% for the private rate of return and 15.7% for the social rate of return, measured by the internal rate of return. These averages have been underestimated. In the case of the social rate of return, the correction concerning the taxes was underestimated. If the total taxes are considered equal to double those which are listed on the balance sheets, the average of the internal rate of return rises from 15.7% to 22.8%. These percentages show a very large spread. The standard deviation for the private rate of return is 7% and 10% for the social rate of return (*IRR* 2). But, on the other hand, the percentage of investments whose social rate of return exceeds 12%, is approximately 70% and the percentage of investments whose rate exceeds 15%, is 38%.

VI. Other results

It is pertinent to mention the results of three other studies which shed light on the social cost of capital. In 1963, the Ministry of Public Works prepared a report [ref. 14] in which they attempted to measure the social rate of return of the irrigation works constructed by the state. Based on the data contained in the report, a calculation [ref. 29] was made, following guidelines similar to those used in the study of the industrial firms. In the calculation,

---

[2] CAP: Compañía Aceros del Pacífico, only steel mill in Chile.

both a zero social cost of labor and a cost equal to the market price were used. The results of the estimation of the average of the rates of return are, in the case of the social cost of labor equal to the market price, 10.9% and, in the case of the zero social cost of labor, 13.4%.

Regarding the investment distribution according to rates of return (with the cost of labor equal to the market price), it turned out that 15% of the total investment had rates of return in excess of 15% and that 44% of the total investment had rates between 10% and 15%.

In a study written by Harberger and Selowsky [ref. 92] rates of return were determined for the investment in education. The following figures were obtained:

Primary eduction	24%
Secondary education	17%
University education	12% .

The weighted average of these rates of return had a value of approximately 20%, which could be regarded as the rate of return of the investment in education. A study similar to the previous one was made on the rate of return in the training of engineers [ref. 48]. The method used consisted in calculating the profit as the difference in salary achieved by bettering the educational level. The result obtained was an internal rate of return of 19%.

In the same study by Harberger and Selowsky, an attempt was made to measure the marginal productivity of the capital for the Chilean economy, based on the Cobb—Douglas production function with constant returns to scale. Considering an output—capital ratio equal to $\frac{1}{3}$ for the whole economy, with a distribution of the gross product between capital and labor of 50%, for each one (based on the National Accounts 1941—62), it has been concluded that the marginal productivity corresponds to 15%.

This last figure was also confirmed by a study made by the Economic Institute of the University of Chile [ref. 100] in which the approximate figure of 10% is cited as the average of the private rate of return[3] of the 44 firms included in the survey. Introducing corrections concerning indirect taxes, direct taxes and depreciations, the approximate value of 15% is obtained, confirming the initial figure, reached in the study by Harberger and Selowsky.

---

[3] The private rate of return was calculated as the ratio between profits and equity capital plus reserves.

VII. Conclusions

The estimation of a reference value for the rate of discount can be accomplished by means of the social rate of return of the industrial investments. These values can be complemented by studying the rates of return obtained for the investments made in public works and by the data obtained from the estimation of the marginal productivity of capital in the global production operations.

Some calculations already carried out on the rates of return of industrial investments and irrigation, show an average of values for the social rates of return, which fluctuate between 12% and 15%. Other more inaccurate calculations, using macroeconomic models, produce rates around 15%.

These figures can provide a basis for indicating the value of the rate of discount which must be used in the calculations. The figure adopted is conditioned, nevertheless, by other factors, and its selection is a political decision.

R.S. Eckaus, P.N. Rosenstein-Rodan (eds.), Analysis of development problems,
© North-Holland Publishing Company

INVESTMENT PROJECT ANALYSIS IN TERMS OF
A MODEL OF OPTICAL GROWTH*

THE CASE OF CHILE

Lance TAYLOR

Harvard University, Cambridge, Mass, U.S.A.

I. Introduction

When the wave of Ramsey analysis was getting underway a few years ago, there was implicit in the literature the idea that these models could be used to calculate interest rates and other shadow prices for use in investment project analysis. More recently, a number of theoretical works discussed this possibility explicitly:[1] Nonetheless, empirical tests of the usefulness of this idea have to date been lacking.[2] The purpose of this paper is to report on one such attempt.

The test case presented here is a two-sector open economy model of Chile, a semi-industrialized country specialized in the export of copper. In sections III—V (following a general description in section II of the economic problems faced by an 'externally strangled' economy like Chile's) some of the salient characteristics of the Chilean economy and the model's attempt to capture them are discussed. Subsequent sections summarize the results obtained with numerical solution of the model, and discuss the specific problems of

(i) specification of functional forms and estimation of the relevant parameters for Chile (sections VI and VII);

(ii) interpretation of the quantity and shadow price solutions of the model, their 'reasonableness' in light of other studies of Chile, and their sensitivity to changes in some of the exogenous data and parameters (sections VIII—X);

* Computational work for this paper in Cambridge, Mass., was supported by the Development Research Group, Center for International Affairs, Harvard University. I am grateful as well to Jorge Fajardo, Steven Black and Jon Eaton for high-powered research assistance.
[1] The most important of these studies is the book by Arrow and Kurz [ref. 4]. See also Little and Mirrlees [ref. 128] and Marglin [ref. 134].
[2] Newbery [ref. 145] describes some interesting hypothetical calculations of shadow wage rates in a labor surplus model, but stops short of specific empirical applications.

(iii) implementation of a computer algorithm based on the differential dynamic programming algorithms of Jacobson and Mayne [ref. 101] to solve the optimal growth model and evaluation of the sensitivity of the shadow prices to 'large' investment projects, i.e. analysis of the second order effects of large projects on the optimal valuation of resources within the economy [3] (appendix).

II. Open economy development constraints

Two coherent theories about the constraints on growth with which developing countries must deal have consolidated themselves in recent years. The first of these (stemming from the seminal work of Lewis, Nurkse, and Rosenstein—Rodan) stresses the institutional barriers to the transformation of 'surplus' agricultural labor into an urbanized, industrial work force. The existence of these constraints leads to valuation of new industrial labor at a shadow wage below the institutionally fixed market wage. Using the tools of optimal growth theory, Little and Mirrlees [ref. 128], Marglin [ref. 134] and Newbery [ref. 145] have attacked the problem of calculating the shadow wage rate in a labor surplus economy.

The second theory — with which we will be concerned in this paper — has its intellectual roots in the writings of the Latin American structuralist economists of the 1950's,[4] but received formal treatment only in the 1960's in the two-gap models of Chenery and other economic programmers. The two-gap thesis is that additional foreign exchange has dual effects on a developing economy: it both supplements domestic savings *and* permits the importation of goods which cannot be produced domestically during the early stages of industrialization for reasons such as economies of scale in production and technological backwardness. Using the mordant terminology often employed around ECLA, one may say that two-gap economies are subject to 'external strangulation' resulting from their dependence on a growing foreign exchange supply.

In practice the structuralists' remedy for strangulation was import substitution, although they still wrote about the need to develop exports as a 'quasi-

---

[3] A related problem is the choice between first order and slower but more accurate second order algorithms for the solution of optimal growth problems. This is also discussed in the appendix.
[4] Most of these economists were associated with Raul Prebisch at the U.N. Economic Commission for Latin America (ECLA). Their work has been ably summarized by Bianchi [ref. 27].

capital goods industry'. Nonetheless, the policy emphasis on import substitution led to the erection of high protective walls around many Latin and other
developing economies, consequent overvaluation of the domestic currency and
an associated handicap to exportation of anything but the primary products
in which these countries had (and have) overwhelming comparative advantage.
The two-gap solution to this problem stressed foreign aid as a short run pallia-
tive; a more long-term approach would be gradual reduction of trade barriers
and devaluation to foment exports. In any case, the inability of domestic industry to produce a full range of sophisticated goods will persist in many developing countries (especially the small ones) for decades. The resulting 'external
dependence' (another ECLA slogan) leads logically to concern about correctly
evaluating the foreign exchange gains and losses of investment projects. The
shadow exchange rate is the appropriate tool of evaluation when it is calculated from an optimizing model taking trade restrictions into account.

Clearly, most developing economies face both surplus labor and external
dependence problems to some extent (and a fusion of the two models might
therefore be called for). Nonetheless, in the case of Chile, the foreign exchange
constraints are more important. The country displays all the classic signs of
high tariffs, overvalued currency, extreme export specialization, frequent gluts
of excess capacity, etc. Although labor problems exist as well (the unemployment rate is usually around 6%, the agricultural sector has for years been semi-
stagnant, and the service sector is unduly large), most economists who have
studied Chile agree that the foreign exchange problem is paramount. For this
reason, a two-gap-like model of the Chilean economy is developed in this
paper — first in general terms in the next three sections, and then in somewhat
specialized form for numerical solution in succeeding sections.

III. A model for Chile

The basic hypothesis (which is most similar to that of McKinnon [ref. 136]
among authors published in the English-language literature) is that domestic
production depends on two types of capital goods — plant which is produced
domestically, and equipment which must largely be imported.[5]

For purposes of the model, we identify the plant-type capital stock with
the output of a non-traded sector of the economy. This sector's product is
also used to satisfy final consumption demands (for services, outputs of the

---

[5] In recent years Chile has imported more than 80% of its equipment.

utilities, etc.) and exogenous demands such as government consumption and residential housing construction.

The product balance equation for the non-traded sector number one can be written as follows:

$$\dot{x}_1 = f^1(x_{01}, x_{11}, L_1, t) - c_1 - z_1 - \delta_1 x_1 , \tag{1}$$

where $\dot{x}_1$ (= dx_1/dt) is the accumulation of domestic-type capital; $f^1(x_{01}, x_{11}, L_1, t)$ is the production function, dependent on the sector's use of foreign-type capital (x_{01}), domestic-type capital (x_{11}), labor (L_1), and technical progress indexed by time (t); c_1 is the consumption of the non-traded product; z_1 is exogenous demand; and δ_1 is the rate of depreciation of domestic-type capital.

In terms of the traditional foreign-trade model, we should now specify two additional sectors, one exporting and one competing with imports. Unfortunately, Chilean data do not permit any real distinction to be drawn among industries which do compete with imports and those (aside from copper and iron mining) which are actual or potential exporters. For this reason, we work with only one traded goods sector, whose output can be consumed, used to satisfy exogenous demands and transformed to foreign exchange through substitution of competitive imports or exportation. In practice, this last 'trade-improvement' destination of product will be identified with non-traditional exports, for reasons to be discussed shortly. The balance equation of the traded goods sector is

$$f^2(x_{02}, x_{12}, L_2, t) - c_2 - z_2 - e_2 = 0 , \tag{2}$$

where the notation is as above, with the addition of the term e_2, the non-traditional export volume.

The foreign exchange constraint faced by the Chilean economy can be written as

$$\dot{x}_0 = (1/\pi_0)[e_{\text{trad}} + g(e_2, t) - \pi_{\text{int}}(\mu_1 f^1 + \mu_2 f^2) - \pi_c c_0 - \delta_0 \pi_0 x_0 - r] , \tag{2a}$$

where $\dot{x}_0$ is accumulation of foreign type capital, μ_i is a coefficient relating non-competitive intermediate imports to production levels in sector i, c_0 is consumption of non-competitive imports, $g(e_2, t)$ is the revenue function giving foreign exchange receipts from exportation of e_2 units of non-traditional exports, e_{trad} is foreign exchange generated by traditional mineral exports (exogenous), δ_0 is the depreciation rate on foreign-type capital, and r is the outflow of capital (calculated basically as repatriation of copper mine profits, less foreign aid).[6] We assume that world prices of imports of capital goods (π_0), intermediate inputs (π_{int}) and consumption goods (π_c) are fixed, while the export price varies with the volume traded via the function $g(e_2, t)$.

An alternative formulation of the foreign exchange constraint is in terms of domestic prices which take into account the effects of tariffs and subsidies, quotas and dumping on resource allocation. Often planners (particularly in externally strangled countries) inherit all manner of such distortions from the past, and it is impossible to think of moving from a highly protected situation to an optimal commercial policy in the short run. Hence, existing trade restrictions have to be included among the constraints on planners' decisions.

Concentrating on tariffs as proxies for all types of commercial interventions, we can express total tariff collections less subsidies as

$$- t_2 \pi_2 e_2 + t_{int} \pi_{int} (\mu_1 f^1 + \mu_2 f^2) + t_c \pi_c c_0 + t_0 \pi_0 (\dot{x}_0 + \delta_0 x_0) \ .$$

Adding and subtracting this quantity (call it R) from eq. (2a), we rewrite the balance of payments restriction as

$$\dot{x}_0 = (1/\tau_0 \pi_0)[e_{trad} + \tau_2 g(e_2, t) - \tau_{int} \pi_{int} (\mu_1 f^1 + \mu_2 f^2)$$

$$- \tau_c \pi_c c_0 - \tau_0 \pi_0 \delta_0 x_0 - r + R] \ , \tag{2b}$$

where $\tau_j = 1 + t_j$ is the 'force' of tariff j. The quantity R, when fixed exogenously, may be viewed as a forecast of the amount of tariffs-less-subsidies which planners suppose is to be collected from all sources. Along with the τ's, R will decline exogenously over time as commercial policy eases.

Adopting the usual optimal growth format, we assume that the planning office is interested in finding the maximum of the following functional

$$\int_{t_0}^{t_f} \exp(-\rho t) L(t) \sum_{i=0}^{2} u_i [c_i(t)/L(t)] \, dt, \tag{3}$$

where ρ is the social rate of discount; the μ_i are components of a separable instantaneous 'felicity' function, defined per capita, then aggregated again over the whole population (assumed proportional in size to the labor force) at time t; t_0 is the initial time in the planning horizon, and t_f is the terminal time.[7] (In the computations t_0 was set to zero and t_f to 30 years.)

---

[6] We do not include foreign borrowing as a control variable in the model since many developing countries (including Chile) do not have very free access to world capital markets. Also, Michael Bruno has elegantly dealt with this problem in a model very similar to the one here [ref. 34], and there is no point in repeating his work.

[7] The program is phrased in terms of finite time maximization for reasons of computational feasibility, and also because we will not be concerned with the subtle implications of infinite programs in any case.

The constraints which the planning office faces are then the supply-demand balances (1) and (2), the foreign exchange constraint in one of its two forms (2a) or (2b), three factor use equations,

$$x_1 - \sum_i x_{1i} = 0 \tag{4}$$

$$x_0 - \sum_i x_{0i} = 0 \tag{5}$$

$$L - \sum_i L_i = 0 , \tag{6}$$

(where $L(t)$ is the exogenously growing labor force), initial values of the capital stocks

$$x_0(t_0) \text{ and } x_1(t_0) \text{ given} , \tag{7}$$

and the necessity to reach terminal capital stock targets (whose derivation is discussed below):

$$x_0(t_f) \text{ and } x_1(t_f) \text{ specified} . \tag{8}$$

In schematic form, these equations complete the statement of the model. Before we enter into discussion of the optimality conditions and explicit specification of the various functions, a few observations are in order:

(i) Treating mineral exports e_{trad} as exogenous appears justified as a first approximation in Chile. The *Gran Minéria,* which produces most of the copper, employs less than 1% of the labor force, is geographically isolated from the main population centers, and has few input—output connections with the rest of the economy. Further, copper prices have fluctuated widely in the past, and are largely beyond Chilean control. These reasons, plus the fact that expansion of copper production requires major, non-marginal investments, justifies leaving this sector outside the year-to-year workings of the model.

(ii) Imports, as noted, are all treated as non-competitive. Mainly, this can be blamed on lack of data identifying production characteristics of separate import-competing and export sectors. We might note, however, that import substitution possibilities are often alleged by ECLA and other economists to have 'run out' in countries like Chile. If by this they mean that costs of production for new import substitutes are high, they are correct in most cases,[8] and it is reasonable to assume that imports are not likely to be reduced below their current 15% of GDP in the near future. Conversely, they are not likely to rise

[8] See [ref. 185] for empirical verification.

much above 15%, either, since there is too much social consensus against closing or even not expanding already established, though costly, production operations. For these reasons, the proportionality assumptions adopted here seem realistic.

(iii) As we will see in the solutions, production from sector 2 for exportation (or trade improvement) grows rapidly. As a general policy prescription, this rapid non-traditional export growth is unassailable. However, the solution does not tell which sectors should have their exports pushed. In part this is a computational problem, but data availability has also limited the specification of production functions for a few more disaggregated export sectors.

(iv) The model as stated marks a break with the two-gap tradition from which it is largely derived by not explicitly including a savings constraint. In part, optimization of a non-linear welfare functional replaces this omission, but one would still like some representation of the apparent (from the National Accounts) fact that wage-earners in Chile do not save. This harks back to the problem of duality which we previously decided to ignore, but it still would make a useful extension of this type of model to include behavioral savings restrictions.

(v) The model is set up with sectoral allocations of factors and consumption, investment, and export levels as control variables. In principle, one would want to replace these aggregates with explicit policy variables, controlled by the government. Unfortunately, this is empirically impossible in an aggregate model. However, the government certainly can control investment allocations to sectors (mainly through its control of the foreign exchange market) and has various means of influencing consumption and industry production levels. For this reason, I feel quite certain that designing policies to implement the model's solutions (assuming that one believes the functional and empirical specification!) would not prove impossible, particularly since the model's 'future' is similar to past observed behavior of the Chilean economy.

(vi) Finally, as mentioned previously but worth repeating here, tariffs and other instruments of commercial policy are not treated as control variables. At best, planners can hope to have some control of the changes (hopefully equalizations) of trade restrictions, with more rapid changes presumably leading to higher political costs from plant failures, worker relocations, and so on. There is no conceptual problem in modelling these costs explicitly, but the practical difficulties one foresees point immediately to the alternative of parametric tariff reduction adopted here.

IV. Optimality conditions, and their interpretation

Let demand prices for foreign-type capital stock, the domestic good, and the export good be defined respectively as P_0, P_1, and P_2. Also, let the rentals on the two types of capital be r_0 and r_1, let the wage of labor be w, and use the notation $(\tau_i \pi_i)^+$ to mean $(\tau_i \pi_i / \tau_0 \pi_0)$, i.e. the price of any type i of non-capital traded good expressed in terms of the capital good price.[9] Finally, for the two domestic sectors, let a net price P_i^* be defined as

$$P_i^* = P_i - P_0 (\tau_{int} \pi_{int})^+ \mu_i \quad (i = 1, 2). \tag{9}$$

Using this notation, plus dynamic programming, the minimum principle, or simple common sense, we can write out a number of equations describing instantaneous equilibrium in the economy. They are as follows:

Consumption equilibrium relationships:

$$e^{-\rho t} L u_i'(c_i/L) = P_i \quad (i = 1, 2)$$

$$e^{-\rho t} L u_0'(c_0/L) = P_0 (\tau_c \pi_c)^+ . \tag{10}$$

These equations in the first derivatives of the components of the additive felicity function (the u_i' terms) can be viewed as setting a scale for the demand prices in terms of instantaneous felicity.

Production equilibrium relationships:

$$P_i^* f_0^i = r_0 \quad (i = 1, 2) \tag{11}$$

$$P_i^* f_1^i = r_1 \quad (i = 1, 2) \tag{12}$$

$$P_i^* f_L^i = w \quad (i = 1, 2) \tag{13}$$

These relationships involving the marginal products of the three factors would be valid for cost-minimizing firms in a competitive economy, and determine allocation of the three scarce factors in the model.

World price/domestic price relationships:

$$P_2 = P_0 \tau_2 g' / (\tau_0 \pi_0), \tag{14}$$

where g' is the derivative of the export revenue function.

[9] The definition of $(\tau_i \pi_i)^+$ clearly presupposes that we are considering maximization subject to the balance of payments expressed in terms of domestic prices. Setting τ_i and τ_0 to unity covers the case of maximization subject to world prices.

This relationship scales the domestic demand price for sector two in terms of the shadow exchange rate P_0, and the subsidies given. Note that eq. (14) is written assuming that planners accept present commercial policy as given, i.e. they seek to maximize welfare subject to the foreign exchange constraint in domestic prices, eq. (2b). Since the price factor $\tau_2/(\tau_0 \pi_0)$ in Chile exceeds unity, this means that domestic shadow prices of traded goods will *exceed* the marginal foreign exchange gains from or losses in trade, multiplied by the shadow exchange rate P_0. On the other hand, if planners maximized welfare subject to the world price foreign exchange constraint, eq. (2a), the tariff factors would disappear from eq. (14), so that the traded good's price P_2 and the exchange rate P_0 would be more nearly equal. Because a neoclassical production technology provides little freedom for relative price shifts between the traded and non-traded good (section VII), the exchange rate will also rise relative to the non-traded good's price under trade liberation. Thus, the shadow exchange rate from the model solution subject to the domestic price foreign exchange constraint will be undervalued in comparison to its level in the world price constrained solution.

Dynamic price relationships:
Finally, the changes in shadow prices of the two capital goods are just equal to their net rentals,

$$-\dot{P}_0 = r_0 - P_0 \delta_0 \tag{15}$$

$$-\dot{P}_1 = r_1 - P_1 \delta_1 . \tag{16}$$

This is a standard result from optimal growth theory, and can be rewritten in standard fashion in terms of own rates of interest, capital gains, and social rates of discount, by judicious substitutions from eqs. (10) − (13). We leave this to the reader, and will solely concentrate on explicating certain consequences of eqs. (15) − (16) for investment project analysis, in the next section.

V. Project evaluation in the optimal growth model

An investment project in the context of optimal growth models is just a perturbation. That is, we can imagine that we have an optimal solution to the model (1) − (8) and then perturb it in the following way:
   (i) Add the amounts $h_i(t)$ − which may be of either sign − to the balance eq. (1) and the foreign exchange constraint (2a) or (2b). These $h_i(t)$, when positive, are just the quantities of goods and foreign exchange produced by

some investment project. When negative, they are the amounts of goods and exchange used up by the project.

(ii) Add the amounts $z_i(t)$ to the three factor balance eqs. (4)–(6). These $z_i(t)$, which will normally be negative, are the amounts of capital and labor tied up in the project at any time t.

Now it is reasonable to assume (and is proved in [ref. 19], among other places), that the project will be economically desirable if its shadow value over its lifetime from its time of initiation t_I to its time of closure t_c is positive, i.e. if

$$0 < \int_{t_I}^{t_C} \left[\sum_i P_i(t) h_i(t) + \sum_{j=0}^{1} r_j(t) z_j(t) + w z_3(t) \right] dt. \tag{17}$$

Economically desirable is here understood in terms of welfare: the value of the welfare functional eq. (3) will be increased if we perturb the without-project model solution by $h(t)$ and $z(t)$, when the criterion (17) is satisfied.[10]

Two comments are in order about this rule:

First, the P_i and r_j decline over time, so eq. (17) gives more weight to effects of the project/perturbation in the near than in the far future. However, prices and factor rentals in a multi-capital goods model need not (and in general will not) decline in fixed proportion according to simple exponential decay functions. For this reason, 'discounting' in the traditional sense is not an appropriate decision rule, although in particular models the decreases in prices and factor rentals over time may be approximated by exponential function. We will see in section VIII to what extent such approximations apply in the present model. For the moment, we stick with writing eq. (17) in general form.

Second, eq. (17) shows that the project should be evaluated with tariff-ridden shadow prices, when welfare is optimized with respect to the tariff-inclusive foreign exchange constraint, eq. (2b). This means – somewhat counter to intuition – that when project analysts really accept current tariffs as binding, they should value capital inflows or foreign exchange revenues from export projects at a price which is *low* relative to the prices of currently traded

---

[10] Strictly speaking, this is a first order result since we have not considered the effect of the project itself on the equilibrium prices of the model. However, this effect is likely to be empirically irrelevant, as is shown in the appendix.

Note that the services of capital in eq. (17) are valued at each moment of the project's life by their respective rentals r_0 and r_1. If a constant amount of some type of capital is used by the project, charging its shadow rentals over the life of the project in evaluation can through the use of eqs. (15) and (16) be shown to be approximately the same as the more common practice of charging its shadow purchase price at the moment the project begins.

goods.[11] The low valuation on foreign exchange reflects the fact that consumption patterns and associated marginal welfare valuations adapt themselves to high tariffs and low foreign exchange content. If free-traders in the planning office do not want to accept this tariff-ridden consumption (and marginal utility) pattern, then it is appropriate for them to try to impose the use of world relative prices for traded goods and appropriately scaled domestic prices for non-traded goods, in investment project analyses and elsewhere. One can view a world-price solution of the optimal growth model as an attempt to indicate the appropriate relative prices.

In more general terms, planners can also try to calculate prices corresponding to welfare maximization subject to politically feasible tariff reductions. To my mind, this is more representative of what is possible in planning operations, and some of the solutions presented here are calculated for various plausible patterns of trade liberation in Chile.[12]

---

[11] Normally, one expects a relatively high shadow price for foreign exchange when there are numerous trade restrictions. In fact, some calculations of exchange rates for use in investment project are constructed to fit this preconception in the following way: we know from eq. (10) that any domestic price index will also be an index of instantaneous felicity gains from additional consumption. But from eq. (14) we can express this index as some weighted average of tariffs, multiplied by P_0. If we make a similar index of foreign exchange gains and losses from trade in world prices, and divide it into the domestic price index, then we end up multiplying P_0 by a factor exceeding unity, to 'correct' for the tariff-caused undervaluation of the exchange rate. As indicated in the text, this is not an appropriate correction if planners choose to respect tariffs as given. If tariffs are not to be respected, it is better not to use an ad hoc correction, but to solve the model subject to the world prices of eq. (2a), calculate the corresponding P_0, and evaluate traded goods at their marginal foreign exchange cost or revenue times P_0. As mentioned above, P_0 under free trade will be higher relative to traded goods prices, than under restricted trade. As we will see below, the same is true for P_0 relative to the non-traded good's price.

[12] This can be considered as an attempt to implement a procedure which Bacha and I judged impractical in [ref. 8]. On concluding this paper, the reader may decide whether the opinion expressed there or the attempt made here is the more appropriate. One might note in passing that people who write articles proposing formulae for calculating the shadow price of foreign exchange sometimes treat either eqs. (2a) or (2b) as *the* appropriate restriction, and then steadfastly and unswervingly carry out their analysis and polemics without considering the alternative. Since running the economy according to world prices is not the sort of thing that one usually recommends to the Minister, while blindly accepting tariffs is sub-optimal economically, some compromise — such as shadow-pricing in light of expected future tariff reductions — might seem desirable.

VI. Functional specifications

(i) Most international evidence and some early returns from Chile [ref. 19] indicate that elasticities of substitution in production between labor and aggregate capital are somewhat less than unity. However, the received wisdom on the substitutability between plant and equipment (or domestic-type and foreign-type capital) is much less developed and persuasive. Two-gap and programming models have assumed that the relevant (direct partial) elasticity of substitution is either zero or infinite. In these circumstances, an agnostic position has been adopted. Production possibilities in each sector are supposed to be described by a two-level C.E.S. production function, the upper level reflecting the trade-offs between aggregated capital stock x_i^* and effective labor L_i

$$f^i = A_i \exp{(\xi_i t)} \, [\gamma_{1i}(x_i^*)^{-\beta_{1i}} + (1 - \gamma_{1i})(L_i)^{-\beta_{1i}}]^{(-1/\beta_{1i})} \quad (i = 1, 2) \,, \quad (18)$$

where A_i is the scale parameter in the upper-level C.E.S., ξ_i is the rate of technical progress, γ_{1i} is the distribution parameters and β_{1i} ($= (1/\sigma_{1i}) - 1$) represents substitution possibilities between aggregate capital and labor. The capital aggregate x_i^* is itself based on a C.E.S. index,

$$x_i^* = [\gamma_{2i}(x_{1i})^{-\beta_{2i}} + (1 - \gamma_{2i})(x_{0i})^{-\beta_{2i}}]^{(-1/\beta_{2i})} \quad (i = 1, 2) \,, \quad (19)$$

where the interpretation of the parameters is as in the upper level function.

(ii) Welfare functional: the theoretical literature is none too explicit about the appropriate from for the functions u_i in eq. (3). The most natural choice. from the point of view of interpretation at least, is one of the utility indices which have been proposed to justify complete systems of demand functions. Among these, the most readily interpretable is the utility function of the Stone-Geary linear system of demand functions [ref. 78]:

$$\sum_i u_i(c_i/L) = \sum_i a_i \log{[(c_i/L) - b_i]}$$

$$(c_i/L) > b_i \,, i = 0, 1, 2; \; \sum_i a_i = 1; \; a_i > 0, i = 0, 1, 2) \,. \quad (20)$$

If q_0, q_1, and q_2 are the prices faced by the consumer, then this 'subsistance income' y^* can be defined as $\Sigma_i b_i q_i$. If his income is just y^* (the utility function is not defined for income levels below y^*), he consumes b_i of each good. Any supernumerary income $y - y^*$ is divided among the goods in proportions $a_i - a_i$ being larger as the income elasticity of demand for good i is higher.

In the model solutions described below, parameters in the base year were estimated to correspond to observed Chilean income and price elasticities of demand. However, the parameters b_i were generally increased as a function of time. This increase in (psychological) subsistence income corresponds to rising expectations on the part of consumers, and is appropriate for a growing economy.

(iii) Export revenue is assumed to be determined by a demand function with constant elasticity η:

$$g(e_2, t) = C \exp (r_{\exp} t) \, e_2^{(1/\eta)+1} , \tag{21}$$

where e_2 is the volume of non-traditional exports, and the time trend allows for growth of world trade.

(iv) World prices are inferred using base year tariff factors τ, on the assumption that base year domestic prices are all equal to unity:

$$\pi_j = 1/\tau_j , \tag{22}$$

where j indexes types of traded goods. The τ_j's (including τ_e, which represents the cost differential the domestic producers face in placing their goods in the world market) are assumed to decline over time in radioactive form:

$$\tau_j(t) = 1 + [\tau_j(t_0) - 1] \cdot \exp [-r_j(t - t_0)] . \tag{23}$$

In some of the numerical exercises described below, it is assumed that tariffs are equal to zero throughout the planning period (the world price foreign exchange constraint binds). When the domestic-price foreign exchange constraint is used, the τ_j's are assumed to decline from their initial levels with halving times of 5 or 15 years.

VII. Base year specification and parameter values

Data for the model were to a large extent drawn from projections made by ODEPLAN, the Chilean National Planning Office, for the economy in a 'full employment' year 1970 [ref. 150]. In reality, 1970 was far from being a full employment year because of pre- and post-election economic uncertainty. However, the ODEPLAN projections are still a fairly realistic indicator of what a full employment base year would look like, and were used (stylistically) for this reason.

The first non-traded sector of the model was identified with services, commerce, transportation and communication, and the utility industries. Of course, some trade is carried out in these sectors (notably in transportation) but to a first approximation, they do not play a major role in the international com-

Table 1
Base year production conditions[a]

	Non-traded goods (sector 1)	Traded goods (sector 2)
Output	6.15	11.70
Employment	1.618	1.324
Domestic capital		
amount	14.19	11.61
relative to output	2.31	0.99
relative to labor	8.77	8.77
Foreign capital		
amount	8.74	9.46
relative to output	1.42	0.81
• relative to labor	5.40	7.15
Capital aggregate		
amount	11.96	10.61
relative to output	1.94	0.91
relative to labor	7.39	8.01
Average labor		
productivity	3.80	8.84

[a] Monetary magnitudes in billions of 1965 escudos. Employment in millions of workers.

merce of most countries. Remaining sectors were treated as traded, and to a large extent this is realistic. (A number of manufacturing industries in Chile are not in fact traded, because of prohibition of imports of their products. However, they are tradeable and were aggregated into sector two for this reason.)

Table 1 shows production conditions corresponding roughly to the ODEPLAN base year. About two-thirds of gross output is assumed traded (or tradeable), the rest non-traded. Capital-labor ratios in the traded sector are clearly higher than in the non-traded sector, and average labor productivity is much higher as well. These relationships correspond to what one expects in a developing country.

Table 2 shows the parameter values assumed for the model. These again are stylized, but based as far as possible on empirical studies, as follows:

(i) Jere Behrman's production function estimates [ref. 19] show that elasticities of substitution in Chile are rather low, as is the rate of technical progress. Hence rates of technical progress of one percent and elasticities of substitution of two-thirds (traded sector) and one-third (non-traded sector)

Table 2.
Values of the parameters for the basic solution

Definition	Parameter symbol	Value
Rate of technical progress in non-traded sector	ξ_1	0.01
Rate of technical progress in traded sector	ξ_2	0.01
Upper level elasticity substitution: non-traded sector	σ_{11}	0.3333
Upper level elasticity of substitution: traded sector	σ_{12}	0.6667
Elasticity of substitution between foreign and domestic capital	$\sigma_{21} = \sigma_{22}$	0.50
Non-competitive intermediate import coefficients	μ_1	0.05
	μ_2	0.20
Capital depreciation rates		
domestic type	δ_1	0.02
foreign type	δ_0	0.04
Supernumerary income allocation parameters in Stone–Geary expenditure function (1: non-traded good; 2: traded good; 0: non-competitive imports)	a_1	0.13
	a_2	0.75
	a_0	0.12
'Subsistence' consumption levels in Stone–Geary function (base year, multiplied by base year labor force of 2.942 million)[a]	$b_1 \cdot L$	2.971
	$b_2 \cdot L$	10.885
	$b_0 \cdot L$	0.530
Rates of growth of all 'subsistence' levels b_i		0.011
Social rate of discount	ρ	0.06
Demand elasticity of sector 2 exports	η	−10.0
Time trend in export demand function	r_{exp}	0.01
World prices[b]:		
foreigen-type capital goods	π_0	0.75
Non-competitive consumption goods	π_c	0.45
Non-competitive intermediate inputs	π_{int}	0.62
Non-traditional exports (base year)	π_2	0.6667
Initial levels of exogenous demands[a]:		
sector 1		1.75
sector 2		0.20
Growth rate of exogenous demands		0.05
Rate of decline of all tariffs per year		0.13863 (five-year halving time)
Capital inflows from abroad ('foreign aid')		U.S. $50 million per year
Labor force growth rate		0.02

[a] Billions of 1965 escudos.
[b] Domestic prices in base year all assumed to be 1.

are probably not far from the mark. The value 0.5 for the elasticity of substitution between the two types of capital was simply assumed. Sato's estimates for the U.S.A. [ref. 170] are higher, but the lower value seemed appropriate in view of the lower flexibility demonstrated by the Chilean economy in most respects. The distribution parameters for the C.E.S. functions were calculated using observed labor shares and estimates of the gross rates of return to domestic and foreign capital of 9% and 11% (non-traded sector) and 24% and 26% (traded sector). The latter rates in turn follow from a study of Chilean manufacturing returns [ref. 31]; the former were based on rough calculations using ODEPLAN value-added and production data. Depreciation rates were based on ODEPLAN estimates, as were the non-competitive intermediate import coefficients.

(ii) The a_i parameters for the Stone–Geary function were chosen on the basis of shares of the three consumption goods (from sectors 1 and 2, and noncompetitive imports) in total consumption, and estimated expenditure elasticities of 0.625, 1.05, and 1.45 respectively. The b_i parameters and their growth rates were chosen initially to correspond to ODEPLAN's crudely estimated own-price elasticities, and then adjusted along with their growth rates to give a relatively credible evolution of aggregate savings in the model solutions. The value of 0.06 for the discount rate was chosen in line with values used in a number of economic programming models, but variations in its value had little effect on the solution.

(iii) The export demand elasticity of −10 is arbitrary (although similar values have been used in other studies). In any case, it is the subject of sensitivity analysis below. World prices were inferred by dividing domestic unit-values by estimated aggregate price differentials. The actual differentials are arbitrary, although based on ODEPLAN estimates and a variety of other estimates described in [ref. 185].

(iv) The exogenous demands correspond mainly to residential construction (assumed exogenous because of the difficulties involved in incorporating it into static utility functions) and government consumption in the non-traded sector, and to government consumption in the traded sector. The assumed growth rate of 5% in these demands is consistent with Chilean experience in the 1960's. The other exogenous entries in the balance of payments, mineral exports and capital outflows, were set equal to ODEPLAN estimates for 1970–80, and extrapolated past 1980 according to their growth rates in the latter part of the decade.

(v) Finally, terminal capital stock levels were chosen by an informal iteration, with different values being tried until significant decumulations or rapid accumulations of capital near the terminal time were avoided. Although this model does not strictly satisfy the conditions under which consumption turn-pike theorems are proved (technical progress is not Harrod neutral, and the exogenous variables grow at non-exponential or differing exponential growth rates), steady exponential growth in the capital stocks was usually observed after a 3 to 5 year initial adjustment period.[13] The steady growth path was used as a reference point, and terminal capital stocks (and their shadow prices) manipulated until growth in the last 5 years of the 30-year horizon was 'quite' steady, on a graph. The initial 10−20 years of the optimal price and quantity programs were essentially unaffected by these terminal adjustments.

There are two additional features of these data that merit explicit comment.

First and not surprising, the base year production data do not conform to the principles of static neoclassical resource allocation embodied in eqs. (9) − (14). The average productivity of labor and rates of return to capital in the non-traded sector are clearly far too low relative to the same magnitudes in the traded sector for there to be any equalization of marginal products of factors. In the real world, this is an expected occurrence for these particular sectors. In an optimizing model without a built-in distortion prohibiting equalization of marginal products in the two sectors, the discrepancy must vanish. This can happen via a resource shift from the non-traded to traded sector, or an increase in the relative price of non-traded goods from our assumed value of unity. We can see immediately which of these two possible shifts away from the base year situation provides more flexibility from the second salient feature of the technological specification, the relative flatness of the model's production possibility curve.

This is illustrated in fig. 1, which shows transformation surfaces corresponding to initial and final factor endowments in the basic solution to the model. Clearly, in any given year, only a small range of relative prices is permitted if we insist, as we must, on a solution with both goods produced. Hence, factor shifts between the two sectors must bear the main burden of static adjustment in this model.[14] Moreover, we can also see that supply of the traded

---

[13] Similar results have been observed for activity analysis models of the Japanese economy, solved by methods essentially the same as those used here [ref. 186]. It is extremely difficult to prove that a turnpike exists in the Japanese models with trending input−output and productivity coefficients, but steady-state disaggregated growth is usually observed in the numerical solutions.

[14] Harry Johnson pointed out long ago that the transformation surface generated by a neoclassical production specification, Cobb−Douglas in his case, is very flat [ref. 105]. Chenery and Raduchel [ref. 40] also observed that large factor shifts among sectors play the main role in accommodating planning models with neoclassical production specifications to various forcing factors such as demand shifts, etc. Over time, of course, the admissible range of relative prices can shift with capital accumulation. The final year transformation curve in fig. 1 is noticeably steeper than the initial year curve.

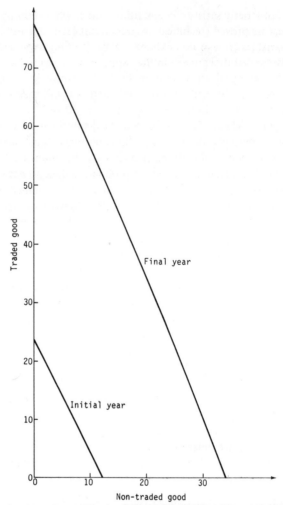

Fig. 1. Product transformation curves for basic solution (billions of 1965 escudos).

good is highly price elastic. This has implications for the numerical solution of the model (see appendix) and also for the magnitude of the adjustments the exchange rate must make from its tariff-ridden value when the model is solved subject to a world price foreign exchange constraint.

VIII. A basic solution

In a low order system of the type considered here, probably the best way to get a feel for the characteristics of the solution is via graphical presentation.

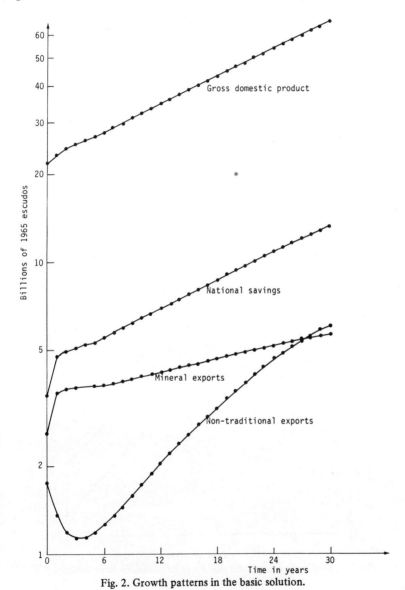

Fig. 2. Growth patterns in the basic solution.

In our particular case, figs. 2 – 4 illustrate a number of interesting characteristics of the model's basic 30-year solution (subject to the specifications of table 2).

It is apparent from figs. 2 and 3 that growth of the major aggregate variables is remarkably steady in the basic solution. After a slight initial spurt, Gross Domestic Product in 1965 prices grows steadily at 3.4% per year from year 6 until year 30. Over the same period, both types of capital stock (fig. 3) grow

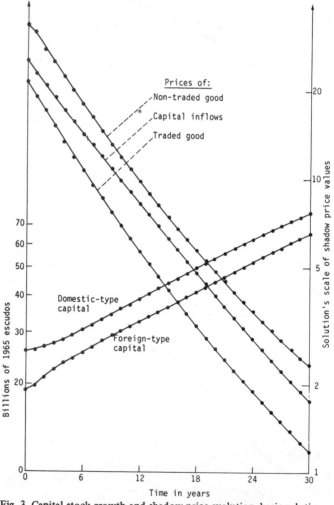

Fig. 3. Capital stock growth and shadow price evolution, basic solution.

at 3.7%. From figs. 2 and 3, it can be seen that the arrival on stream of new copper production capacity in 1971 (which causes the big jump in mineral exports) is used to finance a substantial increase in the amount of foreign-type capital, relative to the domestic type. After this readjustment of the

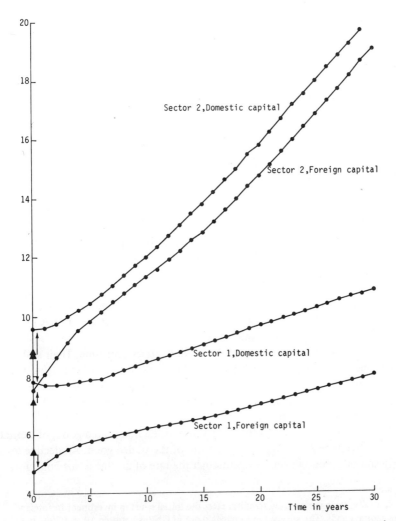

Fig. 4. Capital–labor ratios, basic solution (thousands of 1965 escudos per man; points marked ▲ indicate ODEPLAN's projected 1970 ratios in table 1).

capital stocks to 'turnpike proportions', their aggregate amounts grow proportionately.[15]

Many of the flow variables, however, do not show steady growth. In particular, the volume of non-traditional exports first drops off in response to the spurt in mineral exports, and then grows rapidly until it amounts to nine percent of GDP (8.6% in value terms) by the final year. Although the total export share in GDP is approximately the same in the initial and terminal years, the large proportionate rise of non-traditional exports marks a substantial structural change in the economy. If realistic (and it clearly depends on the accuracy of the copper forecasts), this projection of export growth leads naturally to questions about which specific industries should grow to make up the aggregate total. We can not pursue such issues here, but they seem well worth investigating.

Fig. 4 indicates that growth of non-traditional exports and other products from the traded goods sector requires fairly substantial resource shifts. Capital-labor ratios in sector 2 more than double over the 30-year planning period. In addition, there is an initial shift of resources from the ODEPLAN projections (which as noted above do not embody a fully efficient neoclassical allocation); both capital-labor ratios in the traded goods sector increase relatively to the non-traded sector. After this initial jump, the rapid build-up of foreign-type capital in the first years of the solution is also diverted to sector 2. Once the build-up is complete, capital-labor ratios remain in approximately fixed ratio in both sectors, with foreign capital being more important for the traded good. However, by far the largest proportions of incremental labor and capital stocks are assigned to sector two at any time. Rapid export growth has its costs in terms of domestic resources.

Fig. 3 also shows the behvior of the shadow prices over time. Their scaling is in terms of the total welfare integral, and is difficult to interpret. However, only relative prices are of interest for investment project analysis, since eq. (17) shows that a shadow price evaluation of a project would be unaffected by an arbitrary scaling constant.

The three prices shown in fig. 3 are those of the non-traded good, of capital inflows (the price P_0 divided by $\tau_0 \pi_0$) and of the traded good. All decline in fairly smooth fashion over time, although the rate of decline is *not* constant;

---

[15] Naturally, savings also grow steadily, after the initial spurt in investment in foreign-type capital goods. The steady state savings share of GNP is between 19 and 20%, high by historical standards in Chile, but by no means inconceivable under a growth-oriented socialist government. One might add the GDP growth rate also lies within the range which history would indicate as 'reasonable' for Chile.

strictly speaking, discounting with a constant interest rate is not admissible according to this solution. Depending on your point of view, however, it might be a pretty good approximation. The rentals on the two types of capital for selected years (relative to the price of the non-traded good) are as follows:

Year	Domestic type capital:	Foreign type capital:
0	0.121	0.141
5	0.129	0.104
10	0.120	0.096
15	0.110	0.090
20	0.101	0.083
25	0.093	0.075
30	0.087	0.069

Given that the worthwhileness of an investment project is often insensitive to a narrow range of interest rates, discounting at, say, 10% might not be completely inappropriate.

We have already seen that given the lack of curvature of the transformation curve, relative net prices cannot vary much in this model (see eqs. $(9) - (14)$ and section VII). This is confirmed by fig. 3, which indicates a slight decline in the price of the non-traded good relative to that of the traded good at the beginning of the solution (corresponding to the rapid build-up of the traded capital stock), and then a very slight relative decline of the traded good prices thereafter (resulting from falling marginal revenues as exports expand). However, the overall variation is small.

More interesting is the fact that the two foreign prices (the traded good and capital inflows) are *below* the non-traded good's price. We have already pointed out two reasons for this — the undervaluation of the exchange rate resulting from protection and the fact that both resource reallocations and price shifts from the ODEPLAN base year specification (which had both prices equal to one) were made necessary by the latter's inefficient resource allocation. As fig. 1 indicates, the goods prices must stick fairly closely to their ratios in the basic solution. However, there is room for exchange rate shifts relative to the home good's price as levels of protection change. We explore the importance of this and other responses to alternative specifications in the following section.

IX. Variant solutions

Subject to the search procedure described in section VII for terminal capital stock levels, a number of variant solutions were run. Their specific parameter changes are as follows:

(i) Setting all τ_j to unity throughout the solution period, i.e. generating a 'free trade' solution;

(ii) making the halving time of the τ_j 15 years instead of the 5 years of the basic solution;

(iii) setting exogenous capital inflows to $ 200 million per year instead of $ 50 million;

(iv) changing the export demand elasticity from -10 to -5;

(v) setting the social rate of discount to 0.03, instead of 0.06.

In general the effects of the variant specifications on the real variables are not important. This is demonstrated in table 3, which shows the values of a number of macroquantities in years 10 and 20 of the various solutions. The changes between the solutions are all quite small, and usually comprehensible in terms of the different specifications involved.[16] By all counts, the biggest changes take place in the solution permitting $ 200 million of capital inflow, but even here the differences relative to the basic solution are not large, except that the welfare integral is much less negative with the extra dollars. In general, we conclude along with Harberger [ref. 91] and others that changes in the amount of distortion in a neoclassical system do not have a large percentage impact on macro-economic welfare measures. This is not to deny, of course, that the *absolute* gains from abolishing tariff or getting more foreign aid may be large.

Table 4 illustrates the effects on the shadow prices of the different specifications. In all cases, the relative shifts of the two goods prices are extremely small. However, the value of capital inflows (the shadow exchange rate P_0 divided by the foreign capital good's post-tariff price) does move relatively to the home good's price P_1. The movements subject to the different specifications can be understood easily in light of the non-shifting net prices P_j^*. At any

---

[16] For example, table 3 indicates that the effect of free trade is to permit more rapid capital accumulation without great consumption sacrifices relative to the restricted trade solutions.Along the same lines, less accumulation takes place in the solution with 5-year halving times. High capital inflow permits both higher consumption and more rapid accumulation, while the lower export demand elasticity leads to welfare loss and a shift in accumulation toward the domestic-type capital. The lower discount rate raises consumption and lowers accumulation, but not much.

Table 3
Aggregate magnitudes for variant solutions

		Basic solution	'Free trade' solution	15-year tariff halving time	$ 200 mil-lion capital inflow	Export elastici-ty of −5.0	Discount rate of 0.03
Gross domes-tic product	year 10	32.18	32.31	32.19	32.70	32.06	32.21
	year 20	46.30	46.73	46.10	46.99	45.63	46.25
Total consumption	year 10	19.91	19.85	19.89	20.67	19.81	19.97
	year 20	27.31	27.09	27.24	28.52	27.03	27.63
Welfare integral	year 10	− 85.55	− 92.21	− 91.17	−56.83	− 96.38	− 99.80
	year 20	−136.62	−147.35	−143.83	−87.37	−155.29	−169.72
Domestic capital	year 10	36.01	37.25	35.91	36.72	37.25	36.09
	year 20	53.80	57.05	52.39	54.80	56.23	52.88
Foreign capital	year 10	30.28	30.15	30.51	31.65	29.15	30.32
	year 20	44.71	46.25	44.63	46.24	41.03	44.18

Table 4
Prices relative to the non-traded good's price, various solutions

Solution and year	Capital inflow price	Export good's price	Rent on domestic capital	Rent on foreign capital
Basic solution				
0	0.747	0.629	0.121	0.141
5	0.777	0.596	0.129	0.104
10	0.831	0.581	0.120	0.096
15	0.848	0.565	0.110	0.090
20	0.835	0.549	0.101	0.083
25	0.803	0.531	0.093	0.075
'Free trade' solution				
0	1.055	0.618	0.121	0.139
5	0.960	0.593	0.124	0.108
10	0.933	0.579	0.114	0.098
15	0.901	0.562	0.103	0.089
20	0.859	0.543	0.092	0.079
25	0.810	0.522	0.084	0.070
15-year tariff halving time				
0	0.743	0.628	0.121	0.140
5	0.703	0.598	0.129	0.103
10	0.722	0.583	0.121	0.095
15	0.731	0.569	0.113	0.089
20	0.728	0.553	0.106	0.083
25	0.715	0.538	0.100	0.076

Table 4 (continued)

Solution and year	Capital inflow price	Export good's price	Rent on domestic capital	Rent on foreign capital
$ 200 million capital inflow				
0	0.723	0.625	0.121	0.140
5	0.742	0.588	0.127	0.098
10	0.798	0.573	0.118	0.090
15	0.823	0.558	0.107	0.084
20	0.815	0.544	0.099	0.079
25	0.795	0.532	0.094	0.075
Discount rate of 0.03				
0	0.748	0.630	0.121	0.141
5	0.778	0.596	0.129	0.103
10	0.831	0.580	0.120	0.096
15	0.848	0.566	0.109	0.090
20	0.834	0.550	0.104	0.085
25	0.805	0.535	0.099	0.079
Export elasticity of − 5.0				
0	0.829	0.641	0.120	0.137
5	0.912	0.615	0.122	0.109
10	1.022	0.605	0.112	0.103
15	1.099	0.596	0.100	0.099
20	1.131	0.585	0.091	0.096
25	1.126	0.572	0.085	0.093

time point during the solutions, the flat production possibility surface means
that the two net prices will have to be in some almost constant ratio K:

$$\frac{P_1^*}{P_2^*} = \frac{P_1 - (\tau_{int}\pi_{int}/\tau_0\pi_0)\mu_1}{P_2 - (\tau_{int}\pi_{int}/\tau_0\pi_0)\mu_2} = K \, . \tag{24}$$

Substituting eq. (14), which expresses P_2 in terms of P_0 and the export marginal revenue g', into eq. (24) and rearranging gives

$$P_1 = \frac{[\tau_2 g' - \tau_{int}\pi_{int}\mu_2] + \tau_{int}\pi_{int}\mu_1}{\tau_0\pi_0} P_0 \, . \tag{25}$$

Since μ_1 is quite small (non-traded goods require few imported intermediate
inputs), eq. (25) shows that the home goods price is essentially the value added
of the traded goods sector (taking account of whatever tariffs exist, and expressed relatively to the capital goods price) times the exchange rate. As marginal effective protection of the traded good falls, the exchange rate must rise.

The values of P_0 relative to P_1 in the 'free trade' and 15-year tariff halving
time solutions illustrate this point, being respectively higher and lower than
the values in the basic solution (with a 5-year tariff halving time). The free
trade and basic solutions converge over time, as the tariffs in the latter approach zero at the end of the 30-year planning period.

A similar increase in the value of the exchange rate shows up in the solution
where the elasticity of export demand is reduced to -5.0. Here the exchange
rate is higher than in the basic solution, and markedly appreciates as marginal
revenue falls with export expansion.

In the two other variant solutions, effects are much as might be expected.
Quadrupling capital inflows reduces the exchange rate by about 2.5%, another
example of the great stability of neoclassical models. And reducing the social
rate of discount from 6% to 3% has virtually no effect on either the price or
quantity solution — a result which has been observed in other models.[17]

X. Comparisons to other approaches and conclusions

There are two other studies of shadow prices in Chile to which the results
of this exercise may be directly compared — the rate of return estimates of

[17] The slight differences between the low discount rate and basic solutions toward the
end of the period are due to the fact that I stopped running the former model before
generating a smoothly growing solution at the end of the planning horizon.

Bitar and Trivelli [ref. 31] and the foreign exchange shadow price estimates made by Bacha and me [ref. 185]. The former study gives a number of different estimates of the rate of return to capital in Chile, mostly lying in the $10 - 20\%$ range. This can be compared to the rental rates (relative to the non-traded good's price) shown in table 4, and also to the rate at which the shadow prices decline in fig. 3. These in general are around 10%, two points higher in the initial years of the solution and two points lower at the end. Given the rough nature of all calculations involved, I would say that Bitar—Trivelli and the current study tend to confirm each other's results. In both cases, rental rates are determined from production conditions and appear to be far from the guesses as to the social rate of discount made herein. For a developing country, this is a reassuring result.

Bacha and I estimated from a partial equilibrium model (developed in [ref. 8]) a value for the exchange rate which would rule under free trade conditions in Chile. Competitive imports played the role of a protected traded good that exports play in this model, and our estimating formula was

$$\bar{P}_0 = P_0 \tau^{\eta_m/(a+\eta_m)} , \tag{26}$$

where $\bar{P}_0$ is the free trade exchange rate, P_0 is the current exchange rate, τ is the force of protection given imports, a is a constant and η_m is the demand elasticity of imports. We used a value of -2.0 for η_m, and concluded that the exponent in eq. (26) had a value of something like one-half. Thus, the exchange rate rose less (in percentage terms) than τ fell in its approach to its equilibrium value of unity. With a higher value of η_m (resulting, for example, from highly elastic domestic supply of the import good and 'normally' elastic demand) this of course would not be true, for eq. (27) would in the limit become

$$\bar{P}_0 = \tau P_0 . \tag{27}$$

According to this limiting formula, the product of exchange rate and tariff is constant. But this is just what eq. (25) says about the product of value added in the traded goods sector and the exchange rate. Thus, in both approaches, a highly elastic domestic supply of the traded goods (implicit in the present model) in the almost constant ratio K of net prices in eq. (25) leads to an inverse proportionality relationship like eq. (27) between exchange rate and tariff (or effective tariff). In econometric terms, the lower trade elasticities undoubtedly have more support. But the present neoclassical formulation surely is neater theoretically, and may be more valid in the long run. Flat transformation surfaces and neoclassicism *do* go hand-in-hand, however, and the non-responsiveness of the present model to parameter variations and its strong implications for relative price relationships are also part of this nexus.

I suppose I should say that only further research will demonstrate which specification better approximates the 'true' state of the world, and in the long run I believe it. For the moment, however, I would stick with a discount rate of 10% and an exchange rate more-or-less inversely proportional to tariffs, for Chile.

Appendix: Computation and second order effects

The model stated here can be solved quite easily with existing control theory (or dynamic decomposition) algorithms. The algorithm actually used follows Jacobson and Mayne [ref. 101] and can be summarized as follows:

(i) At the beginning of the solution procedure, an initial nominal control history $\bar{u}_i(t)$ (where i indexes control variables) is used to integrate eqs. (1a), (2a) or (2b), and a differential equation version of eq. (3) forward in time, using a fourth-order Runge–Kutta procedure with half-year time steps.

(ii) Values of the final costate variables, corresponding to P_1 and P_0 in previous notation, and also to $V_{x_1} (\partial V/\partial x_1)$, where V is the value of the optimized welfare functional (3)) and V_{x_0} are chosen, and used as initial conditions to integrate eqs. (15) and (16) backward (for P_0 and P_1, or the vector V_x) in time. Equations for V_{xx}, the matrix of second derivatives of V with respect to the state variables, are also integrated backwards. These integrations are made with state variables set to their nominal values from the forward integration, but with new control variables $u_i^*(t)$ calculated at each time point by maximizing the Hamiltonian evaluated using the V_x.[18] Finally, the difference between the Hamiltonian functions evaluated at the maximizing $u_i^*(t)$ and the nominal $\bar{u}_i(t)$ is also integrated backwards. The result at time t_0 of this qua-

---

[18] The Hamiltonian is maximized by (i) evaluating output levels along the transformation curve at a number of points close to the previous time point's output vector by varying factor allocations subject to eqs. (11) – (13) expressed in ratio form; (ii) numerically differentiating the transformation curve to find the ratio between the net prices P_1^* and P_2^* of eqs. (9); (iii) solving the ratio explicitly for P_2, using the current values from the integration of P_0 and P_1; (iv) using P_2 to calculate the consumption demand for the traded good from eq. (10) and export demand from eq. (14); (v) comparing total demand for the traded good with total supply from step (i), and iterating further by expanding the transformation curve about the demand point if the values are not close. The stability of this cobweb-like iteration in the export good market is guaranteed by the very high supply elasticity of the export good noted in section VII, and convergence is fast.

drature can be shown to be prediction of the gain in welfare resulting from using controls u_i^* in place of $\bar{u}_i$.

(iii) A new forward integration is made, using new nominal control variables calculated by expanding about u_i^* to second order in the changes of state variables from the previous nominal solution, using the vector V_x and matrix V_{xx} as the basic ingredients for deriving the weights in the expansion.

(iv) This forward/backward integration sequence is continued until the predicted welfare gain mentioned in point (ii) is small. Another second order procedure is then used to modify the final values of the V_x vector to try to bring the terminal capital stock levels closer to their specified levels, and the process continues until this latter convergence is achieved.

The first part of this algorithm usually converged within two or three backward integrations, after a successful choice of the terminal values of P_0 and P_1. This choice was initially not simple, given the very small range of relative net prices permitted by the flat transformation surfaces exemplified in fig. 1. Moreover, the algorithm's correction of the final prices often led to corner solutions, and it was often necessary to guess the final price ratio several times to get solutions without rapid accumulations or decumulations of capital as the terminal time was approached. (This problem was no doubt exacerbated by the flatness of the transformation curve, but it often occurs in any case, according to the oral tradition of control theorists.)

I think that the good overall performance of the algorithm was due to minimizing the Hamiltonian at all times. This was one of two major differences between the present algorithm and a more slowly converging one used in some previous numerical analysis of similar problems with David Kendrick [ref. 111]. The other difference was incorporation of second order information via the

Table 5
Values of the first and second derivatives of the optimized welfare functional with respect to state variables (basic solution)

Time	$\dfrac{\partial V}{\partial x_1}(=P_1)$	$\dfrac{\partial V}{\partial x_0}(=P_0)$	$\dfrac{\partial^2 V}{\partial x_1 \partial x_1}$	$\dfrac{\partial^2 V}{\partial x_1 \partial x_0}$	$\dfrac{\partial^2 V}{\partial x_0 \partial x_0}$
0	34.120	25.512	−8.263	−5.727	−5.009
5	20.115	13.675	−2.906	−1.721	−1.485
10	11.924	8.050	−0.946	−0.538	−0.512
15	7.413	4.913	−0.312	−0.166	−0.184
20	4.829	3.086	−0.100	−0.046	−0.067
25	3.277	1.995	−0.026	−0.008	−0.023
30	2.305	1.325	−0.000	−0.000	−0.000

matrix V_{xx}. The numerical values of this matrix were relatively small (as is shown in table 5). It can be [19] shown that the product of the V_{xx} terms and the vector of capital rentals measures the impact which one unit of additional capital stock would have on the vector of capital rentals — in effect the interest on the interest generated by a new investment project. Given this economic interpretation, it is not surprising that the second order terms in the expansion of a new $\bar{u}_i(t)$ have little effect. The same is of course true regarding the importance of (second order) effects of investments on interest rates in project evaluations. In a neoclassical world, such niceties need not be taken into account.

[19] See [ref. 184], eq. (27) and surrounding text.

R.S. Eckaus, P.N. Rosenstein-Rodan (eds.), Analysis of development problems,
© North-Holland Publishing Company

PROJECT EVALUATION
WITHIN A MACROECONOMIC FRAMEWORK *

Peter B. CLARK
*International Bank for Reconstruction and Development,
Washington, D.C., U.S.A.*

Alejandro FOXLEY R.
Catholic University of Chile, Santiago, Chile

and

Anna Maria JUL
University of Pennsylvania, Philadelphia, Penn., U.S.A.

I. Introduction

Planning theory as applied to problems of resource allocation has been developed from both a macro and microeconomic point of view. The distinction between the two approaches is drawn in terms of the sources and tests of data employed, the assumptions and theory underlying the analysis and the application of results for policy formation.

The macroplanner starts usually with the national income accounts, requiring a consistent system to explain aggregate price changes, production growth or resource allocations. When trying to study these, the macroplanner attempts to disaggregate his macrovariables to incorporate as many sectors as he is capable of manipulating, always maintaining the consistency control that all variables may be reaggregated to the macrolevel of the national accounts.

On the other hand, the microplanner is not obligated by this aggregate consistency constraint since he views the world in strictly partial equilibrium

---

* Computation for this paper was carried out under the direction of Adriana Francos on an IBM computer 360 at the Empresa de Computacion del Estado (EMCO). The authors wish to thank the supporting organizations for their help, while at the time emphasizing that this paper does not necessarily reflect the viewpoints of these organizations.

terms. The microeconomic data is usually collected in the market economy. The analysis is often developed in terms of cost and benefit studies at the level of the firm. Project analysis may incorporate average costs generalized to give industry supply and demand schedules by adding together sample data drawn from the firm. Seldom would raw material or factor supplies be considered inelastic for a given project. Therefore, the microplanner frequently does not concern himself with indirect effects of the project on other costs and resource uses.

The decision unit for the microplanner traditionally has been the project. The desire to rank projects according to a variety of investment criteria and to implement as many as can be financed within some global budget constraint has caused this planning process to be called 'bottom-up' planning.[1] On the other hand, the macroplanner with his concern for balanced programs of sectoral investment and the most efficient use of resources among all alternative allocations has been described as a 'top-down' planner. The conflicting assumptions, data requirements and applications of the two methods has led to considerable debate as to which approach is more appropriate for development planning.

As a result of the debate over the 'project approach' as compared to the 'macromodels approach' both the micro and macroplanners have been forced to compromise their initial positions and incorporate aspects of the other's approach in their analytical technique. It has forced macroplanners to decompose their aggregates to account for nonhomogeneous factors, nonsubstitutable import supplies and a variety of other sectorally differentiable phenomena. Economies of scale and externalities which are given important consideration by microeconomists now receive much greater attention in the development of new macroeconomic methods.

As a result of the same controversy we find that as microplanners have perfected cost-benefit analysis they have become preoccupied with the measurement of indirect effects. These may be imputed now to individual projects although never with a satisfactory method for the evaluation and assignment of indirect effects among interdependent projects where economies of scale and externalities may be important.[2] General equilibrium results from macro-

---

[1] See A.R. Prest and R. Turvey, 'Cost-benefit analysis: a survey', *Economic Journal*, December 1965, pp. 683–735, and United Nations, *Manual de proyectos de desarrollo económico*, New York 1958, for a description of techniques of cost-benefit analysis and other partial equilibrium methods used in the evaluation of projects. The theory underlying cost-benefit analysis is found in E.J. Mishan, *Cost-benefit analysis*, (Praeger, 1971).
[2] The influence of Chenery has been important in this respect; 'Interdependence of investment decisions', in: M. Abramoritz et al., *Allocation of economic resources* (Stanford University Press, Stanford, 1959).

econometric studies have also led planners to give greater emphasis to the divergence between private and social costs and benefits which should be imputed to the project. Thus project evaluation now employs shadow prices for factors and particularly scarce goods, both on welfare grounds and to reflect real resource scarcities.[3]

Both approaches to project analysis have tended to converge rapidly. Microplanners now use inverse input—output coefficients to measure indirect effects (calling them backward and forward linkages) and highly aggregate models to estimate a single 'representative' shadow price for a homogeneous factor such as capital, labor or foreign exchange.[4] Similarly, as computer systems have become faster and capable of handling larger quantities of data, the macroplanner has begun experimenting with highly disaggregated general equilibrium models. Optimizing systems allow for the specification of a variety of welfare goals and economic targets to be maximized as part of the test of macroeconomic consistency. Choices between production or imports, between export promotion or import substitution, among alternative techniques, among alternative resource allocations, and between different time profiles of consumption and saving enter the models. Regional models permit the selection and location of projects to minimize transport costs while taking advantage of the special disparities in resource supply and mobility. Single-valued scarcity prices for aggregates have given way to vectors of shadow prices for many subclassifications of goods and factors (for example, various skills of labor, patterns of import use, or capital capacities) which change over time to reflect variations in resource availability.

Dynamic models furnish estimates of the time paths of the shadow prices associated with these nonhomogeneous, multisectoral factor constraints. This technique is more sensitive to intertemporal questions of project phasing and resource exploitation than is the standard procedure of discounting as employed in project analysis.[5] The time pattern of allocations and shadow prices taken

[3] A method for the microeconomic estimation of the principal shadow prices used in project analysis can be found in Papanek and Qureshi [ref. 156]. In recent years cost-benefit methods have been revised to include more of the focus of macroeconomic programming. The works of Little and Mirrlees [ref. 128] and especially Marglin in *Public Investment Criteria* (MIT, Cambridge, Mass., 1968) are based on models of optimization. This has now been formulated as a UNIDO manual, *Guidelines for project evaluation,* U.N. 1972. In the case of Chile, the principal shadow prices have been estimated by partial equilibrium techniques in the studies (found in this book) of foreign exchange by Bacha and Taylor (Chapter 1), for capital by Bitar and Trivelli (Chapter 5), and for labor by Seton (Chapter 3).
[4] An example of this type of estimation is found in Taylor (Chapter 6) in this book.
[5] For other aspects of discounting see Chapter 2 of this book.

from a macroeconomic programming model's solution is a function of the set of sectors operating in the system and their relative rates of growth. Thus the set of shadow prices derived from a general equilibrium framework is sensitive both to the expected factor availability and to the subset of projects selected by the model from the complete set specified. The more complete is the project set specified, the better will be the measure of the opportunity cost of the factors employed.[6] Consequently, shadow prices are also sensitive to the degree of aggregation found in the model's specification.[7]

Thus, neither the micro nor the macroeconomic technique of project evaluation has proved to be a panacea. Elements of both approaches are important and should be incorporated in the analysis of the other. Only recently has it become possible to bridge the gap between the two types of analysis using programming models whose sectors build up from individual projects. In this study we apply the macroeconomic method to a specific project evaluation, utilizing a static linear programming model.[8] In this manner we demonstrate the possibility of analytical continuity between the microeconomic evaluation of projects and models of macroeconomic consistency. The experiment is made in this case with only one project, but this technique can be applied to a large number of projects simultaneously.[9]

II. Description of the macroeconomic model

The economic feasibility of a cellulose plant will be evaluated in this study using a multisectoral linear programming model.[10] We shall demonstrate the use of a multisectoral model for project selection in a fairly aggregate form (15 sectors, 116 variables, and 104 constraints) in order to simplify the pre-

---

[6] Inefficient projects will raise the shadow price of some resources as demonstrated by Clark, *Planning import substitution* (Amsterdam, North-Holland Publishing Co., 1970) chapter 10, section 1.

[7] See Clark, *ibid.*, chapter 9, section 4.

[8] A good presentation of the continuity between project analysis and aggregate planning using a programming model is provided by Bruno [ref. 33].

[9] See Clark, *ibid.*, for a description of experiments with large numbers of projects selected simultaneously.

[10] Other applications of the same model may be found in Clark and Foxley, 'Target shooting with a multisectoral model', chap. 13 of this book, and in Foxley, 'Structural disequilibria and alternatives for growth in the Chilean economy, 1970–1980', Ph. D. Thesis, University of Wisconsin, February, 1970.

sentation and computation.[11] The model allocates the primary factors of
capital (initial capacity plus domestic savings), foreign exchange and labor
among alternative production activities. The supply of these factors is restricted by an upper limit to the marginal savings rate, an upper limit to the
foreign exchange deficit of the balance of payments, and a minimum percentage of the fixed labor force which must be employed.

Domestic savings is utilized to finance the replacement of depreciated
capacity and capital accumulation as required by different sectors. Net investment depends upon the increment in future sectoral production needed to
satisfy the growth of final demand, the productivity of capital in each sector,
and the gestation period for net investment distinguished both by sector and
by type of capital good. On the other hand, we assume that depreciated capital is always replaced and that the amount of sectoral depreciation is proportional to the capital stock of that sector.

The supply of foreign exchange is equal to the value of exports plus the
balance of payments gap. This foreign exchange is assigned to finance non-
competitive imports (for which there is no domestic substitution permitted
during the period of the study), net factor payments abroad, and competitive
imports. The former are fixed requirements determined as functions of the
change in production, consumption, and sectoral investment. The model does
permit a limited amount of import substitution among competitive imports.
Sectoral supply is not allowed to specialize in trade since competitive imports by sector of origin are restricted to a maximum deviation from the
historical trend of foreign exchange use shown by competitive imports.

Labor is allocated among sectors depending upon the level of sectoral production, labor's productivity in each sector, and the global restriction that
the solution must exceed a minimum unemployment level for the economy
as a whole. The resource allocation of the model is restricted not only by the
total resource availability, by the level and composition of demand, but also
by the interrelationship of the restrictions placed on the sectoral production
and import activities.

The level and composition of demand is determined as a function of expenditure elasticities for private consumption, a fixed proportioned expenditure
pattern for government consumption of goods and services, the range of likely
export levels for each sector (fixed and variable) and the demand for capital
goods which is generated as a function of the requirement for additional

---

[11] The model may of course be disaggregated to any number of sectors. We have also
developed a 36-sector version of the same model. The equations of the model may be
found in the appendix to this chapter.

capacity in each sector of destination. Intermediate demand is generated also as a function of sectoral production levels using input–output coefficients.

The model has some degree of freedom to select activities and to shift activities between upper and lower bounds. This flexibility permits the allocation of resources which is consistent with the efficiency criterion for the whole economic system (maximum social welfare).[12] The model will select the most

Table 1
The structure of production and the activity levels of the cellulose project (in millions of 1965 E^O)

Sectors	Input–output coefficients	Value
1. Agriculture and fishing	0.2301	14.220
2. Copper mining	–	–
3. Other mining	0.0452	2.790
4. Food, clothing, textiles	–	–
5. Wood, paper, furniture	0.0004	0.027
6. Non-metallic mineral products	–	–
7. Basic metals	–	–
8. Chemicals and petroleum	0.1060	2.600
9. Mechanical and metallurgical	0.0245	1.510
10. Construction	–	–
11. Electricity, gas, water	–	–
12. Housing and building rents	0.0004	0.021
13. Transport and communications	0.0550	3.360
14. Education and health	–	–
15. Commerce and services	0.0384	2.440
Total inputs	0.5000	30.968
Value added	0.5000	30.776
Gross value of production	1.0000	61.744
Investment		71.300
National		54.200
Imported		17.100
Exports		61.700
Direct employment		374

Source: Data from ODEPLAN, 'Evaluación económica de proyectos de inversión del sector público', May, 1969, and CADE, 'Estudio de factibilidad de una planta de celulosa sulfato en la provincia de Arauco', June, 1966.

[12] The model gives a consistent and efficient allocation of resources in agreement with the primary factor availability. The parametric variation of the supply of these factors provides an illustration of the sensitivity of the system as demonstrated in ODEPLAN [ref. 150] and in the appendix below, which explains the equation of the programming model.

efficient pattern of supply from all possibility sets that are consistent with the demand generated endogenously. The model is free to select within a restricted range the use of foreign exchange for financing competitive imports. This in turn influences the pattern of import substitution among domestic production activities. Finally, the model also selects when to promote exports within a predetermined set of bounds (minimum and maximum) for the sectoral export activities.

The objective function chosen for maximization subject to the restrictions specified in the model is the terminal year consumption level. Given the structure of the model, this is equivalent to maximizing the rate of growth of GDP. The sectors of the model are listed in table 1. The model is static, providing a solution for the year 1975, taking 1970 as the initial year.

The evaluation of an industrial project within the multisectoral macroeconomic framework is accomplished by introducing into the model a new sector which corresponds to the potential project. The model then has the possibility of selecting the project for incorporation in the solution as a new productive activity or the model may reject the project as an inefficient use of resources (sections III and IV). Since the viability of the project will be influenced by the total availability of resources in the economy and by the price at which the new project's output can be sold, we test the sensitivity of this project evaluation method to both of these conditions (section V).

III. Evaluation of the Arauco cellulose project

The methodology of project evaluation made within the macroeconomic framework is illustrated by the feasibility study of the cellulose plant which has been designed for the Province of Arauco, Chile. The viability of the project will depend in this method not only on the structure of direct and indirect costs assigned to the project but also on the assumptions which have been made about the availability of scarce resources in the economy (domestic savings, foreign exchange, and the labor force). In this section we will evaluate the project assuming that the capacity to generate savings in the economy is maintained at the same level as the traditional tendency (a marginal savings rate of about 0.15) and that the gap in the balance of payments may not exceed E° 298 millions (about $ 92 million in 1965 prices) in the terminal year 1975.

[13] The project data has been assembled from the studies of CADE, 'Estudio de factibilidad de una planta de celulosa sulfato en la Provincia de Arauco', June, 1966, and ODEPLAN, Evaluacion economica de proyectos de inversion del sector publico', May, 1969. Its transformation into parameters of the linear programming model is described in the appendix 2 to Clark et al. [ref. 45].

Table 2
Macroeconomic effects of the project (in millions of 1965 E^O and thousands of workers)

Gross value of production	(1) Without the project	(2) With the project	(3) Difference
1. Agriculture and fishing	4260.7	4261.6	0.9
2. Copper mining	3220.9	3220.9	–
3. Other mining	996.9	996.9	–
4. Food, clothing, textiles	9913.1	9892.0	– 21.1
5. Wood, paper, furniture	3226.5	3222.0	– 4.5
6. Non-metallic mineral products	511.8	510.0	– 1.8
7. Basic metals	785.3	785.3	–
8. Chemicals and petroleum	2803.4	2792.6	– 10.8
9. Mechanical and metallurgical	3209.0	3167.1	– 41.9
10. Construction	2431.6	2442.0	10.4
11. Electricity, gas, water	859.4	859.0	–
12. Housing and building rents	1059.4	1058.7	– 0.7
13. Transport and communications	1954.9	1946.9	– 8.0
14. Education and health	2224.3	2225.3	1.0
15. Commerce and services	9527.2	9549.1	21.9
16. Cellulose project	0.0	62.0	62.0
Gross domestic product:	28468.5	28488.9	20.4
Private consumption	20588.5	20605.7	17.2
Government consumption	2936.0	2936.0	–
Gross investment plus stock accumulation	4598.1	4602.0	3.9
Exports (variable prices)	5165.3	5227.0	61.7
Imports	4819.3	4881.0	61.7
Balance of payments gap	400.0	400.0	–
Domestic savings	4300.1	4303.2	3.1
Marginal savings rate	0.15	0.15	–
Unemployment rate	0.071	0.071	–
Employment	3398.745	3399.890	1.145
Exports of Arauco cellulose	0.0	61.7	61.7

Under these conditions, the project (introduced as a 16th sector in the model with its own cost structure, demand, production capacity, and level of exports)[13] appears as a profitable activity. This is evident because in order to reach an optimum solution the model selects the level of production, exports, employment, and investment for the project corresponding to the specifications of the cellulose plant found in the consultant feasibility study. These are set forth in table 1.

Without analyzing completely the project investment criteria of the model (this will be developed in section IV of this study), it is interesting to observe the impact that the project in question will have upon the overall behaviour of the economy. The multisectoral model is a consistent representation of the economy within which the new project has been inserted. In table 2 are shown the levels which will be achieved by the principal macroeconomic variables if the project is not implemented (column 1), if the project is carried out (column 2) and the project's impact as revealed by the difference between both of these situations (column 3).

Although the variations do not appear to be extraordinarily significant since the project has been tried at the medium scale design, there are some interesting conclusions that may be drawn from the comparison. In the first place, it may be observed that the project's implementation implies a growth in the output of three sectors: commerce and services; construction; and agriculture (especially the first). The reason is simple: the project generates a derived demand for inputs of commerce and service, of construction, and of forest products which cause these sectors to expand to a greater extent than they would without the project.

More interesting than these points, however, is to observe that the realization of the project implies a reduction in the output of other sectors: food and textiles, chemicals, and metallurgical products representing the most important. In an economy where there are limited amounts of resources (internal savings and foreign exchange) which may be utilized in a variety of alternative activities, we find that a new project calls for resource *shifts*, not simply a net addition to gross output. At the margin allocating resources to the cellulose project implies necessarily a reduction in alternative uses of these resources. Some of the resources which would otherwise be employed by sectors 4, 8 and 9 are transferred for use in the new project. In spite of these reductions, the project provides a better alternative allocation of resources since the model by selecting the project is able to raise the value of its objective function, consumption and gross domestic product.

The total (direct and indirect) change in employment resulting from the project's implementation would be an increase of 1,145 persons. Against this we must note that the direct employment effect of the project is only 374 persons. The remainder are generated principally in the agricultural sector (forestry), in construction and in the special services required as inputs to the project. The total employment shift attributable to the project is precisely the type of indirect effect which is so difficult to quantify in microeconomic studies of project feasibility.

Finally, it can be observed that the project increases the capacity to import in the economy by E^0 61.7 million (in 1965 prices). This can be explained since the project we are testing happens to export 100% of its product. The use of the new foreign exchange generated by the project has an effect on the structure of supply which also explains in part the changes observed in the pattern of domestic production. The project could equally well have been one of import substitution which would have freed (as a direct consequence of the project) an amount of foreign exchange equivalent to the imports being replaced by the project's new domestic production. However, without a model permitting the selection of both export expansion and import substitution it would be difficult to judge which would be the least cost strategy to conserve foreign exchange while simultaneously encouraging the maximum growth of gross domestic product and personal consumption.

IV. Criteria for selecting a project as evaluated within the framework of a multisectoral programming model

In the programming model there is an implicit criterion for investment which is very similar to those found in the literature of microeconomic analysis. The model compares the social costs with the social benefits derived from each activity.[14] The benefits must always be greater or equal to the costs if an activity is to be chosen for implementation. These activities will be called profitable or viable since they represent an efficient use of resources. The feasibility of each activity can be measured in two different forms: (1) by means of the valuation of all inputs and outputs at their shadow prices as determined by the dual solution of the programming model (defined the 'direct analysis of inputs'), and (2) by means of the valuation of the total primary resource requirements, both direct and indirect, at the shadow prices of these factors (called the 'total analysis of primary factors').

In these two approaches, the shadow price of each product can be interpreted as the value which is required in order to cover the total direct and indirect input costs when valued at their shadow prices (the shadow prices which are consistent with the specification of the activities in the linear program) or as the value of the total direct and indirect primary resources utilized

---

[14] A detailed description of the selection process in programming models can be found in Clark, 'Experimentaciones con la estructura de los modelos de insumo-producto y programacion', ODEPLAN, Santiago, June, 1970, or the appendix to Clark, *Planning import substitution* (Amsterdam, North-Holland Publishing Co., 1970).

Table 3
Evaluation of the profitability of the cellulose project (sector 16) (measured in terms of consumption units)

	Production				Net investment			
	(1) Complete term	(2) Shadow price	(3) Parameter of model	(4) Total value	(5) Complete term	(6) Shadow price	(7) Parameter of model	(8) Total value
1	P_p	1.24966	1.00000	1.24966	P_p^C	0.49892	1.00000	0.49892
2	$P_p k_p^S S_p$	1.17840	-0.00456	-0.00537	$P_9 k_9^I B_{9,p}$	0.99303	-0.01963	-0.01949
3	$P_3 a_{3,p}$	0.98808	-0.04520	-0.04466	$P_{10} k_{10}^I B_{10,p}$	0.72826	-0.25037	-0.18233
4	$P_1 a_{1,p}$	1.52989	-0.23050	-0.35264	$P_9^M \tilde{m}_9 k_9 B_{9,p}$	0.19895	-0.01580	-0.00314
5	$P_8 a_{8,p}$	1.08281	-0.10600	-0.11478	$P_{10}^M \tilde{m}_{10} k_{10}^I B_{10,p}$	1.30033	-0.02480	-0.03226
6	$P_9 a_{9,p}$	0.99303	-0.02450	-0.02433	$P^A k_p^I$	-1.14030	-0.27000	-0.30788
7	$P_{12} a_{12,p}$	4.45072	-0.00040	-0.00178	$P^{PGB} k_p^I$	0.17104	0.27000	0.04618
8	$P_{13} a_{13,p}$	2.58071	-0.01950	-0.05032	π			0.00000
9	$P_{15} a_{15,p}$	0.88839	-0.00540	-0.00480				
10	$P_p^C b_p$	0.49892	-1.15537	-0.57644				
11	$P_p^R r_p$	1.91694	-0.02700	-0.05176				
12	$P_{13}^M \tilde{m}_{13,p}^A$	-0.55213	-0.03550	-0.01960				
13	$P_{15}^M \tilde{m}_{15,p}^A$	1.14021	-0.03300	-0.03763				
14	$P^E I_p$	0.0	-0.00606	0.00000				
15	$P^A k_p^S s_p$	-1.14030	0.00456	-0.00520				
16	$P^{PGB} k_p^S s_p$	0.17104	0.00456	0.00078				
17	π_p			0.00000				

Table 3 (continued)
Evaluation of the profitability of the cellulose project (sector 16) (measured in terms of consumption units)

	Replacement				Exportation			
	(9) Complete term	(10) Shadow price	(11) Parameter of model	(12) Total value	(13) Complete term	(14) Shadow price	(15) Parameter of model	(16) Total value
1	P_p^r	1.91694	1.00000	1.91694	P_p	1.24966	-1.00000	-1.24966
2	$P_1 B_{1,p}$	1.52989	-0.00190	-0.00291	$P^F f_p$	2.50035	1.00000	2.50035
3	$P_9 B_{9,p}$	0.99303	-0.13100	-0.13008	$P^{GDP} f_p$	0.17104	1.00000	0.17104
4	$P_{10} B_{10,p}$	0.72826	-0.86710	-0.63147	$P^S f_p$	1.14030	-1.00000	-1.14030
5	$P_9^M \tilde{m}_9 B_{9,p}$	0.19895	-0.11786	-0.02345	π			0.28143
6	$P_{10}^M \tilde{m}_{10} B_{10,p}$	1.30033	-0.12287	-0.15977				
7	P^A	-1.14030	1.00000	-1.14030				
8	P^{PGB}	0.17104	1.00000	0.17104				
9	π			0.00000				

in the production of the good, also valued at their shadow prices. In almost all solutions of models for the Chilean economy we find unemployed labor existing in the economy which results in a shadow price of zero for this factor. Therefore, with this specification there remain only two primary factors which are scarce in the economy: (1) foreign exchange, which is obtained from exports and from the inflow of foreign capital, and (2) domestic savings which are required to finance capacity expansion or replacement of depreciated capital.[15]

This study will present only the analysis of the direct use of inputs because this presentation will follow most closely the specification of costs as are normally found in the microeconomic analysis of project feasibility.[16]

Table 3 shows the social profitability of each of the activities associated with the selection of the cellulose project. Given that the only demand for the output of this project will be export sales; a project of this type does not represent a potential import substitution and there exists no possibility of competitive import supply. Therefore, if the exportation of cellulose is efficient there would be a joint decision to invest, to replace capital, to produce cellulose domestically, as well as to export it. These four activities must simultaneously be socially profitable if the project is to be implemented.

The first four columns of table 3 set forth the components of the calculation of the viability of the cellulose production activity which can be expressed in the following manner:

$$\pi_p = P_p - \sum_i P_i a_{ip} - \sum_i P_i^f f_{ip}, \tag{1}$$

where π_p = social profitability of project p, P_p = shadow price of output from project p (i.e., the social benefit of project p), P_i = shadow price of ith good, a_{ip} = input–output coefficient of the ith good utilized in project p, P_i^f = shadow price of all other inputs used directly in the production of project p (normally primary factors), and f_{ip} = input coefficients of factors and other inputs of project p.

---

[15] The 'analysis of total primary factors' depends upon the coefficients estimated for the use of the primary resources in each activity. These may be estimated by calculating import coefficients, sectoral capital coefficients, and sectoral labor productivity. These coefficients represent the rate at which the three primary factors are employed and are expressed as rows in the matrix of production inputs. The inverse of this modified transactions matrix provides sectoral coefficients for the total use of foreign exchange, capital and labor, respectively.

[16] See the study of A. Castillo and A. Vasquez as the microeconomic counterpart to the evaluation of the Arauco Cellulose Project; 'Evaluación de los proyectos de celulosa', ODEPLAN, mimeo.

The social profitable of project p is evaluated as the difference between the shadow price of the output from this project (the social benefit attributed to the project) and the sum of the direct intermediate inputs valued at their shadow prices and all other direct inputs of factors valued at their opportunity costs. The analysis of the direct inputs is a valuation of the project's production function where all intermediate inputs (rows 3–9 of table 3) and direct factor inputs (row 2 and 10–16) are measured in terms of their opportunity cost. Among the direct factor costs are included: the cost of capital used for productive capacity (row 10), replacement of capital (row 11), and the cost of stock accumulation (rows 2, 15 and 16 combined); the cost of foreign exchange associated with the fixed requirements for noncompetitive imports (rows 12 and 13); and the cost of labor (row 14).

The first column of table 3 gives the algebraic notation of all terms required to calculate the social profitability of the production activity. In column 2 appears the value of each of the shadow prices associated with a binding constraint. In column 3 is given the parameter values of the input coefficients for the production function. Finally, in column 4 there appears the scarcity value of each of the inputs valued as the product of the input coefficient times its respective shadow price. The social profitability of the production activity appears below column 4 and is the difference between the shadow price of cellulose production and the sum of the production costs of the cellulose project where the shadow prices reflect the direct and indirect resource costs of the factors and inputs embodied in the production.

In an economy where resources can be moved freely among alternative employments, the shadow price will reflect the opportunity cost of all alternative uses of the resources both real and potential such that the profitability of all activities chosen by the model will be reduced to zero. Any project showing positive profits would be substituted by the simplex algorithm of the linear program for a project already with zero profits. An optimum set of projects is reached when there are no projects with positive profits left outside the optimal basis. This fact will be taken as a criterion determining when an activity should be chosen as efficient.

Table 3 also contains the evaluation of the social profitability of the net investment, replacement investment, and export promotion activities. As was pointed out previously, all of the activities associated with the cellulose project must be simultaneously efficient. This condition is required only when there are no imports of cellulose because exports are the single unique source of demand for the product in question. That is, if the good were already being produced domestically or could be supplied as a competitive import, then the activities related to (tied together) by the shadow price of the good might be partially independent. So long as there are alternative sources of supply, a subset of activities involving the good being produced by the project may be selected without the others. However, in the case of an export project, the social evaluation of the product may be thought of as the true resource cost of producing foreign exchange. This cost must be equal to or less than the net benefits derived from the expansion of exports (as shown in the last four columns of table 3).

The criterion used to measure the efficiency of export promotion for a given product may be expressed in the following manner:

$$(1/d_p)P_p \lessgtr (P^F + P^{GDP} - P^S)f_p, \tag{2}$$

where $1/d_p$ = one over one plus the 'drawback rate' for the export subsidy to project p, P_p = shadow price for the output of project p, P^F = shadow price of foreign exchange, P^{GDP} = shadow price of gross domestic product, P^S = shadow price of domestic savings, and f_p = parameter simulating the effect of the international price elasticity of cellulose exports upon the foreign exchange revenue function of the economy.[17]

The expansion of exports will be efficient whenever the price of the good to be exported when depreciated by the drawback coefficient is less than or equal to the sum of the prices of foreign exchange and gross domestic product minus the price of domestic savings (assuming f_p = 1). This rule of thumb may be explained as comparing the opportunity cost of the factors needed to produce the new exports with the potential benefits to the economy that would be derived from additional exports. The opportunity cost is implicit in the price of the good which reflects the direct and indirect costs of its production, including all primary factor inputs as well as imported and domestically produced raw materials. Similarly, the export activity represents a production function for the supply of foreign exchange. It will be efficient to produce foreign exchange whenever the shadow price of the potential export is less than or equal to the net benefits derived by producing the extra foreign exchange. For example, the benefits derived by producing more GDP represent an indirect benefit because each unit of GDP will be saved in proportion to the marginal savings rate and therefore reduce the capital costs of the system (as reflected in the shadow price of savings).

---

[17] f_p may be interpreted as a function of the price elasticity of the export. See for example Foxley and Clark's study of Chilean copper, 'Social profitability of future expansions of Chilean copper production', in: R.S. Eckaus and P.N. Rosenstein-Rodan (eds.) *Sectoral studies of trade and growth for the Chilean economy* (Cambridge, Mass., MIT, 1971), or as the direct revenue effect resulting from the need to sell abroad at a price less than the domestic unit value.

The calculation of the net benefits resulting from the exportation of cellulose can be observed in table 3. In this example, the international price and
the internal price are set equal because the project has been given no subsidy
(that is, the drawback rate is zero, d_p = 1.0). In this case the cost of production is given by the shadow price of the project's output and is equal to 1.24966.
The benefits derived from the greater availability of foreign exchange are
equal to 2.50035; the benefit derived from GDP is 0.14104. The savings required to expand capacity in order to produce this extra amount of foreign
exchange are valued at a shadow price equal to 1.14030. Therefore, the net
benefits derived from the expansion of these exports is equal to 1.53109.
The difference between the cost of a unit of a foreign exchange produced
by this activity (that is, 1.24966) and the net benefits (1.53109) is 0.28143.
The model selects to include this project in its solution because the benefits
derived from additional foreign exchange outweigh the costs represented
by this project. Positive profits remain and are not reduced to zero because
the export activity has an upper bound equal to the planned level of output
for the Arauco plant.

V. Sensitivity of the evaluation method to changes in the availability of total resources and in the international price of cellulose

The analysis in sect. III has referred to an evaluation of the cellulose project under a particular set of macroeconomic assumptions. We have supposed
that the maximum achievable marginal rate of saving for the country would
be equal to 0.15 and that there would be an upper limit on the net flow of
external resources available to Chile equivalent to 92 million dollars in the
terminal year, 1975. We have also supposed that the price of cellulose in
the world market would be sufficient to cover the Chilean costs of production
without requiring an export subsidy.[18]

All of the macroeconomic conditions set forth above are estimates subject
to variation. It is convenient therefore to examine in what form the feasibility
of the project would be affected by changes in these conditions. First we will
analyze the effect of changes in the total amount of external resources available and then in the capacity of the country to raise domestic savings. Finally,
we shall examine the effect on the feasibility of the project which a more
competitive international price would induce.

[18] See the projections made by CADE, op. cit. of the range of possible world prices.

A. Changes in the supply of foreign capital and domestic saving

The project selection criterion implicit in the model will be sensitive to the availability of foreign exchange and domestic savings. Factor supplies will affect the viability of the project by means of altering their shadow prices. If foreign exchange were to be more abundant, for example, its shadow price would lower and the profitability of the export project would decrease. On the other hand, increased savings would result in a more profitable export project because the unit cost of savings would be reduced. Likewise the profitability would be reduced if savings were scarcer and increased if the supply of foreign exchange were more limited. The export project is a special case where the price of foreign exchange is taken as a benefit derived from the project, the import cost of production having already been counted as a cost (pushing up the shadow price of foreign exchange) in the production activity.

Experiments to measure the sensitivity of the project selection with respect to changes in the resource availability can be made by parametric variation of the external debt (F) maintaining the marginal savings rate constant at 0.15. We shall vary the foreign debt between 0 and E^o 2,000 million as measured in 1965 prices. Throughout this range the model continues to select the project. Thus the profitability of the export activity for this project is always positive throughout a very broad range of foreign capital inflow.

Table 4
The sensitivity of the project and factor shadow prices to changes in the supply of foreign exchange

Specification	(1) p^F	(2) p^{GDP}	(3) p^S	(4) $p^F + p^{GDP} - p^S$	(5) Price of project	(6) Value of exportation
$F = 2000.0$, $\Delta S/\Delta Y = 0.15$, $C = 24464.2$	2.278	0.135	0.900	1.513	↑ 1.061	61.7
$F = 1648.9$, $\Delta S/\Delta Y = 0.15$, $C = 23664.2$	2.300	0.136	0.906	1.530	↑ 1.070	61.7
$F = 1647.2$, $\Delta S/\Delta Y = 0.15$, $C = 23660.5$	2.407	0.141	0.941	1.607	↑ 1.117	61.7
$F = 1170.6$, $\Delta S/\Delta Y = 0.15$, $C = 22513.5$	2.414	0.143	0.956	1.601	↑ 1.122	61.7
$F = 1146.6$, $\Delta S/\Delta Y = 0.15$, $C = 22455.6$	2.439	0.151	1.009	1.581	↑ 1.138	61.7
$F = 798.3$, $\Delta S/\Delta Y = 0.15$, $C = 21606.1$	2.500	0.171	1.140	1.531	↑ 1.178	61.7
$F = 394.4$, $\Delta S/\Delta Y = 0.15$, $C = 20596.1$	2.502	0.171	1.143	1.530	↑ 1.179	61.7
$F = 377.8$, $\Delta S/\Delta Y = 0.15$, $C = 20554.7$	2.514	0.174	1.161	1.528	↑ 1.179	61.7
$F = 229.1$, $\Delta S/\Delta Y = 0.15$, $C = 20180.7$	2.560	0.184	1.227	1.517	↑ 1.183	61.7
$F = 99.6$, $\Delta S/\Delta Y = 0.15$, $C = 19849.3$	2.586	0.189	1.258	1.517	↑ 1.199	61.7

F = External gap in the balance of payments, $\Delta S/\Delta Y$ = Marginal savings rate, C = Personal consumption in millions of escudos.

Table 5
The sensitivity of the project and sectoral shadow prices with respect to changes in the marginal savings rate ($\Delta S/\Delta Y$)

Specification	(1) p^F	(2) $pGDP$	(3) p^S	(4) $\frac{p^F + pGDP}{-p^S}$	(5) P_1	(6) P_2	(7) P_3	(8) P_4
$F = 0$, $\Delta S/\Delta Y = 0.0000$, $C = 18818.4$	2.581	0.000	1.459	1.122	↓ 1.672	↓ 1.323	↑ 0.655	↓ 1.223
$F = 0$, $\Delta S/\Delta Y = 0.0038$, $C = 18836.5$	2.479	0.005	1.319	1.165	↓ 1.580	↓ 1.272	↑ 0.741	↕ 1.165
$F = 0$, $\Delta S/\Delta Y = 0.0163$, $C = 18892.5$	2.496	0.022	1.326	1.192	↓ 1.585	↓ 1.282	↑ 0.771	↑ 1.171
$F = 0$, $\Delta S/\Delta Y = 0.0273$, $C = 18942.8$	2.534	0.037	1.361	1.210	↓ 1.609	↓ 1.301	↑ 0.782	↑ 1.188
$F = 0$, $\Delta S/\Delta Y = 0.0514$, $C = 19063.7$	2.579	0.071	1.388	1.262	↓ 1.629	↓ 1.324	↑ 0.836	↑ 1.206
$F = 0$, $\Delta S/\Delta Y = 0.0559$, $C = 19087.1$	2.523	0.073	1.307	1.289	↓ 1.585	↕ 1.289	↑ 0.832	↑ 1.177
$F = 0$, $\Delta S/\Delta Y = 0.0992$, $C = 19322.9$	2.517	0.123	1.242	1.398	↓ 1.567	↑ 1.273	↑ 0.862	↑ 1.167
$F = 0$, $\Delta S/\Delta Y = 0.1804$, $C = 19786.1$	2.627	0.227	1.258	1.596	↓ 1.604	↑ 1.337	↑ 1.035	↑ 1.208
$F = 0$, $\Delta S/\Delta Y = 0.1977$, $C = 19903.8$	2.685	0.257	1.300	1.642	↑ 1.642	↑ 1.367	↑ 1.061	↑ 1.236
$F = 0$, $\Delta S/\Delta Y = 0.1995$, $C = 19916.7$	2.690	0.260	1.303	1.647	↑ 1.646	↑ 1.369	↑ 1.063	↑ 1.239
$F = 0$, $\Delta S/\Delta Y = 0.2158$, $C = 20037.4$	2.664	0.258	1.195	1.727	↑ 1.572	↑ 1.362	↑ 1.044	↑ 1.197
$F = 0$, $\Delta S/\Delta Y = 0.2385$, $C = 20202.5$	2.715	0.286	1.201	1.801	↑ 1.577	↑ 1.391	↑ 1.060	↑ 1.208
$F = 0$, $\Delta S/\Delta Y = 0.2400$, $C = 20213.2$	2.708	0.284	1.183	1.809	↑ 1.565	↑ 1.388	↑ 1.056	↑ 1.200
$F = 0$, $\Delta S/\Delta Y = 0.3285$, $C = 21065.3$	2.398	0.306	0.931	1.773	↕ 1.773	↑ 1.273	↑ 1.151	↑ 1.296
$F = 0$, $\Delta S/\Delta Y = 0.3302$, $C = 21078.6$	2.388	0.305	0.923	1.770	↓ 1.775	↑ 1.269	↑ 1.149	↑ 1.296
$F = 0$, $\Delta S/\Delta Y = 0.3305$, $C = 21080.5$	1.413	0.053	0.160	1.306	↓ 1.698	↑ 0.828	↑ 0.858	↑ 1.157
$F = 0$, $\Delta S/\Delta Y = 0.3317$, $C = 21082.1$	1.208	0.000	0.000	1.208	↓ 1.681	↑ 0.735	↑ 0.797	↑ 1.128

F = External gap in the balance of payments, $\Delta S/\Delta Y$ = Marginal savings rate, C = Personal consumption in millions of escudos.

Table 5 (continued)

The sensitivity of the project and sectoral shadow prices with respect to changes in the marginal savings rate ($\Delta S/\Delta Y$)

Specification	(9) P_5	(10) P_6	(11) P_7	(12) P_8	(13) P_9	(14) Project P_p	E_p
$F = 0$, $\Delta S/\Delta Y = 0.0000$, $C = 18818.4$	↓1.230	↑0.665	↑0.850	↑1.032	↑0.647	↕1.122	0
$F = 0$, $\Delta S/\Delta Y = 0.0038$, $C = 18836.5$	↓1.184	↑0.748	↑0.837	↑1.007	↑0.728	↕1.165	0
$F = 0$, $\Delta S/\Delta Y = 0.0163$, $C = 18892.5$	↕1.192	↑0.777	↑0.848	↑1.018	↑0.756	↕1.192	0
$F = 0$, $\Delta S/\Delta Y = 0.0273$, $C = 18942.8$	↕1.210	↑0.788	↑0.861	↑1.034	↑0.768	↑1.210	61.7
$F = 0$, $\Delta S/\Delta Y = 0.0514$, $C = 19063.7$	↑1.232	↑0.840	↑0.883	↑1.058	↑0.819	↑1.230	61.7
$F = 0$, $\Delta S/\Delta Y = 0.0559$, $C = 19087.1$	↑1.213	↑0.836	↑0.880	↑1.047	↑0.814	↑1.192	61.7
$F = 0$, $\Delta S/\Delta Y = 0.0992$, $C = 19322.9$	↑1.227	↑0.863	↑0.911	↑1.069	↑0.841	↑1.165	61.7
$F = 0$, $\Delta S/\Delta Y = 0.1804$, $C = 19786.1$	↑1.282	↕1.596	↑1.094	↑1.135	↑1.040	↑1.232	61.7
$F = 0$, $\Delta S/\Delta Y = 0.1977$, $C = 19903.8$	↑1.312	↓1.788	↑1.120	↑1.162	↑1.066	↑1.264	61.7
$F = 0$, $\Delta S/\Delta Y = 0.1995$, $C = 19916.7$	↑1.315	↓1.819	↑1.123	↑1.165	↑1.068	↑1.268	61.7
$F = 0$, $\Delta S/\Delta Y = 0.2158$, $C = 20037.4$	↑1.306	↓1.777	↕1.727	↑1.143	↑1.140	↑1.243	61.7
$F = 0$, $\Delta S/\Delta Y = 0.2385$, $C = 20202.5$	↑1.332	↕1.801	↓2.023	↑1.160	↑1.197	↑1.262	61.7
$F = 0$, $\Delta S/\Delta Y = 0.2400$, $C = 20213.2$	↑1.329	↑1.793	↓2.095	↑1.155	↑1.204	↑1.257	61.7
$F = 0$, $\Delta S/\Delta Y = 0.3285$, $C = 21065.3$	↑1.321	↑1.697	↓1.953	↑1.141	↑1.189	↑1.190	61.7
$F = 0$, $\Delta S/\Delta Y = 0.3302$, $C = 21078.6$	↑1.320	↑1.692	↓1.947	↑1.139	↑1.188	↑1.187	61.7
$F = 0$, $\Delta S/\Delta Y = 0.3305$, $C = 21080.5$	↑1.026	↑1.169	↕1.306	↑0.858	↑0.910	↑0.823	61.7
$F = 0$, $\Delta S/\Delta Y = 0.3317$, $C = 21082.1$	↑0.965	↑1.059	↑1.171	↑0.799	↑0.852	↑0.747	61.7

F = External gap in the balance of payments, $\Delta S/\Delta Y$ = Marginal savings rate, C = Personal consumption in millions of escudos.

The results of this parametric variation are shown in table 4, where we see that for all values of F examined the net benefits of the export of cellulose (column 4) are greater than the shadow price of the good (the cost of production as shown in column 5). So long as the price of the primary factors embodied in the project is less than the net benefits derived from the export of cellulose, the project will continue to be selected at its rated export level of E^{o} 61.7 million. The different levels of foreign capital (F) shown in the column headed 'Specification' represent the levels of foreign capital at which other activities enter or leave the optimal basis (activities other than the project under consideration). Other types of export activities move from their upper limit to a lower limit in this range of F but the viability of the cellulose project is not affected.

The parametric variation of the marginal savings rate maintaining F constant at a value of 0 shows that the project is profitable under almost all conditions. We can see in table 5 that the project remains feasible when all resources are considered very scarce (the deficit in the balance of payments is zero, and when the marginal savings rate is greater than or equal to 0.027). It is only when the marginal savings rate falls below or equals 0.027 that the model no longer selects the cellulose project for export promotion. The last column of table 5 shows a zero export level for the project which occurs when the net benefits of the marginal export activity are equal to the cost of production of cellulose (column 4 minus column 14 are equal to zero).

Another interesting aspect of the parametric analysis is that it permits one to determine a priority among export projects from other sectors. Since the cellulose project is oriented exclusively for exportation we were able to compare the cellulose export activity with export activities from other sectors. This comparison gives a ranking of export activities relative to the availability of internal resources (domestic savings).[19] The model will select export activity according to their resource cost for increasing the supply of foreign exchange. The model therefore elects to run certain export activities at their upper limit and others at their lower limit depending upon the availability of savings and the growth of gross domestic product as well as the overall supply of foreign exchange. It is useful to evaluate the sensitivity of the cellulose project in the same context.

[19] When internal savings are scarce, internal demand grows slowly because income increases at a very low rate. As the model begins with a certain installed capacity in each of the sectors, there is a tendency to export in those sectors where excess capacity exists because these exports do not require the direct cost of net investment. This condition prevails in sectors such as nonmetallic minerals (sector 6) and basic metals (sector 7). The marginal cost of earning foreign exchange by using excess capacity is considerably less than the case where new capacity must be installed to promote exports.

In table 5 the production costs of each of the sectors (P_1 for sector 1, P_2 for sector 2, etc.) are compared with the net benefits ($P^F + P^{GDP} - P^S$) from the marginal generation of foreign exchange by additional exports. The direction of the arrows shown in table 5 indicate if the export is at an upper limit (↑), at a lower limit (↓), or in between the two limits (↕). As can be seen in the first row of table 5, the exports of other mining (sector 3), chemical industries (sector 8), basic metals (sector 7), nonmetallic minerals (sector 6), and metallurgical and mechanical industries (sector 9), are all at the upper limit when the marginal savings rate is close to zero. Of these, the exports of non-metallic mineral products and basic metals are viable only because at the lower level of savings there is a high degree of excess capacity in these sectors and exporting to gain foreign exchange is a socially productive form of utilizing this capacity. In the other sectors (3, 8 and 9) the profitability of the exports is maintained regardless of the amount of savings available; they are always at their maximum value.[20]

By raising the marginal rate of saving, we find that the exports of the traditional industry such as food and clothing (sector 4) are made profitable (beginning at a marginal savings rate equal to 0.0163), followed by the cellulose project (beginning with a marginal savings rate equal to 0.0273) and followed by sector 5, wood, furniture and paper (at the marginal savings rate equal to 0.0514). As the marginal savings rate continues to rise we find that the export of copper moves to an upper limit at approximately a marginal savings rate of 0.10 and later agricultural exports go to an upper limit when the marginal savings rate reaches 0.20.

We ought to emphasize once again before leaving this section that our analysis has not considered the subsidies which are received by exporting industries in some of the industries mentioned above. We have supposed that there is no price differential between internal and external prices. Thus the order in which the activities have become profitable for exportation would have to be altered if the subsidies were explicitly introduced as cost factors in the analysis.

[20] These results must be interpreted with care. The model is evaluating the feasibility of exporting from these sectors supposing that there are no differences between the domestic price and the international price. Thus it is supposed that there is no export subsidy active for all of the products being exported. In reality, the tax drawbacks are important as subsidies. In the industries such as chemicals and mechanical manufactures the subsidies are on the order of 20–30% (see Bacha and Taylor, Chapter 4). To introduce these explicitly into the calculation would show that the exports are no longer profitable and the order in which the exports would be expanded would be different. This would not occur in sector 3 (other mining) because the drawback there is set at zero.

B. Changes in the international price of cellulose

The international price of cellulose has shown significant variation in different markets. The price of bleached cellulose, for example, in the European market is almost 40% lower than that which would obtain in the Latin American market.[21] The preliminary study of the project has supposed a gradual absorption of the cellulose exports by the Latin American market, lowering the proportion sold in Europe to zero. Let us suppose that this change in the market structure cannot be produced. Would the cellulose project still be viable if the production of the project had to be sold principally in Europe?

The expected value of the international price would be important in the final decision regarding the viability of the project. Here we turn the problem around in order to estimate a 'break-even price' for cellulose exports given the opportunity cost of Chilean resources in 1975. The expected international price of cellulose can be introduced into the evaluation by making a parametric variation of f_p (the factor representing the international price effect of cellulose) up to the point at which the activity is no longer profitable. In the model this occurs when the price of cellulose has fallen by 19% from that used for the feasibility study by CADE. The losses which would accrue directly to the project if the price received were greater than 19% below the Chilean costs might be offset by providing a production subsidy (such as the drawback) to the export industry. If the effective price in the world market were to fall below that set forth in the feasibility study (which assumed Chilean sales to protected market of Latin-America), planners could use the macroeconomic model to study over what range of foreign exchange availability and internation price decline would it be efficient to extend subsidies to a potential export project.

VI. Conclusions

This study has demonstrated a procedure for evaluating an industrial project within a macroeconomic framework. The analysis ought to be extended to the evaluation of a large number of projects simultaneously. The technique provides a guide for determining the relative priorities given to the projects that would be consistent with the availability of resources as projected for the period of time during which the projects are being implemented. The macroeconomic model is used in order to: (1) measure the indirect effects of the project; (2) to select that set of projects and sectors which constitute the most efficient use of resources that are likely to be available in the future,

[21] See CADE op. cit., appendix II-J.

that is, Chile's comparative advantage given her resource endowments; (3) to examine the sensitivity of the project evaluation with respect to changes in the expected resource availability, and (4) to evaluate certain requirements of policy consistent with the growth objectives set forth by policy makers. Among the policy instruments that are incorporated in the analysis, special attention has been paid to the role of export subsidies (tax drawbacks) and international price differentials. It is possible to determine the rates of subsidy that would be economically efficient under different projections or world prices.

This has been an experimental study which has utilized information available in Chile's industrial and national economic planning offices (CORFO and ODEPLAN) for project evaluation. The implementation of this method in the future will depend essentially on the capacity to develop a multisectoral model with a greater degree of disaggregation. Large numbers of potential projects can be evaluated simultaneously in a manner that is consistent with the macroeconometric framework being used to allocate resources among competing uses within the rest of the economy. In this sense the opportunity cost of the resources is made explicit endogenously in the project evaluation in a manner only partially realized by microeconometric analysis.

Appendix: Equations and restrictions of the multisector linear programming model

$$X_i + d_i \cdot \tilde{M}_i + d_i \hat{M}_i \geqslant \sum_j a_{ij} \cdot X_j + C_i + G_i + I_i + \Delta S_i + E_i + \sum_j d^M_{15j} \cdot M_j$$

$$(1.0)$$

$$C_i = - \bar{c}_i + y_i C \tag{2.0}$$

$$\sum_i C_i + \bar{c}_d + y_d C = C \tag{2.1}$$

$$G_i = g_i \cdot \bar{G} \tag{3.0}$$

$$I_i = N_i + R_i \tag{4.0}$$

$$N_j \geqslant b_j [X_j \cdot (1 + P_j)_{\theta j} - \bar{X}^0_j \cdot (1 + i_j)_{\theta j}] \tag{4.1}$$

$$N_i = \sum_j k^I_j \cdot B_{ij} \cdot N_j \tag{4.2}$$

$$K^i_j = P_j (1 + P_j)^{\theta j - 1} - (1 + i_j)^{\theta j - t} \tag{4.3}$$

$$R_j = r_j \cdot X_j \tag{4.4}$$

$$R_i = \sum_j B_{ij} \cdot R_j \tag{4.5}$$

$$\Delta S_i = k_i^S [\sum_j (S_j^P + S_j^T) \, \Delta X_j + S_j^T \Delta M_i \,] \tag{4.6}$$

$$\widetilde{M}_i = \sum_j \widetilde{m}_{ij}^A \cdot X_j + \widetilde{m}_i^C \cdot C_i + \widetilde{m}_i^B \cdot I_i + \widetilde{m}_i^G \cdot \overline{G} \tag{5.0}$$

$$V = F + \sum_j f_j E_j - \overline{Y}^E - \sum_j \widetilde{M}_j - \sum_j \overline{e}_j \tag{5.1}$$

$$\hat{M}_i \leqslant \hat{m}_i \cdot V \tag{5.2}$$

$$M_i = \widetilde{M}_i + \hat{M}_i \tag{5.3}$$

$$\overline{E}_{i \, \text{MIN}} \leqslant E_i \leqslant \overline{E}_{i \, \text{MAX}} \tag{6.0}$$

$$\sum_j M_j - F - \sum_j f_j E_j \leqslant -\overline{Y}^E + \overline{E}^T - \sum_j \overline{e}_j \tag{7.0}$$

$$F \leqslant \overline{F} \tag{7.1}$$

$$A = \sum_j k_j^I \cdot N_j + \sum_j R_j + \sum_j k_j^S (S_j^P + S_j^T) \, \Delta X_j$$

$$\sum_j k_j^S \cdot S_j^T \cdot \Delta M_j - F + \overline{E}^T \tag{8.0}$$

$$A - t^N \cdot Y \leqslant \overline{A} - t^N \cdot \overline{Y}^0 \tag{8.1}$$

$$L_j = l_j \cdot X_j \tag{9.0}$$

$$\sum_j L_j \geqslant (1-u)\overline{L} \tag{9.1}$$

$$Y = C + \overline{G} + \sum_j k_j^I \cdot N_j + \sum_j R_j + \sum_j k_j^S (S_j^P + S_j^T) \, \Delta X_j$$

$$+ \sum_j k_j^S \, s_j^T \, \Delta M_j - \sum_j M_j + \sum_j f_j E_j + \bar{E}^T + \sum_j ej \tag{10.0}$$

Max: C (0.0)

Parameters:

a_{ij}	Input–output coefficients for domestic plus imported intermediate goods.
b_j	Average capital = output coefficient in sector b_{ij}.
$\bar{c}_i$	The constant term of the consumption function for expenditure on good i. A rearrangement of the definition of the expenditure elasticity gives the following expression: $\bar{P}\,[\bar{C}_i^0/\bar{P}^0]\,(q_i - 1)$
$\bar{c}_d$	Constant term for the non-worker's expenditure for domestic servants.
d_i	Coefficient of distribution (one plus the tariff plus the commercialization cost) of imports of type i.
$d_{15,j}^M$	Aggregate commercialization coefficient for all imports estimated as a fixed proportion of the total c.i.f. value of imports.
$\bar{e}_i$	Constant term of the linear function approximating the price elastic foreign exchange revenue function for exports of sector i.
f_2, f_i	Marginal coefficient of the foreign exchange revenue function used especially to reflect the effect of a change in the price of copper ($i = 2$) and other new goods (i) exported to new markets (e.g., f_p is used for the cellulose project).
g_i	Fixed proportion government expenditure for goods from sector i (where government expenditures for factor payments – value added – is denoted by $g_g \cdot v_g$).
i_j	Vector of intra-plan rates of growth of production (i.e., in the first years).
k_j^I	Stock-flow conversion factor, as defined by eq. (4.3).
k_i^{IS}	Stock-flow conversion coefficient for the inventory level of national goods in sector i.
l_j	Inverse of the productivity of labor employed in sector j.
$\hat{m}_i$	Distribution coefficient of foreign exchange, among different sectors of origin for competitive imports measured in c.i.f. prices.

$$\sum_i \hat{m}_i > 1.0$$

This allows a certain amount of positive substitution of imports in some sectors, negative in others.

$\widetilde{m}_{ij}^A$ — Technical coefficient of noncompetitive intermediate imports, measured in c.i.f. prices.

$\widetilde{m}_i^B, \widetilde{m}_i^C, \widetilde{m}_i^G$ — Coefficient for noncompetitive imports of capital goods, consumption goods and government expenditure for goods from sector i, measured in c.i.f. prices.

θ_j — Average gestation period (lag) for capital formation by sector j.

p_j — Vector of post-terminal rates of growth of production in sector j.

q_i — Expenditure elasticity per capita (or per family) for goods from sector i.

r_j — Replacement coefficient estimated as a proportion of the gross value of production in each sector j.

r_j' — Reciprocal of the average useful life of the stock of capital in sector j. This parameter implies linear depreciation of the stock of capital assuming that the utilization of installed capacity does not vary much and that depreciated capital is always replaced. In effect one could write:

$$R_j = r_j' \cdot K_j = r_j' \cdot b_j \cdot X_j$$

and therefore $R_j = r_j \cdot X_j$ if $r_j = r_j' \cdot b_j$

s_i^P — Stock to output coefficient of goods in process or finished products from sector i.

s_i^T — Stock to output coefficient of transactions stock held by retailers and wholesalers.

t — Number of years in the plan.

t^N — Maximum marginal savings rate for aggregate national savings.

u — Maximum unemployment rate.

y_d — Marginal propensity to consume domestic services.

y_i — $= q_i \left[\dfrac{\overline{C}_i^0}{\overline{C}^0} \right]$

Endogenous variables:

A	Gross national (internal) savings.
C_i	Private consumption of goods from sector i.
C	Total consumption expenditure in the terminal year.
E_i	Total exports of goods from sector i constrained between the minimum and maximum values.
F	Foreign capital inflow, equal to the deficit on current account of the balance of payments at constant prices.
G_i	Total government consumption expenditure for goods from sector i. Payments to factors (wages, salaries, rent and interest payments) are included in a special sector as G_v.
I_i	Gross investment demand for capital goods of sector i.
L_j	Employment in sector j.
M_i	Total imports, at c.i.f. prices, of goods from sector i.
$\tilde{M}_i$	Non-competitive imports of goods from sector i, at c.i.f. prices ($i = j$).
M_i	Competitive imports at c.i.f. prices.
N_j	Net investment by destination accumulated during the planning period (5 years).
R_j	Replacement investment destined for sector j.
ΔS_i	Change of stocks of national origin for goods of sector i.
V	Balance of foreign exchange remaining after financing the noncompetitive imports, at c.i.f. value.
X_i	Gross value of production in sector i.
ΔX_i	Change in the gross value of production in sector i during the period of the plan.
Y	Gross domestic product in the terminal year in variable prices, i.e., including the effect of variable prices in the foreign sector.

Exogenous variables:

$\bar{A}^0$	Gross national (internal) savings in the initial year.
$\bar{C}^0$	Total consumption expenditure in the initial year.
$\bar{C}_i^0$	Consumption of goods from sector i in the initial year.
$\bar{F}$	Maximal external financing at constant prices in the terminal year.
$\bar{G}$	Total government spending in the terminal year.

$$\bar{G} = \sum_i G_i \ (i = \text{number of sectors plus payment to factors used by}$$

the government).

$\overline{L}$ Available labor force in terminal year.

$\overline{P}$ Population in the terminal year.

$\overline{P}^0$ Population in the initial year.

$\overline{X}_j^0$ Value of production in the base year of sector j.

$\overline{Y}^0$ Gross domestic product in the initial year.

$\overline{Y}_E$ Net remissions (interest, profits) paid abroad.

$\overline{E}^T$ Terms of trade factor.

PART III

SECTORAL STUDIES

R.S. Eckaus, P.N. Rosenstein-Rodan (eds.), Analysis of development problems,
© North-Holland Publishing Company

AGGREGATIVE MARKET RESPONSES IN
DEVELOPING AGRICULTURE:
THE POSTWAR CHILEAN EXPERIENCE *

Jere R. BEHRMAN
University of Pennsylvania, Philadelphia, Penn., U.S.A.

I. Introduction

The assumption that agricultural market responses are very limited is basic
in a broad range of models underlying economic analysis and policy prescriptions for the developing economies. Fixed coefficients are used in most of the
long range planning models and the two-gap models.[1] One of the basic assumptions of the Latin American 'structuralist' school is that agricultural elasticities are very low.[2] The same assumption underlies much of the analysis of the

* The author wishes to thank the supporting organizations for their help while at the
same time emphasizing that this paper in no way necessarily reflects the viewpoints of
these organizations. The author also wishes to thank, but not implicate, Juan de la Barra,
Peter B. Clark, Eduardo García, Jorge García, Arnold Harberger, Ricardo Lira, Jozé
Mencinger, Christían Ossa, Joseph Ramos, and Lance Taylor.

[1] For examples see UNECAFE (United Nations Economic Commission for Asia and the
Far East), *Programming techniques for economic development.* Bangkok, 1960; and
UNCTAD (United Nations Conference on Trade and Development), *Trade prospects and
capital needs of developing countries.* New York, United Nations, 1968 (and Jere R.
Behrman, 'Review article: trade prospects and capital needs of developing countries',
International Economic Review 12 (October, 1971) 519–525.
[2] See Jorge Ahumada, *En vez de la miseria.* Santiago, Editorial del Pacífico, 1958;
Roberto de Oliviera Campos, 'Two views on inflation in Latin-America', in: *Latin-American issues,* ed. by A.O. Hirschman. New York, Twentieth Century Fund, 1961, 69–73;
David Felix, 'Structural imbalances, social conflict and inflation: an appraisal of Chile's
recent anti-inflationary effort', *Economic Development and Cultural Change* 8, no. 2
(January, 1960) 133–147; Joseph Grunwald, 'The 'structuralist' school on price stability
and development: the Chilean case', in: *Latin-American issues, ed.* by Albert O. Hirschman, New York, Twentieth Century Fund, 1961; Dudley Seers, 'A theory of inflation
and growth in underdeveloped countries', *Oxford Economic Papers*, June, 1962, 173–
195; Osvaldo Sunkel, 'Inflation in Chile: an unorthodox approach', *International Economic Papers* 10; and UNECLA (United Nations Economic Commission for Latin America), 'Inflation and growth', unpublished (Santiago, n.d.).

impacts of P.L. 480 disposals, agricultural export taxes, food zones, and food price ceilings.[3]

In recent years this assumption has been subjected to considerable empirical testing primarily in the form of the estimation of the price elasticities of the supplies of a number of individual crops.[4] The conclusion from these studies is that the price elasticities of supplies of individual crops in developing countries generally are significantly non-zero and often are not significantly lower than in more developed economies. This conclusion questions quite directly the assumed lack of supply responses in individual markets in some of the discussions about policies which affect individual markets.[5] But these studies do not provide much evidence about the aggregate agricultural response, which is what is relevant for much of the analysis referred to above since total agricultural real product may remain basically constant even though the composition thereof is changing considerably due to different allocations

---

[3] For example see R.O. Olson, 'The impact and implications of foreign surplus disposal on underdeveloped economies', *The Journal of Farm Economics* 42 (December, 1960) 1042 – 1045.

[4] Many of these studies are summarized in Jere R. Behrman, *Supply response in underdeveloped agriculture: A case study of four major annual crops in Thailand, 1937 – 1963.* Amsterdam, North-Holland Publishing Co., 1968, 1 – 19; and Raj Krishna, 'Agricultural price policy and economic development', in: *Agricultural development and economic growth*, ed. by H.M. Southworth and B.F. Johnston. Ithaca, Cornell University Press, 1967, 497 – 540. More recent studies of supply elasticities of individual crops include Jere R. Behrman, 'Econometric model simulations of the world rubber market, 1950 – 1980', in: *Essays in industrial econometrics*, ed. by L.R. Klein, Vol. III. Philadelphia, Economics Research Unit, University of Pennsylvania, 1969, 1 – 96; Jere R. Behrman, 'Monopolistic cocoa pricing', *American Journal of Agricultural Economics* 50 (August, 1968) 702 – 719; Jere R. Behrman, 'Supply response and the modernization of peasant agriculture: a study of four major crops in Thailand', in: *Subsistence agriculture and economic development*, ed. by C.R. Wharton, Jr. Chicago, Aldine, 1969, 232 – 243; Roberto Echeverria, *Repuesta de los productores agrícolas ante cambios en los precios.* Santiago, ICIRA, 1967; and D. Fitchett, 'The price responsiveness of cereals and potato producers', in: *The economic policy gap and Chilean agricultural development.* Santiago, University of Chile, Institute of Economics and Planning, 1968 (the last two of which are concerned with the Chilean experience). Jere R. Behrman, 'Price elasticity of the marketed surplus of a subsistence crop', *Journal of Farm Economics* 48 (November, 1966), 875 – 893, and Raj Krishna, 'A note on the elasticity of the marketable surplus of a subsistence crop', *the Indian Journal of Agricultural Economics* 57 (July–September, 1962) 79 – 84 also have presented estimates of the elasticities of the marketed surplus (as opposed to total production) of individual crops. John Wise and Pan A. Yotopoulos, 'The empirical content of economic rationality: a text for a less developed economy', *Journal of Political Economy*, 77 (November–December, 1969) 976 – 1004 recently have attempted an overall test of economy efficiency in less developed agriculture.

[5] See the last sentence of the previous paragraph.

of the same factors in response to changing relative agricultural product prices.[6] Studies of the aggregate agricultural market responses in developing economies, however, are practically non-existent.[7] The present study is devoted to an examination of such aggregate responses on the basis of annual data from the postwar Chilean experience.[8] This Chilean experience is of special interest because much of the structuralist argument referred to above was developed in Chile in this period and because the reputed lack of market responses in Chilean agriculture in this period is one of the reasons given for the post-sample period attempts to change the structure of Chilean agriculture. The availability of reasonably consistent estimates of relevant relations for each of eight non-agricultural Chilean sectors,[9] moreover, makes possible cross sectoral comparisons.

For ease of exposition the remainder of this study is divided into five sections. Long and short run market responses are considered separately. In section II the long run responses are considered within the framework both of a

---

[6] M.L. Dantwala, 'International planning to combat the scourge of hunger throughout the world', *Annals of Collective Economy* 34 (January–March, 1963) 87, and W.P. Falcon, 'Real effect of foreign surplus disposal in underdeveloped economies: further comment', *The Quarterly Journal of Economics* 77 (May, 1963) 324, and C.R. Wharton, Jr., 'The issues and a research agenda', in: *Subsistence agriculture and economic development*, ed. by C.R. Wharton, Jr. Chicago, Aldine, 1969, 463 all emphasize this point.

[7] Eduardo García D'Acunia, 'Inflation in Chile: a quantitative analysis', Ph.D. diss., Massachusetts Institute of Technology, 1964, p. 96, has presented several estimates of the Chilean aggregate agricultural supply function to which reference will be made below in the discussion of the short run capacity utilization estimates.

[8] The sample used is for 1945–1965. Comparable data is not available before 1940 and after 1965. The war years were excluded because of the need for lags and because special conditions of the war may have had some impact on the structure. Data sources are given in the appendix.

[9] The sectors are mining, construction, manufacturing, transportation, utilities, housing services, government, and other service. The nonagricultural estimates are presented in Jere R. Behrman, 'Cyclical sectoral capacity utilization in a developing economy', chapter 11 in this volume (hereinafter referred to as Chapter 9); Jere R. Behrman, 'The determinants of the annual rates of change of sectoral money wages in a developing economy', *International Economic Review*, 12 (October, 1971) 431–447, (Spanish version forthcoming in Cuadernos de Economia, (hereinafter referred to as 'Sectoral money wages'); Jere R. Behrman, 'Price determination in an inflationary economy: the dynamics of Chilean inflation revisited', Chapter 14 in this volume (hereinafter referred to as Chapter 14), Jere R. Behrman, 'Sectoral elasticities of substitution between capital and labor in a developing economy: time series analysis in the case of postwar Chile', *Econometrica* (in press) (hereinafter referred to as 'Substitution between capital and labor'); and Jere R. Behrman, 'Sectoral investment determination in a developing economy', *American Economic Review* (in press) (hereinafter referred to as 'Sectoral investment determination').

CES production function for the capacity of agricultural value added and of a neoclassical investment function. In section III the short run utilization of this capacity is explored. Given the evidence of the degree of market response which is presented in these two sections, the logical question then seems to be what are the determinants of price changes in the relevant markets. Therefore, section IV is devoted to an examination of the determination of the rate of change of aggregate agricultural product market price changes, and section V is devoted to an examination of the determination of the rate of change of aggregate agricultural wage rates. Finally, conclusions are presented in section VI.

II. Long run Chilean aggregate agricultural market responses

In this section long run Chilean aggregate agricultual market responses are investigated in two respects. First, some of the coefficients of a CES production function for the capacity of value added are estimated. Second, the coefficients of a neoclassical investment function are estimated.

The dependent variable in the first part of the investigation of long run responses is the capacity of real value added in agriculture. The trend through the peaks method is used to define the capacity levels.[10] The underlying technology is assumed to include fixed coefficients for all intermediate inputs and a CES production function for the capacity of real value added with homogeneity of degree one and with factor augmenting technological change:[11]

$$GDPC = [(E_L L)^{-\rho} + (E_K K)^{-\rho}]^{-\frac{1}{\rho}}, \tag{1}$$

[10] L.R. Klein and R. Summers, *The Wharton index of capacity utilization*. Philadelphia, Economic Research Unit, University of Pennsylvania, 1966. For qualifications in respect to this procedure see Behrman, Chapter 9; Almarin Phillips, 'An appraisal of measures of capacity', *American Economic Review* 53 (May, 1963) 275–292; Almarin Phillips, *Measuring industrial capacity in less developed countries*. Philadelphia, University of Pennsylvania, Department of Economics, 1969; and Robert Summers, 'Further results in the measurement of capacity utilization', *Proceedings of the business and economics section of the American statistical Association* (1968), 25 – 34.

[11] The seminal article on this production function, of course, is K. Arrow et al., 'Capital-labor substitution and economic efficiency', *The Review of Economics and Statistics* 45 (August, 1961) 225 – 250. P.A. David and Th. van de Klundert, 'Biased efficiency growth and capital-labor substitution in the U.S.', *American Economic Review* 55 (June, 1965) 357 – 394, discuss factor augmenting technical change.

Other available estimates of elasticities of substitution generally suffer from this same specification problem.

where $GDPC$ = capacity of real value added, L = secular trend in labor, K = = capital stock (including all non labor primary factors), E_L = level of efficiency of labor (assumed equal to be^{rt}), E_K = level of efficiency of capital (assumed equal to $b'e^{r't}$), and t = time trend.

Given the concern of this study, the assumption of fixed coefficients for all intermediate inputs is regrettable but unavoidable due to the absence of relevant data.[12] Despite this probable misspecification, however, the estimation of the elasticity of substitution between labor and capital (broadly defined) in Chilean agriculture should be of interest given the frequent assumptions about its value. The absence of data on the capital stock [13] and on the rate of return for capital preclude the direct estimation of relation (1) or of a number of relations that can be derived from it. Under the assumption that the value of the marginal product is equated to the nominal wage, however, an estimable relation can be derived:[14]

$$\log \frac{GDPC}{L} = \frac{1}{1+\rho} \log \frac{PL}{PGDP} + \frac{\rho}{1+\rho} rt + \frac{\rho}{1+\rho} \log b , \qquad (2)$$

where PL = the nominal wage (including employer social security payments), and $PGDP$ = nominal product price (gross domestic product deflator).

In order to better represent the long run phenomenon under investigation, finally, relation (2) is assumed to represent the desired log $(GDPC/L)$ towards which the actual log $(GDPC/L)$ adjusts in a Koyck–Cagan–Nerlovian distributed lag process, and $PL/PGDP$ is replaced by the expected long run value of $PL/PGDP$ as is represented by a weighted average of past experience:

$$\log \frac{GDPC}{L} = (1-\lambda) \log \left(\frac{GDPC}{L}\right)_{-1} + \sigma \log E\left[\frac{PL}{PGDP}\right] + \sigma \rho rt + \text{constant}, \quad (3)$$

where $\sigma = 1/(1+\rho)$ is the elasticity of substitution between capital and labor, λ = adjustment coefficient, and $E[PL/PGDP]$ = expected $PL/PGDP$ as repre-

[12] The sources for data utilized in this study are presented in the appendix to this chapter.

[13] The investment data used in the estimation of the second relation discussed in this section could be used with some assumption about depreciation and the initial capital stock in order to generate a series for capital stock. An attempt to use such a procedure (in which the assumed constant depreciation rate and the initial capital stock were maximum likelihood estimates together with the other parameters in relation (1)), however, did not lead to very satisfactory results. The investment data, moreover, refer to only part of the capital stock.

[14] Note that a relation of exactly the same form would result if all the same assumptions made except that Hicks neutral technological change (i.e., $r = r'$) were assumed instead of factor augmenting technical change.

sented by weighted average the past values of $PL/PGDP$ in which the pattern of such weights is geometric for lags of from 2 to 5 years (i.e., δ for 2 years, $\delta(1-\delta)$ for 3 years, etc.) with a residual weight for 1 year so that the sum of the weights equals one (i.e., $1-\delta \sum_{i=1}^{4}(1-\delta)^{i-1}$), and zero weights for all other lags.[15]

Under the assumption that least squares procedures are appropriate, the following estimates were obtained:[16]

$$\log \frac{GDPC}{L} = \frac{0.579}{(3.58)} \log \left(\frac{GDPC}{L}\right)_{-1} + \frac{0.129}{(2.26)} \log E\left(\frac{PL}{PGDP}\right) + \frac{1.38}{(2.63)}$$

$$
\begin{aligned}
&\bar{R}^2 = 0.89 \qquad\qquad F = 78.8 \\
&SE = 0.037 \qquad\qquad \sigma = 0.31
\end{aligned}
\tag{4}
$$

$\delta = 0.94$ (lag weights for $1-5$ years are $0.00, 0.94, 0.06, 0.00, 0.00$).

The model apparently is reasonably satisfactory on an overall basis in that the F-test indicates that the estimated relationship is significantly non-zero at the 1% level and in that the coefficient of determination indicates that the model is consistent with almost 90% of the variance in the dependent variable over the sample period. Higher coefficients of determination were obtained for only three of the other eight sectors (manufacturing, government and services).[17] Thus the underlying assumed behavior of responding to product and factor market prices in profit maximizing ways is supported not only in an absolute sense but also in a relative sense in comparison with other Chilean sectors. Even though there is evidence of labor-augmenting or Hicks neutral technological change in half of the other sectors (mining, services, manufacturing, and transportation), however, there is no evidence of such change in agriculture. In this respect, therefore, apparently agriculture has not been among the more progressive sectors. In respect to the flexibility of the response to market pressures, the rapidity of the adjustment of actual towards desired values, the ra-

---

[15] This weighting scheme allows somewhat more flexibility than the usual geometric pattern in that the maximum weight can be for a lag of one or of two years, but still only one parameter is estimated. Because a maximum likelihood scanning procedure was used to estimate δ the statistics and significance tests relating to relation (4) are asymptotic.

[16] Absolute values of the t statistics are given in parentheses beneath the point estimates throughout this paper.

For further discussions of some of the problems in estimating such a relation, see Behrman, 'Substitution between capital and labor'; and Marc Nerlove, 'Recent empirical studies of the CES and related production functions', in: *The theory and empirical analysis of production* 31. New York, National Bureau of Economic Research, Studies in Income and Wealth, 1967, 55–122 (hereinafter referred to as 'Empirical studies of the CES').

[17] Behrman, 'Substitution between capital and labor', 10.

pidity of adjustment of expectations of the wage price ratio, and the magnitude of the elasticity of substitution are all important. On the first two counts the estimates indicate that agricultural flexibility is at least as great as is the modal flexibility across Chilean sectors. The adjustment of actual towards desired values is quicker in agriculture than in half of the other sectors (government, housing services, manufacturing and construction), and the adjustment in the expectations of the wage price ratio is quicker in agricultural than in all but two of the other sectors (utilities and services). In respect to the elasticity of substitution, however, the results are somewhat surprising. The estimate of the elasticity of substitution is significantly non-zero in the short run (0.13) and in the long run (0.31), which does call into question the frequently encountered assumption of complete rigidity. But, contrary to the assumptions of many,[18] this estimate implied that the technical possibility of substituting labor for capital is relatively low in agriculture in comparison to some 'modern' sectors (manufacturing, mining and utilities). If the relative magnitudes of these estimates do reflect the real sectoral substitution possibilities, incidently, more dynamic flexibility and higher growth rates for the total economy may be gained if the product shares of these 'modern' sectors expand at the expense of agriculture.[19]

The second aspect of this empirical investigation of the long run response of Chilean agriculture is the estimation of a neoclassical investment function. The model which is used is basically that which Jorgenson has used widely,[20] except that the production function is assumed to be CES instead of Cobb–Douglas, and the neoclassical desired capital stock is assumed to be modified by considerations relating to the utilization of capacity and to the standard deviation of agricultural prices relative to the gross domestic product deflator. The utilization rate is included to test the hypothesis that low utilization reduces the desired capital stock and vice versa. The standard deviation of agricultural prices relative to the gross domestic product deflator is included to represent one aspect of risk. Following Jorgenson, gross investment is composed of replacement investment and net investment:

$$I = I^R + I^N \, , \tag{5}$$

[18] For example see J.W. Mellor, *The economics of agricultural development.* Ithaca, Cornell University Press, 1966; and Nerlove, 'Empirical studies of the CES', 57.

[19] Nerlove ('Empirical studies of the CES', 57) reaches the opposite conclusion because he assumes relatively high elasticities of substitution to exist in agriculture.

[20] For example see D.W. Jorgenson and C.D. Siebert, 'A comparison of alternative theories of corporate investment behavior', *The American Economic Review* 57 (September 1968) 681–712.

where I = gross investment, I^R = replacement investment, and I^N = net investment.

Replacement investment is assumed to be proportional to the existing capital stock, which is represented in the present estimation by the existing capacity of value added:[21]

$$I^R = aGDPC. \tag{6}$$

Net investment is assumed to depend on the change in desired capital stock:

$$I^N = \Delta K^d \tag{7}$$

where K^d = desired capital stock.

The desired capital stock is assumed to depend upon neoclassical considerations for a CES production function, as modified by the above discussed considerations in respect to capacity utilization and the standard deviation of agricultural prices relative to the gross domestic deflator over the past three years:[22]

$$K^d = cGDP\left(\frac{PGDP}{PK}\right)^\sigma + d\,\frac{GDP}{GDPC} + e\,SD\left[\frac{PGDP}{PGDP^t}\right], \tag{8}$$

where PK = cost of capital,[23] GDP = real value added, $SD[X]$ = standard deviation of X over three years, and $PGDP^t$ = gross domestic product deflator (total economy).

---

[21] If capital augmenting or Hicks neutral technological changes are occurring, replacement needs may be lessened (see Behrman, 'Sectoral investment determination'). In the present case capital augmenting technological change is assumed not to be important, and the results presented above suggest that Hicks neutral technological change is not important. – Note that the treatment of replacement investment differently from net investment implies that neoclassical considerations determine the latter but not the former. This may be justified if replacement investment means replacing a particular piece of equipment in a process in which the connections to other stages of the same process are fixed so that replacement options are limited while in adding a whole process options are more flexible (i.e., a 'putty-clay' type consideration). If the same flexibility for replacement as for net investment is assumed in the present case, the results seem to be less satisfactory.

[22] If capital augmenting or Hicks neutral technological change is occurring, once again the effects should be incorporated. See the penultimate note.

[23] The cost of capital is defined in Jorgenson and Siebert, 618–712. Included in the construction of this variable are considerations relating to the cost of investment goods, taxes, interest rates, and depreciation allowances.

Substitution of relation (8) into (7) and of the result together with relation (6) into (5) leads to the expression actually estimated:

$$I = aGDPC + c\Delta \left(GDP\left(\frac{PGDP}{PK}\right)^{\sigma}\right) + d\Delta\left(\frac{GDP}{GDPC}\right) + e\Delta SD\left[\frac{PGDP}{PGDP^t}\right]. \qquad (9)$$

In order to better account for lags in expectations in the decision making process and in deliveries, however, each of the right-hand side variables is represented by distributed lags over 4 years in a method proposed originally by Hall and Sutch [ref. 83]: In this method a 'Zi' variable is included for each of the 'ith' degrees of the polynomial in the lagged weights.[24] In order to explore the effects of different elasticities of substitution, moreover, σ was allowed to take value of zero, one, and of the estimate in relation (4) above. If σ equals zero, of course, the neoclassical model collapses to an accelerator model. If σ equals one, the Jorgenson Cobb–Douglas form results.

Under the assumption that least squares procedures are appropriate, a number of alternatives were explored. The most successful alternative is as follows:

$$I = \frac{183.}{(3.1)} Z1GDPC \ \frac{-39.1}{3.3} Z2GDPC = -13.9 \ Z1\Delta GDP$$

$$+ \frac{0.621}{1.3} Z1\Delta SD\left[\frac{PGDP}{PGDP^t}\right] \frac{-145.}{(5.7)} \qquad (10)$$

$\bar{R}^2 = 0.83$ $F = 24.9$

$SE = 16.$ $DW = 1.33$

	Weights				
	−0	−1	−2	−3	Σ
GDPC	−0.106	0.038	0.103	0.091	0.126
Δ*GDP*	0.055	0.042	0.028	0.014	0.139
Δ*SD*[*PGDP/PGDP^t*]	−2.5	−1.9	−1.3	−0.6	−6.2

These results suggest that the model apparently is satisfactory on an overall basis in that the F-test indicates that relation (10) is significantly non-zero at the 1% level, in that the coefficient of determination indicates that the model

[24] Polynomials up to the third degree were investigated. The 'tail' which Robert E. Hall and Richard C. Sutch, in: *A flexible infinite distributed lag*. Berkeley, University of California, Institute of Business and Economics Research, Center for Research in Management Science, 1969, include, however, was constrained to zero in the present study.

is consistent with over 80% of the variance in the dependent variable over the sample period, and in that the Durbin–Watson statistic indicates that there is not a problem of serial correlation. The model is relatively consistent with the variation in the dependent variable in the case of agriculture in comparison with real investment relations for other Chilean sectors.[25] In this one sense, thus, these results again support the assumption that Chilean agriculture responds to long run conditions in a manner which is more consistent with the models used for the U.S.A. than do most other Chilean sectors. On the other hand, only in the case of the real investment function for agriculture among the Chilean sectors is there *not* evidence of a response to the relative price part of the neoclassical term. This finding reinforces the result presented above of a very low elasticity of substitution in Chilean agriculture and implies that this technical rigidity precludes long run responses to relative prices. Instead the apparently important real investment determinants are replacement needs, an accelerator term, and risk aversion in respect to the variance of relative product prices. Only in the last of these three factors is there included any response to prices.

III. Short run Chilean aggregate agricultural market responses

An important determinant of actual real agricultural output is the capacity of real agricultural output, which has been discussed in the previous section. Over the sample period, however, not insignificant variations in the degree of agricultural capacity utilization have occurred. Utilization rates have ranged from 0.88 to 1.00, with a mean value of 0.95 and a standard deviation of 0.05.[26] In this section the determinants of these short run variations are explored. Actual real agricultural value added is hypothesized to be proportional to capacity, but the utilization rate is hypothesized to be a linear function of the product price relative to the gross domestic product deflator, the product price relative to wages adjusted for productivity and for employer social security contributions, the product price relative to intermediate input prices, the economy wide level of inventories relative to the economy wide value added (as a proxy for aggregate economic conditions), imports of intermediate goods relative to total value added, credit relative to value added, and a weather index related to rain-

[25] Only in transportation and housing was more consistency obtained. This comparison must be qualified, however, due to the questionable nature of the investment data for many of the sectors. See Behrman, 'Sectoral investment determination'.

[26] Over the sample, however, agriculture has been one of the Chilean sectors with the least foregone output relative to capacity so measured. See Behrman, chapter 11.

fall. The underlying rationale for the inclusion of most of these variables is an ad hoc consideration of the level of the demand curve relative to the marginal cost curve or the availability of some more or less critical factor. Under the assumption that least squares estimates are appropriate, the following estimates were obtained:

$$GDP = \left(\frac{0.883}{(7.0)} + \frac{0.228}{(1.7)} \left(\frac{PGDP}{PGDP^t} \right)_{-1} + \frac{0.00316}{(1.9)} \left(\frac{P}{PL^a} \right) - \frac{0.913}{(2.1)} \left(\frac{INV^t}{GDP^t} \right)_{-1} \right) GDPC$$

$$\bar{R}^2 = 0.91$$
$$SE = 79.6 \qquad DW = 1.55,$$

where INV^t/GDP^t = total inventories relative to total value added, and PL^a = adjusted wages (wages adjusted for productivity in addition to employer social security contributions) or unit labor costs.

On an overall basis once again the estimates seem relatively satisfactory. The model is consistent with over 90% of the invariance in the dependent variable, and the Durbin–Watson statistic indicates that the null hypothesis of no serial correlation is not rejected at the 5% level. The variables which have significant coefficient estimates in the determination of the capacity utilization rate are the aggregate agricultural price relative to the gross domestic product deflator (lagged one year), the aggregate agricultural price relative to the adjusted agricultural wage, and the economy-wide level of inventories relative to the economy wide value added (also lagged one year).[27] The elasticities at the point of sample means with respect to these three variables are 0.24, 0.15, and −0.32.[28] The first two variables refer quite directly to specific market responses, and the third refers to responses to general economic conditions. These estimates suggest that substantial aggregate agricultural short run supply response occurs in Chile, either in comparison with available estimates for individual crops in

---

[27] No significant coefficient estimate was obtained for the weather index. This lack of success may reflect difficulties in constructing such an index in Chile where the runoff from melting snow in the Andes may be much more important than rainfall in the crop lands. See the next note for reference to some other results in respect to the effect of rainfall on agricultural supply.

[28] For comparison, García (p. 95) presents elasticities of 0.27 when the ratio of agricultural to nonagricultural prices is used and of 0.52 when the ratio of agricultural to industrial prices is used. Logarithmic forms are used for his estimates, and his two models are consistent with 25% and 50% of the variance in the dependent variable over the 1929–1961 sample period. The only other variable which he includes is the lagged value of rainfall, for which he obtained significantly negative coefficients.

other developing and developed economies[29] or in comparison with similar estimates for other Chilean sectors. In respect to the latter comparison, only for mining and for transportation have significantly higher elasticities been obtained.[30] Moreover, for many of the nonagricultural Chilean sectors (including mining and transportation) adjustment of actual to desired real value added is slower than in agriculture or the formation of expectations is based primarily on price ratios with greater lags than is the case in agriculture. The structuralist (and other) characterization of Chilean agriculture as being relatively unresponsive in the short run, thus, is clearly not supported by these results.

IV. The determination of the rate of change of Chilean aggregate agricultural prices

Given the evidence in the previous two sections of significant and substantial short and long run market responses in Chilean aggregate agriculture, some pertinent questions arise. What are the determinants of the relevant prices? Do these prices give appropriate signals? In order to obtain some insight into the answers to these questions, this section is devoted to an examination of the determination of aggregate agricultural prices, and the next section is devoted to an examination of the determination of aggregate agricultural wages. In both cases the investigations are conducted in terms of the rates of change of the variables of interest because the high rate of Chilean inflation in the sample period[31] precludes useful examination of price levels due to the very high multicollinearity.

Because of the large number of relevant variables of both a general and a sector—specific nature and because of the large number of lagged values of the monetary variables that are required in order to capture the total response of the rate of change of prices to the rate of change of the monetary supply, the investigation proceeds in two stages. In the first stage are investigated the general pressures on the rate of change of the gross domestic product deflator due

---

[29] See the references in note four and in G.T. Jones, 'The response of the supply of agricultural products in the United Kingdom to price', *The Farm Economist* 10 (January, 1962) 1–28; and Marc Nerlove, *The dynamics of supply: estimation of farmers' response to price*. Baltimore, The Johns Hopkins University Press, 1958. Of course, a priori one would expect the individual crop elasticities to be higher than the aggregate elasticity.

[30] Behrman, chapter 9.

[31] Over the sample period the annual rate of change of the gross domestic price deflator ranged from 0.04 to 0.74 with a mean of 0.296 and a standard deviation of 0.19.

to the rate of change of the per capita nominal money supply, the rate of change
of per capita real income, and the rate of change of the exchange rate.[32] In the
second stage various lags of the systematic part of the rate of change of the
gross domestic product deflator as estimated in the first stage are used to represent the combined effects upon the rate of change of agricultural prices of the
rates of change of nominal per capita money supplies, real per capita income,
and the exchange rate. In addition, a number of more sector—specific variables
are included: the rate of change of private consumption relative to the capacity
of agriculture, the rate of change of intermediate demands for agricultural products relative to the capacity of agriculture, the rate of change of the wage share
of national income, an accelerator variable (i.e., the lagged first difference of
the rate of change of agricultural prices),[33] the rate of change of the price of
agricultural exports in domestic currency, the rate of change of the average indirect tax rate, the rate of change of the price of agricultural inputs, and the
rate of change of wages (adjusted for average labor productivity in addition to
employer's social security contributions). The following estimates seem most
satisfactory for this second stage:

$$r[PGDP] = \frac{0.345}{(3.1)} r[P\hat{G}DP^t]_{-1} \frac{-0.396}{(3.5)} r[P\hat{G}DP^t]_{-2} + \frac{0.163}{(2.0)} r[P\hat{G}DP^t]_{-3}$$

$$+ \frac{0.806}{(4.3)} r\left[\frac{CPRV^t}{GDPC}\right] + \frac{0.838}{(13.2)} r[PINP]$$

$$\bar{R}^2 = 0.93 \qquad DW = 1.20$$
$$SE = 0.049 \qquad F = 70.5 \ , \qquad\qquad\qquad (11)$$

where $r[X]$ = annual rate of change of X, $P\hat{G}DP^t$ = systematic part of stage
one, which represents the effects of nominal per capita monetary balances,
real per capita income, and the exchange rate, $CPRV^t$ = level of total real private consumption expenditure, and $PINP$ = price of intermediate inputs used
by agriculture.

On an overall level, once again, the results appear quite satisfactory. The
F-test indicates that the estimates are significant at least at the 1% level, and
the coefficient of determination indicates that the model is consistent with
over 90% of the variance in the dependent variable. The Durbin—Watson test,

---

[32] For details see Behrman, chapter 14.
[33] Arnold Harberger, 'The dynamics of inflation in Chile', in:*Measurement in economics:
studies in mathematical economics in memory of Yehuda Grunfeld*, ed. by Carl Christ.
Stanford, Stanford University Press, 1963, 219—250, suggests such a variable.

however, is inconclusive. Relative to similar estimates for other Chilean sectors,[34] the coefficient of determination for agriculture is at about the modal value (although substantially above the mean). The key role in the determination of the rate of change of agricultural prices is played by the general nominal per capita monetary, real per capita income, and exchange rate pressures which are transmitted by the lagged values of the systematic part of the rate of change of the gross domestic product deflator from the first stage and by the rate of change of the agricultural input prices.[35] The response to such pressures is significantly less than complete in the current period, but then significant overshooting occurs, which is necessary if agricultural price levels are not to lag permanently behind the overall price level after a once and for all change. Subsequently, a negative coefficient occurs so that the sum of the relevant coefficients is not significantly different from one at the 5% level.[36] Consequently, in the long run the rate of change of agricultural prices adjusts proportionately to the impact of the rates of change of the monetary-real income-exchange rate considerations.[37] In fact, over the sample period the mean rate of change of agricultural prices was 0.301, which was slightly higher than the mean rate of change of the gross domestic price deflator.[38] Agricultural prices thus seem to adjust quite adequately to these general pressures [39] despite claims to the contrary.[40] Although the general pressures are most important in the determination of the rate of change of agricultural prices, sector specific factors also have significant roles. The rate of change of real private consumption expenditures relative to agricultural capacity evidently is representing the degree of excess demand in the product market. That some of the general pressures discussed above are best represented by the rate of change of the price of inputs,

[34] Behrman, chapter 14.

[35] The only difference between the gross domestic product deflator and the index of agricultural input prices is that the weights of the same sectoral prices are different. Over the sample the correlation coefficient between the rates of change of the two is over 0.90.

[36] The sum of the four relevant coefficients is 0.95 with a standard deviation of 0.043.

[37] For further discussion of such lag patterns see Behrman, chapter 14.

[38] The mean rate of change of prices for other Chilean sectors over the sample period were 0.339 for mining, 0.270 for construction, 0.296 for manufacturing, 0.308 for transportation, 0.305 for utilities, 0.252 for housing services, and 0.304 for other services.

[39] In contrast, the sums of the relevant weights for similar estimates for construction and manufacturing are significantly less than one at the 5% level, and the pattern of adjustment for housing services does not include overshooting to compensate for less than complete instantaneous adjustment. See Behrman, chapter 14.

[40] After the end of the sample, however, the use of price ceilings (which are largely on agricultural goods) was extended substantially, so agricultural prices may have lagged behind the general price level.

moreover, suggests that sector-specific cost push factors enter in. At least to some extent, therefore, the rate of change of agricultural prices does give signals in the right direction for resource allocation by reflecting excess demand and intermediate factor cost considerations. This conclusion must be qualified, however, because only for agriculture and construction among the Chilean sectors has no evidence been presented of significant effects of wages and/or labor productivities on the sectoral prices.[41]

V. The determination of the rate of change of Chilean aggregate agricultural wages

The determination of the rate of change of Chilean aggregate agricultural wages is investigated within considerations relating to the level and the rate of change of excess demand in the labor market. Among the variables considered are the rate of change of nominal and of real average agricultural labor productivities, the rate of change of economy-wide human capital per capita, the rate of change of economy-wide nonwage income relative to product (as a proxy for general economic conditions), the rate of change of credit relative to product, the inverse of the capacity utilization rate (as a proxy for Phillips curve phenomena), the rate of change of the minimum wage, the expected rate of change of consumer goods prices (as represented by lagged rates of change of the deflator for private consumption), a representation of frustration in the previous years expected rate of change of consumer goods prices (as represented by the rate of change of the deflator for private consumption lagged two years minus the same variable lagged one year), and the level and the rate of change of non-manufacturing unionization.[42] Under the assumption that least squares estimates are appropriate, the following estimates were obtained:[43]

$$r[PL] = \frac{0.461}{(2.5)} r\left[\frac{YNW}{GDP^{t*}PGDP^t}\right] + \frac{0.661}{(3.0)} r[PCPRV]_{-1} \frac{-0.343}{(1.4)} (r[PCPRV]_{-2}$$

$$-r[PCPRV]_{-1}) + \frac{2.66}{(2.4)} \frac{UNION}{L-LI} + \frac{0.888}{(1.9)} r \frac{[UNION]}{L-LI}$$

$$\bar{R}^2 = 0.68 \qquad DW = 1.82$$
$$sE = 0.15 \qquad\qquad\qquad\qquad\qquad\qquad (12)$$

---

[41] Behrman, chapter 14.
[42] For a discussion in more detail of the model, see Behrman, 'Sectoral money wages'.
[43] The dependent variable does *not* include employer social security contributions.

where $YNW/(GPD^t*PGDP^t)$ = nonwage share of total gross domestic product, $PCPR\,V$ = deflator for private consumption expenditures, and UNION/$L-LI$ = non-manufacturing union membership relative to non-manufacturing labor force.

On an overall basis this model does not appear to be as satisfactory as those discussed in the previous sections. The model is consistent with somewhat less than 70% of the variance in the dependent variable as contrasted with percentages around 90 for the previous estimates. On the other hand the Durbin–Watson statistic indicates that the null hypothesis of no serial correlation is not rejected at the 5% level, and the coefficient of determination is higher than the coefficients of determination obtained for a similar model for all but one of the other Chilean sectors.[44] At least in comparison with the rest of the Chilean economy, therefore, the results generally do not support the frequently encountered hypothesis for developing economies that wages in agriculture are much more determined by traditional institutional considerations than are wages in other sectors.[45] The explicit determinants of the rate of change of agricultural wages appear to be expectations of the general economic conditions (as represented by the rate of change of total non-wage income relative to product), expectations of consumer goods prices, including a correction for the frustration of past such expectations,[46] and the level and rate of change of non-manufacturing unionization. The first variable is significant for half of the Chilean sectors, and the second and third (or related variables) are significant in almost every sector, which is not surprising given the Chilean inflationary history. The significance of these three variables also for the agricultural sector, thus, does not seem surprising. The significance of the unionization variables in the agricultural wage change determination, however, is somewhat surprising since very little of the non-manufacturing unionization actually occurred in agriculture during the sample period, and it would seem unlikely that the spillover effects from other sectors were very strong. In terms of the question as to whether or not agricultural wages give appropriate signals for resource allocation, however, perhaps the most important aspect of the estimates is the

---

[44] For transportation a coefficient of determination of 0.70 was obtained, See Behrman, 'Sectoral money wages'.

[45] For example see W.A. Lewis, 'Economic development with unlimited supplies of labour', *The Manchester School* 22 (May, 1954) 139–191; and G. Ranis and J.C.H. Fei, 'A theory of economic development', *The American Economic Review* 51 (September, 1961) 533–565.

[46] Given the high rate of inflation and the associated multicollinearity, it is not really possible to distinguish between expectations of the rate of change of agricultural product prices which act primarily through the demand side of the agricultural labor market and expectations of the rate of change of consumer prices which act primarily through the supply side.

lack of significance of either the labor productivity variables or the proxy for the Phillips curve term. In contrast, some evidence of a response in the determination of the rates of change of sectoral wages to the first consideration exists for every other Chilean sector except for mining, and some evidence for a response to the second consideration exists for manufacturing and for utilities.[47] Despite the relatively high consistency of the model with the rate of change of agricultural wages, thus, the results do not suggest that these wage changes reflect either absolutely or relatively well the specific conditions in the agricultural labor market. Therefore, Chilean agricultural wages do not seem to be giving particularly useful signals for resource allocation.

VI. Conclusions

For the macro and micro models underlying a vast amount of the analysis and policy prescriptions for developing economies, almost complete rigidity for the agricultural sector is assumed. Recent empirical studies have brought into question this assumption in the case of individual agricultural products, but almost no relevant empirical evidence exists in respect to aggregate agriculture. The present study has attempted to provide such evidence on the basis of the postwar Chilean experience. The basic result of this investigation is that there is considerable evidence of both short and long run flexibility in Chilean agriculture in comparison with other Chilean sectors and in comparison with estimates for other developing and developed countries. In respect to the creation and the utilization of capacity, models based upon the assumption of profit maximizing aggregate responses are very consistent with Chilean aggregate agricultural experience. In comparison with the other Chilean sectors, the agricultural market responses tend to be at least as rapid and at least as pervasive. In respect to the technical possibilities of substitution between capital and labor, on the other hand, the estimates suggest that such possibilities may be less in Chilean agriculture than in some of the modern Chilean sectors. The examination of the determination of the rates of change of product prices and of agricultural wages, moreover, suggests that (especially in the latter) prices may not be reflecting sector-specific conditions as well as might be desired for allocation reasons.

---

[47] Behrman, 'Sectoral money wages'. For another exploration of the effect of the Phillips term for a Chilean sample for which unemployment data exists, see Jere R. Behrman and Jorge García, 'A study of quarterly nominal wage change determinants in an inflationary developing economy', chapter 15 in this volume.

The major conclusion that follows if these empirical results can be believed is that the assumption of almost complete technical and market rigidity in the agricultural sector of the developing economy of Chile is untenable. If used in analysis, such an assumption may lead to an underestimation of the growth possibilities.[48] If used as the basis for policy prescriptions, such an assumption will lead to distorted market signals, responses to which may reduce both levels and rates of growth of real income. In fact, the Chilean government has made such an assumption both for analysis and for policy decisions. Examples of the former include the planning models currently in use in the Central Bank and the Office of National Economic Planning.[49] Examples of the latter include the establishment of ceilings on many agricultural prices, the maintenance of agricultural input prices (e.g., nitrogen fertilizer) high above international levels in order to protect domestic production, the introduction of other distortions in agricultural product and factor markets by foreign trade policy, legal rationing of certain agricultural commodities, and the assertion that a lack of historical agricultural market responsiveness is one reason that a restructuring of agriculture is needed. Given the evidence of considerable aggregate agricultural market responses and the evidence that market prices have not always tended to give correct signals for allocation, policy devoted to improving such signals rather than to introducing further distortions may have a relatively high payoff in terms of the level and rate of growth of real national income.

Appendix: Notational conventions and variable definitions and sources

Notational conventions and operator definitions:

$E[X]$ ≡ expected value of X

e ≡ natural number

$$r[X] \equiv \frac{X - X_{-1}}{X_{-1}}$$

---

[48] Starting from a point of initial full utilization and ignoring any effects of technical change, if the elasticity of substitution between capital and labor is assumed to be zero, the estimate of the growth of capacity will be constrained by the slower growing primary factor. If, in fact, the elasticity of substitution between capital and labor is greater than zero, growth of capacity at least in the medium run can exceed the growth rate of the slower growing primary factor.

[49] See, for example, Jorge Cauas, 'Stabilization policy – the Chilean case', *Journal of Political Economy* 78 (part II) (July/August, 1970) 815–825.

$SD[X]$ ≡ standard deviation of X over years 0, −1, and −2   ·
$Zi[X]$ ≡ Hall–Sutch polynomial of ith degree in parameters (where
$\quad\quad i$ = 1, 2, 3 or 4)
$\Delta X \quad\equiv X - X_{-1}$
$\Sigma_{i=n}^{m} X_i \equiv X_n + \ldots + X_m$
$X * Y \quad\equiv X$ multiplied by Y
$X_{-i} \quad\equiv X$ with lag of i years (i= 1, 2, 3, 4 or 5)

Last letter or superscript on $GDPC\_$, $L\_$, $PL\_$, $PGDP\_$, $GDP\_$, $PINP\_$, $DINT\_$, $PINV\_$, and PK refers to sectors defined as follows: A = agriculture, fishing, hunting and forestry, M = mining and quarrying, C = construction. I = manufacturing, T = transportation, communications and storage, E = electricity, gas and water, H = housing services, S = other services (excluding G), G = public administration and defense.

Variable definitions and sources:[50]

$C\_$ real consumption for private sector (PRV) or total (TOT).

$CPIT$ consumer price index for total with 1965 = 100 (Banco Central b).

$CR\_$ real credit to private sector (PRI), public sector (PUB), and total (TOT) (Fuenzalida and Undurrage).

$DINT\_$ real sectoral intermediate demand calculated from $GDP\_$ and 1962 input output table (ODEPLAN 1970).

$EXRAT$ average national accounts exchange rate in escudos per dollar.

$GDIA\_$ real sectoral gross domestic investment in physical capital in agriculture equal to sum of real gross agricultural investment in machinery and equipment (ODEPLAN 1968a) and real gross investment in public irrigation works (1940–1953 from Contraloria, 1954–1965 from MOP).

$GDP\_$ real sectoral gross domestic product (nominal national accounts value deflated by appropriate $PGDP\_$).

---

[50] All variables are flows over the year or annual averages unless otherwise noted. The last letters on $DINT\_$, $GDI\_$, $GDP\_$, $GDPC\_$, $L\_$, $PGDP\_$, $PINP\_$, $PINV\_$, $PK\_$, and $PL\_$ refer to sectors as indicated immediately preceding these definitions. Unless otherwise noted, all nominal quantities are measured in 10^6 escudos, all real quantities are measured in 10^6 1965 escudos, all labor numbers are measured in 10^3 people, all price and unit value indices and deflators have a value of 1.00 in 1965, and all prices of labor are measured in 10^3 escudos per laborer. Unless otherwise indicated, all data for 1940–1957 are from CORFO 1963, all data for 1958–1963 are from CORFO 1964, and all data for 1964–1965 are from ODEPLAN 1966. Most of these data and other relevant historical data on the Chilean economy may also be found in Mamalakis. The full citations for these and for other sources are given subsequent to the variable definitions.

*GDPC_*   real sectoral capacity of gross domestic product constructed from *GDP_* and trend through peak method (see Klein and Summers for discussion of this method).

INV   see STOCK.

*L_*   sectoral tendency in labor force distribution (Spottke).

*M_*   real imports of intermediate goods (*INT*) or total (*TOT*).

MSUP   nominal money supply (Banco Central b).

*P_*   implicit deflators for private consumption (*CPRV*), exports (*EXP*), gross domestic product (*GDP*), or imports (*IMP*).

PEST   first stage estimate of *PGDP* (Behrman).

*PGDP_*   sectoral deflators for gross domestic product. *A* = agricultural component of wholesale price index (Banco Central b). *M* = constructed on basis of unit value of mineral exports (Banco Central a) and *EXRAT*. *C* = cost of square meter of construction in 13–60 communes (Banco Central b). *I* = industrial component of wholesale price index (Banco Central b). *T* = (ODEPLAN 1969a). *E* = (CHILECTRA). *H* = housing component of consumer price index (Banco Central b). *S* = defined so total index consistent with all of above sectoral indices. *G* = same as *S*.

*PINP_*   sectoral prices of intermediate inputs defined on basis of 1962 input–output table (ODEPLAN 1970), *PGDP_*, *UVMIN*, and *EXRAT*.

*PINV_*   sectoral price of investment goods defined as weighted average of deflators for construction, domestic machinery and equipment, and imported machinery and equipment with weights of the average relative values for 1960–1966 from Meza 1968.

*PK_*   sectoral cost of capital (as defined in Jorgenson and Siebert) which depends on *PINV_*, *RINT*, *TXDB/GDP*PGDP* and sectoral depreciation rates.

*PL_*   sectoral prices of labor for 1944–1946 and for 1948–1951 from Caja de Seguro Obligatoria, for 1952–1965 from Servicio de Seguro Social, missing years estimated from regressions of above data on 1940–1952 data from CORFO 1954.[51] All sectoral labor prices adjusted proportionately so total wage bill equals *YWS* for each year.

RINT   average bank rate of interest (Banco Central b).

STOCK   level of year and stock calculated from *DSTCK* and estimate for 1965 from ODEPLAN 1969b.

---

[51] Missing observations included 1940–1943 and 1947 for all sectors and 1940–1951 for *T* and *E* (in which cases the 1940–1951 values estimated on basis of relations among economy-wide average labor prices and prices of labor for these two sectors for 1952–1965).

SUBT   total real subsidies.

TX__   nominal taxes: direct business (*DB*) indirect total (*IT*), and social security paid by employers (*SSE*), from Banco Central b (except last one from Caja Empleados Particulares), all adjusted proportionately so total, total direct and total indirect consistent with national accounts.

UNION   non-industrial union membership measured in 10^3 workers for 1940– 1959 from Morris and Oyaneder 1962 and for 1960–1965 from Direction General del Trabajo.

*UV X   unit value of total exports.

YNWS   nominal non-wage income (*NWS*).

Data sources:

Banco Central de Chile, *Balanza de Pagos*, Santiago 1945–1969a.

——————— , *Boletin Mensual*, Santiago 1945–1971b.

Behrman, Jere R., 'Price determination in an inflationary economy: the dynamics of Chilean inflation revisited', Chapter 15 in this volume.

Caja de Seguro Obligatoria, *Anuario estadístico*. Santiago 1944–1951.

CHILECTRA, *Memorias anuales*, Santiago 1945–1966.

Contraloría, *Memorias anuales*, Santiago 1953–1965.

CORFO, 'Cuentas nacionales de Chile, 1940–1952' (mimeo.), Santiago, 1954.

——————— , Dirección de Planificación, Departamento de Investigaciones Económicas, 'Cuentas Nacionales de Chile, 1940–1962' (provisional, mimeo.). Santiago 1963.

——————— , ——————— , 'Cuentas nacionales de Chile, 1958–1963' (provisional, mimeo.), Santiago 1964.

Dirección Gerneral del Trabajo, Sección Organizaciones Sindicales, unpublished figures on union membership, Santiago 1969.

Fuenzalida and S. Undurraga, 'El crédito y su distribución en Chile' (mimeo.), Santiago 1968.

Jorgenson, D., and C.D. Siebert, 'A comparison of alternative theories of corporate investment behavior', *American Economic Review* 58 (September, 1968), 681–712.

Klein, L.R. and R. Summers, *The Wharton index of capacity utilization*. Philadelphia, University of Pennsylvania, Economic Research Unit, 1966.

Mamalakis, M., *Historical statistics of Chile (four volumes)*, New Haven, Yale Economic Growth Center (forthcoming, Yale University Press).

Meza, W., 'Inversión geográfica bruta en capital fijo por sectores de destino, período 1962–1966', Santiago, ODEPLAN, División de Programación Financiera (mimeo.), 1968.

MOB (Minestéreo de Obras Públicas), *Memorias anuales.* Santiago 1953–1965.

ODEPLAN, 'Cuentas nacionales de Chile, 1964–1965'. Santiago (mimeo.) 1966.

——————, unpublished agricultural machinery and equipment gross investment series for 1940–1965. Santiago 1968a (?).

——————, División Programación Financiera, unpublished public investment series for 1961–1965. Santiago 1968c.

——————, División Transporte, unpublished price index for transportation sector for 1940–1965. Santiago 1969a (?).

——————, División de Planificación Global, unpublished total stock estimates at end of 1965. Santiago 1969b.

——————, División de Planificación Global, unpublished estimates of gross industrial investment for 1958–1965. Santiago 1969d (?).

——————, *Cuadro de transacciones intersectoriales para la economía Chilena – 1962.* Santiago 1970 (?).

Servicio de Seguro Social, *Estadísticas.* Santiago, Editorial Universitaria, 1957, 1960, 1964, 1968.

Spottke, Alberto, 'Estimaciones y proyecciones mediante interpolación y extrapolación de los datos censales corregidos de la población ocupado a mediados de cada año, 1940–1970'. Santiago, CORFO, Department of Economic Investigations (mimeo.), 1965.

R.S. Eckaus, P.N. Rosenstein-Rodan (eds.), Analysis of development problems,
© North-Holland Publishing Company

CYCLICAL SECTORAL CAPACITY UTILIZATION IN A DEVELOPING ECONOMY [*]

Jere R. BEHRMAN

University of Pennsylvania, Philadelphia, Penn., U.S.A.

I. Introduction

In the postwar literature on the developing economies the major focus has been on the expansion of productive capacity through the expansion of the physical capital stock. Harrod—Domar growth models and the Chenery two-gap model have been used widely as the basis for analysis and for policy prescriptions.[1] In these models productive capacity is assumed to depend on the stock of physical capital, and output is assumed to equal capacity. The first of these assumptions has been questioned more and more recently both on the basis that other factors (e.g., the quality of the labor force) may be important and on the basis that the elasticity of substitution between physical capital and other factors may be significantly non-zero and even not substantially less than in the developed economies.[2] The second assumption also has been questioned re-

---

[*] The author wishes to thank the supporting organizations for their help while at the same time emphasizing that this paper in no way necessarily reflects the viewpoints of these organizations. The author also wishes to thank, but not implicate, Juan de la Barra, Eduardo García, Ricardo Lira, Jozé Mencinger, Christian Ossa, and Almarin Phillips.
[1] For a typical recommendation for the use of the former type models see UNECAFE (United Nations Economic Commission for Asia and the Far East), *Programming techniques for economic development.* Bangkok 1960. For a review of a recent extensive UNCTAD (United Nations Conference on Trade and Development), *Trade prospects and capital needs of developing countries.* New York, United Nations, 1968, study based on the latter type model and for references to other uses thereof, see Jere R. Behrman, 'Review article: trade prospects and capital needs of developing countries', *International Economic Review* 12 (October, 1971) 519–525.
[2] For examples of empirical investigations that support these two points in respect to Chile see Arnold Harberger and Marcelo Selowsky, 'Key factors in the economic growth of Chile: analysis of the sources of past growth and of prospects for 1965–1970' (Paper presented at Conference on the Next Decade of Latin-American Economic Development, Cornell University, April 20–22, 1966), and Jere R. Behrman, 'Sectoral elasticities of substitution between capital and labor in a developing economy: time series analysis in the case of postwar Chile', *Econometrica* (in press) hereinafter referred to as 'Substitution between capital and labor').

cently, primarily because the utilization rates of something like rated capacity in the manufacturing sectors of many developing economies are substantially below the utilization rates for the developed economies.[3] The very procedure of comparing such utilization rates between less and more developed economies, however, seems to reflect the assumption that the really important constraint on production is the stock of physical capital (on which the rated capacity depends), and other currently binding constraints can be loosened relatively cheaply and should be loosened. But as Winston has emphasized in respect to the possibility of increasing rated capacity utilization through an increase in the number of shifts, the costs of loosening the non-physical capital constraints may be considerable at least in the short run.[4] The question of fluctuations in the degree of capacity utilization within these (short run, at least) binding non-physical capital constraints in developing countries is a question on which relatively little attention has been focused. The pervasive assumption in the development literature is that the benefits likely to be obtained from attention to fluctuations in the utilization of historically attained capacity are not sufficient

---

[3] See Ruy Aguiar da Silva Lerne, 'Excess capacity in Brazilian industry', mimeo., UNIDO (ID/WG. 29/12, February 5, 1969); Mario S. Brodersohn, 'The utilization of production capacity in Argentine industry', mimeo. (Centro de Investigaciones Económicas, Instituto Torcuato Di Tella, November, 1968); Aníbal Gómez, 'Utilization of productive capacity in the Latin-American iron and steel industry', mimeo. UNIDO (IG/WG. 29/13, February 5, 1969); Meir Merhav, 'Excess capacity – measurement, causes and uses: a case study of selected industries in Israel', mimeo. UNIDO (ID/WG. 29/7, January 20. 1969); ODEPLAN (Office of Chilean National Economic Planning), 'Capacidad utilizada de la industria manufacturera, 1964–1965–1966', mimeo. Santiago, ODEPLAN, July, 1968; Almarin Phillips, 'Measuring industrial capacity in less developed countries'. Philadelphia, University of Pennsylvania, Department of Economics, 1969 (hereinafter referred to as 'Measuring industrial capacity'); K.L. Saxsena, 'Excess industrial capacity in India and the possibility of its utilization for export purposes', mimeo. UNIDO (ID/WG. 29/5, January 27, 1969); UNIDO (United Nations Industrial Development Organization), 'The causes of excess capacity in the manufacturing industry', mimeo. UNIDO (ID/WG. 29/10, January 24, 1969), (hereinafter referred to as 'Causes of excess capacity'); UNIDO, 'Industrial excess capacity and its utilization for export', mimeo. UNIDO (ID/WG .29/8, January 21, 1969) (hereinafter referred to as 'Industrial excess capacity'); UNIDO, 'The special nature of the fertil - izer industry in developing countries', mimeo. UNIDO (ID/WG .29/11, February 3, 1969) (hereinafter referred to as 'Fertilizer industry'); UNIDO, 'Utilization of excess capacity for export: report of the expert group meeting on excess capacity, Rio de Janeiro, 3–12 March 1969'. New York, United Nations (ID/38), 1969 (hereinafter referred to as 'Utilization of excess capacity'); and Gordon C. Winston, 'Capacity utilization in economic development', mimeo. Williamstown, Mass., Williams College, August, 1969.

[4] L.R. Klein, 'Some theoretical issues in the measurement of capacity', *Econometrica 28* (April 1960) 274, is making the same point when he points out that rated capacities refer to technical limitations and not to economic considerations.

to warrant the costs. Instead, attention has been focused on physical capital accumulation, on removing non-physical capital constraints so that higher utilization of rated capacity can be attained, on 'big pushes', and on 'minimum critical efforts'.[5] In this study attention is focused on the question of fluctuations in the degree of utilization of historically attained levels of production in the developing economy of postwar Chile in an attempt to expand the emprical evidence relevant to the issues discussed above. The extent of fluctuations in the level of sectoral utilization of historically attained capacity in postwar Chile and cross-sectoral patterns therein are examined in section II. An attempt to test hypotheses about the causes of fluctuations in sectoral outputs is described in section III. Conclusions are presented in section IV.

II. Patterns of sectoral utilization of historically attainable capacity in postwar Chile

Historically attainable capacities of real gross domestic product were estimated by the trend through the peaks method[6] in each of the following nine Chilean sectors for the 1945—1965 period:[7] agriculture, mining, construction, manufacturing, transportation, utilities, housing services, government, and other services. This method of estimating capacity does take into account the non-physical capital considerations which historically have limited peak production to levels substantially below rated values. This method also has the advantage

[5] In addition to the references above, see Ken-ichi Inada, 'Development in monocultural economies'. Stanford, Stanford University, Institute for Mathematical Studies in the Social Sciences, April 15, 1968; H. Leibenstein, *Economic backwardness and economic growth: studies in the theory of economic development.* New York, John Wiley & Sons, 1957; V.K.R.V. Rao, 'Investment, income and the multiplier in an underdeveloped economy', *The Indian Economic Review,* 1952; reprint ed., *The economics of underdevelopment,* ed. by A.N. Agarwala and S.P. Singh. New York, Oxford Book Co., 1963; and Paul N. Rosenstein-Rodan, 'Notes on the theory of the 'big push' ', in: *Economic development for Latin-America,* ed. by Howard S. Ellis. New York, St. Martin's Press, 1961.
[6] See L.R. Klein and Robert Summers, *The Wharton index of capacity utilization.* Philadelphia, Economics Research Unit, University of Pennsylvania, 1966; Almarin Phillips, 'An appraisal of measures of capacity', *American Economic Review* 53 (May 1963) 275—292 (hereinafter referred to as 'Measures of capacity'); and Phillips, 'Measuring industrial capacity'.
[7] Data and data references are given in the appendix to chapter 8. This time period was selected because it was considered desirable to exclude the World War II years in which constraints were somewhat different and because consistent data are not available for years before 1940, or after 1965.

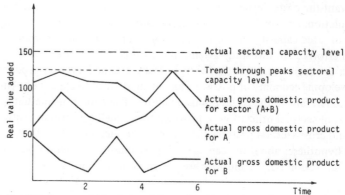

Fig. 1. Possible downward bias in trend through peaks method of measuring capacity utilization due to aggregation problems.

of not demanding nearly as extensive data as do most alternatives[8] and thus of being applicable over a fairly long time period and of being applicable to sectors other than manufacturing. On the other hand, even for the purpose at hand, this method has several limitations. First, there is an aggregation problem because even at a sectoral peak some components of a particular sector may not be operating at their peak level. For example, suppose that a given sector is composed of two components A and B that have full capacity outputs of 100 and 50, respectively, but whose time paths of utilization are not highly correlated, as is illustrated in fig. 1. The trends through the peaks method of estimation of the level of capacity utilization for the sector, therefore, may be biased downward considerably, as is indicated in this figure, even though it would be fine for measuring the capacity of the components of the sector.[9] If the rates of utilization of the subcomponents of each sector are not more highly correlated than are the rates of utilization of the sectoral aggregates (see the discussion of table 2 below) this bias may be quite substantial.[10] Second, even ignoring the aggregation problems, as Phillips[11] notes there is no

---

[8] Alternative measurements of capacity are discussed in Phillips, 'Measures of capacity'; and Phillips, 'Measuring industrial capacity'.
[9] As should be clear, aggregation problems might lead to errors in the measurement of directions of trends of capacity levels and not only in the levels themselves.
[10] For further discussion of aspects of the aggregation problem in the use of such a procedure see Robert Summers, 'Further results in the measurement of capacity utilization', *Proceedings of the business and economics section of the American Statistical Association*, 1968, 26–29.
[11] Phillips, 'Measures of capacity', 290.

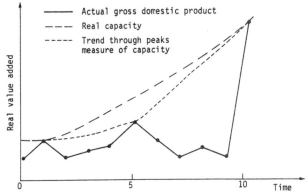

Fig. 2. Possible downward bias in trend through peaks capacity measure due to false identification of peak in period five with full utilization.

reason to believe that every peak in the time series necessarily reflects full capacity utilization in the sense desired. For example, suppose that the real capacity level is given by the dashed line in fig. 2, but that the trend through the peaks measure of capacity is given by the dotted line because period five is wrongly thought to be a year of full capacity utilization by the appropriate criteria.[12] Once again a downward bias in the estimated level of capacity may result. Third, in a somewhat different vein, efficiency implications of full capacity utilization so defined are not clear. In a world without external effects, production by each firm at the minimum point of its long run average cost curve would be efficient, but (ignoring the aggregation problem) there is no reason for a specific relation to exist between full utilization as defined by the trend through the peaks method and any particular point on long run average cost curves. These limitations—especially in regard to the probable downward bias in the estimation of the capacity levels — should be kept in mind in the discussion below.

In tables 1 and 2 are summarized characteristics of Chilean total and sectoral capacity utilization rates based on the trend through the peaks method for annual data for the 1945–1965 period. On the global level the rates of utilization have ranged from 0.88 to 1.00, with a mean of 0.93 and a standard deviation of

---

[12] Such a downward bias is especially liable to occur for periods near the end of the sample. In the case of the Wharton 'trends through the peaks' capacity utilization index for the U.S.A., Summers (31–32) found that the estimate of the capacity level has been biased down near the end of the sample, but the estimates of changes in the utilization rates have not been so biased.

Table 1
Ranges, means and standard deviations of Chilean sectoral real gross domestic product capacity utilization rates over the 1945–1965 period and the ratios of the accumulated unutilized real gross domestic product capacity over the period to the mean actual real gross domestic product[a]

| Sector | Characteristics of capacity utilization rates | | | Total unused capacity |
	Range	Mean	Standard deviation	Mean real gross domestic product
Agriculture	0.88–1.00	0.95	0.05	1.00
Mining	0.53–1.00	0.86	0.15	3.20
Construction	0.80–1.00	0.93	0.08	1.36
Manufacturing	0.83–1.00	0.95	0.05	1.10
Transportation	0.71–1.00	0.88	0.11	2.69
Utilities	0.65–1.00	0.88	0.12	3.11
Housing services	0.75–1.00	0.91	0.09	2.29
Government	0.82–1.00	0.93	0.07	1.85
Other services	0.83–1.00	0.96	0.05	0.94
Total Economy	0.88–1.00	0.93	0.01	1.45

[a] Data sources are given in the appendix to chapter 8.

Table 2
Simple correlation coefficients among Chilean sectoral real gross domestic product utilization rates over the 1945–1965 period[a]

	A	M	C	M	T	U	H	G	O	Total
Agriculture	1.00									
Mining	−0.20	1.00								
Construction	0.08	−0.21	1.00							
Manufacturing	0.02	−0.14	−0.04	1.00						
Transportation	0.14	−0.23	−0.41	−0.13	1.00					
Utilities	0.09	−0.22	−0.12	0.54	0.00	1.00				
Housing services	−0.09	0.17	−0.38	0.31	0.09	0.53	1.00			
Government	−0.14	0.04	−0.08	0.24	−0.04	−0.03	0.22	1.00		
Other services	0.08	0.61	−0.10	−0.22	0.11	−0.24	0.23	0.27	1.00	
Total	0.19	0.52	−0.05	0.27	0.27	0.14	0.55	0.41	0.80	1.00

[a] Data sources are given in the appendix to chapter 8. A correlation coefficient with an absolute value of 0.42 or greater is significantly non-zero at the 5% level.

0.01. If capacity had been fully utilized at historically attainable levels, therefore, actual output could have been an average of 8% per year higher than it actually was. Or, alternatively, the foregone output over the 21 years was equal to the actual mean production of over 17 months (1.45 years). Given that these estimates of the output foregone probably are biased downwards, the benefits of fully utilizing the available capacity would have been considerable. Even ignoring the probable downward bias in this estimate of the benefits, the increased national product that could be obtained if capacity utilization were increased from its mean actual value of 0.93 to full utilization would be greater than the increase in national product that could be obtained if the same rate of capacity utilization were maintained and capacity expanded for 2 years at the mean annual exponential growth rate of capacity actually experienced over the period.[13] In the previous sentence the once and for all gains of an increase in the rate of capacity utilization are emphasized. But one should not conclude that the gains are limited to those of a once and for all nature. A simple Harrod–Dowar framework provides a strong example to the contrary. Within this framework an increase in the average rate of capacity utilization is like an increase in the marginal savings rate or a decrease in the marginal capital/output ratio in that it increases the equilibrium rate of growth permanently.[14]

On the sectoral level rates of capacity utilization have ranged much more than on the global level because the sectoral fluctuations have tended to cancel each other out. This tendency is reflected in the fact that only 3 of the 35 correlation coefficients (in table 2) among the sectoral utilization rates are significantly nonzero at the 5% level.[15] This apparent independence among current sectoral rates of capacity utilization suggests that the conditions which cause underutilization of capacity vary considerably (at least in respect to lags) across sectors. This independence also suggests that an aggregate measurement of unused Chilean capacity calculated directly from the time series of aggregate product by the trend through the peaks method (such as Okun[16] used for the U.S.A.) would substantially understate the actual unused capacity because of the counterbalancing sectoral fluctuations. Likewise, if Chilean subsectoral fluctuations in current rates of capacity utilization are nearly as independent as are the Chilean sectoral fluctuations in current rates of capacity utilization, then the present study understates substantially the extent of unused Chilean capacity. Of course, one would not expect as much independence on the more disaggregate subsectoral level because of greater homogeneity, but the possibility of significant downward bias in the estimates of unused capacity due to lack of

[13] The mean annual exponential growth rates of actual output and of capacity over the 1945–1965 period are both about 3.5%.
[14] Winston, 2–3.
[15] The three exceptions are between mining and other services, between utilities and manufacturing, and between housing services and utilities.
[16] A.M. Okun, 'Potential GNP: its measurement and significance', *Proceedings of the business and economics section of the American Statistical Association,* 1962.

complete correlation among subsectoral utilization rates should not be discounted too heavily.

In order of decreasing foregone product relative to capacity (and in order of the standard deviations of the rates of capacity utilization, except that government and construction are interchanged) the Chilean sectors rank as follows: mining, utilities, transportation, housing services, government, construction, manufacturing, agriculture, and other services (table 1). The first four sectors have had substantially more unutilized capacity than the national average, and the last three sectors have had substantially less. Several characteristics of the individual sectors and of this ordering merit mention. First, mining is a somewhat unique sector in that almost all of Chile's exports originate therein, largely (at least over the sample) under the control of a few foreign companies. Because the exchange rate has been overvalued for most of the period, the estimate given in table 1 probably underestimates the true resource cost to Chile of the substantial underutilization in this sector. Moreover, an alternative method of estimating rates of capacity utilization in this sector (based on the utilization of electric energy sources) suggests that the mean rate of utilization has been only 0.80 and the foregone production has been equal to 5 years of the mean actual production.[17] Most of the low rates of capacity utilization (as calculated by the trend through the peaks method) underlying the low mean value for this sector occurred in the 1952–1958 period in which considerable uncertainty existed about the future course of relations between the Chilean government and the major mining companies.[18] To the extent that the uncertain nature of relations between the government and these companies did underlie the historically low utilization rates, one would expect higher utilization rates in the future because of the recent Chileanization and nationalization of the leading mining companies. Of course, substantial fluctuations may still occur because of fluctuations in the international copper market.

Second, three of the sectors in which fluctuations in capacity utilization generally are hypothesized to be relatively large have had relatively limited fluctuations and relatively high mean levels of capacity utilization. The first of these three sectors is agriculture, for which fluctuations generally are thought to be

[17] This calculation is based on the extension of results for the dominant Gran Minería to all of the sector. The series of rates of capacity utilization so calculated, however, are not significantly correlated at the 5% level with the series calculated by the trend through the peaks method.

[18] For details about the relations between the government and these mining companies, see Markos Mamalakis, 'The American copper companies and the Chilean government, 1920–1967: profile of an export sector'. New Haven, Yale University, Economic Growth Center, 1967.

large because of variations in natural conditions. The other two sectors are construction and manufacturing, in which fluctuations have been hypothesized to be relatively large because of relatively great sensitivity to variations in aggregate demand.[19] Of course the recent upsurge in interest about the existence of unused capacity in the last of these three sectors, manufacturing, is based on the discrepancies between actual utilization and *rated* capacities, not historically attained levels of production.[20]

Third, an examination of interindustry and final demand flows indicates that there is limited support for Hirschman's[21] assertion that 'the risk of excess capacity is lowest when the project's output is widely spread as an input over many sectors (or regions) or when output goes overwhelmingly to final consumption demand; the risk is bigger the greater the concentration of the project's output in a few final consumers or on a few cells of the interindustry matrix'. For agriculture, manufacturing, and other services outputs are relatively widely distributed, but final consumption demand absorbs a fairly large share. All three of those sectors have high mean capacity utilization rates. On the other end of the spectrum as far as mean utilization rates are concerned, the output from mining is sold to a few (mostly foreign) buyers so that risks are relatively high due to this concentration. On the other hand, the results for utilities, transportation, and construction do not seem to support Hirschman's hypothesis. The outputs of utilities and transportation are fairly widespread among final and intermediate uses with substantial portions going to final consumer demand, and yet mean utilization rates are low. In contrast, output from construction is very concentrated in gross investment (which itself is usually considered quite volatile), and the mean utilization rate for construction is about the same as for the economy as a whole.

[19] For an example in the case of another Latin-American country, see Karsten Lawrsen and Lester D. Taylor, 'Unemployment productivity and growth in Columbia'. Cambridge, Mass., Development Advisory Service, Harvard University, 1968, 10.

In section III below the question of the causes of variations in real output in these and in the other sectors will be further examined.

[20] For evidence of this interest and measures of levels of capacity utilization in manufacturing in developing countries, see Aguiar; Brodersohn; Gómez; Merhav; Phillips, 'Measuring industrial capacity'; Saxsena; UNIDO; 'Causes of excess capacity'; UNIDO, 'Industrial excess capacity'; UNIDO, 'Fertilizer industry'; UNIDO, 'Utilization of excess capacity'; and Winston. For Chilean manufacturing ODEPLAN gives estimates for capacity utilization in 1964–1965, which (under the assumption of a proportional relation between the ODEPLAN estimates and the trend through the peak estimates) imply a mean rate of capacity utilization in this sector of from 0.54 to 0.76. The underlying definition of capacity, however, is not clear.

[21] Albert O. Hirschman, *Development projects observed*. Washington, D.C., The Brookings Institute, 1962, 73.

III. The determination of Chilean sectoral outputs of annual real gross domestic product, 1945–1965

In this section the determinants of Chilean sectoral real gross domestic product are explored by the use of regression analysis. The underlying model that is used is given in relations (1) – (3). Relation (1) states that actual real gross domestic product equals actual real gross domestic product for the previous period plus the product of an adjustment coefficient and the difference between currently desired real gross domestic product and lagged actual real gross domestic product:

$$GDP = GDP_{-1} + \gamma(GDP^d - GDP_{-1}) = (1 - \gamma)GDP_{-1} + \gamma GDP^d \qquad (1)$$

Relation (2) states that the desired real gross domestic product is proportional to the capacity of real gross domestic product:

$$GDP^d = \alpha GDPC. \qquad (2)$$

Substitution of relation (2) into relation (1) gives relation (3), which was actually estimated (under the assumption that least squares techniques are applicable):

$$GDP = (1 - \gamma)GDP_{-1} + \gamma \alpha GDPC. \qquad (3)$$

The capacity of real gross domestic product is assumed to be determined by past decisions in respect to stocks of capital, technological change, and available labor force.[22] The question of primary interest for this study is what determines the proportionality factor or desired utilization rate (i.e., α). The primary group of determinants discussed by most observers relates to conditions in the relevant product and factor markets. Frequently mentioned possible causes of low utilization of capacity within this group include that product prices are not remunerative, that demand is inadequate, that primary and intermediate inputs (especially imported ones) are not available or are too expensive, and that labor unrest disrupts normal functioning.[23] In order to represent these considerations, the proportionality factor is hypothesized to be a linear function of a number of variables: the product price relative to the

---

[22] CES production functions for these sectoral capacities of real gross domestic product are presented and discussed in Behrman, 'Substitution between capital and labor'.

[23] Aguiar, pp. 17, 19, 24, 27; Brodersohn, p. 33; M. ErSeleuk, 'Case studies on the problem of industrial excess capacity and its utilization', mimeo. UNIDO (ID/WG .29/14, February 6, 1969), 4, 9–10; Gómez, 14, 17; Merhav, 9; ODEPLAN, 5; Saxsena, 38; UNIDO, 'Causes of excess capacity', 4–7, 10; UNIDO, 'Industrial excess capacity', 28; and Winston, 4.

gross domestic price deflator, the product price relative to unit labor costs (i.e., wages adjusted for productivity and for employer social security contributions), the product price relative to intermediate input prices, the economy-wide level of inventories relative to the economy-wide gross domestic product (as a proxy for aggregate demand conditions), imports of intermediate goods relative to gross domestic product, and total imports relative to gross domestic product, (included only for the other services sector because trade margins from imports are a significant part of the gross domestic product for this sector). A second group of determinants which is frequently mentioned is the availability of short term funds from bank credit or other sources.[24] To represent this condition the proportionality factor is hypothesized to be a linear function also of total credit from the banking system relative to the total gross domestic product. A third group of determinants which merits consideration is related to various natural conditions. Of course, these conditions probably are most important in the case of agriculture, but other sectors — such as utilities (to the extent that hydroelectric electricity production and water distribution are important) — may also be affected. To represent these natural conditions the proportionality factors are hypothesized to be a linear function also of indices related to rainfall and to the intensity of earthquakes.

Relation (3) with the proportionality factor hypothesized to be a linear function of the factors mentioned in the previous paragraph, was estimated for all of the sectors except for the government.[25] The results of these estimations are presented in table 3, and the implied elasticities at the point of the sample means are given in table 4. For the elasticities in table 4 'short run' includes only the current adjustment in the dependent variables while 'long run' includes complete adjustment. Although the title of table 4 suggests that the included elasticities are of the real gross domestic product with respect to capacity and with respect to the variables in the proportionality factor, it should be clear that (given the underlying model discussed above) the elasticities of capacity utilization with respect to the variables in the proportionality factor are identical with the elasticities of real gross domestic product with respect to the same variables. The major characteristics of tables 3 and 4 can be summarized under five general observations.

First, on an overall level the results suggest that the underlying model is reasonably successful. The coefficients of determination indicate that this

---

[24] Aguiar, 17; ErSeleuk, 11; Gómez, 17; ODEPLAN, 5; and UNIDO, 'Causes of excess capacity', 8–9.
[25] The government was excluded because the provision of government services seems to be determined by factors much different from those that are discussed in the text.

Table 3
Determination of sectoral gross domestic product in Chile, 1945–1965[a]

Sector	Capacity of real gross domestic product multiplied by:								$\bar{R}^2$ SE	DW
	Gross domestic product (−1)	Price i GDP deflator (−2)	Price i Unit labor cost in i (−2)	Price i Inter. input price in i (−1)	Inventories Gross domestic product (−1)	Credit Gross domestic product (−0)	Inter. imports Gross domestic product (−1)	Total imports Gross domestic product (−1)		
Agriculture	0.883 (7.03)	0.228[f] (1.71)[b]	0.00316[e] (1.91)		−0.913 (2.13)				0.91 79.6	1.55
Mining	0.560 (4.02)	0.318 (3.45)			−1.23 (3.00)		12.7 (3.61)		0.86 89.6	2.53[d]
Construction	1.08 (8.64)			0.0700 (0.88)[c]	−0.695 (1.97)				0.97 28.1	1.91
Manufacturing	0.893 (20.5)					0.352 (1.35)[b]			0.93 267.7	1.39
Transportation	0.593 (5.07)			0.441[g] (3.89)					0.89 98.6	2.41[d]
Utilities	0.579 (3.17)	0.277 (1.73)	0.00131 (2.53)						0.84 21.1	1.76[d]
Housing services	0.956 (6.24)	0.216 (2.63)			−1.08[g] (1.84)				0.93 100.8	1.81
Other services	0.253 (1.08)[c]	0.629 (2.72)	0.00367 (0.77)[c]					0.231 (1.33)[b]	0.94 299.1	1.58[d]

[a] Data sources are given in the appendix. Absolute values of t-statistics are given in parentheses beneath point estimates. All point estimates are significantly nonzero at least at the 5% level unless otherwise noted. Lags are indicated at the column heads unless otherwise noted. Price i represents the price of the ith sector.
[b] t-test indicates that this estimate is significantly nonzero at the 10% level.
[c] t-test indicates that this estimate is significantly nonzero at the 25% level.
[d] Durbin–Watson statistic is biased towards two because of inclusion of lagged dependent variable.
[e] Lag of zero years.
[f] Lag of 1 year.

Table 4

Elasticities (at point of sample means) of sectoral real gross domestic product with respect to relevant variables, Chile, 1945–1965ᵃ

Sectors	Capacity of real gross domestic product	Elasticities (at point of sample means) of actual gross domestic product with respect to:						
		Price i GDP deflator	Price i Unit labor costs in i	Price i Inter. input price in i	Inventories Gross domestic product	Credit Gross domestic product	Inter. Imports Gross domestic product	Total Imports Gross domestic product
Agriculture	0.95	0.24	0.15		-0.32			
Mining – short run	0.45	0.30			-0.46		0.61	
– long run	1.02	0.68			-1.05		1.39	
Construction	0.93			0.08	-0.23			
Manufacturing	0.95					0.06		
Transportation – short run	0.43			0.43				
– long run	0.70			0.70				
Utilities – short run	0.41		0.09					
– long run	0.95		0.21					
Housing services	0.99	0.33			-0.39			
Other services – short run	0.76		0.04					0.06
– long run	1.02		0.05					0.08

ᵃ Based on estimates in table 3. Price i represents the price of the ith sector. 'Short run' includes only the current adjustment of actual towards desired sectoral real gross domestic product. 'Long run' includes complete adjustment.

model is consistent with from 84 to 97% of the variations in real gross domestic product at the sector level. The Durbin–Watson values do not lead to a rejection of the null hypothesis of no serial correlation.[26]

Second, for four sectors (agriculture, construction, manufacturing, and housing services) the adjustment of actual towards desired real gross domestic product apparently is basically complete in 1 year and in a fifth sector (housing services) evidence of longer adjustment is relatively weak (the relevant point estimate is significantly non-zero at only the 25% level). However for the other three sectors (mining, transportation, and utilities), the evidence for a longer period of adjustment is much stronger, and the point estimates imply that five years are required before adjustment is 95% complete. This longer adjustment period to the desired level of capacity utilization, which in turn depends upon the monotonically increasing actual capacity, apparently underlies the relative low mean utilization rates obtained for these same three sectors (table 1).[27]

Third, the results support the hypothesis that the conditions in the product and factor markets significantly influence the rates of capacity utilization and, therefore, real gross domestic product. For all sectors except manufacturing there is evidence of some response to relative prices.[28] The implied elasticities are all less than unitary and are quite low in construction, utilities, and other services.[29] Nevertheless, the evidence of widespread significant responses to relative prices even at the sectoral level [30] is important because of the widespread assumption of the existence of effectively complete rigidities in the developing economies.[31] In addition to the widespread response to relative prices, moreover, there is evidence of significant responses to overall aggregate demand conditions (as represented by levels of inventory relative to levels of product)

[26] But this statistic is biased towards a value of two in the case of the four sectors in which a lagged value of the dependent variable is included.
[27] In respect to the expansion of capacity itself, in contrast, the results reported in Behrman ('Substitution between capital and labor') suggest that in these same three sectors adjustment of actual towards desired value is relatively quick.
[28] The relevant point estimates for construction and other services, however, are significantly non-zero only at the 25% level.
[29] In contrast to frequently encountered assertions (including those made by the 'structuralist' school in Latin-America), the elasticity of response to relative prices in agriculture does not seem to be relatively low. For examples of such assertions see Jere R. Behrman, *Supply response in underdeveloped agriculture: a case study of four major annual crops in Thailand, 1937–1963.* Amsterdam, North-Holland Publishing Co., 1968, 1–8.
[30] Because intrasectoral factory mobility may be greater, at least in some sectors (e.g., agriculture), than intersectoral factor mobility, one might expect to find higher elasticities at a more disaggregate level of analysis.
[31] See the related discussion in the introduction above and the references therein.

in four sectors (agriculture, mining,[32] construction, and housing services), to the availability of imported intermediate inputs in mining, and to the extent of total import activity (representing part of the demand for commercial services) in other services. The responses to various aspects of product and factor market conditions, thus, seems to be widespread[33] and often substantial. Policies that are based on analysis which ignores such responses to market conditions may be quite misleading.

Fourth, only in the case of manufacturing is there any evidence of a significant response to the availability of short-term credit, and the implied elasticity in this case is very small. Given the concentration of credit flows to this sector, that significant responses do not occur in any other sectors probably is not surprising. The limited magnitude of the response in manufacturing, however, is somewhat surprising given the importance that Chilean manufactures seem to place on the availability of credit in informal explanations of the low rate of capacity utilization.[34] One might think that the cost, not the quantity of credit, would be an important consideration, but for much of the sample period the rate of inflation exceeded the nominal bank credit rates. Credit rationing, therefore, was accomplished by non-price means. In such a situation the desire for increased credit is understandable, but the results in tables 3 and 4 suggest that changes in the availability of credit apparently did not affect utilization rates substantially (whatever effects they may have had on income distribution or on other variables).

Fifth, in no sector – including agriculture – is there evidence of a significant response to the variables used to represent natural conditions. This somewhat surprising result may only reflect the difficulties of constructing a good index of natural conditions.[35] Nevertheless, the model used is consistent with over 90% of the variance in agricultural real gross domestic product without including any index of natural conditions, and when any one of several alternative indices were included, the apparent explanatory power of the model did not improve.

---

[32] The response of mining to aggregate demand conditions may seem surprising because production is largely exported. However, in the early 1960's, one quarter of this sector's production went to domestic uses, so some response to domestic aggregate demand conditions may be realistic.

[33] Manufacturing stands out as an exception to this statement.

[34] See also ODEPLAN, 5.

[35] For more extensive attempts to construct an appropriate index see Michael K. Evans, 'An agricultural submodel for the U.S. economy', in: *Essays in industrial econometrics* 2. Philadelphia, Economics Research Unit, University of Pennsylvania, 1969, 63–146; and B. Oury, *A production model for wheat and feedgrains in France*. Amsterdam, North-Holland Publishing Co., 1966.

IV. Conclusions

Despite probable downward biases in the measurement procedure used, on the bases of comparisons with historically attained levels of output (and *not* with rated capacities) apparently significant excess capacity has existed in the Chilean economy during the postwar period. The utilization of this excess capacity could have resulted in a significant increase both in the level and in the growth rate of national product.[36] The primary determinants of fluctuations in the rates of sectoral capacity utilization in most sectors seem to be the conditions in factor and product markets (including the state of aggregate demand). The policy conclusions that follow for the case of Chile and for any other similar developing economies are as follows. First, substantial gains may be obtained from increasing capacity utilization by following appropriate market and anticyclical policies. These gains may or may not warrant the cost of following the necessary policies, but the possibility that the benefits do outweigh the costs should not be rejected casually without further investigation. Second, the widespread response to market conditions suggest that markets do play an allocative role in such an economy. Policies should not distort the signals transmitted by such markets under the false assumption that they will have no significant effects on allocation. Policies that distort the market conditions (e.g., the Chilean price ceilings) *may* be justified, but the existence of costs in terms of resource allocation should not be ignored. Third, for short and medium term policy, recommendations based on fixed capital coefficients and full capacity utilization assumptions (such as in the Harrod–Domar and Chenery models) may be misleading not only because of the probable importance of other factors and the possibility of some substitution but also because of the existence of unutilized capacity.

---

[36] In Jere R. Behrman ('Sectoral investment determination in a developing economy', *American Economic Review* (in press)), furthermore, evidence of some response in investment decisions to the capacity utilization rates so measured is present for agriculture, industry, utilities, and housing services.

PART IV

INTERNATIONAL TRADE AND DEVELOPMENT
STRATEGIES

R.S. Eckaus, P.N. Rosenstein-Rodan (eds.), Analysis of development problems,
© North-Holland Publishing Company

PREFERENCE FOR INDUSTRY AND COMMERCIAL POLICY
THEORY IN INDUSTRIALIZING COUNTRIES*

Edmar BACHA

University of Brasilia, Brasilia, Brasil

I. Introduction

Throughout the underdeveloped world and in particular in Latin-America, economists and policy makers are trying to devise new strategies of commercial policy which would permit acceleration of the growth process of less developed countries.

At the same time, appreciation of the importance of rationality in resource allocation grows when it is observed that the process of indiscriminate import-substitution is leading one country after the other into economic stagnation.

This paper proposes an analytical scheme designed to compare the various options in commercial policy in terms of their differential impacts on the levels of real output and income of an industrializing country.

In the hypotheses of the model we introduce a new element, a preference for industry on the part of the government of the country. This addition could be justified by arguments found in the literature on infant industries, but here it is taken simply as an additional restriction to be met by the economic system when allocating resources.

After a summary description of the basic model, we analyze the following alternatives of commercial policy one by one: free trade, partial import substitution, 'autarky', tariff preferences in the markets of developed countries, subsidies to industrial exports, and economic integration. Certain aspects of the controversy 'trade vs. aid' are discussed in the appendix. We place more emphasis on the discussion of customs unions because this alternative seems analytically more difficult and politically more significant than the other topics.

---

* The author is indebted for comments to Carlos Diaz-Alejandro, Arnold Harberger, Milton da Mata and Lance Taylor. A version of this paper appeared in *Ensaios economi cos – homenagen a Octavio Gouvea Bulhões*, ed. by Micrea Buescu. APEC Editora. Rio de Janeiro, 1972.

If the preference for industry were ignored, we would arrive at the usual conclusion that free trade is the solution which reaches the highest level of real income, for it is assumed that the economy has a 'static' comparative advantage in agriculture. However, when we impose the preference for industry restriction, free trade is no longer feasible. Tarriff preferences in developed countries, subsidies to industrial exports, and economic integration (under specified conditions) become the more desirable alternatives, in that order.

II. The economy described

Consider an economy with three sectors: agriculture (A), industry-one (I_1), and industry-two (I_2). With a fixed endowment of production factors, the outputs of A, I_1 and I_2 can be related to one another by a *production possibilities curve* with the general form:

$$A = A(I_1, I_2).$$

This function gives the maximum output of the agricultural good which can be obtained with the available resources, for given values of I_1 and I_2. Without loss of generality we will work with a specific form of this function, where alternative costs or transformation rates are constant:

$$A = A^0 - p_1' I_1 - p_2' I_2, \tag{1}$$

where A^0 indicates the maximum agricultural output which can be attained, defined as the output obtained when all available resources are allocated to agriculture; and where p_1' and p_2' are the rates of domestic transformation be tween the agricultural good and the goods of industries one and two, respectively. Under perfect competition and other well-known conditions, p_1' and p_2' define the domestic prices of industrial goods in terms of the agricultural good.

The *structure of comparative advantage* of the economy with respect to the rest of the world is specified by the following relationships between the international and domestic prices of I_1 and I_2:

$$\left. \begin{array}{l} p_1 < p_1' \\ p_2 < p_2' \\ p_1/p_2 < p_1'/p_2', \end{array} \right\} \tag{2}$$

where p_1 and p_2 are the international prices of I_1 and I_2 in terms of agricultural good.

The equations in (2) specify that the economy produces both industrial goods, I_1 and I_2, at higher costs than international market prices. Within the industrial sector, however, the economy produces I_1 at higher relative costs. That is, the 'comparative disadvantage' of the economy is higher in the production of I_1.

It is assumed that the government of this country has a preference for industry.[1] That is, despite the comparative disadvantage of the economy in industrial production, the government wishes to reach a certain degree of industralization. It is irrelevant for the following analysis to inquire on the 'rationality' or 'irrationality' of this preference for industry. In the short-run, there is a trade-off between the level of real income and the degree of industrialization which would suggest irrationality. Given the comparative advantage of the country in agriculture, the higher the industrial output, the lower the level of real income. On the other hand, the preference for industry could be justified if we could show that such preference leads to higher real income in the future. In this rational interpretation of industrial preference, there would be a positive degree of industrialization in the present which would maximize the present value of the future stream of real incomes, appropriately discounted.

This could occur in spite of the present inefficiency of industry because of market imperfections, external effects, learning effects and other socio-cultural arguments related to the impact of modernization of society as a result of the industrialization of the country.[2]

Without discussing the merit of this argument in the present paper, the preference for industry can be taken as observed characteristic of government behavior not only in Chile but in nearly all developing countries. In this paper we study the influence of this industrial preference on the government's evaluation of the commercial policy alternatives open to the country.

Formally, the preference for industry can be represented by a *governmental preference function* of the form:

$$U = U(N, I),$$

---

[1] The present formulation of the preference for industry is based in the presentation of C. Cooper and B. Massel, 'Towards a general theory of customs unions for developing countries', *Journal of Political Economy* 73 (October, 1965) 461–476.

[2] Cf. H.B. Chenery, 'Comparative advantage and development policy', in: American Economic Association/Royal Economic Society, *Surveys of economic theory, II: Growth and development*. St. Martin's Press, New York, 1966, 125–155; and H. Myint, 'Infant industry argument for assistance to industries in the setting of dynamic trade theory', in: *International trade theory in a developing world* ed. by R.F. Harrod and D. Hague. MacMillan, London 1963.

where U is an utility index; N is the total output of the country measured in terms of the agricultural good at international prices:

$$N = A + p_1 I_1 + p_2 I_2 \tag{3}$$

and I is the value of industrial output at international prices:

$$I = p_1 I_1 + p_2 I_2. \tag{4}$$

It is assumed that both $\delta U/\delta N > 0$ and $\delta U/\delta I > 0$ hold true. In other words, the utility level can be raised by an increase in industrial output even when the level of total output remains constant. This means that the level of utility enjoyed by society increases even if a decrease in agricultural output exactly compensates the increase in industrial production leaving the total output unchanged. For mathematical convenience, it is assumed that the function U is defined over the values, in international prices, of N and I. The general nature of the results derived in this paper, however, can be shown to hold under the more realistic assumption that U is defined over N and I when expressed in domestic prices.

One possible form of the index U is illustrated by the family of 'indifference curves' between N and I presented in fig. 1. The different functions U_1, $U_2, U_3, \ldots$, represent successively higher utility levels. Along a given function, U_2 for example, the utility level is constant. This means that the government is indifferent between the position indicated by point D and the position given by point B, where the first point offers more total output but less industry than the second point. However, comparing points D and C, the government will have a clear preference for the second position, which offers the same level of output and more industry than the first one.

One other typy of relationship necessary for this paper is the *transformation between total output and industry*, which is obtained substituting eq. (1) in eq. (3):

$$N = A^0 - (p_1' - p_1) I_1 - (p_2' - p_2) I_2. \tag{5}$$

From this expression we can define two relationships between N and I, the first holding I_1 constant and the second holding I_2 constant. It is sufficient to consider the first relationship: $N = N(I/I_1)$. From the definition of I, we have in terms of changes:

$$\Delta I = p_2 \Delta I_2,$$

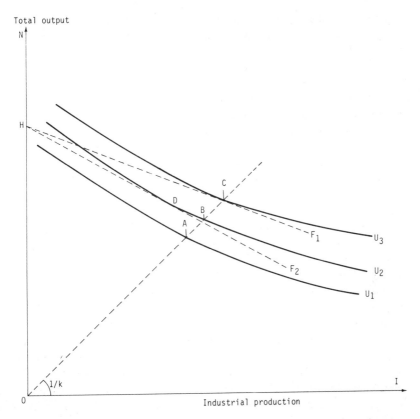

Fig. 1.

and from the definition of N:

$$\Delta N = -(p_2' - p_2)\,\Delta I_2 = -[(p_2'/p_2) - 1]\Delta I.$$

Since $p_2' > p_2$, the higher I, the smaller N will be.

Two transformation curves between N and I are shown in fig. 1, both starting from an arbitrary point, H, which depends on the preassigned output level of I_1. The curve HF_2 indicates a cost of industrialization, that is, a value of the ratio p_2'/p_2, which is higher than that indicated by HF_1.

The analytical task of the following sections is simplified because one needs to work with only one particular point of the preference function which a government might have. This point is determined by the tangency of U with the transformation curve between N and I. Normally, this will be a point such as A, B, or C, located on a ray from the origin. Thus, one can keep U in the background and identify the preference for industry with the inverse of the slope of the ray from the origin which has the following functional form:

$$I = kN, \tag{6}$$

where k expresses the degree of industrialization desired by the government. Actually, this degree is a variable which depends on the shapes of U and the transformation function. The higher industrial costs in the country, the more one will have to sacrifice N in order to obtain additional units of I. This means that the higher industrial costs, the more to the left the tangency point between the transformation curve and the preference function will be. Thus, if the transformation rate between N and I is expressed by HF_1, the relevant point would be C along the ray $OABC$. Should industrial costs be higher, and the transformation curve be expressed by HF_2, then the relevant point would be D along the ray OD (not drawn). Once U and the particular transformation curve which characterize the country are known, the relevant tangency point and the reference ray can be found. Hereafter, we assume that both the preference curve and the transformation function are given. Thus, we can reason as if the reference ray also were given and, as consequence, we can treat k as a parameter which is identified as the fixed degree of industrialization desired by the government.

The last basic hypothesis refers to the *distribution of domestic consumption* between A, I_1 and I_2. Restricting the analysis to the limits of traditional models of international trade, it is assumed that the three goods are final consumption goods and problems of capital formation and input—output relationships are ignored. It is also assumed that the different goods are consumed in fixed proportions:

$$I_1'' = bI_2'', \text{ and:}$$
$$A'' = cI_2'', \tag{7}$$

where the superscript $('')$ indicates consumption levels.

Within certain limits, we could allow for substitution in the consumers' preference function for A, I_1 and I_2 without affecting the results below. The assumption that consumers' preferences are fixed is used to generate an inconsistency between the balance of payments constraint and the degree of industrialization desired by the government. The same inconsistency could have been generated without fixed preferences, as long as the field of substitution among products in the consumers' preference function were limited, as shown in fig. 2. Production and consumption of the agriculture good are indicated in the vertical axis and production and consumption of industry-two

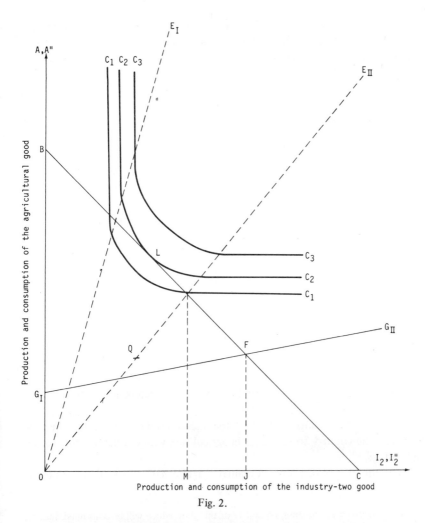

Fig. 2.

good are indicated in the horizontal axis. Assuming again that the output level of I_1 is given, the production opportunities curve $A = A(I_2/I_1)$ represented by the straight line BC can be drawn. A series of indifference curves $C_1, C_2, C_3 \ldots$, are also drawn indicating the degree of substitutability in consumption between the agricultural good and the good of industry-two for successively higher consumers' utility levels. The rays OE_1 and OE_2 mark the substitution field between A'' and I_2''. The competitive equilibrium position in a closed economy with no 'imperfections' (such as discriminatory indirect taxes) is given by point L, in the curve C_2. The straight line G_IG_{II}, however, indicates the values that the outputs of A and I_2 must have in order to satisfy government preference for industry, for a given value of I_1. This line is derived from eqs. (3), (4) and (6), and it has the following analytical expression:

$$A = p_1 I_1 (1 - k)/k + p_2 I_2 (1 - k)/k.$$

In order to satisfy the preference of government for industry, the output of industry-two must be equal to OJ. However, the maximum quantity of this good, which will be consumed domestically under full employment of resources, is OM. Moreover, the consumption will not even reach the level of OM, unless consumer's price of I_2, in terms of A, falls to zero.[3] Thus, the only way of 'closing' the system is by exportation of I_2, which is impossible since the country produces this good at prices higher than the international market.

The dilemma outlined in the last paragraph is fully explored in the following section, where the problem of resource allocation is analyzed in the context of the alternatives of commercial policy which are open to an economy with the characteristics described in this section.

III. Commercial policy alternatives

A. Case 1: free trade

Obviously, free trade is the first option of commercial policy which must be examined for the economy described above.

The free trade solution produces the highest level of total output because it forces the country to specialize in agriculture, where it has a comparative advantage.

The equation of total output evaluated at alternative costs, that is, in interna-

---

[3] The qualification 'maximum quantity of this good which will be consumed domestically *under full employment of resources'* is important. Consumers may be induced to absorb the quantity OJ of the industry-two good combined with a consumption of FJ of the agricultural good. However, this consumption mix, given by point F, offers the consumers the same satisfaction level as the mix given by point Q, located in the same parallel to the horizontal axis as point F. This point Q is located *inside* the production possibilities frontier, BC; that is, it is a point where full employment of resources is lacking, The analysis here is analogous to the classical case of markets failure in underdeveloped countries as presented in R.S. Eckaus, 'The factor-proportions problem in underdeveloped areas', in: *The economics of underdevelopment*, ed. by A.N. Agarwala and S.P. Singh. Oxford University Press, London, 1958, 348–378.

tional prices, is written:

$$N = A + p_1 I_1 + p_2 I_2.$$

Substituting the value of A given by the transformation function (1), one obtains eq. (5), or:

$$N = A^0 - (p_1' - p_1) I_1 - (p_2' - p_2) I_2.$$

Clearly, given assumptions (2), the maximum value of N is A^0. However, at point A^0, the government's preference for industry is not satisfied. Thus, this production point cannot be reached and the free trade solution cannot be applied.

B. Case 2: partial import substitution

In order to overcome the difficulty found in case 1, the most natural attempt at solution is the internal production of I_2 but not of I_1 because, in the latter product, the country has a bigger comparative disadvantage. The question is whether this is a viable solution.

Consider the case of equilibrium in the balance of payments:

$$A - A'' = p_1 I_1'' + p_2 (I_2'' - I_2).$$

This equation means that the exports of A pay for the imports of I_1 which equal the domestic consumption of this industrial good, plus the imports of I_2, which equal the difference between consumption and domestic production of I_2. If national income (N'') is defined as the sum of consumption levels at world prices, then:

$$N'' = A'' + p_1 I_1'' + p_2 I_2''. \tag{8}$$

It can be easily seen that equilibrium in the balance of payments implies that income = output, or:

$$N'' = N = A + p_2 I_2. \tag{9}$$

Consider fig. 3. In the vertical axis, total income and output are marked. In the horizontal, consumption and output levels of I_2 are indicated.

The curve *preference for industry when* $I_1 = 0$ (ON) is derived from eqs. (4) and (6), letting $I_1 = 0$:

$$N = (p_2/k) I_2. \tag{10}$$

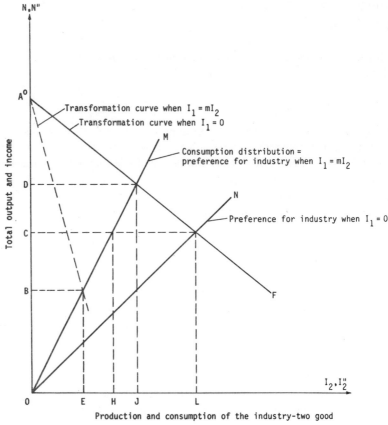

Fig. 3.

The curve *consumption distribution* (*OM*) derives from eqs. (7) and (8), and it is given by:

$$N'' = (c + p_1 b + p_2) I_2''. \tag{11}$$

The *transformation curve when* $I_1 = 0$ ($A^0 F$) is obtained from eq. (5), letting $I_1 = 0$:

$$N = A^0 - (p_2' - p_2) I_2. \tag{12}$$

The meaning of the other curves in the figure will be explained later.

In the intersection of eqs. (10) and (12), the equilibrium points for N and I_2 are determined. In the figure, these are represented by OC and OL, respectively. Balance of payments equilibrium requires that $N'' = N$. It follows that the value of I_2'' can be obtained from eq. (11). This value is measured by OH in the figure.

Thus, we obtain the result that $I_2 > I_2''$ (or: $OL > OH$). The presumed imports of I_2 must, in fact, be exports in order to satisfy the system. However, $p_2' > p_2$, that is, domestic prices of I_2, are higher than international market prices and I_2 cannot be exported in a free market.

We must conclude that the preference for industry condition can be inconsistent with equilibrium in the balance of payments when the domestic demand structure is rigid. In order words, when equilibrium in the balance of payments is required, the desired industrialization level may not be attainable with domestic production of I_2 only. The higher the desired industrialization level and the smaller the domestic market for industry-two, the more likely is this to occur.[4]

C. Case 3: the 'autarkic' solution

One way out of the dilemma of the second case is that imports may also be substituted in industry-one. In such a case, one should produce I_1 until exports of I_2 are not required any longer for balance of payments equilibrium, that is, until $I_2'' = I_2$. For lack of a better term, this solution will be called 'autarkic'.

The production of I_2 per unit of N needed to satisfy the desired degree of industrialization will be smaller the higher the domestic production of I_1. In terms of fig. 3, the preference for industry curve in the plane (I_2, N) will rotate towards the left around the origin. When this curve coincides with the consumption distribution curve, which does not move, I_2 will be equal to I_2'' and consistency between equilibrium in the balance of payments and the preference for industry will be attained.

However, the transformation curve in fig. 3 will also rotate when I_1 is produced domestically. It will rotate towards the left around A^0. This can be proved with the assumption that, at the new eqiulibrium point, the domestic production of I_1 is equal to mI_2, where m is a real number. Then, from eq. (5) we immediately obtain:

---

[4] · The argument above is hypothetical and established only the possibility of a contradiction. In the real world, however, it is believed that the possibility indicated above holds true for a number of Latin-American countries in the 1950's.

$$N = A^0 - [(p_1' - p_1) m + (p_2' - p_2)] I_2. \tag{13}$$

Clearly, the slope of eq. (13) is steeper than in eq. (12). The resulting level of output can then be found by intersecting the preference for industry curve with the production possibilities curve when $I_1 = mI_2$. It can be seen that the new level of output (OB) is smaller than before (OC). This result is also intuitively obvious, since scarce resources in this case are dedicated to the production of I_1, whereas in the last section, they were employed only in the two more efficient sectors, A and I_2.

In order to prove that OB is smaller than OC, consider the following. Substitute the value of I, given by eq. (4), in eq. (6), and change this and eq. (5) into differences:

$$p_1 \Delta I_1 + p_2 \Delta I_2 = k \Delta N$$

and:

$$\Delta N = - (p_1' - p_1) \Delta I_1 - (p_2' - p_2) \Delta I_2.$$

Solving for ΔN as a function of ΔI_1:

$$\Delta N = - \frac{p_1 [(p_1'/p_1) - (p_2'/p_2)]}{1 + k[(p_2'/p_2) - 1]} \Delta I_1. \tag{14}$$

It can be seen, given assumptions in eq. (2), that $\Delta N < 0$. Note that $\Delta I_1 = I_1$ and that $N = OB - OC$ in the figure. Eq. (14) measures the cost of an

Table 1
Gains in output by shifting from 'autarky' to partial import substitution

	Agriculture	Industry-two	Industry-one	Percentual gain in total output as measured by eq. (14)
Initial share in total output ($k = 0.5$)	0.50	0.25	0.25	
World prices	1.0	1.0	1.0	
Domestic prices (alternative hypotheses):				
(i)	1.0	1.2	1.5	0.07
(ii)	1.0	1.2	2.0	0.18
(iii)	1.0	1.5	2.0	0.10
(iv)	1.0	1.5	2.5	0.20

'autarkic' solution compared to partial import substitution. Since the solutions analyzed in the following sections will allow the country to reach output level OC, it is of interest to calculate the losses measured by eq. (14).

For this purpose, consider an economy which has opted for the 'autarkic' solution and measure the gains obtained by changing to the partial import substitution solution under alternative price assumptions (see table 1).

Taking Chile as an example, it is our feeling that Chilean conditions are reflected either by price hypothesis (ii) or (iv).[5] This implies that a customs union with other Latin-American countries could bring a short-run gain of nearly 20% to the tradable part of Chile's national product. Assuming that 50% of the GNP of a country like Chile could enter international trade, these figures imply a gain of the order of 10% of GNP. This figure should be compared with those estimates of possible gains through 'trade creation' in common markets among developed countries, which are always put at levels under 1% of GNP.[6]

D. Case 4: tariff preference in the markets of developed countries

We reached the conclusion in last section that the 'autakic' solution to the problem of resource allocation would lead to substantial losses in output levels. However, one alternative to this solution would be that the home country obtain tariff preferences for exports of manufactured products. Normally, these preferences would be granted by industrial countries as illustrated by the UNCTAD scheme.[7]

Should this tariff preference be important enough to cover the difference $p_2' - p_2$, the home country could specialize in I_2 without creating an inconsistency between the industrialization objectives and the constraints in the balance of payments.

Thus, the output level measured by OC could be reached and, since industrial exports would be made, not at world prices but at domestic prices, total income would be above OC or equal to OD.

In order to illustrate this result, consider the new balance os payments equilibrium conditions.

[5] For comparisons of Chilean and international prices, see L. Taylor and E. Bacha, 'Growth and trade distortions in Chile and their implications in calculating the shadow price of foreign exchange', this volume, 000–000.

[6] Cf. R. G. Lipsey, 'The theory of customs unions: a general survey', *Economic Journal* 70 (September, 1960) 496–513.

[7] Cf. R. Prebish, *Hacia una nueva politicia comercial en pro del desarrollo*. United Nations, New York, 1964.

$$A - A'' + p_2'(I_2 - I_2'') = p_1 I_1'',$$

where the difference with case 2 lies in that I_2 is being exported at domestic prices.

The other equations in the system remain the same, or:

total output:	$N = A + p_2 I_2$	
production of I_2:	$I_2 = (k/p_2) N$	
production of A:	$A = A^0 - p_2' I_2$	
total income:	$N'' = A'' + p_1 I_1'' + p_2 I_2''$	(20)
consumption of I_1:	$I_1'' = b I_2''$	
consumption of A:	$A'' = c I_2''$.	

The following relation can then be immediately derived:

$$N'' = N + (p_2' - p_2)(I_2 - I_2'')$$

Geometrically, given $N = OC$ and $I_2 = OL$, it can be seen in fig. 3 that the only combination of N'' and I_2'' which satisfies this equation is $N'' = OD$ and $I_2'' = OJ$.

It will become clear after the next two alternatives are analyzed that this solution is the one which produces the highest income level among all solutions except free trade, which, as we have seen, is not feasible because it does not satisfy the preference for industry constraint.

There is a practical difficulty with this solution: it is the problem of obtaining tariff concessions which are high enough to permit exports of I_2. On the one hand, industrial countries are reluctant to open their markets to labor intensive manufactured goods from developing countries because the prospect of unemployment resulting from such competitive imports could cause social unrest among workers. On the other hand, even a complete tariff cut might not be enough to overcome the difference between p_2' and p_2 because it is possible that the countries which make the tariff consessions are the same ones which are the lowest cost producers in the world, and thus determine the international price, p_2.

E. Case 5: subsidies to industrial exports

The second alternative to the 'autarkic' solution, which would permit the country to specialize in I_2, would involve subsidizing the exports of this industry. In the case, the exports of I_2 are made at the international price, p_2, but the producers receive the domestic price, p_2', with the difference $p_2' - p_2$ being covered by the government. If the subsidies are financed by taxes, this must be done in such a way as not to disturb the relationships between the domestic prices of the different goods (now dependent on the tax system) and the domestic transformation rates of these goods. If these relationships are disturbed, the determination of the supply structure of the model, which is given by the intersection of the production possibilities curve with the preference-for-industry curve, would not coincide with the equilibrium point reached by private entrepreneurs acting in a competitive market. Without taxes, the points $N = OC$ and $I_2 = OL$ could be reached because private producers are indifferent among all points along the transformation curve A^0F as long as the domestic price of I_2 is p_2'. However, it the export subsidies of I_2 were to be financed by, say, a tax on agricultural production, then the relevant price for producers' decisions would be $p_2'/(1 - t)$, where t is the tax rate paid by farmers. In this case, a competitive system would tend to eliminate agricultural production because the costs at which the home country could produce I_2 in terms of the agricultural good, measured by the slope of the transformation curve and equal to p_2', would always be less than the receipts in terms of the agricultural good derived from the production of I_2, equal to $p_2'/(1 - t)$.

In the model, all goods are consumer goods and the factor endownment is fixed. Hence, any proportional and uniform indirect tax will leave domestic price ratios unchanged and thus will meet the proposed criterion.

By means of a subsidy to exports, the country will specialize in I_2 and thus will reach output level OC. The subsidy will imply some internal income redistribution, but will not interfere with the equality between income and output because exports are made at international prices.

One difficulty with this strategy, however, is that the implied income redistribution may become unmanageable if the difference to be covered by subsidies, $p_2' - p_2$, is large or if the exportable surplus $I_2 - I_2''$ is too big. In this case, serious political impasses may have to be resolved to implement this resolution.

F. Case 6: economic integration

The last possibility to be analyzed is the formation of a customs union with a country that has a similar economic structure to the home country, i.e., a country with a preference for industry as well as a comparative advantage in agriculture. It is assumed, however, that within the industrial sector the partner country has smaller costs in industry-one than in industry-two.

If this union is formed, the home country can export I_2 to the partner country at domestic prices, but it will have to import I_1 from the partner country at its own domestic prices which are higher than international prices.

When the home country specializes in I_2, it reaches output level OC. It is a more complex task than in previous cases to calculate the income level attained, however, since no diagramatic representation can be made. Mathematically, the only required change in the equation system presented in case 4 is in the balance of payments equilibrium condition, which will now become:

$$A - A'' + p_2'(I_2 - I_2'') = p_1 I_1^w + p_1''(I_1'' - I_1^w). \tag{16}$$

That is, the home country exports of A and I_2 are now compensated by imports of I_1 from the rest of the world (I^w) at the world price of this good and by imports of I_1 from the partner country, which are equal to the difference between consumption and imports of the home country from the rest of the world. Intra-unions imports, however, are acquired at our partner's price, p_1''.

If the system (15)–(16) is combined with the corresponding system of the partner country we will end up with fourteen equations in sixteen variables. The whole system is closed by two identities specifying:

exports of I_2 from the home country to the partner country	≡	imports of I_2 of the partner country from the home country

and:

imports of I_1 of the home country from the partner country	≡	exports of I_1 from the partner country to the home country

Assuming the existence of a viable economic solution to this set of equations, the resulting income levels can be determined. Manipulation of eqs. (15)–(16) yields the following expressions:

$$N'' = N + [(p_1/p_1'')p_2' - p_2] (I_2 - I_2'') + [(p_1/p_1'') - 1] S, \tag{17}$$

where

$$S = (A - A'') - p_1 I_1^w$$

is the superavit of the home country transactions with the rest of the world. Consider the second term in the right-hand side of eq. (17). Clearly:

$[(p_1/p_1'') p_2' - p_2] (I_2 - I_2'') \gtreqqless 0$, according to $p_2'/p_2 \gtreqqless p_1''/p_1$.

That is, if the home country is less efficient in I_2 than the partner country in I_1 (i.e.: if $p_2'/p_2 > p_1''/p_1$), then the income level of the home country, N'', will tend to be higher than the output level, N. If the home country is more efficient, the opposite will hold true.

Consider now the last term of eq. (17). Clearly:

$[(p_1/p_1'') - 1] S \gtreqqless 0$, according to $S \lesseqqgtr O$, since $p_1'' > p_1$.

Thus, if the home country shows a deficit with the rest of the world ($S < 0$), corresponding to a superavit with the union, the income level will tend to be higher than output.

The results can be expressed more synthetically by the manipulation of eq. (17), from which, using eq. (16), one can obtain:

$$N'' - N = (p_2' - p_2) (I_2 - I_2'') - (p_1'' - p_1) (I_1'' - I_1^w). \tag{17a}$$

As eq. (17a) shows the home country will benefit from intra-union trade as long as the difference between the home country exports and the value of these exports at international prices is larger than the difference between the home country imports and the value of these imports at international prices. Of course, the exports and imports specified here refer only to those resulting from intra-union trade.[8]

Observe that for the union as a whole these differences are zero sum gains or losses. If one country has income higher than product, the partner will have product higher than income. Moreover, the home country income + partner's income = the home country output + partner's output, simply because the balance of payments of the union with the rest of the world is balanced in world prices. Thus, from the point of view of the customs union, the only gains compared with an 'autarkic' solution are those measured by the displacement of the output from OB to OC, due to the elimination of the less efficient industrial production.

[8.] A formula similar to eq. (17a) is proposed by Ffrench–Davis and Griffin to obtain the value of compensation payments, which would assure that the 'reciprocity principle' is respected in the context of commercial flows induced by the Latin American Free Trade Association. Cf. R. Ffrench–Davis and K.B. Griffin, *Comercio internacional y politicas de desarrollo economico*, Fondo de Cultura Economica, Mexico 1967, 196–198. See also: D.C. Mead, 'The distribution of gains in a customs union between developing countries', *Kyklos*, 1968, fasc. 4; and also: Carlos F. Diaz-Alejandro, 'The Andean common market: gestation and outlook', this volume, 000–000.

In this way, it can be concluded that a customs union could solve the problem of resource allocation satisfactorily. However, inequalities in the benefits enjoyed by the partner countries will ineviably arise if the countries are at different stages of industrial efficiency. The same thing will happen if intra-union trade is unbalanced at those points where the partner countries are specialized in their more efficient activities.

The political problems involved in creating a compensation mechanism to cancel possible discrepancies between output and income, as measured by eq. (17), are well known. Thus, it must be concluded that the only solution to the problem of equity in a customs union is by means of association of countries which have a similar degree of industrial efficiency and for which intra-union trade equilibrium can be expected at the specialization points.

If intra-union trade equilibrium is imposed, then, in general, only one of the two countries will completely specialize in its more efficient industry and the other will continue to produce both industrial goods. Formally, what happens can be visualized by the substitution of eq. (16) by two equilibrium conditions:

$$p_2'(I_2 - I_2'') = p_1''(I_1'' - I_1^w) \tag{18}$$

and

$$A - A = p_1 I_1^w.$$

The first equation imposes equilibrium in intra-union trade; the second equation can be derived from the first, when eq. (16) is taken into account.

Equation counting will reveal that, in this case, there are seventeen equations in the whole system (recalling that eq. (18) serves both countries) with the same sixteen variables as before. This system is overdetermined. It can be made consistent only if one of the countries activates its less efficient industry. In this case, we would have one additional variable to be determined — the domestic production of I_1 for example — and the system would present as many equations as variables.

Two additional points deserve consideration.

One of the initial assumptions was that the home country would export I_2 to his patner and import only I_1, from him. However, it might occur within our price assumptions that:

$$p_1' < p_1'',$$

and:

$$p_2' < p_2'',$$

even when:

$$p_1'/p_2' > p_1''/p_2''.$$

That is, relative to the price of the agricultural good, the home country could have both industrial prices lower than its partner's even when it produces I_1 at costs measured in relation to the price of the industry-two good, which are higher than those of the partner country.

If this occurred, the home country would tend to export both I_1 and I_2 to the partner, importing from him the agricultural good, A.

Obviously, such a situation would be uninteresting to the home country in terms of real output and would hurt the partner country in two ways: first by not satisfying its industrial preference and second by forcing it to buy industrial goods from a relatively expensive source.[9]

The best alternative for the partner country under these conditions would be to subsidize the intra-union exports of I_1 in order to cover the difference $p_1'' - p_1'$ and thus give competitive conditions to its industry in the home country's market. The creation of a payments union with flexible exchange rates between the two countries and valid only for industrial goods, or the institution by the partner country of a dual exchange rate system favoring industrial exports in general would have effects comparable to those of subsidies. Such commercial policies could 'artificially' reduce the price of I_1 produced in the partner country to levels below the home country's domestic price and thus induce 'correct' commercial flows within the union.

One might ask if it would be easy to find, for any given home country, a partner country with a comparative advantage exactly in the home country's less efficient industry. When one remembers that in the real world there are numerous industries instead of only two, however, it becomes clear that it would be difficult to find two countries with exactly the same structure of comparative advantage. Obviously, the more distinct these structures are, the more the union gains since the number of inefficient industries in the home country would be reduced according to the extent to which the partner's market is open to a large number of the home countries' cheaper industrial goods.

Finally, it would be interesting to compare the results obtained in this paper with those derived using the approaches of the Viner and Meade variety,

---

[9] Incidentally, in the context of the proposed Andean Group, the role of the partner country would be played by Venezuela, which has higher industrial costs than Chile and Colombia. This would explain Venezuela's reluctance to enter such a customs union. Cf. E.L. Bacha, 'Venezuela y el grupo andino: el problema y las alternativas', *El Trimestre Economico*, January–March, 1970.

which focus upon 'trade creation' and 'trade diversion' in the context of partial equilibrium models.

The present work, in viewing the customs union as an alternative to the 'autarkic' solution, distinguishes between a *production effect* and *a consumption effect*. The production effect, measured by eq. (14), is always positive if we ignore the perverse cases of specialization in the higher-cost industries. The consumption effect, measured by eqs. (17) or (17a), can be positive or negative depending on the relative industrial efficiency of the home country as compared to the partner and on the balance of trade situation within the union. For all partners taken together, however, the sum of the consumption effects is zero. Thus, from the point of view of the union, economic integration is *always* a good thing.

This result can be contrasted with the conclusion derived from a comparison of the benefits of 'trade creation' with the costs of 'trade diversion'. Based on this comparison it is frequently concluded that the costs will be higher than the benefits in the context of customs unions among developing countries.[10] The fundamental difference between the two approaches is that the alternative to integration, in the case of Viner and Meade, is seen as free trade whereas in the present approach, the alternative to integration is the 'autarkic' solution.[11] This difference, in turn, is linked to the introduction of the preference-for-industry assumption discussed in this paper.

IV. Ordering the alternatives

In conclusion, the different cases studied here can be ordered according to the level of income attained without constraints and according to the level of income reached along the preference-for-industry curve. Table 2, considering only customs unions for which the income level is equal to the output level, summarizes the conclusions.

The following comments about the results shown in table 2 can be made:

(i) The classification of 'free trade' and 'partial import substitution' as the less desirable alternatives with the preference for industry constraint is explained by the fact that the only income level compatible with the preference-for-industry constraint is 0. Perhaps one could also say that these alternatives are *not applicable* when a preference for industry exists rather than try to classify them.

[10] Cf. R.L. Allen, 'Integration in less developed areas', *Kyklos*, 1961, fasc. 3.

[11] The type of approach of this paper is also employed by S. Dell, *A Latin-American common market?* Oxford University Press, London, 1967.

Table 2
Ordering of the commercial policy alternatives

Alternative	Ordering according to unconstrained income level		Ordering according to income level along the preference for industry curve	
Free trade	1	$(OA°)$	4	(O)
Partial import substitution	2	(OD)	4	(O)
'Autarky'	4	(OB)	3	(OB)
Tariff preferences in industrial countries	2	(OD)	1	(OD)
Industrial exports subsidies	3	(OC)	2	(OC)
Economic integration	3	(OC)	2	(OC)

(ii) The 'partial import substitution' solution is placed second, according to the unconstrained income level attained, on the assumption that the country becomes self-sufficient in I_2 and does not produce I_1 at all. In this case, $N = N'' = OD$ and $I_2 = I_2'' = OJ$ in fig. 3.

(iii) 'Economic integration' has the same rank order as 'industrial exports subsidies' whether or not a preference for industry exists. However, taking into account the difficulties of creating an intra-union compensation mechanism and the fact that, in principle, it is uncertain whether or not the country would be hurt or helped by intra-union trade, it can be anticipated that a government with risk aversion would rank 'export subsidies' higher than 'economic integration'.

Appendix: a note on the 'trade vs. aid' controversy

Recent macroeconomic analysis of the development process and of the potential contribution of external aid makes a distinction between two alternative limits to the growth rate of output: one given by the domestic savings potential, and the other by the capacity to import.[12] Empirically, it has been observed that many underdeveloped countries have their growth rates limited not by the savings potential but by the capacity to import intermediate and capital goods.[13]

[12] This is the well-known Chenery's two gap model which is discussed by R. McKinnon, 'Foreign exchange constraints in economic development and efficient aid allocation', *Economic Journal*, June, 1964.
[13] Cf. H.B. Chenery and A. Strout, 'Foreign assistance and economic development', *American Economic Review* 56 (September, 1966) 679–733.

In the above situation, an additional dollar of foreign aid would have the same effect on the growth rate as an additional dollar of exports because in both cases the external bottleneck would be reduced by the same proportion. Thus from a developing country's view point, trade and aid would be perfect substitutes.

Such a conclusion, argues Harry Johnson,[14] is fallacious because foreign aid can eliminate a prospective trade gap without any additional savings effort, whereas the elimination of the same gap through exports would not only require that the country supply the goods, but also that it increase its domestic savings by the same amount as its new exports receipts.

More specifically, Prof. Johnson maintains that:

'As a first approximation, foreign aid serves two functions in the development process. First, it provides real resources additional to what can be extracted from the domestic economy, increasing the total available for investment; second, since the resources are foreign it averts the real income losses to the country involved in transforming domestic into foreign resources. The opening of additional opportunities to trade differs from the provision of additional aid in that, again as a first approximation, it does not provide additional real resources for investment. Instead, it provides the opportunity to convert additional domestic resources into foreign resources without the losses that would ensue on the country's own efforts to effect this transformation. The contribution of resources is obviously to be measured, not by the value of the additional trade, but by the losses the opportunity permits the country to avoid.'[15]

Thus, from the point of view of a developing country, dollar per dollar foreign aid is always more valuable than the export opportunity. It is also concluded that the higher the costs of import substitution, the more attractive exports promotion becomes.

The analysis of Prof. Johnson is irrefutable in its own terms; it simply reafirms the common sense observation that an additional domestic saving unit has a positive alternative cost even when the country's propensity to save is not an effective constraint on its growth rate.

However, for an economy such as that described by the model in this paper, it can be shown that Prof. Johnson's conclusion does not hold as long as tariff preferences for manufactured exports provide additional trade opportunities.[16]

[14.] Cf. H.C. Johnson, *Economic polices towards less developed countries.* Frederick A. Praeger, New York, 1967, 52 ff.
[15.] H.G. Johnson, *op. cit.,* 55–56.
[16.] This is the context in which the controversy trade vs. aid is discussed in UNCTAD. See: R. Prebish, *Hacia una nueva politicia comercial en pro del desarrollo.* United Nations, New York, 1964.

The conclusion of the two gap model is not verified and preferential trade, dollar per dollar, appears as inequivocally better than foreign aid.

This conclusion can be obtained from the model presented in this paper because the opportunity to export manufactures allows the country to specialize in its more efficient industry. In the case of foreign aid, although the country is allowed to live with a deficit in its foreign accounts, it becomes necessary to operate the industry in which the country is less efficient in order to meet its government industrial preference.

Let us consider fig. 4 for a geometric proof of the superiority of preferential trade over aid. From the text, we know that, under preferential trade, the output level will be OC and the income level will be OD. CD measures not only the difference between income and product, but also the potential deficit in the trade balance of the country if its exports of I_2 were made not at the do-

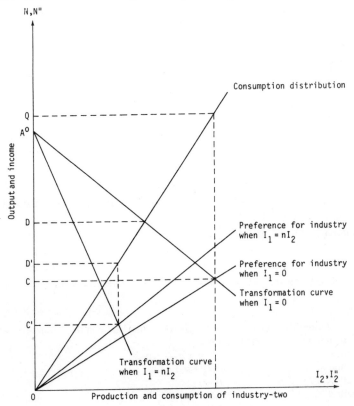

Fig. 4.

mestic prices, as they are, but at world prices, as they would have to be in the absence of tariff preferences. Thus, CD is identifiable as 'foreign aid'. Suppose that this same value, CD, were given as a continuous flow of donations rather through tariff preferences. Then the question is; what levels of output and income can be reached when CD is given as a donation?

In the first place, it can be seen in fig. 4 that an amount of aid equal to CD is inconsistent with specialization of the country in I_2. For, in the case of specialization, the output level would be OC generating a supply of I_2 equal to OL. OL would be totally consumed only if the income level were equal to OQ, implying a flow of aid equal to CQ, which is much higher than CD.

Thus, it is necessary to manufacture I_1 in the country. In this case (according to eq. (14) in the text), the output level would be less than OC. Graphically, the new levels of output and income can be found by simultaneously rotating the transformation locus (clockwise around A^0) and the preference for industry locus (counterclockwise around the origin) until the vertical distance between the crossing point of these two loci and the consumption distribution line is equal to the aid amount $CD = C'D'$. At this point it is assumed in the figure that domestic production of I_1 is given by $I_1 = nI_2$, where n is an auxiliary variable found by the solution of the equation system in the text.[17]

It can be seen that the income level reached with preferential trade, OD, is above that level, OD', attained with a foreign aid equivalent dollar-per-dollar to the tariff preference. Actually, it is conceivable that the distance OD' is even less that OC, if the country is not very inefficient in the production of I_1. In this case, and external aid equal to CD would be even less desirable than a domestic policy of export subsidies, which would permit the country to specialize in I_2 (in this case income and output levels would be equal to OC as shown in the text).

Finally, it is unimportant whether any positive level of aid will permit the country to reach an income level superior to that under an "autarkic" policy, as described in the text. This is true, because as long as it is positive, foreign aid will lead to an output of I_1 smaller than that obtained under the "autarkic" solution.

[17.] The equations are the same as in the 'autarkic' solution, with the difference that a deficit is allowed in the trade balance:

total output:	$N = A + p_1 I_1 + p_2 I_2$
production of I_1:	$p_1 I_1 + p_2 I_2 = kN$
production of I_2:	$I_2 = I_2''$
production of A:	$A = A^0 - p_1' I_1 - p_2' I_2$
total income:	$N'' = A'' + p_1 I_1'' + p_2 I_2''$
consumption of I_1:	$I_1'' = b I_2''$
consumption of A:	$A'' = c I_2''$
balance of payments:	$A - A'' + \text{AID} = p_1 (I_1'' - I_1)$,

where AID $= CD$ in the figure.

R.S. Eckaus, P.N. Rosenstein-Rodan (eds.), Analysis of development problems,
© North-Holland Publishing Company

THE ANDEAN COMMON MARKET:
GESTATION AND OUTLOOK *

Carlos F. DIAZ-ALEJANDRO

Yale University, New Haven, Conn., USA

I. Introduction

By the mid-1960's the dissatisfaction of several middle-sized Latin American countries with the Latin-American Free Trade Association (LAFTA) became acute. Some complained that the three Latin-American giants (Argentina, Brazil and México) were reaping most of the advantages of the group. That argument centered on trade balances within the association. Others, eager for a faster integration pace, saw in a sub-regional approach, bringing together countries of roughly equal economic dimension, a useful complement (and goad) to LAFTA and a necessary steppingstone in the construction of a Latin American Common Market.[1]

The formal birth of the Andean group as a sub-region of LAFTA may be dated with the Declaration of Bogotá of August 1966, signed by Chile, Colombia, Ecuador, Perú and Venezuela. The treaty creating the Andean Common Market was only signed nearly three years later, in May 1969. Laborious negotiations have failed to persuade Venezuela to accept the final treaty; Bolivia, which had joined the Andean group during 1967, joined the other four countries in this 'Treaty of Cartagena'.

---

* Earlier drafts of this paper have benefitted from comments by Charles P. Kindleberger, Osvaldo Sunkel and Raúl Sáez. Several of the ideas presented in this paper were sketched in my 'El Grupo Andino en el proceso de integración latinoamericana', Estudios Internacionales 2, No. 2 (July–September, 1968) 242–57. Important Andean events have occurred between the writing of this paper (May 1970) and stylistic revision of its page proofs; the reader must go elsewhere for a discussion of such matters as the impact on the Andean group of the election of President Allende in Chile, the details of Decision 24, and the Ecuadorian oil boom.

[1] For a discussion of LAFTA history see: Economic cooperation in Latin-America, Africa and Asia: a handbook of documents, ed. by Miguel S. Wionczek, The M.I.T. Press, Cambridge, Mass., 1969, Chapter 1.

This paper will examine the gestation of the Andean Common Market during 1966 through 1969, paying particular attention to issues generally relevant to the formation of customs unions among developing countries. The outlook for the economic impact of Andean integration, as it appeared during the first semester of 1970, will be discussed. Most of the arguments which will be developed would apply, a fortiori, to the analysis of the economic effects of a hypothetical Latin-American Common Market. This is particularly true for the central thesis of this paper, which argues that the possible trade-creating effects of Latin-American integration are substantial, and much larger than commonly assumed in the literature on customs unions among developing countries.[2]

Before turning to these matters, it will be useful to outline the major characteristics of the five Andean countries (Bolivia, Chile, Colombia, Ecuador and Perú) and contrast them with the rest of Latin-America.

II. Some characteristics of the Andean Five

The Andean Five in 1966 had a population of 49 million, representing 20% of the population of the twenty Latin-American republics, and exceeding that of México, and by far those of Argentina and the Central American Common Market.[3]

As shown in table 1, the Andean population extends over an area covering 23% of the Latin-American domain. Total Andean Gross Domestic Product is similar to that of Argentina; had Venezuela stayed in the group the combined GDP would have been roughly comparable to those of Brazil and México.

---

[2] See, for example, C.A. Cooper and B.F. Massell, 'Towards a general theory of customs unions for developing countries', *The Journal of Political Economy* 73 (October, 1965) 461–76; and Donald C. Meade, 'The distribution of gains in customs unions between developing countries', *Kyklos* 21 (1968) 713–36. As Meade puts it: '. . . we would agree with the appraisal of R.L. Allen that customs unions among developing countries 'are all fundamentally protectionist', in the sense that they are designed to facilitate the expansion of output in lines where money costs of production are now and are likely to remain above world prices' (p. 718). It should be noted that Meade writes on the basis of African experience.

[3] Compare also with the 1966 populations of the proposed Maghreb group (32 million, including Morocco, Algeria, Tunisia and Lybia), that for East Africa (29 million, including Kenya, Uganda and Tanzania), Nordek (17 million, including Denmark, Iceland, Norway and Sweden), and the Caribbean Free Trade Association (CARIFTA, including several of the smaller Antilles, about 5 million).

Table 1
Basic data on the Andean countries and other Latin-American republics, 1966

	Five Andean countries	Vene-zuela	Argen-tina	Brazil	México	Central-American Common Market	Other republics
Population (million)	48.5	9.4	22.7	83.2	44.1	13.2	22.2
Area (million Km.^{2})	4.6	0.9	2.8	8.5	2.0	0.4	0.9
GDP (billion $)	23.0	8.8	22.5	34.4	33.1	5.3	9.1
GDP per capita $	470	940	990	410	750	400	410
Merchandise Exports (Bill $)	2.5	2.4	1.6	1.7	1.2	0.8	1.2
Merchandise Imports (Bill $)	2.6	1.3	1.1	1.5	1.6	0.9	1.6
Mining output:							
Coal (mill. tons)	4.0	0.03	0.4	2.4	2.1	nil	nil
Iron (mill. tons)	12.9	11.4	0.1	15.8	1.5	nil	nil
Copper (000 tons)	837.7	nil	nil	3.0	74.4	9.9	12.0
Lead (000 tons)	186.1	nil	30.0	20.0	182.1	10.0	nil
Zinc (000 tons)	328.9	nil	26.6	nil	219.2	9.0	nil
Tin (000 tons)	25.6	nil	1.0	1.2	0.8	nil	nil
Crude oil (mill. m^3)	18.0	195.8	16.7	6.4	20.5	nil	nil
Agricultural output:							
Rice (mill. tons)	1.4	0.2	0.2	5.8	0.4	0.2	0.7
Maize (mill. tons)	2.1	0.6	7.0	11.4	9.1	1.7	1.0
Wheat (mill. tons)	1.6	nil	6.4	0.6	1.6	nil	0.4
Sugar (mill. tons)	1.7	0.4	1.0	4.4	2.1	0.5	5.4
Cocoa (000 tons)	72.0	22.0	nil	173.3	23.8	9.1	32.1
Coffee (000 tons)	583.7	61.0	nil	1365.6	185.8	335.1	99.4
Cotton (000 tons)	204	16	114	622	619	230	33
Wool (000 tons)	43.4	nil	200.0	29.0	8.0	nil	86.2
Tobacco (000 tons)	64.3	9.8	42.3	228.3	68.9	11.0	84.6
Beef and veal (000 tons)	713	165	2653	1460	385	151	615
Pork (000 tons)	162	31	252	590	147	33	110
Milk (mill. tons)	3.8	0.6	4.7	6.5	2.6	0.8	2.5
Hen eggs (000 tons)	124	30	175	510	201	31	62
Industrial output:							
Electricity (000 GWH)	20.0	8.9	16.5	35.3	20.9	2.4	7.9
Finished steel (mill. tons)	0.8	0.3	1.3	2.6	2.2	nil	nil
Steel ingots (mill. tons)	1.0	0.7	1.3	3.7	3.0	nil	nil
Pig iron (mill. tons)	0.61	0.35	0.52	2.89	1.40	nil	nil
Cement (mill. tons)	5.0	2.1	3.5	5.5	4.9	0.5	1.8
Sheet glass (mill. m^2)	5.6	nil	7.0[a]	6.2	12.5	nil	1.9
Caustic soda (000 tons)	55	10	63	100[b]	128	nil	3
Soda ash (000 tons)	46	nil	nil	85	175	nil	nil

Table 1 (continued)

	Five Andean countries	Vene-zuela	Argen-tina	Brazil	México	Central American Common Market	Othe repu
Industrial output:							
Sulphuric acid (000 tons)	270	52	168[b]	301[b]	579	11	150[a]
Tubes (mill. units)	1.1	0.8	2.7	3.7	1.3	nil	0.
Tires (mill. units)	1.7	1.3	2.9	5.2	2.3	nil	0..
Paper and board (000 tons)	329	155	479	695	610	11	148
Pulp (000 tons)	422	20	135	619[b]	353	nil	38
Synthetic fibers (000 tons)	7.9	5.5	14.8	15.4	11.9	nil	0.!
Beer (mill. liters)	1144	297	226	766	1166	63	221
Gasoline (mill. m^3)	5.2	8.5	4.6	6.6	5.6	nil	1..

Sources: GDP determined by ECLA, Estudio económico de la América Latina, 1968, mimeo.
All other statistics from Statistical Bulletin for Latin-America 5, No. 1.
[a] Refers to 1963.
[b] Refers to 1965.

Latin-American mineral production is dominated by Andean countries, even without Venezuela. Of total regional output, for example, they account for 90% of tin, 89% of copper, 56% of zinc, 45% of coal, 43% of lead, 31% of iron (58% including Venezuela), and 7% of oil (83% including Venezuela). Andean output of tungsten, molybdenum, antimony, nitrate and bismuth also dominate Latin-American production of those products. Joint policies could give these countries substantial bargaining power and control over the exploitation and marketing of their natural resources, as for several mining products they represent important shares of world trade. Even where those shares are small, a minimum of solidarity can expand the options open to individual countries when dealing with non-Andean firms, as illustrated in the dispute between Bolivia and Gulf Oil Company. But more on this below.

Per capita Andean food and fiber production, on the other hand, is below that of the rest of Latin-America taken as a whole, as suggested in table 1. Andean output of rice and wheat accounts for about 15% of the Latin-American total, and the proportion is even less for maize, sugar and beef and veal. Although the subregion has been a net exporter of coffee, fruits and fish, it is a net importer of meat, cereals (especially wheat) and dairy products. The help which Andean countries will be able to give each other in making their food and fiber supply more flexible will be limited, although not zero. For example, Perú is an efficient producer and exporter of sugar, while Chile is an inefficient producer and importer of that good. Rich fishing along the Pacific coast, hardwood forests in southern Chile and tropical woods elsewhere also contribute to the Andean natural resource base.

The Andean Five generate 18% of Latin-American electricity and account for 21% of cement output, figures roughly in line with their population share. But the Andean manufacturing sector clearly lags behind those of Argentina, Brazil and México in 'heavy' branches, such as metallurgy, petrochemicals and machinery and equipment. The Andean output of iron and steel, for example, represents only about 11% of Latin-American production. The desire to overcome this lag is one of the motivations for the creation of a subregion which allows for larger markets (and economies of scale), but still keeps out the large Latin-American countries which are more advanced in 'dynamic' activities. Andean countries with 'insufficient markets' prefer to face Brazilean competition in, say, steel, after they have had a chance to expand their own activities within the larger subregional market.

The post-war growth of Andean economies, although not spectacular, has been respectable. Manufacturing output has grown at an average annual rate of 5.6% during 1950—68. Output of electricity has expanded at a yerly rate of 7.4% during 1960—68. With the exception of Ecuador, the GDP of all Andean countries grew as fast or faster than the Latin-American average for 1960—66. Merchandise imports and exports, measured in current dollars, grew at a healthy 7.0% per annum during 1959—68. In contrast with the bigger Latin-American countries, the participation of foreign trade in Andean GDP has risen since 1950. Intra-Andean trade, however, remains a tiny fraction (3%) of total Andean foreign trade. The relative Andean dynamism could be an important factor in smoothing the frictions and facilitating the adjustments which rapid trade liberalization programs may generate and call for. Note that an annual growth rate of 6% will *double* industrial output in less than 12 years, roughly the period foreseen as transition to a full customs union.[4]

Andean development problems are similar to those of many other Latin-American countries: a population expansion larger than 3% per annum, nearly half of the labor force in primary production (typically at low levels of productivity), skewed income distribution and limited availability of education, health and other social services, especially in rural areas.

---

[4] Data in this paragraph obtained from several issues of Economic Commission for Latin-America (ECLA). *Notas sobre la economía y el desarollo de América Latina,* and *International financial statistics.* During 1967—70, however, Andean growth seems to have declined relative to that of the rest of Latin-America.

The subregion is far from homogeneous, creating many possibilities for further imbalances and frictions on the way to a customs union. Chile has a per capita GNP three times that of Bolivia, for example. (But contrast this with an Argentine per capita GNP ten times that of Haiti.) Chile and Colombia have had many years of tight protectionist measures and overvalued exchange rates, which have brought down the ratio of imports of goods and services in GNP to between 12 and 14%. Perú has maintained a more open economy, and has an import coefficient around 21% of GNP, although it also has a substantial manufacturing sector. Ecuador and Bolivia, the smallest and least developed members of the group, have weak manufacturing sectors and import coefficients far above those of Chile and Colombia. Reluctant Venezuela, with its oil resources, presents many sharp structural contrasts vis-a-vis the five Andeans. To differences in per capita income, manufacturing development and foreign trade participation one should add the heterogeneity of Andean historical experiences with inflation and exchange rate stability. For example, during 1963–68, Chilean consumer prices rose at an annual rate of 28%, those of Perú at 13%, in Colombia at 11%, while smaller rates were registered in Ecuador and Bolivia. Venezuela, of course, has a long tradition of price and exchange stability

During its early years, the Andean group had more 'constitutionalist' political structures than most other South-American countries. Presidents Frei, of Chile, and Lleras Restrepo, of Colombia, provided dynamic leadership. Elections to replace both took place during 1970, while military governments rule Perú and Bolivia. On the whole, Andean political leadership tends to be more nationalistic and populistic than the Latin-American average. Together with the (often exaggerated) fear of becoming industrial satellites of the three big Latin-American countries, this fact has been an important force strengthening the political will to create an Andean community within LAFTA.

III. The road to Cartagena

The implementation of broad agreements reached in the Declaration of Bogotá was first held up by postponements in the publicized meeting of the Presidents of the Americas. In February 1967, Raúl Sáez, chief Chilean representative to the Andean group at that time, visited the Presidents of Colombia, Perú and Venezuela, trying to speed up action on Andean matters. The meeting of the American Presidents, finally held on April 1967, recognized the desirability of subregional agreements, like that of the Andean coun-

tries.[5] In June 1967, a Mixed Commission was created by personal representatives of the Andean Presidents, in a meeting at Viña del Mar, at which time
a first draft for the Andean Corporation was also prepared. The second and
third meetings of the Mixed Commision were held in Quito (July 1967) and
Caracas (August 1967), respectively. In the latter meeting, the entrance of
Bolivia into the Andean group and the bases for the subregional treaty were
approved. During August/September 1967 the LAFTA foreign ministers
approved guidelines for the creation of subregional groups within LAFTA,
following proposals by the Andean group. At the same meeting, LAFTA gave
new signs of weakness. At the fourth meeting of the Mixed Commission, held
in Lima in November 1967, it was decided to create the Andean Corporation
by public treaty, requiring legislative ratification, thus postponing the date
when this institution could start operating. The fifth meeting, held in Bogotá
in February 1968, produced a finished treaty creating the Andean Corporation,
and drafts for the treaty creating the common market.

While the treaty creating the Andean Development Corporation was formally signed by the Andean five plus Venezuela in Bogotá, on February 1968,
disagreements arose over the draft customs union treaty. During the sixth
meeting of the Mixed Commission, held in Cartagena during July 1968, only
Bolivia, Colombia and Chile expressed willingness to sign that treaty as drafted.
Perú and Venezuela objected to what they regarded as too fast a pace of trade
liberalization. Nearly a year later, and after some dilution of the trade-libera-
lizing provisions and a bit of horsetrading,[6] the treaty creating an Andean
customs union was signed in Bogotá, in May 1969. Venezuela, however, could
not be persuaded, and was given until the end of 1970 to join without the
need of special negotiations. On July 1969 LAFTA formally approved the
treaty as compatible with that organization, and by October 1969 the Treaty
of Cartagena had been ratified by enough countries to be formally in effect.

The architects of the Andean group considered that an efficient and rapid
path toward economic integration had to rely not only on automatic trade
liberalization, but also on institutions which could guide, smooth and plan
that process. Thus the importance given to the Andean Development Corporation.

[5] The meeting of the Presidents also solemnly pledged that a Latin-American Common
Market would be created within no more than 15 years, starting in 1970. Neither then nor
now was that pledge taken seriously by either the signataries nor anybody else. The Alice-
in-Wonderland atmosphere of pan-American meetings reached an all time high at those sessions.
[6] For example, it is said that Perú finally decided to sign only after Lima was chosen as
the headquarters for the treaty secretariat. Colombia had very much hoped Bogotá would
be chosen.

A. The Andean Development Corporation

Venezuelan reluctance to sign the Treaty of Cartagena has left the Andean Development Corporation (ADC), as created in February 1968, in a somewhat anomalous situation. Among other things, this first multinational long-term financial institution wholly controlled by Latin-Americans is supposed to be located in Caracas. On January 1970 the required minimum of ratifications of the ADC treaty had reached the community's authorities, clearing legal requirements for the beginning of operations of that institution. Whatever the final outcome of Venezuelan relations with the Andean Five, however, the nature of the ADC is unlikely to depart much from what was foreseen in the treaty of February 1968. The institution is supposed to start with suscribed capital of $ 25 million, wholly supplied by the six Andean countries.[7] The Corporation has the power to issue a wide variety of securities, and counts with great legal flexibility to obtain credits and issue guarantees, if it so wished. The organizers of the Corporation expect to tap new private and public sources of funds, inside and outside the region. Although the instrument creating the Corporation foresees the possibility of having the private sector represented in its board of directors, a possibility which aroused concern in some parliaments, majority control is assured for the six governments. Prodded by Chile, the community authorities have emphasized the dominant role of the public sector in the ADC, and have committed themselves to limit the participation of the *foreign* private sector in the equities of the corporation.

The Andean Development Corporation is supposed to accelerate integration with its investment policy. It will give special attention to multinational projects and those benefitting the least developed members, Ecuador and Bolivia. (The first president of the ADC is a Bolivian.) It will not have to wait for projects to be presented for their consideration, as it has the power to study, prepare and carry out projects on its own initiative. As in the case of some national development institutions, it will be able to promote the creation or modernization of enterprises. In short, instead of becoming one more financial institution, it could act as a dynamic engine of integration and development, with an impact far superior to that suggested by its original capital.

[7] The shares of Bolivia and Ecuador are smaller than the (equal) shares of Colombia, Chile, Perú and Venezuela. An earlier proposal establishing shares according to contributions to the Interamerican Development Bank, which would have meant that Venezuela provided the largest share, was dropped at the request of Perú, which in the IDB has a smaller contribution. Earlier proposals to speed up the creation of the ADC by circumventing the need to obtain Congressional approvals were also shelved.

Together with the executive regional authority, created by the Treaty of Cartagena and with whom it should have close coordination, the ADC should help plan regional growth. It would help coordinate national investments in social overhead capital, especially regarding 'physical integration', and in key industrial branches where economies of scale are very pronounced. The corporation could also be used in some circumstances as the sole representative of the Andean community, as when negotiating with foreign investors and institutions. By issuing Andean bonds in world capital markets it could help diversify the external sources of funds to the region, while perhaps improving the credit terms each country faces in isolation. The ADC may also receive concessional loans (aid) from industrialized countries (east and west) and international lending institutions, to be devoted to encouraging integration. While non-Andean participation should remain limited in the creation of an Andean common market, even under the most optimistic assumptions regarding external willingness to help, such foreign cooperation could play a modest positive role if it serves to strengthen and partly finance the budding Andean community institutions, such as the ADC and balance-of-payments clearing mechanisms.

Frictions and disequilibria created by the trade liberalization program could be smoothed by special loans from the ADC for retraining of workers or to give a new start for some entrepreneurs. A wise distribution of loans could also (temporarily) offset politically dangerous regional trade imbalances.

B. The Treaty of Cartagena

Throughout the negotiations leading to the Treaty of Cartagena, the exact role and speed of trade liberalization has been a source of disagreement, although few, if any, saw in such liberalization the only instrument of integration. Integration of new vs. established industries, planning integration vs. trade liberalization, etc., were some of the forms in which the arguments took shape. To an economist, the substance of much of the debate could be summarized under the pro's and con's of trade diversion and creation.

The final version of the Treaty of Cartagena, while allowing considerable flexibility in the program of trade liberalization and embodying substantial concessions to those fearful of rapid reduction of intra-Andean trade barriers, sets up a non-trival integration pace, so long as the numerous escape clauses are used with moderation. Complete freedom for most intra-Andean trade is scheduled for no later than the end of 1980; all barriers to such trade, including those under exchange control and import licensing, should be permanently eliminated by then. It may be noted that Colombia and Chile had advocated a shorter deadline for total freedom of trade.

Trade in goods included under sectorial complementation agreements (like petrochemicals) will be freed according to the pace specified in such agreements, typically involving new industries. Trade in goods not now produced in any of the Andean five should have been freed totally by February 1971. Trade in about 85 products already included in LAFTA's 'Common List', many rural products with slight processing, were scheduled to be freed totally during April 1970. Duties on the intra-Andean trade of all other commodities will be reduced every year by 10% of the starting duty, which will be the lowest duty for each product now found in Colombia, Chile or Perú, and in no case exceeding 100% ad valorem. By the end of 1970 duties were brought down, for each product, to the lowest duty found in Colombia, Chile or Perú; the 10% cuts from that duty start at the end of 1971, so that by the end of 1980 they will reach zero. In other words, contrary to cumbersome LAFTA procedures, trade liberalization could be automatic, irreversible and across-the-board.

The liberalization program also commits the countries to the 'stand-still' principle, i.e., no new restrictions of any kind may be introduced in intra-Andean trade.

This program is qualified in several ways to take into account sundry fears of trade liberalization. Each country can present 'lists of exceptions'. These escape clauses are least generous to Chile and Colombia, the champions of trade liberalization. Rural products have their own special escape clauses. Bolivia and Ecuador will not have to start cutting tariffs by 10% until the end of 1976, dragging cuts until the end of 1985, although their exports to other Andean countries will benefit from an accelerated program of liberalization. The production of some goods may be 'reserved' for Ecuador and Bolivia, in which case the liberalization of their trade may be delayed. And so on; clearly, the pace of trade liberalization will depend on the use or abuse which will be made of escape clauses of various kinds.

The Treaty of Cartagena foresees the approach toward a common external Andean tariff in two steps. By the end of 1975 a *minimum* common external tariff should be established; by the end of 1980 the countries should have completed the transition toward the same tariff. As in the liberalization program, Bolivia and Ecuador are covered by special provisions, allowing them a more leisurely schedule. The Treaty says little about the target level of the common external tariff.

The Treaty also touches upon industrial and rural programming, physical integration and social overhead capital, financial and monetary cooperation, and the coordination of development plans and of policies toward local and foreign capital. It stresses the need to distribute fairly gains from integration and reduce regional income inequalities (special provisions for Bolivia and Ecuador take a good share of the Treaty). But, perhaps wisely, nothing very concrete is said on these matters. Rather, a good deal of decision-making power is given to institutions created by the Treaty. The burden of work will fall on a technical body (the Junta), made up of three members with their own staff, charged with acting only on behalf of Andean community interest, and who will receive no instructions from individual countries. The first members of the Junta have already been named, and are installed in Lima. They are responsible to a Commission made up of representatives of each of the member governments, most of whose decisions will require the affirmative vote of 4 out of the 5 Commissioners. Consultative groups, including representatives of entrepreneurs and trade unions, will advise the Commission and the Junta.

These community authorities, together with those of the ADC, will face the difficult task of defining clearly, and finding a workable equilibrium among, the several community goals, such as economic efficiency, geographical balance, integration, a fair income distribution and greater regional autonomy, while minimizing the sovereignty each country yields to the new decision makers. Community authorities will be supported in their efforts by specialized regional agencies, such as the United Nations' Economic Commission for Latin-America and the Latin-American Institute of Economic and Social Planning.

IV. Outlook for the Andean customs union: trade creation

Although it is commonly asserted that analysis focusing on trade diversion and creation is irrelevant for integration among less developed countries, arguments given to support such assertions are unconvincing in a Latin-American context. At best they indicate the need to supplement the analysis with other considerations regarding economies of scale, bargaining power, etc.

It is also important to specify the alternative to which a customs union outcome is being compared. Ideally, trade diversion and creation should be measured with respect to, not the pre-customs union situation, but the conditions which would have existed in each country without a customs union. It does not seem unreasonable to suppose that in the Andean case the most likely alternative to a customs union is the continuation in each country of protectionist policies not very different from those now in effect.

Even granting this basic assumption, the precise economic impact of the customs union will depend, among other things, on the actual speed and nature of trade liberalization (i.e., which products are freed first), and of course on the level and structure of the new common tariff.

An optimistic scenario would include across-the-board trade liberalization, with few exceptions, with the Andean countries taking this opportunity to reshape and rationalize their system of protection. A common external tariff with duties averaging, say, around 30% ad valorem, and the elimination of most quantitative restrictions over foreign trade could be foreseen in this scenario.[8] Under these circumstances, which would also require a more flexible exchange rate policy, the Andean customs union would become a politically feasible way to improve overall foreign trade policies, as trade would be liberalized not only among Andean countries, but also, on balance, with the rest of the world.

It is more likely that the subregion will move faster in liberalizing commodities produced by activities new to the zone (as already indicated in the Treaty of Cartagena), and that the eventual common tariff will be closer to an average of present direct and indirect levies on imports, weighted in favor of the higher duties.[9] However, even under these circumstances, but assuming that the 1980 target for 'nearly' complete trade liberalization is kept, the gross trade-creating effect of the Andean customs union will be large. The basic reason is that these countries have already come close to achieving self-sufficiency in a number of 'light' manufacturing activities, such as food-processing, textiles, leather products, etc. Most of the trade on these goods was long ago diverted from foreign suppliers toward domestic producers; each country carried out this process on its own, although with different degrees of efficiency.

---

[8] The following are simple arithmetic means of the approximate incidence in ad valorem terms of duties and charges applied by Andean countries (except Bolivia) to imports during the early 1960's:

	Chile	Colombia	Ecuador	Perú
Primary commodities and capital goods	58	64	35	18
Semi-manufactured and durable consumer goods	96	48	56	25
Non-durable consumer manufactures	328	247	117	72
Overall average	138%	112%	62%	34%

Data obtained from Santiago Macario, 'Protectionism and industrialization in Latin-America', *Economic Bulletin for Latin-America* 9 (March, 1964) 75, table 5. In recent years Venezuela has relied heavily on quantitative restrictions to promote import substitution. In the petrochemical complementation agreement, signed in August 1968 by Bolivia, Colombia, Chile and Perú, *minimum* preference margins vis-a-vis third countries of 15%, 25% and 50% were agreed upon for primary, intermediate and final petrochemical products, respectively.

[9] The Central-American Common Market has ended up with a tariff higher than the average of the individual countries' pre-integration duties.

Table 2
Imports of Manufactures expressed as percentages of total supplies of manufactured
products

	Bolivia 1960	Colombia 1965	Chile 1965	Ecuador 1960	Perú 1965
Total	58	10	17	41	25
I. Foodstuffs, beverages tobacco, textiles clothing, wood and leather products	40	1	8	11	10
II. Paper and rubber and their products chemicals, non-metallic minerals, basic metals	66	22	11	65	27
III. Petrochemicals	56	5	14	15	19
IV. Machinery and equipment, metal-working	79	46	51	95	70
V. Printing and publishing, other manufacturing	65	10	26	51	33

Source: Adapted from Edmar L. Bacha, 'Venezuela y el grupo Andino. El problema y
las alternativas', *El Trimestre Económico* 37 (1), No. 145 (January–March, 1970) 160,
table III. 'Total Supplies' refer to imports plus domestic output.

Table 2 shows the extent to which import substituting industrialization has
advanced, especially in Colombia, Chile and Perú. By 1970, the participation
of imports in total manufactured supplies must have been around 15% for the three
countries taken as a whole. It has been estimated that in 1968 the share of
domestic manufacturing in the GDP of the Andean five reached 21%, ranging
from 27% in Chile to 14% in Bolivia. Clearly, common market discussions
which neglect the industrialization already accomplished are seriously
flawed.

Sketchy data indicate that there exists a great variation from country to
country in the prices and costs of many of the goods already produced
within the Andean community, suggesting that there is considerable room

for a more efficient pattern of regional production and trade.[10] In other words, regarding most of manufacturing the Andean countries, especially the major ones, are actually very similar, but potentially very complementary. As trade restrictions sometimes have shut out completely from one Andean country a commodity which it does not produce, but which is produced in another country of the subregion, the liberalization of regional trade will also allow

[10] Some examples of price disparities within the Andean group may be given. The following indices refer to prices for different goods in the Andean countries where the Chilean price is set equal to 100 for each product. The indices are based on dollar prices, obtained by applying a purchasing power parity exchange rate to the prices expressed in local currencies. The prices refer to 1962.

	Bolivia	Colombia	Ecuador	Perú
Beer	102	64	111	98
Footwear	85	77	88	134
Cotton cloth	55	48	53	88
Woolen cloth	195	100	175	114
Soap	154	49	127	76
Light bulbs	123	119	70	107
Washing machines	94	77	100	56
Radios	71	50	121	80
Aspirin	138	194	244	581

These data do not necessarily reflect costs as they may be biased by different tax systems and mark-ups; furthermore, using other exchange rates, different results will be obtained. But together with other bits of information, they suggest a rich pay-off to specialization and increased trade within the Andean group. Indices computed from United Nations, *El proceso de industrialización en América-Latina,* statistical appendix, 89–92. The main body of that publication also notes price and cost differences among Latin-American countries; see its pp. 107, 121 and 253. See also Edmar L. Bacha, 'Venezuela y el grupo Andino', *op. cit.* 157, table 1. Price disparities are also marked in such basic inputs as steel and chemicals. It is at first sight breathtaking that the Andean five have plunged ahead with their plans in spite of the lack of exact data on cost differences, effective rates of protection, economies of scale, etc. The not-unreasonable counter to this timidity is that the flexibility of the Treaty coupled with strong policy-making community institutions are more efficient weapons in handling uncertainty than time-consuming studies. It may be noted that while the prices of most Andean 'light' industries compare unfavorably with world prices at going exchange rates, it is not clear how they would perform under exchange rates corresponding to free trade conditions, which would also allow them access to their inputs at world prices. In other words, some of these activities may be quite efficient, even at world market prices, but several domestic price distortions make them appear otherwise.

consumers wider choice. Colombians may be able to enjoy Chilean wine while Chileans may purchase Colombian textiles of a type not available in Chile. The same may be said about trade in services, from tourism to shipping and air freight.

By 1980, then, the share of imports from non-Andean sources in total supplies of 'light' manufacturing products is unlikely to be lower than it is now (excepting Bolivia), but the share of imports from Andean partners in such supplies for each Andean nation is likely to be substantially higher. This, of course, will be a clear indication that trade creation has taken place in these commodities.[11] This aspect of the Andean customs union may be viewed as consolidating and rationalizing the industrialization accomplished during the last 30 years, especially in 'light' industries. It could signal that these activities and their entrepreneurs are no longer infants, and that they are ready to face Latin-American competition and are *almost* ready to face world markets. In some lines the larger Andean base may induce larger exports to the rest of the world.

It would be a mistake to regard the present low figures of intra-Andean trade[12] as evidence of the low potential trade creating effects of the common market. That they reflect to a large extent past national policies of import-substitution, which have artificially depressed intra-Andean trade by inefficient duplication of production facilities, is dramatically illustrated by massive smuggling along several Andean borders, such as those between Colombia and Venezuela, Colombia and Ecuador, Colombia and Perú, and Perú and Bolivia. Part of that smuggling deals with non-Andean goods, but a substantial part

---

[11] See Edwin M. Truman, 'The European Economic Community: trade creation and trade diversion'. *Yale Economic Essays* 9 (Spring, 1969) especially pp. 202–208. Existing data do not warrant a precise quantification of the likely static grains from trade-creation. But to the argument that quantification of such gains inevitably has yielded meagre results the following observations can be made: (a) differences in effective rates of protection among Andean countries are large, and suggest differences in costs greater than those found elsewhere; and (b) it should be recalled that expressions approximating these welfare gains have as one of their terms the *squared* values of the taxes removed as a result of the creation of the common market. As already noted, these taxes are quite high in most Andean countries. In the case of the total removal of a tax on goods already imported from a country in the common market, the welfare gain can be approximated by:

$$\tfrac{1}{2}[(pq) \cdot t^2 \cdot E],$$

where t represents the ad valorem tax removed, E the absolute value of the price elasticity of demand, and (pq) the value of expenditures on the imported good.

[12] Footnote: see next page.

handles Andean textiles and other consumer goods. Indeed, market pressures along these borders have motivated during the post-war schemes for 'border integration', especially along the Colombo–Venezuelean and Colombo–Ecuadorian frontiers.[13] It may be noted that these market pressures have been potent in spite of the neglect of economic overhead facilities near frontier zones, a neglect arising from old and petty suspicions and fears. If the trade liberalization program foreseen in the Treaty of Cartagena comes off anywhere near schedule, officially recorded intra-Andean trade is very likely to witness phenomenal growth rates during the 1970's.

Trade liberalization is also likely to have other positive effects on welfare, some, but not all, related to the static trade-creation gains. Greater competition among established 'light' activities, most of which produce goods weighing heavily on working class budgets, should reduce their relative prices, contributing toward a better income distribution.[14] In more than one Andean country, important wage-goods are often produced under near-monopolistic conditions. The new competitive climate may also induce entrepreneurs in these activities, who often have been lulled into a fat oligopolistic tranquility by excessive protection, to become truly modern managers on the lookout for cost reducing innovations, and who will be able to operate succesfully not only in large Latin-American markets, but also in new export markets in the rest of the world. The time has come for the Latin-American entrepreneur

[12] According to data obtained from the International Monetary Fund, *Direction of Trade* (several issues), the following are the percentages of intra-Andean trade (excluding Venezuela) in the total merchandise trade of each country:

	Exports		Imports	
	1961–63	1964–66	1961–63	1964–66
Bolivia	0.5	1.2	4.3	3.1
Chile	1.1	1.2	5.2	4.6
Colombia	1.2	2.1	1.3	2.6
Ecuador	7.0	6.2	2.3	3.7
Perú	4.8	4.0	1.9	2.6
Total Andean	2.8%	2.7%	2.8%	3.3%

The annual value of intra-Andean trade (exports plus imports) was about $ 140 million during 1964–66. These data do not attempt an estimation of smuggling.

[13] These schemes have been actively discussed since the late 1950's. But it has proved very difficult to plan for 'border integration' in isolation from a full customs union among participating countries.

[14] But the net effect of integration on income distribution is ambiguous.

in 'vegetative' activities to become a leader in the introduction of new technology and new management techniques, if necessary by creating new pan-Andean
multinational firms. It may turn out that greater competitive pressures may
keep previously overprotected entrepreneurs and trade unions from capturing,
as in the past, most of the productivity advantages of the modern sectors of
the economy, thus leading to a wider distribution of the gains from modern
technology, and higher employment-output growth elasticities.

In some Andean entrepreneurial and academic circles the program of automatic and general liberalization of intra-Andean trade raises fears and resistan-
ces. Many prefer to limit the activities of the common market to agreements
regarding the establishment of new regional import-substituting (or trade-
diverting) activities. It is feared that freeing trade in goods produced by 'vegetative' and other established activities could lead to disorderly competition
and unemployment and excess capacity in many branches of production. This
is the same type of fear which existed in France and Italy when the European
Common Market was proposed.[15] Often these fears are inconsistent, as when
all Andean producers of a given good claim to be less competitive than other
producers in the zone, and they are usually grossly exaggerated. Relatively
capital-rich countries complain about cheap foreign labor, while labor-rich
countries complain about cheap foreign machinery. Relatively open economies complain that they are at a disadvantage because they started late in
their industrialization, while entrepreneurs in relatively closed economies ask
for more time to get used to competition.

No doubt the elimination of barriers to Andean trade will increase competitive pressures on *all* producers, even if it also expands their markets. But
the transition toward a new situation will not be as violent and destructive
as it is often painted. In the first place, the reduction of tariffs will be gradual,

---

[15] See Bela Balassa, 'Integration and resource allocation in Latin-America' (forthcoming).
This paper also stresses the gains to be achieved by greater competition among already established Latin-American industries. See also Tibor Scitovsky, *Economic theory and
western European integration*. Unwin University Books, London, 1962, for an analysis
stressing the gains to be achieved by greater degrees of competition within a Western
European context. While that experience is not directly applicable to Latin-America, it
is not irrelevant to the area either. The Chilean and Colombian industries of 1970 were
not far behind those of Italy in 1957. It is curious that, within a pan-Latin-American
context, the small countries fear that the big three will reap most benefits from integration, while Argentina and Brazil also show reluctance to press for a common market,
sometimes arguing the primacy of 'national integration', a label which at best refers
to a geopolitical concept and at worst is a meaningless semantic trick.

perhaps too much so, and gradual enough to allow for the maturing of any 'infant industries' which may remain, especially in Perú, Ecuador and Bolivia. Secondly, neither entrepreneurs nor consumers change their plans quickly, either because of capacity limits and marketing delays, or because of habit and inertia. Thus the early years of the common market will give entrepreneurs a change to adapt to the new conditions, without the threat of an immediate catastrophe. Finally, as has been noted, Andean manufacturing has been expanding at a fast rate. In this environment adjustment is easier than in a context of stagnation; many relatively inefficient firms may simply have to reduce their expansion and change their output mix, sometimes without having to face reductions in their *absolute* level of aggregate output and employment. The marginal increments to output will thus be produced by the more efficient plants, without necessarily creating excess capacity. The threat of competition may often lead to gains in efficiency without being accompanied by actual increments in trade flows.

In spite of these arguments, fears about trade liberalization will persist. Indeed, in some cases, and in spite of fast growth, economic efficiency may indicate the advisability of closing down plants and reallocating their labor force. As the Andean authorities seem to be aware, it will be useful to have generous programs set up by the ADC to grant credits and retraining facilities to entrepreneurs and workers severely hurt by intra-Andean competition and willing to shift to other activities.

This insurance against excessive adjustment costs to trade liberalization, and against an unequitable distribution of that burden, seems preferable to the pleas for detailed 'planning' often heard from critics of the trade liberalization program. It is only superficially paradoxical that after a decade characterized by the acceptance of planning in Latin-America, the Andean group should propose a rapid and automatic liberalization of subregional trade in many products. It is precisely because in mixed economies planning, whether national or regional, should concentrate on priority activities where market forces operate either weakly or perversely, that the market should be given a large share of the responsibility for accelerating integration in activities, such as 'light' industries, where market forces can be expected to work reasonably well. One of the surest ways of stopping economic integration is to insist that before each step is taken, exhaustive and detailed studies should be prepared industry by industry, so that some central authority can take a decision on the basis of such studies. (Data in most of those studies are likely to be obsolete by the time they are completed.) Given the difficulties Latin-American countries have had building up planning at the national level, the project of guiding each step of integration from a master plan covering five countries is foolhardy. It should also be borne in mind that in most cases it is difficult to predict ex ante which country should specialize in which activity. Economic history teaches us that often socially profitable specialization comes from bold initiatives of (private and public) entrepreneurs, which may not have met with the approval of central authorities. The executive regional authority directing the steps of the Andean group would, therefore, do well to limit its regional planning to a few critical sectors and policies, establishing for the rest general 'rules of the game'.[16] This 'modest' agenda will keep them quite busy.

V. Trade diversion

As shown in table 2, imports still weigh heavily in the total Andean supply of goods produced by 'dynamic' industries. For the countries taken individually, import substitution in these industries has been or could be very expensive, due to smallness of market. The effort will be less costly when new plants produce for the whole Andean community; in some cases, the larger market may in fact make regional production competitive with foreign goods even without protection.[17] In any case, it is to be expected that protection will be given to these infant industries by the common external tariff, and that the regional output of paper, pulp, petrochemicals, metals, machinery, equipment, etc., will expand at a faster rate than their imports from non-Andean sources. Because of the economies of scale which characterize many of these activities, a proliferation of plants would not be desirable. Joint regional planning plus a common external tariff which does not wholly elimi-

---

[16] It could be argued that price and costs distortions are so great within Andean economies that partial trade liberalization may lead to intra-Andean trade flows unrelated to *real* cost advantages and disadvantages. This argument can be used to propose either strict central planning of integration or its postponement until after the distortions are reduced or eliminated. The empirical underpinning of this thesis, however, is shaky. Nevertheless, trade flows arising from the early rounds of tariff-cutting should be scanned by the community's secretariat for evidence on this point.

[17] It may be argued that in that case any one country could have started producing the commodity in large scale, exporting the surplus to world markets, without the need for a regional group. But this argument neglects the smaller risk involved in producing for a regional group in contrast with producing for the world market. On the other hand, one should be on guard against overly optimistic ex ante engineering studies, which almost always turn out, ex post, to have underestimated the competitive disadvantage of domestic output vis-a-vis the world market, or to have overestimated the ability of new activities to keep up with productivity increases in the rest of the world.

nate foreign competitive pressures may be the best instruments available to avoid excessive regional costs in those new industries. The presumption in favor of the central planning of many of these 'heavy' activities (e.g., steel), is strengthened by the fact that already they are handled by public enterprises in Andean countries.

Some trade diversion is bound to occur in the dynamic branches of manufacturing. Such trade diversion, or regional import substitution going beyond that which would occur under ideal neo-classical assumptions (free trade, equilibrium exchange rates, etc.), is a cost which the Andean countries appear willing to pay for having a more diversified industrial structure and for achieving non-economic goals. These targets are seldom spelled out carefully, but they go beyond a naive 'desire for industry'. They are motivated partly by a wish for greater autonomy vis-a-vis the powerful world economic centers, partly by a desire to avoid the uncertainties of international trade, and also by an intuitive preference for 'heavy' intermediate and capital goods industries, which are supposed to accelerate capital formation, technological change and 'backward linkages'. A fundamental task for subregional planning will be to spell out clearly what long run benefits are expected to flow from different kinds of trade diversion, and to minimize, for a given desired degree of diversification and subregional autonomy, the costs of that trade diversion, by careful selection of industries to be given special protection. This new stage of import substitution at the regional level should avoid the mistakes made in the old stage of import substitution at a national level. This is of particular importance due to the nature of the goods subject to the new import substitution. As pointed out, they are intermediate and capital goods. Inefficiencies in those activities will also affect all other Andean industries relying on them for inputs, including exporters. White elephants of Andean dimensions could be monstrous.

Import substitution at the regional level will be guided mainly by complementation agreements in key industrial areas, such as petrochemicals, basic metals, automotive industry, etc. Most progress up until now has been registered in petrochemicals, electronics, and metals in general. The agreement on petrochemicals, already signed by Bolivia, Colombia, Chile and Perú, covers 23 important products, whose production is allocated among the participating countries.[18] Petrochemicals offered a promising area for this type of arrangement, as Andean countries had not yet invested heavy sums in their production, although several were at the verge of doing so. As here the choice appears to be only between national and regional import substitution, clauses of the

[18] For details of the petrochemical agreement see Banco Nacional de Comercio Exterior, *Comercio Exterior* (México, D.F.), January, 1968, 10–11.

agreement limiting entry are a small price to pay to avoid proliferation of very uneconomical small plants, so long as the community authorities keep common tariff levels which maintain some foreign competitive pressure, beyond a reasonable margin of protection. Given the politico-economic dynamics of tariff setting, it may turn out that the starting restrictions on firm entry will result in the long run in smaller tariffs; the open entry policy followed by many Latin-American countries in the automotive industry certainly does not provide a good model to follow, meretricious sloganeering about 'free competition' notwithstanding.

An Andean group limited to promoting subregional trade only for new industries would reap exiguous gains from that customs union. Gains may still exist compared with a situation in which each country carried out that import substitution in isolation. But the growth of intra-Andean trade and its impact on Andean overall expansion would remain relatively minor; note that for the Andean Five taken as a whole imports are already only about 11% of GDP, according to table 1, and that only part of those imports can 'reasonably' be substituted for local output during the next ten years. Brazil and México, with GDP's larger than that for the Andean Five, have import coefficients of about 5% of GDP (also according to table 1), and even with their large markets import substitution has not always yielded satisfactory results.[19] In short, it is difficult to visualize significant Andean economic integration without trade liberalization across the board; without it the whole impetus toward the creation of an economic and political community will wither.

VI. Outlook for Andean policies toward intra-Andean factor movements

Discussion so far has been limited to commodity trade. One may wonder whether it is desirable for the subregion to liberalize also movements of labor and capital within the area. The Treaty of Cartagena is vague on this point, and does not set up a time table for factor movement liberalization comparable to that for trade. This is wise.

Based on the historical experience of Southern Italy and the U.S.A.'s South some observers point out the danger that a common market could lead to the immiseration of a member country. But those examples refer to situations

[19] Cf. Edmar L. Bacha, 'Venezuela y el Grupo Andino . . . ', *op. cit.* 159–162. Bacha also stresses the difficulties to be expected in negotiating complementation agreements for new industries, noting the experience of the Central-American Common Market on this matter, and the inflationary cost-push arising from inefficient import substitution.

where the common market was accompanied by a free flow of labor and capital. In a customs union including only trade in goods and services, mindful of the dangers of excessive trade-diversion, and where the balance of payments constraint limits how much a country can import from its partners and the rest of the world, the possibility of immiseration is negligible. A flexible exchange rate can always insure balance in the international accounts, and export taxes can handle the danger of unfavorable terms of trade effects. But with completely free flows of labor and capital, no such rapid adjustment mechanisms exist. This is why, given present nationalisms and while political and social Andean solidarity is still in its infancy, the flow of factors across frontiers should be limited (and controlled). Note the frictions which legal and illegal Colombian migrations into Venezuela have created. Other examples include Chilean, Bolivian and Paraguayan migrations into Argentina, and Bolivian migration into northern Chile. Even under controls fears of 'dismemberment' (in the sense that with integration some regions of the country may become economically linked more closely with regions of other countries than with their own national capital), as well as fears of invasion of cheap foreign labor, may persist. And indeed new economic patterns are likely to emerge, say along the Chile—Perú and Colombia—Ecuador frontiers as a result of trade liberalization.

Community authorities could nevertheless profitably encourage certain types of intra-Andean factor movements. While none of the member countries suffers from shortages of unskilled labor, specific bottlenecks in skilled categories often develop, and could be relieved by pooling Andean availabilities of such skills into one common market. Fresh investments into 'human capital' could be jointly planned, especially in the fields of higher education and scientific and technological research, and this will call for some labor mobility within the zone. Regional 'centers of excellence' for research into matters of special Andean interest, such as geology, copper and tin technology, etc., could be established with the help of the ADC, and by pooling Andean talents.

The Treaty of Cartagena refers to the importance of creating Andean-owned multinational corporations, able to operate with similar ease in the five countries. These are likely to include public, private and mixed enterprises, and will of course require, as in the case of the ADC, some intra-Andean capital movements. In some cases, joint ventures could be undertaken with non-Andean Latin-American companies,[20] or with those of industrialized countries (more on this

---

[20] Andean efforts to set up a regional electronics industry (mainly in radios and television sets) are reported to include a joint venture with the Mexican Majestic group, which in return for a minority interest will supply the technical backing. See *Business Week,* March 21, 1970, 49. The multiplication of contacts among Andean entrepreneurs during the last few years, it may be observed, has been remarkable.

below). Andean planners are conscious of the failure of the European common market authorities to provide leadership in the creation of all-European firms; they do not want to repeat their weak performance. Before December 1971 the Commission, following the advice of the Junta, was scheduled to adopt a uniform regime for the creation of Andean multinational firms. As put by Paul N. Rosenstein-Rodan: 'One measure of wealth is the waste one can afford. Latin-America is not as rich as Europe. In the field of multinational corporations it can and it should do better.'[21]

If trade liberalization proceeds as scheduled, it will be desirable to start preparing the way, during the 1970's for a closer post-1980 economic union. An important element in such a union will be an active and increasingly free Andean capital market, open primarily to Andean public and private enterprises. It will also be desirable to create Andean financial assets which will be able to attract funds from medium- and small-sized savers, thus offering alternatives to foreign assets, such as mutual funds, which threaten to become an important drain of Andean investable funds. Gradual harmonization of fiscal, monetary, and social security policies, as well as ad hoc mechanisms, also vaguely pledged in the Treaty of Cartagena, will encourage such a trend.

But harmonization of such policies need not receive the top priority which should be given to creating Andean multinational firms and to coordinating Andean policies toward foreign traders and investors. In other words, it would be premature, and potentially harmful, to attempt during the 1970's to transform the Andean subregion into a single currency area, with free factor movements and common monetary and fiscal policies. In particular, it would be a mistake to try to freeze exchange rates, *even if all countries in the region had rates of inflation similar to each other and to those of 'the rest of the world'.* It is clear that, given unequal inflationary conditions in different countries, it would be foolhardy to attempt making the region into a unified currency area, while waiting for the end of inflation, say in Chile, is likely to postpone indefinitely and unnecessarily the integration efforts. But even without inflation, trade liberalization and the convergence toward a common external tariff may induce structural changes requiring adjustments in the real exchange rate of several countries. At a time when these countries are giving up national control over policy instruments (i.e., tariffs and import controls) much used in the past for balance of payments adjustments, there will be a greater need, at least

[21] Paul N. Rosenstein-Rodan, 'Multinational investment in the framework of Latin-American integration', in: Inter-American Development Bank, *Multinatinal investment in the economic development and integration of Latin-America* (Round Table, Inter-American Development Bank, Bogotá, Colombia, April 1968, 87).

during a transition period, for a more flexible exchange rate policy in each country. It should be borne in mind that the Andean integration process will hopefully be accompanied, at least in countries such as Chile and Colombia, by a rationalization and lowering of protection vis-a-vis the rest of the world. The Junta, of course, should adopt general guidelines to reconcile national exchange rate flexibility with community needs.

VII. Outlook for Andean policies toward non-Andean traders and investors

One of the expected benefits from the creation of the Andean subregion is typically summarized by the expression 'increase in bargaining power'. For example, in the commercial field it is to be expected that the Andean Five acting in unison will be in a stronger position when dealing, say with the European Common Market, than if each country negotiated in isolation.[22]

A very important application of the principle of greater bargaining power by joint action is expected to take place in dealing with direct foreign investors. Here the objectives are not only economic and in the narrow sense, but also include obtaining greater Andean control over its economy.

Many in the Andean countries, and in the rest of Latin-America, fear that the creation of a common market will lead to a massive inflow of foreign multinational corporations, which are better equipped than national firms, and even Andean multinational firms, to take advantage of the broader economic space. Such a massive inflow, even when favorable to economic growth, will have undesirable political and social effects.[23] This fear has been partly responsible for delaying Latin-American integration efforts. The Treaty of Cartagena meets this issue openly, and established that by the end of 1970 the Community should adopt a common policy toward direct foreign investment, as well as toward foreign patents, licenses and royalty agreements.

Comprehensive data on 1970 direct foreign investment in the Andean Five are lacking, but it is clear that most of it was in petroleum, mining and smelting, continuing a tradition going back to the early days of the Spanish conquest of the Andean highlands. Of the total 1968 book value of U.S. direct foreign investment in the three largest Andean countries (Chile, Colombia and

[22] There was talk of joint Andean participation in the 1970 World Fair at Osaka, Japan. This idea, however, was abandoned.
[23] For a more detailed discussion of the issues raised by direct foreign investment in Latin-American development see my 'Direct foreign investment in Latin-America', in: The international corporation, ed. by Ch.P. Kindleberger, M.I.T. Press, Cambridge, Mass., 1970.

Perú), at least 60% was in those activities.[24] Japanese investors have recently
also shown keen interest in the mineral resources of these countries, which
could be labelled Pacific as well as Andean. U.S. Department of Commerce
data, however, indicate that U.S. direct investment in manufacturing has grown
faster than other items; while such investments amounted to only 8% of total
book value of U.S. direct investments in Chile, Colombia and Perú in 1950,
their share had reached 16% by 1968. It is noteworthy that in spite of the
smaller national markets in those countries compared to Argentina, Brazil and
México, during 1950–68 U.S. manufacturing investments in the two groups
of countries grew at roughly the same average annual rates (9.5% for Chile,
Colombia and Perú, and 9.0% for Argentina, Brazil and México).[25] For both
groups of countries, the rate of expansion in the book value of those manufacturing investments was faster during the 1960's than during the 1950's,
in spite of the fears provoked by the Cuban Revolution. Recent experience
in Perú, where the Southern Peru Copper Corporation was willing to sign an
agreement with a government which shortly before had nationalized, allegedly
without 'prompt and adequate' compensation, assets of the International
Petroleum Company also indicates that in spite of the public diffidence shown
by foreign investors and their demands for 'favorable climate', the Andean
countries are regarded as attractive places where to invest. The bargaining
power and room to manoeuvre of these countries is, therefore, greater than
what one would think by reading business and popular journals.

That bargaining power is probably strongest in the field of natural resources. It could be further strengthened by a closer coordination and eventual
merger of the national public enterprises which now act in minerals, oil, transport, communications and electricity. Programs such as 'Chileanization' and
'Peruanization' of copper could probably gain in bargaining strength, as well
as efficiency, by their joint planning. The fact that several industrialized regions,
such as Japan, the U.S.A., and Western and Eastern Europe are each interested
in obtaining access to raw materials naturally strengthens the Andean hand.

New forms of association with foreign investors in manufacturing and
other enterprises can also be developed under better conditions if Andean
countries act jointly and/or establish common 'rules of the game'. These are
likely to be closer to those of, say, México than to the more liberal regulations

---

[24] Data obtained from U.S. Department of Commerce, *Survey of current business*,
October 1969. The 1968 book value of all U.S. direct investments in those three countries
is put at $ 2.3 billion. Of all U.S. direct investments (book value) in mining and smelting
in Latin-America, 72% were in Chile and Perú.
[25] The book value of *all* U.S. direct investments in Chile, Colombia and Perú grew during
1950–68 at an annual rate of 5.5%.

of Argentina and Central America, and they are also likely to include a closer look at the accounting arrangements on such matters of royalty and other fee payments between subsidiaries and head offices abroad. The curious phenomenon of continued foreign investment into branches which show persistent accounting losses has caused considerable interest in Andean circles. The Foreign ministers of the Andean Five, meeting in Lima on November 1969, reaffirmed that it will be Andean policy to encourage preferentially Andean entrepreneurs, and to control foreign investment. It is likely that certain fields, such as most 'vegetative' and key 'dynamic' branches of manufacturing, as well as banking, communications, etc., will be increasingly reserved for public and private Andean entrepreneurs. This trend is already marked in Perú, Bolivia, Chile and Colombia.

As noted earlier, the trade field also offers potential rewards to joint Andean policies, not only when dealing with trade blocs such as those of Western and Eastern Europe, but also in dealing with the larger LAFTA countries, and with the rapidly expanding Japanese and Australian markets, which share with the Andean countries the Pacific basin.[26] One may ask whether Andean (and Latin-American) bargaining power should be used to obtain *regional* trade preferences from the U.S.A. On this point Colombia and her partners appear to have different views. It should be noted that during the 1960's Andean international trade has become geographically more diversified; schemes for U.S. regional preferences would jeopardize such gains and would also hamper Andean freedom to bargain with direct foreign investors. It is difficult to visualize, for example, the political feasibility of a situation where, say, Italian investors within the Andean group would export to the U.S. market taking advantage of U.S. regional preferences.

[26] According to the International Monetary Fund, *Direction of trade,* the recent geographical percentage structure of Andean foreign trade has been as follows (excluding Venezuela):

	Exports (f.o.b.)			Imports (c.i.f.)		
	1961–63	1964–65	1966–67	1961–63	1964–65	1966–67
U.S.A.	41.7	38.3	36.3	43.2	42.5	40.8
United Kingdom	10.4	8.9	9.7	6.5	5.9	5.2
Japan	5.1	6.7	7.4	3.9	4.5	5.1
European Common Market	25.6	27.5	28.3	21.8	19.5	20.7
Latin-America	7.1	7.7	7.4	11.7	14.2	14.9
Others	10.1	11.0	10.9	13.0	13.6	13.3

The figures for 'Latin-America' include intra-Andean trade; compared with those given earlier for that trade they indicate greater flows between Andean and other LAFTA countries than within the group. But they also reveal the large and growing deficit between the Andeans and the rest of LAFTA, which has troubled the subregion.

Pooling of Andean foreign exchange reserves, combined with expanded cooperation among the five Central Banks, could decrease Andean vulnerability to fluctuations in foreign exchange earnings from the rest of the world. A first step may be the pooling of the newly created Special Drawing Rights.

Andean documents and declarations have been careful to emphasize that their activities and actions are compatible with the march toward a pan-Latin-American common market, and they often assert that the creation of the subregion will accelerate such march. Yet it is clear that the Andean working hypothesis is that no such market is yet in sight, and that LAFTA will continue developing at a very slow pace. On the other hand, the Andean group is often eyed with misgivings by other LAFTA members.

While it is unlikely that the Andean group will be joined in the immediate future by other countries (excepting Venezuela), it is possible that it will develop special links with Central America and the Caribbean region; Colombia has shown particular interest in these areas, having shores both on the Pacific and the Caribbean.[27]

VIII. Possible future difficulties and dangers of the Andean Group

Looked at from the viewpoint of each participating country, expected benefits from the creation of the subregion are of two major types. One group of benefits will arise from the favorable long run effects of trade creation, greater bargaining power vis-a-vis the rest of the world, possible improvements in subregional external terms of trade, etc. These benefits are *not* obtained at the expense of partners in the subregion. The other type of benefits will, for a substantial period of time, be obtained at the expense of subregional partners. When an industry, heavily protected by the common external tariff, is set up in a given country, such country may benefit from having that activity, but only at the expense of consumers (and/or public revenues) of custom union partners. The benefit to that country, neglecting for a moment quid pro quos, is equivalent to an improvement in its terms of trade exactly matched by a worsening of partners' terms of trade. Unless such 'infant industries' mature so as to make its regional protection superfluous, the situation will persist indefinitely.

[27] See Rodrigo Botero, *La Comunidad Económica Caribe – Andina.* Ediciones Tercer Mundo, Bogotá, 1967. See also Marcos Kaplán E., *Problemas del desarollo y de la integración de America Latina.* Editorial de la Universidad de Chile, Escuela de Derecho de Valparaiso, 1967.

Naturally, each country will be expected to return the favor regarding the second type of benefit, and thus incur in corresponding costs to subsidize the protected regional industries located in partner countries. But there are likely to be other costs, mainly of a short- or medium-run nature. These can be summarized under the label of 'burden of adjustment', and are usually neglected in textbook discussions of long-run economic mechanisms. They include possible costs of resource reallocation arising from trade creation and balance of payments adjustments, as well as induced changes in national tax and policy-making systems. Throughout history, the politically powerful have tended to thrust the burden of adjusting to changing world economic conditions onto the politically weak; when supply and demand conditions favor the strong, the adjustment burden is proclaimed to be the inevitable price of progress exacted by a blind market, an argument brushed aside on grounds of 'political realism', to be accepted by all 'reasonable' men, when economic trends threaten to hurt the interests of the strong.[28] This argument, rather than vague fears of cumulative tendencies toward uneven development, provides substance to the suspicions of the politically weakest countries within common markets.

Providing even a general accounting framework to keep track, for each participating country, of all these possible costs and benefits of a common market is a most difficult task. Hence the high probability of frictions, complaints, delays and arduous negotiations in the formation of custom unions, especially among developing countries. Strong political leadership and solidarity is needed if the project is to advance significantly; it is not yet obvious that such leadership and solidarity will be steadily applied in the Andean context. It could be argued that most of the leadership of participating countries has not yet fully realized the full implications of the Treaty of Cartagena, and they may back down when the time comes for concrete actions, such as the lowering of important protective tariffs. Colombia and Chile have new Presidents since 1970, and the Andean political picture and enthusiasm for integration looks quite different from that at the time of the Declaration of Bogotá. Both LAFTA and the Central American Common Market have shown, unfortunately, the relative political weakness of signed and sealed economic pacts, which are no match for the furies of petty and archaic chauvinism. Unfortunately, there are plenty of old quarrels and animosities among Andean nations (to name but a few, the borders between Chile and

---

[28] Consider in this light the asymmetrical reactions of the U.S.A. and Western Europe to increases and decreases in the prices of coffee, copper, textiles, etc. Aid flows from the strong to the weak can then be viewed as partial compensation for trade asymmetrics.

Bolivia and Perú, and between Perú and Ecuador, can still arouse strong emotions), which could be manipulated to generate severe frictions. Furthermore, it is possible that some of the countries within the subregion will take a sharply more leftward course than their neighbors, especially regarding central planning of economic activity. In that case, the meshing together of economies with very different degrees of private market activity will further tax regional ingenuity and solidarity.

The potential difficulties of the Andean scheme have been foreshadowed by the unsuccessful negotiations to convince Venezuela to sign the Treaty of Cartagena. Venezuelan objections to that Treaty involve fear of *both* trade creation and diversion, coupled with preoccupation with the possibility of large and chronic deficits of Venezuela vis-a-vis the Andean Five. This preoccupation is rooted in the peculiar price-cost structure of the oil-rich Venezuelan economy; indeed, calculations using recent exchange rates confirm across-the-board Venezuelan competitive disadvantages with respect to at least Chile.[29] But even assuming that somehow (perhaps using dual exchange rates, or similar schemes), the Venezuelan–Andean Five trade could be equilibrated, it is likely that Venezuelan misgivings would persist. Vis-a-vis the Andean Five Venezuela is likely to have comparative disadvantage in labor-intensive activities, such as textiles, which have expanded behind import controls only relatively recently. Firms in such industries, nearly all private, take a dim view of the threat of Colombian and Chilean competition. But many Venezuelan firms, public and private, also have a more economically legitimate case against the Cartagena program. Traditionally, they have imported capital and intermediate goods at prices prevailing in world markets (duties being generally low on those products); moves toward a common external tariff are almost certain to raise those prices for Venezuelan buyers, to induce diversion of their purchases toward Andean producers of those goods, not all of which would be Venezuelan. Adding to the opposition of Venezuelan private entrepreneurs to the Treaty of Cartagena is their estimation that Venezuelan activities likely to benefit from trade diversion are partly or totally publicly owned, such as in petrochemicals and steel. Some Andean observers have also remarked that the large influence of foreign investors in the Venezuelan economy presents an additional reason for Andean–Venezuelan incompatibility, echoing British-Continental difficulties in Western Europe.

The Andean common external tariff is also likely to imply an increase in many Peruvian, Bolivian and Ecuadorian tariffs (or of import controls expressed as equivalent tariffs), even if they result in decreases in tariffs or tariff-

[29] See Edmar L. Bacha, 'Venezuela y el Grupo Andino', *op. cit.,* especially table II.

equivalencies for Chile and Colombia. Indeed, for a while Peruvian agreement to the Treaty of Cartagena was in doubt, for reasons similar to those given by Venezuela for rejecting the Treaty. The two weakest countries, Ecuador and Bolivia, face potential trade diversion not only in products of 'dynamic' or new industries, but also, as suggested by table 2 especially for Bolivia, in simpler manufactured products. But these two countries, comprising only 19% of the Andean Five population, have received a considerable number of theoretical safeguards and assurances in both the Treaty of Cartagena and the ADC. Indeed, there is a danger that the ADC may neglect socially profitable actions elsewhere for the sake of concentrating on projects benefitting Bolivia and Ecuador. Integration, as noted by C.P. Kindleberger, calls for contributions according to ability to pay (and here Bolivia and Ecuador have a smaller burden), and investments according to some calculation of pay-off. Offsetting trade diversion costly to Ecuador and Bolivia with inefficient investments in those countries will not encourage growth in the subregion.

While it may be difficult to be precise about all of the costs and benefits of integration for each Andean country, certain aspects may be roughly quantified. The real costs of regional trade diversion, for example, should be distributed in a conscious fashion among the member countries. Reciprocity should *not* be defined with respect to an equal expansion of regional imports and exports in each member country, nor with equal expansion of trade in manufactured goods. Rather, it should refer partly to a fair distribution of the real costs arising from trade diversion. For example, suppose that Peruvian imports and exports to the Andean group increase by the same amount, but that its exports are made up by goods which it could sell in world markets at the same prices it receives from Andean customers (e.g., cotton), while its imports are made up by goods which Perú previously imported from world markets at lower prices (e.g., machinery). Although its regional trade is balanced, it could hardly be said that Perú is benefitting from the common market or that it is receiving reciprocity for its purchases of Andean products, whose prices (at least for a while) are higher than those in world markets. Reciprocity could be reestablished, ceteris paribus, if Perú exported to the subregion goods whose prices were also above those in world markets, in an amount which compensated the real costs of diverting its imports from world to Andean exporters.[30]

Using this approach to reciprocity, and combining it with estimates of adjustment costs, regional authorities could make rough calculations of what each country obtains, net, from integration. Even if rough-and-ready, such

---

[30] Footnote: see next page.

calculations may help to foresee difficulties and avoid frictions. In particular, by keeping tabs on the costs of trade diversion, it may avoid some of the situations obtained in the Central-American Common Market, where, for example, Nicaragua has felt victimized by subregional import substitution.

Indeed, the biggest danger of the Andean project is that, under pressure from vested interests, it may be turned into a mercantilistic mechanism to promote *exclusively* import substitution at the regional level, perhaps with the excuse of supporting overvalued exchange rates (disguised under the argument of closing the foreign exchange gap). Although economies of scale will help to reduce the real costs of some new industries, it may still leave unit costs in many activities way above world market costs. Under these circumstances rapid and efficient Andean growth will require an expanding volume of exports to the rest of the world, to finance growing imports of capital and intermediate goods whose production in the region may still be uneconomical. As the experience of import substitution at the national level shows, the creation of inefficient intermediate and capital goods industries will have negative cost-push effects throughout the economy, and especially on non-traditional exports. Countries with a long tradition of export promotion, such as Perú, will do well to keep a sharp eye on the level and structure of the common external tariff.

Excessive emphasis on inefficient Andean import substitution will also create vested interests which will later oppose a wider Latin-American common market. If an Andean steel industry develops without reaching the efficiency of, say, that of Brazil, it will generate pressures opposing further integration. (Ceteris paribus, the smaller the economic space covered by a common market, the greater the danger that it will lead to costly trade diversion; thus the pity of not having the rich Venezuelan market within the agreement.) In the same way that the old import substitution at the national level created vested interests now opposing regional trade liberalization, there is the risk that the new

[30] This way of viewing reciprocity may also be found in R. French-Davis and K.B. Griffin, *Comercio internacional y políticas de desarrollo económico,* Fondo de Cultura Económica, México, 1967, 196–198. If Δp is the difference between Andean prices and those in world markets (assumed to be a positive amount), then:

$$q_1 \cdot \Delta p_1 = q_2 \cdot \Delta p_2$$

is the condition for true reciprocity, where the q's represent quantities imported from the region (subscript 1) and quantities exported to the region (subscript 2), for any country in the group. See also D.C. Meade, 'The distribution of gains in customs unions between developing countries', *Kyklos* 21 (1968) 713–734, where the same formula is proposed as a guide for true reciprocity.

regional import substitution will generate interests which later on will oppose a wider Latin-American integration. The best way to guard against this risk is to promote regional import substitution only in activities where one can reasonably be sure that acceptable levels of efficiency will be reached after a few years of 'learning by doing'.[31]

A quick look at a map will show that the Andean group is not, prima facie, the most reasonable one which could have been devised from a viewpoint of economic efficiency. For example, it makes more economic sense to accelerate integration of the Chilean automobile industry with that of Córdoba in Argentina, rather than with those of Colombia or Venezuela. Only one of the Andean countries (Perú) has frontiers with all of its four partners. As a group, the Andean Five have more trade with other LAFTA countries than with each other.

Besides these long run preoccupations, the Andean group faces difficult adjustment problems in the short and medium run. As trade restrictions are lifted, there is no assurance that the regional trade flows forthcoming will be balanced. Some countries will develop surpluses and others deficits vis-a-vis the region. This (very likely) possibility arouses considerable anxiety among the member countries. Several devices have been proposed to deal with it: faster-than-scheduled duty reductions in surplus countries and the opposite for deficit countries, the creation of a payments union with generous swing credits, a system of different exchange rates for intra- and extra-regional trade, special lending policies by the ADC, etc. Many of these devices will be useful in decreasing the negative political impact of severe regional imbalances in trade flows, especially if they also involve sharp disparities in the expansion of intra-Andean manufactured exports. But more fundamentally, it should be recalled that true reciprocity need not necessarily involve balanced regional trade flows (nor balanced trade in manufactured goods), and that so long as the overall *global* balance of payments of a country is kept in equilibrium, a deficit with a region will be compensated by a surplus with the rest of the world. Old-fashioned mercantilistic notions should be discarded when dealing with these issues, as attempts to force strictly balanced regional flows could lead to severe inefficiencies. It remains true, however, that the Andean countries will have to rely on exchange rate variations as a tool to maintain *global*

---

[31] It has been suggested that the Andean countries at their first integration efforts avoid a common external tariff, essentially creating a free trade zone coupled with ad hoc complementation agreements. If the latter are well planned, this proposal could avoid many of the dangers of trade diversion, especially for Perú and Venezuela.

balance of payments equilibrium, to a much greater extent than it was done in the past. In the future, each Andean country will lose independent control over tariffs and other trade restrictions, which in the past were often used to secure balance of payments equilibrium. Leaving aside painful income mechanisms of adjustment, only exchange rate policy is left to bring about a desired global target in the balance of trade. It is to be hoped that exchange rate movements will be preferred to a slowdown in the trade liberalization agreements, or to extreme and sustained efforts to force regional trade balance. At any rate, intra-regional trade starts at such a low fraction of total international trade of these countries, that even (proportionally) very large deficits or surpluses with the region will have a small impact on the overall balance of payments of each country, at least during the early years of the common market.

Trade liberalization and the movement toward a common external tariff are likely to have a negative impact on public revenues, at least in some of the Andean countries. But this development should not be difficult to handle, and could motivate much needed fiscal reforms. A fair division of funds collected under the common external tariff, a subject on which the Treaty of Caratagena is silent, should not be difficult to devise.

The low present figures for intra-Andean trade indicate that great efforts will have to be made in establishing new trade and commercialization contacts and channels. The transportation, financial and psychological 'overhead' of trade will have to be built almost from scratch, often with the help of the ADC. On the other hand, intra-Andean transport should be facilitated by a wide 'road' formed between the countries by the Pacific, the Panama Canal and the Caribbean. Most of the Andean population centers are located on or near one of those bodies of water.

IX. Some conclusions

Because of their journalistic visibility and glamour, there is a tendency to expect too much from integration efforts. Even with Venezuela, the Andean group would only come to about the economic size of México and Brazil. One must remember that the great 'common markets' of Brazil and India have contributed only modestly to solving the development problems of those countries. In particular, the Andean integration effort is unlikely to change significantly the welfare of the poorest half of the Andean population, whether located in the bigger or smaller countries. It may lower the prices of some wage-goods, but it may also, by itself, tend to concentrate income in some new sectors. National planning offices, rather than subregional authorities, will remain responsible for monitoring what is happening to the incomes of the lowest half within each country, and for trying to improve them. The less important target of reducing the income gaps among the Andean countries will of course remain a preoccupation of subregional bodies.

While not a panacea for all of the economic and social ills of the subregion, a properly handled Andean customs union can raise the growth rate of each of the participant countries significantly above what those rates would be if each country followed in isolation an import substitution policy similar to those of the 1950's and early 1960's. It could do this by increasing the efficiency of already established industries, by taking advantage of larger scale in selected new import substituting efforts, by increasing Andean bargaining power in world commerce and finance, and by creating a climate conducive to faster technological change, improved management and a bolder attitude toward foreign markets.

It is difficult at this stage to be precise about the addition to the growth rate which the Andean plans could bring about. It may be guessed that it could be as high as one percentage point, on average, throughout the next fifteen years, although its beneficial effects will be felt most strongly during the latter part of that period. But even if the per capita growth rate with integration is only 2.5% per annum, compared with a 2.0% rate without integration, by 1985 that difference would mean a per capita GDP of $ 680 rather than one of $ 630. Contrary to the situation in most of Africa and Asia, the Latin-American per capita income base is such that apparently small changes in per capita growth rates can make the difference between breaking into the income category of, say, Italy, within a reasonable time span, or remaining in the semi-industrialized stage Argentina has been for the last forty years. It should also be remembered that the Andean scheme should bring these countries closer to their non-economic goals, such as greater regional autonomy vis-a-vis the rest of the world.

So with all of its limitations and dangers, the Andean program appears as a worthwhile and exciting undertaking, which should be politically feasible. One can apply to it what Paul N. Rosenstein-Rodan has written about Latin-American integration: 'It is an idea that once launched will not and cannot perish. It may suffer agonizing delays, create many difficulties, but it offers such obvious advantages to all that we should despair of human reason if narrow nationalistic instincts were to stop it.'[32]

---

[32] Paul N. Rosenstein-Rodan, 'Multinational investment in the framework of Latin-American integration', *op. cit.* 33.

R.S. Eckaus, P.N. Rosenstein-Rodan (eds.) Analysis of development problems,
© North-Holland Publishing Company

NEOCLASSICAL PROJECTIONS OF
FOREIGN EXCHANGE NEEDS IN CHILE*

L. TAYLOR

Harvard University, Cambridge, Mass., U.S.A.

The purpose of this paper is to work out some rough forecasts of the required growth of non-traditional exports over the next decade in Chile — 'required' being taken in the sense of those exports necessary to equilibrate the Balance of Payments under various assumptions about the rate of growth of GDP or aggregate consumption. The basic result — that non-traditional exports will have to grow at rates of 7–10% annually — is by no means surprising, and complements the results of Foxley et al. [ref. 72] and others. However, in some sense the forecasts here are less open to criticism than those of other authors, since I have been at some pains to construct a very neo-classical projection model, which allows relatively more opportunity for substitution against exports than other models. If exports are required to grow rapidly in the substitution-rich economy considered here, then one can be fairly sure that they will have to grow rapidly in any 'reasonable' forecast for Chile. This insensitivity of the export projections to forecasting technique is why Bacha and I place such emphasis on export-oriented investment in our paper on calculating foreign exchange shadow prices [ref. 185].

The projection model itself is a cross between Johansen's prescient *Multisector study of economic growth* [ref. 103] and McKinnon's two-gap model [ref. 136]. I follow Johansen in his general equilibrium analysis of the economy, with full consideration of all price-quantity relationships (but with a much less disaggregated equation structure), and add McKinnon's important distinction between domestically produced and imported capital goods. The McKinnon approach (which was anticipated by the Latin American structuralist economists) treats exports as a 'quasi-capital goods' sector; export revenues must grow constantly to finance growing capital goods imports. The play in the model therefore centers in part on the degree of substitutability

* Thanks are due Edmar Bacha and Marcelo Selowsky for helpful comments.

327

between domestic and imported capital. And from this follows the interest of the neo-classical specification, which in detail is as follows:

I. A neoclassical model for projecting foreign exchange requirements

Let x_1 be the output for final purposes of the economy, not including mineral production for export, which is labelled x_2. Assume that x_1 is produced according to the following production function,

$$x_1 = Ae^{\epsilon t}L^\alpha (K^*)^{1-\alpha} , \tag{1}$$

where A is a scaling constant, ϵ is the rate of technical progress, L is labor input, α is the exponent in the Cobb–Douglas function (1) and K^* is an index of the productivity of the capital stock. This index is assumed to be of the C.E.S. type, constructed as follows:

$$K^* = [\gamma(K^D)^{-\beta} + (1-\gamma)(K^F)^{-\beta}]^{-1/\beta} , \tag{2}$$

where γ is the distribution parameter in the C.E.S. index function, and β is equal to $(1/\sigma) - 1$, with σ being the 'Direct' partial elasticity of substitution between domestic-type capital K^D and foreign-type capital K^F in the 'production' of the capital-aggregate K^*.[1] If the elasticity σ is close to zero, the two types of capital are poor substitutes, while if it is large, they are virtually perfect substitutes. Since K^D corresponds essentially to plant and K^F to equipment, the results of Sato [ref. 170] for the U.S.A. would indicate that σ has a value of about 2. In the numerical examples discussed below, σ is set to this value, and also to the much lower value of 0.5.

It is assumed that the production of x_1 requires intermediate imports in the amount m, where

$$m = \mu x_1 , \tag{3}$$

where μ is a *fixed* coefficient. One could in principle allow the intermediate imports m to be related to x_1 by some more flexible arrangement than eq. (3), but this is uninteresting for the following reasons: (i) the general impression is that further import substitution of intermediate goods in Chile is likely to be a costly process, and will not (or perhaps 'should not') be pursued with great intensity; (ii) allowing more than the current quota of intermediate imports is counter-productive in a model which is supposed to be biased against

---

[1] The production-function given by eqs. (1) and (2) is a special case of the two-level C.E.S. function proposed by Sato [ref. 170].

export growth, and in any case is not a likely policy when jobs and other vested interests in intermediate import-competing industries are at stake.

There are two kinds of consumption in the model, C^D of domestic goods, and C^F of foreign goods. They are functionally specified as follows:

$$C^D = Vg_1(s_c, p, y) \tag{4}$$

$$C^F = Vg_0(s_c, p, y), \tag{5}$$

where V is population, g_0 and g_1 are *per capita* demand functions, s_c is the domestic price of imported consumption goods, p is the price of the domestic-ally-produced consumption good, and y is total consumption per capita at the going prices,

$$y = s_c g_0 + p g_1. \tag{6}$$

As usual, only two of the three eqs. (4)–(6) are independent.

Capital stocks are assumed to depreciate 'radioactively',

$$D^D = \delta^D K^D, \tag{7}$$

$$D^F = \delta^F K^F, \tag{8}$$

where D^D and D^F represent physical depreciation of the two types of capital goods. Net investments are defined in the usual way as follows:

$$I^D = \dot{K}^D \tag{9}$$

$$I^F = \dot{K}^F, \tag{10}$$

where the dot means differentiation with respect to time.

Domestic production is supposed to satisfy demand for domestic-type goods,

$$x_1 = C^D + I^D + D^D + Z + E. \tag{11}$$

where Z stands for the government and other exogenous expenditures, and E is production for export or import substitution. At the same time, there must be balance of trade in world prices,

$$\pi_e E + \pi_2 x_2 + F = \pi_m m + \pi_c C^F + \pi_k (I^F + D^F), \tag{12}$$

where the π's stand for the appropriate world prices, and F is the sum of foreign capital inflows. World prices are assumed to vary independently of the other variables of the model — probably a realistic assumption even in the case of the copper-plus-iron price π_2.

We now have in hand a complete production-side description of the economy, except for the factor markets. Here, following Johansen, perfect competition is assumed as the only well-specified alternative. Literally speaking, this condition does not obtain in Chile, but on the other hand its simplicity dominates other possible specifications.

In any case, cost minimization under the production assumptions (1)–(3) gives the following equations (which close the production-side description of the economy):

$$\alpha(p-\mu s_m)x_1 = wL \tag{13}$$

$$(1-\alpha)(p-\mu s_m)(x_1/K^*)\ \gamma(K^*/K^D)^{1+\beta} = (R+\delta^D)p \tag{14}$$

$$(1-\alpha)(p-\mu s_m)(x_1/K^*)\ (1-\gamma)(K^*/K^F)^{1+\beta} = (R+\delta^F)s_k\ . \tag{15}$$

These equations all specify the equality of marginal value products of the three production factors (after deduction for the costs per unit of output of intermediate imports, μs_m) to their costs. In the case of labor, this cost is just the wage w; in the case of each of the two capital goods, it is the economy-wide net rate of return to capital R, plus an appropriate allowance for depreciation, multiplied by the prices p or s_k of domestic or foreign capital respectively.

From the specification of the foregoing equations, it is apparent that they 'should' determine an equilibrium for the economy, provided enough variables are specified independently. For example, eqs. (1)–(5) and (7)–(15) are independent, and will determine the 14 variables K^D, K^F, K^*, m, x_1, E, D^D, D^F, w, R, C^D, C^F, K^D, and K^F, provided that the labor force (L), domestic and foreign prices of traded goods (the s and π terms), the domestic price level (p), total consumption per capita (y), investments (I^D and I^F) and exogenous demands and outputs (Z,x_2,F) are specified. We will take for granted the existence of this type of equilibrium and explore feasible patterns of evolution of the system over time from the original equilibrium point. To do this, we will work out a system of differential equations, *linearized* about the initial equilibrium point, relating the growth rates of key variables of the system. Taking advantage of the linearity of the equations, it will be easy to specify a sufficient number of these growth rates exogenously, and examine how the remaining growth rates vary as functions of the exogenous ones.[2]

---

[2] An alternative procedure would be to solve a non-linear set of differential equations forward through time from the initial point, subject to different assumptions about the evolution of the exogenous variables. For the model considered here (with eight to ten differential equations), this exercise would be easily within the capacity of computing equipment available in Chile.

For example, we will use this method to find growth rates of non-traditional exports required to support different growth rates of per capita consumption, subject to various hypotheses about the rate of technical progress, rate of growth of mineral exports, etc.

Starting with eq. (2) for the capital stock index, straightforward differentiation gives

$$\dot{K}^*/K^* = \gamma(K^*/K^D)^\beta \dot{K}^D/K^D + (1-\gamma)(K^*/K^F)^\beta \dot{K}^F/K^F , \qquad (16)$$

while logarithmic differentiation of the production function (1) itself gives,

$$\dot{x}_1/x_1 = \alpha \dot{L}/L + (1-\alpha)\dot{K}^*/K^* + \epsilon . \qquad (17)$$

At the same time, inspection of the intermediate import function (3) assures us that

$$\dot{m}/m = \dot{x}_1/x_1 . \qquad (18)$$

Turning to the production equilibrium relationships, we adopt the convention that all domestic prices in the base year are equal to one, so that the 'net price' of domestic output (after deduction for intermediate non-competitive imports) is

$$p^* = p - \mu s_m = 1 - \mu .$$

With this convention, logarithmic differentiation of the labor market equilibrium condition (13) gives

$$\dot{p}^*/p^* + \dot{x}_1/x_1 = \dot{w}/w + \dot{L}/L ,$$

or in other terms,

$$(1/(1-\mu))\dot{p}/p - (\mu/(1-\mu))\dot{s}_m/s_m + \dot{x}_1/x_1 = \dot{w}/w + \dot{L}/L , \qquad (19)$$

where once again the initial equality of the prices p and s_m to unity has been used.

The production equilibrium conditions for capital are treated in a similar fashion. Differentiation of eq. (14) gives

$$\dot{p}^*/p^* + \dot{x}_1/x_1 + \beta \dot{K}^*/K^* - (1+\beta)\dot{K}^D/K^D = [\dot{R}p+(R+\delta^D)\dot{p}]/(R+\delta^D p) .$$

After substitution from above to remove the expression for $\dot{p}^*/p^*$ and some manipulation, this equation reduces to

$$\dot{w}/w + \dot{L}/L + \beta \dot{K}^*/K^* - (1+\beta)\dot{K}^D/K^D = \dot{p}/p + (R/(R+\delta^D))\dot{R}/R . \qquad (20)$$

The equivalent expression for foreign-type capital goods is

$$\dot{w}/w + \dot{L}/L + \beta\dot{K}^*/K^* - (1+\beta)\dot{K}^F/K^F = \dot{s}_k/s_k + (R/R+\delta^F))\dot{R}/R \ . \tag{21}$$

Finally we turn to the demand-supply balance equations for the two types of goods in the model. Note first that we can write, say, $\dot{C}^D$ as

$$\dot{C}^D = V\dot{g}_1 + g_1\dot{V}$$

$$= Vg_1(\dot{g}_1/g_1) + Vg_1(\dot{V}/V)$$

$$= C^D[g_{10}(\dot{s}_c/s_c)+g_{11}(\dot{p}/p)+G_1(\dot{y}/y)] + C^D(\dot{V}/V) \ ,$$

where g_{10} and g_{11} are the elasticities of consumption of domestic goods per capita with respect to the prices of foreign and domestic consumer goods, respectively, and G_1 is the income elasticity. Differentiating eq. (11) and substituting the expression for $\dot{C}^D$ gives

$$x_1(\dot{x}_1/x_1) = \dot{I}^D + \delta^D K^D(\dot{K}^D/K^D) + \dot{Z} + E(\dot{E}/E)$$

$$+ C^D[g_{10}(\dot{s}_c/s_c)+g_{11}(\dot{p}/p)+G_1(\dot{y}/y)] \tag{22}$$

$$+ C^D(\dot{V}/V) \ .$$

Similar manipulation of the balance of trade eq. (12) gives

$$\pi_e E(\dot{E}/E) + \pi_2 x_2(\dot{x}_2/x_2) + \pi_2 x_2(\dot{\pi}_2/\pi_2) + \dot{F} = \pi_m m(\dot{m}/m)$$

$$+ \pi_k(\dot{I}^F+\delta^F K^F(\dot{K}^F/K^F)) + \pi_c C^F[g_{00}(\dot{s}_c/s_c) \tag{23}$$

$$+ g_{01}(\dot{p}/p)+G_0(\dot{y}/y)] + \pi_c C^F(\dot{V}/V) \ ,$$

where variation in both the price π_2 and quantity x_2 of mineral exports is explicitly allowed for.

II. Numerical projections

The eight eqs. (16)–(23) will determine the relative growth rates of eight variables in the system, when the growth rates of the other variables are specified exogenously. In the numerical experiments reported below, we usually treat growth rates of the following variables as endogenous (although other combinations are clearly possible):

Domestic-type capital K^D
Foreign-type capital K^F
Total capital index K^*
Domestic production x_1

Intermediate imports m
Wage rate w
Rate of return R
Non-traditional exports E

The majority of the coefficients in the model depend on both technical parameters of the production functions, etc., and base-year values of the variables. Table 1 presents a summary of the values elected for the former. The justifications for these illustrative values are as follows:

The Cobb–Douglas coefficient α has a value roughly consistent with the observed share of wage income (but does not take into account whatever part of earnings of non-corporate enterprise should be imputed to labor).[3]

The depreciation rates, in connection with a capital-output ratio of 3.0, imply total depreciation is about 7% or 8% of GDP, as shown below. This is consistent with the recorded data, and the rates themselves seem consistent with usually postulated lifetimes for capital in Chile.

Table 1
Basic parameter values

Name	Description	Value
α	Exponent in Cobb–Douglas function	0.5
σ	Elasticity of substitution between domestic and foreign capital	0.5 or 2.0
δD	Depreciation rate, domestic capital	0.02
δF	Depreciation rate, foreign capital	0.04
μ	Intermediate import coefficient	0.15
G_1	Income elasticity, domestic consumption	1.0
g_{11}	Own-price elasticity, domestic consumption	-1.0
g_{10}	Cross-price elasticity, domestic consumption	0.0
G_0	Income elasticity, import consumption	1.0
g_{01}	Cross-price elasticity, import consumption	0.0
g_{00}	Own-price elasticity, import consumption	-1.0
π_m	World price, intermediate imports	0.62
π_c	World price, consumption imports	0.45
π_k	World price, capital goods imports	0.65
π_e	World price, non-traditional exports	1.0

[3] Acceptance of this value for α in effect amounts to accepting a neo-classical theory of distribution in addition to our neo-classical capital theory – having accepted half the Devil's bargain regarding capital stock, there seems less harm in accepting the rest on the distribution side!

The income and price elasticities correspond to those of a Cobb–Douglas utility function, which is more or less appropriate to such aggregated consumption categories. In addition, the values are consistent with those observed in recent time series.

The world prices (calculated with domestic prices all set to unity) are based on estimates for 1970 made by ODEPLAN's global programming group.[4] The price of production for trade improvement (mainly export) assumes drawback payments will be negligible in the 1970's.

To calculate base-year values for the variables of the model, liberal use was made of the ODEPLAN projections of the situation in 1970 (treated as a 'full employment' year). Table 2 gives details on some of these estimates. The main comments to be made about them are as follows:

(i) The mineral export price π_2 was assumed to be at its 1965 value in making the accounts balance.

(ii) A capital-output ratio of 3.0 was assumed, and 60% and 40% of capital stock were assumed to be of domestic and foreign origin, respectively. Together with the rates of depreciation from table 2, these assumptions serve to

Table 2
Base year values of the variables

Name	Description	Value (10^9 Escudos of 1965)
K^D	Stock of domestic-type capital	33.984
K^F	Stock of foreign-type capital	22.656
K^*	Index of total capital stock	28.213 ($\sigma = 2.0$)
		29.069 ($\sigma = 0.5$)
γ	Distribution parameter – capital index	0.516 ($\sigma = 2.0$)
		0.662 ($\sigma = 0.5$)
x_1	Domestic production	18.88
x_2	Production for export (mineral)	2.6
m	Intermediate imports (domestic prices)	2.832
F	Capital inflows on current account	−0.18
E	Non-traditional exports	0.9
C^D	Consumption of domestic-types goods	14.8
C^F	Consumption of imports (domestic prices)	1.3
R	Rate of return	0.1137
	Gross domestic product	20.966

[4] These prices are roughly consistent with those estimated from other sources; see [ref. 185] for details.

determine the rate of return R. Its value is consistent with actual rates of return estimated by Bitar and Trivelli [ref. 30] and Gavan [ref. 77]. The index of aggregate capital stock was calculated from eq. (2). The value or γ, the distribution parameter in eq. (2), depends on the assumed value for the elasticity of substitution σ. It was calculated previous to the capital stock index by using eqs. (14) and (15).

With the parameters and base-year values of tables 1 and 2, the model's equations can be evaluated numerically. This set of equations can be written as

$$Mu + Nv = 0 \, ,$$

where u is the vector of growth rates of eight endogenous variables, and v is a similar vector for fourteen exogenous variables. This system can be solved in the form

$$u = -M^{-1}Nv \, ,$$

which expresses the endogenous growth rates in terms of the exogenous growth rates. For the two cases of σ equaling 2 and 0.5, the matrices $-M^{-1}N$ are shown in tables 3 and 4. Each row in these tables shows the multipliers giving rates of growth of the endogenous variables as functions of rates of growth of the exogenous variables. Thus, in table 3, a growth rate of 1% in mineral production for export $(\dot{x}_2/x_2)$ implies a growth rate of -3.45133% in non-traditional exports $(\dot{E}/E)$.

In perusal of tables 3 and 4, a number of points stand out. These include: (i) the elasticity of substitution between the two types of capital enters as a second-order parameter in the determination of the growth rates of the 'real' variables. Thus, most of the multipliers have similar values in the two tables. However, the effects of changes in the domestic price p and the capital import price s_k on the accumulation of the two types of capital stock *are* significantly different. Since relatively little is known econometrically about the value of σ in Chile, this suggests that a change in the relative prices of domestic and foreign capital goods would have fairly unpredictable effects on the rate at which the two types of capital are accumulated. On the other hand — and always accepting the assumption of a Cobb–Douglas production function — raising or lowering the domestic price of imported capital goods would have little influence on the growth of the real wage and/or employment. (ii) The rate of growth of non-traditional exports is very much influenced by the growth of mineral exports (or their price), growth of per capita consumption, the domestic price level and population. If consumption growth is taken as a welfare goal, growth of non-traditional exports appears as something of a pre-

Table 3
Multiplier matrix for endogenous growth rates ($\sigma = 2$)

	$\dot{L}/L$	$\dot{y}/y$	$\dot{p}/p$	$\dot{x}_2/x_2$	$\dot{F}$
$\dot{K}^D/K^D$	-1.30236	2.23405	-3.07774	-0.37754	-0.14521
$\dot{K}^F/K^F$	-1.00277	1.94334	-0.63133	-0.32842	-0.12631
$\dot{K}^*/K^*$	-1.17237	2.10792	-2.01630	-0.35623	-0.13701
$\dot{m}/m$	-0.08619	1.05396	-1.00815	-0.17811	-0.06851
$\dot{x}_1/x_1$	-0.08619	1.05396	-1.00815	-0.17811	-0.06851
$\dot{w}/w$	-1.08619	1.05396	0.16832	-0.17811	-0.06851
$\dot{R}/R$	1.35367	-1.31351	2.01707	0.22198	0.08538
$\dot{E}/E$	-0.82446	3.97814	-2.38005	-3.45133	-1.32743
$G\dot{D}P/GDP$	-0.08556	0.92433	-0.83297	-0.02643	-0.05786

	$\dot{s}_m/s_m$	$\dot{s}_c/s_c$	$\dot{s}_k/s_k$	$\dot{\pi}_2/\pi_2$	$\dot{j}^D$
$\dot{K}^D/K^D$	0.02085	-0.08495	0.90779	-0.37754	0.14521
$\dot{K}^F/K^F$	-0.02779	-0.07389	-1.21033	-0.32842	0.12631
$\dot{K}^*/K^*$	-0.00026	-0.08015	-0.01121	-0.35623	0.13701
$\dot{m}/m$	-0.00013	-0.04008	-0.00560	-0.17811	0.06851
$\dot{x}_1/x_1$	-0.00013	-0.04008	-0.00560	-0.17811	0.06851
$\dot{w}/w$	-0.17660	-0.04008	-0.00560	-0.17811	0.06851
$\dot{R}/R$	-0.21977	0.04994	-0.53374	0.22198	-0.08538
$\dot{E}/E$	-0.01844	-0.77655	-0.80310	-3.45133	0.21632
$G\dot{D}P/GDP$	-0.00053	-0.06795	-0.02289	-0.02643	0.05786

	$\dot{j}^F$	$\dot{V}/V$	$\dot{Z}$	ϵ
$\dot{K}^D/K^D$	0.09439	2.23405	0.14521	-2.60472
$\dot{K}^F/K^F$	0.08210	1.94334	0.12631	-2.00553
$\dot{K}^*/K^*$	0.08906	2.10792	0.13701	-2.34475
$\dot{m}/m$	0.04453	1.05396	0.06851	-0.17237
$\dot{x}_1/x_1$	0.04453	1.05396	0.06851	-0.17237
$\dot{w}/w$	0.04453	1.05396	0.06851	-0.17237
$\dot{R}/R$	-0.05549	-1.31351	-0.08538	2.70735
$\dot{E}/E$	0.86283	3.97814	0.21632	-1.64892
$G\dot{D}P/GDP$	0.05431	0.92433	0.05786	-0.17113

requisite for this goal. This will show up clearly in the numerical experiments reported below. (iii) The rates of growth of domestic production (x_1) and of GDP in base year prices (shown in the bottom line) are also strongly influenced by consumption growth and the growth of population. The domestic price p, which enters in a complex way in substitution on both demand and supply sides of the model, influences both x_1 and E negatively.

Table 4
Multiplier matrix for endogenous growth rates ($\sigma=1/2$)

	$\dot{L}/L$	$\dot{y}/y$	$\dot{p}/p$	$\dot{x}_2/x_2$	$\dot{F}$
$\dot{K}^D/K^D$	−1.20607	2.14062	−2.29151	−0.36176	−0.13914
$\dot{K}^F/K^F$	−1.13114	2.06791	−1.67958	−0.34947	−0.13441
$\dot{K}^*/K^*$	−1.17356	2.10907	−2.02601	−0.35642	−0.13709
$\dot{m}/m$	−0.08678	1.05453	−1.01300	−0.17821	−0.06854
$\dot{x}_1/x_1$	−0.08678	1.05453	−1.01300	−0.17821	−0.06854
$\dot{w}/w$	−1.08678	1.05453	0.16346	−0.17821	−0.06854
$\dot{R}/R$	1.35441	−1.31423	2.02312	0.22210	0.08542
$\dot{E}/E$	−0.90964	4.06079	−3.07560	−3.46529	−1.33281
$\dot{GDP}/GDP$	−0.08799	0.92669	−0.85279	−0.02683	−0.05802

	$\dot{s}_m/s_m$	$\dot{s}_c/s_c$	$\dot{s}_k/s_k$	$\dot{\pi}_2/\pi_2$	$\dot{i}^D$
$\dot{K}^D/K^D$	0.00521	−0.08140	0.22707	−0.36176	0.13914
$\dot{K}^F/K^F$	−0.00695	−0.07863	−0.30275	−0.34947	0.13441
$\dot{K}^*/K^*$	−0.00006	−0.08020	−0.00280	−0.35642	0.13709
$\dot{m}/m$	−0.00003	−0.04010	−0.00140	−0.17821	0.06854
$\dot{x}_1/x_1$	−0.00003	−0.04010	−0.00140	−0.17821	0.06854
$\dot{w}/w$	−0.17650	−0.04010	−0.00140	−0.17821	0.06854
$\dot{R}/R$	−0.21989	0.04997	−0.53897	0.22210	−0.08542
$\dot{E}/E$	−0.00461	−0.77969	−0.20089	−3.46529	0.22170
$\dot{GDP}/GDP$	−0.00013	−0.06804	−0.00572	−0.02683	0.05802

	$\dot{i}^F$	$\dot{V}/V$	$\dot{Z}$	ϵ
$\dot{K}^D/K^D$	0.09044	2.14062	0.13914	−2.41215
$\dot{K}^F/K^F$	0.08737	2.06791	0.13441	−2.26227
$\dot{K}^*/K^*$	0.08911	2.10907	0.13709	−2.34712
$\dot{m}/m$	0.04455	1.05453	0.06854	−0.17356
$\dot{x}_1/x_1$	0.04455	1.05453	0.06854	−0.17356
$\dot{w}/w$	0.04455	1.05453	0.06854	−0.17356
$\dot{R}/R$	−0.05552	−1.31423	−0.08542	2.70883
$\dot{E}/E$	0.86632	4.06079	0.22170	−1.81928
$\dot{GDP}/GDP$	0.05440	0.92669	0.05802	−0.17598

To add flesh to these necessarily superficial observations about the role of the exogenous growth rates in influencing changes in the endogenous variables, it is necessary to undertake numerical experimentation with the model. There are many possible experiments which could be undertaken, but only two are presented here — a small exploration of the sensitivity of the rates of growth of non-traditional exports to certain key exogenous growth rates, and

Table 5
Values of exogenous growth rates

Symbol	Description	Value
$\dot{L}/L$	Labor growth	0.02
$\dot{p}/p$	Domestic price level	0.0
$\dot{F}$	Capital inflow	0.0
s_m/s_m	Domestic price $-$ int. imps.	0.0
s_c/s_c	Domestic price $-$ cons. imps.	0.0
s_1/s_1	Domestic price $-$ cap. imps.	0.0
$\dot{\pi}_2/\pi_2$	Mineral export price	0.0
$\dot{i}D$	Change in domestic-type investment	0.06
$\dot{i}F$	Change in foreign-type investment	0.03
$\dot{V}/V$	Population	0.02
$\dot{Z}$	Exogenous demand	0.05

some analysis of the response of demand for labor to changes in the wage rate.

For both of these experiments, the majority of the exogenous growth rates were kept constant at the values of table 5. In this table, it is seen that both labor force and population are assumed (for the export projections) to grow at two percent annually, while exogenous demand (mainly from government) grows the equivalent of 50 million escudos from its initial value of 1.3 billion. The rates of change of investment were set by assuming 5% growth rates from the net investment levels of the ODEPLAN 1970 projections. No experiments with changes in relative prices were undertaken, as all the zero entries for price changes in table 5 testify, although this could be a potentially fruitful use of the model.

Table 6 gives the projections for rates of growth of non-traditional exports under variations in the rate of growth of total consumption, mineral exports and technical progress. In addition, the share of gross investment in GDP is included as a measure of the feasibility of the various projections from the savings side. The two values of the per capita consumption growth rate suffice to double this quantity in 23.5 and 17.5 years, respectively, while the two values of technical progress which appear in the table $-$ 2.5% and 1.25% $-$ roughly correspond to the estimates of Harberger and Selowsky [ref. 92] and Michapolous [ref. 140], respectively. The growth rates of mineral exports were chosen arbitrarily, but the reader can make his own modifications in the results by using the multipliers in table 3.

It is apparent from table 6 that growth rates of per capita consumption of 3% and 4% would seem to be feasible within historical limits on gross invest-

Table 6
Growth of non-traditional exports ($\sigma = 2$)

Non-trad. exports	Total con-sumption	Growth rates of Mineral exports	Technical change	Investment share
0.05282	0.03	0.04	0.025	0.15
0.07343	0.03	0.04	0.0125	0.21
0.12185	0.03	0.02	0.025	0.16
0.09260	0.04	0.04	0.025	0.20
0.11321	0.04	0.04	0.0125	0.25
0.16163	0.04	0.02	0.25	0.21

ment. However, it is obvious that these consumption growth rates must be ac-companied by a healthy expansion of non-traditional exports. On the best as-sumptions about technical progress and the growth of traditional exports, a growth rate of non-traditional exports of 10% is required to support 4% growth in per capita consumption. The growth rate increases to more than 16% when it is assumed that traditional exports grow at 2% per year (or that the sum of the rates of growth of the volume and the price of these exports is 2%).

At least from the neo-classical point of view, it seems obvious that strong efforts in export fomentation will be necessary over the ensuing few years.

As another exercise with the model, I undertook some exploration of the labor demand implicit in it. In this case, wages were taken as exogenous, and the labor force growth rate as endogenous. Thus, as wages are increased, sub-

Table 7
Growth of labor force and growth of wages[a]

Labor force growth	Wage rate growth	Consumption growth
0.02774	0.02	0.03
0.01854	0.03	0.03
0.00933	0.04	0.03
0.00012	0.05	0.03
0.03745	0.02	0.04
0.02824	0.03	0.04
0.01903	0.04	0.04
0.00983	0.05	0.04

[a] Calculated for $\sigma = 2$ and $\epsilon = 0.025$.

stitution against labor is induced, and the labor force employed by the non-mineral sector grows correspondingly more slowly. Table 7 shows the ranges of values for these growth rates produced by the model. With 4% consumption growth, it appears that growth in employment on the order of 2% or more annually is consistent with wage increases of between 3% and 4% per year. The extent to which one is willing to accept these values depends on the degree of one's neoclassical optimism. It remains to be seen whether a buoyant performance in the 1970's will support faith in the flexibility of the Chilean economy or not.

R.S. Eckaus, P.N. Rosenstein-Rodan (eds.), Analysis of development problems,
© North-Holland Publishing Company

TARGET SHOOTING WITH A MULTISECTORAL MODEL

Peter B. CLARK

International Bank for Reconstruction and Development, Washington, D.C., U.S.A.

and

Alejandro FOXLEY R.

Catholic University of Chile, Santiago, Chile

I. Introduction

In a recent article [ref. 116], Janos Kornai has described plan formulation
as a mutual learning process which must occur between political decisionmakers and technical planners. The former define a set of desired goals for
the economy within which an aspiration level for the principle objective of
the plan is initially selected. The latter explore the technical feasibility of
achieving simultaneously the set of goals, given the willingness of the political
level to mobilize resources. This paper describes how multisectoral models
taught Chilean planners about technical trade-offs in the economy.

The planners are faced with the task of exploring feasible alternatives of
target achievement which are as close as possible to the aspiration levels defined by the political decisionmakers. For this purpose, planners have developed econometric models. Models are an abstract and imperfect representation
of reality. An abstraction is required in part because of the computational
limitations which restrict the planners to fewer sectors and variables than might
be wished by officials charged with the task of choosing investment projects
or implementing policy. The models are also imperfect because of limitations
imposed by technique (for example, linearity restrictions) or because reality
itself is also changing. In an historic period of time it might be possible for a
model builder to estimate exactly the parameter values which would result in
endogenous variables equivalent to the statistician's perception of reality
However, in future time, parameters can always be changed, sometimes by the
decisions of policymakers due to their revised estimate of what is politically
feasible. Therefore, improved planning will result from the increased interaction of political policymakers and technical planner.

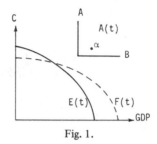

Fig. 1.

The previous description of an efficient planning process may be represented graphically by fig. 1. We assume for simplification that two goals are both desired by policymakers; the growth of gross domestic product (*GDP*) and the growth of private consumption (*C*). $A(t)$ represents the set of acceptable targets for policymakers with boundary conditions fixed by lower limits A and B. The point α is the particular initial set of goals which have been selected. Planners estimate and explore a feasibility surface $E(t)$ which is generated by all the production possibility sets for the producing sectors, given the resources policymakers are willing to mobilize. $E(t)$ is only an approximation of the 'true' feasible target range described by the set $F(t)$ representing the real world.

The process of plan formulation is one where information is exchanged between planners and policymakers. The planners demonstrate by the use of models what are the policy trade-offs, quantifying the opportunity costs of attaining one target vis-a-vis others and the influence of the resource constraints that will be faced by the economy during the plan period. On the other hand, decisionmakers elaborate on the political variables which can shift upwards (or downwards) the feasibility set $E(t)$. $E(t)$ will approach $F(t)$ during the planning process because of technical improvements in the models and the refinement of politically determined limitations previously considered inflexible. Given the aspiration levels of the politicians and the best performance estimates of the planners, policymakers may endorse new programs. For example, in Chile we have observed new trade agreements within the Andean Group, the nationalization of the copper industry, enforced savings policies as part of the annual wage adjustment process, initiation of export subsidies, tariff liberalization, new employment policies, changes in investment credits, tax reforms, adjustments in the social security system, land reform and new foreign investment codes.

The interaction of policymakers and planners causes the movement of $E(t)$ towards $F(t)$, of both schedules outwards due to broad policy reforms, and a redefinition of the bounds A and B of the target space $A(t)$. An interactive

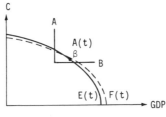

Fig. 2.

process of mutual education, policy revision and technical adjustment, will lead $E(t)$ and $A(t)$ to intersect so that a set $U(t) = E(t) \cap [A(t)]$ represents a surface of acceptable and feasible targets among which decisionmakers are able to make their choices. See fig. 2. Point β represents a case where the policymaker's revised aspiration level is coincident with the planner's estimate of the target trade-off surface, but still short of that which reality would permit.

The description of the planning process we have given is a useful conception to better understand the degree of success of plan implementation achieved in many countries. In many cases ex post studies show chosen targets to be outside of $F(t)$, although some economies (for example the Japanese) have fixed targets well inside of $F(t)$. Moreover, it often happens that: (a) the desired target set $A(t)$ as defined by decisionmakers is completely out of range with respect to the economically feasible set $F(t)$; and (b) the exploration of technically feasible trade-offs of objectives by planners is too divergent from the feasibility limits as they exist in reality. The latter is of course a function of the kind of tools used by planners to describe real trade-offs in the economy.

One could say that planning in Chile, as in most countries, has suffered from both problems (a) and (b). We do not attempt to examine and analyse here all the factors which explain why this has been so. Instead, we shall concentrate this study on the practical experience of Chile's National Planning Office (ODEPLAN) during that part of the planning process when modelling techniques were being improved and information revised. ODEPLAN's experience in trying to develop and use better techniques effectively to empirically explore target alternatives is equivalent, using our previous definitions, to ensuring that $E(t)$ is as good a representation of $F(t)$ as the existing data and political assumptions will permit.

II. Multisectoral programming models

Multisectoral models have been used frequently in developing countries to check the consistency of targets embodied in national development plans, but only occasionally have they been used in the planning process to *set* targets. In some sense, this represents a waste of resources, since, in principle, programming models can take into account a wide range of alternative policy goals and illustrate the trade-offs among them. Static linear programming (LP) models are well suited to incorporate large numbers of overlapping and alternative policy functions which may act under varying circumstances as constraints on the economic system.[1] Raising the number of policy instruments and resource restrictions included in an LP model increases the dimensions of the transformation surface representing the production possibility set for the economy. Increasing the number of endogenous policy variables has been the direction of recent extensions of the Chilean programming models as illustrated by Foxley and Clark [ref. 43], Clark et al. [ref. 45].

Parametric variation of the technical coefficients of LP models permits one to simulate the general effects of policy changes, similar to impact multipliers in econometric systems, but does not simulate the precise consequences on all microeconomic elements throughout the system. The advantage of this type of modelling is that it furnishes planners with a tool to test out the feasibility of attaining complex sets of conflicting goals.

An example of target definition by means of multisectoral models is provided by the planning exercises carried out in ODEPLAN during the late 1960's. In 1969, a Leontief system was used to predict feasible production, investment, and import levels in 1970. These projections served as a base year for studies designed to test trade-offs among development targets for 1975 and 1980. Initial sets of targets were calculated using optimizing linear programming (LP) models of the type described in section III below. In terms of fig. 1, planners used parametric variations to trace out policy trade-offs equivalent to initial estimates of $E(t)$. The multisectoral model also served as a useful framework to measure economic interactions whose component parts were checked individually by specialists and sector planners controlling groups of projects. The model's solutions helped the national accounts specialists to test the consis-

---

[1] The 'on and off' nature of linear constraints may seem unrealistic to the planner who would prefer to think in terms of 'more or less' effective policies rather than effective (binding) or redundant (non-binding) policies. This is the weakness of linear models which is tolerated for their computational advantages. The weakness is overcome by the artful planner who uses step functions or piece-wise linear approximations to non-linear functions.

tency of the underlying data required to estimate the parameters of the model. Analysis of solutions caused planners to make explicit many of their implicit assumptions about the behavior of the Chilean economy. The numerous revisions of the model, which took approximately 10 months, presumably resulted in the movement of $E(t)$ towards $F(t)$. After final consultation with sector specialists and after using the revised programming model for further evaluations of possible policy trade-offs, revised alternative medium term projections for the decade of the 1970's finally appeared in an official perspective policy study, ODEPLAN [ref. 148]. This document was prepared by ODEPLAN as the first step of the planners' interaction with political policymakers.

The use of quantitative models in Chile as part of the process initiated in ODEPLAN to set medium term targets has laid a foundation for effective planning in the future. Once planners have presented to the policymakers and politicians the gross alternative targets and some of the trade-offs among them, the mutual education process derived from their increased communication should result in a convergence of the politicians' goal aspiration set $A(t)$ and the planners' technical feasibility set $E(t)$. We set forth below the experience gained in Chile with the use of programming models to define reasonable target trade-offs for presentation to political policymakers as part of medium term planning. When decisionmakers do not heed the best possible estimates of the limits of technical feasibility and trade-offs among conflicting goals, as described by $E(t)$, they may find themselves attempting to implement totally inconsistent policies.

III. Description of the model

All the programming models used for the target-setting exercises were static, providing consistent solutions for only one period at a time. The 15 sector static linear programming model spans a planning period from 1970 to 1975, although all variables are measured in constant 1965 prices. The numbers in parentheses below refer to the equations and lists of variables as given in the appendix to this paper. We shall now describe briefly the reasons for choosing the current specification of the model and the sources for some of the key variables.

The model allocates three resources whose supplies are restricted: domestic savings (8.0), which is subject to a maximum rate of marginal savings obtainable during the plan period (8.1); foreign exchange, as defined in the current account of the balance of payments (7.0), which originates from the exporting activities (6.0) and from the foreign capital inflow which is limited to an exogenously determined maximum annual total (7.1); and lastly, labor (9.0), which is considered homogeneous and whose employment depends on labor's sectoral productivity and on sectoral output. The employment of labor is restricted furthermore by the size of the labor force available, by the sectoral trend in labor productivity and by the requirement to employ a minimum percentage of the labor force (9.1).

A fundamental restriction of any consistency model is that total supply (in this case, domestic production plus competitive and non-competitive imports) must be greater than or equal to intermediate plus final demand in each sector (1.0). All domestic relationships are expressed in user's prices which is the unit of measure for Chile's national accounts and for the input—output table. The latter, based on the technology of 1962,[2] was transformed by the RAS method[3] to be consistent with the sectoral intermediate and final demands as well as the import, value added and production estimates for 1965. This relationship, after some modifications for technical change known to be occurring, was used in 1969 as an input—output model to predict the 1970 production, import and demand levels. In this manner a set of base year estimates were obtained for use in all subsequent studies.

The elements of final demand found in the model are estimated endogenously by the following specifications. Sectoral consumption expenditure elasticities (table 1) are estimated by ODEPLAN [ref. 149] from time series data (1960— 1968) and used to form linear approximations (2.0) to the implicit Engel curves. In those sectors where regressions were not significant (Non-metallic Minerals, Education and Health, as well as Commerce and Services) expenditure elasticities were estimated from cross-sectional data collected by CIEUC [ref. 39]. Total consumption is defined to include not only the final demand for all 15 producing sectors, but also the demand for domestic services (2.1). Government expenditure is set exogenously, although distributed among sectors according to fixed proportions (3.0). These proportions can be altered at any time as policy parameters.

Gross capital formation is composed of net and replacement investments identified by sectors of origin (4.0). Sectoral net investment requirements for the duration of the plan are estimated by sector of destination as a function of the lagged capacity adjustments needed to fulfill endogenously determined output levels for post-terminal years (4.1). The net investment demand by sector of destination is transformed into demand by sector of origin for the terminal year by means of an intersectoral capital distribution matrix and stock-flow

[2] See ODEPLAN [ref. 147].
[3] The method of Stone and Brown [ref. 177] was adapted to Chile by Gomez [ref. 80].

Table 1
Consumption elasticities used in the model

Sector	Period 1970 – 1975
1. Agriculture, fishing	0.52
2. Copper mining	–
3. Other mining	1.01
4. Food, clothing, textiles	0.55
5. Wood, furniture, paper	0.60
6. Non-metallic minerals	0.75
7. Basic metals	–
8. Chemicals, petroleum	3.20
9. Mechanical, metallurgical	2.90
10. Construction	–
11. Electricity, gas, water	2.20
12. Housing rentals	0.10
13. Transport, communications	1.28
14. Education, health	1.10
15. Commerce, services	0.70
16. Domestic services	1.10

conversion factors (4.2). The latter are sector specific depending on the average gestation period found in each sector,[4] and the interplan and post-plan growth rates of sectoral capital stocks (4.3). The equilibrium values of these parameters are often difficult to obtain. We are not even sure if there is a unique set of values of the stock-flow conversion factors which will cause the realized interplan sectoral growth rates to be consistent with target post-terminal rates and the average lag structure found in each sector's capital formation. Empirical tests of the convergence to equilibrium values demonstrated to us that no simple rules of thumb would assure that the system would reach consistent sectoral equilibrium in a finite or predictable number of iterations.[5]

The replacement of depreciated capital stock of each sector is assumed to be a function of its use and is therefore related to sectoral production (4.4). The transformation of demand estimates from sector of destination to sector of origin is also made by means of the intersectoral capital matrix (4.5). Estimates of the average life of different types of capital goods were used to set

---

[4] Studies of the gestation period required for different types of investments were based on an inventory of projects collected by CORFO [ref. 49] and on the principal types of construction works expected in the period 1968–1974.
[5] Frustration with the unrealistic aspects of these parameters led to experiments designed to introduce the more familiar accelerator specification into static programming models using a complementary open Leontief model to generate capacity expansion and demand for net investment. See Clark and Taylor [ref. 46].

the replacement parameters as derived from engineering studies and technical feasibility studies of CORFO (Chile's industrial development agency). Finally, inventory coefficients were estimated from survey data and statistical reports of wholesalers and retailers for the period from the mid-1950's to 1967. The relationships derived for stock investments (4.6) appear relatively stable which led us to use fixed proportion coefficients. In this model we have assumed that the volume of inventories (raw materials, goods in process and finished stocks) maintained by producers in each sector are proportional to output and that commercial inventories are a function of the total supply of each good, including imports.

The model is specified to divide imports into competitive and non-competitive (or non-substitutable) categories (5.3). A complete enumeration of all imports making assignment into competitive and non-competitive categories both by sectors of origin and destination was made by ODEPLAN's Foreign Trade Division. This study reclassified the customs and Central Bank data for the years 1962–1966.[6] Non-competitive import parameters are estimated to be proportional to their intermediate use and to the final demand categories of personal consumption, government consumption and gross capital formation (5.0).

The fixed requirements for non-competitive imports deplete the total supply of foreign exchange leaving a residual quantity of foreign exchange available to finance competitive imports (5.1). This foreign exchange balance can be used for any single competitive import or can be distributed among sectors reflecting some of the institutional rigidities or non-price determinants of the pattern of trade. These options are determined in the model by a set of competitive import constraints (5.2). Since it is unlikely that Chile will take up free trade policies during the 1970's, alternative vectors of competitive import boundary coefficients are specified to test the implications of changes from the historical pattern of foreign exchange use for competitive imports. Table 2 shows the different parameters used for experimentation. When the coefficient values sum to more than 1.0, the model is free to change directly the structure of supply by import substitution rather than only indirectly by variation in the pattern of demand.

It is similarly desirable to permit the sectoral pattern of exports to change in response to variations in the structure of Chile's comparative costs. Accordingly, ODEPLAN's Foreign Trade Division made projections of the exports expected in 1975. To these projections we added maximum and minimum expansion rates to set up upper and lower bound restrictions for 1975 exports (6.0). These values are shown in table 3.

---

[6] The method, implicit assumptions, and analysis of aggregate results may be found in Rodriguez [ref. 168].

Table 2
Distribution of limits imposed on competitive imports

Sector	(1) Average distribution Period 1962–1966	(2) Average distribution Readjusted for policy	(3) Distribution 1.25 maximum Period 1962–1966	(4) Distribution 1.25 times Readjusted for policy
1	0.159	0.120	0.120	0.120
2	0.000	0.000	0.000	0.000
3	0.051	0.040	0.087	0.050
4	0.164	0.164	0.226	0.205
5	0.023	0.060	0.034	0.075
6	0.015	0.015	0.024	0.019
7	0.037	0.037	0.060	0.046
8	0.092	0.092	0.121	0.115
9	0.218	0.269	0.320	0.300
10	0.000	0.000	0.000	0.000
11	0.006	0.006	0.006	0.006
12	0.007	0.007	0.007	0.007
13	0.118	0.080	0.118	0.080
14	0.001	0.001	0.001	0.001
15	0.109	0.109	0.109	0.109
Total	1.000	1.000	1.233	1.133

The demand for copper exports is specified as a function of the price elasticity of demand for copper which confronts Chile. The foreign exchange revenue is found to be non-proportional to increased copper exports and is included in the model as a linear function:[7]

$$Y_N = e_2 + f_2 \ddot{E}_2 .$$

The system is finally specified by defining GDP with an identity taken from the expenditure side of the national income accounts (10.0). This is the variable price definition which includes a terms of trade adjustment for the difference between the average 1965 copper price obtained by Chilean exports and the expected price for 1970. This variable price concept is carried over into the balance of payments restriction (7.0) and the definition of gross national savings (8.0). Hence, the average copper price attained by Chilean exports enters directly into the primary resource constraints affecting the future behavior

[7] A full explanation of the transformation of an estimate of the world price elasticity of demand into the Chilean copper export function is given in Clark and Foxley. [ref. 43].

Table 3
Export limits 1975 (millions of E^O)

(1)	(2)	(3) 1970–75	(4) 1975	(5) 1970–75	(6)	(7) 1970–75
Sector	Lower limits	Minimum rates	Predic- tion	Annual rate	Upper limits	Maximum rates
1	128.0	2.0%	139.0	3.5%	156.0	6.0%
2	2821.0	5.0%	2992.0	6.1%	3102.0	7.0%
3	400.0	−2.0%	422.0	0.9%	444.0	2.0%
4	160.0	0.0%	219.0	6.3%	224.0	7.0%
5	227.0	12.0%	278.0	15.7%	386.0	25.0%
6	2.0	−21.3%	2.0	− 21.3%	15.0	21.0%
7	80.0	10.0%	97.0	13.3%	124.0	20.0%
8	63.0	15.0%	106.0	24.3%	116.0	30.0%
9	76.0	5.0%	112.0	12.6%	120.0	15.0%
10	–	–	–	–	–	–
11	2.0	10.3%	2.0	10.3%	2.0	10.3%
12	9.0	3.9%	9.0	3.9%	9.0	3.9%
13	172.0	0.0%	217.0	4.7%	230.0	6.0%
14			2.0	1.0%	2.0	1.0%
15	209.0	0.0%	236.0	2.5%	266.0	5.0%
Total	4349.0		4833.0		5196.0	
Difference		−484.0		+363.0		
Total when adjusted for terms of trade effect:	4451.0		4935.0		5298.0	

(the production possibility set) of the economy as well as indirectly affecting the foreign exchange earned by copper exports due to the impact of Chilean copper sales on the world copper price.

Given the concern here with the definition of economic goals, one approach might be to describe a large number of alternative objective functions for the LP model. These targets could be tested one at a time or in a complex weighted average of the individually selected targets. The parametric variation of the weights would then test the feasible trade-offs of the goals specified. Instead, we prefer to select a single numeraire as a global objective to be maximized, in this case personal consumption (0.0). All other potential goals have been included within the system of constraints. These include increased employment (9.1), increased labor productivity (9.0), the redistribution of income by means of changes in the consumption expenditure elasticities (2.0), the substitution of imports (5.2), the expansion and diversification of exports (6.0), the mobi-

Table 4
Tableau of primal problem of the multisectoral model

	X	M	$\hat{M}$	$\tilde{M}$	N	R	C	Y	L	A	F	E	V		RHS
Distribution	$[a_{ij}]$	$[k_j^S s_j^T + a_{15}]$	$\{-d_j\}$	$\{-d_j\}$	$[b_{ij}k_j^I]$	$[b_{ij}]$	$\{y_i\}$					$[1]$		$\leqslant$	$\{k_i^S S_i^o + \bar{c}_i - \bar{G}_i\}$
Capacity	$[b_j(1+r_j)^{\theta}]$													$\leqslant$	$\{b_i\bar{X}_i^o(1+i_i)^{\theta}\}$
Replacement	$\{r_j\}$			$\{-1\}$		$[-1]$								$\leqslant$	$\{0\}$
Non-competitive imports	$[\tilde{m}_{ij}^A]$			$\{-1\}$	$[\tilde{m}_i^B b_{ij}k_j^I]$	$[\tilde{m}_i^B b_{ij}]$	$\{\tilde{m}_i^C y_i\}$							$=$	$\{\tilde{m}_i^C \bar{c}_i - m_i^G \bar{G}\}$
Balance of payments		$\langle 1\rangle$									-1	$\langle -1\rangle$		$\leqslant$	$-\bar{Y}^E$
Employment	$\langle l_j\rangle$								-1					$=$	0
Total imports		$[1]$	$[-1]$	$[-1]$	$[-1]$									$=$	$\{0\}$
Total saving	$\langle -k_j^S s_j^T - k_j^S s_j^P\rangle$	$\langle 1-k_j^S s_j^T\rangle$			$\langle -k_j^I\rangle$	$\langle -1\rangle$				1	1	$\langle -1\rangle$		$=$	$\bar{E}^T - \bar{Y}^E - \bar{S}^o$
Marginal saving								$-{}_t^N$		1				$\leqslant$	$\bar{A}^o - {}_t N(\bar{Y}^o)$
Gross domestic product	$\langle -k_j^S s_j^T - k_j^S s_j^P\rangle$	$\langle 1-k_j^S s_j^T\rangle$			$\langle -k_j^I\rangle$	$\langle -1\rangle$	-1	1				$\langle -1\rangle$		$=$	$\bar{E}^T + \bar{G} - \bar{S}^o$
Maximum external gap											1			$\leqslant$	$\bar{F}$
Maximum employment									1					$\leqslant$	$\bar{L}$
Minimum employment									-1					$\leqslant$	$-(1-u)\bar{L}$
Balance of foreign exchange				$\langle -1\rangle$							1	$\langle 1\rangle$	-1	$=$	$\bar{Y}^E$
Competitive imports													$\{-\tilde{m}_i\}$	$\leqslant$	$\{0\}$
Maximand			$[1]$				1								

lization of increased savings (8.1), the reduction of dependence on foreign capital inflows (7.1), a reduction in the investment lag in key sectors (4.3), slowing the rate of public sector expenditures (3.0), the rationalization of the tariff structure (1.0), or a limited expansion of copper exports in order to not depress the world price (7.0).

The variation of the goals described above and other policy objectives implicit in the system may all be expressed in terms of their effects upon the single objective of the model. This incremental relationship is a shadow price which describes the change in the objective function resulting from a unit change in a restricted variable. For example, the shadow price of foreign exchange is defined as $\partial C/\partial F$. It is the slope of the transformation surface described by the cutting plane of the concumption-foreign trade gap axes.

The relationships given in the specification of the model may be written as a tableau (table 4) to be solved by the simplex algorithm using an LP code. We have used the following vector and matrix notation to simplify the representation of the model:

$\{x_i\}$ = a column vector of the parameter X.

$\langle x_j \rangle$ = a row vector of the parameter X.

$[a_{ij}]$ = a square matrix of the parameters a.

$\lfloor a_{ij} \rfloor$ = a diagonal matrix of the parameters a.

IV. Aggregate adjustments of the models

In this section we will demonstrate some of the aggregate adjustments which can be made in key parameters to reflect policy alternatives or in primary resource availabilities. The examples given are simply illustrative of the procedures followed by ODEPLAN technicians as they traced out, improved and recalculated hundreds of variations of the basic multisectoral model's structure. It is our objective here to give examples and a general explanation of the potential for quantification of target trade-offs but not to make recommendations for revisions in Chile's development policies.

The most important variations in the basic specification involve competitive imports, exports and employment. With respect to the first, there are three basic variations where the foreign exchange remaining after financing all noncompetitive import requirements is distributed among sectors according to: (a) the historical pattern observed during the period from 1962 to 1966, (b) the same pattern but where the sectors of agriculture and transport have been reduced to reflect policymakers' aspirations to induce greater import substitution and stimulation in these sectors, and (c) the same pattern as (b) except that all parameters for sectors 3 to 9 have been increased by 25%. In the latter form, the model has a certain degree of freedom to assign foreign exchange according to its own efficiency criteria rather than the potentially inconsistent preferences of policymakers. This is permitted because $\Sigma_i \hat{m}_i > 1$. The three sets of coefficients used in these three alternatives are shown in table 2, columns 1, 2, and 4 and will hereafter be referred to as 'historical', 'historical corrected' and 'variable' competitive import coefficients.

Two alternative export specifications have been used. The first is where export values for 1975 are 'fixed' according to ODEPLAN's projections, as shown in column 4 of table 3. The second specification permits the model to adjust sectoral exports between the minimum and maximum values also shown in table 3. The model will choose to expand exports of a given sector to the maximum, fix them between the specified limits or reduce them to the minimum according to the opportunity cost of producing an additional unit of that sector's output for export as compared with the increment in benefits obtained from employing the additional foreign exchange generated by the new exports. This last export specification will be referred to as the 'variable' specification.

In the case of employment, a full employment limit is fixed when the projected 1975 labor force has been completely distributed among sectors. The full employment limit can be kept active or left inactive if one expects increased labor productivity to occur in dynamic sectors whenever the economy approaches full employment. This only occurs when the growth rate of GDP exceeds 6 percent annually.

The model is also specified to include a minimum employment restriction to ensure that unemployment does not grow above unacceptable limits. The deviation of solutions when this restriction is not active from those when it is included furnishes a measure of the social cost, in terms of consumption forgone, of implementing programs to increase employment. The solutions will include the maximum and minimum employment constraints as 'active' or 'inactive' in the examples given below.

In the first exercise we suppose that the maximum foreign capital inflow in 1975 will not exceed $ 80 million, that is, E° 298 million as calculated in 1965 prices. In terms of a constant copper price, this figure represents a gap of $ 120 million or E° 400 million at 1965 prices. We also assume that the marginal savings rate will not exceed the historical average of 0.15. Both the full employment and minimum employment restrictions are left inactive which means that the unemployment rate given by the model's solution will depend heavily on the trend in sectoral labor productivity observed during the period 1960–1968. No sectors have been induced to increase production in order that the economy might absorb more labor.

We give three variations of the first experiment. In Test 1, the specification

Table 5
The effect of alternative specifications on the solution of the model (E^O millions of 1965)

Specification		1	2	3
Deficit b. of pay.	Variable price	298	298	298
	Constant price	400	400	400
		fixed	variable	variable
Imports, competitive		historical	historical	historical
		corrected	corrected	
Employment, maximum		active	active	active
Employment, minimum		not active	not active	not active
Marginal saving limit		0.15	0.15	0.15
Export limit		fixed	variable	variable

Results		1	2	3
GDP	value	27766	28471	28491
	rate	0.0415	0.0465	0.0467
Consumption	value	19992	20541	20607
	rate	0.0438	0.0497	0.0498
Investment	value	4492	4598	4602
	rate	0.0512	0.0559	0.0560
Imports	value	4586	4837	4861
	rate	0.0643	0.0749	0.0759
Exports	value	4935	5183	5207
	rate	0.0656	0.0754	0.0764
National saving	value	4194	4300	4304
	S/GDP	0.1500	0.1500	0.1510
$\Delta S/\Delta GDP$		0.1500	0.1500	0.1500
Rate of unemployment		0.0900	0.0720	0.0710
M compet/total M		0.6361	0.6630	0.6510
Balance of supply $\frac{\Delta X}{X+M}$		−0.0145	−0.0240	−0.0218
Inv/GDP		0.1618	0.1615	0.1615
Marg. coeff.	Capital (Net)	2.1298	1.9311	1.9227
	Output (Gross)	3.8747	3.4673	3.4468

of exports and the competitive import coefficients are fixed. In this case, there is a high degree of rigidity in the resource allocation which is determined by historical patterns. In Test 2 all exports and competitive imports in sectors other than agriculture and transport are permitted to vary from historical patterns in accordance with more efficient resource allocations selected by the model's solution. Agriculture and transport sectors in this case are being managed by policymakers' perceptions of efficient policies. Test 3 differs from the second because now policymakers' aspirations are omitted which permits a greater degree of flexibility in the model's choice of competitive imports (column 4 of table 2). The macroeconomic variables given by these comparative static solutions appear in table 5.

One observes that when the model has more flexibility that the average growth of GDP from 1970 to 1975 increases from 4.15% annually to 4.67% which reduces the unemployment rate from 9.0% in the rigid case to 7.1% in the more flexible solution.

How can these results be interpreted? In the first place, part of the effect is obtained by means of the greater economic efficiency derived from the increased supply of foreign exchange once exports become variable. In this case the model elects to augment imports to achieve faster growth. The decision to expand exports is not automatic in all sectors (this can be observed in the difference between Tests 2 and 3) depending upon the greater freedom of resource allocation permitted in Test 3. A specification with increased capacity to select the sectoral competitive import pattern allows the model to satisfy efficiency criteria not possible with the rigid historical parameter structure.[8]

These factors are reflected in the import substitution decisions made by the model when the structure is flexible as compared to the more rigid version. Table 6 shows the changing structure of sectoral supply from 1970 to 1975. The change in the domestic share of total supply in each sector is used as a measure of the degree of import substitution occurring during the plan period.

When we compare Tests 1 and 3, we observe that there is more import substitution when the specification is flexible; that is, domestic production as a share of total supply for all sectors is increased in Test 3 by 2.18% rather than only 1.45% in Test 1. The structure of import substitution by sector (table 6) shows an increased dependence on imports of basic metals and mechanical and metallurgical products, the maintenance of the same degree of substitution in petroleum and chemical products, while import substitution is complete in the commerce and services sector when the import specification is more flexible.

Finally, it is also important to note that the productivity of investment tends to increase in Test 3 as shown by the ex post measurement of the aggregate capital-output ratio. The net incremental coefficient falls from 2.13 to 1.92 while the gross coefficient drops from 3.87 to 3.45. Behind the aggregate behavior of the model is a great variation in sectoral behavior. The interpretation of these changes in sectoral patterns and an interpretation of the efficiency criterion implicit in the model is of great importance to the planner but will not be described here.[9] We turn now to the resource variations which will help quantify target trade-offs.

---

[8] This is obvious from other solutions not reported here where the export specification alone is varied while competitive imports remain fixed. The result is significantly less than the change observed between Tests 1 and 3.

[9] See Clark and Foxley [ref. 43] for a full discussion of the sectoral planning criteria.

Table 6
The degree of import substitution

Test no. 1		$\left(\dfrac{X^0}{X^0+M^0}\right)$	$(\dfrac{X}{X+M})$	$(\dfrac{\Delta X}{X+M})$	ΔX
01	Agriculture, fishing	0.8648	0.8509	−0.0139	− 70.1
02	Copper mining	1.0000	1.0000	−0.0000	− 0.1
03	Other mining	0.8677	0.8084	−0.0594	− 77.1
04	Food, clothing, textiles	0.9187	0.9172	−0.0015	− 17.1
05	Wood, furniture, paper	0.8276	0.8106	−0.0170	− 59.9
06	Non-metallic minerals	0.8794	0.8478	−0.0315	− 21.2
07	Basic metals	0.7656	0.7439	−0.0217	− 25.9
08	Chemicals, petroleum	0.7646	0.7101	−0.0545	−184.5
09	Mechanical, metallurgical	0.5589	0.5296	−0.0294	−190.1
10	Construction	1.0000	1.0000	0.0	0.0
11	Electricity, gas, water	0.9885	0.9785	−0.0100	− 8.5
12	Housing rentals	0.9736	0.9806	0.0070	7.6
13	Transport, communications	0.9265	0.8953	−0.0312	− 72.4
14	Eduaction, health	0.9967	0.9986	0.0019	4.2
15	Commerce and services	0.9762	0.8544	−0.1218	−109.9
	Total	0.8729	0.8584	−0.0145	−781.7

Test no. 3		$\left(\dfrac{X^0}{X^0+M^0}\right)$	$(\dfrac{X}{X+M})$	$(\dfrac{\Delta X}{X+M})$	ΔX
01	Agriculture, fishing	0.8648	0.8441	−0.0207	−104.8
02	Copper mining	1.0000	1.0000	0.0	− 0.1
03	Other mining	0.8677	0.7586	−0.1091	−143.4
04	Food, clothing, textiles	0.9187	0.8931	−0.0256	−287.4
05	Wood, furniture, paper	0.8276	0.7773	−0.0503	−186.8
06	Non-metallic minerals	0.8794	0.8050	−0.0743	− 50.4
07	Basic metals	0.7656	0.6814	−0.0842	− 97.3
08	Chemicals, petroleum	0.7646	0.7073	−0.0573	−201.4
09	Mechanical, metallurgical	0.5589	0.4962	−0.0627	−419.8
10	Construction	1.0000	1.0000	0.0	0.0
11	Electricity, gas, water	0.9885	0.9775	−0.0110	− 9.6
12	Housing rentals	0.9736	0.9788	0.0052	5.6
13	Transport, communications	0.9265	0.8872	−0.0392	− 91.1
14.	Education, health	0.9967	1.0000	0.0033	7.3
15	Commerce and services	0.9762	1.0000	0.0238	225.9
	Total	0.8729	0.8484	−0.0244	−1344.7

X = Production, M = Importation, $X+M$ = Supply total, 0 = Initial year.

V. Target trade-offs described by policy variations

Let us consider three different strategies of growth — one dominated by a policy of increased domestic saving, a second characterized by export expansion and increased foreign capital inflows to expand the foreign exchange supply, and a third designed to reduce overt unemployment without expanding the resources at hand. Parametric variations of the basic model which simulate changes in the primary resource availability are used to define trade-offs between the basic objective, the maximal expansion of personal consumption, and each of these three strategies. Once the basic strategies and policy options have been described, each of the trade-off curves may be again altered by policymakers' changes in key parameters such as those described in the previous section. The successive iterations of model solutions and policy revision will approximate the convergence process illustrated by the movement from fig. 1 to fig. 2.

We shall first explore growth strategies dominated by a shortage of domestic savings. To test the effect of an increased determination to raise internal savings, the model is programmed to give solutions where the marginal savings rate varies from zero to an upper limit reached when labor is fully employed (at a rate of 0.27). All of these variations are made with the foreign capital inflow constant at E^o 400 in 1965 prices.

The results in table 7 indicate a variation in the potential growth rate of GDP from an annual average of 3.4% at the lowest saving rate to 6.2% when full employment is achieved. When the absolute level of saving is unchanged from 1970 to 1975, the unemployment rate increases to 12.2%. One can observe that in those cases where savings are very scarce (Tests 5, 6 and 7) the model always chooses to expand exports to their upper limits. This expansion is viable because at low levels of savings and investment there is no excess capacity in the economy. The maximum value of exports is the only way to assure an abundant supply of imports sufficient to diminish the need to expand domestic production in order to satisfy the growth of demand. In this way, the model uses the least amount of the scarce factor.

One may also note in table 7 that the share of domestic production in total supply decreases from 2.5% to 2.7% in Tests 5 and 6 but thereafter the amount of negative import substitution (as compared with 1970) decreases steadily as the marginal rate of saving is augmented. Exports are no longer increased to their maximum value in Tests 8, 9 and 10. The reasons for these choices are best explained at the sectoral level in terms of the changing profitability of different activities shown as columns of table 4.[10] If one maps the relationship between the objective function, private consumption, and savings one can obtain the first trade-off among targets. Fig. 3 traces out the relationship between

---

[10] The essay describing project analysis within a macroeconomic framework, chapter 7 of this book, gives an example of an analysis of changing sectoral patterns.

Table 7

Growth dominated by the availability of national savings (E° millions of 1965)

Specification		5	6	7	8	9	10	11
Deficit b. of pay.	Variable prices	298	298	298	298	298	298	298
	Constant prices	400	400	400	400	400	400	400
Imports: competitive		variable	variable	variable	variable	variable	variable	variable
Employment, maximum		active	active	active	active	active	active	active
Employment, minimum		inactive	→	→	→	→	→	→
Marginal savings limit		0.0	0.05	0.10	0.15	0.20	0.25	0.2688
Export limit		variable	→	→	→	→	→	→

Results		5	6	7	8	9	10	11
G.D.P.	value	26781	27260	27811	28491	29318	30318	30744
	rate	0.0343	0.0378	0.0418	0.0467	0.0524	0.0591	0.0619
Consumption	value	19787	20031	20292	20607	20972	21385	21551
	rate	0.0417	0.0442	0.0468	0.0498	0.0534	0.0572	0.0588
Investment	value	3712	3947	4237	4602	5064	5651	5911
	rate	0.0131	0.0253	0.0395	0.0560	0.0752	0.0971	0.1061
Imports	value	4710	4866	4866	4861	4839	4850	4866
	rate	0.0695	0.0761	0.0761	0.0759	0.0749	0.0754	0.0761
Exports	value	5056	5212	5212	5207	5185	5196	5212
	rate	0.0705	0.0765	0.0765	0.0764	0.0755	0.0759	0.0765
National saving	value	3414	3649	3939	4304	4766	5353	5613
	S/GDP	0.1275	0.1339	0.1416	0.1510	0.1625	0.1766	0.1826
$\Delta S / \Delta GDP$		0.0	0.0500	0.1000	0.1500	0.2000	0.2500	0.2688
Rate of unemployment		0.122	0.110	0.094	0.071	0.043	0.012	0.000
M Compet./M		0.6894	0.6850	0.6688	0.6510	0.6285	0.6009	0.5882
Balance of supply $\dfrac{\Delta X}{X+M}$		-0.0250	-0.0274	-0.0252	-0.0218	-0.0175	-0.0135	-0.0122
Inv/GDP		0.1386	0.1448	0.1524	0.1615	0.1727	0.1864	0.1923
Marg. coeff.	Capital (net)	1.9591	1.9348	1.9290	1.9227	1.9246	1.9379	1.9454
	Output (gross)	4.0230	3.8065	3.6253	3.4468	3.2871	3.1512	3.1061

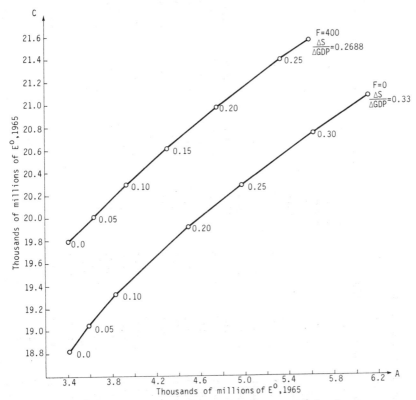

Fig. 3. The trade-off between consumption and national savings.

national savings and personal consumption for two values of the constant foreign exchange gap ($F = E^o$ 400 million and $F = E^o$ 0). The slope of this curve at each point gives the shadow price of national savings, that is, the partial derivative of consumption with respect to savings ($\partial C / \partial S$).

In the lower range of the curves the shadow price of saving is relatively low. This is explained because the supply of domestic demand is met, at the low rates of growth, to a large extent by means of imports. The existence of excess capacity now makes it convenient to expand exports so that imported supply may increase in order to satisfy internal demand most efficiently. At higher growth rates, the shadow price of savings rises. Given that demand also expands, the excess capacity is now utilized to satisfy demand directly and new investments must be incurred to satisfy the larger demand. This implies that savings become scarcer (as the marginal savings rate increases from 0.05

Table 8
Growth dominated by the availability of foreign exchange (E° millions of 1965)

Specification	18	19	20	21	22	23	24	25
Deficit b. of pay. Constant prices	0.0	400.0	800.0	1200.0	0.0	400.0	800.0	1200.0
Imports: competitive	variable	→	→	→	fixed hist.	→	→	→
Maximum employment	active	→	→	→	active	→	→	→
Minimum employment	not active	→	→	→	not active	→	→	→
Marginal saving limit	0.15	→	→	0.15	0.15	→	→	→
Export limit	variable	→	→	→	variable	→	→	→

Results		18	19	20	21	22	23	24	25
GDP	value	27292	28491	29666	30658	26788	27878	28962	30036
	rate	0.0381	0.0467	0.0548	0.0613	0.0343	0.0423	0.0500	0.0572
Consumption	value	19588	20607	21607	22508	19160	20086	21008	21921
	rate	0.0397	0.0498	0.0593	0.0675	0.0353	0.0447	0.0537	0.0622
Investment	value	4022	4602	5178	5668	3946	4510	5072	5633
	rate	0.0291	0.0560	0.0796	0.0977	0.0253	0.0520	0.0755	0.0965
Imports	value	4466	4861	5279	5666	4409	4809	5237	5637
	rate	0.0589	0.0759	0.0924	0.1065	0.0563	0.0737	0.0908	0.1055
Exports	value	5212	5207	5225	5212	5155	5155	5183	5187
	rate	0.0765	0.0764	0.0771	0.0765	0.0744	0.0744	0.0754	0.0754
National saving	value	4124	4304	4480	4570	4048	4212	4374	4535
	S/GDP	0.1511	0.1510	0.1510	0.1491	0.1511	0.1511	0.1510	0.1510
$\Delta S/\Delta GDP$		0.1500	0.1500	0.1500	0.1428	0.1500	0.1500	0.1500	0.1500
Rate of unemployment		0.111	0.071	0.031	0.000	0.128	0.092	0.054	0.019
M compet./M total		0.6526	0.6510	0.6523	0.6538	0.6323	0.6325	0.6352	0.6352
Balance of supply $\frac{\Delta X}{X+M}$		-0.0165	-0.0218	-0.0271	-0.0321	-0.0095	-0.0150	-0.0206	-0.0252
Inv/GDP		0.1474	0.1615	0.1745	0.1849	0.1473	0.1618	0.1751	0.1876
Marg. coeff. $\left(\frac{\text{Capital (net)}}{\text{Output (gross)}}\right)$		1.9770	1.9227	1.8857	1.8606	2.1315	2.0713	2.0281	1.9942
		3.8498	3.4468	3.1821	3.0156	4.2236	3.7673	3.4637	3.2462

to 0.15) and the shadow price rises to reflect the new opportunity cost of savings. The rate of return to additional savings remains constant in the range of marginal savings rates from 0.15 to 0.20. Hence, the shadow price remains constant over this range but drops to zero once the economy achieves full employment.

The process of tracing out the other two strategies is quite similar to the case where savings are varied. Let us assume that the marginal savings rate is maintained at the historical rate of 0.15 while the external gap is increased from zero to E° 1,200 millions in 1965 prices. The results of these calculations are recorded at intervals of E° 400 million in table 8 both in the case where competitive imports are fixed in the historical pattern and when they are left variable.

It is instructive to examine the full employment solution (Test 21) of table 8 and compare it to Test 11 of table 7. Both solutions incorporate precisely the same variable structure of imports and exports. Moreover, both exhibit the same aggregate growth rate of GDP, 6.1%, while the composition of final demand is entirely different. For example, personal consumption grows at 9.7% annually in Test 21 but in Test 11 only at the rate of 5.9%. This is the result of the greater abundance of foreign exchange and the relative shortage of domestic savings in Test 21. Savings being at a low level, consumption is permitted to grow more. In Test 11, on the other hand, savings must substitute for scarce foreign exchange resulting in the slower growth of consumption. In contrast, the greater availability of foreign exchange in Test 21 permits an extensive expansion of imports at an annual growth rate of 10.6% compared to 7.6% in Test 11. See table 9.

It is especially instructive to recognize that the shadow prices are the same in both tests. Although one encounters a pattern of production, imports and investment which is very different in each case, the shadow prices of the primary factors are exactly the same because, at the margin, the limiting factor is labor which has reached full employment.

Table 9
Shadow prices of primary factors

	Test 11		Test 21	
	$F = 400$		$F = 1200$	
BOP limit				
Saving limit	$\Delta S / \Delta Y =$	0.30	$\Delta S / \Delta Y =$	0.15
Effective rate	$\Delta S / \Delta Y =$	0.2688	$\Delta S / \Delta Y =$	0.1428
Employment (labor)		3.534		3.534
Foreign exchange		1.196		1.196
National savings		0.0		0.0

Internal savings are redundant in both solutions. Only primary factors whose increased supply would expand consumption have a positive shadow price. In addition, one should note that in Test 11 the effective marginal savings rate is 0.2688, although the upper limit was fixed at 0.30 and in Test 21, the effective rate was 0.1420.

We conclude our analysis of the foreign-exchange-dominant strategies by pointing out that the combination of a marginal saving rate of 0.27 and a foreign gap of E^o 400 has exactly the same growth effect as a marginal saving rate of 0.14 and a foreign gap of E^o 1,200. The first case represents the strategy of large augmentation of domestic saving with a great reduction of Chile's foreign dependence as compared with the opposite situation as illustrated by Test 21.

The trade-off between consumption growth and lessening the foreign trade gap is drawn in fig. 4 for two constant savings rates of 0.15 and 0.25. The inclusion of increased numbers of policy constraints and the decomposition of primary factors into several types (for example, different skill groups of labor) give the trade-off schedules greater and more continuous curvature.

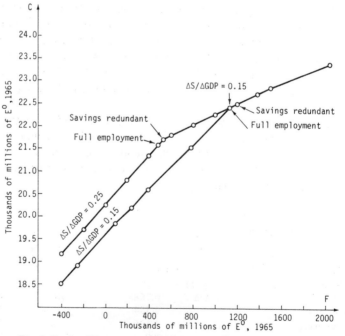

Fig. 4. Trade-off between consumption and foreign capital inflow.

An employment-creating growth strategy might be implemented under two different conditions. First a limit may be imposed by the size of the work force on the potential growth rate of GDP, while all other resources are still relatively underutilized. Second, the economy is incapable of spontaneously generating an acceptable employment rate so it would be preferable to reallocate resources in an effort to absorb more labor even if this strategy should reduce the overall growth of the economy. In the example which follows we shall deal only with the second situation.

We begin with Test 3 which represents a general case in terms of the other two development strategies: a balance of payments deficit of E^o 400 million, a marginal saving rate of 0.15 and an unemployment rate of 7.1% expected in 1975. We should like to trace out the consequence of a strategy which reduces the unemployment rate to 6%, 5% or 4% without changing the magnitude of the other resource expenditures. This strategy requires the structure of production to adjust as if the government were implementing a policy to induce producers to use larger amounts of labor, at their fixed sectoral productivity rates. This will only occur if low productivity sectors expand production while imports replace potential domestic production in high productivity sectors.

Since it is obvious that this strategy involves some grossly inefficient allocations, we place the following restrictions on the experiment: no sector will be permitted to increase production by more than 5% above the levels originally observed in the solution of Test 3; this policy spreads the social cost of increased employment among all sectors. In addition, the total amount of domestic savings which can be mobilized for investment is fixed in absolute terms at the value determined in Test 3. If the marginal rate were to remain at 0.15, the inefficiency imposed by the unproductive job-creation strategy would lower the growth of GDP and therefore of savings.

The results of tests in which the acceptable unemployment rate is steadily reduced are given in table 10. They may be compared to Test 3 in order to evaluate the social cost of increasing employment where labor substitution for other factors occurs only in the aggregate results due to the changing sectoral composition of supply given the fixed sectoral productivities. The aggregate growth of GDP falls from 4.67% annually to 4.08% when unemployment is reduced from 7.1% to 4.0% in 1975. We may observe the degree of inefficiency in the growth of the capital coefficients even when the investment rate remains unchanged.

Fig. 5 illustrates the target trade-off curve between consumption increases and employment creation. The shadow price of labor employment which is indicated at each of the kinks in the trade-off curve represents the increased marginal social cost of absorbing an additional worker at each higher level of em-

Table 10
Growth with restricted unemployment (E⁰ millions of 1965)

Specification	26	27	28	29
Deficit b. of payments	400	→	→	→
Imports: competitive	variable	→	→	→
Employment maximum	active	→	→	→
Employment minimum	active	→	→	→
Marginal saving limit	0.06 fixed absolute value	0.05 →	0.04 →	0.03 →
Export limit	variable	→	→	→

Results		26	27	28	29
GDP	value	28467	28152	27660	23377
	rate	0.0465	0.0443	0.0408	0.0070
Consumption	value	20584	20269	19777	15495
	rate	0.0496	0.0465	0.0416	−0.0070
Investment	value	4601	4601	4601	4601
	rate	0.0560	0.0560	0.0560	0.0560
Imports	value	4884	4670	4583	4379
	rate	0.0708	0.0678	0.0641	0.0550
Exports	value	5230	5016	4929	4725
	rate	0.0772	0.0689	0.0654	0.0569
National saving	value	4303	4303	4303	4303
	S/GDP	0.1510	0.1528	0.1556	0.1841
$\Delta S/\Delta GDP$		0.1506	0.1591	0.1744	1.0894
Rate of unemployment		0.060	0.050	0.040	0.030
M compet /M		0.6653	0.6546	0.6526	0.6521
Balance of supply $\frac{\Delta X}{X+M}$		−0.0226	−0.0167	−0.0138	−0.0040
Inv/GDP		0.1620	0.1634	0.1663	0.1968
Coeff. marg. $\frac{Capital}{Output}$: Net		1.939	2.0641	2.2955	14.778
Gross		3.467	3.6845	4.0790	26.504

ployment.[11] Under these conditions the changing shadow prices cause the expansion of copper exports to fall to a minimum, since copper mining is very capital intensive, so that any available savings and foreign exchange obtained from other sources may be allocated to sectors which will absorb the maximum amount of labor.

[11] This is not a shadow wage rate and cannot be used for project analysis. For a complete analysis of the problem of reduced unemployment by job-creation see Clark [ref. 42].

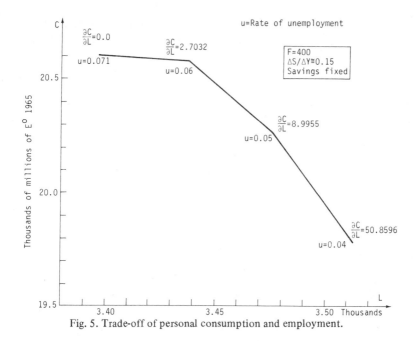

Fig. 5. Trade-off of personal consumption and employment.

VI. Conclusions

We have illustrated the use of a multisectoral model to quantify target trade-offs for communication with policymakers. The method has been one of comparative statics where only one policy variable or resource constraint has been altered at a time. The solutions reported are in the range of low, but historically consistent, growth rates. This has only provided crude, but controlled, illustrations of the potential use of the model framework. Nonetheless, these same constraints might be adjusted simultaneously to demonstrate higher growth potentials for the economy. For example, an average annual growth of GDP of 6.2% is feasible during the period from 1970 to 1975 under either of the following two strategies:

(a) a large foreign debt and a low savings rate, that is, with a balance of payments deficit of E^o 1,100 million, the historical marginal saving rate of 0.15 with full employment of labor whose sectoral productivities are consistent with the trend established during the 1960—1968 period; or

(b) by means of a higher savings rate with a reduction in the external dependence, that is, when the marginal saving rate increases to 0.27 and the foreign gap is reduced to E^o 300 million which also produces full employment.

Chilean planners have continued to evaluate a wide range of alternative development strategies which they categorized into low, medium and high growth strategies. The quantitative results of their analysis was prepared for the evaluation of political decisionmakers. ODEPLAN [ref. 148] includes a full discussion of the trade-offs among the three general development strategies we have illustrated here plus a number of additional options. All of the other development goals described above in the section explaining the choice of the objective function for the model also could be tested by further parametric variation. Foxley [ref. 71] expands the analysis to include tests of an export diversification strategy and the impact of income redistribution by changing the expenditure elasticities of table 1.

The planner could go on indefinitely testing hundreds of development poli-cy options with his multisectoral modelling system because the possible com-binations are infinite. Nonetheless, models cannot compute an optimal devel-opment program. Once one realizes that the number of target trade-offs is very great and that planners are always attempting to improve their estimates of reality by making small changes in the specification and parameter estimates of their model, it becomes clear that optimality is a useful distinguishing char-acteristic of one solution compared to another – but not a description of the most feasible or most suitable strategy. Policy choices can only be narrowed by the involvement of the political policymakers in the planning process. This group will determine the limits of the goal aspiration set. They will also rede-fine what policy adjustments are politically acceptable and what new programs can be implemented. It is not only the task of the technical planner to provide policymakers with a large menu of alternative development strategies, but these must be restricted to a politically feasible range of options. This process calls for increased interaction between planners and policymakers which we have termed a process of mutual education. However, until planners can pro-duce realistic alternatives at a time when policymakers are concerned about the consequences of their medium term policies, this interactive process is not likely to be initiated.

PART V

STUDIES OF THE EFFECTS OF INFLATION

R.S. Eckaus, P.N. Rosenstein-Rodan (eds.), Analysis of development problems,
© North-Holland Publishing Company

PRICE DETERMINATION
IN AN INFLATIONARY ECONOMY:
THE DYNAMICS OF CHILEAN INFLATION REVISITED*

Jere R. BEHRMAN

University of Pennsylvania, Philadelphia, Penn., U.S.A.

I. Introduction

Substantial controversy exists over the relative importance and the lag structures of monetary and non-monetary factors in the determination of price changes. One very important aspect of this controversy is whether or not sectoral prices give appropriate signals for allocation decisions. The purpose of this study is to provide new empirical evidence relevant to this controversy by examining the determination of the rate of change of prices in an inflationary economy. Because of econometric problems related to the large number of variables suggested by alternative hypothesis and because of the existence of data of both a general nature and of a sector-specific nature in the case considered, this examination is divided into two parts. In section II is discussed the relationship between the demand for real per capita monetary balances and the adjustment of aggregate prices to changes in nominal per capita money supplies, in real per capita gross domestic product, in the exchange rate, and in the cost to the employer of a unit of labor relative to the average product of labor. The inconsistency of the available estimates of the former relationship with the pattern of adjustment required for the latter is noted, and new estimates of the latter relationship are presented and discussed. In section III the determination of the rates of changes of sectoral deflators in response to both aggregate and sectoral-specific variables is exam-

* The author wishes to thank the supporting organizations for their help while at the same time emphasizing that this paper in no way necessarily reflects the viewpoints of these organizations. The author also wishes to thank, but not implicate, Juan de la Barra, Jorge Cauas, Eduardo García, Jorge García, Arnold Harberger, Ricardo Lira, Carlos Massad, Cristían Ossa, and Lance Taylor.

ined. Most important among the aggregate variables is the combined effect of changes in the nominal per capita monetary balances, in real per capita income and in the exchange rate, all of which are represented together by a variable constructed from the results of the first section.[1] Other aggregate variables included are the level of inventories relative to gross domestic product in order to represent the pressures of aggregate real final demand and changes in the wage share of national income, in the indirect tax rate, and in the subsidy rate. The most important sector-specific variables are changes in intermediate input costs and in labor costs relative to productivity. The sectoral results suggest that changes in factor costs may play a more important role at least in the transmission of pressures for price changes than the results of section II imply and that sectoral prices do tend to give signals at least in the right direction for allocation purposes. Other sectoral-specific variables include the changes in the export price in terms of the domestic currency (the primary determinant in the case of the major export sector), in components of final and of intermediate demand relative to capacity, and expectational or 'acceleration'[2] effects as represented by the lagged first difference of the rate of change in prices.

The data used for the empirical tests are from the postwar Chilean experience (1945–1965).[3] As Harberger has noted, the Chilean economy provides a promising case for such a study for a number of reasons.[4] The data are relatively good. The economy has a long and practically continuous inflationary history, and the relevant variables have sufficient variance in their rates of changes to permit the testing of hypotheses in which the rates of change are used (see table 1). A number of related studies are available.[5]

---

[1] The contribution of changes in the aggregate cost to the employer of a unit of labor relative to the average product of labor is not included in the construction of this variable because changes in a similar variable at the sectoral level of aggregation are included.

[2] See Arnold Harberger, 'The dynamics of inflation in Chile', in: *Measurement in economics: studies in mathematical economics in memory of Yehuda Grunfeld,* ed. by Carl Christ. Stanford, Stanford University Press, 1963, 225–227 (hereinafter referred to as 'Dynamics of inflation').

[3] Data series and sources are given in the appendix to chapter 8. Consistent national income data are not available before 1940, or after 1965, and the inclusion of lags eliminated several initial observations. Furthermore, Allan Hynes has presented evidence that the desired real money balances were altered significantly by portfolio substitution during the war. See Allan Hynes, 'The demand for money and monetary adjustments in Chile', *Review of Economic Studies* 34 (June, 1967) 285–293.

[4] Harberger, 'Dynamics of inflation', 219.

[5] For footnote, see next page.

[5] Harberger, 'Dynamics of inflation'; Hynes; Jere R. Behrman, 'Cyclical sectoral capacity utilization in a developing economy', chapter 9 in this volume (hereinafter referred to as chapter 9); Jere R. Behrman, 'The determinants of the annual rates of change of sectoral money wages in a developing economy', *International Economic Review* 12 (October, 1971) 431–447 (Spanish version forthcoming in *Cuadernos de Economia*) (hereinafter referred to as 'Sectoral money wages'); Jere R. Behrman, 'Sectoral elasticities of substitution between capital and labor in a developing economy: time series analysis in the case of postwar Chile', *Econometrica* (in press) (hereinafter referred to as 'Substitution between capital and labor'); Jere R. Behrman, 'Sectoral investment determination in a developing economy', *American Economic Review* (in press) (hereinafter referred to as 'Sectoral investment determination'); Jere R. Behrman, 'Short-run flexibility in a developing economy', *Journal of Political Economy* 80 (March/April, 1972) 292–313; Jere R. Behrman and Jorge García M., 'A study of quarterly nominal wage change determination in an inflationary developing economy', chapter 15 in this volume; Jorge Cauas, 'Stabilization policy – the Chilean case', *Journal of Political Economy* 78 Supplement (July/ August, 1970) 815–825; John Deaver, 'The Chilean inflation and the demand for money', Ph.D. diss., University of Chicago, 1960; Eduardo García D'Acuna, 'Inflation in Chile: a quantitative analysis', Ph.D. dis., M.I.T., 1964; Peter Gregory, *Industrial wages in Chile*. New York State School of Industrial and Labor Relations, Cornell University, Ithaca, 1967; Cristían Ossa, 'The relative stability of monetary velocity and the investment multiplier in Chile', mimeo. (unpublished, no date); Joseph Ramos, 'Politicas de remuneraciones en Chile', mimeo., Universidad de Chile, Instituto de Economia y Planificacion, Santiago, September 1968; and Tomas Reichmann M., *La demanda de diner – un intento de cuantificacion*. Instituto de Economía, Universidad de Chile, Santiago, 1965.

Table 1
Means, ranges and standard deviations of annual percentage rates of change over 1945–1965 period: gross domestic product deflator, nominal per capita money supply, real per capita gross domestic product, and the exchange rate[a]

Variable	Annual percentage rates of change, 1945–1965		
	Mean	Range	Standard deviation
Gross domestic product deflator	29.6	3.8–74.0	19.3
Per capita nominal money supply[b]	28.9	6.7–57.5	13.0
Per capita real gross domestic product	1.8	−8.1–10.4	4.1
Exchange rate	27.7	0.0–93.9	28.4

[a] Data sources are given in the appendix to chapter 2.
[b] Currency and demand deposits (except interbank deposits).

Finally, the economy is sufficiently modernized so that the principal results of such a study might be generalizable to 'modern' economies. Financial instituions are relatively well developed, the industrial sector is fairly large (manufacturing accounted for about 20% of national income throughout the period of interest), and the 'non-monetary' sector is very small (agriculture declined from 15 to 10% of national income in the period of the study and is largely commercial, not subsistence, in nature).

II. The demand for per capita real monetary balances and aggregate price determination

A number of studies of the Chilean demand for real monetary balances are available.[6] These studies vary in details, but the basic approach is the same. The nominal supply of money is assumed to be exogenous, and thus the demand for real per capita monetary balances is assumed to be identified. Actual per capita holdings of real monetary balances are assumed to adjust toward desired per capita holdings which depend upon per capita wealth and the opportunity cost of holding real balances. Per capita wealth is represented by a weighted average of past and present real per capita national income (i.e., permanent income). The opportunity cost of holding real monetary balances is composed of (1) the expected rate of change of prices, and (2) the real rate of return on capital. The expected rate of change of prices is represented by a weighted average of past and present rates of change of prices, but the real rate of return on capital cannot be represented explicitly given in the available data, so this component of the opportunity cost is excluded at the cost of some misspecification.[7]

The adjustment process of actual real per capita balances toward desired real per capita balances is of considerable interest here. Assume an initial state of equilibrium (in which actual and desired real per capita balances are identical) that is interrupted by a once and for all exogenous increase in the money supply. What then will occur so that actual real per capita monetary balances adjust to equal desired real per capita monetary balances? Several (not necessarily exclusive) possibilities are suggested by the previous para-

---

[6] Deaver, Hynes; and Reichmann. For a related study in the case of another Latin American country with a substantial inflationary history, see Adolfo Cesar Diz, 'Money and prices in Argentina, 1935–1962', Ph.D. diss., University of Chicago, 1966.

[7] The data summarized in table 1, however, suggest that a large fraction of the variance in the nominal rate of interest has been a result of variation in the first component of this opportunity cost.

graph. First, interest rates could adjust downward with the result that desired real per capita monetary balances would be increased. Over most of the period of this and the aforementioned studies, however, the role of changes of interest rates in the adjustment towards desired real per capita monetary balances apparently was quite limited.[8] Second, real per capita wealth or real per capita permanent income could adjust. However, substantial adjustment through this determinant seems unlikely for several reasons. Changes in real per capita income have been quite small in comparison with changes in per capita nominal monetary balances (see table 1), and the real income elasticity of the demand for real monetary balances is not hypothesized to be sufficiently large so as to allow for the possibility that the former variable has caused most of the variations in the latter.[9] Moreover, no statistical support for a substantial response to discrepancies between actual and desired real per capita monetary balance has been found.[10] Third, prices might increase in order to reduce actual real per capita balances toward desired real per capita balances. In the Chilean case, in fact, price changes apparently have been the primary means for adjusting actual toward desired real per capita monetary balances. Of the alternatives included in the demand for real per capita balances hypotheses, only variations in prices have been sufficient to possibly have changed substantially any real balance discrepancy.

Now focus, therefore, on the price adjustment relationship. Following Harberger,[11] formulate the relationship in terms of rates of change in order to

---

[8] For most of this period the Central Bank was required by law to rediscount all eligible commercial paper offered to it by commercial banks at a discount rate fixed by law at a level that generally was far below the inflation rate. Instead of using interest rates as a rationing device for bank credit, the Central Bank used quantitative limits on the rate of expansion of commercial bank loans. See Harberger, 'Dynamics of inflation', 248.

[9] The evidence in table 1, of course, pertains directly to changes in real per capita current income and not in real per capita permanent income, nor in real per capita wealth. Presumably, however, the latter two variables are determined in large part by the time path of the former.

[10] In the larger project of which this study is a part the possibilities of such responses have been explored.

[11] Harberger, 'Dynamics of inflation', passim. Harberger also included an 'acceleration' variable (see section III below), did not adjust the wage rate (he used the minimum wage) for employers' social security payments nor for productivity changes, and did not include the exchange rate. Subsequently, however, he argued for the inclusion of the last variable. See Arnold Harberger, 'Some notes on inflation', in: *Inflation and growth in Latin-America,* ed. by Werner Baer and Isaac Kerstenetzky. Richard D. Irwin, Homewood, Ill., 1964) 336–351 (hereinafter referred to as 'Notes on inflation'). Gregory (p. 49) and Ramos (p. 60) present some aggregate results in which basically the same model as above is used, but in which very short lags are included.

lessen the multicollinearity which occurs among all nominal variables in an
economy with an inflationary history like that of Chile, and hypothesize that
the determination of the rate of change of prices may be approximated by a
linear function of the relevant variables:[12]

$$r[PGDP^t]_t = \sum_{i=0}^{m} a_i r \left[\frac{MSUP}{POPUL} \right]_{t-i} + \sum_{i=0}^{n} b_i r \left[\frac{GDP^t}{POPUL} \right]_{t-i}$$

$$+ \sum_{i=0}^{p} c_i r [EXRAT]_{t-i} + \sum_{i=0}^{q} d_i r \, \frac{PL^t(1+TXRSSE)}{GDP^t/L^t}$$

$$+ \text{ constant} + u \, , \tag{1}$$

where

$r[X]$	= annual rate of change of X,
$PGDP^t$	= annual average deflator for total gross domestic product,
$\dfrac{MSUP}{POPUL}$	= nominal average annual per capita money supply,
$\dfrac{GDP^t}{POPUL}$	= real average annual per capita total gross domestic product,
$EXRAT$	= average annual exchange rate,
$\dfrac{PL^t(1+TXRSSE)}{GDP^t/L^t}$	= average annual wage rate, adjusted for average employer's social security contribution, relative to average value added per domestic laborer,
a_i, b_i, c_i, d_i	= parameters to be estimated, and
u	= disturbance term.

The constant term is included because of possible misspecification, but in
the nonstochastic discussion immediately following it will be assumed to be
zero. For generality each of the right-hand side variables is shown to be represented by lags of different lengths. What can one say about the patterns of
lagged responses? First, concentrate on the response in the rate of change of
prices to a change in the rate of change of the nominal per capita money supply. Fig. 1 provides an illustration of the continuous case for which eq. (1) is
a discrete representation. Assume that initially an equilibrium steady state
prevails in which the rates of growth of the last three right-hand variables and
of population are zero, and the rate of growth of the nominal per capita supply of money is g_0. In order to be in equilibrium the actual real per capita

---

[12] Attempts to include (in addition to the variables in eq. (1) terms that related to the
difference between actual and desired real per capita monetary balances were unsuccessful because of great problems of multicollinearity.

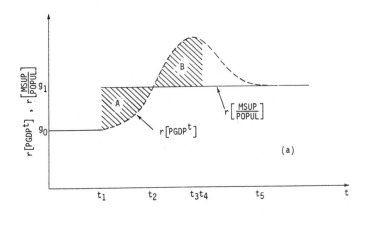

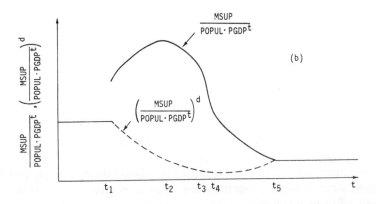

Fig. 1. Adjustments from an initial equilibrium in which the rate of change both of prices and of nominal per capita monetary balances are g_0 to another equilibrium in which rates of change are g_1. The rates of change of all other relevant variables are assumed to be zero. The initial equilibrium is disturbed by an instantaneous and permanent change in the rate of growth of the nominal per capita money supply from g_0 to g_1. (a) Rates of change of prices and of nominal per capita monetary balances. (b) Levels of actual and desired real per capita monetary balances.

monetary balances must be equal to the desired real per capita monetary balances, which implies that prices also must be growing at a rate of g_0 and in the discrete case that

$$\sum_{i=0}^{m} a_i = 1 .\tag{2a}$$

Assume that at time t_1 the rate of growth of the nominal per capita money supply increases to g_1 and remains at that level thereafter, but that the rate of growth of prices adjusts with a lag. Assuming that a new equilibrium is reached, eventually the rate of growth of prices also must be g_1. But before that new equilibrium is reached the rate of growth of prices must overshoot g_1 not only because of the lag in the adjustment of prices but also because in the adjustment process the level of prices must increase more than does the level of nominal per capita money supply in order that actual real per capita monetary balances may adjust to the final lower equilibrium level desired.[13] Why is the final equilibrium desired real per capita monetary balance lower than the initial equilibrium value? It is because in the final equilibrium the opportunity cost of holding real balances is larger than initially due to the increased equilibrium rate of increase in prices. To allow for this overshooting of the rate of changes in prices in the discrete case, the following condition must hold:

$$\sum_{i=0}^{k} a_i > 1 ,\tag{2b}$$

where $k(<m)$ is the number of periods after the disturbance of the initial equilibrium in which the maximum rate of change of prices occurs (i.e., the discrete approximation to $t_3 - t_1$).

What happens to real per capita monetary balances during this adjustment process? Actual real per capita monetary balances increase discontinuously at t_1 and continue to increase at a decreasing rate until the rate of growth of prices reaches g_1 at t_2. Then these balances start to decline with the maximum rate of decline occurring at t_3 when prices increase at their maximum rate. The actual balance would then continue to decline at a decreasing rate,[14] equaling the original equilibrium actual real per capita balances at t_4 (which is not necessarily after t_3) when the integral of the overshooting of the rate of

[13] This basic insight is due to Diz, 63. The author wishes to thank Arnold Harberger, who first brought this point to his attention.

[14] After overshooting g_1 and reaching a maximum, the rate of growth of prices may decrease monotonically towards g_1 (as is illustrated in fig. 1a) or approach g_1 in a damped cyclical adjustment. In the latter case the time paths of $M/(N \cdot P)$ and $(M/N \cdot P)^d$ would adjust accordingly (and conceivably could cross), and the rates of change and desired real per capita balances would not change monotonically.

change of prices (area B) is sufficiently large to offset the integral for the initial lag in the adjustment of prices (area A) and obtaining the new equilibrium level of desired real per capita monetary balances at t_5. Desired real per capita monetary balances, in contrast, begin to decline at t_1 because of the higher opportunity cost of holding real balances due to the higher rates of increases of prices. These desired balances reach a minimum at t_3 where the rate of increase of prices is a maximum and then subsequently increase to the new equilibrium level that is obtained at t_5.[15]

The pattern of lagged responses to the other three right-hand side variables can be discussed more rapidly. Consider, for example, the case in which all rates of growth of right-hand side variables in eq. (1) are zero except those related to the level of real per capita gross domestic product. Assume an initial equilibrium in which prices are changing at a constant rate of g_2, and real per capita income is changing at a constant rate of g_3. The ratio of g_2 to g_3 is equal to $\Sigma_{i=0}^{n} b_i$ and is the estimate of the elasticity of price with respect to real per capita gross domestic product. If. eq. (1) is basically a linear expansion of the demand for real per capita monetary balances relation discussed at the start of this section, then the ratio of g_2 to g_3 also is the elasticity of real per capita monetary balances with respect to real per capita gross domestic product. The continuous case in which the elasticity of prices with respect to real per capita gross domestic product is less than unity is depicted in fig. 2.

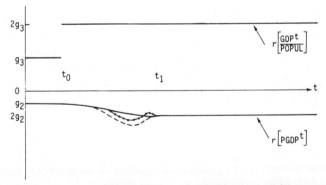

Fig. 2. Adjustments from an initial equilibrium in which the rate of change of prices is g_2, the rate of change of real per capita gross domestic product is g_3, and all other rates of change are zero to a new equilibrium in which all rates of change are doubled. The initial equilibrium is disturbed by an instantaneous and permanent doubling of the rate of change of real per capita gross domestic product.

[15] See the previous note.

At time t_0 the rate of change of real per capita gross domestic product instantaneously doubles and remains at this new level. The rate of change of prices adjusts with a lag to the new equilibrium level of $2g_2$, which is reached at time t_1. The time path of the adjustment of the rate of growth of prices may be monotonic (solid line), may have damped cyclical fluctuations (dotted line), or may simply overshoot (dashed line).[16] In the discrete approximation of the last two cases some of the b_i have positive values although the sum of the b_i have negative values. But note that such overshooting and the related change of signs of the coefficients in eq. (1) are only a possibility but are not necessary as in the case discussed first. The comments of this paragraph, appropriately modified to allow for the expectation that $\Sigma_{i=0}^{p} c_i > 0$ and $\Sigma_{i=0}^{q} d_i > 0$, apply to the patterns of lagged adjustment to the other two right-hand variables in eq. (1).

Before examining empirical estimates of eq. (1) consider what is the relationship of the adjustment portrayed in fig. 1 to the adjustment of actual real per capita monetary balances towards desired real per capita monetary balances. Hynes suggests that there is no direct relation;[17] but if the adjustment in prices is responsible for most of the adjustment in the real per capita monetary balances, relation would seem to have to be consistent with the considerations discussed in relation to fig. 1. None of the available studies of the Chilean demand for real monetary balances includes an adjustment that is consistent with such considerations.[18] All of these functions, thus, seem to be misspecified in this respect.

Consider now the estimates of eq. (1) on the basis of annual Chilean data for the 1945–65 period. Ordinary least squares estimation results are summarized in table 2. In fig. 3 are presented the time patterns of adjustments in the rate of change of prices to once and for all alternations in the rates of change of nominal per capita money supplies and of real per capita gross domestic product. For purposes of comparison also are presented the lag patterns obtained with an alternative representation of the distributional lag

---

[16] For a brief discussion of the analogous case in respect to the response to changes in the nominal per capita money supply, see note 13 above.

[17] Hynes, 293.

[18] Deaver assumes immediate adjustment (i.e., $a_0 = 1$, $a_i = 0$ for $i > 0$). Hynes assumes that the rate of change of actual real per capita monetary balances is proportional to the difference between desired and actual real per capita monetary balances, which clearly is inconsistent with fig. 1a. Reichmann assumes that the price in $t + 1$ is the equilibrium price (i.e., $a_1 = 1$, $a_i = 0$ for all $i \neq 1$). Interestingly, in his Argentinian study Diz also makes the same assumption as does Deaver.

Table 2
Ordinary least squares estimates of the annual price adjustment relation for Chile, 1946–1965

Lag	Coefficients of			
	$r\left[\dfrac{MSUP}{POPUL}\right]$	$r\left[\dfrac{GDP^t}{POPUL}\right]$	$r[EXRAT]$	$r\left[\dfrac{PL^t(1+TXRSSE)}{GDP^t/L^t}\right]$
−0	0.847 (5.49)	−1.488 (3.84)	0.260 (3.34)	0.151a (1.42)
−1	−0.272a (1.61)	−0.453b (1.05)		
−2	−0.200b (1.12)	1.579 (4.44)	$\bar{R}^2$ = 0.94 SE = 0.0464	
−3	0.797 (4.63)		DW = 1.52	
−4	−0.844 (4.39)		F = 33.6	
−5	0.316 (2.10)		Absolute values of t-statistics are in parenthesis beneath the point estimates. All point estimates are significantly non-zero at the 5% level unless otherwise indicated. Data sources are given in the appendix to chapter 2.	
Σ coefficients	0.644 (4.70)	0.362c (0.48)		

a Significantly non-zero at the 10% level.
b Significantly non-zero at the 25% level.
c Not significantly non-zero at the 25% level.

response suggested by Robert E. Hall and Richard C. Sutch[19] and the lag patterns obtained by Harberger.[20]

[19] Robert E. Hall and Richard C. Sutch, 'A flexible infinite distributed lag', Berkeley, University of California, Institute of Business and Economics Research, Center for Research in Management Science, no date). Polynomial patterns of lags up to the fourth degree over a 5-year period were explored using the Hall-Sutch method. Multicollinearity did not seem to be much less of a problem than in the case presented in table 2 and the maximum $\bar{R}^2$ obtained was 0.82, so the results are neither presented nor discussed here.
[20] Harberger, 'Dynamics of inflation', 233, 235. These results are not based on per capita right-hand side variables. The wholesale and consumer prices indices used by Harberger are based largely on the same underlying data as is the gross domestic product deflator used in this study, so his results should be somewhat comparable to those of this study.

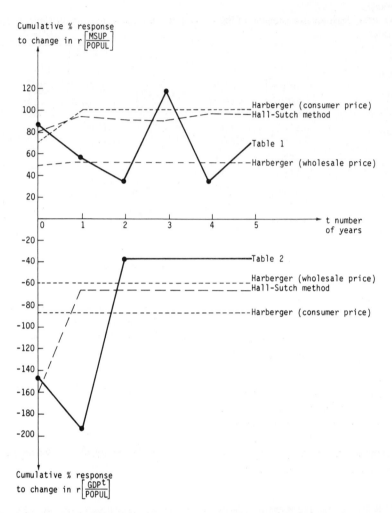

Fig. 3. Estimated time patterns of adjustment of the rate of change of prices in response to a once and for all change in the rates of change of nominal per capita money supply and of real per capita gross domestic product.

Under the assumption that least squares estimates are appropriate, in an overall sense the model in eq. (1) seems to be quite consistent with the Chilean experience despite some apparent problem of multicollinearity due to the large number of variables included. The coefficient of determination (corrected for degrees of freedom) indicates that the model is consistent with 94% of the variation in the rate of change of the gross domestic product deflator;[21] the F-test indicates that this relation is significantly non-zero at the 0.1% level; and the Dubin–Watson statistic suggests that there are not serious problems of autocorrelation. The long run equilibrium considerations discussed above suggest that the constant term should be zero if the model is properly specified so that the equilibrium rate of change of prices will be zero (except for random disturbances) if the values of all the right-hand side variables are zero in equilibrium. In fact, the constant term obtained was not significantly non-zero at the 10% level and thus was suppressed.

The lagged responses of the specific right-hand side variables in eq. (1) are best considered by examining table 2 column by column. The first column refers to the response to changes in the rate of change of nominal per capita money supplies. The mixture of positive and negative coefficients results in the response indicated in fig. 3. The current response is positive and not different from one at the 5% level of significance. In the next two periods the response is dampened somewhat, and the cumulative response is less than one at the 5% level of significance by the end of the second period. In the third period there is a strong reversal of response, and the accumulated response overshoots the value of one, although not significantly so at the 5% level. In the fourth period the response again is dampened so that the accumulated response is less than one at the 5% level of significance. In the fifth period there is some recovery, but the total accumulated response remains less than one at the 5% (although not at the 1%) level. How does this pattern compare with the a priori discussion above? First, the initial dampening is not anticipated in the discussion above although it does not seem to be inconsistent with it. Second, both significant negative and positive coefficients are obtained, as is suggested above. Third, overshooting in respect to the expected value of the accumulated response occurs, as is anticipated, but such overshooting is not significant and is not sufficient to offset the dampening of the initial response in respect to total effects on the actual real per capita monetary balances held. Fourth, the total accumulated response is significantly less than that predicted (at the 5% level although not at the 1% level).[22]

---

[21] Harberger ('Dynamics of inflation') obtained coefficients of determination (it is not clear whether or not they are corrected for degrees of freedom) of 0.87 and 0.80 for the annual rate of change of consumer and of wholesale price indices, respectively.

[22] Diz also obtained estimates for some time periods in which the total accumulated response apparently is significantly less than the a priori expected value. For example, see his table 7.

The second column in table 2 refers to the response to changes in the rate of change of real per capita gross domestic product. The estimates imply a strong initial response that is significantly greater than unity at the 5% level in the current period. In the subsequent period this response is dampened, however, so that it is not significantly greater than unity at the end of the first period nor significantly non-zero at the end of the second period. Assuming that eq. (1) is an approximate linear transformation of the demand for real per capita monetary balances, the same pattern of an initial elastic, but long run insignificant response to those balances to changes in real per capita gross domestic product is implied. This result is in sharp contrast to the long run real per capita permanent income elasticity of 2 estimated by Hynes.[23] This result is not inconsistent, however, with a permanent income hypothesis for real per capita *consumption*. For example, assume that the marginal propensity to consume out of transitory real per capita income is small and that the only alternative to consuming such income in the short run is holding larger real per capita monetary balances. Assume, furthermore, that if any change in real per capita income that persists for, say, 3 years is considered permanent and that the marginal propensity to consume out of permanent real per capita income is almost unitary. Under these assumptions a pattern of responses to changes in the rate of change of real per capita income similar to that presented in table 2 and in fig. 3 might result.[24] The assumptions of this example do not hold exactly in Chile (e.g., transitory balances might be held in alternative forms), but the basic thrust of the example may be relevant.

The third column in table 2 refers to responses in the rate of change of prices to changes in the rate of change of the exchange rate. The estimated response is rapid (no evidence of any lagged response was found) and substantial. The rapidity presumably reflects the almost immediate transmission of news about exchange rate alternatives to the relevant sectors of the economy. The size of the response reflects the substantial role of exports and imports (and close substitution for both) in the Chilean economy.[25]

The fourth column in table 2 refers to responses in the rate of change of prices to changes in the rate of change of wages (adjusted to include employer

---

[23] Hynes, 290. Reichmann (p. 67) presents estimates that imply an inelastic response, but the level of significance of these estimates is not clear from his study. Harberger's results are discussed below.

[24] The coefficients of the rates of change of real per capita gross domestic product, however, are relatively sensitive to changes in the rest of the specification of the model. These results, therefore, must be interpreted with some caution.

[25] See Harberger ('Notes on inflation') for a detailed examination of the effects of devaluation on the domestic price level.

social security contributions) relative to average labor productivity. No significant lagged response to this variable was obtained, and the current response is significantly non-zero only at the 10% level. If the wage variable is not corrected for variations in average labor productivity, moreover, the coefficient obtained is significantly non-zero only at the 25% level.[26] The evidence of a major direct causal role of wage changes in the determination of the aggregate rate of change of prices, therefore, is not strong. However, the sectoral results presented below in section III and other work on the determination of the rate of change of wages in Chile suggest that wages may play a more important transmission role in the determination of more disaggregate price changes.[27] Of course, an alternative interpretation of the wage variable as it is included in eq. (2) is as a representation of the distribution of gross domestic product between labor and non-labor. In the case of this interpretation a positive coefficient would imply that a redistribution of product towards labor results in a higher rate of change of prices, ceteris paribus, presumably because laborers tend to hold relatively smaller real per capita monetary balances.

The only directly comparable study of a relation such as eq. (1) of which the author is aware is Harberger's study of the rate of change of Chilean annual wholesale and consumer prices.[28] How do the results in table 2 compare with Harberger's results? First, the estimated relation in table 2 is more consistent with the variation in the overall rate of change of prices than are Harberger's estimates.[29] This difference could reflect primarily differences in variable definitions and sources and whether or not the exchange rate is included, but stepwise regressions suggest that the major improvement results from the inclusion of more lags for the rate of change of nominal per capita monetary balances. Second, Harberger also obtained constant terms that are not significantly non-zero at the 5% level. Third, the pattern of lagged response to changes in the rate of change of nominal monetary balances which Harberger obtained is considerably different from that implied by table 2. Harberger used a stepwise procedure in which he included additional lags until coefficients insignificantly different from zero resulted. Using this procedure he

---

[26] If the wage variable is not corrected for productivity changes, moreover, productivity improvements would result in increased prices since wages do increase in response to productivity increases. See Behrman, 'Sectoral money wages'.

[27] See Behrman, 'Sectoral money wages'; Behrman and Garcia; Gregory, p. 49; Harberger, 'Dynamics of inflation', 246–248; and Ramos, 57–67.

[28] Harberger, 'Dynamics of inflation', 233, 235. Harberger also presents results for the components of these estimates and for quarterly rates of change.

[29] See note 21 above.

obtained 'complete' adjustment after a lag of one period in the case of the consumer price index and at the end of the current period in the case of the wholesale price index. For the former the sum of the coefficients (0.95) apparently is not significantly different from one at the 5% level, but for the latter the sum (0.47) is significantly different from one at this level.[30] In neither case did Harberger obtain evidence of overshooting nor significantly negative coefficients. This latter point illustrates an interesting example of the effects of a priori expectations on applied econometric procedures. Because Harberger did his study long before Diz made his observation about the necessity for having some negative coefficients, he did not expect to have them. He, therefore, apparently did not consider the possibility that the insignificant coefficients he obtained for a lag of one or two periods might be followed by significant coefficients if more lags were included. Yet table 2 and stepwise regressions with the data in this study suggest that is exactly what occurs. As a result Harberger not only obtained a function in which the estimates imply that after complete adjustment to an increase in nominal monetary balances real desired monetary balances are higher, but he also concluded that the major effects of changes in the monetary supply have occurred in 1 or 2 years. The results in table 2 suggest that the lag may be substantially longer, which probably is reflected in the real world difficulties of reducing the rate of Chilean inflation in the short run through limiting the expansion of the monetary supply because of the considerable lagged responses to past expansion.[31] Fourth, Harberger obtained a substantially different pattern of lagged responses to changes in the rate of growth of real product. He obtained a much smaller current response, no evidence of a lagged response (apparently this possibility was not investigated) and a larger long run response (although in the case of wholesale prices this response is not significantly non-zero at the 5% level). His lack of attention to longer responses or some representation of permanent income excludes a very direct comparison with the results of this study. Fifth, Harberger did not include the effect of the rate of change of the exchange rate on the domestic price level.[32] Sixth, Harberger included an acceleration variable (see section III below) that was not significantly non-zero at the 10% level and that is not included in eq. (1) above.

---

[30] If one includes the relatively insignificant (i.e., t value of 0.25) coefficient of the lagged rate of change in this sum, the total is 0.53, and this sum is not significantly different from one at the 5% level if the variance between the coefficients is greater than −0.0106. However, the same sum also is not significantly non-zero if this covariance is greater than −0.0076.

[31] For further evidence on this point, see Behrman and García.

[32] Gregory (49), however, did include such a variable and also found that it was significant.

Seventh, Harberger also found only limited evidence of a response to the rate of change of wages[33], and this response also apparently is concentrated in the current period. For the consumer price index the coefficient he obtained is not significantly non-zero at the 25% level, but for the wholesale price index the coefficient which he obtained is substantially bigger (10.77) than that in table 2 and is significantly non-zero at the 5% level.

III. The determination of the rate of change of sectoral Chilean prices, 1945–1965

The existence of substantial sector-specific data in the Chilean case allows a more disaggregate investigation of the determination of the rate of change of prices. Given the nature of these data, the best disaggregation seems to be by production sectors.[34] In eq. (3) is presented the basic model for the investigation discussed in this section. Both general and sector-specific pressures operating on the demand and on the supply side are represented as well as is possible given the available data and the author's imagination. For simplicity of presentation, lags are not indicated explicitly (as in eq. (1) above), but current and lagged values are explored in the actual estimation.

$$r[PGDP] = a\frac{STOCK^t}{GDP^t} + br[P\hat{G}\hat{D}P^t] + cr\left[\frac{CPRV^t}{GDPC}\right] + dr\left[\frac{DINT}{GDCC}\right] + er\left[\frac{PL^*L}{Y}\right]$$

$$+ f(r[PGDP]_{-1} - r[PGDP]_{-2}) + gr[UVX] + hr\left[\frac{TXI}{GDP^t}\right]$$

$$+ jr\left[\frac{SUB^t}{GDP^t}\right] + kr[PINP] + mr\left[\frac{PL(1+TXRSSE)}{GDP/L}\right]$$

$$+ \text{constant} + u \,, \tag{3}$$

where
$r[X]$ = annual rate of change of X,

---

[33] He actually used the legal minimum wage (*sueldo vital*) uncorrected for changes in the social security system and in average labor productivity. Gregory (p. 49) and Ramos (pp. 57–67) present somewhat stronger evidence for the role of wages (also uncorrected for changes in the social security system and in average labor productivity).
[34] Harberger ('Dynamics of inflation') instead presents disaggregated results for four components of consumer and wholesale price indices. He did not, however, use the sector specific data utilized in this study.

$PGDP$	= annual average sectoral price deflator,
$\dfrac{INV^t}{GDP^t}$	= level of total year end inventory stocks relative to total annual gross domestic product,
$P\hat{G}DP^t$	= average annual price level estimated from table 2 and including the effects of nominal per capita monetary balances, real per capita gross domestic product, and the exchange rate,
$\dfrac{CPRV^t}{GDPC}$	= level of annual total real private consumption expenditures relative to annual real sectoral capacity,
$\dfrac{DINT}{GDCC}$	= level of annual real indirect demands for product of sector (based on input–output table and the level of production for all sectors) relative to annual real sectoral capacity,
$\dfrac{PL^{*}L}{Y}$	= total annual wage bill relative to annual national income,
UVX	= average annual unit value of sectoral exports in domestic currency,
$\dfrac{TXI}{GDP^t}$	= average annual effective indirect tax rate for the total economy,
$PINP$	= price of intermediate inputs used by the ith sector (based on input–output table and all sectoral prices),
$\dfrac{PL(1+TXRSSE)}{GDP/L}$	= average annual wage rate for ith sector, adjusted for employer's social security contribution, relative to average gross domestic product per domestic worker in that sector,
$a-m$	= parameters to be estimated,
u	= disturbance term.

For economy of presentation it seems best to discuss the above specification together with the estimates that are presented in table 2. Examination of this table suggests that in a general sense the above model is consistent with a considerable fraction of the variance in the dependent variables. Only in the case of construction is the coefficient of determination below 0.80, and in five of the eight cases the estimated relations are consistent for the sample with over 90% of the variance in the rate of change of the relevant sectoral price.[35] Moreover, the Durbin–Watson statistic does not indicate rejection of the null

---

[35] For comparison, in none of the disaggregated estimates that Harberger presents is the coefficient of determination (corrected for degrees of freedom?) as high as 0.80. Of course, his basis for disaggregation is different. See the previous note.

Table 3
Estimates of the determination of the rate of change of sector GDP deflators in Chile, 1945–1965[a]

Sector	$\dfrac{STOCK^t}{GDP^t}$		$P\hat{G}DP^t$ In rate of change form			
	−0	−1	−0	−1	−2	−3
1	2	3	4	5	6	7
Agriculture				0.345 (3.13)	−0.396 (3.47)	0.163 (1.97)
Mining						
Construction		−0.671[c] (1.04)	0.613 (3.53)			
Manufacturing				0.152[b] (1.49)	−0.104[b] (1.53)	
Transportation			0.835 (6.03)		−0.239[b] (1.51)	
Utilities	−0.413 (3.45)		0.703 (16.9)		−0.148 (2.04)	
Housing services			0.295 (1.78)	0.309 (1.58)		0.390 (2.49)
Other serives			1.250 (10.08)	−0.445 (3.46)		0.205 (2.39)

Sector	In rate of change form					
	$\dfrac{CPRV^t}{GDPC}$	$\dfrac{DINT}{GDCC}$	$\dfrac{PL^{*}L}{Y}$	$\Delta PGDP$	UVX	$\dfrac{TXI}{GDP^t}$
	−0	−0	−0	−1	−0	−0
1	8	9	10	11	12	13
Agriculture	0.806 (4.27)					
Mining					0.815 (17.50)	
Construction		0.226[c] (1.04)				
Manufacturing						0.127[c] (1.15)
Transportation		0.873 (2.38)				
Utilities			0.371 (5.83)	0.295 (6.42)		
Housing services						
Other serives		0.572 (2.04)				

Table 3 (cont.)

Sector	$\dfrac{SUB^t}{GDP^t}$	PGDP		$\dfrac{PL(1+TXRSSE)}{GDP/L}$		$\dfrac{GDP}{L}PL(1+TXRSSE)$	
	-0	-0	-1	-0	-1	-0	-0
	14	15	16	17	18	19	20
Agriculture		0.838 (13.22)					
Mining			0.0744 (1.76)	0.111 (2.69)			
Construction							
Manufacturing		0.809 (10.08)		0.141 (2.63)			
Transportation	-0.090 (2.03)		0.337 (2.44)			-0.969 (7.32)	
Utilities			0.443 (8.38)		0.0735 (3.39)	-0.349 (8.08)	
Housing services							0.207 (2.58)
Other services				0.223 (2.94)		-0.572 (3.15)	

Sector	Constant	$\bar{R}^2$ / SE	DW / F	Sum of coefficients in columns 4–7, 15–16	Mean, standard deviation of dep. variables
	21	22	23	24	25
Agriculture		0.93 (0.049)	1.20 / 70.5	0.951 (22.1)	0.301 / 0.188
Mining		0.98 (0.044)	2.87 / 203.4	0.0744 (1.77)	0.339 / 0.280
Construction	0.340^{b} (1.47)	0.42 (0.125)	3.16 / 5.78	0.613 (3.52)	0.270 / 0.164
Manufacturing		0.96 (0.041)	2.30 / 123.7	0.857 (13.8)	0.296 / 0.164
Transportation	0.0857 (2.22)	0.88 (0.071)	2.75 / 24.8	0.943 (6.42)	0.308 / 0.204
Utilities	0.145 (3.21)	0.99 (0.023)	2.31 / 249.4	0.998 (10.3)	0.305 / 0.226
Housing services	-0.057^{b} (1.40)	0.80 (0.086)	2.42 / 20.7	0.994 (5.48)	0.252 / 0.192
Other services		0.95 (0.051)	2.00 / 81.3	1.010 (10.1)	0.304 / 0.234

[a] Variable definitions at column heads are given in the text. Data sources are given in the appendix to chapter 8. Absolute values of t-statistics are given beneath the point estimate of the parameters. All point estimates are significantly non-zero at the 5% level unless otherwise indicated.
[b] Significantly non-zero at the 10% level.
[c] Significantly non-zero at the 25% level.

hypothesis of no serial correlation at the 5% level in any case (although the test is inconclusive in several cases). One might also note that the constant terms are not significantly non-zero even at the 25% level (and, therefore, have been suppressed) in half of the sectors. The relatively large constant terms for two sectors — Construction and Utilities — are related to the inclusion of the *level* of total inventories relative to gross domestic product in the relations for those two sectors. The negative constant term in the housing services sector probably reflects secularly increasing rent control (and possibly some biases in the sample used to construct the price index) which has resulted in a lower rate of increase in the price index for that sector than for any of the other seven (see the last column of table 3). The author has no specific explanation for the significantly positive constant in the case of transportation.

In respect to the remainder of the point estimates, subdivision into general and sector-specific variables related only to demand and only to supply is useful. The general demand related variables are three. The first such variable is the level (*not* the rate of change) of total year-end inventory stocks relative to total gross domestic production that is included as a summary measure of the state of aggregate demand relative to aggregate supply under the assumption that non-proportional stock changes largely reflect unanticipated discrepancies between these aggregates.[36] Under this hypothesis one a priori would expect negative coefficients, as is the case for the two sectors (i.e., construction and utilities) in which non-zero coefficients estimates were obtained at the 25% level of significance. In the case of construction, however, the coefficient estimate is not significantly nonzero at the 10% level. With the possible exception of utilities (for which product industrial demands may immediately reflect changes in production decisions due to unanticipated inventory stock changes), thus, the results do not support a hypothesis that the discrepancy between aggregate demand and supply (at least as measured by this variable) plays a major role in the rate of change of prices. A second general demand variable included is the rate of change of income distribution between labor and non-labor. In the case of utilities the significant positive coefficient estimate suggests that increases in the income share of labor result in increased demand pressures. For all other sectors no evidence of a significant response to this variable was obtained. The third and most important general demand variable is the general pressure on the rate of change of prices which results from the rate of change of nominal per capita monetary supplies, of real per

---

[36] Attempts to explain Chilean measured inventory stock behavior by other hypothesis have not proved to be very consistent with the data. The inventory stock data themselves, however, are probably relatively weak.

capita gross domestic product, and/or of exchange rates and which is represented by the estimated impacts of these variables on the rate of change of the deflator for total gross domestic product in table 2.[37] In this sense, thus, the estimates in table 3 are two stage estimates. A problem of maintaining the distinction between demand and supply pressures for price changes arises in the evaluation of the impact of this variable because of the high correlations among this variable and the sector specific rates of change of intermediate input prices. The existence of such a problem should not be surprising since all of these variables are only differently weighted averages of the same rates of change of the various sectoral prices. The comments following immediately, therefore, refer to sets of coefficients for both variables (columns 15 and 16 as well as 4–7 in table 3). A number of interesting characteristics are evident upon examination of the lag structures of the responses to these variables. First, given that the rate of change of the overall gross domestic product deflator is a weighted average of the rates of change of the sectoral prices and that the proxy variables for the impact of alterations in the rate of change of nominal per capita monetary balances – real per capita gross domestic product – exchange rate considerations are highly correlated with the rate of change of the gross domestic product deflator, if the accumulated change in the rate of change of prices of any one sector is significantly less than 1, then the accumulated change in the rate of change of prices of at least one other sector must be significantly greater than 1.[38]

In fig. 4 are presented the accumulated responses for all of the sectors except mining, in which most of the product is exported and the rate of change of prices logically is determined primarily by the rate of change of the export price in domestic currency. At the 5% level of significance the accumulated response of the rate of change of the construction price is less than one at all times; at the end of the current period the response is significantly less than one for four other sectors (Housing services, Utilities, Manufacturing, and Agriculture); at the end of the first period the same holds for two other sectors (Housing services and Other services); at the end of the third period the

[37] The effect of changes in the wage rate relative to labor productivity is not included in the construction of this variable because sector-specific data about this variable are included separately.

[38] This statement must be qualified (a) to the extent that the relevant pressures are transmitted by the wage variables (see the discussion below), (b) to the extent that non-zero constants are not offset by the level of inventories relative to gross domestic product, and (c) to the extent that the correlation between $[PG\hat{D}P^t]$ and $r[PINP]$ is less than 1. These correlations range from 0.86 to 0.98 with the exception of a value of 0.72 for the case of housing services.

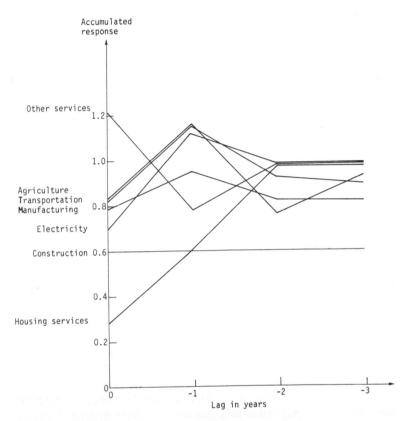

Fig. 4. The accumulated response of the rates of change of sectoral prices to a once and for all change in the nominal monetary — real gross domestic product — exchange rate considerations embodied in $PG\hat{D}P^t$ and $PINP$.

same holds for two sectors (Agriculture and Manufacturing), and the long run accumulated response for manufacturing is less than one. To offset the above accumulated responses that are less than one, the rate of change of the price of mining on the average is greater than the rate of change of the gross domestic price deflator (see table 1 and column 25 in table 3); in the current period the response in the case of other services is greater than one; and at the end of the first period the accumulated responses of three sectors (Agriculture, Transportation, and Utilities) are significantly greater than one. Thus, in the short run the patterns of adjustment are seen to be complex with various sectors overshooting and undershooting. In the long run all sectors adjust proportionally to the general inflationary pressure except manufacturing and construction adjust less than completely with the relatively large changes in the price of mining serving as an offset in the sample. An unanswered question is why are construction and industry prices characterized by this relative inertia? Second, given that $r[P\hat{GD}P^t]$ has been positive throughout the period under study, if the path of adjustment of the rate of change of a given sectoral price indicates a response significantly less than one for the current period, then even if the sum of the coefficients for this sector is not significantly different from one, the rate of change of the sectoral prices will on the average be less than for the gross domestic deflator unless significant overshooting occurs. Housing services provides an example of such a pattern without overshooting, which (together with the negative secular trend represented by the constant) largely explains why this sector had the lowest mean rate of growth of prices over the sample period (see column 25 in table 3).[39] With the exception of construction and manufacturing (which had the next lowest mean rates of growth of prices over the sample), all the other nonmining sectors are characterized by some overshooting in such responses. Third, the relative speed of adjustment across sectors varies substantially depending on the criteria used. If complete adjustment to the long run level of response is used, then construction adjusts most rapidly, agriculture adjusts most slowly, and all other nonmining sectors are tied between. If the response in the current period is used, the sectors may be ordered as follows: other services, agriculture, transportation, manufacturing, utilities, construction, housing services. If the attainment of an accumulated response not significantly different from one is used, the ordering changes to transportation, manufacturing, and other nonmining sectors except construction. For any reasonable criterion, however, adjustment in the rate of change of prices in housing services seems to be relatively slow, which apparently reflects in part the existence of numerous annual (or longer) rental contracts and of rent control.[40] Fourth, independent of the degree of relative sluggishness, the responses in general are distributed over a considerably longer period than those suggested by Harberger. For most sectors long run equilibrium is not attained before the end of the second

[39] One might also note that, despite many comments to the contrary, the rate of growth of agricultural prices has not been the lowest of all the sectors but has been on the average slightly higher than the rate of growth of the deflator of gross domestic product. The existence of price controls especially in this sector suggests that, if anything, the actual rate of growth is higher than the reported rate.
[40] Harberger ('Dynamics of inflation', 233–234, 238–239) also characterized house rents to be relatively sluggish.

period, and, given the two stage procedure, a once and for all change in the equilibrium rate of expansion of the nominal per capita money supply may still be causing adjustment from 5 to 8 years later. Fifth, that in five sectors the use of the rate of change of input prices results in a better fit than the use of $r[PG\hat{D}P^t]$ with the same lag suggests that some of the pressures due to alterations in the rate of change of per capita monetary balances — real per capita gross domestic product — exchange rate variables are transmitted through intermediate input prices in what might be called a cost push phenomenon.

The sector-specific demand related variables may be divided into three groups. The first group of sector-specific demand variables are the rates of changes of components of real demand important to a sector relative to the real production capacity of that sector. A priori one would expect any significant coefficients of these variables to be positive since the expansion of real demand relative to capacity would seem to lead to pressure for increased prices (and vice versa). For the four sectors for which significantly non-zero (although only at the 25% level for construction) coefficients were obtained, all the estimates are positive. Only in the case of agriculture, however, is a component of *final* demand (i.e., real private consumption) apparently important. For each of the other three sectors (Construction, Transportation, and Other services) real intermediate demands are important. The relative importance of intermediate demands in such sectoral rates of change of price determination relations should not be surprising given the importance of intermediate flows in the absorption of total product for these sectors.[41] This fact, together with the role of the rate of changes of input prices, points to the importance of specifying the interconnections among sectors in a study of this type. The second sector-specific demand variable is the first difference of the lagged rate of change of the sector price or what Harberger calls the 'accelerator',[42] which is included as a measure of expectations regarding the rates of change of future prices. In the case of electricity there does seem to be a significant positive accelerator effect, but no such evidence is found in the other sectors. The very limited role apparently played by this variable according to the results of this study is not unlike that found by Harberger in his full model. The third sector-specific demand variable is the rate of change

---

[41] According to the 1962 input—output table, the percents of total product originating in the following sectors (including imports) and delivered as intermediate inputs for other sectors are 11% for construction, 57% from transportation, and 62% from other services.

[42] Harberger, 'Dynamics of inflation', 225—227, 240—241.

of unit values of exports in domestic currency. As is noted above this variable is of primary importance in the determination of the rate of change of the price in the primary exporting sector (i.e., mining). However, no other link to international prices through exports or imports is indicated to be significant by the results in table 3 except in so far as imported input prices are included in the input price indices.

The general supply related variables are the rate of change of the average effective indirect tax rate and the rate of change of the average effective subsidy rate. The former variable has a positive coefficient estimate that is significantly non-zero at the 25% level in the case of industry, and the latter variable has a negative coefficient estimate that is significantly non-zero at the 5% level in the case of transportation. That only for manufacturing is there even limited evidence that the former variable is significant is not unreasonable because indirect taxes probably are more effectively collected on industrial than on nonindustrial goods. That only for transportation is there evidence that the latter variable is significant again is not surprising because this sector is probably relatively the most subsidized in the economy. In any case the evidence of any wide impact due to changes in either of these average rates is very limited, and even in the case of the two sectors in which the rates of change of prices apparently are affected, the absolute value of the coefficients suggests that only about one-tenth of any percentage change is passed on to buyer in the form of different prices.

The sector-specific supply variables also are divided into two groups. The first is related to the rate of change of the price of intermediate inputs, which is discussed above. The second is related to the rate of change of wages (adjusted for average employer's actual social security contributions) relative to the average value added per laborer in the sector. A priori one would expect the pressure for price increases to be greater the greater the rate of increase of wages and the less the increase of average labor productivity. The estimates in columns 17–20 of table 3 provide support for the hypothesis that these labor cost variables do affect the rate of change of sectoral prices significantly..Only for construction and agriculture is there not such evidence, and for agriculture this absence is somewhat illusionary in that the labor cost variable in column 20 can be used to replace the $r[P\hat{G}DP^t]$ variables in columns 5–7 at almost no cost in terms of the extent to which the estimates are consistent with the variance in the dependent variable.[43] In contrast, only in his quarterly regression for the import price component (sic) of the wholesale price index does Harberger present evidence of significant (at the 5% level) influence of labor

[43] For footnote, see next page.

costs on the rate of change of disaggregate prices. This difference between the present results and those of Harberger probably reflects his use of the rate of change of the government minimum wage (*sueldo vital*) instead of sector-specific wage data. In any case the results in respect to labor costs in table 3, just as these in respect to intermediate costs, suggest a much larger role for cost push factors in the determination of sectoral price changes than Harberger seems to allow. In agreement with Harberger's interpretation, however, the present author sees this role as being one of transmitting overall pressures for price increases to specific product prices. The determination of the rate of change of wages, for example, apparently depends substantially on expectations as to the future rate of inflation, and such expectations probably largely reflect recent experience.[44] One final comment seems in order in respect to the estimates of the response to rates of change in unit labor costs in table 3. For two sectors (Utilities and Other services) estimates of the coefficients of the rate of change of wages relative to average labor productivity *and* of average labor productivity are both significantly nonzero. One might question the justification for including the latter variable in addition to the former in such an estimation. Including both of these variables is justified if one considers eq. (3) to be the rate of change form of a linear approximation to a process in which the production function is CES with the elasticity of substitution unequal to one and in which the price is set so that the value of the marginal product of labor is equal to the exogenously determined wage rate.[45]

IV. Conclusions

This study has examined models which are shown to be consistent with a very high percent of the variances in the rate of change of aggregate and sectoral prices in Chile. The estimates of these models have provided support

[43] $r[PGDP] = \dfrac{0.671}{(3.12)} r\left[\dfrac{CPRI^t}{GDPC}\right] + \dfrac{0.819}{(11.96)} r[PINP] + \dfrac{0.119}{(2.09)} r\left[\dfrac{PL(1+TXRSSE)}{GDP/L}\right]$

$\bar{R}^2 = 0.91$
$SE = 0.066$
$DW = 1.80$
$F = 104.6$

[44] This relationship probably underlies the high multicollinearity between the rate of change of agricultural wages relative to labor productivity and various lagged values of $r[PG\dot{D}P^t]$. See the previous note and table 3. Further evidence exists in Behrman, 'Sectoral money wages'; Behrman and Garcia; and Ramos.

[45] For footnote, see next page.

for hypotheses that non-monetary factors have played a significant role in sustaining the substantial rate of inflation which Chile has experienced in the postwar period. Cost push factors operating through intermediate and unit labor costs apparently have been more important in transmitting overall inflationary pressures (including those that arise from the role of expectations in the wage bargaining process) than earlier studies have maintained. Real changes in transitory per capita gross domestic product,[46] in labor productivity, and in demands (especially of an intermediate nature) facing sectors relative to capacity have had significant impacts. Exchange rate policy (which, of course, is ultimately related to domestic price changes) apparently has been very relevant in determining at least the time path of overall inflation and particularly of price changes in the export sectors. Subsidy, indirect tax, and social security tax decisions may have played more minor roles.

Given the existence of other empirical evidence that significant responses to sectoral prices do occur in both short run and long run Chilean allocation decisions,[47] however, the most important characteristic of these results about the role of non-monetary factors is that sector specific prices do respond significantly to sector specific costs and capacity utilization considerations. Thus, at least signals in the right directions are given for allocation decisions. The price system apparently is playing to some degree a role that probably leads to greater efficiency.[48] To ignore this role when conducting analysis and giving policy prescriptions may be costly in terms of foregoing

[45] In standard or previously defined notation the production function is given in

$$GDP = \gamma[\delta K^{-\rho} + (1-\delta)L^{-\rho}]^{-1/\rho} \tag{4a}$$

Setting the value of the marginal product of labor equal to the wage and solving for the price gives eq. (4b)

$$PGDP = \frac{PL}{(GDP/L)^{-1/\sigma}}. \tag{4b}$$

The point of the comment in the text is that PL and GDP/L are raised to different powers if the elasticity of substitution between capital and labor ($=\sigma$) is unequal to one. For direct estimates of the Chilean sectoral elasticities of substitution, see Behrman, 'Substitution between capital and labor'.

[46] That permanent income may be relatively unimportant in the desired demand for real per capita monetary balances because it is important in the desired demand for real per capita consumption is an interesting suggestion that arises out of the estimates of section II.

[47] See Behrman, Chapter 9; Behrman, 'Substitution between capital and labor'; and Behrman, 'Sectoral investment determination'.

[48] Gregory, Harberger, and Ramos do not investigate the determination of sectoral prices and, therefore, do not explore this important question.

the use of some policy tools and in terms of creating incentives for misallocations. Yet this role is ignored in much analysis and in many policy recommendations.[49]

Despite such evidence of the significance of non-monetary considerations, however, the results of this study support the position that the rate of change of nominal per capita monetary balances has been the primary force behind the Chilean inflationary experience.[50] Earlier studies of the demand for real per capita monetary balances in Chile by Deaver, Hynes, and Reichmann and in Argentina by Diz as well as studies of price determination in Chile by Gregory, Harberger, and Ramos, however, have all been misspecified in that they have not been consistent with Diz's observation about the necessity for overshooting in the rate of change of price adjustment. The estimated rate of change of the deflator for gross domestic product relation which is discussed in section II suggests that the Chilean experience is basically consistent with the pattern of adjustment implied by Diz although the estimated overshooting and the long run accumulative response both are somewhat less than expected a priori..The results in section III suggest that the patterns of adjustment of the rate of change of sectoral prices differ considerably from sector to sector (with some additional overshooting) in ways that reflect the interconnectedness of the sectors (through input prices and intermediate demands) and institutional constraints (such as the contractual relations in the ownership of dwellings sector). A very important characteristic of the patterns of adjustment discussed in sections II and III is that the lags in adjustment are much longer than previous studies have maintained. Rather than basically complete adjustment at the end of the current year or after one more year as is suggested by Gregory, Harberger, and Ramos, significant responses are estimated to occurring 5–8 years later. These substantially greater lags obviously imply much greater difficulties in eliminating inflation. The failures of three substantial Chilean anti-inflationary programs in the last 15 years attest to those difficulties.

---

[49] For example, see the models recommended for use by ECAFE (*Programming for economic development*. Bangkok 1960) or the Chenery two gap model which is used in UNCTAD, *Trade prospects and capital needs of developing countries*. United Nations, New York, 1968 (a review of which by the present author is in *International Economic Review* 12 (October, 1971).519–525.

[50] Of course, one can also ask what are the causes of the changes in nominal monetary supplies, but to do so is beyond the scope of this study. See, however, García (186–213) for an argument that most of the variation in money supplies is not exogenous but dependent upon government deficits and redistributive concerns to offset wage increases.

R.S. Eckaus, P.N. Rosenstein-Rodan (eds.), Analysis of development problems,
© North-Holland Publishing Company

A STUDY OF QUARTERLY NOMINAL WAGE CHANGE DETERMINATION IN AN INFLATIONARY DEVELOPING ECONOMY *

Jere R. BEHRMAN

University of Pennsylvania, Philadelphia, Penn., U.S.A.

and

Jorge G. MUJICA

Oficina de Planificacion Nacional, Santiago, Chile

I. Introduction

Since Phillips'[1] seminal work of more than a decade ago, there have been numerous studies of the rates of change of nominal wages in developed and relatively non-inflationary economies.[2] One point of controversy in the re-

* An earlier version of this paper was presented to a seminar on Chilean labor economics at the *Instituto de Economía y Planificación.* The authors wish to thank, but not implicate, the sponsoring organizations, the members of the above-mentioned seminar, and Eduardo García, Gree Lewis, Ricardo Lira, Joze Mencinger, and Joseph Ramos.

[1] A.W. Phillips, 'The relation between unemployment and the rate of change of money wage rates in the United Kingdom, 1861–1957', *Economica,* New Series, 25 (November, 1958) 283–299.

[2] For example, see L.A. Dicks-Mireaux, 'The interrelationship between cost and price changes, 1946–1959: a study of inflation in post-war Britain', *Oxford Economic Papers,* New Series, 13 (October, 1961) 267–292; H.G. Hines, 'Trade unions and wage inflation in the United Kingdom, 1893–1961', *Review of Economic Studies* 31 (October, 1964) 221–252; H.G. Hines, 'Unemployment and the rate of change of money wages in the United Kingdom: a reappraisal', *Review of Economics and Statistics* 40 (February, 1968) 60–67; E. Kuh, 'A productivity theory of wage levels – an alternative to the Phillips curve', *Review of Economic Studies* 34 (October, 1967) 333–362; Richard G. Lipsey, 'The relation between unemployment and the role of change of money wage rates in the United Kingdom, 1862–1957: a further analysis', *Economica,* New Series, 27 (February, 1960) 1–31; Richard G. Lipsey and M.D. Steuer, 'The relation between profits and wage rates', *Economica,* New Series, 38 (May, 1961) 137–155; G.L. Perry, 'The determinants of wage rate changes and the inflation-unemployment trade-off for the United States', *Review of Economic Studies* 31 (October, 1964) 287–308; N.J. Simler and Alfred Tella, 'Labor reserves and the Phillips Curve', *Review of Economics and Statistics* 40 (February, 1968) 32–49; and Mahmood A. Zaidi, 'The determination of money wage rate changes and unemployment – inflation 'trade-off' in Canada', *International Economic Review* 10 (June, 1969) 207–219.

sulting literature is whether or not the rate of change of prices (either of consumption goods or of products) has had a significant role in the determination of money wage changes. For economies with a long history of inflation, in contrast, there probably would be widespread a priori agreement that the rate of change of prices (or expectations thereof) has had a significant role in this process. However, a number of questions about this role have not been explored empirically. To what extent in such an economy do rates of changes of prices (or expectations thereof) dominate the determination of the rate of change of wages? What are the lengths and the natures of the lags in the process (whether due to adjustment or due to expectations)? Have real wages declined because nominal wage changes have had a delayed adjustment to price changes? Have variations in the seasonal patterns of price changes (or expectations thereof) had a role? To what degree have Phillips' curve phenomena (in the form of the inverse of the unemployment rate) been important? Have productivity changes and, therefore, changes in the unemployment rates been significant determinants as Kuh has argued is the case in less inflationary economies?

   Chile has had a long history of substantial inflation and provides an interesting data base for the exploration of such questions.[3] The availability of quarterly data makes possible such an exploration for the twenty-eight quarters of the 1961–1967 period for manufacturing (two data sources for wages), electricity and transportation, construction, and commerce, and for Santiago and the total country.[4] Because many wages are set on annual contractual bases and many other wages apparently tend to follow the pattern of such contractual wages, in the regressional analysis below the dependent variable is the rate of change of wages from the same quarter of the previous year (and not from the previous quarter), and the expected rate of change of prices likewise is based upon annual (and not quarterly) rates of change in the level of the price index.[5] The distributions of the dependent variables over the sample period

---

[3] In the two postwar decades the rate of change of the gross domestic product deflator has ranged from 0.038 to 0.740, with a mean of 0.296 and a standard deviation of 0.193. For discussions of the dynamics of the Chilean price determination process, see Jere R. Behrman, 'Price determination in an inflationary economy: the dynamics of Chilean inflation revisited', chapter 14 in this volume (hereinafter referred to as chapter 14); and Arnold Harberger, 'The dynamics of inflation in Chile', in: *Measurement in economics: studies in mathematical economics in memory of Yehuda Grunfeld*, ed. by Carl Crist. Stanford University Press, Stanford, 1963, 219–250.
[4] Data sources are given in the appendix to this chapter.
[5] For the same reasons L.R. Klein and R.J. Ball, in: 'Some econometrics of the determination of absolute prices and wages', *Economic Journal* 49 (September, 1965) 465–482, followed a similar approach (although they worked with levels, not with the rates of change).

Table 1

Characteristics of the distributions of annual rates of change of nominal wages over the 28 quarters of the 1961–1967 period[a]

Sector	Range	Mean	Standard deviation	Correlation coefficients						
				Manufacturing I	Manufacturing II	Electricity and transportation	Construction	Commerce	Santiago	Total
Manufacturing I	0.03 – 0.69	0.35	0.19	1.0						
Manufacturing II	0.06 – 0.57	0.33	0.13	0.73	1.0					
Electricity and transportation	−0.14 – 0.85	0.29	0.30	0.66	0.68	1.0				
Construction	−0.14 – 0.66	0.33	0.24	0.86	0.85	0.71	1.0			
Commerce	0.05 – 0.58	0.30	0.11	0.57	0.44	0.50	0.57	1.0		
Santiago	−0.27 – 0.62	0.28	0.26	0.82	0.67	0.67	0.68	0.56	1.0	
Total	0.08 – 0.61	0.33	0.15	0.95	0.78	0.79	0.91	0.61	0.87	1.0

a Data sources are given in the appendix to this chapter. All correlation coefficients are significantly non-zero at the 1% level except that between manufacturing II and commerce (which is significantly non-zero at the 5% level).

for the seven data cells are summarized in table 1. The ranges and standard deviations of the rates of change of nominal wages have been substantial (although somewhat less for commerce, manufacturing and the total than for the other three data cells). For every cell except commerce the maximum rate of change occurred in the second or third quarter of 1964, and the minimum rate of change occurred between the second quarter of 1961, and the last quarter of 1962.[6] The movements among the dependent variables of the various cells have been significantly correlated at the 1% level (except between manufacturing II and commerce), but a number of the correlation coefficients are substantially below 1.[7] The means are concentrated between 0.28 and 0.35, with manufacturing, construction, and the total having increases in real wages over the period while the other cells experienced slight decreases in real wages.[8]

The remainder of this paper is devoted to an econometric examination of the rates of change of nominal wages for the seven cells in table 1 in hopes of illuminating some of the questions posed above. In section III the degree of consistency between the rates of change of nominal wages and expected rates of changes of prices is explored. In section III the effects of including (in addition to expected rates of change of prices) some of the other possible determinants mentioned above are examined. In section IV concluding comments are presented.

II. The role of expectations of the rate of change of price levels in the determination of sectoral rates of change of nominal wages

Because of the long inflationary history which Chile has experienced, one would expect both suppliers and demanders of labor to use some notion of an expected or normal rate of inflation as an important component in the determination of their respective labor market behavior.[9] More specifically, from

---

[6] For commerce, local maximums and minimums occurred at the same times as in the other cells, but global maximums and minimums occurred, respectively, in the third quarter of 1966, and in the second quarter of 1967.

[7] Of the twenty-one correlation coefficients, two are greater than 0.90, four are between 0.80 and 0.90, four are between 0.70 and 0.80, six are between 0.60 and 0.70, four are between 0.50 and 0.60, and one is between 0.40 and 0.50. Note that the correlation coefficient between the two sources of data for the rate of change of nominal wages in manufacturing (0.73) is about in the middle of this distribution.

[8] The mean annual increase in the consumer price index level over the period was 0.31.

[9] For an extensive discussion of the possibility of a substantial equilibrium rate of inflation (with associated expectations, see Jorge García Mujica, 'Inflation como un procest de equilibrio'. Universidad de Chile, Instituto de Economía y Planificacíon, Santiago, December 1968.

the point of view of suppliers of labor, expectations of the rates of change of consumer prices and of returns from their ownership of other factors would seem to be important while from the point of view of demanders of labor, expectations of the rates of change of product prices and of other input prices would seem to be important. If one could distinguish among the effects of these various expectations, one might be able to distinguish usefully between cost push and demand pull considerations (although clearly problems of simultaneity would remain). In the present case data limitations and multicollinearity preclude such a possibility, so expectations of the rate of change of the consumer price index are used in a reduced form manner to represent the effects of inflation expectations held by both suppliers and demanders. For the purpose of estimation such aggregate expectations are represented by a distributed lag of past rates of change. Given that Chile has had a long inflationary history with substantial variance in year to year rates, one might expect that the experience of a number of years would be incorporated into expectations of normal rates of change. Therefore, the possibilities that such expectations are based upon periods of two, four, seven, and ten years are examined below. Consideration of what would happen to real wages in such a case if the long run equilibrium rate of change of prices were to increase once and for all from one level to a higher level is suggestive in respect to a priori expectations about the lag pattern. If real wages were to remain basically constant in the long run, the sum of all of the lagged weights of the rates of change of the price level in the expectation model must be insignificantly different from one.[10] If the weight of the current rate of change of prices in the expectation model is significantly less than one, however, in order for the level of real wages to be maintained constant the weights in subsequent periods must be such that the sum of the weights at some point in the adjustment period for expectation is significantly greater than one; and then subsequently some significantly *negative* weights must be present in order that the total sum not be significantly different from one.[11] In other words, in order to maintain real wages constant in the long run, if the instantaneous weight is significantly less than one, the sum of the weights over the first k periods (where k is less than the number of

---

[10] If there were constant exponential changes in productivity that resulted in constant exponential changes in real wages, a significantly non-zero constant term would result, but the statements in the text about the pattern of the weights would still hold.
[11] The partial analogy to the pattern of adjustment of the rate of change of prices to the rates of change of the money supply suggested by Aldofo Cesar Diz, 'Money and prices in Argentina, 1935–1962', Ph.D. diss., University of Chicago, 1966, should be clear. For some support in respect to the existence of such a pattern in the case of Chilean price adjustments, see Behrman, chapter 14 in this volume.

periods for complete adjustment) must be significantly greater than one in order to make up for the delayed response even though the total sum of the weights must not be significantly different from one. Of course, factors other than price expectations also affect the determination of wages, so the above patterns might not occur exactly in the estimations. Over a period as short as seven years with the inflationary experience that Chile has had, however, one might well expect that the role of price expectations would be sufficiently strong so that some evidence of such patterns would be obtained.

The results which were obtained when the rates of change of wages were postulated to be functions only of the expected rate of change of prices are summarized in table 2.[12] In order to limit problems of multicollinearity and to allow the possibility of lag patterns such as those discussed in the previous paragraph, the lag pattern of the expected rates of change of prices was represented by one variable constructed from the historical rates of change for each degree of the polynomial allowed in the lag patterns.[13] The first three columns in the table are the coefficients of the constructed variables (i.e., $Z1$, $Z2$, and $Z3$) for first, second, and third degree polynomials.[14] The next ten columns are the weights of various lagged values of the rates of change of prices that are implied by the polynomial coefficients, and the next column is the sum of these weights. The last two columns are the coefficients of determination (corrected for degree of freedom), the standard errors of the estimate, and the Durbin–Watson statistics.

The coefficients of determination indicate, that, with the expection of commerce, the model of expected rates of change of prices by itself is consistent with a substantial portion (from 67 to 85%) of the variance in the rate of change of nominal wages over the sample period in every data cell. The Durbin–Watson statistics indicate that the null hypothesis of no serial correlation is

[12] For the estimates presented in this table even the constant terms have been suppressed. If the constant terms are not suppressed, the estimates thereof are not significantly non-zero at the 5% level, and the other point estimates are not significantly altered in the majority of the data cells. For electricity and transportation and Santiago, however, large significantly negative constants (−0.93 and −1.11, respectively) are obtained, and the pattern of weights of the lagged rates of change of prices is shifted up so that the sums are substantially greater than one (4.0 and 5.2, respectively). For the second alternative for manufacturing, the composite results are obtained.

[13] This method is suggested by Robert E. Hall and Richard C. Stuch in 'A flexible infinite distributed lag', University of California, Institute of Business and Economics Research, Center for Research in Management Science, Berkeley, 1968, to whom the interested reader is referred for details.

[14] The use of fourth degree polynomials was also investigated but was not successful.

Table 2

Estimates of the role of the expected rate of change of prices in the determination of sectoral rates of change of annual nominal wages over the 28 quarters in 1961–1967 period[a]

Sector	Z rate of change of price level			Weights in expectation model for various lags for rates of change of prices											$\bar{R}^2$ SE	DW
	1	2	3	-0	-1	-2	-3	-4	-5	-6	-7	-8	-9	Σ		
Manufacturing I	-4.29 (7.1)	0.722 (5.5)	-0.0367 (4.7)	0.75	0.33	0.15	0.01	-0.05	-0.06	-0.02	0.02	0.05	0.05	1.29	0.67 0.111	1.65
Manufacturing II	-3.05 (8.8)	0.470 (6.2)	-0.0226 (5.1)	0.62	0.36	0.18	0.06	0.00	-0.02	-0.01	0.01	0.02	0.03	1.24	0.77 0.063	1.06
Electricity and transportation	-6.91 (7.7)	1.29 (6.6)	-0.0693 (6.0)	0.93	0.36	0.01	-0.17	-0.21	-0.16	-0.07	0.04	0.12	0.12	0.96	0.70 0.164	1.63
Construction	-6.45 (11.6)	1.19 (9.8)	-0.0632 (8.8)	0.92	0.38	0.05	-0.12	-0.17	-0.14	-0.05	0.04	0.11	0.11	1.12	0.83 0.100	1.30
Commerce	-1.66 (3.4)	0.250 (2.4)	-0.0123 (2.0)	0.39	0.25	0.15	0.08	0.05	0.03	0.03	0.03	0.03	0.02	1.07	0.29 0.089	2.56
Santiago	-4.42 (5.9)	0.611 (3.8)	-0.0259 (2.7)	0.90	0.52	0.24	0.05	-0.06	-0.11	-0.11	-0.09	-0.05	-0.02	1.27	0.73 0.135	0.78
Total	-3.87 (12.1)	0.672 (9.7)	-0.0351 (8.5)	0.65	0.33	0.12	0.00	-0.04	-0.04	-0.01	0.04	0.06	0.06	1.18	0.85 0.058	1.91

[a] Data sources are given in the appendix to this chapter. The absolute value of t ratios is given under the point estimates of $Z1, Z2,$ and $Z3$. These t ratios suggest that all of these point estimates are significantly non-zero at least at the 5% level. The $Z1, Z2, Z3$ variables are polynomial of degree one, two, and three, respectively, constructed from the lagged rates of change of prices as is suggested by Robert E. Hall and Richard C. Stuch, 'A flexible infinite distributed lag'. University of California, Institute of Business and Economics Research, Center for Research in Management Science, Berkeley, 1968.

rejected at the 5% level only in the case of the Santiago cell although the test is inconclusive in the case of the alternative series for manufacturing and in the case of construction. An examination of the residuals of each equation suggests that there is some tendency for the relatively large absolute values of the errors of prediction to be concentrated in the first and last two years of the sample. These concentrations may reflect the effects of the Alessandri and Frei stabilization programs.[15] The residuals do not seem to be very highly correlated across cells, however, except that in five of the seven cells (excluding Manufacturing II and the total) the rates of change of nominal wages are overestimated in the first quarter and underestimated in the second quarter of 1962, and that in five of the seven cells (excluding Manufacturing II and Electricity and transportation) the rates of change are overestimated for the first quarter of 1966, and underestimated for the first quarter of 1967. Once again, these exceptions may reflect the effects of the two stabilization programs.

The patterns of weights estimated for the lagged rates of change of prices in the expectations model show surprising conformity across cells (with commerce being the greatest exception) and generally reflect the characteristics anticipated in the a priori discussion above. In every cell a third order polynomial[16] over 10 years resulted in a lag pattern that is most consistent with the variance in the dependent variable. The current period response is relatively large but significantly less than one. The sum of the weights for the first two periods (except for commerce) is significantly greater than, or not different from, one. The sum of the weights reaches a maximum substantially greater than one after a lag of 2–4 years and then declines for the next 2–6 years (again excepting commerce). The total sum of the weights (even including commerce) is not substantially different from one.[17]

[15] For details about these programs, see Jorge Cauas, 'Stabilization policy – the Chilean case', *Journal of Political Economy* 78, part II (July/August, 1970) 815–825; Ricardo Ffrench-Davis, 'Three stabilization programs', Paper presented at University of Chicago, 8 August 1967; Peter Gregory, *Industrial wages in Chile*. New York State School of Industrial and Labor Relations, Cornell University, Ithaca, 1967; Joseph Ramos, 'Políticas de renumeraciones en Chile', mimeo. Universidad de Chile, Instituto de Economía, Santiago, September 1968; and Enrique Sierra C., 'Políticas de estabilización', mimeo. Instituto Latinoamericano de Planificación Económica y Social, Santiago, October 1967.
[16] The first critical point (excepting commerce) is at the minimum algebraic value of the weights in the fourth through sixth periods. The second critical point generally is a local maximum near the end of the response period. Even though this second critical point generally is discernible only in the third significant figure of the estimated weights, replacement of the third order polynomials by second order polynomials results in a significant reduction in the coefficient of determination.
[17] However, see note 12 above.

With the exception of commerce, therefore, the expected rate of change of price model seems quite satisfactory. Although the responses are relatively large in the first several years, significant responses occur over a decade apparently in part because of the great variation in the historical rates of inflation. The pattern of lags, moreover, generally allows overshooting to compensate for the less than proportional instantaneous response and to maintain the real wage basically constant in the long run.

III. Some possible additional determinants of the rate of change of Chilean sectoral nominal wages

In an economy with such a substantial inflationary history as that which Chile has experienced, the primary determinant of the rate of change of nominal wages would seem to be the expected rate of inflation. The results reported in the previous section provide support for such a supposition. However, a number of other determinants might also have significant roles: the rate of change of productivity, the rate of change of non-labor income, the level and rates of change of unemployment, the rate of change of legislated minimum wages, the level and rates of change of union strength, higher moments of the probability distribution in respect to future inflation.[18] Data are not available ·to represent adequately most of these variables in the sample period (which in the case of variables such as those related to productivity and union strength probably does not distort substantially the analysis because only very limited variance apparently occurred in the seven years of the sample).[19] However, data are available to explore three additional possible determinants, each of which is now briefly discussed.

First, the existence of unemployment data allows the possibility of exploring the extent of response to the Phillips curve phenomenon by including the inverse of the unemployment rate. To the extent that this variable reflects well excess demand in the labor market[20], it would seem also to represent

[18] Various such variables are included in the studies of wage rate determination listed in note 2 above.

[19] In a study over a 21-year period, however, Jere R. Behrman in 'The determinants of the annual rates of change of sectoral money wages in a developing economy', *International Economic Review*, 12 (October, 1971) 431–447 (Spanish version forthcoming in *Cuadernos de Economia*) (hereinafter referred to as 'Sectoral money wages') has found some evidence of significant responses in the rate of change of Chilean wages to rates of change of productivity, of unionization, of profits, of credit, and to levels of unionization and of capacity utilization.

[20] If participation rates are a function of unemployment, then ideally this variable should be adjusted for this interaction. See Simler and Tella.

some of the considerations mentioned above (such as productivity changes) that would result in shifts in real demand and real supply. One might hope, therefore, that the inclusion of this variable would add the representation of the effects of the real market environment to the representation of the inflationary effects discussed above.

Second, the existence of the unemployment data also permit the testing of Kuh's[21] hypothesis that the change of the employment rate, not the level, should be included in the rate of wage change determination because of productivity considerations.

Third, the same data that are used for the rate of change of prices above also can be used to test the hypothesis that the rate of change of nominal wages responds to expectations about changes in the seasonal pattern of price changes. The theoretical justification for the inclusion of such a variable is simple. For a given nominal wage assumed to hold throughout the next year and for a given increase in the prive level between the date of the wage determination and a date one year later, the level of real wages is greater the more the pattern of price level changes approximates path one in fig. 1 rather than path two. Changes in the path of seasonal fluctuations of prices, thus, affect real wages and therefore, the supply (and the demand) for labor. Assuming that consumption expenditures are spread evenly throughout the year, the integral of the area under the relevant path represents the extent to which the real wage is reduced by inflation. The index of seasonality which is used, therefore, is a discrete approximation to this integral that was constructed by calculating the ratio of the mean of the monthly price index levels over the year relative to the average of beginning and year end price levels.[22] Expectations

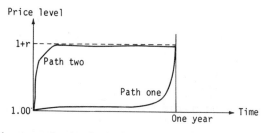

Fig. 1. Alternative seasonal paths of price level changes with substantially different effects on real wages.

[21] p. 336.

[22] Alternatively and more customarily, one could combine the seasonal effect with the effect of the change in the price level over the contract year by using the changes in yearly average prices rather than in the level of the index on the first and last date of the contract year. The attempt to separate these two effects seems interesting in the present case, however, so such a separation is explored.

Table 3
Estimates of the determination of sectoral rates of change of annual nominal wages over the 28 quarters in the 1961−1967 period as functions of expectations of price level changes, expectations of price seasonality changes, the inverse of the unemployment rate, and the change in the unemployment rate[a]

Sector	X = rate of change of price	ZX			Weights for various lagged values of X				
		1	2	3	−0	−1	−2	−3	−4
Manufac- turing I-1	Level	−1.71 (2.2)	0.112 (1.9)		0.59	0.43	0.30	0.18	0.09
	Season- ality	−0.0358 (2.2)	0.00331 (1.3)[b]		0.075	0.042	0.016	−0.003	−0.016
-2	Level		−0.0148 (1.5)[b]		0.07	0.07	0.07	0.06	0.05
	Season- ality		−0.0243 (4.3)		0.12	0.12	0.11	0.10	0.08
Manufac- turing II-1	Level	−2.50 (7.5)	0.432 (6.6)	−0.0220 (5.7)	0.38	0.17	0.03	−0.04	−0.07
-2	Level	−1.16 (1.2)[c]	0.696 (1.9)	−0.0737 (2.1)	−0.07	−0.13	−0.08	0.01	0.01
	Season ality	0.257 (1.5)[b]	−0.0396 (1.8)		0.014	0.036	0.050	0.055	0.053
Electri- city and transpor- tation -1	Level	2.29 (2.0)	−0.366 (2.7)			0.19	0.38	0.50	0.55
	Season- ality	1.12 (2.5)	−0.186 (3.1)		0.13	0.22	0.28	0.30	0.28
Con- struc- tion -1	Level	6.10 (6.2)	−1.27 (6.1)		−0.40	0.08	0.31	0.28	
	Season- ality	0.802 (5.5)	−0.212 (7.0)		0.019	0.078	0.094	0.068	
-2	Level	−5.52 (10.3)	0.989 (8.6)	−0.0513 (7.5)	0.76	0.30	0.01	−0.15	−0.20
Santiago -1	Level	−0.208 (12.9)			0.21	0.19	0.17	0.15	0.13
	Season- ality		−0.0308 (8.5)		0.20	0.19	0.18	0.17	0.15
Total -1	Level	−1.20 (3.1)	0.0742 (2.5)		0.46	0.34	0.25	0.16	0.10
	Season- ality	−0.293 (4.1)	0.026 (2.4)		0.067	0.041	0.019	0.003	−0.008
-2	Level	−1.76 (6.4)	0.0891 (5.8)		0.87	0.70	0.55	0.42	0.31

Table 3 (continued)

Sector	Weights for various lagged values of X						$\dfrac{1}{\text{unemployment rate}}$		Constant	R^2 SE	DW
	−5	−6	−7	−8	−9	Σ	−0	−1			
Manufacturing I-1	0.02	−0.03	−0.06	−0.06	−0.04	1.42				0.65 / 0.114	1.76
	−0.022	−0.021	+0.014			0.058					
−2	0.04	0.02				0.37			3.30 (3.0)	0.57 / 0.127	1.62
	0.06	0.03				0.61					
Manufacturing II-1	−0.07	−0.04	−0.01	0.02	0.03	0.38	1.24 (3.9)			0.84 / 0.053	1.97
−2	0.17	0.15				0.15	1.22 (3.0)			0.78 / 0.062	2.06
	0.044	0.026				0.28					
Electricity and transportation -1	0.52	0.42	0.25			2.82	0.137 (1.3)[b]		−0.824 (2.5)	0.69 / 0.165	2.18
	0.22	0.13				1.55					
Construction -1						0.27	0.157 (3.2)		2.00 (1.9)	0.91 / 0.071	2.24
						0.26					
−2	−0.17	−0.10	−0.02	0.05	0.06	0.53			2.39 (3.5)	0.88 / 0.84	1.66
Santiago -1	0.10	0.08	0.06	0.04	0.02	1.15				0.74 / 0.133	1.09
	0.12	0.09	0.05			1.15					
Total -1	0.04	0.00	−0.02	−0.03	−0.02	1.29				0.79 / 0.070	1.78
	−0.014	−0.015	−0.010			0.084					
−2	0.21	0.13	0.07	0.03	0.01	3.30	1.47 (1.6)[b]	1.94 (2.2)	−1.06 (3.0)	0.66 / 0.089	1.49

[a] Data sources are given in the appendix to this chapter. The absolute value of t ratios are given in parenthesis under the point estimates of the parameters of variables in the estimating equations. All such point estimates are significantly non-zero at the 5% level unless otherwise noted. The Z1, Z2, and Z3 variables are polynomials of degree one, two and three constructed from lagged rates of change of price levels or of the price seasonality index by the method suggested by Robert E. Hall and Richard C. Stuch, 'A flexible infinite distributed lag'. University of California, Institute of Business and Economics Research, Center for Research in Management Science, Berkeley, 1968. All weights for the seasonality variables have been multiplied by ten for ease of presentation.
[b] Significantly non-zero at the 10% level.
[c] Significantly non-zero at the 15% level.

of the rate of change of this variable were represented by polynomials in the lagged weights just as was done for expectation of the rate of price levels. Prima facie the concern with expected fluctuations in the paths of price changes may seem somewhat esoteric, but the fluctuations or the rate of change of the index have been considerable (from −19 to +40% in the 1953–1967 period), and the mass communications system monthly informs the populace about the current pattern of seasonal price changes as compared with recent years.

The results obtained for the rate of change of nominal wages when any of the three variables just discussed are included in addition to expectations of the rate of change of prices are summarized in table 3. For commerce, in no case did any of these additional variables have a significant coefficient. For electricity and transportation and for Santiago, one such relation each appeared interesting and is presented. For the other four data cells, two estimates each are presented. The characteristics of the ten sets of estimates in table 3 may be summarized by five general comments.

First, on an overall level the results are basically satisfactory, but at least one qualification is appropriate. The coefficients of determination indicate that the alternative specifications are consistent with from 57–91% of the variance in the dependent variables, and the Durbin–Watson statistics indicate that the null hypothesis of no serial correlation cannot be rejected at the 5% level of significance except possibly in the case of the Santiago cell. Examination of the residuals period by period once again reveals some concentration of the larger absolute values in the first two and last two years, but no apparent high overall correlations across cells except for a fairly widespread tendency (with Manufacturing II again the most consistent exception) to overestimate the rates of change in 1962.4, 1963.1, 1966.1, 1967.3 and 1967.4. This last tendency is somewhat different from that observed in the case of the residuals for table 2, but probably also is related to the stabilization programs. The qualification which must be made is that on the basis of looking only at the coefficients of determination (without worrying about point estimates, lag patterns, etc.), the results in table 3 apparently are significantly more consistent with the variation in the dependent variable than those in table 2 in only two cells (Manufacturing II and Construction [23]) and apparently are significantly less consistent with such variations in two other cells (Commerce and the Total cell). The additional considerations of this section, thus, cannot be said generally to add considerably to the explanatory power of the model.

---

[23] The apparent relative success of the model for the construction cell is in sharp contrast to the lack of success for construction reported in Behrman, 'Sectoral money wages'.

Second, the inclusion of one or more of the three additional variables generally has a substantial impact on the pattern of weights for the expected rate of change of prices. Except for manufacturing II and construction -2, the coefficients of the third order polynomials are no longer significantly non-zero and for Santiago and manufacturing I only the coefficient of one polynomial term is significantly non-zero. The length of the adjustment period which maximizes the coefficient of determination, moreover, is cut to seven or even 4 years for four of the ten sets of estimates. The general lag pattern described above in section II is evident in about half of the cases (i.e., manufacturing I-1, manufacturing II-1, construction-2, total-1 and -2), but even in many of these cases the sum of the weights is significantly different from one. In those cases in which the constant term has been suppressed because it was insubstantial and insignificant and in which the inverse of the unemployment rate is included, the initial lagged values of the rate of change of prices apparently assume the role that one would have thought a negative constant term would serve by offsetting to a degree the always positive impact of the Phillips term. As a result in such cases the initial weights and the total sum of weights of the lagged rates of change of prices are significantly less than in the results of table 2.[24] In those cases in which the constant term has not been suppressed because it is significantly non-zero (i.e., electricity and transportation and total-2), the constant estimate is negative and very large in absolute value. In part these constant estimates serve to offset the always positive impact of the Phillips term which is mentioned above, but they are so large in absolute value that their inclusion also seems to result in an upward shift of the whole pattern of weights for the lagged value of the rate of change of prices.[25] The fact that the constant term assumes more than just the roles of representing exponential changes in productivity and of partially offsetting the Phillips term suggests that there is a specification problem which has considerable impact upon the estimated lag pattern of the weights for the rates of change of prices. The exact nature of this apparent misspecification, however, is not clear.

Third, the evidence of the impact of the inverse of the unemployment rate is somewhat mixed. For every cell except commerce and Santiago there is some evidence of a significant impact of this variable, thus suggesting that wages do

---

[24] Manufacturing II-2 and construction-1 provide the most extreme examples of this phenomenon, but manufacturing I-2, manufacturing II-1, and construction-2 also are illustrations. In manufacturing II, however, the constant estimate, if included, is almost significantly non-zero at the 5% level and is substantial and positive in value, with the same result as that described in note 12 above.

[25] If a constant term is included in the Santiago cell estimate, the same result is obtained. See note 12 above.

respond to real excess demands so measured. The question as to whether or not such responses occur is important because empirical evidence has been presented which suggests that both the creation and the utilization of Chilean sectoral capacity respond significantly to wages.[26] Therefore, it would be preferable from the point of view of efficiency if wage changes reflected real conditions in labor markets. The interpretation of the coefficients of the Phillips term, however, must be heavily qualified because only in manufacturing II and construction does the inclusion of this term apparently increase significantly the consistency of the model with variations in the rate of change of wages and because of the perplexing situation in respect to the constant term that is discussed in the previous paragraph.[27]

Fourth, no evidence was obtained of a significant impact of the change of the unemployment rate. In no data cell was the coefficient of this variable significantly non-zero even at the 15% level.

Fifth, in every cell except commerce some evidence is presented for a significant role for expectations of the rate of change of seasonal price patterns. The total impact of this variable tends to be substantially less than that for the expectations of the rate of change of prices [28] and tends to occur over a period which is no longer than that for expectations of the rate of change of prices. The sums of the weights of lagged values of the rate of change of the seasonal index are small but still imply fairly substantial effects for electricity and transportation and for Santiago.[29] Why these two cells should have evidence of

---

[26] Jere R. Behrman, 'Cyclical sectoral capacity utilization in a developing economy', chapter 9 in this volume (hereinafter referred to as chapter 9); and Jere R. Behrman, 'Sectoral elasticities of substitution between capital and labor in a developing economy: time series analysis in the case of postwar Chile', *Econometrica* (in press) (hereinafter referred to as 'Substitution between capital and labor').

[27] Considering only the Phillips curve term and the constant (if any), at the point of means the estimated effects on the rate of change of nominal wages is as follows: manufacturing I-2 (0.62), manufacturing II-1 and -2 (0.23), electricity and transportation-1 (−0.71), construction-1 (0.17) and -2 (0.19), and total -2 (−0.54). To offset exactly the negative constant terms for the electricity and transportation cell and for the total cell would require unemployment rates, respectively, of 0.002 and 0.035 as compared with mean values over the sample of 0.013 and 0.068. Such calculations illustrate in another way the problem discussed in the text.

[28] Note that all weights for this variable in table 3 have been multiplied by 10 for ease in presentation.

[29] The mean absolute value of the rate of change of the seasonality index over the sixty quarters in the 1953−1967 period is 0.16. The implied impact on the rate of change of wages at this value for the various estimates is manufacturing I-1 (0.001) and -2 (0.01), manufacturing II-2 (0.004), electricity and transportation-1 (0.03), construction-1 (0.004), Santiago -1 (0.02) and total-1 (0.001).

relatively large responses to expectations of the rate of change of seasonal patterns of prices in contrast with the other cells is not clear except that (in the case of Santiago) the concentration of communications media and the government offices in Snatiago probably results in greater awareness of changes in the seasonal patterns there than elsewhere.

IV. Conclusions

The dominant factor in accounting for the rate of change of nominal wages in the seven Chilean data cells examined in this study is the expectation of rates of change of the price level. This factor by itself is consistent with from 67—85% of the variance in the rate of change of nominal wages (excluding commerce). The estimated pattern of weights of lagged rates of change of price level that enter into the expectations of future inflation are distributed over a decade (but with the larger values concentrated near the beginning), apparently allow overshooting to compensate for the less than complete instantaneous response (excluding commerce, once again), and sum approximately to one so that real wages are maintained approximately constant in the long run.

The other three factors considered have much less clear roles (if any) in the determination of wage changes. Some evidence exists for a response to the inverse of the unemployment rate in five of the seven cells, but the evidence is cloudy because of some apparent misspecifications that result in a perplexing interaction among this variable, the polynomials for the formulation of expectations of the rate of change of the price level, and the constant. The extent to which wage changes are reflecting excess demand conditions in the labor markets, thus, is left unclear, which is unfortunate in that other studies suggest that wages do affect capacity creation and utilization.[30] A perhaps more positive aspect of this result, on the other hand, is that there is little evidence of a trade-off between unemployment and inflation in Chile. No evidence was found for a response to the change in the unemployment rate. Evidence was found for a significant response to expectations regarding changes in seasonal paths of price changes in all data cells except for commerce, but the magnitudes of the estimated responses are small.

The Chilean government has embarked on a number of price stabilization attempts, two of which overlapped the start and the end of the sample period. In both of these stabilization programs there has been an attempt to influence the rate of change of wages, primarily through minimum wage (i.e., *sueldo vital*)

---

[30] Behrman, chapter 9 and Behrman, 'Substitution between capital and labor'.

adjustments. In some quarters the rate of change of the minimum wage is thought to be the primary determinant of the rate of change of nominal wages.[31] An examination of the residuals of the relations estimated in this study sug-* gests that the stabilization programs (through the adjustments in the *sueldo vital*) well may have had some impact on the rate of change of nominal wages. A much more important factor, however, has been the nature of inflation expectations which apparently are based primarily upon past experience over a considerable period of time and, therefore, are not highly correlated with changes in the *sueldo vital* (which in recent years have been related to the rate of change of the consumer price index of the previous year). The government can lower relative wages in the fiscal sector that it directly controls, but decreasing the rate of inflation substantially will be very difficult unless the link between past experience and expectations of future inflation can be severed widely in the determination of the rates of change of wages and of other prices. Unless this link is severed, there will be strong pressure for wages to play a transmitting role in the inflationary process almost independent of current government policies.[32] In both of the stabilization attempts of the 1960's, the government attempted to sever the link with historical experience, and the estimates of this study suggests that both times the government failed to do so. These failures will make any future attempt to sever this link all the more difficult. The Frei government had the largest political mandate ever at the polls, was based on a political party which was not tied too closely to the traditional power centers, had created wide expectations of change, had as one of its major goals the stopping of inflation according to a preannounced time-table.[33] Given that that government was unable to succeed in its stabilization program, under what conditions might any future stabilization attempt seem sufficiently credible so the link to the past could be severed? In the near future only some drastic change in the domestic or international environment could possibly make yet another stabilization attempt widely credible.

Appendix: data sources

The wage data (except for manufacturing II) are from the social security administration (*Estadísticas, Servicio de Seguro Social*). These data may under-

---

[31] For suggestions that such a viewpoint is widespread, see Gregory, pp. x, 40–43; and Ramos.
[32] Harberger and Behrman (chapter 14) discuss the role of wages as a transmitter of inflationary pressures in Chile.
[33] Cauas and Ffrench-Davis.

estimate levels of wages systematically because of the incentive for employers to underreport wage levels and, therefore, social security payments. It is not clear that any such underreporting leads to any systematic bias in the rates of nominal wages. The alternative wage series for manufacturing (i.e., manufacturing II) are from quarterly surveys conducted by the Bureau of Statistics and the Census (*Dirección de Estadística y Censos*). Gregory [34] discusses the latter data, and Ramos discusses both sources.

The consumer price index is based on monthly surveys conducted by the *Dirección de Estadística y Censos* and is published in the monthly bulletin of the central bank (*Boletín Mensual de Banco Central*).

The unemployment rates are based on the results of the quarterly survey of employment and unemployment conducted by the Economies Institute of the University of Chile (*Encuesta de Ocupación y Desocupación, Instituto de Economía, Universidad de Chile*).

[34] Gregory, 7–33.

REFERENCES

[1] Adams, N., Import structure and economic growth: a comparison of time-series and cross-section data, Economic Development and Cultural Change 15 (January, 1967) 143–162.

[2] Aguiar da Silva Lerne, Ruy, Excess capacity in Brazilian industry, mimeo, UNIDO (ID/WG .29/12), February 5, 1969.

[3] Ahumado, Jorge, En vez de la miseria, Editorial du Pacifico, Santiago, 1958.

[4] Arrow, K.J. and M. Kurz, Public investment, the rate of return, and optimal fiscal policy. Johns Hopkins Press, Baltimore, 1970.

[5] Arrow, K.J., M. Kurz, H. Chenery, B. Minhas and R. Solow, Capital–labor substitution and economic efficiency, Review of Economics and Statistics 45 (August, 1961) 225–250.

[6] Athans, M. and P.L. Falb, Optimal control. McGraw-Hill, New York, 1966.

[7] Bacha, E.L., Taxas de cambio de equilibrio: formulacao e exemplificacao, Revista Brasileira de Economia, March, 1970.

[8] Bacha, E.L. and L. Taylor, Foreign exchange shadow prices: a critical review of current theories, Quarterly Journal of Economics 85 (May, 1971).

[9] Bacha, E.L. and L. Taylor, Foreign exchange shadow prices in Chile: conflicting theories and comparative evaluations. ODEPLAN, Santiago, 1969.

[10] Balassa, B., The purchaging power parity doctrine: a reappraisal, Journal of Political Economy 72 (December, 1964) 584–596.

[11] Balassa, B. and D. Schydlowsky, Effective tariffs, domestic cost of foreign exchange and the equilibrium exchange rate, Journal of Political Economy 76 (May/June, 1968) 348–360.

[12] Balassa, B. et al., Studies in trade liberation. Johns Hopkins University Press, Baltimore, 1967.

[13] Behrman, J.R., Cyclical sectoral capacity utilization in a developing economy, chapter 9 in this volume.

[14] Behrman, J.R., Econometric model simulations of the world rubber market, 1950–1980, in: Essays in industrial economics, 3. Economics Research Unit, University of Pennsylvania, Philadelphia. Studies in Quantitative Economics No. 5, 1969, 1–96.

[15] Behrman, J.R., Monopolistic cocoa pricing, American Journal of Agricultural Economics 50 (August, 1968) 702–719.

[16] Behrman, J.R., Price determination in an inflationary economy: the dynamics of Chilean inflation revisited, chapter 14 in this volume.

[17] Behrman, J.R., Price elasticity of the marketed surplus of a subsistence crop, Journal of Farm Economics 48 (November, 1966) 875–893.

[18] Behrman, J.R., Review article: trade prospects and capital needs of developing countries, International Economic Review 12 (October, 1971).

[19] Behrman, J.R., Sectoral elasticities of substitution between capital and labor in a developing economy: time series analysis in the case of postwar Chile. University of Pennsylvania, Department of Economics, Philadelphia, Discussion Paper No. 153, 1970; also forthcoming in Econometrica.

[20] Behrman, J.R., Sectoral investment determination in a developing economy, American Economic Review, in press.

[21] Behrman, J.R., Short run flexibility in a developing economy, American Economic Review, in press.

[22] Behrman, J.R., Supply response and the modernization of peasant agriculture: a study of four major crops in Thailand, in: Subsistence agriculture and economic development, ed. by C.R. Wharton, Jr., Aldine, Chicago, 1969.

[23] Behrman, J.R., Supply response in underdeveloped agriculture: a case study of four major annual crops in Thailand, 1937–1963. North-Holland Publishing Co., Amsterdam, 1968.

[24] Behrman, J.R., The determinants of the annual rates of change of sectoral money wages in a developing economy, International Economic Review 12 (October, 1971) 431–447 (Spanish version forthcoming in Cuadernos de Economia).

[25] Behrman, J.R., P.B. Clark and L. Taylor, Studies on the integration of models for development planning, forthcoming.

[26] Behrman, J.R. and Jorge Garcia M., A study of quarterly nominal wage change determinants in an inflationary developing economy, chapter 15 in this volume.

[27] Bianchi, A., Introduction: notas sobre la teoria del desarollo economica Latino Americano, in: America Latina: ensayos de interpretation, ed. by A. Bianchi. Editorial Universitaria, Santiago, 1969.

[28] Bischoff, C.W., Lags in fiscal and monetary impacts on investment in producers durable equipment. Yale University, New Haven, Cowles Foundation Discussion Paper No. 520, 1968.

[29] Bischoff, C.W. and J. Seefeldt, Rentabilidad social de obras de regadio. Centro de Planeamiento, Universidad de Chile, mimeo., 1968.

[30] Bitar, S. and H. Trivelli, Calculado de rentabilidades financieras y economicas de empresas industriales Chilenas, Cuadernos de Economia, No. 19, Universidad Catolica de Chile, December, 1969, Annexes 1, 2, 3.

[31] Bitar, S. and H. Trivelli, The cost of capital in Chile, chapter 5 in this volume.

[32] Brodersohn, M.S., The utilization of production capacity in Argentine industry. mimeo., Centro de Investigaciones Economicas, Instituto Torcuato Di Tella, November, 1968. Circulated in English by UNIDO (ID/WG .29/9), February 12, 1969.

[33] Bruno, M., The optimal selection of export-promoting and import-substituting projects, in: United Nations, Planning the external sector: techniques, problems and policies (ST/TAO/SERC/91. New York, 1967).

[34] Bruno, M., Trade, growth, and capital. mimeo., Department of Economics, MIT, Cambridge, Mass., 1970.

[35] Bruton, H.J., Productivity growth in Latin America, American Economic Review 57 (December, 1967) 1099–1116.

[36] Bryson, A.E. and Y.C. Ho, Applied optimal control. Blaisdell, Waltham, Mass., 1969.

[37] Campos, Roberto de Oliviera, Two views on inflation in Latin America, in: Latin-American issues, ed. by A.O. Hirschman. Twentieth Century Fund, New York, 1961, 69–73.

[38] Cauas, Jorge, Stabilization policy – the Chilean case, Journal of Political Economy 78 (July–August, 1970) 815–825.

[39] Centro de Investigaciones Economicas, Universidad Catolica (CIEUC), Algunos resultados de la encuesta de presupuestos familiares, 1963–1964. Santiago, 1967.

[40] Chenery, H.B. and A. MacEwan, Optimal patterns of growth and aid: the case of Pakistan, in: The theory and design of economic development, ed. by I. Adelman and E. Thorbecke. Johns Hopkins University Press, Baltimore, 1966.

[41] Chenery, H.B. and W. Raduchel, Substitution in planning models, in: Studies in development planning, ed. by H. Chenery. Harvard University Press, Cambridge, Mass., 1971.

[42] Clark, P.B., The social cost of make-work employment programs, paper presented to Second World Congress of Econometric Society in Cambridge, England, Sept., 1970.

[43] Clark, P.B. and A. Foxley, Export concentration and diversification in a developing economy: the case of Chilean copper, forthcoming.

[44] Clark, P.B. and A. Foxley, Usos alternativos de divisas, ahorro interno y mano de obra en un processo de crecimiento acelerado. ODEPLAN, June, 1970.

[45] Clark, P.B., A. Foxley and A.M. Jul, Project evaluation in a macroeconomic framework', chapter 6 in this volume.

[46] Clark, P.B. and L. Taylor, Dynamic input—output planning with optimal end conditions: the case of Chile, paper presented to the European Econometric Society Meetings, Budapest, September 5, 1972.

[47] Coddington, S. and N. Levinson, Theory of ordinary differential equations. McGraw-Hill, New York, 1955.

[48] Cordoba, Julio, La evaluacion economica de la formacion de ingeneiro, Facultad de Ciencias Fisicas y Naturales, Tesis de Graduado, Universidad de Chile, 1966.

[49] Corfo, Division de Planificacion Industrial, Inventario de projectos del sector industrial manufacturero. Santiago, April, 1969.

[50] Dantwala, M.L., International planning to combat the scourge of hunger throughout the world, Annals of Collective Economy 34 (January—March 1963) 71—96.

[51] David, P.A. and Th. van de Klundert, Biased efficiency growth and capital labor substitution in the U.S., American Economic Review 55 (June, 1965) 357—394.

[52] Deaver, J., The Chilean inflation and the demand for money, Ph.D. Dissertation, University of Chicago, 1960.

[53] Dicks-Mireaux, L.A., The interrelationship between cost and price changes, 1946—1959: a study of inflation in postwar Britain, Oxford Economic Papers, New Series 13 (October, 1961) 267—292.

[54] Diz, A.C., Money and prices in Argentina, 1935—1962, Ph.D. dissertation, University of Chicago, 1966.

[55] Dorfman, R., P.A. Samelson and R.M. Solow, Linear programming and economic analysis. McGraw-Hill, New York, 1958.

[56] Dreyfus, S., Dynamic programming and the calculus of variations. Academic Press, New York, 1965.

[57] Echeverria, R., Respuesta de los Productores agricolas ante cambios en los precios. ICIRA, Santiago, 1967.

[58] Eckstein, O., Investment criteria for economic development and the theory of international economics, Quarterly Journal of Economics 81 (February, 1957) 56—85.

[59] Eckstein, O., A survey of the theory of public expenditures criteria, Public Finances: Needs, Sources and Utilization, National Bureau of Economic Research, 1961.

[60] Er Seleuk, M., Case on the problem of industrial excess capacity and its utilization. mimeo., UNIDO (ID/WG .29/14), February 6, 1969.

[61] Ethier, W.J., General equilibrium theory and the concept of the effective rate of protection. Discussion Paper 170, Department of Economics, University of Pennsylvania, 1970.

[62] Evans, M.K., An agricultural submodel for the U.S. economy, in: Essays in industrial econometrics, 3, ed. by L.R. Klein, Economics Research Unit, University of Pennsylvania, Philadelphia, 1969, 63—146.

[63] Falcon, W.P., Real effect of foreign surplus disposal in underdeveloped economies: further comment, Quarterly Journal of Economics 77 (May, 1963) 323—326.

[64] Feldstein, M.S., The social time preference discount rate in cost benefit analysis Economic Journal 74 (June, 1964) 364.

[65] Felix, David, Structural imbalances, social conflict, and inflation: an appraisal of Chile's recent anti-inflationary effort, Economic Development and Cultural Change 8 (January, 1960) 113–147.

[66] Fitchett, D., The price responsiveness of cereals and potato producers, in: The economic policy gap and Chilean agricultural development. University of Chile, Institute of Economics and Planning, Santiago, Discussion Document No. 19, 1968.

[67] Fleming, J.M., On making the best of balance of payments restrictions on imports, Economic Journal 61 (March, 1951) 48–71.

[68] Floyd, J.E., The over-valuation of the dollar, Amercian Economic Review 55 (March, 1965) 95–106.

[69] Fontaine, E.R., El precio sombra de la divisas in la evaluacion social de proyectos. Universidad Catolica de Chile, Santiago, 1969.

[70] Foxley, A., Experiencias in la utilizacion de modelos economicos para la planificacion de mediano plazo en Chile. Paper presented at the International Seminar on Social and Economic Planning Techniques, Ambers, Belgium, 1968.

[71] Foxley, A., Opciones de desarollo bajo condiciones de reduccion in la dependencia externa – un analisis cuantitavo, Documento 11, CEPLAN, Santiago, Chile, October 1971 and presented to Conference on the Role of the Computer in Economic and Social Research in Latin-America, Cuernavaca, Mexico, October, 1971.

[72] Foxley, A., M. Gomez and R. Infante, Desequilibrios de financiamento en el proceso de desarrollo: resultados para Chile en el decenio 1970–1980. ODEPLAN, 1969.

[73] Ffrench-Davis, R., Three stabilization programs. mimeo., paper presented August 8, 1967, at University of Chicago.

[74] Frisch, R., Dynamic Utility, Econometrica 32 (July, 1964).

[75] Garcia D'Acunia, Eduardo, Inflation in Chile: a quantitative analysis, Ph.D. dissertation, MIT, 1964.

[76] Garcia-Mujica, J., Inflacion como un proceso de equilibrio. Universidad de Chile, Instituto de Economia y Planificacion, Santiago, Document de Discusion No. 15, December. 1968.

[77] Gavan. J., Sobre la distribucion funcional de ingreso en Chile, Cuadernos de Economia 5 (August, 1968) 34–48.

[78] Goldberger, A.S., Functional form and utility: a review of consumer demand theory. mimeo., Social Systems Research Institute, University of Wisconsin, Madison, 1967.

[79] Gomez, A., Utilization of productive capacity in the Latin-American iron and steel industry. mimeo., UNIDO (ID/WG .29/13), February 5, 1969.

[80] Gomez, P.M., Actualizacion de matrices de insumo producto – el metodo RAS, Memoria para optar al grado de Licenciado en Ciencias Economicas y al titulo de Ingenero Comercial, Santiago, 1969.

[81] Gregory, P., Industrial wages in Chile. Cornell University, New York State School of Industrial and Labor Relations, Ithaca, 1967.

[82] Grunwald, Joseph, The 'structuralist' school of price stability and development: the Chilean case, in: Latin-American issues, ed. by A.O. Hirschman. Twentieth Century Fund, New York, 1961.

[83] Hall, R.E. and R.C. Sutch, A flexible infinite distributed lag. Univeristy of California, Institute of Business and Economics Research, Center of Research in Management Science, Berkeley, Working Paper No. 124, 1969.

[84] Harberger, A.C., On measuring the social opportunity cost of public funds. Paper presented at Annual Meeting of Water Resources Research Committee, Western Agricultural Research Council, Denver, Colo., December, 1968.

[85] Harberger, A.C., Investment in men or investment in machines. The case of India, in Education and economic development, ed., C.A. Anderson and M.J. Bowman, Aldine Publ. Co., Chicago, 1969.

[86] Harberger, A.C., On the discount rate in cost benefit analysis. Instituto de Economia, Universidad de Chile, 1963.

[87] Harberger, A.C., Professor Arrow on the social discount rate. Comments presented at a Symposium on Cost-Benefit Analysis, Madison, Wisconsin, May, 1969,

[88] Harberger, A.C., Some Notes on Inflation, in: Inflation and growth in Latin-America, ed. by W. Baer and I. Kerstenetzky. Richard D. Irwin, Homewood, Ill., 1964, pp. 336–351.

[89] Harberger, A.C., Survey of literature on cost-benefit analysis for industrial project evaluation. Paper presented at the United Nations Inter-Regional Symposium in Industrial Project Evaluation, Prague, 1965.

[90] Harberger, A.C., The dynamics of inflation in Chile, in: Measurement in economics: studies in mathematical economics in memory of Yehuda Grunfeld, ed. by Carl Christ. Stanford University Press, Stanford, 1963, 219–250.

[91] Harberger, A.C., Using the resources at hand more effectively, American Economic Review (papers and proceedings) 49 (May, 1959) 136–146.

[92] Harberger, A.C. and M. Selowsky, Key factors in the economic growth of Chile. Paper presented at the Conference on the Next Decade in Latin-American Economic Development, Cornell University, Paril, 1966.

[93] Henderson, P.D., Investment criteria for public enterprises, in: Public enterprise, ed. by R. Turvey. Penguin Books, Harmondsworth, Middlesex, 1968.

[94] Hines, H.G., Trade unions and wage inflation in the United Kingdom, 1893–1961, Review of Economic Studies 31 (October, 1964) 221–252.

[95] Hines, H.G., Unemployment and the rate of change of money wages in the United Kingdom: a reappraisal, Review of Economics and Statistics 40 (February, 1968) 60–67.

[96] Hirschman, A.O., Development projects observed. The Brookings Institution, Washington, 1967.

[97] Hufbauer, G.C., West Pakistan exports: effective taxation, policy promotion and sectoral discrimination. Economic Development Report No. 118, Development Advisory Service, Cambridge, Mass., 1968.

[98] Hynes, A., The demand for money and monetary adjustments in Chile, Review of Economic Studies 34 (June 1967) 285–293.

[99] Inada, K., Development in monocultural economics. Stanford University, Institute for Mathematical Studies in the Social Sciences, Stanford, Technical Report No. 12, April 15, 1968.

[100] Instituto de Economia, Universidad de Chile, Formacion de capital en impresas industriales Chilenas. Santiago, 1964.

[101] Jacobson, D.H. and D.Q. Mayne, Differential dynamic programming. American Elsevier, New York, 1970.

[102] Jeanneret, T., The structure of protection in Chile. mimeo., 1969.

[103] Johansen, L., A multi-sectoral study of economic growth. North-Holland Publishing Co., Amsterdam, 1964.

[104] Johnson, H.G., A model of protection and the exchange rate, Review of Economic Studies 33 (April, 1966) 159–163.

[105] Johnson, H.G., Factor market distortions and the shape of the transformation curve, Econometrica 34 (July, 1966).

[106] Johnson, L., Problems of import substitution: the Chilean automobile industry, Economic Development and Cultural Change 5 (January, 1967) 202–216.

[107] Jones, G.T., The response of the supply of agricultural products in the United Kingdom to price, Farm Economist 10 (January, 1962) 1–28.

[108] Jorgenson, D.W. and C.D. Sibert, A comparison of alternative theories of corporate investment behavior, American Economic Review 57 (September, 1968) 681–712.

[109] Jul, A.M., Diversificación de exportaciones: el caso Chileno. Honors Thesis, Faculty of Economic Sciences, University of Chile, 1969.

[110] Kemp, M., The pure theory of international trade. Prentice-Hall, Englewood Cliffs, N.J., 1964.

[111] Kendrick, D. and L. Taylor, Numerical solution of nonlinear planning models, Econometrica 38 (May, 1970) 453–467.

[112] Klein, L.R., Some theoretical issues in the measurement of capacity, Econometrica 28 (April, 1960) 272–286.

[113] Klein, L.R. and R.J. Ball, Some econometrics of the determination of absolute prices and wages, Economic Journal 49 (September, 1965) 465–482.

[114] Klein, L.R. and R. Preston, Some new results in the measurement of capacity utilization, American Economic Review 57 (March, 1967) 34–58.

[115] Klein, L.R. and R. Summers, The Wharton index of capacity utilization. Economic Research Unit, University of Pennsylvania, Philadelphia (Studies in Quantitative Economics No. 1) 1966.

[116] Kornai, J., A general descriptive process of plan formulation, Economics of Planning, Oslo, 1971.

[117] Krishna, Raj, Agricultural price policy and economic development, in: Agricultural development and economic growth, H.M. Southworth and B.F. Johnston, ed. by Cornell University Press, Ithaca, 1967, 497–540.

[118] Krishna, Raj. A note on the elasticity of the marketable surplus of a subsistence crop, Indian Journal of Agricultural Economics 57 (July–September, 1962) 79–84.

[119] Krueger, A.O., Some economic costs of exchange control: the Turkish case, Journal of Political Economy 74 (October, 1966) 466–480.

[120] Krueger, A.O., The role of home goods and money in exchange rate adjustments. University of Minnesota, Minneapolis, 1969.

[121] Kuh, E., A productivity theory of wage levels – an alternative to the Phillips curve, Review of Economic Studies 34 (October, 1967) 333–362.

[122] Laursen, K. and L.D. Taylor, Unemployment, productivity and growth in Colombia. Development Advisory Service, Harvard University, Cambridge, Mass., Economic Development Report No. 121, November, 1968.

[123] Leibenstein, H., Economic backwardness and economic growth: studies in the theory of economic development. Wiley & Sons, New York, 1957.

[124] Lewis, Jr., S.R. and S.E. Guisinger, Measuring protection in a developing country: the case of Pakistan, Journal of Political Economy 76 (November/December, 1968) 1170–1198.

[125] Lewis, W.A., Economic development with unlimited supplies of labour, Manchester School 22 (May, 1954) 139–191.

[126] Lipsey, R.G., The relation between unemployment and the role of change of money wage rates in the United Kingdom, 1862–1957: a further analysis, Economica, New Series 27, (February, 1960) 1–31.

[127] Lipsey, R.G. and M.D. Steuer, The relation between profits and wage rates, Economica, New Series 38 (May, 1961) 137–155.

[128] Little, I.M.D. and J.A. Mirrlees, Manual of industrial project analysis in developing countries, Vol. II: Social cost benefit analysis. OECD, Paris, 1969.

[129] Malinvaud, E., Capital accumulation and efficient allocation of resources, Econometrica 21 (April, 1953) 233–268.

[130] Malinvaud, E., Critères de choix des invertissements, in: Choix et efficience des invertissements, ed. by Charles Bettlehelm. Paris, 1965.

[131] Mallon, R.M. and A. Urdinola, Policies to promote Colombian exports of manufactures. Paper presented at the Harvard Development Advisory Service Conference, Sorrento, Italy, 1967.

[132] Mamalakis, M., Historical statistics of Chile, 4 vols. Yale University Press, New Haven, forthcoming.

[133] Mamalakis, M., The American copper companies and the Chilean government, 1920–1967: profile of an export sector. Yale University, Economic Growth Center, New Haven, Discussion Paper No. 37, September 22, 1967.

[134] Marglin, S.B., Industrial development in the labor-surplus economy: an essay in the theory of optimal growth. Harvard University, Cambridge, Mass., 1966.

[135] Marglin, S.B., Intemporal choice: the social rate of discount, in: Manual on Formulation and Evaluation of Industrial Projects. UNIDO, 1970.

[136] McKinnon, R.I., Foreign exchange constraints in economic development and efficient aid allocation, Economic Journal 74 (June, 1964) 388–409.

[137] Mellor, J.W., The economics of agricultural development. Cornell University Press, Ithaca, 1966.

[138] Merhave, M., Excess capacity – measurements, causes and uses: case study of selected industries in Israel. mimeo., UNIDO (FD/WG .29/7), January 20, 1969.

[139] Metzler, L.A., The theory of international trade, in: A survey of contemporary economics, ed. by H.S. Ellis and L.A. Metzler. Blakiston, Philadelphia, 1948.

[140] Michalopoulos, C., Productivity growth in Latin-America: comment, American Economic Review 59 (June, 1969) 435–439.

[141] Ministerio de Obras Publicas, Rentabilidad de obras de regadio en explotacion construidas por el estado. Chile, 1963.

[142] Negishi, I., Approaches to the analysis of devaluation, International Economic Review 9 (June, 1968) 219–227.

[143] Nerlove, M., The dynamics of supply: estimation of farmers' response to price. Johns Hopkins Univeristy Press, Baltimore, 1958.

[144] Nerlove, M., Recent empirical studies of the CES and related production functions, in: The theory and empirical analysis of production, 31. National Bureau of Economic Research, New York, 1967, 55–122.

[145] Newbery, D., The choice of techniques in a dual economy. mimeo., New Haven, Cowles Foundation Discussion Paper No. 278, 1969.

[146] ODEPLAN (Office of Chilean National Economic Planning), Capacidad utilizada de la industria manufacturera, 1964–1965–1966. mimeo., Santiago, July, 1968.

[147] ODEPLAN, Cuadro de transacciones intersectoriales para la economía Chilena – 1962. Santiago, 1969.

[148] ODEPLAN' El desarollo económico y social de Chile en la década 1970–1980. Santiago, July, 1970.

[149] ODEPLAN, Investigación de las serias de tiempo de consumo. Santiago, 1969.

[150] ODEPLAN, Marco de referencia cuantitativo preliminar para la elaboracion del programa 1970–1980. Santiago, 1970.

[151] Okun, A.M., Potential GNP: its measurement and significance, in: Proceedings of the business and economics section of the American Statistical Association. 1962.

[152] Olivier, R., Techniques modernes d'établissement des programmes de développement, Série planification en Afrique. Ministère de Coopération, Paris, 1963.

[153] Olson, R.O., The impact and implications of foreign surplus disposal on underdeveloped economies, Journal of Farm Economics 42 (December, 1960) 1042–1045.

[154] Ossa, C., The relative stability of monetary velocity and the investment multiplier in Chile, mimeo., unpublished, no date.

[155] Oury, B., A production model for wheat and feedgrains in france. North-Holland Publishing Co., Amsterdam, 1966.

[156] Papanek, G. and A. Quereski, The use of accounting prices in planning, Organization, planning and programming for economic development (1963). United States paper prepared for UN conference on the application of science and technology for the benefit of the less developed areas.

[157] Pérez, V., Estimación del costo social de la divisa, Honors Thesis, Centro de Planeamiento, University of Chile, 1970.

[158] Perry, G.L., The determinants of wage rate changes and the inflation-unemployment trade-off for the United States, Review of Economic Studies 31 (October, 1964) 287–308.

[159] Phillips, A.W., An appraisal of measures of capacity, American Economic Review 53 (May, 1963) 275–292.

[160] Phillips, A.W., Measuring industrial capacity in less developed countries. University of Pennsylvania, Department of Economics, Philadelphia, Duscussion Paper No. 110, 1969.

[161] Phillips, A.W., The relation between unemployment and the rate of change of money wage rates in the United Kingdom, 1951–1957, Economica, New Series 25 (November, 1958) 283–299.

[162] Ramos, J., Políticas de remuneraciones en Chile. mimeo., Universidad de Chile, Instituto de Economía y Planificacion, Santiago, September, 1968.

[163] Ranis, G. and J.C.H. Fei, A theory of economic development, American Economic Review 51 (September, 1961) 533–565.

[164] Reichmann, M.T., La demanda de diner – un intento de quantificacion. Instituto de Economía, Universidad de Chile, Santiago, 1965.

[165] Rao, V.K.R.V., Investment, income and the multiplier in an underdeveloped economy, in: The economics of underdevelopment, ed. by A.N. Agarwala and S.P. Singh. Oxford Book Co., New York, 1963; originally in Indian Economic Review, 1952.

[166] Rihtman, Ivo, Capacity utilization in some African countries. mimeo., UNIDO (ID/WG .29/6), January 27, 1969.

[167] Robinson, J., The foreign exchanges, in: A survey of contemporary economics, ed. by H.S. Ellis and L.A. Metzler. Blakiston, Philadelphia, 1948.

[168] Rodriguez, L., Importaciones competitivas y complementarias: un analysis cuantitivo. Honors Thesis, Faculty of Economic Sciences, University of Chile, 1967.

[169] Rosenstein-Rodan, P.N., Notes on the theory of the 'big push', in: Economic development for Latin-America, ed. by H.S. Ellis. St. Martin's Press, New York, 1961.

[170] Sato, K., A two-level constant elasticity of substitution production function, Review of Economic Studies 34 (April, 1967) 201–218.

[171] Saxsena, K.L., Excess industrial capacity in India and the possibility of its utilization for export purposes, mimeo., UNIDO (ID/WG .29/5), January 27, 1969.

[172] Schydlowsky, D.M., On the choice of a shadow price for foreign exchange. Economic Development Report No. 108, Development Advisory Service, Cambridge, Mass., 1968.

[173] Seagraves, J.A., More on the social rate of discount, Quarterly Journal of Economics 84 (August, 1970) 430–450.

[174] Seers, D., A theory of inflation and growth in underdeveloped countries, Oxford Economic Papers; June, 1962, 173–195.

[175] Siena, C.E., Políticas de estabilizacíon, mimeo., Instituto Latino Americano de Planificación Economica y Social, Santiago, October, 1967.

[176] Simler, N.J. and A. Tella, Labor reserves and the Phillips curve, Review of Economics and Statistics 40 (February, 1968) 32–49.

[177] Stone, R. and J.A.C. Brown, A computer model of economic growth. Department of Applied Economics, University of Cambridge, Cambridge, England, 1963.

[178] Summers, R., Further results in the measurement of capacity utilization, in: Proceedings of the business and economics section of the American Statistical Association, 1968, 25–34.

[179] Sunkel, Osvaldo, Inflation in Chile: an unorthodox approach, International Economic Papers, 10.

[180] Taylor, L., Development patterns: A simulation study, Quarterly Journal of Economic 83 (May, 1969) 220–241.

[181] Taylor, L., Investment project analysis in terms of a model of optimal growth: the case of Chile, chapter 6 in this volume.

[182] Taylor, L., On the non-optimality of discounting, and its correct generalizations in investment project analysis. Economic Development Report No. 157, Project for Quantitative Research in Economic Development, Cambridge, Mass., 1970.

[183] Taylor, L., Projecciones neoclasicas del crecimiento economico en Chile, Cuadernos de Economia, forthcoming.

[184] Taylor, L., Two generalizations of discounting, chapter 2 in this volume.

[185] Taylor, L. and E. Bacha, Growth and trade distortions in Chile, and their implications in calculating the shadow price of foreign exchange, chapter 4 in this volume.

[186] Tsukui, J., Application of a turnpike theorem to planning for efficient accumulation: an example for Japan, Econometrica 36 (January, 1968) 172–186.

[187] UNCTAD, Trade prospects and capital needs of developing countries. UN, New York, 1968.

[188] U.N., CAFE, Programming techniques for economic development. Bangkok, 1960.

[189] U.N., ECLA, Inflation and growth. Santiago, unpublished and undated.

[190] U.N., ECLA, Medición del nivel de precios y el poder adquisitivo de la moneda en América-Latina, 1960–1962. E/CN .12/653, Santiago, 1967.

[191] U.N., ECLA, La medición del ingreso real Latinoamericano en dólares estaouni-
dense, Boletín Económico para América Latina 12 (October, 1967) 221–249.

[192] UNIDO, The causes of excess capacity in the manufacturing industry. mimeo.,
UNIDO (FD/WG .29/10), January 24, 1969.

[193] UNIDO, Industrial excess capacity and its utilization for export. mimeo., UNIDO
(JD/WG .29/8), January 21, 1969.

[194] UNIDO, The special nature of the fertilizer industry in developing countries.
mimeo., UNIDO (ID/WG .29/11), February 3, 1969.

[195] UNIDO, Utilization of excess capacity for export: report of the expert group
meeting on excess capacity, Rio de Janeiro, 3–12 March, 1969. U.N. (ID/38),
New York, 1969.

[196] Wharton, Jr., C.R., The issues and a research agenda, in: Subsistence agriculture
and economic development. ed. by C.R. Wharton, Jr., Aldine, Chicago, 1969,
455–468.

[197] Winston, G.C., Capacity utilization in economic development. mimeo., Williams
College, Williamstown, Mass., August, 1969.

[198] Wise, J. and P.A. Yotopoulos, The empirical content of economic rationality: a
test for a less developed economy, Journal of Political Economy 77 (November–
December, 1969) 976–1004.

[199] Zaidi, M.A., The determination of money wage rate changes and unemployment
inflation 'trade-off' in Canada, International Economic Review 10 (June, 1969)
207–219.

SUBJECT INDEX